International Accounting

Sixth Edition

Timothy Doupnik
University of South Carolina

Mark Finn
Northwestern University

Giorgio Gotti
University of Texas Rio Grande Valley

INTERNATIONAL ACCOUNTING

To my wife, Birgit, and children, Stephanie and Alexander

—TSD

To Kaori, Alisa, Monica, and George

—MF

To my parents, and to Alan, Martina, Maurizio, Nicola, and Sara[2]

—GG

About the Authors

Timothy S. Doupnik *University of South Carolina*

Timothy S. Doupnik is a Distinguished Professor Emeritus of Accounting at the University of South Carolina, where he joined the faculty in 1982. He served as director of the School of Accounting from 2003 until 2010, and then as Vice Provost for international affairs until 2013. He has an undergraduate degree from California State University-Fullerton and received his master's and PhD from the University of Illinois.

Professor Doupnik has published exclusively in the area of international accounting in various academic journals, including *The Accounting Review; Accounting, Organizations, and Society; Abacus; Journal of International Accounting Research; Journal of Accounting Literature; International Journal of Accounting;* and *Journal of International Business Studies.*

Professor Doupnik is a past president of the International Accounting Section of the American Accounting Association, and he received the section's Outstanding International Accounting Educator Award in 2008. He has taught or conducted research in international accounting at universities in a number of countries around the world, including Austria, Brazil, China, Dominican Republic, Finland, Germany, and Mexico.

Mark Finn *Northwestern University*

Mark Finn is a Clinical Professor of Accounting at the Kellogg School of Management, Northwestern University, having served on the Kellogg faculty since 1996. Prior to Kellogg, Professor Finn was on the faculty of the University of Chicago's Booth School of Business. He has been affiliated with the Sasin School of Management, Chulalongkorn University (Bangkok, Thailand) since 2003 and the Birla Institute of Technology and Science's School of Management (Mumbai) since 2020. Professor Finn has also served as a visiting professor at the Indian School of Business (Hyderabad and Mohali) and Keio University (Hiyoshi, Japan). From 2001 to 2008 he was director of Kellogg's Global Initiatives in Management (GIM) program. He received a PhD from Cornell University and a BA with honors from Stanford University.

Professor Finn teaches core financial accounting and advanced classes in financial reporting, taxation, international accounting, and sustainability reporting. He received Kellogg's Chairs' Core Teaching Award in 1999, 2005, 2008, 2012, 2014, and 2021 and the Indian School of Business's Teacher of the Year award in 2003, 2008, and 2009. Within the GIM program, he served as a faculty adviser to classes on China, Japan, India, and South Africa. His primary research interests are related to the quality and credibility of financial disclosures, especially in non-U.S. settings. His research articles include "Market Rewards for Increasing Earnings Patterns," published in the *Journal of Accounting Research.*

Giorgio Gotti *University of Texas Rio Grande Valley*

Giorgio Gotti is the Director of the School of Accountancy and Professor at the Robert C. Vackar College of Business & Entrepreneurship, University of Texas Rio Grande Valley. He received his PhD in Business Administration and his Master of Accountancy from the University of Tennessee and a Laurea in Economics from Bocconi University, Italy. He is a Chartered Accountant and Statutory Auditor in Milan, Italy.

Professor Gotti's research and teaching interests are in international and financial accounting. His papers have been published in the *International Journal of Accounting; Journal of Accounting, Auditing & Finance; Journal of International Accounting Research; Management International Review; Journal of Business Ethics; Research in Accounting Regulation; Journal of Management and Governance; Management Decision;* and *Review of Accounting and*

Finance. He has taught international accounting to graduate students at various universities in Italy, Brazil, and the United States.

Professor Gotti is Director focusing on International in the Board of Directors of the American Accounting Association, and past president of the International Accounting Section of the American Accounting Association. He is a member of the Editorial Board of the *International Journal of Accounting* and Associate Editor of the *Journal of International Accounting, Auditing & Taxation.* He has been a member of the Scientific Committee of the European Accounting Association Annual Congress since 2016. He served as Associate Editor of the *Journal of International Accounting Research* in 2014–2017 and is now a member of the Editorial Board.

Preface

ORIENTATION AND UNIQUE FEATURES

International accounting can be viewed in terms of the accounting issues uniquely confronted by companies involved in international business. It also can be viewed more broadly as the study of how accounting is practiced in each and every country around the world, learning about and comparing the differences in financial reporting, taxation, and other accounting practices that exist across countries. More recently, international accounting has come to be viewed as the study of rules and regulations issued by international organizations—most notably International Financial Reporting Standards (IFRS) issued by the International Accounting Standards Board (IASB). This book is designed to be used in a course that attempts to provide an overview of the broadly defined area of international accounting. It focuses on the accounting issues related to international business activities and foreign operations and provides substantial coverage of the IASB and IFRS.

The unique benefits of this textbook include its up-to-date coverage of relevant material; extensive numerical examples provided in most chapters; two chapters devoted to the application of IFRS; and coverage of nontraditional but important topics such as management accounting issues in multinational companies, international corporate governance, and corporate social reporting. This book contains several important distinguishing features:

- Numerous excerpts from recent annual reports to demonstrate differences in financial reporting practices across countries and financial reporting issues especially relevant for multinational corporations.
- Incorporation of research findings into the discussion of many issues.
- Extensive end-of-chapter assignments that help students develop their analytical, communication, and research skills.
- Detailed discussion on the most recent developments in the area of international convergence of financial reporting standards.
- Two chapters on IFRS that provide detailed coverage of a wide range of standards and topics. One chapter focuses on the financial reporting of assets, and the second chapter focuses on liabilities, financial instruments, and revenue recognition. (IFRS related to foreign currency translation is covered in other chapters.) The IFRS chapters also include numerical examples demonstrating major differences between IFRS and U.S. GAAP and their implications for financial statements.
- Separate chapters for foreign currency transactions and hedging foreign exchange risk, and translation of foreign currency financial statements. The first of these chapters includes detailed examples demonstrating the accounting for foreign currency derivatives used to hedge a variety of types of foreign currency exposure.
- Separate chapters for international taxation and international transfer pricing, with detailed examples based on U.S. tax law. The chapter on international taxation covers the international tax provisions in the new U.S. tax law (Tax Cuts and Jobs Act of 2017).
- A chapter devoted to a discussion of the management accounting issues facing multinational corporations, with a focus on issues important for strategy formulation and implementation.
- Coverage of the importance of corporate governance in an international context and the role of auditing (external and internal) in enhancing it.
- A chapter on sustainability reporting, which is becoming increasingly more common among global enterprises and is now a mandatory part of the corporate reporting model in many countries.

CHAPTER-BY-CHAPTER CONTENT

Chapter 1 introduces the accounting issues related to international business by following the evolution of a fictional company as it grows from a domestic company to a global enterprise. This chapter provides the context into which the topics covered in the remaining chapters can be placed.

Chapters 2 and 3 focus on differences in financial reporting across countries and the efforts at converging accounting standards internationally.

- Chapter 2 presents evidence of the diversity in financial reporting that exists around the world, explores the reasons for that diversity, and describes the problems that are created by differences in accounting practice across countries. In this chapter, we also describe several major models of accounting used internationally, discuss the potential impact that culture has on the development of national accounting systems, and present a simplified model of the reasons for international differences in financial reporting. The next to last section of this chapter uses excerpts from recent annual reports to present additional examples of some of the differences in accounting that exist across countries. The final section introduces the facts that some countries require parent company-only financial statements in addition to consolidated financial statements, and that most companies in the world are privately held. In both cases, local GAAP often is required to be followed.
- Chapter 3 focuses on the major efforts worldwide to converge financial reporting practices, with an emphasis on the activities of the IASB. We explain the meaning of convergence, identify the arguments for and against convergence, and discuss the use of the IASB's IFRS internationally.

The universal recognition of IFRS as a set of global accounting standards is one of the most important trends in modern accounting. IFRS are used as the primary set of reporting standards in a majority of the world's economies. In countries that continue to use national standards, including the U.S. and India, IFRS provide a set of benchmarks toward which the national standards converge over time. The chapter surveys the status of IFRS adoption or convergence in each of the world's major economies: the European Union, China, India, Japan, and the United States. Chapters 4 and 5 introduce financial reporting under IFRS for a wide range of accounting issues.

- Chapter 4 summarizes the major differences between IFRS and U.S. GAAP. It provides detailed information on selected IFRS, concentrating on standards that relate to the recognition and measurement of assets—including inventories; property, plant, and equipment; investment properties; biological assets; and intangible assets. The chapter also provides a discussion of accounting for business combinations and the scope of consolidation. Numerical examples demonstrate the application of IFRS, differences between IFRS and U.S. GAAP, and the implications for financial statements.
- Chapter 5 focuses on current liabilities, provisions, employee benefits, share-based payment, income taxes, revenue recognition, financial instruments, and leases, including major differences between IFRS and U.S. GAAP. This chapter also describes the requirements of IFRS in a variety of disclosure and presentation standards.

Chapters 6 and 7 deal with financial reporting issues that are of particular importance to multinational corporations. Two different surveys of business executives indicate that the most important topics that should be covered in an international accounting course are related to the accounting for foreign currency.[1] Because of its importance, this topic is covered in two separate chapters (Chapters 6 and 7).

---

[1] T. Conover, S. Salter, and J. Price, "International Accounting Education: A Comparison of Course Syllabi and CFO Preferences," *Issues in Accounting Education* 9, no. 2 (Fall 1994); and T. Foroughi and B. Reed, "A Survey of the Present and Desirable International Accounting Topics in Accounting Education," *International Journal of Accounting* 23, no. 1 (Fall 1987), pp. 64–82.

- Chapter 6 begins with a description of the foreign exchange market and then illustrates the accounting for foreign currency transactions. Much of this chapter deals with the accounting for derivatives used in foreign currency hedging activities. We first describe how foreign currency forward contracts and foreign currency options can be used to hedge foreign exchange risk. We then explain the concepts of cash flow hedges, fair value hedges, and hedge accounting. Finally, we present examples of accounting for forward contracts and options used as cash flow hedges and fair value hedges to hedge foreign currency assets and liabilities, foreign currency firm commitments, and forecasted foreign currency transactions.

- Chapter 7 focuses on the translation of foreign currency financial statements for the purpose of preparing consolidated financial statements. We begin by examining the conceptual issues related to translation, focusing on the concept of balance sheet exposure and the economic interpretability of the translation adjustment. Only after a thorough discussion of the concepts and issues do we then describe the manner in which these issues have been addressed by the IASB and by the U.S. FASB. We then illustrate application of the two methods prescribed by both standard-setters and compare the results. We discuss the hedging of balance sheet exposure and provide examples of disclosures related to translation. The appendix to this chapter covers the translation of foreign currency financial statements in hyperinflationary environments.

In terms of importance, business executives rank international taxation second only to foreign currency as a topic to be covered in an international accounting course.[2] International taxation and tax issues related to international transfer pricing are covered in Chapters 8 and 9.

- Chapter 8 begins with a discussion of the types of taxes and different tax rates imposed on corporations by countries around the world. We describe different approaches countries take with respect to tax jurisdiction, the problem of double taxation due to overlapping tax jurisdictions, and mechanisms through which countries provide relief from double taxation, focusing on foreign tax credits. We summarize the U.S. approach to taxing income earned by foreign operations of U.S. corporations and provide an example to demonstrate application of this approach. We also discuss benefits of tax treaties and the translation of foreign currency amounts for tax purposes. The appendix to this chapter describes several issues related to U.S. taxation of expatriate individuals.

- Chapter 9 covers the topic of international transfer pricing, focusing on tax implications. We explain how discretionary transfer pricing can be used to achieve specific cost minimization objectives and how the objectives of performance evaluation and cost minimization can conflict in determining international transfer prices. We also describe government reactions to the use of discretionary transfer pricing by multinational companies, focusing on the U.S. rules governing intercompany pricing.

Chapter 10 covers management accounting issues of particular relevance to multinational corporations. This chapter covers multinational capital budgeting as a vital component of strategy formulation and operational budgeting as a key ingredient in strategy implementation, and it discusses issues that must be addressed in designing a process for evaluating the performance of foreign operations.

Chapter 11 explains the importance of corporate governance internationally and the role of auditing in enhancing it. This chapter discusses the meaning of corporate governance and both external and internal auditing issues as they relate to corporate governance. Chapter 11 also describes international diversity in external auditing and the international harmonization of auditing standards.

---

[2] T. Conover, S. Salter, and J. Price, "International Accounting Education: A Comparison of Course Syllabi and CFO Preferences," *Issues in Accounting Education* 9, no. 2 (Fall 1994); and T. Foroughi and B. Reed, "A Survey of the Present and Desirable International Accounting Topics in Accounting Education," *International Journal of Accounting* 23, no. 1 (Fall 1987), pp. 64–82.

Chapter 12 introduces sustainability reporting, a system of measuring and disclosing an entity's social and environmental performance using well-defined, internationally agreed-upon standards. Sustainability reporting is now required of all large companies in the European Union. Elsewhere, most large companies voluntarily publish annual sustainability reports that are analogous to traditional financial reports. Chapter 12 describes the structure of the sustainability reporting system, including the Global Reporting Initiative at the international level and the Sustainability Accounting Standards Board in the United States.

CHANGES IN THE SIXTH EDITION

Chapter 1

- Updated statistics in the section titled "The Global Economy."
- Updated end-of-chapter assignments based on annual reports and replaced other dated material with the most current information available.
- Added two end-of-chapter exercises and problems related to the sections titled "International Income Taxation" and "International Auditing."

Chapter 2

- Updated excerpts from corporate annual reports in the section titled "Evidence of Accounting Diversity" and added to the discussions of those excerpts.
- Updated and reworded some of the explication and discussion in the "National Culture" subsection of "Reasons for Accounting Diversity." For example, in the interest of clarity, Hofstede's original use of the term "masculinity" as a cultural dimension is now described as "competitiveness."
- Updated excerpts from corporate annual reports in the section titled "Further Evidence of Accounting Diversity" and added to the discussions of those excerpts.
- Added a section titled "Parent Company-Only Financial Statements and Private Company Financial Reporting" with a new, related learning objective.
- Added a new question in the end-of-chapter assignments related to private company financial reporting.
- Replaced one exercise in the end-of-chapter assignments related to accounting families with a new exercise related to identifying financial reporting differences across countries.

Chapter 3

- Updated annual reports excerpts from various companies.
- Added a discussion of convergence with IFRS in India and China.
- Added a discussion of the expansion of IFRS in Japan.
- Added a discussion of *IFRS for Small and Medium Size Entities.*
- Added a new questions and new exercises and problems to the end-of-chapter material to reflect the updated focus on convergence in large economies.
- Replaced Case 3-1 to examine the difference between Indian Accounting Standards (Ind AS) and IFRS at Dr. Reddy's Laboratories.

Chapter 4

- Updated annual reports excerpts from various companies.
- Revised the discussion of biological assets to present the financial statements of *Stora Enso Oyj.*
- Revised and updated the discussion of capitalized development costs in the German auto industry.

- Added and/or modified problems to reflect the above changes.
- Revised and updated the *Jaguar Land Rover plc* case.

Chapter 5

- Updated annual reports excerpts from various companies.
- Added a comparison of IFRS 9 and ASC Topic 326 covering the current expected credit loss model (CECL).

Chapter 6

- Updated statistics, annual report excerpts and the related discussions.
- Updated Exhibits 6.1 and 6.2 and related discussions to provide recent exchange rates.
- Added information on IFRS 9, *Financial Instruments.*
- Updated Case 6-2 to be based on more recent exchange rates.
- Updated Case 6-3, Jaguar Land Rover, related to 2020 Brexit.
- Introduced 2020 Brexit example and discussed the consequences for UK firms related to sudden devaluation of the British pound without proper hedging.

Chapter 7

- Updated corporate annual report excerpts and related discussions.
- Updated information about hyperinflationary countries in the appendix.
- Added an exhibit to the appendix containing an excerpt from a company's annual report disclosing its treatment of foreign currency financial statements in countries with hyperinflationary economies.
- Changed the facts provided in several end-of-chapter exercises and problems.

Chapter 8

- Updated information related to income tax, withholding tax, and tax treaty rates in several exhibits and also updated related discussions.
- Changed the source of information in the exhibit on tax havens in the section "Types of Taxes and Tax Rates."
- Added anecdotal information on the impact of the deemed repatriation of foreign earnings tax for several companies in "U.S. Tax Reform 2017: Other International Tax Provisions."
- Updated the amounts that may be excluded from U.S. taxable income in the sections titled "Foreign Earned Income Exclusion" and "Foreign Housing Cost Exclusion" in the appendix to this chapter.
- Changed the facts provided in several end-of-chapter exercises and problems.

Chapter 9

- Updated statistics related to the incidence of cross-border intercompany transfers, the implementation of country-by-country reporting, and the use of advance pricing agreements.
- Added anecdotal information on the "Enforcement of Transfer Pricing Regulations" in the United States.

Chapter 10

- Added a footnote referencing recent professional journal articles that provide further insights into budgeting in a multinational corporation.
- Streamlined the discussion of culture and management control.

Chapter 11

- Updated corporate annual report excerpts and related discussions.
- Added a discussion and end-of-chapter problems on Germany's Corporate Governance Code.
- Added a discussion of reforms outside the United States that were inspired by the Sarbanes-Oxley Act.
- Added a short discussion of the PCAOB's framework for inspecting auditors in non-U.S. settings and the controversy over inspections in China.
- Revised and expanded Cases 11-1 and 11-2.

Chapter 12

- Updated corporate annual and sustainability report excerpts and related discussions.
- Added a discussion of the Global Sustainability Standards Board, its merger with the Sustainability Accounting Standards Board, and the future direction of IFRS Sustainability Disclosure Standards.
- Added a discussion of the Task Force on Climate-related Financial Disclosure and the ESG rating system introduced by Institutional Shareholder Services.
- Expanded the discussion of the SEC's climate reporting rules.
- Added and/or modified problems to reflect the above changes.

NEW! ONLINE ASSIGNMENTS

NEW for the 6th edition, *International Accounting* is accompanied by Connect, McGraw-Hill's teaching and learning platform. Connect helps students learn more efficiently by providing feedback and practice material when they need it, where they need it. Connect grades homework automatically and gives immediate feedback on any questions students may have missed. End of chapter material has been incorporated in Connect.

Connect also incorporates SmartBook, an adaptive reading experience that actively tailors the content of the eBook to the needs of the individual student. Smartbook's adaptive technology provides precise, personalized instruction on what the student should do next, guiding the student to master and remember key concepts, targeting gaps in knowledge, and driving the student toward comprehension and retention.

INSTRUCTOR LIBRARY

The Connect Instructor Library and Online Learning Center contains supplementary items for both students and instructors. The Online Learning Center (www.mhhe.com/doupnik6e and available through Connect) is a book-specific website that includes the following supplementary materials.

For Students:

- PowerPoint Presentation

For Instructors:

- Access to all supplementary materials for students
- Instructor's Manual
- PowerPoint Presentation
- Test Bank

Instructors
The Power of Connections

A complete course platform

Connect enables you to build deeper connections with your students through cohesive digital content and tools, creating engaging learning experiences. We are committed to providing you with the right resources and tools to support all your students along their personal learning journeys.

65%
Less Time
Grading

Laptop: Getty Images; Woman/dog: George Doyle/Getty Images

Every learner is unique

In Connect, instructors can assign an adaptive reading experience with SmartBook® 2.0. Rooted in advanced learning science principles, SmartBook 2.0 delivers each student a personalized experience, focusing students on their learning gaps, ensuring that the time they spend studying is time well-spent.
mheducation.com/highered/connect/smartbook

Affordable solutions, added value

Make technology work for you with LMS integration for single sign-on access, mobile access to the digital textbook, and reports to quickly show you how each of your students is doing. And with our Inclusive Access program, you can provide all these tools at the lowest available market price to your students. Ask your McGraw Hill representative for more information.

Solutions for your challenges

A product isn't a solution. Real solutions are affordable, reliable, and come with training and ongoing support when you need it and how you want it. Visit **supportateverystep.com** for videos and resources both you and your students can use throughout the term.

Students
Get Learning that Fits You

Effective tools for efficient studying

Connect is designed to help you be more productive with simple, flexible, intuitive tools that maximize your study time and meet your individual learning needs. Get learning that works for you with Connect.

Study anytime, anywhere

Download the free ReadAnywhere® app and access your online eBook, SmartBook® 2.0, or Adaptive Learning Assignments when it's convenient, even if you're offline. And since the app automatically syncs with your Connect account, all of your work is available every time you open it. Find out more at **mheducation.com/readanywhere**

"I really liked this app—it made it easy to study when you don't have your text-book in front of you."

- Jordan Cunningham, Eastern Washington University

iPhone: Getty Images

Everything you need in one place

Your Connect course has everything you need—whether reading your digital eBook or completing assignments for class—Connect makes it easy to get your work done.

Learning for everyone

McGraw Hill works directly with Accessibility Services Departments and faculty to meet the learning needs of all students. Please contact your Accessibility Services Office and ask them to email accessibility@mheducation.com, or visit **mheducation.com/about/accessibility** for more information.

Acknowledgments

We extend our sincere thanks to Hector Perera—gentleman, scholar, and true world citizen. As an original author of this text, Hector was instrumental in making *International Accounting* the market leader that it is today. We want to thank the many people who participated in the review process and offered their helpful comments and suggestions:

Wagdy Abdallah
Seton Hall University

Kristine Brands
Regis University

Bradley Childs
Belmont University

Teresa Conover
University of North Texas

Burak Dolar
Western Michigan University

Orapin Duangploy
University of Houston-Downtown

Gertrude Eguae-Obazee
Albright College

Emmanuel Emmenyonu
Southern Connecticut State University

Christine Errico
Champlain College

Charles Fazzi
Saint Vincent College

Leslie B. Fletcher
Georgia Southern University

Paul Foote
California State University-Fullerton

Mohamed Gaber
State University of New York at Plattsburgh

Julie E. Glittelman
Salisbury University

Shiv Goyal
University of Maryland University College

Rita H. Grant
Grand Valley State University

Robert Gruber
University of Wisconsin

Andrew Holt
Metropolitan State University of Denver

Marianne James
California State University-Los Angeles

Agatha E. Jeffers
Montclair State University

Cynthia Jeffrey
Iowa State University

Craig Keller
Missouri State University

Victoria Krivogorsky
San Diego State University

Junghun (Jay) Lee
University of Massachusetts Boston

Daphne Main
Loyola University New Orleans

John R. McGowan
St. Louis University

Britton McKay
Georgia Southern University

Jamshed Mistry
Suffolk University

James N. Mohs
University of New Haven

Gregory Naples
Marquette University

Cynthia Nye
Bellevue University

Randon C. Otte
Clarion University

Obeua Persons
Rider University

Felix Pomeranz
Florida International University

Grace Pownall
Emory University

Juan Rivera
University of Notre Dame

Kurt Schulzke
Kennesaw State University

Mary Sykes
University of Houston-Downtown

Elaine (Ying) Wang
University of Massachusetts Amherst

Sung Wook Yoon
California State University-Northridge

We also pass along many thanks to all the people at McGraw-Hill Education who participated in the creation of this book. In particular, we extend our thanks to Executive Portfolio Manager Rebecca Olson, Product Developer Destiny Hadley, and Marketing Manager Lauren Schur.

Brief Contents

Contents

Chapter **One**

Introduction to International Accounting

Learning Objectives

After reading this chapter, you should be able to

- Discuss the nature and scope of international accounting.
- Describe accounting issues confronted by companies involved in international trade (import and export transactions).
- Explain the reasons for, and the accounting issues associated with, foreign direct investment.
- Describe the practice of cross-listing on foreign stock exchanges.
- Explain the notion of global accounting standards.
- Understand the importance of international trade, foreign direct investment, and multinational corporations in the global economy.

INTRODUCTION

Most accounting students are familiar with financial accounting and managerial accounting, but many have only a vague idea of what international accounting is. Defined broadly, the *accounting* in international accounting encompasses the functional areas of financial reporting, managerial accounting, auditing, and taxation.

The word *international* in international accounting can be defined at three different levels.[1] At the *first level,* international accounting can be viewed as the study of the standards, guidelines, and rules of accounting, auditing, and taxation that exist within each country as well as comparison of those items across countries. Examples would be cross-country comparisons of rules related to the financial reporting of property, plant, and equipment; income and other tax rates; and the requirements for becoming a member of the national accounting profession.

At the *second level* is supranational accounting, which denotes standards, guidelines, and rules of financial reporting, auditing, and taxation issued by supranational organizations. Such organizations include the International Accounting Standards Board (IASB), the International Federation of Accountants (IFAC), and the Organization for Economic Cooperation and Development (OECD).

---

[1] This framework for defining international accounting was developed by Professor Konrad Kubin in the preface to *International Accounting Bibliography 1982–1994,* distributed by the International Accounting Section of the American Accounting Association (Sarasota, FL: AAA, 1997).

At the *third level,* the company level, international accounting can be viewed in terms of the accounting standards, guidelines, and practices that a company follows that are *specifically related to its international business activities and foreign investments.* These would include standards for accounting for transactions denominated in a foreign currency, tax rules related to international transfer pricing, and techniques for evaluating the performance of foreign operations.

Clearly, international accounting encompasses an enormous amount of territory—both geographically and topically. It is not feasible or desirable to cover the entire discipline in one course. This book is designed to be used in a course that provides an overview of the broadly defined area of international accounting, including certain supranational guidelines, but that focuses on the accounting issues related to international business activities and foreign investments. In other words, this book focuses on international accounting issues at the company level that are specifically relevant to multinational corporations.[2]

The next section of this chapter introduces accounting issues that are important to multinational corporations by describing the evolution of a fictitious company as it becomes increasingly more multinational. To provide justification for the importance of these issues, the following section highlights the importance of international trade, foreign direct investment, and multinational corporations in the global economy. The final section of this chapter summarizes the major topics covered in this book.

EVOLUTION OF A MULTINATIONAL CORPORATION

To gain an appreciation for the accounting issues related to international business, let us follow the evolution of Magnum Corporation, a fictional auto parts manufacturer headquartered in Detroit, Michigan.[3] Magnum was founded in the early 1950s to produce and sell rearview mirrors to automakers in the United States. For the first several decades, all of Magnum's transactions occurred in the United States. Raw materials and machinery and equipment were purchased from suppliers located across the United States, finished products were sold to U.S. automakers, loans were obtained from banks in Michigan and Illinois, and the common stock was sold on the New York Stock Exchange. At this stage, all of Magnum's business activities were carried out in U.S. dollars, its financial reporting was done in compliance with U.S. generally accepted accounting principles (GAAP), and taxes were paid to the U.S. federal government and the state of Michigan.

Sales to Customers

In the 1980s, one of Magnum's major customers, Normal Motors Inc., acquired a production facility in the United Kingdom, and Magnum was asked to supply this operation with rearview mirrors. The most feasible means of supplying Normal Motors UK (NMUK) was to manufacture the mirrors in Michigan and then ship them to the United Kingdom, thus making export sales to a foreign customer. If the sales had been invoiced in U.S. dollars, accounting for the export sales would have been no different from accounting for domestic

---

[2] There is no universally accepted definition of a multinational corporation. Rugman and Collinson define a multinational corporation as a company that is "headquartered in one country but has operations in other countries" (Alan M. Rugman and Simon Collinson, *International Business,* 6th ed., Essex, England: Pearson Education Limited, 2012, page 7). The United Nations defines multinational corporations as "enterprises which own or control production or service facilities outside the country in which they are based" (United Nations, *Multinational Corporations in World Development,* 1973, page 23).

[3] The description of Magnum's evolution is developed from a U.S. perspective. However, the international accounting issues that Magnum is forced to address would be equally applicable to a company headquartered in any other country in the world.

sales. However, Normal Motors required Magnum to bill the sales to NMUK in British pounds (£), thus creating foreign currency sales for Magnum. The first shipment of mirrors to NMUK was invoiced at £100,000 with credit terms of 2/10, net 30. If Magnum were a British company, the journal entry to record this sale would have been:

Dr. Accounts Receivable (+ Assets)............................... £100,000	
Cr. Sales Revenue (+ Equity)	£100,000

However, Magnum is a U.S.-based company that keeps its accounting records in U.S. dollars (US$). To account for this export sale, the British pound sales revenue and account receivable must be translated into US$. Assuming that the exchange rate between the £ and the US$ at the time of this transaction was £1 = US$1.35, the journal entry would have been:

Dr. Accounts Receivable (£) (+ Assets)......................... US$135,000	
Cr. Sales Revenue (+ Equity)	US$135,000

This was the first time since its formation that Magnum had found it necessary to account for a transaction denominated (invoiced) in a currency other than the U.S. dollar. The company added to its chart of accounts a new account indicating that the receivable was in a foreign currency, "Accounts Receivable (£)," and the accountant had to determine the appropriate exchange rate to translate £ into US$.

As luck would have it, by the time NMUK paid its account to Magnum, the value of the £ had fallen to £1 = US$1.30, and the £100,000 received by Magnum was converted into US$130,000. The partial journal entry to record this would have been:

Dr. Cash (+ Assets).. US$130,000	
Cr. Accounts Receivable (£) (– Assets)...........................	US$135,000

This journal entry is obviously incomplete because the debit and the credit are not equal and the balance sheet will be out of balance. A question arises: How should the difference of US$5,000 between the original US$ value of the receivable and the actual number of US$ received be reflected in the accounting records? Two possible answers would be (1) to treat the difference as a reduction in sales revenue or (2) to record the difference as a separate loss resulting from a change in the foreign exchange rate. This is an accounting issue that Magnum was not required to deal with until it became involved in export sales. Specific rules for accounting for foreign currency transactions exist in the United States, and Magnum's accountants had to develop an ability to apply those rules.

Through the British-pound account receivable, Magnum became exposed to foreign exchange risk—the risk that the foreign currency will decrease in US$ value over the life of the receivable. The obvious way to avoid this risk is to require foreign customers to pay for their purchases in US$. Sometimes foreign customers will not or cannot pay in the seller's currency, and to make the sale, the seller is obliged to accept payment in the foreign currency. Thus, foreign exchange risk arises.

Hedges of Foreign Exchange Risk

Companies can use a variety of techniques to manage, or hedge, their exposure to foreign exchange risk. A popular way to hedge foreign exchange risk is through the purchase of a foreign currency option that gives the option owner the right, but not the obligation, to sell foreign currency at a predetermined exchange rate known as the strike price. Magnum purchased such an option for US$200 and was able to sell the £100,000 it received for a total of US$135,000 because of the option's strike price. The foreign currency option was an asset that Magnum was required to account for over its 30-day life. Options are a type of derivative financial instrument,[4] the accounting for which can be quite complicated. Foreign currency forward contracts are another example of derivative financial instruments commonly used to hedge foreign exchange risk. Magnum never had to worry about how to account for hedging instruments such as options and forward contracts until it became involved in international trade.

Foreign Direct Investment

Although the managers at Magnum at first were apprehensive about international business transactions, they soon discovered that foreign sales were a good way to grow revenues and, with careful management of foreign currency risk, would allow the company to earn adequate profit. Over time, Magnum became known throughout Europe for its quality products. The company entered into negotiations and eventually landed supplier contracts with several European automakers, filling orders through export sales from its factory in the United States. Because of the combination of increased shipping costs and its European customers' desire to move toward just-in-time inventory systems, Magnum began thinking about investing in a production facility somewhere in Europe. The ownership and control of foreign assets, such as a manufacturing plant, are known as foreign direct investment. For Magnum, maintaining and increasing sales to European customers, reducing shipping costs, and gaining a foothold in the European Union economic bloc were all relevant reasons for making a foreign direct investment.

Two ways for Magnum to establish a manufacturing presence in Europe were to purchase an existing mirror manufacturer (acquisition) or to construct a brand-new plant (greenfield investment). In either case, the company needed to calculate the net present value (NPV) of future cash flows from the potential investment to make sure that the return on investment would be adequate. Determination of NPV involves forecasting future profits and cash flows, discounting those cash flows back to their present value, and comparing this with the amount of the investment. NPV calculations inherently involve a great deal of uncertainty; this is even more true when the investment is being made in a foreign country.

In the early 1990s, Magnum identified a company in Portugal (Espelho Ltda.) as a potential acquisition candidate. In determining NPV, Magnum needed to forecast future cash flows and determine a fair price to pay for Espelho. Magnum had to deal with several complications in making a foreign investment decision that would not have come into play in a domestic situation.

First, to assist in determining a fair price to offer for the company, Magnum asked for Espelho's financial statements for the past five years. The financial statements had been prepared in accordance with Portuguese accounting rules, which were much different from the accounting rules Magnum's managers were familiar with. The balance sheet did not provide a clear picture of the company's assets, and many liabilities appeared to be kept off-balance-sheet. Footnote disclosure was limited, and cash flow information was not provided. This was the first time that Magnum's management became aware of the significant differences in accounting between countries. Magnum's accountants spent much time and effort restating Espelho's financial statements to a basis that Magnum felt it could use for valuing the company.

---

[4] A derivative is a financial instrument whose value is based on (or derived from) a traditional security (such as a stock or bond), an asset (such as foreign currency or a commodity like gold), or a market index (such as the S&P 500 index). In this example, the value of the British-pound option is based on the price of the British pound.

Second, in determining NPV, cash flows should be measured on an after-tax basis. To adequately incorporate tax effects into the analysis, Magnum's management had to learn a great deal about the Portuguese income tax system and the taxes and restrictions imposed on dividend payments made to foreign parent companies. These and other complications make the analysis of a foreign investment much more challenging than the analysis of a domestic investment.

Magnum determined that the purchase of Espelho Ltda. would satisfy its European production needs and also generate an adequate return on investment. Magnum acquired all of the company's outstanding common stock, and Espelho Ltda. continued as a Portuguese corporation. The investment in a subsidiary located in a foreign country created several new accounting challenges that Magnum previously had not been required to address.

Financial Reporting for Foreign Operations

As a publicly traded company in the United States, Magnum Corporation is required to prepare consolidated financial statements in which the assets, liabilities, and income of its subsidiaries (domestic and foreign) are combined with those of the parent company. The consolidated financial statements must be presented in U.S. dollars and prepared using U.S. GAAP. Espelho Ltda., being a Portuguese corporation, keeps its accounting records in euros (€) in accordance with Portuguese GAAP.[5] To consolidate the results of its Portuguese subsidiary, two procedures must be completed.

First, for all those accounting issues for which Portuguese accounting rules differ from U.S. GAAP, amounts calculated under Portuguese GAAP must be converted to a U.S. GAAP basis. To do this, Magnum needs someone who has expertise in both U.S. and Portuguese GAAP and can reconcile the differences between them. Magnum's financial reporting system was altered to accommodate this conversion process. Magnum relied heavily on its external auditing firm (one of the so-called Big Four firms) in developing procedures to restate Espelho's financial statements to U.S. GAAP.

Second, after the account balances have been converted to a U.S. GAAP basis, they then must be translated from the foreign currency (€) into US$. Several methods exist for translating foreign currency financial statements into the parent's reporting currency. All the methods involve the use of both the current exchange rate at the balance sheet date and historical exchange rates. By translating some financial statement items at the current exchange rate and other items at historical exchange rates, the resulting translated balance sheet no longer balances, as can be seen in the following example:

Assets	€1,000	×	$1.35	=	US$1,350
Liabilities	600	×	1.35	=	810
Stockholders' equity	400	×	1.00	=	400
	€1,000				US$1,210

To get the US$ financial statements back into balance, a translation adjustment of US$140 must be added to stockholders' equity. One of the major debates in translating foreign currency financial statements is whether the translation adjustment should be reported as a gain in consolidated net income or whether it should be treated as a component of other comprehensive income and added to equity with no effect on net income. Each country has

---

[5] Note that in 2005, in compliance with European Union regulations, Portugal adopted International Financial Reporting Standards for publicly traded (i.e., stock exchange listed) companies. However, as a wholly owned subsidiary of a U.S. parent company, Espelho Ltda. continues to use Portuguese GAAP in keeping its books.

rules regarding the appropriate exchange rate to be used for the various financial statement items and the disposition of the translation adjustment. Magnum's accountants needed to learn and be able to apply the rules in force in the United States.

International Income Taxation

The existence of a foreign subsidiary raises two kinds of questions with respect to taxation:

1. What are the income taxes that Espelho Ltda. has to pay in the host country, Portugal, and how can those taxes legally be minimized?
2. What are the taxes, if any, that Magnum Corporation has to pay in its home country, the United States, related to the income earned by Espelho Ltda. in Portugal, and how can those taxes legally be minimized?

All else being equal, Magnum wants to minimize the total amount of taxes it pays world-wide because doing so will maximize its after-tax cash flows. To achieve this objective, Magnum must have expertise in the tax systems in each of the countries in which it operates. Just as every country has its own financial accounting rules, each country also has a unique set of tax regulations.

As a Portuguese corporation doing business in Portugal, Espelho Ltda. is required to pay income tax to the Portuguese government on its Portuguese source income. Magnum's management began to understand the Portuguese tax system in the process of determining after-tax net present value when deciding to acquire Espelho. At the time Magnum acquired Espelho, the United States taxed corporate profits on a worldwide basis, which meant that Magnum also has to pay tax to the U.S. government on the income earned by its Portuguese subsidiary. However, because Espelho is legally incorporated in Portugal (as a subsidiary), U.S. tax was not owed until Espelho's income was repatriated to the parent in the United States as a dividend. If Espelho were registered with the Portuguese government as a branch, its income would be taxed currently in the United States regardless of when the income is remitted to Magnum. Thus, income earned by foreign operations can be subject to double taxation.[6]

Some home countries provide parent companies with foreign operations relief from double taxation through a credit for the amount of taxes already paid to the foreign government. Tax treaties between two countries might also provide some relief from double taxation. Other countries eliminate double taxation by exempting income earned by foreign operations from corporate income taxation. Magnum's tax accountants must be very conversant in both U.S. and foreign tax laws as it pertains to foreign income to make sure that the company is not paying more taxes worldwide than is necessary.

International Transfer Pricing

Some companies with foreign operations attempt to minimize the amount of worldwide taxes they pay through the use of discretionary transfer pricing. Automobile mirrors consist of three major components: mirrored glass, a plastic housing, and a steel bracket. The injection-molding machinery for producing the plastic housing is expensive, and Espelho Ltda. does not own such equipment. The plastic parts that Espelho requires are produced by Magnum in the United States and then shipped to Espelho as an intercompany sale. Prices must be established for these intercompany transfers. The transfer price generates sales revenue for Magnum and is a component of cost of goods sold for Espelho. If the

[6] In 2018, the United States abandoned its worldwide approach in favor of a territorial approach to taxing foreign source income. Beginning that year, income earned by foreign subsidiaries of U.S. companies was no longer subject to U.S. corporate income taxation. However, income earned by foreign branches of U.S. companies remains taxable in the United States.

transfer were being made within the United States, Magnum's management would allow the buyer and the seller to negotiate a price that both would be willing to accept.

This intercompany sale is being made from one country to another. Because the income tax rate in Portugal is higher than that in the United States, Magnum requires these parts to be sold to Espelho at as high a price as possible. Transferring parts to Portugal at high prices shifts gross profit to the United States that otherwise would be earned in Portugal, thus reducing the total taxes paid across both countries. Most governments are aware that multinational companies have the ability to shift profits from high-tax countries to low-tax countries through discretionary transfer pricing. To make sure that companies pay their fair share of local taxes, most countries have laws that regulate international transfer pricing. Magnum Corporation must be careful that, in transferring parts from the United States to Portugal, the transfer price is acceptable to tax authorities in both countries. The United States and several other countries have become aggressive in enforcing their transfer pricing regulations.

Performance Evaluation of Foreign Operations

To ensure that operations in both the United States and Portugal are achieving their objectives, Magnum's top management requests that the managers of the various operating units submit periodic reports to headquarters detailing their unit's performance. Headquarters management is interested in evaluating the performance of the operating unit as well as the performance of the individuals responsible for managing those units. The process for evaluating performance that Magnum has used in the past for its U.S. operations is not directly transferable to evaluating the performance of Espelho Ltda. Several issues unique to foreign operations must be considered in designing the evaluation system. For example, Magnum has to decide whether to evaluate Espelho's performance on the basis of euros or U.S. dollars. Translation from one currency to another can affect return-on-investment ratios that are often used as performance measures. Magnum also must decide whether reported results should be adjusted to factor out those items over which Espelho's managers have no control, such as the artificially high price paid for plastic parts imported from Magnum. There are no universally correct solutions to the various issues that Magnum must address in evaluating performance, and the company is likely to find it necessary to make periodic adjustments to its evaluation process for foreign operations.

International Auditing

The primary objective of Magnum's performance evaluation system is to maintain control over its decentralized operations. Another important component of the management control process is internal auditing. The internal auditor must (1) make sure that the company's policies and procedures are being followed and (2) uncover errors, inefficiencies, and, unfortunately at times, fraud. There are several issues that make the internal audit of a foreign operation more complicated than domestic audits.

Perhaps the most obvious obstacle to performing an effective internal audit is language. To be able to communicate with Espelho's managers and employees—asking the questions that need to be asked and understanding the answers—Magnum's internal auditors should speak Portuguese. The auditors also need to be familiar with the local culture and customs, because these may affect the amount of work necessary in the audit. This familiarity can help to explain some of the behavior encountered and perhaps can be useful in planning the audit. Another important function of the internal auditor is to make sure that the company is in compliance with the Foreign Corrupt Practices Act, which prohibits a U.S. company from paying bribes to foreign government officials to obtain business. Magnum needs to make sure that internal controls are in place to provide reasonable assurance that illegal payments are not made.

External auditors encounter the same problems as internal auditors in dealing with the foreign operations of their clients. External auditors with multinational company clients must have expertise in the various sets of financial accounting rules as well as the auditing standards in the various jurisdictions in which their clients operate. Magnum's external auditors, for example, must be capable of applying Portuguese auditing standards to attest that Espelho's financial statements present a true and fair view in accordance with Portuguese GAAP. In addition, they must apply U.S. auditing standards to verify that the reconciliation of Espelho's financial statements for consolidation purposes brings the financial statements into compliance with U.S. GAAP.

As firms have become more multinational, so have their external auditors. Today, the Big Four international accounting firms are among the most multinational organizations in the world. Indeed, one of the Big Four accounting firms, KPMG, is the result of a merger of accounting firms that originated in four different countries: Germany, Netherlands, United Kingdom, and United States. Each of the Big Four firms, Deloitte Touche Tohmatsu, Ernst & Young, KPMG, and PricewaterhouseCoopers, has offices in more than 120 countries and territories around the world.

Cross-Listing on Foreign Stock Exchanges

Magnum's investment in Portugal turned out to be extremely profitable, and over time the company established operations in other countries around the world. As each new country was added to the increasingly international company, Magnum had to address new problems associated with foreign GAAP conversion, foreign currency translation, international taxation and transfer pricing, and management control.

By the beginning of the 21st century, Magnum had become a truly global enterprise, with more than 10,000 employees spread across 16 different countries. Although the United States remained its major market, the company generated less than half of its revenues in its home country. Magnum eventually decided that in addition to its stock being listed on the New York Stock Exchange (NYSE), there would be advantages to having the stock listed and traded on several foreign stock exchanges. Most stock exchanges require companies to file an annual report and specify the accounting rules that must be followed in preparing financial statements. Regulations pertaining to foreign companies can differ from those for domestic companies. For example, in the United States, the Securities and Exchange Commission (SEC) requires all U.S. companies to use U.S. GAAP in preparing their financial statements. Foreign companies listed on U.S. stock exchanges may use foreign GAAP in preparing their financial statements but generally must provide a reconciliation of net income and stockholders' equity to U.S. GAAP. In 2007, the U.S. SEC relaxed this requirement for those foreign companies that use International Financial Reporting Standards (IFRS) developed by the International Accounting Standards Board (IASB) to prepare financial statements. Foreign companies that file financial statements with the SEC that have been prepared under IFRS need not provide any reconciliation to U.S. GAAP.

Many stock exchanges around the world allow foreign companies to be listed on those exchanges by using IFRS in preparing their financial statements. Magnum determined that by preparing a set of consolidated financial statements based on IFRS, it could gain access to most of the stock exchanges it might possibly want to, including London's and Hong Kong's. With the help of its external auditing firm, Magnum's accountants developed a second set of financial statements prepared in accordance with IFRS, and the company was able to obtain stock exchange listings in several foreign countries.

Sustainability Reporting

As Magnum's managers became more internationally oriented, they discovered that several automotive firms located in foreign countries provide information on their corporate

Web sites related to *sustainability*. In addition to an annual financial report containing traditional financial statements, many companies today prepare a separate report that provides the company's stakeholders with information on the company's sustainability strategy and the progress made in meeting sustainability objectives. Although companies give these reports various names such as *Environmental, Social and Governance (ESG) Report* or *Corporate Responsibility Report,* commonly they are simply titled *Sustainability Report.* Sustainability reports tend to provide information on issues such as environmental impact, labor practices, product safety, and corporate governance. In many cases, companies prepare and publish these reports voluntarily, but sustainability disclosures are actually required in several countries. Seeing a potential benefit to providing stakeholders with this type of information, Magnum's management team developed the framework for a corporate responsibility and sustainability report and began to voluntarily provide this information on the company's Web site.

Global Financial Reporting Standards

Through their experiences in analyzing the financial statements of potential acquisitions and in cross-listing the company's stock, Magnum's managers began to wonder whether the differences that exist in GAAP across countries were really necessary. There would be significant advantages if all countries, including the United States, were to adopt a common set of financial reporting standards. In that case, Magnum could use one set of standards as the local GAAP in each of the countries in which it has operations and thus avoid the GAAP conversion that it currently must perform in preparing consolidated financial statements. It also could use one set of financial statements to facilitate obtaining financing in different countries. In addition, a single set of financial reporting standards used worldwide would significantly reduce the problems the company had experienced over the years in evaluating foreign investment opportunities based on financial statements prepared in compliance with a variety of local GAAP. Over time, Magnum Corporation became a strong proponent of global financial reporting standards.

THE GLOBAL ECONOMY

Although Magnum is a fictitious company, its evolution into a multinational corporation is not unrealistic. Most companies begin by selling their products in the domestic market. As foreign demand for the company's product arises, this demand is met initially through making export sales. Exporting is the entry point for most companies into the world of international business.

International Trade

International trade (imports and exports) constitutes a significant portion of the world economy. In 2020, companies worldwide exported more than $17.5 trillion worth of merchandise.[7] The three largest exporters were China, the United States, and Germany, in that order. The United States, China, and Germany, in that order, were the three largest importers. Although international trade has existed for thousands of years, recent growth in trade has been phenomenal. Over the period 2009–2019, U.S. exports increased from $1,056 billion to $1,645 billion per year, a 56 percent increase. During the same period, Chinese exports more than doubled to $2,499 billion in 2019.[8]

[7] World Trade Organization, *World Trade Statistical Review 2021,* Table A.6, Leading Exporters and Importers in World Merchandise Trade, 2020.

[8] World Trade Organization, *World Trade Statistical Review 2020,* Table A.57, World Merchandise Exports by Region and Selected Economy, 2009–2019.

The number of companies involved in international trade also has grown substantially. The number of U.S. companies making export sales rose by 233 percent from 1987 to 1999, when the number stood at 231,420.[9] In 2019, 288,063 U.S. companies were involved in exporting.[10] The Boeing Company is a U.S.-based aerospace company with billions of dollars of annual export sales. In 2020, 37 percent ($22 billion) of the company's sales were outside of the United States. In addition, some of the company's key suppliers and subcontractors are located in Europe and Japan. However, not only large companies are involved in exporting. Companies with fewer than 20 employees comprise more than 35 percent of U.S. exporters.[11]

Foreign Direct Investment

The product cycle theory suggests that, as time passes, exporters might believe the only way to retain their advantage over competition in foreign markets is to produce locally, thereby reducing transportation costs. Companies often acquire existing operations in foreign countries as a way to establish a local production capability. Alternatively, companies can establish a local presence by founding a new company specifically tailored to the company's needs. Sometimes this is done through a joint venture with a local partner.

The acquisition of existing foreign companies and the creation of new foreign subsidiaries are the two most common forms of what is known as foreign direct investment (FDI). Each year, in its *World Investment Report,* the United Nations publishes data on "cross-border M&A" (acquisition of existing foreign companies) and "greenfield FDI" (creation of new foreign subsidiaries) activity. In 2020, 6,201 cross-border M&A transactions took place, with a total of $475 billion invested. U.S. companies were most often the buyers in these transactions (17.4 percent of the total), followed by UK companies (8.9 percent). U.S. and UK companies also were the most common sellers in these transactions.[12]

In 2020, 12,971 greenfield FDI projects were announced, with a total investment of $564 billion. Europe was the most popular region for new investment (31.3 percent of the total), followed by Asia (30.1 percent). The single most popular country for greenfield FDI was the United States (11.8 percent), with the United Kingdom, China, Germany, and Poland rounding out the top five countries. By far, information and communication was the most popular industry for greenfield FDI (22.4 percent of the total).[13]

The cumulative amount of FDI worldwide has increased substantially over the past several decades. The total stock of FDI was $2.2 trillion in 1990. By 2010, cumulative FDI had increased almost ten-fold to $19.9 trillion, and, by 2020, it had grown to $41.4 trillion. The United States has received more FDI than any other country ($10.8 trillion), followed by the Netherlands ($2.9 trillion), the United Kingdom ($2.2 trillion), China ($1.9 trillion), and Hong Kong ($1.9 trillion). The United States also has the largest amount of cumulative outbound FDI ($8.1 trillion), followed by the Netherlands ($3.8 trillion), China ($2.4 trillion), the United Kingdom ($2.1 trillion), and Japan ($2.0 trillion).[14]

[9] U.S. Department of Commerce, International Trade Administration, "Small and Medium-Sized Enterprises Play an Important Role," *Export America,* September 2001, pp. 26–29.

[10] U.S. Census Bureau, *Profile of Importing and Exporting Companies 2018–2019,* Table 1a, available at www.census.gov (accessed January 15, 2022).

[11] ibid.

[12] United Nations, *World Investment Report 2021,* Web Annex Tables 7–9, available at https://worldinvestmentreport.unctad.org/annex-tables (accessed January 15, 2022).

[13] United Nations, *World Investment Report 2021,* Web Annex Tables 14, 17, and 18.

[14] United Nations, *World Investment Report 2021,* Web Annex Tables 3 and 4.

Multinational Corporations

A multinational corporation is a company that is headquartered in one country but has operations in other countries.[15] In 2009, the United Nations estimated that there were more than 82,000 multinational companies in the world, with more than 810,000 foreign affiliates.[16] At that time, the 100 largest multinational companies accounted for approximately 4 percent of the world's GDP.[17]

Companies located in a relatively small number of countries conduct a large proportion of international trade and investment. These countries include the "triad"—the United States, Japan, and Western Europe—that collectively dominated the world economy until the 1990s. More recently, Chinese companies have emerged as major players in the world economy. As Exhibit 1.1 shows, the triad countries plus China are home to the vast majority of the 100 largest companies in the world. In 2016, 19 of the world's 100 largest companies were Chinese. By 2021, that number had increased to 30, and is second only to the United States.

In 2020, the United Nations measured the multinationality of companies by averaging three factors: the ratio of foreign sales to total sales, the ratio of foreign assets to total assets, and the ratio of foreign employees to total employees. Exhibit 1.2 lists the top 10 nonfinancial companies according to this multinationality index (MNI). Barrick Gold Corporation was the most multinational company in the world, with more than 98 percent of its assets, sales, and employees located outside its home country of Canada. Medtronic Plc is headquartered in Dublin, Ireland, but generates less than 3 percent of its revenue from operations in its home country. Six of the ten companies on this list are headquartered in Western Europe. The five most multinational U.S. companies in 2020, in order, were Mondelez International, Coca-Cola, Johnson & Johnson, Chevron, and IBM. Mondelez had a multinationality index of 75.9 percent.

Many companies have established a worldwide presence. As one example, U.S.-based Nike Inc., the world's largest manufacturer of athletic footwear, apparel, and equipment, has branch offices and subsidiaries in 51 countries, sells products in virtually all countries, and has more than 70,000 employees around the globe. Almost all of Nike's footwear and

EXHIBIT 1.1
Home Country of Largest 100 Companies by Revenues, 2021

Source: Fortune Global 500 2021, available at fortune.com/global500/, accessed on January 15, 2022.

"Triad" Countries		Other Countries	
United States	36	South Korea	2
Japan	9	India	1
Western Europe		Russia	1
Germany	6	Saudi Arabia	1
France	5	Taiwan	1
Netherlands	3		6
Switzerland	2		100
United Kingdom	2		
Italy	1		
	64		
China	30		
	94		

[15] As noted earlier, there is no universally accepted definition of a multinational corporation. The definition used here comes from Alan M. Rugman and Simon Collinson, *International Business,* 6th ed. (Essex, England: Pearson Education Limited, 2012), p. 7.

[16] United Nations, *World Investment Report 2009,* p. 17.

[17] United Nations, *World Investment Report 2009,* p. 17.

EXHIBIT 1.2 **The World's Top 10 Nonfinancial Companies in Terms of Multinationality, 2020**

Source: United Nations, *World Investment Report 2021,* Web Annex Table 19, available at https://worldinvestmentreport.unctad.org/annex-tables/ (accessed on January 15, 2022).

Corporation	Country	Industry	MNI*
Barrick Gold Corporation	Canada	Mining, quarrying and petroleum	98.1
Medtronic Plc	Ireland	Instruments and related products	97.6
Rio Tinto Plc	United Kingdom	Mining, quarrying and petroleum	97.3
Anglo American Plc	United Kingdom	Mining, quarrying and petroleum	94.8
CK Hutchison Holdings	Hong Kong, China	Retail trade	92.1
Takeda Pharmaceutical Company Limited	Japan	Pharmaceuticals	91.3
Hon Hai Precision Industries	Taiwan	Electronic components	90.9
Roche Group	Switzerland	Pharmaceuticals	90.3
Nestlé SA	Switzerland	Food and beverages	90.2
Unilever Plc	United Kingdom	Food and beverages	89.5

* Multinationality index (MNI) is calculated as the average of three ratios: foreign assets/total assets, foreign sales/total sales, and foreign employment/total employment.

apparel products are manufactured outside of its home country of the United States. The company generates approximately 59 percent of its sales outside of North America.[18]

As another example, Unilever Plc is a diversified company headquartered in the United Kingdom. The company operates in more than 190 countries around the world and has significant subsidiaries in countries like Argentina, Australia, Brazil, India, the Netherlands, Switzerland, and the United States, among others. Unilever uses the euro as its reporting currency in presenting financial statements. Because many of its subsidiaries are located outside of the euro zone, Unilever must translate the financial statements from these operations into euros for consolidation purposes. Unilever's management notes that it uses foreign currency borrowings and forward contracts as hedges of the currency risk associated with net investments in foreign subsidiaries.[19]

International Capital Markets

Many multinational corporations have found it necessary, for one reason or another, to have their stock cross-listed on foreign stock exchanges. In addition to its stock being listed on the stock exchange in London, Unilever's shares also are listed on the Euronext Amsterdam exchange in the Netherlands and the New York Stock Exchange (NYSE) in the United States. Large companies in small countries, such as Finland's Nokia OY, might find cross-listing their stock necessary to obtain sufficient capital at a reasonable cost. Nokia's shares are listed on stock exchanges in Helsinki, Paris, and New York. Other companies obtain a listing on a foreign exchange to have an "acquisition currency" for acquiring firms in that country through stock swaps. Several years after obtaining an NYSE listing in 1993, Germany's Daimler-Benz acquired Chrysler in the United States through an exchange of shares. The resulting DaimlerChrysler merger was short-lived, however, with Daimler selling its investment in Chrysler in 2007.

As of May 31, 2021, there were 494 foreign companies from 45 countries cross-listed on the NYSE.[20] More than one-quarter of these companies are Canadian. Likewise, a number of U.S. companies are cross-listed on non-U.S. stock exchanges. For example, approximately

[18] Nike Inc., 2020 Form 10-K, various pages.

[19] Unilever Plc, *Annual Report and Accounts 2020,* various pages.

[20] New York Stock Exchange, *Current List of All Non-U.S. Issuers,* accessed at www.nyse.com on January 15, 2022.

20 U.S. companies are listed on the London Stock Exchange, including Boeing, Honeywell, and Marsh & McLennan. U.S. companies such as Aerkomm, Caterpillar, and GT Biopharma are listed on the Euronext Paris stock exchange.

OUTLINE OF THE BOOK

The evolution of the fictitious Magnum Corporation presented in this chapter highlights many of the major accounting issues that a multinational corporation must address and that form the focus for this book. The remainder of this book is organized as follows.

Chapters 2 and 3 focus on differences in financial reporting across countries and the worldwide convergence of financial reporting standards. Chapter 2 provides evidence of the diversity in financial reporting that has existed internationally, explores the reasons for that diversity, and describes the various attempts to classify countries by accounting system. Chapter 3 describes and evaluates the major efforts to converge accounting internationally. The most important player in the development of global financial reporting standards is the International Accounting Standards Board (IASB). Chapter 3 describes the work of the IASB and introduces International Financial Reporting Standards (IFRS).

Chapters 4 and 5 describe and demonstrate the requirements of selected IASB standards through numerical examples. In addition to describing the guidance provided by IFRS, these chapters provide comparisons with U.S. GAAP to indicate the differences and similarities between the two sets of standards. Chapter 4 focuses on IFRS related to the recognition and measurement of assets, specifically inventories; property, plant, and equipment; investment property; biological assets; and intangibles and goodwill. This chapter also covers business combinations and consolidated financial statements, and borrowing costs. Chapter 5 covers IFRS related to current liabilities, provisions, employee benefits, share-based payment, income taxes, revenue, financial instruments, and leases. IFRS that deal exclusively with disclosure and presentation issues also are briefly summarized.

Chapters 6 and 7 focus on financial reporting issues that are of particular relevance to international business operations (international trade and foreign direct investments). Chapter 6 covers the accounting for international transactions that are denominated in a foreign currency (foreign currency transactions) as well as the accounting for hedges used to minimize the risk associated with these transactions arising from changes in exchange rates (hedges of foreign exchange risk). Chapter 7 demonstrates the translation of foreign currency financial statements of foreign operations for the purpose of preparing consolidated financial statements. An appendix to Chapter 7 covers the translation of financial statements when the foreign operation is located in a hyperinflationary country. Chapters 6 and 7 focus on IFRS and U.S. GAAP related to these topics.

Chapters 8 and 9 cover the topics of international taxation and international transfer pricing. Chapters 8 provides an overview of corporate income taxation worldwide and then focuses on the taxation of foreign operation income by the home-country government. A working knowledge of international taxation issues is important for all students of international business and accounting, not only for tax specialists. Chapter 9 covers the topic of international transfer pricing, focusing on tax implications. This chapter describes rules established by national governments to counteract multinational corporations' use of international transfer pricing to reduce income taxes, with an emphasis on the rules imposed by the U.S. government. These rules are relevant not only for U.S. multinational corporations, but also for foreign corporations that have subsidiaries in the United States.

Chapter 10 focuses on managerial accounting issues of particular relevance to multinational corporations. This chapter covers multinational capital budgeting as a vital component of strategy formulation and operational budgeting as a key ingredient in strategy implementation. Chapter 10 also describes issues that must be addressed in designing a process for evaluating the performance of foreign operations.

Chapter 11 covers auditing and corporate governance from an international perspective. This chapter discusses both external and internal auditing issues as they relate to corporate governance in an international context. Chapter 11 also describes international diversity in external auditing, International Standards on Auditing, and the international harmonization of auditing standards.

Chapter 12 introduces sustainability reporting, a system of measuring and disclosing an entity's social and environmental performance using well-defined, internationally agreed-upon standards. Sustainability reporting is now required of all large companies in the European Union. Elsewhere, most large companies voluntarily publish annual sustainability reports that are analogous to traditional annual financial reports. Chapter 12 describes the structure of the sustainability reporting system, including the work of the Global Reporting Initiative at the international level and the Sustainability Accounting Standards Board in the United States.

Summary

1. International accounting is an extremely broad topic. At a minimum, it focuses on the accounting issues unique to multinational corporations. At the other extreme, it includes the study of the various functional areas of accounting (financial, managerial, auditing, and taxation) in all countries of the world, as well as a comparison across countries. This book focuses on the accounting issues encountered by multinational companies engaged in international trade and making foreign direct investments and also includes coverage of certain supranational guidelines that are relevant for multinationals.

2. The world economy is becoming increasingly more integrated. International trade (imports and exports) has grown substantially in recent years and has even become a normal part of business for relatively small companies.

3. The acquisition of an existing foreign company or the creation of a new foreign subsidiary are the two most common forms of foreign direct investment (FDI). The cumulative amount of FDI has increased substantially in recent decades. The United States has attracted more FDI than any other country.

4. There are tens of thousands of multinational companies in the world. A disproportionate number of the largest multinational corporations are headquartered in the United States, China, Japan, and Western Europe.

5. According to the United Nations, 7 of the top 10 most multinational nonfinancial companies in the world in 2019 were headquartered in Europe, with 4 of these companies located in the United Kingdom.

6. In addition to establishing operations overseas, some multinational companies also cross-list their shares on stock exchanges outside of their home country. There are a number of reasons for doing this, including gaining access to a larger pool of capital.

7. The remainder of this book consists of 11 chapters. Six chapters (Chapters 2–7) deal primarily with financial accounting and reporting issues. Chapters 8 and 9 focus on international taxation and transfer pricing. Chapter 10 deals with management accounting issues specifically relevant to multinational corporations. Chapter 11 provides an international perspective on auditing and corporate governance. The final chapter, Chapter 12, provides an introduction to sustainability reporting at the international level.

Questions

1. How important is international trade (imports and exports) to the world economy?
2. What accounting issues arise for a company as a result of engaging in international trade (imports and exports)?
3. What financial reporting issues arise for a company as a result of making a foreign direct investment?
4. What taxation issues arise for a company as a result of making a foreign direct investment?
5. What are some of the issues that arise in evaluating and maintaining control over foreign operations?
6. Why might a company want its stock listed on a stock exchange outside of its home country?
7. Where might one find information that could be used to measure the "multinationality" of a company?
8. What would be the advantages of having a single set of financial reporting standards used worldwide?

Exercises and Problems

1. Sony Corporation, headquartered in Tokyo, Japan, is one of the largest multinational companies in the world. While Sony's financial reporting currency is the Japanese yen, the company's foreign subsidiaries keep books in a variety of different currencies including the British pound, Euro, Indian rupee, Mexican peso, and U.S. dollar. In addition, Sony engages in international transactions denominated in currencies other than the Japanese yen. As a result, Sony must translate foreign currency receivables and payables into Japanese yen and also must translate each foreign subsidiary's financial statements into Japanese yen to prepare consolidated financial statements.

   Sony is one of the foreign companies listed on the NYSE, and therefore files an annual report on Form 20-F with the U.S. Securities and Exchange Commission (SEC) each year. Search the internet to access Sony Corporation's Form 20-F for the fiscal year (FY) ended March 31, 2020, and refer to "Translation of foreign currencies" in the "Summary of significant accounting polices" on page F-17.

   Required:
   Explain in your own words the policies that Sony uses to reflect the impact of changes in foreign exchange rates in its consolidated financial statements.

2. The Tax Foundation provides data on "Corporate Tax Rates Around the World" on its Web site. To complete this exercise, visit https://taxfoundation.org/publications/corporate-tax-rates-around-the-world/ and download the PDF file containing corporate tax rate data for the most recent year available.

   Required:
   a. Identify countries with a statutory corporate income tax rate larger than 35 percent.
   b. Identify countries with a statutory corporate income tax rate smaller than 10 percent.
   c. Identify five countries without a general corporate income tax.
   d. Which region of the world has the largest average corporate income tax rate?
   e. Which region of the world has the smallest average corporate income tax rate?
   f. What is the average corporate income tax rate across all countries in the world?
   g. All else equal, would a multinational corporation pay a smaller amount of corporate income tax to the local government by establishing a subsidiary in Italy or in Switzerland?

3. The president of Modular Office of Brazil (MOB), the wholly owned Brazilian subsidiary of U.S.-based Modular Office Corporation receives a compensation package that consists of a combination of salary and bonus. The annual bonus is calculated as a predetermined percentage of the pre-tax income earned by MOB. Brazil's national currency is the Brazilian real (BRL), which has been falling in value against the U.S. dollar. A condensed income statement for MOB for the most recent year is as follows (amounts in thousands of BRL):

Sales	BRL 10,000
Expenses	9,500
Pre-tax income	BRL 500

MOB's production is highly automated and depreciation on machinery is the company's major expense. After translating the BRL income statement into U.S. dollars (USD), the condensed income statement for MOB appears as follows (amounts in thousands of USD):

Sales	USD 2,500
Expenses	2,850
Pre-tax income (loss)	USD (350)

Required:

a. Speculate as to how MOB's BRL pre-tax income became a USD pre-tax loss.

b. Discuss whether the president of MOB should be paid a bonus or not.

4. PricewaterhouseCoopers (PwC), one of the world's largest accounting firms, has offices in more than 150 territories. To complete this exercise, access information on PwC office locations available at https://www.pwc.com/gx/en/about/office-locations.xhtml#/.

Required:

a. Determine the number of cities in which PwC has offices in each of the following countries: Australia, France, India, Mexico, Poland, Saudi Arabia, Vietnam, Zimbabwe.

b. Identify in which of the following countries PwC has one or more offices: Iran, Iraq, Israel, Jordan, Lebanon, Oman, Syria, Yemen.

c. Does PwC have offices in more cities in Brazil or in Mexico? Speculate as to the reason why this is the case.

5. The New York Stock Exchange (NYSE) provides a PDF file on its Web site (www.nyse.com) that discloses the non-U.S. companies listed on the exchange. This document can be accessed either by using a web browser to search for "NYSE Current List of All Non-U.S. Issuers" or by searching within the NYSE Web site.

Required:

a. Determine the number of non-U.S. companies listed on the NYSE and the number of countries they represent.

b. Determine the five countries with the largest number of non-U.S. companies listed on the NYSE.

c. Speculate as to why non-U.S. companies have gone to the effort to have their shares listed on the NYSE.

6. The London Stock Exchange (LSE) provides a downloadable Excel file on its Web site (www.londonstockexchange.com) containing a list of all companies traded on the exchange. This document can be found by searching the internet for "London Stock Exchange Issuer List." The issuer list is located on the LSE Web site under "News and Prices," "Reports," "Issuers and instruments," "Issuers," "Issuer list."

Required:

a. Determine the number of foreign companies listed on the LSE and the number of countries they represent.

b. Determine the number of companies listed on the LSE from these countries: Australia, Brazil, Canada, France, Germany, Mexico, and the United States. Speculate as to why there are more companies listed on the LSE from Australia and Canada than from France and Germany.

7. Volkswagen AG and Daimler AG, both based in Germany, are two of the largest automobile manufacturers in the world. The following information was provided in each company's 2020 annual report.

Required:

Calculate an index of multinationality based upon the geographical distribution of revenue and noncurrent assets (employee information is not available) to determine which of these two companies is more multinational.

VOLKSWAGEN AG

Excerpt from 2020 Annual Report

Euro millions	Sales revenue from external customers	Intangible assets, property, plant and equipment, lease assets, and investment property
Germany	42,847	105,630
Europe/Other markets†	90,652	47,680
North America	36,810	23,852
South America	8,632	2,323
Asia-Pacific	44,288	3,611
Hedges sales revenue	− 345	—
Total	**222,884**	**183,096**

† Excluding Germany

DAIMLER AG

Excerpt from 2020 Annual Report

In millions of euros	Revenue	Noncurrent assets
Europe	64,226	68,456
thereof Germany	25,262	49,819
North America	42,937	24,764
thereof United States	37,801	21,979
Asia	39,944	4,189
thereof China	21,343	474
Other markets	7,202	1,788
	154,309	**99,197**

Case 1-1

Besserbrau AG

Besserbrau AG is a German beer producer headquartered in Ergersheim, Bavaria. The company was founded in 1842 and is publicly traded, with shares listed on the Frankfurt Stock Exchange. Manufacturing in strict accordance with the more than 500-year-old German Beer Purity Law, Besserbrau uses only four ingredients in making its products: malt, hops, yeast, and water. While the other ingredients are obtained locally, Besserbrau imports hops from a company located in the Czech Republic. Czech hops are considered to be among the world's finest. Historically, Besserbrau's products were marketed exclusively in Germany. To take advantage of a potentially enormous market for its products and expand sales, Besserbrau began making sales in the People's Republic of China three years ago. The company established a wholly owned subsidiary in China (BB Pijiu) to handle the distribution of Besserbrau products in that country. In the most recent year, sales to BB Pijiu accounted for 20 percent of Besserbrau's sales, and BB Pijiu's sales to customers in China accounted for 10 percent of the Besserbrau Group's total profits. In fact, sales of Besserbrau products in China have expanded so rapidly and the potential for continued sales growth is so great that the company recently broke ground on the construction of a brewery in Qingdao, China. To finance construction of the new facility, Besserbrau negotiated a listing of its shares on the Hong Kong Stock Exchange to facilitate an initial public offering of new shares of stock.

Required:

Discuss the various international accounting issues confronted by Besserbrau AG.

Case 1-2

Vanguard International Growth Fund

The Vanguard Group is an investment firm with more than 50 different mutual funds in which the public may invest. Among these funds are several international funds that concentrate on investments in non-U.S. stocks and bonds. One of these is the International Growth Fund. The following information about this fund was provided in the fund's prospectus, dated December 22, 2020:

VANGUARD INTERNATIONAL GROWTH FUND
Excerpts from Prospectus
December 22, 2020

Vanguard Fund Summary

Investment Objective

The Fund seeks to provide long-term capital appreciation.

Principal Investment Strategies

The Fund invests predominantly in the stocks of companies located outside the United States and is expected to diversify its assets across developed and emerging markets. In selecting stocks, the Fund's advisors evaluate foreign markets around the world and choose large-, mid-, and small-capitalization companies considered to have above-average growth potential. The Fund uses multiple investment advisors.

Principal Risks

The Fund could lose money over short or long periods of time. You should expect the Fund's share price and total return to fluctuate within a wide range. The Fund is subject to the following risks, which could affect the Fund's performance:

- *Investment style risk,* which is the chance that returns from non-U.S. growth stocks and, to the extent that the Fund is invested in them, small- and mid-cap stocks, will trail returns from global stock markets. Historically, non-U.S. small- and mid-cap stocks have been more volatile in price than the large-cap stocks that dominate the global markets, and they often perform quite differently.
- *Stock market risk,* which is the chance that stock prices overall will decline. Stock markets tend to move in cycles, with periods of rising prices and periods of falling prices. The Fund's investments in foreign stocks can be riskier than U.S. stock investments. Foreign stocks tend to be more volatile and less liquid than U.S. stocks. The prices of foreign stocks and the prices of U.S. stocks may move in opposite directions.
- *Country/regional risk,* which is the chance that world events—such as political upheaval, financial troubles, or natural disasters—will adversely affect the value of securities issued by companies in foreign countries or regions. Because the Fund may invest a large portion of its assets in securities of companies located in any one country or region, including emerging markets, the Fund's performance may be hurt disproportionately by the poor performance of its investments in that area. Country/regional risk is especially high in emerging markets.
- *Currency risk,* which is the chance that the value of a foreign investment, measured in U.S. dollars, will decrease because of unfavorable changes in currency exchange rates. Currency risk is especially high in emerging markets.
- *Manager risk,* which is the chance that poor security selection will cause the Fund to underperform relevant benchmarks or other funds with a similar investment objective. In addition, significant investment in the consumer discretionary sector subjects the Fund to proportionately higher exposure to the risks of this sector.

PLAIN TALK ABOUT
International Investing

U.S. investors who invest in foreign securities will encounter risks not typically associated with U.S. companies because foreign stock and bond markets operate differently from the U.S. markets. For instance, foreign companies and governments are not subject to the same accounting, auditing, legal, tax, and financial reporting standards and practices as U.S. companies and the U.S. government, and their stocks and bonds may not be as liquid as those of similar U.S. entities. In addition, foreign stock exchanges, brokers, companies, bond markets, and dealers may be subject to less government supervision and regulation than their counterparts in the United States. These factors, among others, could negatively affect the returns U.S. investors receive from foreign investments.

Source: Vanguard International Growth Fund Prospectus, December 22, 2020, pp. 1–10.

The International Growth Fund's annual report for the year ended August 31, 2020, indicated that 97.1 percent of the fund's portfolio by market value was invested in common stock of 123 companies, including 5 U.S. companies. The allocation of the fund's market value by region and individual country is presented in the following table:

Allocation of Fund Market Value by Region and Country (% of market value of net assets)			
Europe		**Pacific**	
Germany	8.1%	Japan	9.7%
Netherlands	7.5	Hong Kong	6.9
France	6.4	South Korea	1.0
United Kingdom	5.1	Australia	0.4
Switzerland	4.7	New Zealand	0.0
Sweden	4.6	Subtotal	18.0%
Denmark	3.4	**Emerging Markets**	
Italy	2.2	China	14.4%
Spain	1.9	Taiwan	1.1
Belgium	1.3	India	1.0
Norway	0.7	Brazil	0.3
Austria	0.3	Indonesia	0.3
Subtotal	46.2%	Subtotal	17.1%
		North America	
		United States	14.4%
		Canada	0.7
		Subtotal	15.1%
		Middle East	
		Israel	0.7%

Source: Vanguard International Growth Fund Annual Report, August 31, 2020, pp. 10–12.

Required:

1. Explain why an individual investor might want to invest in an international growth fund.
2. Describe the risks associated with making an investment in an international growth fund. Identify the risks that would be common to domestic and international funds and the risks that would be unique to an international fund.
3. Refer to the "Plain Talk About International Investing" box. Speculate as to how the fact that foreign companies are not subject to the same accounting, auditing, and financial reporting standards and practices as U.S. companies could negatively affect the returns U.S. investors receive from foreign investments.
4. Consider the Fund's allocation of market value of net assets by region. Speculate as to why the proportions of fund assets are distributed in this manner.
5. Consider the Fund's allocation of market value of net assets by country. Identify the countries in which the fund is most heavily invested. Speculate as to why this might be the case. Are there any countries in which you would have expected the fund to be more heavily invested? Are there any countries in which you would have expected the fund to be invested and it is not?

Chapter Two

Worldwide Accounting Diversity

Learning Objectives

After reading this chapter, you should be able to

- Provide evidence of the diversity that exists in accounting internationally.
- Describe the major factors that influence the development of national accounting systems and lead to cross-national accounting diversity.
- Explain the problems caused by accounting diversity.
- Describe attempts to classify countries by financial reporting system.
- Describe a simplified model of the reasons for international differences in financial reporting.
- Categorize accounting differences that exist internationally and provide examples of each type of difference.
- Explain that, internationally, private company financial reporting often differs from financial reporting required of publicly traded companies.

INTRODUCTION

Historically, considerable differences have existed across countries in the preparation and presentation of financial statements. For example, companies in the United States following U.S. generally accepted accounting principles (GAAP) are not allowed to report property, plant, and equipment (PPE) at amounts greater than historical cost. In contrast, companies in the European Union (EU) and other countries using International Financial Reporting Standards (IFRS) may choose to report assets on the balance sheet at either historical cost or fair value. Both U.S. GAAP and Japanese GAAP stipulate that research and development costs must be expensed as incurred, whereas IFRS require development costs to be capitalized as an intangible asset when certain conditions are met. Companies following Chinese accounting standards must use the direct method in preparing the statement of cash flows, whereas most companies in the United States and the EU use the indirect method.

Differences in accounting can result in significantly different amounts being reported on the balance sheet and income statement. In its 2010 Form 20-F annual report filed with the U.S. Securities and Exchange Commission (SEC), the South Korean telecommunications firm SK Telecom Company Ltd. described 19 significant differences between South Korean and U.S. accounting rules. Under South Korean GAAP, SK Telecom reported 2010 net income of 1,297 billion South Korean won (KRW). If SK Telecom had used U.S. GAAP in 2010, its net income would have been KRW 1,397 billion, approximately 8 percent larger than under South Korean GAAP.[1] Shareholders' equity as stated under South Korean GAAP was KRW 12,479 billion but would have been KRW 14,573 billion under U.S. GAAP, a 17 percent difference.[2]

This chapter presents evidence of accounting diversity, explores the reasons for that diversity, and describes the problems that are created by differences in accounting practice across countries. Historically, several major models of accounting have been used internationally, with clusters of countries following them. These also are described and compared in this chapter.

The final section of this chapter categorizes the types of differences in financial reporting that exist across countries and uses excerpts from annual reports to present examples of those differences. It should be noted that much of the financial reporting diversity that existed in the past has been eliminated as countries have abandoned their local GAAP in favor of IFRS issued by the International Accounting Standards Board (IASB).[3] This chapter provides both a historical and a current perspective on accounting diversity that should allow readers to more fully appreciate the international financial reporting convergence efforts described in the next chapter.

EVIDENCE OF ACCOUNTING DIVERSITY

Exhibits 2.1 and 2.2 present consolidated balance sheets for the British company Vodafone Group Plc and its U.S. counterpart Verizon Communications Inc. A quick examination of these statements shows several differences in format and terminology between the United Kingdom and the United States. Perhaps the most obvious difference is the order in which assets are presented. Whereas Verizon presents assets in order of liquidity, beginning with cash and cash equivalents, Vodafone presents assets in reverse order of liquidity, starting with goodwill. On the other side of the balance sheet, Vodafone presents its equity accounts before liabilities. In the equity section, "Called-up share capital" is the equivalent of the "common stock" account on the U.S. balance sheet. Vodafone includes "Provisions," which represent estimated liabilities related to restructurings, legal disputes, and asset retirements, in both current and noncurrent liabilities. This line item does not appear in the U.S. balance sheet. Similar to many British companies, Vodafone includes a column in its balance sheet in which the company indicates the note relating to many of the balance sheet line items. Verizon does not provide similar information in its balance sheet, and it is uncommon for U.S. firms to do so.

As is the norm for U.S. companies, Verizon includes only consolidated financial statements in its annual report. In addition to consolidated financial statements, Vodafone also includes the parent company's separate balance sheet in its annual report. This is shown in Exhibit 2.3. In the parent company balance sheet, investments in subsidiaries are not

[1] As reported in SK Telecom's Form 20-F filed with the U.S. SEC, the largest adjustments from South Korean GAAP to U.S. GAAP related to "scope of consolidation" and the recognition of losses on "currency and interest rate swap."

[2] Note that SK Telecom adopted International Financial Reporting Standards (IFRS) in 2011 and since then has not provided information on a South Korean GAAP or U.S. GAAP basis in its Form 20-F annual report filed with the U.S. SEC.

[3] As will be discussed in Chapter 3, many countries now require publicly traded (that is, stock exchange-listed) companies to use IFRS in preparing their consolidated financial statements. However, many countries continue to have a national GAAP that must be used by private companies in preparing consolidated financial statements, as well as by publicly traded companies in preparing separate parent company financial statements.

EXHIBIT 2.1

VODAFONE GROUP PLC
Consolidated Statement of Financial Position

at 31 March

	Note	31 March 2021 £m	31 March 2020 £m
Noncurrent assets			
Goodwill	10	31,731	31,378
Other intangible assets	10	21,818	22,631
Property, plant, and equipment	11	41,243	40,113
Investments in associates and joint ventures	12	4,670	5,831
Other investments	13	925	792
Deferred tax assets	6	21,569	23,606
Post employment benefits	25	60	590
Trade and other receivables	14	4,777	10,393
		126,793	135,334
Current assets			
Inventory		676	598
Taxation recoverable		434	278
Trade and other receivables	14	10,923	11,724
Other investments	13	9,159	7,089
Cash and cash equivalents	19	5,821	13,557
		27,013	33,246
Assets held for sale	7	1,257	(412)
Total assets		155,063	168,168
Equity			
Called up share capital	18	4,797	4,797
Additional paid-in capital		150,812	152,629
Treasury shares		(6,172)	(7,802)
Accumulated losses		(121,587)	(120,349)
Accumulated other comprehensive income		27,954	32,135
Total attributable to owners of the parent		55,804	61,410
Noncontrolling interests		2,012	1,215
Total equity		57,816	62,625
Noncurrent liabilities			
Borrowings	21	59,272	62,949
Deferred tax liabilities	6	2,095	2,103
Post employment benefits	25	513	438
Provisions	16	1,747	1,479
Trade and other payables	15	4,909	5,189
		68,536	72,158
Current liabilities			
Borrowings	21	8,488	11,976
Financial liabilities under put option arrangements	22	492	1,850
Taxation liabilities		769	787
Provisions	16	892	1,053
Trade and other payables	15	18,070	17,719
		28,711	33,385
Total equity and liabilities		155,063	168,168

EXHIBIT 2.2

VERIZON COMMUNICATIONS INC.
Consolidated Balance Sheets

(dollars in millions, except per share amounts) At December 31	2020	2019
Assets		
Current assets		
Cash and cash equivalents	$ 22,171	$ 2,594
Accounts receivable	25,169	26,162
Less Allowance for credit losses	1,252	—
Less Allowance for doubtful accounts	—	733
Accounts receivable, net (Note 1)	23,917	25,429
Inventories	1,796	1,422
Prepaid expenses and other	6,710	8,028
Total current assets	54,594	37,473
Plant, property, and equipment	279,737	265,734
Less accumulated depreciation	184,904	173,819
Plant, property, and equipment, net	94,833	91,915
Investments in unconsolidated businesses	589	558
Wireless licenses	96,097	95,059
Goodwill	24,773	24,389
Other intangible assets, net	9,143	9,408
Operating lease right of use assets	22,531	22,694
Other assets	13,651	10,141
Total assets	$316,481	$291,727
Liabilities and Equity		
Current liabilities		
Debt maturing within one year	$ 5,889	$ 10,777
Accounts payable and accrued liabilities	20,658	21,806
Current operating lease liabilities	3,485	3,261
Other current liabilities	9,628	9,024
Total current liabilities	39,660	44,868
Long-term debt	123,173	1100,712
Employee benefit obligations	18,657	17,952
Deferred income taxes	35,711	34,703
Non-current operating lease liabilities	18,000	18,393
Other liabilities	12,008	12,264
Total long-term liabilities	207,549	184,024
Equity		
Series preferred stock ($.10 par value; 250,000,000 shares authorized; none issued)	—	—
Common stock ($.10 par value; 6,250,000,000 shares authorized in each period; 4,242,374,240 shares issued in each period)	429	429
Additional paid in capital	13,404	13,419
Retained earnings	60,464	53,147
Accumulated other comprehensive income (loss)	(71)	998
Common stock in treasury, at cost (155,304,088 and 155,605,527 shares outstanding)	(6,719)	(6,820)
Deferred compensation—employee stock ownership plans and other	335	222
Noncontrolling interests	1,430	1,440
Total equity	69,272	62,835
Total liabilities and equity	$316,481	$291,727

EXHIBIT 2.3

VODAFONE GROUP PLC
Company Statement of Financial Position

at 31 March

	Note	2021 £m	2020 £m
Fixed assets			
Shares in Group undertakings	2	**83,385**	83,466
Current assets			
Debtors: amounts falling due after more than one year	3	**3,128**	8,424
Debtors: amounts falling due within one year	3	**164,149**	225,819
Other investments.	4	**3,107**	1,115
Cash at bank and in hand		**586**	188
		170,970	235,546
Creditors: amounts falling due within one year	5	**(162,761)**	(217,322)
Net current assets		**8,209**	18,224
Total assets less current liabilities		**91,594**	101,690
Creditors: amounts falling due after more than one year	5	**(47,122)**	(54,628)
		44,472	47,062
Capital and reserves			
Called up share capital	6	**4,797**	4,797
Share premium account.		**20,383**	20,382
Capital redemption reserve		**111**	111
Other reserves.		**2,970**	4,865
Own shares held.		**(6,307)**	(7,937)
Profit and loss account.		**322,518**	24,844
Total equity shareholders' funds		**44,472**	47,062

consolidated, but instead are reported as *Shares in Group undertakings* in the *Fixed assets* section. Liabilities are called *Creditors,* and receivables are *Debtors.* Note that *Debtors: amounts falling due after more than one year* are included among *Current assets.*

Many differences in terminology exist in the presentation of shareholders' equity (labeled *Capital and reserves*) in the parent company balance sheet. Additional paid-in capital is called *Share premium account,* treasury stock is titled *Own shares held,* and retained earnings are reflected in the line titled *Profit and loss account.* Perhaps most unusual from a U.S. perspective are the *Capital redemption reserve* and *Other reserves* line items. These accounts reflect appropriations of retained earnings and are virtually unknown in the United States. Appropriated retained earnings are restricted for a specific purpose, such as capital redemption, and therefore are not available for the payment of dividends.

From the perspective of U.S. financial reporting, the UK parent company balance sheet has an unusual structure. Rather than the U.S. norm of Assets = Liabilities + Shareholders' equity, Vodafone's parent company balance sheet is presented as Assets − Liabilities = Shareholders' equity. Closer inspection shows that the balance sheet presents the left-hand side of the equation as Noncurrent assets + Net current assets (or Working capital) − Noncurrent liabilities, which is equal to total Shareholders' equity.

All of these superficial differences would probably cause a U.S. financial analyst little problem in analyzing the British company's financial statements. More important than the format and terminology differences are the possible differences in recognition and measurement rules employed to account for assets and liabilities and to determine net income.

As was noted in the introduction to this chapter, very different amounts of net income and stockholders' equity can be reported by a company depending on the accounting rules that it uses. For example, the following chart summarizes results reported by the Colombian petroleum company, Ecopetrol S.A., in its 2014 Form 20-F annual report filed with the U.S. SEC:

(in millions of Colombian pesos)	Colombian GAAP	U.S. GAAP	Percentage Difference
Net income (A)...........................	7,510,270	6,819,550	+ 10.1%
Average shareholders' equity (B)	69,832,587	44,705,918	+ 56.2%
Return on equity (A ÷ B).................	10.8%	15.3%	− 29.5%

Ecopetrol reported 10.1 percent more income and 56.2 percent more equity under Colombian GAAP than under U.S. GAAP.[4] As a result, return on equity calculated from the company's Colombian GAAP results was 29.5 percent smaller than if calculated from the U.S. GAAP amounts. The company disclosed 27 differences between Colombian GAAP and U.S. GAAP that affected the calculation of net income. The single most important difference related to the accounting for changes in foreign currency exchange rates. Financial statement analysts could come to a very different assessment of Ecopetrol's profitability depending on whether they based their analysis on Colombian GAAP or U.S. GAAP information.

REASONS FOR ACCOUNTING DIVERSITY

Why do financial reporting practices differ across countries? Accounting scholars have hypothesized numerous influences on a country's accounting system, including factors as varied as the nature of the political system, the stage of economic development, and the state of accounting education and research. A survey of the relevant literature identified the following five items as being commonly accepted as factors influencing the development of a country's financial reporting practices: (1) legal system, (2) taxation, (3) providers of financing, (4) inflation, and (5) political and economic ties.[5] In addition to economic and institutional determinants, national culture has long been considered a factor that affects the accounting system of a country.[6]

Legal System

There are two major types of legal systems used around the world: common law and codified Roman law. Common law began in England and is primarily found in the English-speaking countries of the world. Common law countries rely on a limited amount of statute law, which is then interpreted by the courts. Court decisions establish precedents, thereby developing case law that supplements the statutes. A system of code law, followed in most non-English-speaking countries, originated in the Roman *jus civile* and was developed further in European universities during the Middle Ages. Code law countries tend to have relatively more statute or codified law governing a wider range of human activity.

What does a country's legal system have to do with accounting? Code law countries generally have corporation law (sometimes called a commercial code or companies act)

[4] Ecopetrol switched to IFRS in 2015 and no longer reports on a Colombian GAAP or U.S. GAAP basis in its Form 20-F.

[5] Gary K. Meek and Sharokh M. Saudagaran, "A Survey of Research on Financial Reporting in a Transnational Context," *Journal of Accounting Literature,* 1990, pp. 145–82.

[6] One of the first to argue that accounting is determined by culture was W. J. Violet in "The Development of International Accounting Standards: An Anthropological Perspective," *International Journal of Accounting,* 1983, pp. 1–12.

that establishes the basic legal parameters governing business enterprises. The corporation law often stipulates which financial statements must be published in accordance with a prescribed format. Additional accounting measurement and disclosure rules are included in an accounting law debated and passed by the national legislature. In countries where accounting rules are legislated, the accounting profession tends to have little influence on the development of accounting standards. In countries with a tradition of common law, although a corporation law laying the basic framework for accounting might exist (such as in the United Kingdom), specific accounting rules are established by the profession or by an independent nongovernmental body representing a variety of constituencies. Thus, the type of legal system in a country tends to determine whether the primary source of accounting rules is the government or a nongovernmental organization.

In *code law* countries, the accounting law tends to be rather general, does not provide much detail regarding specific accounting practices, and may provide no guidance at all in certain areas. Germany is a good example of this type of country. The German accounting law passed in 1985 is only 47 pages long and is silent with regard to issues such as leases, foreign currency translation, and cash flow statements.[7] When no guidance is provided in the law, German companies refer to other sources, including tax law, opinions of the German auditing profession, and standards issued by the German Accounting Standards Committee, to decide how to do their accounting. Interestingly enough, important sources of accounting practice in Germany have been textbooks and commentaries written by accounting academicians.

In *common law* countries, where there is likely to be a nonlegislative organization developing accounting standards, much more detailed rules are developed. The extreme case might be the Financial Accounting Standards Board (FASB) in the United States, which provides a substantial amount of implementation guidance in its accounting standards codification (ASC) and updates and has been accused of producing a "standards overload."

To illustrate this point, consider the rules related to accounting for leases established by the FASB in the United States and in German accounting law. In the United States, a lease must be classified and accounted for as a finance lease or an operating lease. Additional guidance establishes rules for specific situations such as sales with leasebacks and leveraged leases. In contrast, the German accounting law is silent with regard to leases. The only relevant guidance in the law simply states that all liabilities must be recorded.[8]

Taxation

In some countries, published financial statements form the basis for taxation, whereas in other countries, financial statements are adjusted for tax purposes and submitted to the government separately from the reports sent to stockholders. Continuing to focus on Germany, prior to 2009, the principle of reverse conformity (*umgekehrte Massgeblichkeit*) in that country required that, in most cases, an expense deductible for tax purposes must also be used in the calculation of financial statement income. Well-managed German companies attempted to minimize income for tax purposes, for example, through the use of accelerated depreciation, so as to reduce their tax liability. As a result of the reverse conformity principle, accelerated depreciation also had to be recognized in the calculation of accounting income. In 2009, the accounting modernization law (*Bilanzrechtsmodernisierungsgesetz*) removed the reverse conformity requirement, which has reduced the influence that taxation has on financial reporting in Germany.

---

[7] Jermyn Paul Brooks and Dietz Mertin, *Neues Deutsches Bilanzrecht* (Düsseldorf: IDW-Verlag, 1986).

[8] In compliance with EU regulations, Germany requires publicly traded companies to use IFRS to prepare their consolidated financial statements. German accounting law continues to be used by privately held companies and by publicly traded companies in preparing parent company financial statements.

In contrast, general conformity between the tax statement and the financial statements has never been required in the United States.[9] U.S. companies are allowed to use accelerated depreciation for tax purposes and straight-line depreciation in the financial statements. All else being equal, until 2009, because of the influence of the reverse conformity principle, a German company was likely to report lower accounting net income than its U.S. counterpart.

Providers of Financing

The major providers of financing for business enterprises are family members, banks, governments, and shareholders. In those countries in which company financing is dominated by families, banks, or the state, there will be less pressure for public accountability and information disclosure. Banks and the state will often be represented on the board of directors and will therefore be able to obtain information necessary for decision making from inside the company. As companies become more dependent on financing from the general populace through the public offering of shares of stock, however, the demand for more information made available outside the company becomes greater. It simply is not feasible for the company to allow the hundreds, thousands, or hundreds of thousands of shareholders access to internal accounting records. The information needs of those financial statement users can be satisfied only through extensive disclosures in accounting reports.

There can also be a difference in financial statement orientation, with stockholders being more interested in profit (emphasis on the income statement) and banks more interested in solvency and liquidity (emphasis on the balance sheet). Bankers tend to prefer companies to practice rather conservative accounting with regard to assets and liabilities.

Inflation

Historically, countries experiencing chronic high rates of inflation have found it necessary to adopt accounting rules that require the inflation adjustment of historical cost amounts. This has been especially true in Latin America, which as a region has had more inflation than any other part of the world. For example, throughout the 1980s and 1990s, the average annual rate of inflation rate in Mexico was approximately 50 percent, with a high of 159 percent in 1987.[10] Double- and triple-digit inflation rates render historical costs meaningless. Throughout most of the latter half of the 20th century, this factor primarily distinguished Latin America from the rest of the world with regard to accounting.[11] However, inflation has been successfully brought under control in most countries, and this factor is no longer as important in explaining accounting diversity as it once was.

Adjusting accounting records for inflation results in a write-up of nonmonetary assets (inventory, intangibles, and property, plant, and equipment), with a corresponding increase in expenses related to those assets (cost-of-goods-sold, amortization, and depreciation expenses). Adjusting income for inflation was especially important in those countries in which accounting statements served as the basis for taxation; otherwise, companies would have paid taxes on fictitious profits.

Political and Economic Ties

Accounting is a technology that can be relatively easily borrowed from or imposed on another country. Through political and economic links, accounting rules have been

---

[9] An exception is the so-called "LIFO conformity rule," which stipulates that if the last-in-first-out (LIFO) cost flow method is used to determine taxable income, it must also be used in the financial statements.

[10] Joseph B. Lipscomb and Harold Hunt, "Mexican Mortgages: Structure and Default Incentives, Historical Simulation 1982–1998," *Journal of Housing Research* 10, no. 2 (1999), pp. 235–65.

[11] Mexico continued its use of inflation accounting until 2007.

conveyed from one country to another. For example, through previous colonialism, both England and France have transferred their accounting frameworks to a variety of countries around the world. British-style accounting systems can be found in countries as far-flung as Australia and Zimbabwe. French accounting is prevalent in the former French colonies of western Africa. Perhaps the most striking example of political and economic ties influencing accounting across countries is the adoption of IFRS for publicly traded companies in the 27 countries comprising the European Union.

Correlation of Factors

Whether by coincidence or not, there is a relatively high degree of correlation between legal system, tax conformity, and source of financing. As Exhibit 2.4 shows, common law countries tend to have greater numbers of domestic listed companies per capita than code law countries. This indicates a greater usage of equity as a source of financing in common law countries. Code law countries tend to link taxation to accounting statements, whereas common law countries do not.

National Culture

Using responses to an attitude survey of IBM employees worldwide, Hofstede identified four cultural dimensions that can be used to describe general similarities and differences in cultures around the world: (1) individualism versus collectivism, (2) power distance (high vs low), (3) uncertainty avoidance (high vs low), and (4) competitiveness versus cooperativeness.[12] *Individualism* refers to a preference for a loosely knit social fabric rather than a tightly knit social fabric (*collectivism*). *Power distance* refers to the extent to which hierarchy and unequal power distribution in institutions and organizations are accepted. *Uncertainty avoidance* refers to the degree to which individuals feel uncomfortable with uncertainty and ambiguity. *Competitiveness* refers to an emphasis on values like performance and achievement rather than values like relationships, caring, and nurturing (*cooperativeness*). More recently, two additional cultural dimensions were added: long-term orientation versus short-term orientation and indulgence versus restraint.[13] *Long-term orientation* relates to an emphasis on persistence rather than an emphasis on quick results (*short-term orientation*). *Indulgence* relates to satisfying human needs and desires versus curbing one's desires and withholding pleasures (*restraint*).

EXHIBIT 2.4
Relationship between Several Factors Influencing Accounting Diversity

Source: Number of domestic listed companies and country populations obtained from IndexMundi, www.indexmundi.com.

| Country | Legal System | Domestic Listed Companies | | Tax Conformity |
		Number	Per Million of Population	
Germany	Code	555	6.9	Yes
France	Code	490	7.3	Yes
Japan	Code	3,504	27.7	Yes
United Kingdom	Common	1,858	45.6	No
Australia	Common	1,989	86.5	No
Canada	Common	3,799	107.3	No

[12] G. Hofstede, *Culture's Consequences: International Differences in Work-Related Values* (London: Sage, 1980). Hofstede originally called the fourth cultural dimension *masculinity* (vs femininity), but in the interest of clarity, this text uses the term *competitiveness* (vs cooperativeness).

[13] See G. Hofstede, G.J. Hofstede, and M. Minkov, *Cultures and Organizations: Software of the Mind,* 3rd ed. (New York: McGraw-Hill, 2010).

Accounting Values

From a review of accounting literature and practice, Gray identified four widely recognized accounting values that can be used to define a country's accounting subculture: professionalism, uniformity, conservatism, and secrecy.[14] These accounting values and their opposites can be described as follows:

Professionalism is a preference for the exercise of individual professional judgment in making financial reporting decisions. In contrast, *Statutory Control* is a preference for compliance with prescriptive legal requirements.

Uniformity is a preference for the use of uniform accounting practices across companies. In contrast, *Flexibility* allows for differences in accounting practices across companies to accommodate the specific circumstances of individual companies.

Conservatism is a preference for a cautious approach to accounting measurement. Delaying recognition of assets and income until they are virtually certain, but recognizing liabilities and expense as soon as they are deemed to be probable is consistent with conservatism. In contrast, *Optimism* refers to a more optimistic, risk-taking approach to accounting measurement.

Secrecy is a preference for disclosure of company information only to its management and providers of financing. Providing limited disclosure in notes to financial statements is consistent with secrecy. In contrast, *Transparency* refers to a more transparent approach, with an emphasis on full disclosure to the public at large.

Gray argues that national cultural values affect accounting values, as shown in Exhibit 2.5.

The accounting values of conservatism and secrecy have the greatest relevance for the information content of a set of financial statements. The relationship between culture and each of these two accounting values can be explained as follows.

Conservatism is thought to be most heavily influenced by strong uncertainty avoidance and short-term orientation. Strong uncertainty avoidance leads to a more conservative approach to measurement of income and assets because of a concern with security "and a perceived need to adopt a cautious approach to cope with uncertainty of future events."[15] Short-term orientation results in an expectation of quick results and leads to a less conservative approach to income and asset measurement.

Secrecy is thought to be consistent with strong uncertainty avoidance, high power distance, collectivism, and long-term orientation. Withholding information reduces the

EXHIBIT 2.5
Relationships between Accounting Values and Cultural Dimensions

Source: Adapted from Lee H. Radebaugh and Sidney J. Gray, *International Accounting and Multinational Enterprises,* 5th ed. (New York: Wiley, 2001), p. 49. The relationships posited in this exhibit predate the addition of indulgence as one of Hoftstede's cultural dimensions.

Cultural Dimension	Accounting Values			
	Professionalism	**Uniformity**	**Conservatism**	**Secrecy**
Power distance	Neg.	Pos.	n/a	Pos.
Uncertainty avoidance	Neg.	Pos.	Pos.	Pos.
Individualism	Pos.	Neg.	Neg.	Neg.
Competitiveness	Pos.	n/a	Neg.	Neg.
Long-term orientation	Neg.	n/a	Pos.	Pos.

Pos. = Positive relationship hypothesized between cultural dimension and accounting value.
Neg. = Negative relationship hypothesized between cultural dimension and accounting value.
n/a = No relationship hypothesized.

[14] S. J. Gray, "Towards a Theory of Cultural Influence on the Development of Accounting Systems Internationally," *Abacus,* March 1988, pp. 1–15.

[15] Lee H. Radebaugh and Sidney J. Gray, *International Accounting and Multinational Enterprises,* 5th ed. (New York: Wiley, 2001), p. 47.

likelihood of conflict among stakeholders and reduces uncertainty. It also helps maintain power inequalities, which is consistent with high power distance. Secrecy also is thought to be consistent with collectivism "in that its concern is for the interests of those closely involved with the firm rather than external parties. A long-term orientation also suggests a preference for secrecy that is consistent with the need to conserve resources within the firm and ensure that funds are available for investment relative to the demands of shareholders and employees for higher payments."[16]

Gray's Cultural Accounting Framework

Gray extended Hofstede's model of cultural patterns to develop a framework that identifies the mechanism through which culture influences the development of corporate financial reporting systems on a national level. According to this framework (shown in Exhibit 2.6), the particular way in which a country's accounting system develops is influenced by accountants' accounting values and the country's institutional framework, both of which are influenced by cultural dimensions. Thus, culture is viewed as affecting accounting systems indirectly in two ways: through its influence on accounting values and through its institutional consequences.

Using measures of each of the cultural values for a group of more than 40 countries, Hofstede classified those countries into 10 different cultural areas. A group of countries

EXHIBIT 2.6   **Framework for the Development of Accounting Systems**

Source: Adapted from S. J. Gray, "Towards a Theory of Cultural Influence on the Development of Accounting Systems Internationally," *Abacus,* March 1988, p. 7.

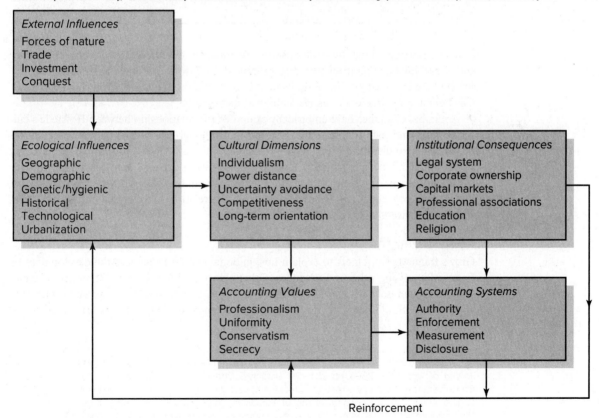

[16] Lee H. Radebaugh and Sidney J. Gray, *International Accounting and Multinational Enterprises,* 5th ed. (New York: Wiley, 2001), p. 48.

that includes Australia, Canada, the United Kingdom, and the United States, for example, is characterized by high individualism, low uncertainty avoidance, low power distance, and moderate competitiveness. Given this pattern of cultural values, Gray hypothesized that this group of countries would rank relatively low on the accounting values of conservatism and secrecy (or high on optimism and high on transparency). Exhibiting the opposite pattern of cultural values, a group of countries that includes Chile, Colombia, Mexico, Panama, Portugal, and Venezuela was hypothesized to rank relatively high in conservatism and secrecy. On a scale of 1 (low secrecy) to 7 (high secrecy) and a scale of 1 (low conservatism) to 5 (high conservatism), the different cultural areas were ranked as follows:

Countries in Different Cultural Areas	Secrecy	Conservatism
Australia, Canada, Ireland, New Zealand, South Africa, United Kingdom, United States	1	1
Denmark, Finland, Netherlands, Norway, Sweden	2	2
Hong Kong, Singapore	2	3
East Africa, West Africa	3	4
Belgium, France, Italy, Spain, Argentina, Brazil	3	5
India, Indonesia, Malaysia, Pakistan, Philippines, Taiwan, Thailand	4	4
Japan	5	5
Arab countries, Greece, Iran, Turkey, Yugoslavia	5	5
Austria, Germany, Israel, Switzerland	6	4
Chile, Colombia, Costa Rica, Ecuador, El Salvador, Guatemala, Mexico, Panama, Peru, Portugal, Uruguay, Venezuela	7	5

These rankings show the strong positive relationship expected to exist between secrecy and conservatism. Countries that require limited disclosures in financial statements (high secrecy) are expected to more strictly adhere to the notion of conservatism (high conservatism) in the measurement of assets, liabilities, and income.

A number of studies have empirically examined the relationship between Hofstede's cultural values and national accounting systems.[17] Although the results of this research are mixed, most studies find a relationship between cultural values and disclosure (secrecy) consistent with Gray's hypothesis. However, these studies are unable to determine whether culture influences disclosure through its effect on accounting values or through its effect on institutional consequences. Research results on the relationship between culture and measurement (conservatism) are less conclusive.

Modified Gray Framework

Gray's framework attempts to explain how national culture influences the development of financial reporting rules and practices. Others have modified Gray's framework to argue that culture not only influences accounting rules but also the manner in which accountants apply those rules.[18] According to this partial refinement of Gray's framework, accountants

[17] See, for example, Joseph J. Schultz and Thomas J. Lopez, "The Impact of National Influence on Accounting Estimates: Implications for International Accounting Standard-Setters," The *International Journal of Accounting*, 2001, pp. 271–90; Timothy S. Doupnik and Edson L. Riccio, "The Influence of Conservatism and Secrecy on the Interpretation of Verbal Probability Expressions in the Anglo and Latin Cultural Areas," The *International Journal of Accounting*, 2006, pp. 237–61; and George T. Tsakumis, "The Influence of Culture on Accountants' Application of Financial Reporting Rules," *Abacus*, 2007, pp. 27–48.

[18] George T. Tsakumis, "The Influence of Culture on Accountants' Application of Financial Reporting Rules," *Abacus*, 2007, pp. 27–48.

are expected to apply financial reporting rules in a fashion consistent with their cultural values. As a result, accountants' financial reporting decisions should differ between countries because of differences in the cultural values of the accountants applying the rules. This is especially true for those financial reporting decisions that require the application of judgment.

Several research studies also have empirically examined the relationship between cultural values and accountants' financial reporting decisions in situations in which professional judgment must be applied.[19] Decisions studied include the estimation of warranty expense and assessing the probability of a future liability. Although the results of this research also are somewhat mixed, most studies do find a relationship between cultural values and the manner in which accountants apply accounting rules that is consistent with the modified Gray model. This suggests that differences in cultural values across countries could result in differences in financial reporting across countries even if a common set of financial reporting standards is being used internationally.

PROBLEMS CAUSED BY ACCOUNTING DIVERSITY

Preparation of Consolidated Financial Statements

The diversity in accounting practice that has historically existed across countries causes problems that can be quite serious for some parties. One problem relates to the preparation of consolidated financial statements by companies with foreign operations. Consider General Motors Corporation, which has subsidiaries in more than 50 countries around the world. Each subsidiary incorporated in the country in which it is located is required to prepare financial statements in accordance with local regulations. These regulations usually require companies to keep books in local currency using local accounting principles. Thus, General Motors de Mexico prepares financial statements in Mexican pesos using Mexican accounting rules, and General Motors Japan Ltd. prepares financial statements in Japanese yen using Japanese accounting standards. To prepare consolidated financial statements in the United States, in addition to translating the foreign currency financial statements into U.S. dollars, the parent company must also convert the financial statements of its foreign operations into U.S. GAAP. Either each foreign operation must maintain two sets of books prepared in accordance with both local and U.S. GAAP or, as is more common, reconciliations from local GAAP to U.S. GAAP must be made at the balance sheet date. In either case, considerable effort and cost are involved; company personnel must develop an expertise in more than one country's accounting standards.

Access to Foreign Capital Markets

A second problem caused by accounting diversity relates to companies gaining access to foreign capital markets. If a company desires to obtain capital by selling stock or borrowing money in a foreign country, it might be required to present a set of financial statements prepared in accordance with the accounting standards in the country in which the capital is

---

[19] See, for example, Joseph J. Schultz and Thomas J. Lopez, "The Impact of National Influence on Accounting Estimates: Implications for International Accounting Standard-Setters," *The International Journal of Accounting,* 2001, pp. 271–90; Timothy S. Doupnik and Martin Richter, "The Impact of Culture on the Interpretation of 'In Context' Verbal Probability Expressions," *Journal of International Accounting Research* 3, no. 1 (2004), pp. 1-20; Timothy S. Doupnik and Edson L. Riccio, "The Influence of Conservatism and Secrecy on the Interpretation of Verbal Probability Expressions in the Anglo and Latin Cultural Areas," *The International Journal of Accounting,* 2006, pp. 237–61; and George T. Tsakumis, "The Influence of Culture on Accountants' Application of Financial Reporting Rules," *Abacus,* 2007, pp. 27–48.

being obtained. Consider the case of the semiconductor manufacturer STMicroelectronics, which is based in Geneva, Switzerland. The company's common shares are listed on the Euronext Paris and Borsa Italiana stock exchanges in Europe and on the New York Stock Exchange (NYSE) in the United States. Historically, to have stock traded in the United States, foreign companies were required to either prepare financial statements using U.S. accounting standards or provide a reconciliation of local GAAP net income and stockholders' equity to U.S. GAAP.

Reconciliation from one set of GAAP to another can be quite costly. In preparing for a New York Stock Exchange listing in 1993, the German automaker Daimler-Benz estimated it spent $60 million to initially prepare U.S. GAAP financial statements, and it expected to spend $15 million to $20 million each year thereafter.[20] The appendix to this chapter describes the case of Daimler-Benz in becoming the first German company to list on the NYSE.[21] As noted in Chapter 1, in 2008, the U.S. SEC eliminated the U.S. GAAP reconciliation requirement for those foreign companies using IFRS to prepare their financial statements. However, foreign companies not using IFRS continue to be required to provide U.S. GAAP information.

Comparability of Financial Statements

A third problem caused by accounting diversity relates to the diminished comparability of financial statements between companies that use different GAAP. This can significantly affect the analysis of foreign financial statements for making investment and lending decisions. There has been an explosion in mutual funds that invest in the stock of foreign companies. As an example, the number of international stock mutual funds increased from 123 in 1989 to 534 by the end of 1995.[22] T. Rowe Price's New Asia Fund, for example, invests exclusively in stocks and bonds of companies located in Asian countries other than Japan. The job of deciding in which foreign companies to invest is complicated by the fact that foreign companies use accounting rules that differ from those used in the United States, and that those rules can differ from country to country. Historically, it was very difficult if not impossible for a potential investor to directly compare the financial position and performance of an automobile manufacturer in Germany (e.g., Volkswagen), Italy (e.g., Fiat), and the United States (e.g., Ford) because these three countries had different financial accounting and reporting standards. This problem has been partially resolved by Germany and Italy through their adoption of IFRS for publicly traded companies. However, comparability issues between German and Italian companies that use IFRS and U.S. companies that use U.S. GAAP continue to exist.

A lack of comparability of financial statements also can have an adverse effect on corporations when making foreign acquisition decisions. As a case in point, consider the experience of foreign investors in Eastern Europe. After the fall of the Berlin Wall in 1989, Western companies were invited to acquire newly privatized companies in Poland, Hungary, and other countries in the former communist bloc. The concepts of profit and accounting for assets in those countries under communism were so different from accounting practice in the West that most Western investors found financial statements useless in helping to determine which enterprises were the most attractive acquisition targets. In many cases, the international public accounting firms were called on to convert financial statements to a Western basis before acquisition of a company could be seriously considered.

---

[20] Allan B. Afterman, *International Accounting, Financial Reporting, and Analysis* (New York: Warren, Gorham & Lamont, 1995), pp. C1-17, C1-22. Note that Daimler-Benz is now called Daimler.

[21] Note that Daimler-Benz, which is now called Daimler, dropped its NYSE listing in 2010.

[22] James L. Cochrane, James E. Shapiro, and Jean E. Tobin, "Foreign Equities and U.S. Investors: Breaking Down the Barriers Separating Supply and Demand," NYSE Working Paper 95–04, 1995.

There was a very good reason why accounting in the communist countries of Eastern Europe and the Soviet Union was so different from accounting in capitalist countries. Financial statements in those countries were not prepared for the benefit of investors and creditors to be used in making investment and lending decisions. Instead, financial statements were prepared to provide the government with information to determine whether the central economic plan was being fulfilled. Financial statements prepared for central planning purposes had limited value in making investment decisions.

Lack of High-Quality Accounting Information

A fourth problem associated with accounting diversity was the lack of high-quality accounting standards in some parts of the world. There is general agreement that the failure of many banks in the 1997 East Asian financial crisis was due to three factors: a highly leveraged corporate sector, the private sector's reliance on foreign currency debt, and a lack of accounting transparency.[23] To be sure, inadequate disclosure did not create the East Asian meltdown, but it did contribute to the depth and breadth of the crisis. International investors and creditors were unable to adequately assess risk because financial statements did not reflect the extent of risk exposure due to the following disclosure deficiencies:

- The actual magnitude of debt was hidden by undisclosed related party transactions and off-balance-sheet financing.
- High levels of exposure to foreign exchange risk were not evident.
- Information on the extent to which investments and loans were made in highly speculative assets (such as real estate) was not available.
- Contingent liabilities for guaranteeing loans, often foreign currency loans, were not reported.
- Appropriate disclosures regarding loan loss provisions were not made.

Because of the problems associated with worldwide accounting diversity, attempts to reduce the accounting differences across countries began in earnest in the 1960s. The ultimate goal is to have all countries converge on a single set of international accounting standards that are followed by all companies around the world. International convergence of financial reporting is the major topic of Chapter 3.

CLASSIFICATION OF ACCOUNTING SYSTEMS

Given the discussion regarding factors influencing accounting practice worldwide, it should not be surprising to learn that historically there were clusters of countries that shared a common accounting orientation and practices. One classification scheme identified three major accounting models: the Fair Presentation/Full Disclosure Model, the Legal Compliance Model, and the Inflation-Adjusted Model.[24] The Fair Presentation/Full Disclosure Model (also known as the Anglo-Saxon or Anglo-American model) described the approach used in the United Kingdom and the United States, where accounting is oriented toward the decision needs of large numbers of investors and creditors. This model was used in most English-speaking countries and other countries heavily influenced by the United Kingdom

---

[23] M. Zubaidur Rahman, "The Role of Accounting in the East Asian Financial Crisis: Lessons Learned?" *Transnational Corporations* 7, no. 3 (December 1998), pp. 1–52.

[24] Helen Gernon and Gary Meek, *Accounting: An International Perspective,* 5th ed. (Burr Ridge, IL: Irwin/McGraw-Hill, 2001), pp. 10–11.

or the United States. Most of these countries follow a common law legal system. The Legal Compliance Model originated in the code law countries of Continental Europe and is sometimes referred to as the Continental European model. It was used by most of Europe, Japan, and other code law countries. Companies in this group usually were tied closely to banks that served as the primary suppliers of financing. Because these are code law countries, accounting was legalistic and designed to provide information for taxation or government-planning purposes. The Inflation-Adjusted Model was found primarily in South America. It resembled the Continental European model in its legalistic, tax, and government-planning orientation. It distinguished itself, however, through the extensive use of adjustments for inflation.

A Judgmental Classification of Financial Reporting Systems

Concentrating on the Anglo-Saxon and Continental European model countries, Nobes developed a more refined classification scheme in the early 1980s that attempted to show how the financial reporting systems in 14 developed countries relate to one another.[25] Exhibit 2.7 presents an adaptation of Nobes's classification.

The terms *micro-based* and *macro-uniform* in Nobes's classification describe the Anglo-Saxon and Continental European models, respectively. Each of these classes is divided into two subclasses that are further divided into families. Within the micro-based class of accounting systems, there is a subclass heavily influenced by business economics and accounting theory. The Netherlands is the only country in this subclass. One manifestation of the influence of theory is that Dutch companies historically were permitted to use current replacement cost accounting to value assets in their primary financial statements. The other micro-based subclass, of British origin, is more pragmatic and is oriented toward business practice, relying less on economic theory in the development of accounting rules. The British-origin subclass is further split into two families, one dominated by the United Kingdom and one dominated by the United States.

On the macro-uniform side of the classification, a "government, economics" subclass has only one country, Sweden. Swedish accounting distinguished itself from the other macro-uniform countries in being closely aligned with national economic policies. The "continental: government, tax, legal" subclass primarily contains Continental European countries. This subclass is further divided into two families. Led by Germany, the law-based family includes Japan. The tax-based family consists of several Romance-language countries. The major difference between these families is that the accounting law is the primary determinant of accounting practice in Germany and Japan, whereas the tax law dominates in the Southern European countries.

The importance of this hierarchical model is that it showed the comparative distances between countries and could be used as a blueprint for determining where financial statement comparability was likely to be greater. For example, comparisons of financial statements between the United States and Canada (which are in the same family) were likely to be more valid than comparisons between the United States and the United Kingdom (which are not in the same family). However, financial statements from the United States and the United Kingdom (which are in the same subclass) were more comparable than statements from the United States and the Netherlands (which are in different subclasses). Finally, comparisons between the United States and the Netherlands (which are in the same class) might be more meaningful than comparisons between the United States and any of the macro-uniform countries.

---

[25] Christopher W. Nobes, "A Judgemental International Classification of Financial Reporting Practices," *Journal of Business Finance and Accounting,* Spring 1983.

EXHIBIT 2.7
Nobes's Judgmental Classification of Financial Reporting Systems

Source: Adapted from Christopher W. Nobes, "A Judgemental International Classification of Financial Reporting Practices," *Journal of Business Finance and Accounting,* Spring 1983, p. 7.

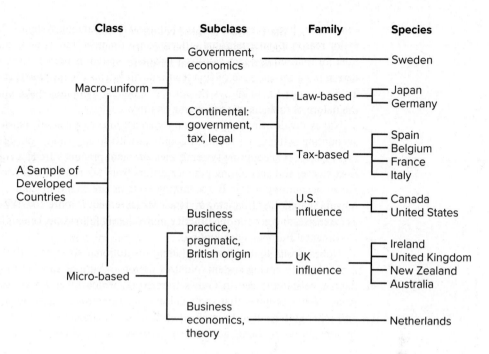

Empirical Test of the Judgmental Classification

The judgmental classification in Exhibit 2.7 was empirically tested in 1990.[26] Data gathered on 100 financial reporting practices in 50 countries (including the 14 countries in Exhibit 2.7) were analyzed using the statistical procedure of hierarchical cluster analysis. The clusters of countries arising from the statistical analysis clearly indicated the existence of two significantly different classes of accounting systems and were generally consistent with the classes, subclasses, and families of Nobes's classification.

The two classes of accounting differed significantly on 66 of the 100 financial reporting practices examined. Differences existed for 41 of the 56 disclosure practices studied. In all but one case, the micro class of countries provided a higher level of disclosure than the macro class of countries. There were also significant differences for 25 of the 44 practices examined affecting income measurement. Of particular importance is the item asking whether accounting practice adhered to tax requirements. The mean level of agreement with this statement among macro countries was 72 percent, whereas it was only 45 percent among micro countries. To summarize, companies in the micro-based countries provide more extensive disclosure than do companies in the macro-uniform countries, and companies in the macro countries are more heavily influenced by taxation than are companies in the micro countries. These results are consistent with the relative importance of equity finance and the relatively weak link between accounting and taxation in the micro countries.

A SIMPLIFIED MODEL OF THE REASONS FOR INTERNATIONAL DIFFERENCES IN FINANCIAL REPORTING

Sifting through the many reasons that have been hypothesized to affect international differences in financial reporting, Nobes subsequently developed a simplified model with two

[26] Timothy S. Doupnik and Stephen B. Salter, "An Empirical Test of a Judgemental International Classification of Financial Reporting Practices," *Journal of International Business Studies,* First Quarter 1993, pp. 41–60.

explanatory factors: culture and the nature of the financing system.[27] Nobes argued that the major reason for international differences in financial reporting is that different purposes exist for that reporting. A country's financing system is seen as the most relevant factor in determining the purpose of financial reporting. Specifically, whether or not a country has a strong equity financing system with large numbers of outside shareholders will determine the nature of financial reporting in a country.

Nobes divides financial reporting systems into two classes, labeled A and B. Class A accounting systems are found in countries with strong equity–outside shareholder financing. In Class A accounting systems, measurement practices are less conservative, disclosure is extensive, and accounting practice differs from tax rules. Class A corresponds to Anglo-Saxon accounting. Class B accounting systems are found in countries with weak equity-outside shareholder financing systems. Measurement is more conservative, disclosure is not as extensive, and accounting practice more closely follows tax rules. Class B corresponds to Continental European accounting.

Nobes posits that culture, including institutional structures, determines the nature of a country's financing system. Nobes's notion of culture appears to go beyond the rather narrow definition used in Gray's framework, which relies on Hofstede's cultural dimensions. Nobes assumes that some cultures lead to strong equity-outsider financing systems and other cultures lead to weak equity-outsider financing systems. His simplified model of reasons for international accounting differences is as follows:

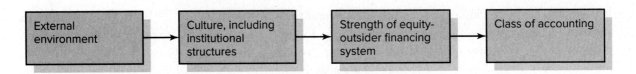

This model can be further refined as follows:

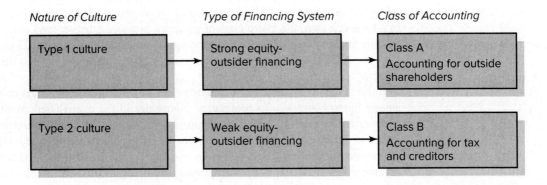

Many countries in the developing world are culturally influenced by another country, often as a result of European colonialism. Nobes argues that culturally influenced countries use the accounting system of their influencing country regardless of the nature of the equity financing system. Thus, countries with a Type 1 culture as well as countries culturally influenced by a Type 1 culture country use Class A accounting systems.

---

[27] Christopher W. Nobes, "Towards a General Model of the Reasons for International Differences in Financial Reporting," *Abacus,* September 1998, p. 166.

Examples of Countries with Class A Accounting

The United Kingdom is a Type 1 culture country with a strong equity-outsider system. It has an outside shareholder-oriented Class A accounting system. New Zealand is culturally influenced by the United Kingdom. It also has a strong equity-outsider financing system, probably because of the influence of British culture. New Zealand also has a Class A accounting system. According to Nobes's model, this can be the result of New Zealand's being culturally influenced by the United Kingdom (a Type 1 culture country), having a strong equity-outsider financing system, or both. The African nation of Malawi has a weak equity-outsider financing system, but as a former British colony (culturally influenced by the United Kingdom), it has adopted a Class A accounting system.

Nobes further suggests that as the financing system in a country evolves from weak outside equity to strong outside equity, the accounting system also evolves in the direction of Class A accounting. He cites China as an example. Finally, Nobes argues that individual companies with strong outside equity financing will attempt to use Class A accounting even if they are located in a Class B accounting system country. He cites the German firms Deutsche Bank and Bayer and the Swiss company Nestlé as examples.

Accounting Change in Europe

The simplified model appears to explain accounting developments that occurred in Europe during the 1990s and 2000s. Because of the desire for companies to be competitive in attracting international equity investment, several European countries (with Class B accounting systems) developed a two-tiered financial reporting system in the late 1990s. Austria, France, Germany, Italy, and Switzerland gave stock exchange–listed companies the option to use IFRS, a Class A accounting system, in preparing their consolidated financial statements.[28] The parent company statements, which serve as the basis for taxation, continued to be prepared using local accounting rules. Large numbers of German and Swiss companies (including Deutsche Bank, Bayer, and Nestlé), in particular, availed themselves of this opportunity to use IFRS.

This desire for companies to be competitive in the international capital market ultimately led the European Commission in 2005 to require all publicly traded companies within the EU to use IFRS in preparing consolidated financial statements. Thus, it is no longer appropriate to think in terms of all German (or all French, all Italian, etc.) companies following the traditional Continental European model of accounting. Publicly traded companies in the EU now use a set of accounting standards based upon the Anglo-Saxon model of accounting in preparing their consolidated statements. However, in most cases, privately held companies in the EU continue to use local GAAP, as do publicly traded companies in preparing parent company financial statements. In these countries, accountants need to develop an expertise in both local GAAP and IFRS; the vast majority of companies in the EU, which are not publicly traded, continue to use local GAAP.

FURTHER EVIDENCE OF ACCOUNTING DIVERSITY

In this section, we provide additional anecdotal evidence of some of the differences in financial reporting that continue to exist across countries. The examples in this section are taken from the consolidated financial statements of publicly traded companies, that is, companies

---

[28] IFRS are issued by the International Accounting Standards Board and are discussed in more detail in Chapters 4 and 5.

whose equity shares are listed on a stock exchange. We categorize accounting differences in the following manner and provide examples of each:

1. Differences in the financial statements included in an annual report.
2. Differences in the format used to present individual financial statements.
3. Differences in the level of detail provided in the financial statements.
4. Differences in terminology.
5. Differences in disclosure.
6. Differences in recognition and measurement.

We illustrate these differences by considering a typical set of U.S. financial statements as a point of reference.

Financial Statements

U.S. companies are required to include an income statement, a balance sheet, a statement of cash flows, a statement of changes in equity, and explanatory notes in a set of financial statements. The income statement must report net income, as well as other comprehensive income; alternatively, an income statement and separate statement of comprehensive income may be presented. IFRS have similar requirements with regard to what must be included in a set of financial statements.

Along with a balance sheet, income statement, cash flow statement, and statement of equity, the Austrian construction firm Strabag SE includes a "statement of changes in noncurrent assets" as one of its primary financial statements. This statement provides detail on the change during the year in the historical cost of noncurrent intangible assets, noncurrent tangible assets, and investment property. Financial statements prepared by German companies also often include a statement of changes in noncurrent assets.

In addition to providing the financial statements required by IFRS, the Brazilian mining company Vale SA includes a *Value Added Statement* in its annual report (see Exhibit 2.8). The top portion of this statement provides a calculation of *Total value added to be distributed.* It begins with *Gross revenue,* to which various other items are added and from which a variety of what appear to be expenses are subtracted. Although this portion of the value added statement appears to calculate an amount similar to net income, this is not the case. Whereas Vale reports *Total value added to be distributed* of 76,876 million Brazilian reais (BRL) in 2020, the income statement reports *Net income* as only BRL 26,713 million.

The lower portion of the *Value Added Statement* indicates how the *Total value added* is distributed and provides some insight into the groups that benefit most from the company's existence. Employees (*Personnel and charges*) received BRL 9,366 million of the value added in 2020, whereas financial institutions (*Interest*) received BRL 29,979 million. Stockholders received none of the value added in 2020. Instead, BRL 26,713 million of total value added was reinvested in the company. In addition, BRL 12,042 million of the value added created by the company went to the government (*Taxes and contributions*).

Format of Financial Statements

U.S. companies list assets and liabilities on the balance sheet in order of liquidity, from most liquid (Cash) to least liquid (often Intangible Assets). The same is generally true in Canada, Mexico, and Japan. Companies in many other countries (including most of Europe) list assets and liabilities in reverse order of liquidity. An example was presented in Exhibit 2.1 for the British company Vodafone.[29]

[29] Note that neither U.S. GAAP nor IFRS (used by Vodafone) stipulates the order in which assets and liabilities are to be presented in the balance sheet. By tradition, U.S. companies report assets in order of liquidity and, by tradition, British companies do the opposite.

EXHIBIT 2.8

VALE SA
Value Added Statement

In millions of Brazilian Reais	Year ended December 31	
	Consolidated	
	2020	2019
Generation of value added		
Gross revenue		
Revenue from products and services	210,108	149,982
Revenue from the construction of own assets	6,064	6,584
Other revenues	2,101	725
Less:		
Cost of products, goods and services sold	(28,250)	(22,780)
Material, energy, third-party services and other	(40,000)	(36,475)
Impairment of non-current assets and others results	(11,819)	(20,762)
Brumadinho event	(27,016)	(28,818)
Other costs and expenses	(18,398)	(11,460)
Gross value added	**92,790**	**36,996**
Depreciation, amortization, and depletion	(16,679)	(14,751)
Net value added	**76,111**	**22,245**
Received from third parties		
Equity results from entities	(5,436)	(2,684)
Financial income	6,201	3,505
Total value added to be distributed	**76,876**	**23,066**
Personnel and charges	9,336	8,183
Taxes and contributions	12,042	4,540
Interest (net derivatives and monetary and exchange rate variation)	29,979	16,702
Other remunerations of third party funds	616	2,338
Reinvested net income (absorbed loss)	26,713	(6,672)
Loss attributable to noncontrolling interest	(1,810)	(2,025)
Distributed value added	**76,876**	**23,066**

In the income statement format commonly used by U.S. companies, sales revenue and cost of goods sold (or cost of sales) are generally reported as separate line items, the difference being gross profit. Callaway Golf Company's income statement, presented in Exhibit 2.9, illustrates the format often used by U.S.-based companies. Cost of sales includes manufacturing costs (materials, labor, and overhead) related to those goods sold during the year. In addition to cost of sales, selling expenses, general and administrative expense, research and development expense, and goodwill and trade name impairment are subtracted to calculate operate income (or income from operations). Other than impairment, each of these operating expense line items also includes costs related to materials (including supplies), labor, and overhead. For example, research and development (R&D) expenses include compensation paid to R&D staff, supplies used in R&D, and depreciation and amortization on R&D assets.

In contrast to the cost of goods sold format income statement commonly found in the United States, many European companies present their income statement using a *type of expenditure* format. An example is presented in Exhibit 2.10 for Südzucker AG, a German sugar manufacturer. Rather than presenting cost of goods sold (or cost of sales) as a single line item, Südzucker presents separate line items for cost of materials, personnel expenses, and depreciation. The line item *Personnel expenses* aggregates the total amount of personnel cost incurred by the company. In contrast, Callaway Golf allocates personnel costs to the

EXHIBIT 2.9

CALLAWAY GOLF COMPANY
Consolidated Statements of Operations

(In thousands, except per share data)

	Year Ended December 31,		
	2020	2019	2018
Net sales	$1,589,460	$1,701,063	$1,242,834
Cost of sales	931,875	934,276	664,465
Gross profit	657,585	766,787	578,369
Operating expenses:			
Selling expenses	391,815	438,238	308,709
General and administrative expenses	150,716	145,302	100,466
Research and development expenses	46,300	50,579	40,752
Goodwill and trade name impairment	174,269	—	—
Total operating expenses	763,100	634,119	449,927
(Loss) income from operations	(105,515)	132,668	128,442
Interest income	492	807	594
Interest expense	(47,424)	(39,300)	(5,543)
Other income, net	24,969	1,594	7,779
(Loss) income before income taxes	(127,478)	95,769	131,272
Income tax (benefit) provision	(544)	16,540	26,018
Net income	126,934	79,229	105,254
Less: Net (loss) income attributable to non-controlling interests	—	(179)	514
Net (loss) income attributable to Callaway Golf Company	$ 189,900	$ 79,408	$ 104,740
Earnings per common share:			
Basic	$ 2.02	$ 0.18	$ 0.21
Diluted	$ 1.98	$ 0.17	$ 0.20
Weighted-average common shares outstanding			
Basic	94,045	83,116	77,559
Diluted	95,845	84,611	78,385

EXHIBIT 2.10

SÜDZUCKER AG
Statement of Comprehensive Income

1 March 2020 to 28 February 2021

€ million	Notes	2020/21	2019/20
Revenues	(6)	6,679.0	6,670.7
Change in work in progress and finished goods inventories and internal costs capitalized	(7)	−35.7	180.4
Other operating income	(8)	111.0	113.2
Cost of materials	(9)	−4,355.5	−4,628.0
Personnel expenses	(10)	−984.0	−978.4
Depreciation	(11)	−366.3	−363.9
Other operating expenses	(12)	−852.8	−897.1
Result from companies consolidated at equity	(13)	−125.7	−48.9
Result from operations	(14)	70.0	48.0
Financial income	(15)	38.2	48.5
Financial expense	(15)	−87.2	−87.6
Earnings before income taxes		21.0	8.9
Taxes on income	(16)	−56.6	−63.4
Net earnings	(18)	−35.6	−54.5
of which attributable to Südzucker AG shareholders		−106.3	−121.5
of which attributable to hybrid capital		12.6	13.0
of which attributable to other non-controlling interests		58.1	54.0
Earnings per share (€)	(18)	−0.52	−0.60

various categories of operating expense (manufacturing, selling, administrative, research and development). Similarly, the line item *Depreciation* in Südzucker's income statement includes depreciation on manufacturing assets, as well as depreciation on assets used in administration, marketing, research, and other departments. The second line in Südzucker's income statement, *Change in work in progress and finished goods inventories and internal costs capitalized,* adjusts for the manufacturing costs included in *Cost of materials, Personnel expenses, Depreciation,* and *Other operating expenses* that are not part of cost of goods sold in the current year. As a result of this adjustment, the amount related to the cost of goods sold subtracted in calculating operating income is the same as if cost of goods sold had been reported as a separate line item. Although much different in appearance, the format Südzucker uses to report *Result from operations* (operating income) does not affect the amount reported. The amount is the same regardless of whether the company uses the type of expenditure format or the cost of goods sold format.

Most companies present revenues, operating income, pre-tax income, and net income as measures of performance in their income statements. Exhibit 2.11 shows the *Consolidated income statement* for Meliá Hotels International S.A., a Spanish hotel chain, which provides several other and different measures of performance. The first performance measure reflected in Meliá's income statement is *Operating income.* Indeed, Meliá presents operating income as the first line item in its income statement. However, the fact that Meliá

EXHIBIT 2.11

MELIÁ HOTELS INTERNATIONAL S.A.
Consolidated Income Statement

(Thousand €)	Note	2020	2019
Operating income		528,398	1,789,537
Results from assets sale		—	11,211
Total operating income and results from assets sale	8.1	**528,398**	**1,800,748**
Supplies	8.2	(58,871)	(199,035)
Staff costs	8.3	(282,106)	(523,918)
Other expenses	8.4	(338,288)	(579,301)
Total operating expenses		**(679,265)**	**(1,302,254)**
EBITDAR		**(150,867)**	**498,494**
Leases	18.2	(664)	(20,584)
EBITDA	7.1	**(151,531)**	**477,910**
Depreciation and impairment	8.5	(111,452)	(122,329)
Depreciation and impairment Right of use	8.5	(225,905)	(137,713)
Bargain purchase	8.6	—	4,926
EBIT		**(557,348)**	**222,794**
Exchange differences		(65)	(12,753)
Borrowings		(33,328)	(33,069)
Financial expense leases		(32,507)	(41,381)
Other financial income		(8,074)	14,417
Net financial income	8.7	**(74,564)**	**(72,786)**
Profit/(Loss) from companies carried by the equity method	13	**(31,859)**	**6,304**
NET INCOME BEFORE TAX		**(663,771)**	**156,312**
Income tax	20.6	51,050	(34,633)
CONSOLIDATED NET INCOME		**(612,721)**	**121,679**
A) Attributed to the parent company	9	(595,928)	112,898
B) Attributed to minority interests	16.6	(16,792)	8,781
BASIC EARNINGS PER SHARE IN EUROS	9	(2.78)	0.50
DILUTED EARNINGS PER SHARE IN EUROS	9	(2.78)	0.50

reports subsequent line items labeled *Supplies, Staff costs,* and *Other expenses,* which are added together to comprise *Total operating expenses,* suggests that *Operating income* actually reflects the company's total revenues. The next measure of performance reported by Meliá is *EBITDAR* (earnings before interest, tax, depreciation, amortization, and rent expenses), which is then followed by *EBITDA* (EBITDAR minus rent expense), and then *EBIT* (EBITDA minus depreciation and amortization expense). Meliá notes that EBITDAR can be directly compared across hotel business units regardless of whether the hotels are owned or leased, and that EBITDA provides an estimate of net cash flow from operating activities.[30]

Note that Meliá provides only two years of comparative information in its consolidated income statement, as does Südzucker. In contrast, Callaway Golf presents three years of data in its income statement, as is required by the U.S. SEC.

Level of Detail

Differences exist in the level of detail provided in the individual financial statements. Many companies provide relatively few line items on the face of the financial statements and then supplement these with additional detail in the notes. The income statements presented thus far in this chapter are cases in point. The level of detail provided by the companies shown in Exhibits 2.9–2.11 can be contrasted with the extremely detailed income statement provided by Thai Airways International Public Company Limited, a portion of which is shown in Exhibit 2.12. Instead of reporting revenues in a single line item as do Callaway Golf and Südzucker, Thai Airways reports revenues in three line items. Whereas Callaway Golf reports operating expenses in four line items, Thai Airways presents 13 separate categories of operating expense.

It should be noted that Exhibit 2.12 provides only a portion of the statement of comprehensive income included in Thai Airways' 2020 financial statements, in effect, only the part showing the calculation of income (loss) from operating activities. The remainder of this statement (not shown in Exhibit 2.12) (a) lists five expenses/losses related to non-operating activities to arrive at net *loss for the years,* (b) lists 10 unrealized gains and losses that make up *other comprehensive income,* (c) reports *profit* and *total comprehensive income attributable to owners of the parent* and *attributable to noncontrolling interests,* and (d) discloses *profit per share.* In addition, the two far right columns in the statement of comprehensive income (not shown in Exhibit 2.12) present *separate financial statements* that indicate the amount in each line item related to the parent company only, excluding amounts related to its subsidiaries. One final aspect of the level of detail provided by Thai Airways is the fact that Thai baht (THB) currency amounts are not rounded to the nearest thousand, million, or billion. *Passenger and excess baggage* revenues in 2020 are presented as THB 34,162,870,829, rather than, for example, as THB 34.1 billion.

Another example of a difference in level of detail (as well as a difference in financial statement format) can be found in the 2020 consolidated income statement of the British grocery store chain, Tesco PLC (see Exhibit 2.13 for an excerpt). For each income statement line item, Tesco reports the amount *Before exceptional items and amortization of acquired intangibles,* the amount related to *Exceptional items and amortization of acquired intangibles,* and *Total.* Tesco does not provide a clear definition of what constitutes an exceptional item, but states that "exceptional items are excluded from our headline performance measures, by virtue of their size and nature, in order to reflect management's view of underlying

---

[30] Melia Hotels International S.A., *2020 Consolidated Management Report and Annual Accounts,* p. 318.

EXHIBIT 2.12

THAI AIRWAYS INTERNATIONAL PUBLIC COMPANY LIMITED AND ITS SUBSIDIARIES
Excerpt from Statements of Profit or Loss and Other Comprehensive Income
For the year ended December 31, 2020

		Unit: Baht	
		CONSOLIDATED FINANCIAL STATEMENTS	
	Note	2020	2019
Revenues	31.1, 31.2		
Revenues from sales or services	25		
Passenger and excess baggage		34,162,870,829	149,044,250,701
Freight and mail.		6,892,792,058	17,783,341,709
Other business		6,660,792,421	14,214,449,444
Total revenues from sales or rendering of services		**47,716,455,308**	**181,042,041,854**
Other income			
Interest income		204,313,537	196,131,554
Net foreign exchange gain		—	4,439,258,477
Gain on changes in ownership interest		205,606,044	273,177,862
Other income—others		594,658,938	3,003,838,936
Total other income		**920,407,740**	**7,912,406,829**
Total Revenues.		**48,636,863,048**	**188,954,448,683**
Expenses			
Aircraft fuel expenses.		12,386,470,504	54,675,194,646
Employee benefits expenses		20,545,806,773	31,171,648,957
Flight service expenses.		6,726,875,952	21,058,256,685
Crew expenses		1,552,405,251	6,241,614,091
Aircraft repair and maintenance expenses		7,872,278,019	19,321,533,731
Depreciation and amortization expenses.		27,704,277,826	17,327,587,865
Lease of aircraft and spare parts		218,838,293	14,489,007,667
Inventories and supplies expenses.		2,111,050,175	9,100,798,414
Selling and advertising expenses		1,952,068,751	10,637,026,412
Impairment loss on aircrafts, right-of-use assets, and rotable aircraft spare. . . .	26	82,702,523,715	633,915,384
Net foreign exchange loss		894,693,377	—
Impairment loss on investment in subsidiary and associate.	11	—	—
Other expenses.		5,873,592,962	10,668,496,728
Total Expenses		**170,540,881,598**	**195,325,080,580**
Loss from operating activities		**(121,904,018,550)**	**(6,379,631,897)**

Group performance."[31] In 2020, exceptional items included "impairment charge on Tesco bank goodwill," "acquisition of property joint venture," and "litigation costs." Note that none of the other companies whose income statements are presented in this chapter present exceptional items in a separate column of information.

One final difference in level of detail to make note of here is the column of information provided in individual financial statements that indicates the note providing additional information related to specific line items. This is common practice in many countries and can be seen in the income statements of Südzucker, Meliá Hotels, Thai Airways, and Tesco presented in this chapter. However, as the income statement of Callaway Golf reflects, this practice is virtually unknown in the United States.

[31] Tesco PLC, *Annual Report and Financial Statements 2021,* p. 22.

EXHIBIT 2.13

TESCO PLC
Excerpt from Group Income Statement

		52 weeks ended 27 February 2021		
Continuing operations	Note	Before exceptional items and amortization of acquired intangibles £m	Exceptional items and amortization of acquired intangibles (Note 4) £m	Total £m
Revenue	2	57,887	—	57,887
Cost sales		(53,921)	383	(53,538)
Impairment loss on financial assets	2	(384)	—	(384)
Gross profit/(loss)		3,582	383	3,965
Administrative expenses		(1,767)	(462)	(2,229)
Operating profit/(loss)		1,815	(79)	1,736

Terminology

The examination of Vodafone PLC's balance sheet earlier in this chapter revealed a number of differences in the terminology used by Vodafone and a typical U.S. company. As another example, Jardine Matheson Holdings Limited, which is incorporated in Bermuda, includes the following current assets on its balance sheet: *Bank balances and other liquid funds, Current tax assets, Current debtors,* and *Stocks and work in progress.* A "translation" of these terms into terminology commonly used in the United States would be: Cash and cash equivalents, Taxes receivable, Accounts receivable, and Inventories. Many non-English-language companies translate their annual reports into English for the convenience of English speakers. These companies often choose between British and American formats and terminology in preparing convenience translations.

Occasionally terms unfamiliar to both British and U.S. accounting are found in English-language reports to reflect business, legal, or accounting practice unique to a specific country. For example, the Brazilian petrochemical firm Braskem SA includes the line items *Judicial deposits* as an asset and *Leniency agreement* as a liability on its December 31, 2020, balance sheet. Note 25 to Braskem's financial statements discloses that the *Leniency agreement* relates to a legal settlement to be paid by the company to Brazilian and foreign legal authorities. However, the financial statements provide no further information with regard to *Judicial deposits.* On its English-language 2016 balance sheet, SK Telecom includes a noncurrent asset called *Guarantee deposits* and a current liability referred to as *Withholdings,* with no further explanation as to what either of these items might be.

Disclosure

Differences exist across countries in the amount and types of information disclosed in a set of financial statements. Many of the disclosures provided by companies are required by law or other regulations. In addition, many companies around the world provide additional, voluntary disclosures, often to better compete in obtaining finance in the international capital markets.

There is an infinite number of differences that can exist in the disclosures provided by companies. To illustrate the wide diversity, we provide several examples of disclosures uncommon in the United States and most other countries. The Swedish appliance manufacturer AB Electrolux includes a note in its financial statements titled *Employees and Remuneration* (see Exhibit 2.14). This note reports the number of employees by geographical area, their gender, and their total remuneration. By splitting total remuneration into the amount paid to boards and senior managers and the amount paid to other employees,

EXHIBIT 2.14

AB ELECTROLUX
Excerpt from Note 27, Employees and Remuneration

Notes, all amounts in SEKm, unless otherwise stated

Average number of employees, by geographical area

	Group	
	2020	**2019**
Europe.	18,727	18,909
North America	6,752	6,640
Latin America	14,113	14,844
Asia-Pacific, Middle East and Africa	7951	8,259
Total	**47,543**	**48,652**

In 2020, the average number of employees was 47,543 (48,652), of which 29,644 (29,747) were men and 17,899 (18,905) women.

Salaries, other remuneration and employer contributions

	2020			2019		
	Salaries and remuneration	Employer contributions	Total	Salaries and remuneration	Employer contributions	Total
Parent Company	1,050	624	1,674	1,063	577	1,640
whereof pension costs	—	294	294	—	243	243
Subsidiaries	14,616	2,785	17,401	15,255	2,861	18,116
whereof pension costs	—	583	583	—	493	493
Total Group	**15,666**	**3,409**	**19,075**	**16,318**	**3,438**	**19,756**
whereof pension costs	—	877	877	—	736	736

Salaries and remuneration for board members, senior managers, and other employees

	2020			2019		
	Board members and senior managers	Other employees	Total	Board members and senior managers	Other employees	Total
Parent Company	75	975	1,050	59	1,004	1,063
Other	326	14,290	14,616	338	14,917	15,255
Total Group	**401**	**15,265**	**15,666**	**397**	**15,921**	**16,318**

Of the board members in Group companies, 80 (91) were men and 15 (14) were women, of whom 5 (6) men and 3 (3) women in the Parent Company. According to the definition of senior managers in the Swedish Annual Accounts Act, the number of senior managers in the Group consisted of 182 (178) men and 78 (75) women, of whom 7 (6) men and 2 (2) women in the parent company. The total pension cost for board members and senior managers in the group amounted to SEK 29m (33).

the statement allows interested readers to see that it is the latter group that receives the vast majority of compensation. The second half of Note 27, which is not shown, provides detailed information on the *ordinary compensation* and *compensation for committee work* for each of Electolux's 16 board members.

The Dutch specialty chemicals company, AkzoNobel N.V., includes two lines in the noncurrent liability section of the balance sheet titled *Post-retirement benefit provisions* and *Other provisions*. Provisions are accrued liabilities that by their nature involve a substantial amount of estimation, such as the obligation related to pensions and other postretirement benefits. In Note 20 to the financial statements, AkzoNobel provides details about the various items included in *Other Provisions* and the change in each of these items during the year (see Exhibit 2.15). This information can be used to assess the quality of the estimates made by the company with respect to expected future liabilities. For example, Note 20 indicates

EXHIBIT 2.15

AKZONOBEL NV
Excerpt from Note 20, Other Provisions and Contingent Liabilities

In € millions	Restructuring of activities	Environmental costs	Liabilities to (former) employees	Sundry	Total
Balance at January 1, 2020	96	75	169	122	462
Additions made during the year	77	6	30	47	160
Utilization	(84)	(9)	(16)	(44)	(153)
Amounts reversed during the year	(14)	(7)	(3)	(18)	(42)
Unwind of discount	—	3	6	—	9
Divestments	—	—	—	(5)	(5)
Changes in exchange rates	(1)	(5)	(8)	(5)	(19)
Balance at December 31, 2020	74	63	178	97	412
Non-current portion of provisions	13	53	114	52	232
Current portion of provisions	61	10	64	45	180
Balance at December 31, 2020	74	63	178	97	412

that for the year 2020, AkzoNobel had a beginning restructuring provision of €96 million and €77 million was added to the provision throughout the year. During 2020, €84 million of the estimated liability related to restructuring was paid and another €14 million was reversed as a result of overestimating the liability in a previous year. Note 20 also discloses that only €9 million of the €75 million, the company expected in environmental cleanup costs as of January 1, 2020, was paid in 2020, while an additional €7 million was reversed during the year. At the end of 2020, estimated environmental costs amounted to €63 million, with a major portion (€53 million) not expected to be paid until after 2021.

An excerpt from the final note in the 2020 consolidated financial statements of French tire maker, Compagnie Générale des Établissements Michelin, is presented in Exhibit 2.16. As part of its set of financial statements, Michelin discloses the amount of audit and

EXHIBIT 2.16

MICHELIN GROUP
Excerpt from Note 37, Statutory Auditors' Fees

(in € thousands)	Deloitte		PricewaterhouseCoopers	
	Statutory Auditor (Deloitte & Associés)	Network	Statutory Auditor (PricewaterhouseCoopers Audit)	Network
	Amount	Amount	Amount	Amount
STATUTORY AUDIT AND HALF-YEAR REVIEW OF THE INDIVIDUAL AND CONSOLIDATED FINANCIAL STATEMENTS				
Issuer	481	—	530	—
Fully consolidated subsidiaries	886	3,657	825	3,516
Sub-total	1,367	3,657	1,355	3,516
NON-AUDIT SERVICES				
Issuer	100	—	214	—
Fully consolidated subsidiaries	3	181	114	502
Sub-total	103	181	328	502
TOTAL	1,470	3,838	1,683	4,018

non audit fees paid to its statutory independent auditors. French law requires the accounts of publicly traded companies to be audited by two statutory auditors. Note 37 discloses that, in 2020, Michelin paid €5.308 million in fees to Deloitte and €5.701 million to PricewaterhouseCoopers. Most of the fees were paid for annual audits and half-year reviews, and most of the fees were paid to the two audit firms' international networks, probably for work done in connection with foreign subsidiaries.

Recognition and Measurement

Perhaps the most important differences that exist in financial reporting internationally are those related to the recognition and measurement of assets, liabilities, revenues, and expenses. *Recognition* refers to the decision as to whether an item should be reported in the financial statements. *Measurement* refers to the determination of the amount to be reported. For example, national accounting standards establish whether costs associated with acquiring the use of a resource should be recognized as an asset on the balance sheet. If so, then guidance must be provided with respect to both the initial measurement of the asset and measurement at subsequent balance sheet dates. Recognition and measurement procedures affect the amounts reported in the balance sheet and income statement. As a result, differences in the national recognition and measurement procedures used by companies can adversely affect the comparability of financial statements across countries.

We close this section by describing the diversity that exists with respect to measuring PPE subsequent to acquisition. Possible values at which these assets can be reported on the balance sheet include:

1. Historical cost (HC),
2. Historical cost adjusted for changes in the general purchasing power (GPP) of the currency, and
3. Fair value (FV).

In most cases, GPP and FV accounting result in PPE being written up to an amount higher than under HC accounting. In turn, the larger asset values under GPP and FV accounting result in the recognition of a higher amount of depreciation expense than under HC accounting. The counterpart to the asset write-up generally is treated as an increase in stockholders' equity, often reflected in a Revaluation Reserve or Revaluation Surplus account.

To better appreciate the impact the measurement of PPE has on financial statements, consider the following example. Assume a company acquires a building with a 10-year life at the beginning of the year for $10,000. The country in which the company is located experiences inflation of 40 percent in the current year, and the building is appraised to have a fair value (replacement cost) at year-end of $15,000. Under HC accounting, the building would be reported on the year-end balance sheet at its cost of $10,000, with accumulated depreciation of $1,000 ($10,000 / 10 years), and $1,000 of depreciation expense would be recognized in measuring net income. Under GPP accounting, the original cost of the building would be written up by the inflation rate of 40 percent and reported on the year-end balance sheet at $14,000, with accumulated depreciation of $1,400 ($14,000 / 10 years), and $1,400 of depreciation expense would be reflected in net income. Under FV accounting, the building would be written up to its fair value of $15,000 at year-end, accumulated depreciation would be $1,500 ($15,000 / 10 years), and depreciation expense would be $1,500. Thus, depending on the method applied in measuring PPE, the building could be reported at a net carrying amount of either $9,000, $12,600, or $13,500 on the year-end balance sheet, and either $1,000, $1,400, or $1,500 of depreciation expense would be subtracted in measuring net income.

U.S. GAAP requires PPE to be carried on the balance sheet at historical cost (HC) less accumulated depreciation. If an asset is impaired, that is, its carrying amount exceeds the amount of cash expected to result from use of the asset, it must be written down to fair value. Upward revaluation of PPE to fair value is not acceptable. HC accounting also is required in Japan. Although the specific rules vary from those in the United States, writing PPE down to a lower value is required if a permanent impairment of value has occurred.

In contrast, in those countries in which publicly traded companies use IFRS, those companies are free to choose between two different models for measuring PPE subsequent to acquisition: a cost model (HC accounting) or a revaluation model (FV accounting). If a company chooses to report assets at FV (rather than HC), it has an obligation to keep the valuations up-to-date, which might require annual adjustments.[32]

Until the early 1990s, publicly traded companies in Brazil were required to use GPP accounting in preparing financial statements. PPE was measured initially at HC and then restated in terms of GPP at subsequent balance sheet dates. The same was true in Mexico until 2008. Even today, IFRS require the use of GPP accounting in those countries experiencing hyperinflation.[33]

PARENT COMPANY-ONLY FINANCIAL STATEMENTS AND PRIVATE COMPANY FINANCIAL REPORTING

As noted earlier, all of the examples of financial reporting in the previous section of this chapter are taken from the consolidated financial statements of publicly traded companies. Most countries have specific accounting and financial reporting requirements for publicly traded companies. For example, in the United States, the Securities and Exchange Commission (SEC) requires publicly traded companies to file annual and quarterly reports in compliance with U.S. GAAP as promulgated by the Financial Accounting Standards Board (FASB). In contrast, publicly traded companies located in countries within the European Union are required by European Commission law to publish consolidated financial statements based on International Financial Reporting Standards (IFRS) issued by the International Accounting Standards Board (IASB).

Some countries also require publicly traded companies to file separate *parent company-only* financial statements (in which subsidiaries are not consolidated) with the appropriate government agency. These separate financial statements often are the basis for corporate income taxation. For example, France, Germany, Italy, and the Netherlands require public companies to file separate parent company-only financial statements. Unlike Italy and the Netherlands, France and Germany do not allow parent company-only financial statements to be prepared in accordance with IFRS, but instead they must be prepared using local GAAP. Thus, French stock exchange–listed companies, for example, prepare a set of consolidated financial statements in accordance with IFRS and a set of parent company-only financial statements using French GAAP. Other countries, such as the United States, do not require public companies to file parent company-only financial statements with a governmental authority, so there is no specific set of accounting rules required in preparing them. Indeed, in these countries, parent company-only financial statements generally are only available to individuals inside the company.

Most companies in the world are not publicly traded, but instead are privately held, often by family members, but increasingly by private investor groups (such as the so-called hedge funds). Some countries, including all members of the European Union (EU), require private companies to file a set of financial statements (balance sheet, income statement, and notes only) with a national registry, usually on an annual basis only, which are then

---

[32] Chapter 4 provides more detail on the revaluation model allowed under IFRS to measure PPE subsequent to acquisition.

[33] The Appendix to Chapter 7 provides more detail on the use of GPP accounting under IFRS.

made available to interested parties. The specific financial statement and disclosure requirements differ based on the size of the company (small, medium, or large), with the amount of information disclosed increasing with size. Small companies in the EU, for example, are only required to file an abridged balance sheet with abridged notes; an income statement is not required. Regardless of size, however, in these countries, private companies generally are required to use local GAAP in preparing their financial statements, and local GAAP generally is established by law. Thus, a family-owned (private) company in Germany must follow German statutory accounting principles in preparing the financial statements that it submits to the Federal Registry each year. Potential users of these financial statements include creditors (banks, suppliers, and so on), employees and their labor unions, and local government authorities.

Other countries have no financial reporting requirement for private companies. Such is the case, for example, in the United States. U.S. private companies must file articles of incorporation, which contain little to no financial information, with the Secretary of State of the state in which they incorporate. Once incorporated, a privately held company is not required to provide any additional information, such as financial statements, to the state. The only requirements related to providing financial information are the quarterly tax estimates and annual tax return filed with the U.S. Internal Revenue Service. However, tax return information is not made available to the public, but is restricted to being used by the U.S. federal government only.

Local GAAP in one country differs from IFRS, U.S. GAAP, and local GAAP in other countries. As an example of how local GAAP can differ from both IFRS and U.S. GAAP, consider the following local German accounting practices:

- Goodwill must be amortized over its useful life. If that life exceeds five years, an explanation must be provided in the notes.
- Construction contracts are accounted for using the completed contract method only; the percentage of completion method is not allowed.
- Derivative financial instruments with a negative fair value are reported on the balance sheet as a liability; derivatives with a positive fair value are not recognized as an asset.
- The concept of functional currency is not used in accounting for foreign currency; in translating foreign currency financial statements, the current rate method is used exclusively.
- A statement of cash flows and statement of changes in equity are not required in a set of parent company-only financial statements.

Each of these practices is inconsistent with both U.S. GAAP and IFRS.

Summary

1. Historically, considerable diversity has existed across countries with respect to the preparation and presentation of financial statements.
2. Many environmental factors are thought to have contributed to differences in financial reporting across countries. Some of the more commonly mentioned factors include legal system, the influence of taxation on financial reporting, corporate financing system, inflation, political and economic ties between countries, and national culture.
3. Several research studies provide evidence of a relationship between national culture and differences in financial reporting rules and practices across countries. Other studies provide some evidence of a relationship between national culture and the manner in which accountants across countries apply financial reporting rules.
4. The diversity that exists in financial reporting across countries creates problems for multinational corporations in preparing consolidated financial statements on the basis of a single set of accounting standards and can result in increased costs for companies

tapping into foreign capital markets. Accounting diversity also can adversely affect an investor's ability to compare financial statements across companies located in different countries.

5. Several accounting scholars have classified countries according to similarities and differences in financial reporting. Two dominant models of accounting used in the developed world are the Anglo-Saxon model and the Continental European model.

6. Concentrating on the Anglo-Saxon and Continental European model countries, Nobes developed a classification scheme that attempts to show how the financial reporting systems in 14 developed countries relate to one another. Nobes breaks down the two major classes of accounting system first into subclasses and then into families. This classification scheme shows how different families of accounting are related.

7. In a simplified model, Nobes suggests that the dominant reason for international differences in financial reporting is the extent to which corporate financing is obtained through the sale of equity securities to outside shareholders. Some cultures lead to a strong equity-outsider financing system and other cultures lead to a weak equity-outsider financing system. In strong equity-outsider financing countries, accounting measurement practices are less conservative, disclosure is extensive, and accounting practice differs from tax rules. This is consistent with the Anglo-Saxon model of accounting. In accounting systems found in countries with weak equity–outside shareholder financing systems, measurement is more conservative, disclosure is not as extensive, and accounting practice follows tax rules. This is consistent with the Continental European accounting model.

8. Differences in financial reporting exist across countries with regard to the financial statements provided by companies; the format, level of detail, and terminology used in presenting financial statements; the nature and amount of disclosure provided in financial statements; and the principles used to recognize and measure assets, liabilities, revenues, and expenses.

9. Some countries require parent companies to publish a set of parent company-only financial statements in addition to consolidated financial statements. In addition, some countries require private companies to publish a set of financial statements. In both cases, local GAAP generally is used.

Appendix to Chapter 2

The Case of Daimler-Benz

Daimler-Benz was the first German company to list on the NYSE, doing so in 1993. This was a major event for the NYSE and the SEC because German companies had previously refused to make the adjustments necessary to reconcile their German law-based financial statements to U.S. GAAP. After some compromise on the part of the SEC and because of Daimler's strong desire to enter the U.S. capital market (and be the first German company to do so), Daimler agreed to comply with SEC regulations.

Subsequent to its NYSE listing, Daimler-Benz filed an annual report on Form 20-F with the SEC.[1] In its 20-F filing, Daimler prepared financial statements in English, in both

---

[1] U.S. companies file their annual reports with the SEC on Form 10-K; foreign companies file their annual reports on Form 20-F.

German deutsche marks (DM) and U.S. dollars, and, until 1996, according to German accounting principles. In the notes to the 1995 financial statements, Daimler provided a "Reconciliation to U.S. GAAP" in which adjustments were made to net income and stockholders' equity prepared in accordance with German accounting law to reconcile to U.S. GAAP. The net effect of these adjustments over the period 1993–1995 is shown in Exhibit A2.1.

The fact that in 1993 Daimler-Benz reported a profit under German GAAP but a loss under U.S. GAAP created quite a stir in the international financial community. Because German companies were well known for intentionally understating income through the creation of hidden reserves, one would have expected German GAAP income to be smaller than U.S. GAAP income (as was true in 1994). In 1993, however, Daimler incurred a net loss for the year (as can be seen from the negative amount of U.S. GAAP income). To avoid reporting this loss, the company "released" hidden reserves that had been created in earlier years, thus reporting a profit of DM 615 million under German GAAP. The difference in German GAAP and U.S. GAAP income in 1993 of some DM 2.5 billion shows just how unreliable German GAAP income can be in reflecting the actual performance of a company. In fact, the German Financial Analysts Federation (DVFA) developed a method for adjusting German GAAP earnings to a more reliable amount (known as DVFA earnings).

In 1996, Daimler-Benz decided to abandon German GAAP and implement a U.S. GAAP accounting system worldwide. The 1996 annual report was prepared using U.S. GAAP and received an unqualified opinion on this basis from KPMG. The rationale for this decision was outlined in the 1996 annual report and is reproduced in Exhibit A2.2. The company indicated that U.S. GAAP figures not only allowed external analysts to better evaluate the company but also served as a better basis for the internal controlling of the company. This clearly points out the differences in orientation between a typical macro-uniform accounting system, which is geared toward minimizing taxes and protecting creditors, and a micro-based accounting system, which has the objective of providing information that is useful for making decisions, not only by external parties but by management as well.

In 1998, Daimler-Benz acquired U.S.-based Chrysler Corporation and the merged firm was named DaimlerChrysler. Upon the sale of Chrysler in 2007, the company's name was changed to Daimler. In 2010, Daimler delisted its shares from the NYSE. Since 2005, the company has followed IFRS in preparing its consolidated financial statements, as is required under EU law.

EXHIBIT A2.1

DAIMLER-BENZ

Excerpt from Form 20-F: Reconciliation to U.S. GAAP 1995

(all amounts in DM)

	1993	1994	1995
Net income as reported in the consolidated income statement under German GAAP.	615	895	(5,734)
Net income in accordance with U.S. GAAP	(1,839)	1,052	(5,729)
Stockholders' equity as reported in the consolidated balance sheet under German GAAP.	18,145	20,251	13,842
Stockholders' equity in accordance with U.S. GAAP	26,281	29,435	22,860

EXHIBIT A2.2

DAIMLER-BENZ
Excerpts from Annual Report 1996

Excerpts from *Value-Based Management, U.S. GAAP, and New Controlling Instruments* (pages 44–45)

1996 Financial Statements Prepared Entirely in Accordance with U.S. GAAP for the First Time Since our listing on the New York Stock Exchange we have increasingly aligned our external reporting in accordance with the information requirements of the international financial world. . . . With our 1996 annual report, we are the first German company to present an entire year's financial statements in accordance with U.S. GAAP while at the same time complying with the German Law to Facilitate Equity Borrowing. The report thus also conforms with EU guidelines and European accounting principles.

Improved External Disclosure
Instead of providing various figures concerning the economic performance of the Company that are derived using the HGB and U.S. GAAP but that in some instances differ significantly from each other because of the distinct accounting philosophies, we supply a complete set of figures in conformance with U.S. GAAP for our shareholders, the financial analysts, and the interested public. In so doing, we fulfill accounting standards of the highest reputation worldwide, and we believe our approach more clearly and accurately reflects the economic performance, financial situation, and net worth of the Company than any other accounting system available at this time. This is not least due to the fact that U.S. accounting principles focus on investor information rather than creditor protection, which is the dominant concern under German accounting principles. Discretionary valuation is greatly limited, and the allocation of income and expenses to the individual accounting period is based on strict economic considerations.

Advantages for All Shareholders
Using U.S. accounting principles makes it significantly easier to internationally active financial analysts or experienced institutional investors to accurately assess the financial situation and development of the Company. Moreover, it improves disclosure at Daimler-Benz as well as comparability on an international scale. This helps promote the worldwide acceptance of our stock.

Internal Controlling on the Basis of Balance Sheet Values in Accordance with U.S. GAAP
The U.S. GAAP not only made Daimler-Benz more transparent from an external perspective. Because the earnings figures as derived with American accounting principles accurately reflect the economic performance of the Company, we are now able to use figures from our external reporting for the internal controlling of the Company and its individual business units rather than relying on the internal operating profit used in the past. We thus make use of the same figures both internally and externally to measure the economic performance of the Company and the business units.

Excerpt from *Letter to the Stockholders and Friends of Our Company* (page 4)
1996 marks the first time we have prepared our accounts in accordance with U.S. accounting principles which gives our investors worldwide the transparency they require. This means that our success as well as our shortcomings will be reported with new clarity. The terms operating profit, return on capital employed, and cash flow have become part of the language of the entire company and part of our corporate philosophy.

Questions

1. What are the two common methods used internationally for the order in which assets are listed on the balance sheet? Which of these two methods is most common in North America? In Europe?

2. What are the two major types of legal systems used in the world? How does the type of legal system affect accounting?

3. How does the relationship between financial reporting and taxation affect the manner in which income is measured for financial reporting purposes?

4. Who are the major providers of capital (financing) for business enterprises? What influence does the relative importance of equity financing in a country have on financial statement disclosure?

5. In general terms, how is financial reporting different in the Anglo-Saxon model of accounting from the Continental European model of accounting?

6. According to Gray, how does national culture affect the development of a country's accounting system?

7. What are the hypothesized relationships between the cultural value of uncertainty avoidance and the accounting values of conservatism and secrecy?

8. How is the group of countries that includes Australia, Canada, Ireland, New Zealand, South Africa, the United Kingdom, and the United States expected to differ from the group of countries that includes Chile, Colombia, Costa Rica, Ecuador, El Salvador, Guatemala, Mexico, Panama, Peru, Portugal, Uruguay, and Venezuela with respect to the accounting values of conservatism and secrecy?

9. What is the implication from the modified Gray framework for the use of a common set of financial reporting standards across all countries?

10. What are the major problems caused by worldwide accounting diversity for a multinational corporation?

11. What are the major problems caused by worldwide accounting diversity for international portfolio investment?

12. According to Nobes's simplified model of accounting diversity, what are the two most important factors influencing differences in accounting systems across countries?

13. In what way does Nobes's simplified model of accounting diversity appear to explain accounting developments that have occurred in Europe over the past three decades?

14. What are the different ways in which financial statements might differ across countries?

15. How are the various costs that comprise cost of goods sold (or cost of sales) reflected in a "type of expenditure" format income statement?

16. What information is provided in a "value added statement"?

17. What are the alternative methods used internationally to measure property, plant, and equipment (PPE) subsequent to acquisition?

18. What accounting rules often are required to be followed by private companies in those countries that require such companies to file a set of financial statements with a government authority?

Exercises and Problems

1. Refer to the income statement excerpts presented in Exhibits 2.9, 2.10, 2.11, 2.12, and 2.13 for Callaway Golf Company, Südzucker AG, Meliá Hotels International S.A., Thai Airways Limited, and Tesco PLC, respectively.

   Required:
   a. Calculate gross profit margin (gross profit/revenues) and operating profit margin (operating profit/revenues) for each of these companies for the most recent year presented. If a particular ratio cannot be calculated, explain why not.

   b. Is it valid to compare the profit margins calculated in part (a) across these companies in assessing relative profitability? Why or why not?

2. Referring to their most recent annual reports, access the financial statements of a foreign company and a domestic company with which you are familiar to complete this assignment.

Required:

a. Determine the GAAP the foreign and domestic companies use to prepare financial statements.

b. Determine whether the financial statements provided by the foreign and domestic companies include the same components (e.g., consolidated balance sheet, consolidated income statement, consolidated cash flows statement, and so on).

c. List any format differences (up to five) in the companies' income statements.

d. List any format differences (up to five) in the companies' balance sheets.

e. Note any terminology differences (up to five) that exist between the two companies' income statements and balance sheets.

f. In very general terms, assess whether the scope and content of the information provided in the notes to the financial statements is similar between the two companies.

g. Provide your overall impression (no detail) of how the two companies' sets of financial statements compare.

3. Using their most recent annual reports, access the financial statements of two foreign companies located in the same country to complete this assignment.

Required:

a. Determine the GAAP the two foreign companies use to prepare financial statements.

b. Determine whether the financial statements provided by the two foreign companies include the same components (e.g., consolidated balance sheet, consolidated income statement, consolidated cash flows statement, and so on).

c. List any format differences (up to five) in the companies' income statements.

d. List any format differences (up to five) in the companies' balance sheets.

e. Note any terminology differences (up to five) that exist between the two companies' income statements and balance sheets.

f. In very general terms, assess whether the scope and content of the information provided in the notes to the financial statements is similar between the two companies.

g. Provide your overall impression (no detail) of how the two companies' sets of financial statements compare.

4. Cultural dimension index scores developed by Hofstede for six countries are reported in the table below.

Required:

Using Gray's hypothesis relating culture to the accounting value of secrecy, rate these six countries as relatively high or relatively low with respect to the level of disclosure you would expect to find in financial statements. Explain your ratings.

Country	Power Distance		Uncertainty Avoidance		Individualism		Competitiveness		Long-Term Orientation	
	Index	Rank[a]	Index	Rank[a]	Index	Rank[a]	Index	Rank[a]	Index	Rank[b]
Belgium	65	20	94	5–6	75	8	54	22	38	18
Brazil	69	14	76	21–22	38	26–27	49	27	65	6
Korea (South)	60	27–28	85	16–17	18	43	39	41	75	5
Netherlands	38	40	53	35	80	4–5	14	51	44	11–12
Sweden	31	47–48	29	49–50	71	10–11	5	53	33	20
Thailand	64	21–23	64	30	20	39–41	34	44	56	8

[a] 1 = highest rank; 53 = lowest rank.
[b] 1 = highest rank; 34 = lowest rank.

5. GlaxoSmithKline plc (GSK), Boehringer Ingelheim AG (BI), and Dr. Reddy's Laboratories Limited (DRL), three of the world's largest pharmaceutical companies, are located in the United Kingdom, Germany, and India, respectively. Use the following links to access the 2020 annual report and consolidated income statement for each company:

    http://gsk.com/media/6662/annual-report-2020.pdf(Annual Report 2020, p. 154)

    http://boehringer-ingelheim.com/sites/default/files/ARPC/AR_2020/Boehringer-Ingelheim_Annual_Report_2020.pdf(Annual Report 2020, p. 53)

    http://drreddys.com/media/1003010/drl-annual-report-fy2021.pdf(Annual Report 2020–21, p. 179)

    Required:

    a. Determine the accounting rules followed by each company in preparing its consolidated financial statements.

    b. Summarize similarities and differences in scope, format, and terminology across the consolidated income statements of the three companies.

6. Five factors are often mentioned as affecting a country's accounting practices: (a) legal system, (b) taxation, (c) providers of financing, (d) inflation, and (e) political and economic ties.

    Required:

    Consider your home country. Identify which of these factors has had the strongest influence on the development of accounting in your country. Provide specific examples to support your position.

7. As noted in the chapter, diversity in accounting practice across countries generates problems for a number of different groups.

    Required:

    Answer the following questions and provide explanations for your answers.

    a. Which is the greatest problem arising from worldwide accounting diversity?

    b. Which group is most affected by worldwide accounting diversity?

    c. Which group can most easily deal with the problems associated with accounting diversity?

8. Various attempts have been made to reduce the accounting diversity that exists internationally. This process is known as convergence and is discussed in more detail in Chapter 3. The ultimate form of convergence would be a world in which all countries followed a similar set of financial reporting rules and practices.

    Required:

    Consider each of the following factors that contribute to existing accounting diversity as described in this chapter:

    - Legal system
    - Taxation
    - Providers of financing
    - Inflation
    - Political and economic ties
    - National culture

    Which factor do you believe is likely to be the greatest impediment to the international convergence of accounting? Which factor do you believe creates the smallest impediment to convergence? Explain your reasoning.

9. The parent company balance sheet for Babcock International Group PLC at March 31, 2021, is as follows:

Company Statement of Financial Position

As at 31 March 2021	Note	2021 £m	2020 £m
Fixed assets			
Investment in subsidiaries................................	5	2,466.5	2,466.5
Current assets			
Trade and other receivables.............................	6	3,764.7	3,944.1
Cash and cash equivalents..............................		115.0	865.0
Creditors: Amounts falling due within one year:			
Trade and other payables...............................	7	(2,270.6)	(2,482.7)
Net current assets.....................................		**1,609.1**	**2,326.4**
Total assets less current liabilities		**4,075.6**	**4,792.9**
Creditors: Amounts falling due after more than one year:			
Trade and other payables...............................	7	(1,322.4)	(2,054.0)
Net assets		**2,753.2**	**2,783.9**
Equity			
Called up share capital	9	303.4	303.4
Share premium account.................................		873.0	873.0
Capital redemption reserve		30.6	30.6
Other reserve..		768.8	768.8
Retained earnings.....................................		777.4	763.1
Total shareholders' funds		**2,753.2**	**2,738.9**

Required:
Transform Babcock's March 31, 2021, company balance sheet to a format and using terminology commonly used by U.S. companies.

CASE 2-1

The Impact of Culture on Conservatism

PART I

The framework created by Professor Sidney Gray in 1988 to explain the development of a country's accounting system is presented in this chapter in Exhibit 2.6. Gray theorized that culture has an impact on a country's accounting system through its influence on accounting values. Focusing on that part of a country's accounting system comprised of financial reporting rules and practices, the model can be visualized as follows:

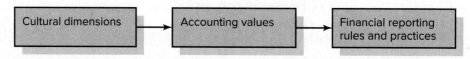

In short, cultural values shared by members of a society influence the accounting values shared by members of the accounting subculture. The shared values of the accounting subculture in turn affect the financial reporting rules and practices found within a country.

With respect to the accounting value of conservatism, Gray hypothesized that the higher a country ranks on the cultural dimensions of uncertainty avoidance and long-term orientation, and the lower it ranks in terms of individualism and competitiveness, then the more likely it is to rank highly in terms of conservatism. Conservatism is a preference for a cautious approach to measurement. Conservatism is manifested in a country's accounting system through a tendency to defer recognition of assets and items that increase net income and a tendency to accelerate the recognition of liabilities and items that decrease net income. One example of conservatism in practice would be a rule that requires an unrealized contingent liability to be recognized when it is probable that an outflow of future resources will arise but that does not allow the recognition of an unrealized contingent asset under any circumstances.

Required:

Discuss the implications for the global convergence of financial reporting standards raised by Gray's model.

PART II

Although Gray's model relates cultural values to the accounting value of conservatism as it is embodied in a country's financial reporting rules, it can be argued that the model is equally applicable to the manner in which a country's accountants apply those rules:

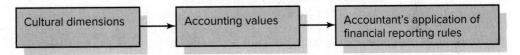

Required:

Discuss the implications this argument has for the comparability of financial statements across countries, even in an environment of substantial international accounting convergence. Identify areas in which differences in cultural dimensions across countries could lead to differences in the application of financial reporting rules.

PART III

Cancan Enterprises Inc. is a Canadian-based company with subsidiaries located in Brazil, Korea, and Sweden. (Hofstede's cultural dimension index scores for these countries are presented in Exercise 4.) Cancan Enterprises must apply IFRS worldwide in preparing consolidated financial statements. Cancan has developed a corporate accounting manual that prescribes the accounting policies based on IFRS that are to be applied by all the company's operations. Each year, Cancan's internal auditors have the responsibility of ensuring that the company's accounting policies have been applied consistently companywide.

Required:

Discuss the implications that the model presented in Part II of this case has for the internal auditors of Cancan Enterprises in carrying out their responsibilities.

CASE 2-2

SKD Limited

SKD Limited is a biotechnology company that prepares financial statements using internally developed accounting rules (referred to as SKD GAAP). To be able to compare SKD's financial statements with those of companies in their home country, financial analysts in Country A and Country B prepared a reconciliation of SKD's current year net income and stockholders' equity. Adjustments were based on the actual accounting policies and practices followed by biotechnology companies in Country A and Country B. The following table shows the adjustments to income and stockholders' equity made by each country analyst:

	Country A	Country B
Income under SKD GAAP	1,050	1,050
Adjustments:		
Goodwill amortization	300	(100)
Capitalized interest.	50	50
Depreciation related to capitalized interest.	(20)	(20)
Depreciation related to revalued property, plant, and equipment . . .	—	(8)
Income under local GAAP	1,380	972
Stockholders' equity under SKD GAAP.	15,000	15,000
Adjustments:		
Goodwill	900	(300)
Capitalized interest.	30	30
Revaluation of property, plant, and equipment	—	56
Stockholders' equity under local GAAP	15,930	14,786

Description of Accounting Differences

Goodwill. SKD capitalizes goodwill and amortizes it over a 20-year period. Goodwill is also treated as an asset in Country A and Country B. However, goodwill is not amortized in Country A, but instead is subjected to an annual impairment test. Goodwill is amortized over a five-year period in Country B.

Interest. SKD expenses all interest immediately. In both Country A and Country B, interest related to self-constructed assets must be capitalized as a part of the cost of the asset.

Property, plant, and equipment. SKD carries assets on the balance sheet at their historical cost, less accumulated depreciation. The same treatment is required in Country A. In Country B, companies in the biotechnology industry generally carry assets on the balance sheet at revalued amounts. Depreciation is based on the revalued amount of property, plant, and equipment.

Required:

1. With respect to the adjustments related to goodwill, answer the following:
   a. Why does the adjustment for goodwill amortization increase net income under Country A GAAP but decrease net income under Country B GAAP?
   b. Why does the goodwill adjustment increase stockholders' equity in Country A but decrease stockholders' equity in Country B?
   c. Why are the adjustments to stockholders' equity larger than the adjustments to income?

2. With respect to the adjustments made by the analyst in Country A related to interest, answer the following:
   a. Why are there two separate adjustments to income related to interest?
   b. Why does the adjustment to income for capitalized interest increase income, whereas the adjustment for depreciation related to capitalized interest decreases income?
   c. Why is the positive adjustment to stockholders' equity for capitalized interest smaller than the positive adjustment to income for capitalized interest?

3. With respect to the adjustments made by the analyst in Country B related to property, plant, and equipment, answer the following:
   a. Why does the adjustment for depreciation related to revalued property, plant, and equipment decrease income, whereas the adjustment for revaluation of property, plant, and equipment increases stockholders' equity?

Chapter **Three**

International Convergence of Financial Reporting

Learning Objectives

After reading this chapter, you should be able to

- Explain the meaning of convergence.
- Identify the arguments for and against international convergence of financial reporting standards.
- Discuss major harmonization and convergence efforts under the IASC and IASB, respectively.
- Explain the principles-based approach to setting accounting standards.
- Describe the difference in approaches taken by the IASC and FASB in setting accounting standards.
- Describe the extent of adoption of IFRS across the world's major economies.
- Examine the issues related to international convergence of financial reporting standards.
- Understand the basis approach taken in the IASB's standard *IFRS for Small and Medium-Sized Entities*.
- Explain the meaning of "Anglo-Saxon" accounting.

INTRODUCTION

In Chapter 2, we discussed worldwide diversity in accounting practices and some of the problems caused by such diversity. Sir Bryan Carsberg, former secretary-general of the International Accounting Standards Committee (IASC), explains how accounting diversity affects international capital markets:

> Imagine the case of an international business, with operations in many different countries. It is likely to be required to prepare accounts for its operations in each country, in compliance with the rules of that country. It will then have to convert those accounts to conform to the rules of the country in which the holding company is resident, for the preparation of group accounts. If the company has listings on stock exchanges outside its home country, these exchanges or their regulators may require the accounts to be filed under some other basis. The extra cost could be enormous. Heavy costs also fall on investors in trying to compare the results of companies based in different countries and they may just be unable to make such

comparisons. . . . But the biggest cost may be in limiting the effectiveness of the international capital markets. Cross border investment is likely to be inhibited.[1]

The accounting profession and standard-setters have been under pressure from multinational companies, stock exchanges, securities regulators, international lending institutions such as the World Bank, and other international bodies such as G20 to reduce diversity and harmonize accounting standards and practices internationally. This chapter focuses mainly on the activities of the International Accounting Standards Board (IASB) and the movement to develop and promote International Financial Reporting Standards (IFRS). IFRS are a set of benchmark accounting standards that have been adopted by many countries and serve as a framework used by the global accounting community. The chapter includes a brief survey of how IFRS are incorporated into the accounting systems of each of the world's largest economies.

INTERNATIONAL HARMONIZATION OF ACCOUNTING STANDARDS

The evolution of the IASC and the IASB shows international accounting standard-setting has been in the private sector with the support of the accounting bodies, standard-setters, capital market regulators, and government authorities in various countries, as well as the preparers and users of financial statements around the world.

International standard-setting is usually associated with the word *harmonization,* which means different things to different people. Sometimes harmonization is viewed as meaning the same thing as standardization. However, whereas standardization implies the elimination of alternatives in accounting for economic transactions and other events, harmonization refers to the reduction of alternatives while retaining a high degree of flexibility in accounting practices. Harmonization allows different countries to have different standards as long as the standards do not conflict. For example, prior to 2005, within the European Union (EU) harmonization program, companies were permitted to use different measurement methods: German companies could use historical cost for valuing assets, while Dutch companies could use replacement cost without violating the harmonization requirements.

Harmonization is a process that takes place over time. Accounting harmonization can be considered in two ways, namely, harmonization of accounting regulations or standards (also known as formal or de jure harmonization), and harmonization of accounting practices (also known as material or de facto harmonization). Harmonization of accounting practices is the ultimate goal of international harmonization efforts. Harmonization of standards may not necessarily lead to harmonization of accounting practices adopted by companies. Other factors, such as differences in the quality of audits, enforcement mechanisms, culture, legal requirements, and socioeconomic and political systems, may lead to noncomparable accounting numbers despite similar accounting standards.

HARMONIZATION EFFORTS THROUGH THE INTERNATIONAL ACCOUNTING STANDARDS COMMITTEE (IASC)

The IASC was established in 1973 by an agreement of the leading professional accounting bodies in 10 countries (Australia, Canada, France, Germany, Ireland, Japan, Mexico, the Netherlands, the United Kingdom, and the United States) with the broad objective of

---

[1] Excerpt from Sir Bryan Carsberg, "Global Issues and Implementing Core International Accounting Standards: Where Lies IASC's Final Goal?" Remarks made at the 50th Anniversary Dinner, Japanese Institute of CPAs, Tokyo, October 23, 1998.

formulating "international accounting standards." The IASC was funded by contributions from member bodies, multinational companies, financial institutions, accounting firms, and the sale of IASC publications.

The "Lowest-Common-Denominator" Approach

The IASC's harmonization efforts from 1973 to 2001 evolved in several different phases. In the initial phase, covering the first 15 years, the IASC's main activity was the issuance of 26 generic International Accounting Standards (IAS), many of which allowed multiple options. The IASC's approach to standard-setting during this phase can be described as a lowest-common-denominator approach, as the standards reflected an effort to accommodate existing accounting practices in various countries. For example, IAS 11, *Construction Contracts,* as originally written in 1979, allowed companies to choose between the percentage-of-completion method and the completed contract method in accounting for long-term construction contracts, effectively sanctioning the two major methods used internationally. A study conducted in 1988 found that all or most of the companies listed on the stock exchanges of the countries included in Nobes's classification (presented in Chapter 2 of this book), except for Germany and Italy, were in compliance with the IAS.[2] Given the lowest-common-denominator approach adopted by the IASC, it is obvious that IASC standards existing in 1988 introduced little if any comparability of financial statements across countries.

The Comparability Project

Two significant activities took place from 1989 to 1993, which can be described as the IASC's second phase. The first was the 1989 publication of the *Framework for the Preparation and Presentation of Financial Statements* (hereafter referred to as the *Framework*), which set out the objectives of financial statements, the qualitative characteristics of financial information, definitions of the elements of financial statements, and the criteria for recognition of financial statement elements. The second activity was the Comparability of Financial Statements Project, the purpose of which was "to eliminate most of the choices of accounting treatment currently permitted under International Accounting Standards."[3] As a result of the Comparability Project, 10 revised International Accounting Standards were approved in 1993 and became effective in 1995. As an example of the changes brought about by the Comparability Project, IAS 11 was revised to require the use of the percentage-of-completion method when certain criteria are met, thereby removing the option to avoid the use of this method altogether.

The IOSCO Agreement

The final phase in the work of the IASC began with the International Organization of Securities Commissions (IOSCO) agreement in 1993 and ended with the creation of the IASB in 2001. The main activity during this phase was the development of a core set of international standards that could be endorsed by IOSCO for cross-listing purposes. This period also was marked by the proposal to restructure the IASC and the proposal's final approval.

IOSCO became a member of the IASC's Consultative Group in 1987 and supported the IASC's Comparability Project. In 1993, IOSCO and the IASC agreed on a list of 30 core standards that the IASC needed to develop that could be used by companies involved in cross-border security offerings and listings. In 1995, the IASC and IOSCO agreed on a

---

[2] International Accounting Standards Committee, *Survey of the Use and Application of International Accounting Standards 1988* (London: IASC, 1988).

[3] International Accounting Standards Committee, *International Accounting Standards 1990* (London: IASC, 1990), p. 13.

work program for the IASC to develop the set of core international standards, and IOSCO agreed to evaluate the standards for possible endorsement for cross-border purposes upon their completion.

With the publication of IAS 39, *Financial Instruments: Recognition and Measurement,* in December 1998, the IASC completed its work program to develop the set of 30 core standards. In May 2000, IOSCO's Technical Committee recommended that securities regulators permit foreign issuers to use the core IASC standards to gain access to a country's capital market as an alternative to using local standards. The Technical Committee consisted of securities regulators representing the 14 largest and most developed capital markets, including Australia, France, Germany, Japan, the United Kingdom, and the United States. IOSCO's endorsement of IASC standards was an important step in the harmonization process.[4]

OTHER HARMONIZATION EFFORTS

Several international organizations have been involved in harmonization efforts either regionally (such as the European Union, and Association of Southeast Asian Nations) or worldwide (such as the United Nations). The IOSCO, the International Federation of Accountants (IFAC), and the International Forum of Accountancy Development (IFAD) also have contributed to the harmonization efforts at the global level.

International Organization of Securities Commissions

IOSCO aims, among other things, to ensure a better regulation of the markets on both the domestic and international levels. It provides assistance to ensure the integrity of the markets by a rigorous application of the standards and by effective enforcement.

As one of its objectives, IOSCO works to facilitate cross-border securities offerings and listings by multinational issuers. It has consistently advocated the adoption of a set of high-quality accounting standards for cross-border listings. To this end, IOSCO supported the efforts of the International Accounting Standards Committee (IASC) in developing international accounting standards that foreign issuers could use in lieu of local accounting standards when entering capital markets outside of their home country.

International Federation of Accountants

IFAC is now a global organization of 160 member bodies and associates in 135 countries, representing over 3 million accountants employed in public practice, industry and commerce, government, and academia. Its mission is to serve the public interest and to strengthen the worldwide accountancy profession and contribute to the development of strong international economies by establishing and promoting adherence to high-quality professional standards on auditing, ethics, education, and training.

In June 1999, IFAC launched IFAD in response to a criticism from the World Bank (following the Asian financial crisis) that the accounting profession was not doing enough to enhance the accounting capacity and capabilities in developing and emerging nations. IFAD's membership includes international financial institutions (such as the World Bank, International Monetary Fund, and Asian Development Bank); other key international organizations (such as IOSCO, IASB, and the Securities and Exchange Commission [SEC]); and the large accountancy firms.[5] The primary aim of this forum is to promote transparent financial reporting, duly audited to high standards by a strong accounting and auditing profession.

---

[4] IOSCO, *Final Communique of the XXIXth Annual Conference of the International Organization of Securities Commissions,* Amman, May 17–20, 2004.

[5] IFAD completed its work with the publication of *GAAP Convergence 2002.*

In May 2000, IFAC and the large international accounting firms established the Forum of Firms, also aimed at raising standards of financial reporting and auditing globally in order to protect the interests of cross-border investors and promote international flows of capital. The forum works alongside IFAD in achieving common objectives.

European Union

The 2004 additions to EU membership are likely to change the dynamics of the group, especially considering that 8 of the 10 new entrants were members of the former Soviet bloc. Until May 2004 all EU countries possessed similar traits in many respects. They all were wealthy industrial nations with similar political goals, comparable standards of living, high volumes of trade within the union, and good transportation links.

From the beginning, the EU's aim has been to create a unified business environment. Accordingly, the harmonization of company laws and taxation, the promotion of full freedom in the movement of goods and labor between member countries, and the creation of a community capital market have been high on its agenda. In July 2002, most EU members adopted a single currency, the euro, as envisaged in the Treaty of Maastricht signed in 1991.[6]

Two directives have been aimed at harmonizing accounting: the Fourth Directive (issued in 1978) deals with valuation rules, disclosure requirements, and the format of financial statements; and the Seventh Directive (issued in 1983) deals with consolidated financial statements. The latter requires companies to prepare consolidated financial statements and outlines the procedures for their preparation. It has had a significant impact on European accounting, as consolidations were previously uncommon in Continental Europe.

The Fourth Directive includes comprehensive accounting rules covering the content of annual financial statements, their methods of presentation, and measurement and disclosure of information for both public and private companies. It established the "true and fair view" principle, which requires financial statements to provide a true and fair view of a company's assets and liabilities and its financial position and profit and loss for the benefit of shareholders and third parties.

The Fourth Directive provides considerable flexibility. Dozens of provisions beginning with the expression "Member states may require or permit companies to . . ." allow countries to choose from among acceptable alternatives. For example, under Dutch and British law, companies could write assets up to higher market values, whereas in Germany this was strictly forbidden. Both approaches are acceptable under the Fourth Directive. By allowing different options for a variety of accounting issues, the EU directives opened the door for noncomparability in financial statements.

Profit measurement across EU countries differed in part because the directives failed to cover several important topics, including lease accounting, foreign currency translation, accounting changes, contingencies, income taxes, and long-term construction contracts.

Notwithstanding the flexibility afforded by the directives, their implementation into local law caused extensive change in accounting practice in several EU member countries. The following are some of the changes in German accounting practice brought about by the integration of the EU's Fourth and Seventh Directives into German law in 1985:

1. Required inclusion of notes to the financial statements.
2. Preparation of consolidated financial statements on a worldwide basis (i.e., foreign subsidiaries no longer could be excluded from consolidation).
3. Elimination of unrealized intercompany losses on consolidation.
4. Use of the equity method for investments in associated companies.

---

[6] Several EU members—namely, Denmark, Sweden, and the United Kingdom—have not adopted the euro as their national currency.

5. Disclosure of comparative figures in the balance sheet and income statement.
6. Disclosure of liabilities with a maturity of less than one year.
7. Accrual of deferred tax liabilities and pension obligations.[7]

Most of these "innovations" had been common practice in the United States for several decades.

Although the EU directives did not lead to complete comparability across member nations, they helped reduce differences in financial statements. In addition, the EU directives served as a basic framework of accounting that had been adopted by other countries in search of an accounting model. With the economic reforms in Eastern Europe since 1989, several countries in that region found it necessary to abandon the Soviet-style accounting system previously used in favor of a Western, market-oriented system. For example, in the early 1990s, Hungary, Poland, and the Czech and Slovak Republics all passed new accounting laws primarily based on the EU directives in anticipation of securing EU membership. This was further evidence of the influence that economic ties among countries could have on accounting practice.

In 1990, the European Commission indicated that there would be no further EU directives related to accounting. Instead, the commission indicated in 1995 that it would associate the EU with efforts undertaken by the IASC toward a broader international harmonization of accounting standards. In June 2000, the European Commission issued the following communication to the European Parliament:

- Before the end of 2000, the Commission will present a formal proposal requiring all listed EU companies to prepare their consolidated accounts in accordance with one single set of accounting standards, namely International Accounting Standards (IAS).
- This requirement will go into effect, at the latest, from 2005 onward.
- Member states will be allowed to extend the application of IAS to unlisted companies and to individual accounts.[8]

The International Forum on Accountancy Development (IFAD)

IFAD was created as a working group between the Basel Committee, the IFAC, IOSCO, the large accounting firms, the Organization for Economic Cooperation and Development (OECD), the United Nations Conference on Trade and Development (UNCTAD), and the World Bank and regional development banks, which flowed from the East Asian crisis in the late 1990s. Its mission was to improve market security and transparency and financial stability on a global basis. With a view to assisting national governments, its objectives highlight the following:

- To promote the importance of transparent financial reporting in accordance with sound corporate governance.
- To help develop the idea that the accountancy profession should take responsibility to support the public interest.
- To inculcate the importance of focusing on the accountancy and auditing needs of developing countries.
- To encourage cooperation among governments, the accountancy and other professions, the international financial institutions, regulators, standard-setters, capital providers, and issuers.[9]

[7] Timothy S. Doupnik, "Recent Innovations in German Accounting Practice Through the Integration of EC Directives," *Advances in International Accounting* 5 (1992), pp. 75–103.
[8] Commission of the European Communities, "EU Financial Reporting Strategy: The Way Forward," Communication from the Commission to the Council and the European Parliament, June 13, 2000.
[9] Source: https://www.iasplus.com.

IFAD promoted the view that the national accounting standards of most countries should be raised, with the IAS as the benchmark. IFAD completed its work with the publication of *GAAP Convergence 2002.*

CREATION OF THE IASB

Responding to these challenges, the IASC appointed a Strategy Working Party in 1996, which issued a discussion document in December 1998 entitled, "Shaping IASC for the Future." This document proposed a vastly different structure and process for the development of international accounting standards.

The final recommendations of the IASC Strategy Working Party were approved at its Venice meeting in November 1999. These recommendations, designed to deal with the issue of legitimacy, attempted to balance calls for a structure based on geographic representativeness with those based on technical competence and independence. Accordingly, it was decided that representativeness would be provided by the geographic distribution of the trustees, who would be essential to ensuring the effectiveness and independence of the Board, but that Board members would be selected based on their expertise.

On April 1, 2001, the newly created IASB took over from the IASC as the creator of international accounting standards, which were to be called IFRS. The process of restructuring the IASC into the IASB took over five years.

The formation of the IASB in 2001, with a change in focus from harmonization to convergence or global standard-setting, marked the beginning of a new era in international financial reporting.

The Structure of the IASB

The IASB is organized under an independent foundation called the IFRS Foundation. As shown in Exhibit 3.1, components of the structure are:

1. IASB.
2. IFRS Foundation (IFRSF).
3. Monitoring Board.
4. IFRS Interpretations Committee (IFRSIC).
5. IFRS Advisory Council (IFRSAC).
6. Working groups (expert task forces for individual agenda projects).

Monitoring Board

The IASC Foundation Constitution was amended in February 2009 to create a Monitoring Board of public authorities. The Monitoring Board consists of representatives from the European Commission, the Growth and Emerging Markets Committee of IOSCO, the U.S. Securities and Exchange Commission, as well as securities regulators from Brazil, Japan, the People's Republic of China, and South Korea. The Monitoring Board oversees the IFRS Foundation trustees, participates in the trustee nomination process, and approves appointments to the trustees. The specific functions of the Monitoring Board include the following:

- To enhance public accountability of the IASC Foundation.
- To participate in the trustee nomination process and approval of appointments to the trustees.
- To carry out oversight responsibilities in relation to the trustees and their oversight of the IASB's activities, in particular the agenda-setting process and the IASB's efforts to improve the accuracy and effectiveness of financial reporting and to protect investors.

EXHIBIT 3.1
The Structure of the
IASB

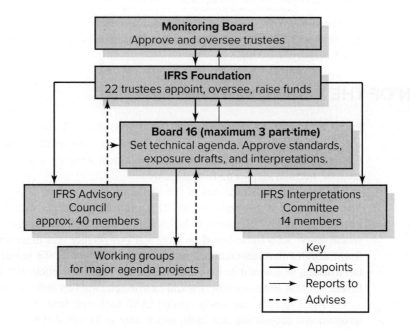

Trustees of the IFRS Foundation

The IFRS Foundation consists of 22 trustees (the number of trustees was increased from 19 to 22 as a result of revisions to the IFRS Foundation in June 2005). These 22 trustees represent different geographical areas (six from North America; six from Europe; six from the Asia/Oceania region; and four from any area, subject to establishing overall geographical balance). With regard to the composition of the trustees, the constitution requires an appropriate balance of professional backgrounds, including auditors, preparers, users, academics, and other officials serving the public interest. Two trustees are normally senior partners of prominent international accounting firms. The trustees of the IFRS Foundation have the responsibility, among other things, to:

*   Appoint the members of the IASB and establish their contracts of service and performance criteria.
*   Appoint the members of the International Financial Reporting Interpretations Committee and the IFRS Advisory Council.
*   Review annually the strategy of the IASC Foundation and the IASB and its effectiveness, including consideration, but not determination, of the IASB's agenda.
*   Approve annually the budget of the IFRS Foundation and determine the basis for funding.
*   Review broad strategic issues affecting accounting standards, promote the IASC Foundation and its work, and promote the objective of rigorous application of IAS and IFRS—provided that the trustees shall be excluded from involvement in technical matters relating to accounting standards.
*   Establish and amend operating procedures, consultative arrangements, and due process for the IASB, the International Financial Reporting Interpretations Committee, and the Standards Advisory Council (SAC).
*   Review compliance with the operating procedures, consultative arrangements, and due process procedures.
*   Approve amendments to the constitution after following a due process, including consultation with the IFRS Advisory Council and publication of an Exposure Draft for public comment and subject to the voting requirements.

- Exercise all powers of the IFRS Foundation, except for those expressly reserved for the IASB, the IFRS Interpretations Committee, and the IFRS Advisory Council.
- Foster and review the development of educational programs and materials that are consistent with the IFRS Foundation's objectives.

International Accounting Standards Board
The IASB has sole responsibility for establishing the IFRS.

The principal responsibilities of the IASB are to:

- Develop and issue IFRS and Exposure Drafts.
- Approve interpretations developed by the International Financial Reporting Interpretations Committee (IFRIC).

The Board consists of 14 members (effective February 1, 2009), of whom at least 11 serve full-time and not more than 3 serve part-time.

The Board members are selected on the basis of professional competence and practical experience. They are expected to represent a geographical mix and to ensure a broad international diversity. Since December 2018, the composition of the board has been:

- Four members from the Asia/Oceania region.
- Four members from Europe.
- Four members from the Americas.
- One member from Africa.
- One member appointed from any area, subject to maintaining overall geographical balance.

Due process procedures followed by the IASB include the following (the steps that are required by the IASC Foundation constitution are indicated by an asterisk*):

1. Ask the staff to identify and review the issues associated with the topic and to consider the application of the *Framework* to the issues.
2. Study national accounting requirements and practice and exchange views about the issues with national standard-setters.
3. Consult the SAC about the advisability of adding the topic to the IASB's agenda.*
4. Form an advisory group (generally called a "working group") to advise the IASB and its staff on the project.
5. Publish for public comment a discussion document.
6. Publish for public comment an Exposure Draft approved by the vote of at least nine IASB members, including any dissenting opinions held by IASB members (in Exposure Drafts, dissenting opinions are referred to as "alternative views").*
7. Publish within an Exposure Draft a basis for conclusions.
8. Consider all comments received within the comment period on discussion documents and Exposure Drafts.*
9. Consider the desirability of holding a public hearing and the desirability of conducting field tests and, if considered desirable, holding such hearings and conducting such tests.
10. Approve a standard by the votes of at least nine IASB members and include in the published standard any dissenting opinions.*
11. Publish within a standard a basis for conclusions, explaining, among other things, the steps in the IASB's due process and how the IASB dealt with public comments on the Exposure Draft.

In March 2006, the trustees of the IFRS Foundation published a new *Due Process Handbook* for the IASB. The *Handbook* describes the IASB's consultative procedures.

IFRS Advisory Council

The IFRS Advisory Council provides a forum for participation by organizations and individuals with an interest in international financial reporting, having diverse geographical and functional backgrounds. Its objectives include: (a) to advise the IASB on its priorities, and (b) to inform the IASB of the views of the Council members on its major standard-setting projects.[10]

The Advisory Council currently has about 40 members. The requirement is to have at least 30 members. Members are appointed by the trustees for a renewable term of three years. They have diverse geographical and functional backgrounds.

IFRS Interpretations Committee

The IFRS Interpretations Committee (initially this committee was known as the Standing Interpretations Committee and later changed its name to the International Financial Reporting Interpretations Committee) has 14 members appointed by the Trustees for terms of three years (in November 2007, the membership was increased from 12 to 14).

The Committee's responsibilities include:

- To interpret the application of IFRS and provide guidance on issues not specifically addressed in IFRS or IASs, in the context of the IASB's framework.
- To publish Draft Interpretations for public comment and consider their comments before finalizing an interpretation.
- To obtain Board approval for final interpretation.[11]

IFRS Foundation Constitution

In January 2009, the trustees voted to revise the constitution for changes resulting from the first phase of the review, including formation of the Monitoring Board. In January 2010, the trustees again voted to revise the constitution for changes resulting from the second phase of the review, including name changes from IASC Foundation to IFRS Foundation, from International Financial Reporting Interpretations Committee to IFRS Interpretations Committee, and from the SAC to IFRS Advisory Council.

International Sustainability Standards Board

In November 2021, the IFRS Foundation launched an initiative to form the International Sustainability Standards Board (ISSB). The ISSB will be a deliberative body that develops and promulgates a globally accepted set of standards in the area of *sustainability reporting,* also referred to as *environmental, social, and governance (ESG) reporting.* As currently envisioned, the ISSB will be a separate, roughly co-equal, board that reports directly to the IFRS Foundation.

The ISSB's establishment will be a major milestone in the development of sustainability reporting. In taking this step, the IFRS Foundation has responded to the rapidly growing demand for ESG disclosures by investors around the world, as well as the need to bring more rigor and standardization to what has been heretofore a chaotic, largely voluntary reporting system. Sustainability reporting is covered in greater detail in Chapter 12.

---

[10] Source: https://www.iasplus.com.

[11] Source: https://www.iasplus.com.

FROM HARMONIZATION TO CONVERGENCE OF FINANCIAL REPORTING STANDARDS

The IASB has earned a great deal of goodwill from many interested parties. Its approach clearly reflected a change of role from a harmonizer to a global standard-setter. The phrase "international convergence of accounting standards" refers to both a goal and the process adopted to achieve it. The goal of "convergence" in accounting standards can be interpreted differently. From a strict viewpoint, it refers to the enforcement of a single set of accepted standards by several regulatory bodies. From a soft viewpoint, it refers to diminishing differences among accounting standards issued by several regulators. According to a third viewpoint, it refers to a situation where two or more jurisdictions agree on a core set of common standards, allowing varying interpretations regarding non-core issues. Similarly, in implementing the international "convergence" process, three fundamental approaches can be adopted. First, the aim could be to merge all standard-setting bodies into a unified "global" body. From a theoretical point of view, it is often argued that the unified solution of a single international standard-setting body is optimal. Second, the aim could be to recognize each of the existing standard-setting bodies as the sole authority in its respective jurisdiction. Accordingly, it could also be argued that discretion and flexibility in accounting standards through mutual recognition are theoretically more desirable than uniformity and rigidity, and when the incentive consequences and the investment effects of accounting standards are taken into consideration, then discretion can be superior to uniformity. Third, the aim could also be to recognize that a national standard-setting body can coexist with international coordination bodies. The IASB's main objective is to achieve international convergence with its standards. In other words, the efforts of the IASB are directed toward developing a high-quality set of standards for use internationally for financial reporting purposes (global standard-setting).[12]

According to its former chairman, the IASB's strategy has been to identify the best in standards around the world and build a body of accounting standards that constitutes the "highest common denominator" of financial reporting. The IASB has adopted a principles-based approach to standard-setting and has obtained the support of U.S. regulators (even though U.S. standard-setters historically have taken a rules-based approach). On the other hand, the IASB's structure is similar to that of the U.S. standard-setter, recognizing that the FASB has the best institutional structure for developing accounting standards.

The major concerns in achieving IFRS convergence include:

- The complicated nature of particular standards, especially those related to financial instruments and fair value accounting.
- For countries with tax-driven national accounting regimes, using IFRS as the basis for taxation may be a problem.
- Disagreement with certain significant IFRS, especially those related to financial statements and fair value accounting.
- Insufficient guidance on first-time application of IFRS.
- For countries with limited capital markets, there is little benefit to be derived from using IFRS.
- Investor/user satisfaction with national accounting standards.
- IFRS language translation difficulties.

---

[12] G. Whittington, "The Adoption of International Accounting Standards in the European Union," *European Accounting Review* 14, no. 1 (2005), pp. 127–53.

The IASB has taken initiatives to facilitate and enhance its role as a global standard-setter. The issuance of IFRS 1 is one such initiative. IFRS 1 was issued in response to the concern about a lack of guidance on first-time application of IFRS. The official language of the IASB is English, and IFRS are written in this language. The IASB has attempted to address the translation issue by permitting national accountancy bodies to translate IFRS into more than 30 languages, including Chinese, French, German, Japanese, Portuguese, and Spanish.

As stated earlier in this chapter, the main objective of the IASB is to achieve international convergence with IFRS. However, as Stephen Zeff has pointed out, some obstacles to comparability are likely to arise in areas of the business and financial culture, the accounting culture, the auditing culture, and the regulatory culture.[13] He also warns that, in addition to the obstacles to convergence due to the problems of interpretation, language, and terminology, the impact of politics could create a "catch-22" situation. He states:

> The more rigorous the enforcement mechanism—that is, the more authority and the larger budget a country gives to its securities market regulator to fortify the effort to secure compliance with IFRS—the more lobbying pressure that will be brought on the IASB, because companies in such countries will know that they have no "escape valve," no way of side-stepping the adverse consequences, as they see them, of a proposed IASB standard or interpretation. If the auditor is strict and the regulator is strict, political lobbying of the standard setter, IASB, may become more intense. If a powerful company or group of companies do not like a draft standard, they will have an incentive to engage in politicking of the standard-setting body. Hence it becomes a Catch-22.

Regardless of the arguments against harmonization/convergence, substantial efforts to reduce differences in accounting practice have been ongoing for several decades. The question is no longer *whether* convergence should be strived for, but *how to achieve* convergence.

PRESENTATION OF FINANCIAL STATEMENTS (IAS 1/IFRS 1)

IAS 1 is a single standard providing guidelines for the preparation and presentation of financial statements. In September 2007, the IASB published a revised IAS 1, effective for annual periods beginning on or after January 1, 2009. It provides guidance in the following areas:

- *Purpose of financial statements.* To provide information for decision making.
- *Components of financial statements.* A set of financial statements must include a balance sheet, income statement, statement of cash flows, statement of changes in equity, and notes, comprising a summary of significant accounting policies and other explanatory notes.
- *Overriding principle of fair presentation.* IAS 1 states that financial statements "shall present fairly the financial position, financial performance and cash flows of an entity. Fair presentation requires the faithful representation of the effects of transactions, other events and conditions in accordance with the definitions and recognition criteria for assets, liabilities, income and expenses set out in the *Framework.*"[14] Compliance with IFRS generally ensures fair presentation. In the *extremely rare* circumstance when management concludes that compliance with the requirement of a standard or interpretation would be so misleading that it would conflict with the objective of financial statements set out in the *Framework,* IAS 1 *requires* departing from that requirement, with extensive disclosures made in the notes. If the local regulatory framework will not allow departing from a requirement, disclosures must be made to reduce the misleading aspects of compliance with that requirement.

[13] S. Zeff, "Political Lobbying on Proposed Standards: A Challenge to the IASB," *Accounting Horizons* 16, no. 1 (2002), pp. 43–54.
[14] IAS 1.

- *Accounting policies.* Management should select and apply accounting policies to be in compliance with all IASB standards and all applicable interpretations. If guidance is lacking on a specific issue, management should refer to (a) the requirements and guidance in other IASB standards dealing with similar issues; (b) the definitions, recognition, and measurement criteria for assets, liabilities, income, and expenses set out in the IASB *Framework;* and (c) pronouncements of other standard-setting bodies and accepted industry practices to the extent, but only to the extent, that these are consistent with (a) and (b). IAS 1 does not indicate that this is a hierarchy. It is important to note that individual country GAAP may be used to fill in the blanks, but only if consistent with other IASB standards and the IASB *Framework.*

- *Basic principles and assumptions.* IAS 1 reiterates the accrual basis and going-concern assumptions and the consistency and comparative information principles found in the *Framework.* IAS 1 adds to the guidance provided in the *Framework* by indicating that immaterial items should be aggregated. It also stipulates that assets and liabilities and income and expenses should not be offset and reported at a net amount unless specifically permitted by a standard or interpretation.

- *Structure and content of financial statements.* IAS 1 also provides guidance with respect to: (a) current/noncurrent distinction, (b) items to be presented on the face of financial statements, and (c) items to be disclosed in the notes.

IAS 1 requires companies to classify assets and liabilities as current and noncurrent on the balance sheet, except when a presentation based on liquidity provides information that is reliable and more relevant. IAS 1 also provides guidance with respect to the items, at a minimum, that should be reported on the face of the income statement or balance sheet. The line items comprising profit before tax must be reflected using either a nature of expense format (common in Continental Europe) or a function of expense format (commonly found in Anglo countries). IAS 1 specifically precludes designating items as extraordinary on the income statement or in the notes.

A PRINCIPLES-BASED APPROACH TO INTERNATIONAL FINANCIAL REPORTING STANDARDS

The IASB uses a principles-based approach in developing accounting standards, rather than a rules-based approach. Principles-based standards focus on establishing general principles derived from the IASB *Framework,* providing recognition, measurement, and reporting requirements for the transactions covered by the standard. By following this approach, IFRS tend to limit guidance for applying the general principles to typical transactions and encourage professional judgment in applying the general principles to transactions specific to an entity or industry. Sir David Tweedie, former chairman of the IASB, explains the principles-based approach of the IASB as follows:

> The IASB concluded that a body of detailed guidance (sometimes referred to as *brightlines*) encourages a rule-based mentality of "where does it say I can't do this?" We take the view that this is counter-productive and helps those who are intent on finding ways around standards more than it helps those seeking to apply standards in a way that gives useful information. Put simply, adding the detailed guidance may obscure, rather than highlight, the underlying principles. The emphasis tends to be on compliance with the letter of the rule rather than on the spirit of the accounting standard. We prefer an approach that requires the company and its auditors to take a step back and consider with the underlying principles. This is not a soft option. Our approach requires both companies and their auditors to exercise professional judgement in the public interest. Our approach requires a strong commitment from preparers to financial statements that provide a faithful representation of all transactions and

strong commitment from auditors to resist client pressures. It will not work without those commitments. There will be more individual transactions and situations that are not explicitly addressed. We hope that a clear statement of the underlying principles will allow companies and auditors to deal with those situations without resorting to detailed rules.[15]

A report published by the Institute of Chartered Accountants in Scotland in early 2006 stated that rules-based accounting adds unnecessary complexity, encourages financial engineering, and does not necessarily lead to a true and fair view or a fair presentation. Further, it pointed out that the volume of rules would hinder the translation into different languages and cultures. The Global Accounting Alliance (GAA) supported a single set of globally accepted and principles-based accounting standards that focused on transparency and capital market needs and would be ideal for all stakeholders.[16] In February 2010, the IOSCO, in a report entitled "Principles for Periodic Disclosure by Listed Entities," provided securities regulators with a framework for establishing or reviewing their periodic disclosure regimes. According to the report, its principles-based format allows for a wide range of application and adaptation by securities regulators.

ARGUMENTS FOR AND AGAINST INTERNATIONAL CONVERGENCE OF FINANCIAL REPORTING STANDARDS

Arguments for Convergence

Proponents of accounting convergence put forward several arguments. First, they argue that comparability of financial statements worldwide is necessary for the globalization of capital markets. Financial statement comparability would make it easier for investors to evaluate potential investments in foreign securities and thereby take advantage of the risk reduction possible through international diversification. Second, accounting convergence would simplify the evaluation by multinational companies of possible foreign takeover targets. Third, convergence would reduce financial reporting costs for companies that seek to list their shares on foreign stock exchanges. Cross-listing of securities would allow companies to gain access to less expensive capital in other countries and would make it easier for foreign investors to acquire the company's stock. Fourth, national differences in corporate reporting cause loss of investor confidence, which affects the availability and cost of capital. Investors often build in a premium to the required return on their investment if there is any uncertainty or lack of comparability about the figures—and such premiums can be as large as 40 percent.[17] Fifth, one set of universally accepted accounting standards would reduce the cost of preparing worldwide consolidated financial statements, and the auditing of these statements also would be simplified. Sixth, multinational companies would find it easier to transfer accounting staff to other countries. This would be true for the international auditing firms as well. Finally, convergence would help raise the quality level of accounting practices internationally, thereby increasing the credibility of financial information. In relation to this argument, some point out that as a result of convergence, developing countries would be able to adopt a ready-made set of high-quality standards with minimum cost and effort.

[15] Excerpt from a speech delivered before the Committee on Banking, Housing and Urban Affairs of the U.S. Senate, Washington, DC, February 14, 2002.

[16] The Global Accounting Alliance was an alliance of 11 leading professional accounting bodies in the United States, the United Kingdom, Canada, Hong Kong, Australia, Germany, Japan, New Zealand, and South Africa formed in November 2005 to promote quality services, share information, and collaborate on important international issues.

[17] David Illigworth, president of the Institute of Chartered Accountants in England and Wales, in a speech at the China Economic Summit 2004 of the 7th China Beijing International High-Tech Expo, May 21, 2004.

Arguments against Convergence

The greatest obstacle to convergence is the magnitude of the differences that exist between countries and the fact that the political cost of eliminating those differences would be enormous. One of the main obstacles is nationalism. Whether out of deep-seated tradition, indifference born of economic power, or resistance to intrusion of foreign influence, some say that national entities will not bow to any international body. Arriving at principles that satisfy all of the parties involved throughout the world seems an almost impossible task. Not only would convergence be difficult to achieve, but the need for such standards is not universally accepted. A well-developed global capital market exists already. It has evolved without uniform accounting standards. Opponents of convergence argue that it is unnecessary to force all companies worldwide to follow a common set of rules. They also point out that this would lead to a situation of "standards overload" as a result of requiring some enterprises to comply with a set of standards not relevant to them. The international capital market will force those companies that can benefit from accessing the market to provide the required accounting information without convergence. Yet another argument against convergence is that because of different environmental influences, differences in accounting across countries might be appropriate and necessary. For example, countries that are at different stages of economic development or that rely on different sources of financing perhaps should have differently oriented accounting systems. Professor Frederick Choi refers to this as the dilemma of global harmonization. According to him, the dilemma is that the thesis of environmentally stimulated and justified differences in accounting runs directly counter to efforts at the worldwide harmonization of accounting.[18]

THE IASB CONCEPTUAL FRAMEWORK

The Need for a Framework

With no conceptual framework, accounting standards are developed unsystematically. As a result, accounting standards may be inconsistent and, according to *Gresham's law,* bad accounting practices will triumph over good practices.[19] In this situation, a principle or practice may be declared to be "right" because it is generally accepted, but it may not be generally accepted because it is "right." Further, it is unwise to develop standards unless there is agreement on the scope and objective of financial reporting, the type of entities that should produce financial reports, recognition and measurement rules, and qualitative characteristics of financial information. Furthermore, by adding rigor and discipline, a conceptual framework enhances public confidence in financial reports, and preparers and auditors can use the conceptual framework as a point of reference to resolve an accounting issue in the absence of a standard that specifically deals with that issue.

The *Framework for the Preparation and Presentation of Financial Statements* was first approved by the IASC Board in 1989 and was reaffirmed by the newly formed IASB in 2001. The objective of the *Framework* is to establish the concepts underlying the preparation and presentation of IFRS-based financial statements. It deals with the following:

1. Objective of financial statements and underlying assumptions.
2. Qualitative characteristics that affect the usefulness of financial statements.
3. Definition, recognition, and measurement of the financial statements elements.
4. Concepts of capital and capital maintenance.

[18] See F. D. S. Choi, "A Cluster Approach to Harmonization." *Management Accounting,* August 1981, pp. 27–31.

[19] Gresham's law is named after Sir Thomas Gresham (1519–1579), an English financier in Tudor times. It means, briefly, "Bad money drives out good."

The purpose of the *Framework* is, among other things, to assist the IASB in developing future standards and revising existing standards. It also is intended to assist preparers of financial statements in applying IFRS and in dealing with topics that have not yet been addressed in IFRS. The *Framework* identifies investors, creditors, employees, suppliers, customers, government agencies, and the general public as potential users of financial statements but concludes that financial statements that are designed to meet the needs of investors will also meet most of the information needs of other users. This is an important conclusion because it sets the tone for the nature of individual IFRS, that is, that their application will result in a set of financial statements that is useful for making investment decisions.

Objective of Financial Statements and Underlying Assumptions

The *Framework* establishes that the primary objective of IFRS-based financial statements is to *provide information useful for decision making.* Financial statements also show the results of management's stewardship of enterprise resources, but that is not their primary objective. To meet the objective of decision usefulness, financial statements must be prepared on an *accrual basis.* The other underlying assumption is that the enterprise for which financial statements are being prepared is a *going concern.*

Qualitative Characteristics of Financial Statements

The four characteristics that make financial statement information useful are *understandability, relevance, reliability,* and *comparability.* Information is relevant if it can be used to make predictions of the future or if it can be used to confirm expectations from the past. The *Framework* indicates that the relevance of information is affected by its nature and its materiality. An item of information is material if its misstatement or omission could influence the decision of a user of financial statements.

Information is reliable when it is neutral (i.e., free of bias) and represents faithfully what it purports to. The *Framework* specifically states that reflecting items in the financial statements based on their economic substance rather than their legal form is necessary for faithful representation. The *Framework* also states that while the exercise of prudence (conservatism) in measuring accounting elements is necessary, it does not allow the creation of hidden reserves or excessive provisions to deliberately understate income, as this would be biased and therefore would not have the quality of reliability.

Elements of Financial Statements: Definition, Recognition, and Measurement

Assets are defined as resources controlled by the enterprise from which future economic benefits are expected to flow to the enterprise. Note that a resource need not be owned to be an asset of an enterprise. This allows, for example, for leased resources to be treated as assets. An *asset should be recognized only when it is probable that future economic benefits will flow to the enterprise and the asset has a cost or value that can be measured reliably.* The *Framework* acknowledges that several different measurement bases may be used to measure assets, including historical cost, current cost, realizable value, and present value.

Liabilities are present obligations arising from past events that are expected to be settled through an outflow of resources. Obligations need not be contractual to be treated as a liability. Similar to assets, *liabilities should be recognized when it is probable that an outflow of resources will be required to settle them and the amount can be measured reliably.* Also as with assets, several different bases exist for measuring liabilities, including the amount of proceeds received in exchange for the obligation, the amount that would be required to settle the obligation currently, undiscounted settlement value in the normal course of business, and the present value of future cash outflows expected to settle the liabilities.

The *Framework* identifies income and expenses as the two elements that constitute profit. *Income,* which encompasses both revenues and gains, is defined as increases in equity other than from transactions with owners. *Expenses,* including losses, are decreases in equity other than through distributions to owners. *Equity* is defined as assets minus liabilities. Income should be recognized when the increase in an asset or decrease in a liability can be measured reliably. The *Framework* does not provide more specific guidance with respect to income recognition. (This topic is covered in IAS 18, *Revenue.*) Expenses are recognized when the related decrease in assets or increase in liabilities can be measured reliably. The *Framework* acknowledges the use of the matching principle in recognizing liabilities but specifically precludes use of the matching principle to recognize expenses and a related liability when it does not meet the definition of a liability. For example, it is inappropriate to recognize an expense if a present obligation arising from a past event does not exist.

Concepts of Capital Maintenance

The *Framework* describes different concepts of capital maintenance (financial capital maintenance vs physical capital maintenance) and acknowledges that each leads to a different basis for measuring assets (historical cost vs current cost). The *Framework* does not prescribe one measurement basis (and related model of accounting) over another, but indicates that it (the *Framework*) is applicable to a range of accounting models.

INTERNATIONAL FINANCIAL REPORTING STANDARDS (IFRS)

The IASC has issued 41 IAS, of which 16 IAS have been superseded mainly by IFRS. As a result, only 25 IAS are still in force in 2022. The IASB has issued 17 IFRS, of which IFRS 4, *Insurance Contracts,* has been superseded by IFRS 17, *Insurance Contracts.* IFRS 1 was issued by the IASB in 2003, providing guidance on the important question of how a company goes about restating its financial statements when it adopts IFRS for the first time. Because the IASB is a private body, it does not have the ability to enforce its standards. Instead, the IASB develops IFRS for the public good, making them available to any country or company that might choose to adopt them.

Adoption of IFRS

There are a number of different ways in which a country might adopt IFRS, including requiring (or permitting) IFRS to be used by the following:

1. *All* companies; in effect, IFRS replace national GAAP.
2. *Consolidated entities* preparing group-level financial statements; national GAAP is used in parent company-only financial statements.
3. *Stock exchange–listed* companies in preparing consolidated financial statements. Nonlisted companies use national GAAP.
4. *Foreign* companies listing on domestic stock exchanges. Domestic companies use national GAAP.
5. Domestic companies that list on *foreign* stock exchanges. Other domestic companies use national GAAP.

Below we will survey the extent to which IFRS has been incorporated into the accounting systems of the world's major economies. Before doing so, we should note that many developing countries have adopted IFRS with little or no amendment to their national standards. For some, it may have been a less expensive option than developing their own standards. The need to attract foreign investment also may have been an influencing factor. Countries changing from centrally planned to market-based economies also have found

IFRS attractive, as they offer a ready-made set of standards to facilitate the development of a market system.

In contrast, larger economies have tended to have already-well-developed capital markets and better resourced regulatory bodies. They may have also had more rigidly established systems of financial reporting. Thus, the costs of migrating to a new accounting system may have been perceived to be higher while the immediate need to do so lower. Each of the foregoing characteristics is certainly true of the United States. We will conclude our survey by chronicling the long, up-and-down relationship American accountants have had with IFRS convergence.

IFRS in the European Union

The single most important milestone in the global dissemination of IFRS occurred in July 2002, when the European Union (EU) issued a directive (Regulation 1606/2002) requiring all listed companies of member states to prepare consolidated financial statements based on IFRS beginning January 1, 2005. The aim was to improve the quality of corporate financial reporting by increasing comparability and transparency and to promote the development of a single capital market in Europe.

Technically, the EU adopts IFRS through the mediation of the European Financial Reporting Advisory Group (EFRAG), a private-sector non-profit. EFRAG plays the dual role of advocating for European perspectives at the IASB and providing technical advice to the European Commission on implementing IFRS. From time to time, EFRAG may suggest amendments to particular IFRS provisions that are necessary for adoption by the EU. Once a standard, including amendments, meets EFRAG's criteria, the EU *endorses* it, thereby giving it the force of law.

The requirement that the EU formally endorse, that is, adopt, IFRS is generally reflected in accounting policy descriptions used by EU companies and auditors. For instance, the Swedish firm AB Electrolux in Note 1, Accounting Principles of the 2021 Annual Report, describes the basis of preparation of its consolidated financial statements as follows:

> The consolidated financial statements are prepared in accordance with International
> Financial Reporting Standards (IFRS) *as endorsed* by the European Union (EU).

Electrolux's auditor, Deloitte AB, uses similar language in its audit opinion.

In addition to consolidated financial statements prepared using IFRS, Electrolux's annual report also presents parent-level statements prepared according to the Sweden's *Annual Accounts Act* (1995). In doing so, Electrolux follows the dominant paradigm in the European Union for publicly listed corporations: group-level consolidated accounts prepared using IFRS and parent-level accounts prepared according to national GAAP.

Swedish company law specifies that even parent-level statements follow IFRS as far as possible within the framework of the Annual Accounts Act. As noted earlier in this chapter, there has been substantial convergence of national GAAP toward IFRS throughout the EU. However, significant differences remain. For instance, Electrolux's IFRS-based consolidated balance sheet categorizes the Electrolux trademark in North America as *indefinitely-lived.* In other words, utilizing the provisions of IFRS, the company carries this asset in its balance sheet without amortization. In contrast, Sweden's national accounting system requires all identifiable intangibles, including trademarks, to be amortized over finite useful lives. Thus, Electrolux discloses the following departure from IFRS accounting in its parent-level financial statements:

> The Parent Company amortizes trademarks in accordance with RFR2 (Accounting for Legal
> Entities). The Electrolux trademark in North America is amortized over 40 years using the
> straight-line method. All other trademarks are amortized over their useful lives, estimated to
> be 10 years, using the straight-line method.

Accounting for intangible assets under IFRS is discussed in greater detail in Chapter 4.

IFRS in China and India

Both the People's Republic of China (PRC) and India maintain their own domestic accounting standards, that is, national GAAP. However, each has undertaken significant convergence initiatives to bring its national standards into conformity with IFRS. In the case of China, the Ministry of Finance enacted 38 Accounting Standards for Business Enterprises in 2007. These Chinese Accounting Standards (CAS) addressed substantially all of the topics covered by IFRS at the time. The primary difference between IFRS and CAS is that IFRS gives companies the option to revalue fixed assets, such as property, plant, and equipment (see Chapter 4), while CAS mandates the use of historical cost for such assets. Note that in this case, companies following CAS would not be in violation of IFRS because IFRS permits historical cost for these assets.

We should also note that 30 percent of Chinese companies by market capitalization use IFRS outright because they have shares that are listed on the Hong Kong Stock Exchange (HKSE). The HKSE requires the use of IFRS. For example, Tencent, the largest Chinese company by market capitalization, lists its share in Hong Kong and discloses in its 2021 annual report:

> The consolidated financial statements of the Group have been prepared in accordance with all applicable International Financial Reporting Standards ("IFRSs").

As is the case with many large Chinese technology companies, the *Group* in Tencent's case consists of a parent holding company domiciled in the Cayman Islands that controls Chinese operating entities through contracts. American accountants would refer to these entities as variable interest entities (VIEs). This sort of corporate organization is used by many of the large Chinese companies that report under IFRS, including Alibaba.

India's adoption of IFRS largely resembles that of China, although lagging by about one decade. Through 2014, Indian companies used Indian Generally Accepted Accounting Principles, or I-GAAP, a set of standards that had its roots in the accounting traditions of the British Commonwealth, but that had already been brought into alignment with IFRS in many respects. Beginning in 2015, Indian companies were allowed to switch to India's new implementation of IFRS, termed Indian Accounting Standards, or *Ind AS*. The use of Ind AS became mandatory for large public and private companies in 2016 and for smaller companies in 2017.

For the purposes of most accountants, Ind AS can be considered a faithful implementation of IFRS in the Indian context. However, there are a number of small differences between the two systems scattered throughout the Ind AS standards. For example, IAS 40, the IFRS standard for investment property (see Chapter 4), allows investment properties to be carried in the balance sheet at either historical cost or fair value. Ind AS 40 also covers investment property but restricts Indian companies to the cost method. Note that as in the Chinese case discussed above, an Indian company applying Ind AS 40 would not violate the relevant provisions of IAS 40.

IFRS in Japan

The vast majority of Japanese companies use Japanese GAAP, a national GAAP system that differs materially from IFRS. However, the Japanese government has long recognized the need for its prominent multinational companies to be able to transact in global markets using financial statements prepared according to internationally recognized standards. As early as the late 1960s, Japanese companies such as Sony and Toyota received permission to use U.S. GAAP in lieu of Japanese GAAP for consolidated financial reporting. Implicitly, the target audience for these U.S. GAAP statements was international investors, creditors, vendors, and customers. A recent example of a Japanese company utilizing this reporting flexibility is Omron, a multinational electronics company based in Kyoto, Japan. Omron's 2021 annual report contained the following passage in its footnote describing significant accounting policies:

> Based upon requirements for depositary receipts issued in Europe, the consolidated financial statements are presented in accordance with accounting principles generally accepted in the United States of America.

Given Japan's longstanding openness to allowing the use by its companies of foreign financial accounting standards, it is no surprise that the Japanese government also allows its companies to use IFRS in lieu of Japanese GAAP for essentially the same reasons that it condoned the use of U.S. GAAP in earlier decades. Beginning in 2010, Japan's Financial Services Agency (FSA) began allowing companies with overseas subsidiaries to use IFRS for consolidated reporting. Over time, the FSA has eased the rules and encourage companies to adopt IFRS. By December 31, 2021, over 200 Japanese publicly listed companies had adopted IFRS representing 40 percent of Japan's stock market capitalization. The most prominent company to have done so is Toyota, which migrated from U.S. GAAP to IFRS in the first quarter of the 2020-21 fiscal year. According to the company's financial statements of that quarter:

> Toyota Motor Corporation has replaced Generally Accepted Accounting Standards in the United States (U.S. GAAP) and adopted International Financial Reporting Standards (IFRS) beginning with the first quarter ended June 30, 2020.

It is worth noting that Japan has not adopted the aggressive measures of China and India to bring Japanese GAAP (J-GAAP), its set of national accounting standards, into alignment with IFRS. Instead, it issued Japan's Modified International Standards (JMIS) in 2015. JMIS was the country's attempt to create an IFRS-aligned national standard. However, granted the flexibility to choose either J-GAAP or IFRS, companies have seen no benefit of adopting JMIS, and the system languishes largely unused.

Japan is unique among the world's economies in allowing large, prominent domestic companies to choose from among three different sets of accounting standards in the preparation of consolidated financial statements. This degree of accounting choice certainly inhibits investors' ability to make comparisons that they would consider relevant. To understand the extent of this problem, review the following table, which contains a sampling of companies that reported under each of the different systems in fiscal 2020-21.

Industry	IFRS	Japanese GAAP	U.S. GAAP
Autos	Toyota Motor	Mazda Motor	
	Honda Motor	Nissan Motor	
Airlines	Japan Airlines	All Nippon Airways	
Equipment Manufacturing	Kubota	Kawasaki	Komatsu
Electronic Components	Nidec	Ibiden	Murata Mfg.
Investment Banking	SBI Holdings	Daiwa Securities	Nomura Securities

Every day, many investors around the world are comparing the operating profit or financial position of, say, Toyota against that of Nissan, or of Kubota against that of Komatsu. The best informed of these investors incorporate into their decision making the fact that financial data about these companies is being prepared under several different sets of rules.

IFRS in the United States

Initially, of the 14 countries represented on IOSCO's Technical Committee, only Canada and the United States did not allow foreign companies to use IAS without reconciliation to local GAAP for listing purposes.[20] In 1996, the U.S. SEC announced three criteria IAS must meet to be acceptable for cross-listing purposes. Namely, IAS must:

- Constitute a comprehensive, generally accepted basis of accounting.
- Be of high quality, resulting in comparability and transparency, and providing for full disclosure.
- Be rigorously interpreted and applied.

Partly in response to the third criterion, the IASC created a Standing Interpretations Committee (SIC) to provide guidance on accounting issues where there is likely to be divergent or unacceptable treatment in the absence of specific guidance in an IAS. The SEC began its assessment of the IASC's core set of standards in 1999 and issued a concept release in 2000 soliciting comments on whether it should modify its requirement that all financial statements be reconciled to U.S. GAAP.

The Norwalk Agreement

In September 2002, at a meeting in Norwalk, Connecticut, the FASB and the IASB pledged to use their best efforts (1) to make their existing financial reporting standards fully compatible as soon as is practicable, and (2) to coordinate their work program to ensure that once achieved, compatibility would be maintained. This became known as the "Norwalk Agreement." Note that this agreement did not mean that the FASB would always try to move in the direction of IASB standards to remove existing differences, but that the opposite also would occur. Significantly, the two standard-setters agreed to work together on future issues to try to develop common solutions. In March 2003, the IASB decided to use identical style and wording in the standards issued by the FASB and IASB on joint projects. The expectation was that through these initiatives, significant progress could be made toward convergence with IFRS over time.

Support for a Principles-Based Approach

A significant undercurrent within the U.S. accounting community that strengthened support for acceptance of IFRS was a growing recognition of the need to move to a principles-based approach in formulating accounting standards. Support for the elevation of *principles* over *rules* came from many quarters, including current and former U.S. regulators. It was pointed out that as part of the commitment to convergence, the FASB and SEC should change their behavior and become more like the rest of the world. For example, a former SEC chairman, expressing preference for the IASB's principles-based standards, referred to the IASB's approach as a "Ten Commandments" approach in contrast to the FASB's "cookbook" approach.[21] The SEC chairman, in a speech made in Puerto Rico in February 2002, also expressed preference for a principles-based set of accounting standards.[22] In addition, in an editorial in the June 27, 2002, edition of *Financial Times,* titled "The World after

---

[20] The SEC allows foreign companies listed on U.S. stock exchanges to file annual reports based on IAS, but only if a reconciliation from IAS to U.S. GAAP for income and stockholders' equity is included in the notes to the financial statements. Many foreign companies find this reconciliation to be very costly and view this requirement as a significant barrier to entering the U.S. capital market.

[21] See: https://www.sec.gov/rules/other/2010/33-9109.pdf.

[22] See: www.sec.gov/news/speech/spch539.htm.

WorldCom," U.S. regulators were urged to move to principles-based standards. The following is an extract from that editorial:

> It is time for U.S. accounting standards to move away from prescriptive rulemaking towards the alternative used in many other countries, which focuses on "substance over form." U.S. regulators have been suspicious of principles-based standards drafted by the International Accounting Standards Board, arguing that the U.S. approach is superior. As the list of U.S. accounting scandals mounts, it is hard to maintain such a position.

The SEC and IFRS Convergence

In November 2007, the SEC decided to remove the requirement that foreign private issuers using IFRS reconcile their financial statements to U.S. GAAP. This reflected the recognition that IFRS had become a high-quality set of accounting standards that is capable of ensuring adequate disclosure for the protection of investors and the promotion of fair, orderly, and efficient markets. This decision was supported by the experience in the European markets, where there had been no market disruption or loss of investor confidence as a result of the introduction of IFRS in 2005. Substantial amounts of capital had been invested by U.S. investors in European companies that report under IFRS, thus suggesting that many U.S. investors already had concluded that IFRS is a fit-for-purpose financial reporting framework. Beginning in 2007, the Form 20-F filed by these companies with the SEC no longer included a reconciliation to U.S. GAAP.

Elimination of the reconciliation requirement for foreign filers who prepare their financial reports in accordance with IFRS created an asymmetric situation, as domestic filers do not have the option of preparing their financial reports in accordance with IFRS. In July 2007, the SEC issued a concept release soliciting public comment on the idea of allowing U.S. companies to choose between the use of IFRS and U.S. GAAP. In October 2007, the AICPA recommended that the SEC should allow American public companies to report financial results using international accounting standards. A survey conducted by Deloitte & Touche LLP in November 2007 showed that approximately 205 CEOs and senior finance professionals (representing approximately 300 U.S. companies) would consider adopting IFRS, if given a choice by the SEC. Even the chairmen of the FASB and the Financial Accounting Foundation (FAF), which oversees the FASB, expressed approval for a move toward the use of IFRS in the United States. They concluded that:

> Investors would be better served if all U.S. public companies used accounting standards promulgated by a single global standard setter as the basis for preparing their financial reports. This would be best accomplished by moving U.S. public companies to an improved version of International Financial Reporting Standards (IFRS).[23]

In November 2008, the SEC issued a rule called "Roadmap for the Potential Use of Financial Statements Prepared in Accordance with International Financial Reporting Standards (IFRS) by U.S. Issuers." Beginning in 2009, the SEC began suggesting that a gradual convergence toward IFRS be engineered by the FASB, stating that a single set of high-quality, globally accepted accounting standards would benefit U.S. investors. In February 2010, the SEC issued a statement supporting global accounting standards and convergence with IFRS. That statement was based on the responses to its November 2008 proposed rule. However, the move to IFRS in the United States would be a complex, multiyear process that would involve making significant changes to the U.S. financial reporting system, including

---

[23] Letter to Ms. Nancy M. Morris, Securities and Exchange Commission, signed by Jeff Mahoney, General Counsel, Council of Institutional Investors, dated November 9, 2007. See: https://www.sec.gov /comments/s7-20-07/s72007-24.pdf.

changes in auditing standards, licensing requirements, and how accountants are educated. Further, for companies and financial professionals that have been using detailed rules associated with U.S. GAAP, the prospect of IFRS presented both opportunities and challenges.

The Great Financial Crisis and its Aftermath

The Great Financial Crisis (GFC) of 2007 and 2008 led to much soul-searching among global standard-setters and regulators for its underlying root causes, as many commentators pointed to inaccurate accounting standards and the need for improvement. Further, standard-setters such as the IASB and FASB came under intense political pressure to accommodate the interests of the banking regulators, who required financial stability and accounting standards that would not result in "credit crunches" by depressing bank capital at a time of falling securities prices.

Following the global financial crisis (GFC), the Financial Crisis Advisory Group (FCAG), a high-level group of recognized leaders with broad experience in international financial markets, was formed at the request of the IASB and FASB to consider financial reporting issues arising from the crisis. The FCAG published in July 2009 a wide-ranging review of standard-setting activities following the global financial crisis. The report articulated four main principles and contains a series of recommendations to improve the functioning and effectiveness of global standard-setting. The main areas addressed in the report are:

- Effective financial reporting.
- Limitations of financial reporting.
- Convergence of accounting standards.
- Standard-setting independence and accountability.

As the co-chairmen of the FCAG stated, accounting was not a root cause of the financial crisis, but it would have an important role to play in its resolution. Improved financial reporting would help restore the confidence of financial market participants and serve as a catalyst for increased financial stability and sound economic growth. The independence and integrity of the standard-setting process, including wide consultation, would be critical to developing high-quality, broadly accepted accounting standards responsive to the issues highlighted by the crisis.

After the GFC, the Dodd-Frank Act (2010) produced little reform to financial reporting, although the GFC emphasized the importance of having common fair value measurement and disclosure requirements in IFRS and U.S. GAAP. During the post-GFC period, there was much debate in the United States over the use of fair value accounting. For example, many companies argued that fair value accounting would exacerbate the financial crisis and complained that they were being asked to value holdings using market prices when there was no functioning market for the controversial kinds of assets in need of pricing. Another thorny issue was revenue recognition.

In 2011, the FASB and IASB completed the *Fair Value Measurement* project and issued SFAS 157 and IFRS 13 (effective from January 2013), respectively. Before 2011, some IFRS had little or no guidance on fair value measurement. IFRS 13 harmonized the disclosures by providing consistent guidance in this respect across nearly all asset and liability classes, and thereby increased the transparency of fair values reported in the financial statements. For example, it clarified which fair values were based on quoted market prices and which were derived from models and gave investors and analysts a better understanding of the relative subjectivity of the measurement. However, IFRS 13 only gave guidance for measuring fair value when other standards required it, and it did not specify which assets or liabilities should be at fair value. Further, the FASB's activities during the aftermath of the GFC were described as "riding two horses." On the one hand, it had to respond to the financial reporting crisis, and on the other hand, it needed to take timely actions to improve U.S. GAAP while also working with the IASB.

Although IFRS 13 was nearly identical to the FASB standard (ASC 820, formerly SFAS No. 157), with an identical definition of fair value, some variations in interpretation would lead to different fair value measurements. For example, depending on the interpretation of the unit of account, the fair value measurement would be significantly different and could also result in an immediate write-down for some investments, such as those held by private equity funds. The unit of account is a key concept in accounting that specifies what is to be measured at fair value and refers to the level of aggregation at which an asset or liability is recognized in the financial statements. In March 2013, the IASB made two tentative decisions in this respect. It stated that (a) the unit of account for investments in subsidiaries, joint ventures, and associates should be the investment as a whole, and (b) the fair value measurement of an investment comprising quoted financial instruments should be the product of the quoted price of the instrument times the quantity held.

The debate about a fair value system between the IASB and FASB was based on these two competing worldviews. The FASB's fair value view assumed that markets were relatively perfect and complete, while the IASB's alternative view assumed that markets were relatively imperfect and incomplete. The FASB argued that in a perfect market setting, financial reports should meet the needs of passive investors and creditors by reporting fair values derived from current market prices. On the other hand, the IASB argued that in a relatively imperfect market setting, financial reports should also meet the monitoring requirements of current shareholders (stewardship) by reporting past transactions and events using entity-specific measurements that would reflect the opportunities actually available to the reporting entity. One of the main features of the FASB's fair value view concerned *usefulness for economic decisions,* which was the sole objective of financial reporting; in contrast, the IASB's alternative view was that *stewardship,* defined as accountability to present shareholders, was a distinct objective, ranking equally with decision usefulness. The implication of the former was that *stewardship* was not a distinct objective of financial statements, although its needs might be met incidentally to others, whereas the latter insisted that the information needs of *present shareholders,* including *stewardship* requirements, must be met. Another feature of the FASB's view was that *present and prospective investors and creditors* were the reference users for general-purpose financial statements, whereas the IASB's alternative view held that *present shareholders* of a holding company had a special status as users of financial statements. The implication of the former was that *present shareholders had no special status* among investors as users of financial statements. Further, according to the FASB's view, *relevance* was the primary characteristic required in financial statements, and *reliability* was less important and better replaced by *representational faithfulness,* which implied a concern for capturing economic substance. In contrast, according to the IASB's view, financial reporting relieved *information asymmetry* in an uncertain world, so *reliability* was an essential characteristic. The implication of the former was that accounting information needed ideally to reflect the *future,* not the past, so *past transactions and events* were only peripherally *relevant,* whereas according to the IASB's view, *past transactions and events* were *relevant* information and, together with *reliability of measurement* and *probability of existence,* were critical requirements for the *recognition* of elements of accounts, in order to achieve *reliability.*

Due to the different interpretations of controversial financial reporting issues, and non-decision on such issues, the efforts to achieve near-term convergence between U.S. GAAP and IFRS were mostly suspended in the decade following the GFC. Chapters 4 and 5 cover a number of significant differences between IFRS and U.S. GAAP that remain today. This is not to say that U.S. GAAP–IFRS convergence has been entirely abandoned. In some areas, notably revenue recognition, the two systems have been brought into very close alignment.

However, in other areas, for instance, lease accounting, standard-setters in the United States have made choices that have widened the gap between the two systems.

In the long-run, several factors make it inevitable that U.S. GAAP and IFRS move into closer alignment. First, there is an ever larger amount of cross-border collaboration and exchange between American accountants and their counterparts outside the United States. In fact, the IASB has two American members, more than any other country. Second, as discussed previously, the rest of the world has moved decisively toward a greater alignment with IFRS. Many countries use IFRS outright. Among those that do not, there has been a dramatic push to align national standards with IFRS, making IFRS the de facto benchmark standards for most of the world. Finally, the demands by investors and other users for high-quality, comparable, principles-based financial statements have only grown stronger over time. These demands will ultimately be met by greater global convergence.

IFRS FOR SMES

IFRS are designed to meet the information needs of the stakeholders of a wide array of companies, all the way up to the largest multinationals. They must be robust enough to capture the performance and financial health of companies as complex and diverse as Alibaba (e-commerce), Toyota (autos), Sanofi (pharmaceuticals), and Credit Suisse (banking). As a consequence, the full set of IFRS (generally termed *full-set IFRS*) must be voluminous and complex.

Often, the information needs of stakeholders of small and medium-sized enterprises (SMEs) are less expansive than what is provided for in full-set IFRS. The business models of SMEs may be simpler and involve fewer complex accounting issues. SMEs also tend to have smaller budgets to spend on accounting systems and staff. Indeed, a common complaint expressed by SMEs throughout the world is that accounting rules and disclosure requirements, often specifically designed with large companies in mind, have become too complex and burdensome. They assert that the benefits that SMEs receive from complying with full-set IFRS do not outweigh the costs.

In response, the IASB issued the *IFRS for SMEs* standard in 2009 and revised it in 2015. IFRS for SMEs incorporate a number of simplifications that are thought to reduce the reporting burden for smaller enterprises. The following two examples illustrate standard's approach to pairing down the choices presented by full-set IFRS:

- *Expensing all R&D expenditures:* As discussed in Chapter 4, one of the most important requirements of full-set IFRS is that companies capitalize development costs (late-stage R&D) when several criteria are met. The spending must be expensed if the criteria are not satisfied. The most important of the criteria is that it be probable that future benefits of the spending outweigh current costs. The determination of when R&D spending crosses the threshold between being expensed to meriting capitalization can be complex and subjective. IFRS for SMEs remove this decision from the accountant's to-do list by requiring that *all* R&D spending be expensed.
- *Requiring the equity method for all investments in associates and joint ventures:* Associates are often termed *affiliates* in the United States. They are entities over which the company has significant influence, but not control. This is often the case with investments in joint ventures. Companies generally apply the equity method to such investments, but not always. Full-set IFRS allow companies to apply the cost or fair value methods in some cases. IFRS for SMEs removes the decision over which method to use from the accountant's to-do list and requires that associates and joint ventures only be accounted for using the equity method.

Who uses IFRS for SMEs in practice? Precise figures are impossible to obtain because many of the users are non-listed and generally small. As of January 2021, the standard was required or permitted in 86 jurisdictions. These would be mainly classified as *emerging markets,* with the notable exceptions of the United Kingdom, Ireland, Switzerland, Israel, Hong Kong, and Singapore. In the UK, the standard has been implemented with adjustments as Financial Reporting Standard (FRS)102. Use of the standard is not allowed in most of the major EU countries, such as France and Germany. European countries where the standard is permitted include Bosnia and Herzegovina, Kosovo, Serbia, and Ukraine. Looking globally, large emerging market countries that allow or require the standard include Brazil, Argentina, and Chile in Latin America; Nigeria and South Africa in Africa; and Pakistan and the Philippines in Asia.

Summary

1. Harmonization and convergence are processes of reducing differences in financial reporting practices across countries.

2. Unlike harmonization, convergence implies the adoption of one set of standards internationally. The major goal of both harmonization and convergence is comparability of financial statements.

3. Harmonization or convergence of accounting standards might not necessarily result in comparable financial statements internationally due to nation-specific factors such as culture.

4. Proponents of international accounting harmonization/convergence argue that cross-country comparability of financial statements is required for the globalization of capital markets. Opponents argue that globalization is occurring without harmonization/convergence and that it might be appropriate for countries with different environments to have different standards.

5. Several organizations have been involved in the harmonization efforts at global and regional levels, including the IASC, the IOSCO, the IFAC, and the EU.

6. To achieve a common capital market, the EU attempted to harmonize accounting through the issuance of the Fourth and the Seventh Directives. Although the EU directives reduced differences in accounting in Europe, complete comparability was not achieved. Rather than developing additional directives, the European Commission decided to require the use of IFRS beginning in 2005.

7. The IASC was formed in 1973 to harmonize accounting at the international level. In 2001, the IASC was replaced by the IASB.

8. The IASB has 14 members (11 full-time and 3 part-time). The IASB adheres to an open process in developing standards, which are principles-based (rather than rules-based). With the establishment of the IASB, there has been a shift in emphasis from harmonization to global standard-setting or convergence.

9. The IASB's main aim is to develop a set of high-quality financial reporting standards for global use.

10. Currently, International Financial Reporting Standards (IFRS) consist of 25 IAS, 16 IFRS, and a number of interpretations. As a private organization, the IASB does not have the ability to require the use of its standards.

11. The IOSCO recommends that securities regulators permit foreign issuers to use IFRS for cross-listing. Most major stock exchanges are in compliance with this recommendation. In addition, a large and growing number of countries either require or allow domestic listed companies to use IFRS in preparing consolidated financial statements. The EU's adoption of IFRS in 2005 was a major boost to the IASB's legitimacy as a global accounting standard-setter.

12. The IASB's *Framework for the Preparation and Presentation of Financial Statements* establishes usefulness for decision making as the primary objective of financial statements prepared under IFRS. Understandability, relevance, reliability, and comparability are the primary qualitative characteristics that make financial statements useful. The *Framework* also provides workable definitions of the accounting elements.

13. IAS 1 is a single standard providing guidelines for the presentation of financial statements. The standard stipulates that a set of IFRS-based financial statements must include a balance sheet, an income statement, a statement of cash flows, a statement of changes in equity, and accounting policies and explanatory notes. IAS 1 establishes the overriding principle of fair presentation and, in the extremely rare case in which management concludes that compliance with a requirement of an IASB standard would be misleading, it permits an override of that requirement.

14. IFRS 1, *First Time Adoption of IFRS,* which replaced IAS 1, provides guidance to companies that are adopting IFRS for the first time. IFRS 1 requires an entity to comply with each IFRS effective at the reporting date of its first IFRS financial statements. However, IFRS 1 provides exemptions to this rule where the cost of complying with this requirement would likely exceed the benefit to users.

15. China and India have each comprehensively revamped their national accounting standards to bring them into alignment with IFRS. These IFRS-aligned standards are called Chinese Accounting Standards (CAS) and Indian Accounting Standards (Ind AS).

16. Thirty percent of Chinese companies use IFRS because their shares are listed on the Hong Kong Stock Exchange, and the HKSE requires IFRS for all listed companies.

17. Japan allows companies to choose from among Japanese GAAP, IFRS, U.S. GAAP, and Japan's Modified International Standards. Examples abound of globally prominent Japanese companies using the first three of these systems, creating problems of interpretation and comparability for investors.

18. In 2002, the FASB and the IASB signed the Norwalk Agreement, in which they agreed to work toward convergence of their two sets of financial reporting standards.

19. In November 2007, the SEC removed the requirement that foreign private issuers using IFRS must reconcile their financial statements to U.S. GAAP.

20. The IASB issued the IFRS for SMEs standard in 2009 to better serve the needs of small and medium-sized businesses. It revised the standard in 2015. The standard is mainly used in emerging market economies, although there are notable exceptions among wealthier economies, including the United Kingdom and Singapore.

Appendix to Chapter 3

What Is This Thing Called "Anglo-Saxon" Accounting?

The term *Anglo-Saxon* or *Anglo-American* is used for a group of countries that includes the United States, the United Kingdom, Canada, Australia, and New Zealand. This group often figures in international accounting textbooks and articles, particularly with regard to international classification of accounting systems and international harmonization of accounting standards. The efforts of the IASB (and its predecessor, the IASC) are usually associated with Anglo-Saxon accounting. Some even criticize the IASB for attempting to promote Anglo-Saxon accounting throughout the world. However, many non-Anglo countries are already using IFRS. Given this, it is important to examine some of the important features of Anglo-Saxon accounting, which are the basis for IFRS.

In a broad sense, the term *Anglo-Saxon accounting* refers to the accounting systems prevalent in the English-speaking countries mentioned in the preceding paragraph. Although the accounting systems in these countries are not identical, they share some fundamental features that distinguish them from other systems of accounting:

- A focus on how businesses operate at the firm level (micro orientation), with an emphasis on the importance of professional judgment (recognition of professional rules and professional self-regulation).
- An investor orientation, with the provision of information for efficient operation of the capital market as the primary aim (recognition of the importance of being transparent).
- Less emphasis on prudence and measurement of taxable income or distributable income, and a willingness to go beyond superficial legal form (substance over form).[1]

There are other recognizable commonalities that are related to the above features. For example, because of the investor orientation and emphasis on transparency in accounting reports, the principle of "true and fair view" or fair presentation is predominant in Anglo-Saxon financial reporting. Auditors are required to report on whether, in their opinion, the financial statements have been prepared in such a way that they adhere to this principle. In the United Kingdom, the concept of *true and fair view* has not been clearly defined in legislation. The courts have placed considerable reliance on expert witnesses in developing a meaning for this concept. The UK government's view has been that this is a highly technical matter and therefore should be dealt with by the profession. This leaves open the possibility for different interpretations. There is no single true and fair view. There are also some differences in how the concept of true and fair view is applied. For example, in the United Kingdom, it is an overriding requirement. In other words, complying with the legal requirements does not necessarily lead to a true and fair view, in which case additional information should be provided. However, in Canada and Australia, a true and fair view override does not apply. Further, the U.S. equivalent to true and fair view, *present fairly,* is defined in terms of conformity with U.S. GAAP. In other words, if the financial statements have been prepared in accordance with U.S. GAAP, then it is assumed that the information is presented fairly. In general, it is recognized that the application of the qualitative characteristics and appropriate accounting standards would normally result in financial statements that convey a true and fair view of such information, or that present it fairly.[2]

The use of a conceptual framework to provide guidance for developing accounting standards is another common feature among these countries. The qualitative characteristics such as understandability, relevance, reliability, and objectivity or representational faithfulness are found in the conceptual frameworks developed by all Anglo-Saxon countries and by the IASB. The IASB's conceptual framework is largely based on that of the U.S. FASB. This has been one of the reasons for the view that the IASB has been heavily influenced by Anglo-Saxon accounting. Another recognizable common feature among Anglo-Saxon countries is that they all have common law traditions rather than code law traditions. This means they all use common law legal systems, which tend to be flexible in terms of legislation and rely heavily on private-sector and market mechanisms for regulation. Related to this, all these countries have private-sector standard-setting bodies recognizing the profession's capacity to self-regulate.[3]

Some differences can be observed among Anglo-Saxon countries with regard to the recognizable common features described in the preceding paragraph. For example, the

[1] Christopher W. Nobes, "On the Myth of 'Anglo-Saxon' Financial Accounting: A Comment," *International Journal of Accounting* 38 (2003), pp. 95–104.

[2] IASC, *Framework for the Preparation and Presentation of Financial Statements* (London: IASC, 1989).

[3] Nobes (2003), op cit.

conceptual frameworks are not always used as the basis for developing accounting standards. As a case in point, in the United States, SFAS 87, *Employers' Accounting for Pensions,* specifically states that it does not follow the FASB's conceptual framework. Further, a common law legal system does not necessarily lead to flexible standards. U.S. accounting standards are increasingly becoming more detailed and rigidly prescriptive as compared to accounting standards developed in the United Kingdom. With regard to private-sector standard-setting, traditionally the U.S. standard-setting system is significantly more public-sector-oriented than the UK system, because the U.S. SEC has the ultimate responsibility for authorizing accounting standards. On the basis of these differences, some commentators have argued that Anglo-Saxon accounting is a myth.[4] However, such differences do not necessarily indicate that these countries cannot usefully be seen as members of the same group.[5]

[4] David Alexander and Simon Archer, "On the Myth of 'Anglo-Saxon' Accounting," *International Journal of Accounting* 35, no. 4 (2000), pp. 539–57.
[5] Nobes (2003), op cit.

Questions

1. How does harmonization differ from convergence?
2. What are the potential benefits that a multinational corporation could derive from the international convergence of accounting standards?
3. Were the EU directives effective in generating comparability of financial statements across companies located in member nations? Why or why not?
4. What were the three phases in the life of the IASC?
5. Why was IOSCO's endorsement of IAS so important to the IASC's efforts?
6. How does the structure of the IASB help to establish its legitimacy as a global standard-setter?
7. What is the IASB's principles-based approach to accounting standard-setting?
8. Are there any major accounting issues that have not yet been covered by IFRS?
9. Do you see a major change of emphasis in the harmonization process since the establishment of the IASB? Explain.
10. What are the different ways in which IFRS might be used within a country?
11. Would the worldwide adoption of IFRS result in worldwide comparability of financial statements? Why or why not?
12. In what way is the IASB's *Framework* intended to assist firms in preparing IFRS-based financial statements?
13. As expressed in IAS 1, what is the overriding principle that should be followed in preparing IFRS-based financial statements?
14. What are the conditions to be satisfied if a firm wants to claim that its financial statements have been prepared in accordance with IFRS?
15. To what extent are IFRS used for domestic financial reporting in the major economies surveyed in the chapter?
16. How has the U.S. SEC policy toward IFRS changed?
17. What is the main difference between the two approaches to accounting standard-setting taken by the FASB and the IASB?
18. Why did the IASB issue *IFRS for Small and Medium-sized Entities,* a special framework designed for SMEs?

Exercises and Problems

1. "The IASB has been repeatedly accused of devising accounting standards that pay insufficient attention to the concerns and practices of companies. . . . Some European banks and insurers complain about poor due process by the IASB, and Frits Bolkestein, European commissioner responsible for accounting matters, endorsed their concerns earlier this month." (*Financial Times,* March 24, 2004, p. 20)

   Required:
   Elaborate on the concerns raised in the preceding quote, and discuss the measures that have been taken to alleviate those concerns.

2. Since 2005, publicly traded companies in the EU have been required to use IFRS in preparing their consolidated financial statements.

   Required:
   a. Explain the EU's objective in requiring the use of IFRS.
   b. Identify and describe two issues that might hamper the EU from achieving the objective underlying the use of IFRS.

3. Assume that you have been invited to advise the accounting oversight body in one of the former Eastern European countries that became a member of the EU in May 2004. The accounting oversight body is charged with the task of identifying the main issues to be addressed in implementing the use of IFRS.

   Required:
   Prepare a report outlining the key points you would include in your advice to this accounting oversight body.

4. Today several countries still do not permit domestic listed companies to use IFRS.

   Required:
   Identify three countries from this group that are likely to have different reasons for not permitting the use of IFRS by domestic listed companies. Describe those reasons.

5. The professional accounting bodies in many countries have taken, or are taking, steps to adopt IFRS.

   Required:
   Go to the website of a professional accounting body of your choice and outline the steps it has taken so far to facilitate adoption of IFRS.

6. The appendix to this chapter describes what is commonly referred to as *Anglo-Saxon accounting.*

   Required:
   Explain why Anglo-Saxon accounting might be of interest to Chinese accounting regulators.

7. In its 2014 annual report, Honda Motor Company states that its manufacturing operations are principally conducted in 22 separate factories, including 3 in Japan; the Japanese factories maintain their books of account in conformity with financial accounting standards in Japan, while the subsidiaries in foreign countries generally maintain their books of account in conformity with accounting standards in the countries of their domicile; and the consolidated financial statements have been prepared in conformity with the accounting principals generally accepted in the U.S. Honda's policy of using U.S. GAAP to prepare its consolidated financial statements extended back to at least 1977, when Honda first listed its American depositary receipts (ADRs) on the New York Stock Exchange.

Required:
a. Discuss the possible reasons for Honda to prepare its consolidated financial statements in conformity with U.S. GAAP.
b. In 2015, Honda switched from using U.S. GAAP to using IFRS. The accounting policy note in the 2015 annual report also eliminated references to the foreign subsidiaries maintaining their books in conformity with local accounting principles. Discuss possible reasons for Honda's migration to IFRS in 2015.

8. A list of foreign companies with shares traded on the New York Stock Exchange (NYSE) can be found on the NYSE's website (www.nyse.com).

Required:
a. Identify a developing country in Asia, Africa, and Latin America and determine how many companies from each of those countries are listed on the NYSE.
b. Describe the manner in which IFRS are used by the companies identified in item (a).

9. The *Financial Times,* on Tuesday, April 13, 2004, made the following comment in its editorial, "Parmalat: Perennial Lessons of European Scandal: Urgent need for better enforcement and investor skepticism":

> After the accounting scandals in the US, there was an unseemly amount of crowing in Europe. As it happens, Parmalat is a much older scandal than Enron or WorldCom. It just took longer to come out at the Italian dairy company. . . . Convergence of standards—in accounting, for instance—will help spread best practice. . . . But we are nowhere near having a world super-regulator. . . . In Italy regulation has been weak because of fragmentation and lack of clout and resources. Attempts to tackle this and to ensure regulators' independence from political interference should be urgently pursued. (p. 12)

Required:
Discuss the lessons referred to above concerning the objectives of efforts to set global standards for accounting and financial reporting.

10. The chapter describes different phases in the harmonization efforts of the IASC.

Required:
Identify one such phase and prepare a brief report describing its importance in the overall scheme of international harmonization of accounting standards. You should consult relevant literature in preparing this report.

11. The IASB's main objective is to develop a set of high-quality standards for financial reporting by companies at the international level.

Required:
Critically examine the possibility of achieving this objective.

12. Toyota Motor is a Japanese auto company based in Toyota City, Japan. Toyota switched from reporting under U.S. GAAP to reporting under IFRS in fiscal 2020–21.

Required:
Provide possible reasons for Toyota's decision to switch to IFRS.

13. Mazda Motor is a Japanese auto company based in Hiroshima, Japan. Mazda continues to use Japanese GAAP despite the trend in Japan to adopt IFRS.

Required:
What are possible reasons for Mazda's reluctance to switch to IFRS?

14. The SEC has lifted its requirement that foreign companies, which have used IFRS as the basis for preparing their financial statements, must reconcile their financial statements using U.S. GAAP in order to be eligible to list their shares on U.S. stock exchanges.

    Required:
    Discuss the possible reasons for this relaxation of rules.

15. A majority of developing economies allow or mandate IFRS for Small and Medium-sized Entities (SMEs), but some have prohibited it. Thailand is in the latter category. Thailand requires its listed companies to use Thai Financial Reporting Standards (TFRS), which are based on full-set IFRS.

    Required:
    Discuss the possible reasons for Thailand's prohibition of IFRS for SMEs.

Case 3-1

Comparing Ind AS and IFRS at Dr. Reddy's Laboratories

Dr. Reddy's Laboratories (DRL) is based in Hyderabad, India, and is one of that country's leading pharmaceutical manufacturers, specializing in generic and biosimilar drugs. DRL is publicly listed on the Bombay Stock Exchange and prepares its primary financial statements, included in the annual report, using Ind AS. However, American depositary shares for DRL stock also trade on the New York Stock Exchange under the ticker RDY. Therefore, in addition to its standard annual report, DRL must file a Form 20-F with the U.S. SEC annually.

Note that like most Indian companies, DRL's fiscal year runs from April 1st to March 31st of the following calendar year.

Required:

Access DRL's annual report and 20-F for the 2019–20 fiscal year on the Investor Relations section of the company's website (www.drreddys.com/investors/reports-and-filings). Answer the following questions using the company's 2019–20 consolidated financial statements. Be sure not to use DRL's parent-level statements, which are also included in the annual report.

1. The consolidated financial statements contained in DRL's annual report were prepared under Ind AS, and not IFRS. Review these to evaluate whether the financial statements presented comply with the presentation requirements in IAS 1, *Presentation of Financial Statements.* Document your evaluation.

2. Compare basic accounting figures in the Ind AS consolidated financial statements of the annual report with the consolidated financial statements of the 20-F prepared using IFRS and answer the following questions:

   • Which system is more conservative in how it reckons profit and loss, operating cash flow, the value of total assets, and the value of shareholders' equity? To answer this question, compare total revenue, after-tax income (profit and loss), and operating cash flow under both systems for fiscal 2019–20 and fiscal 2018–19. Compare the value of total assets and shareholders' equity under both systems as of March 31, 2020 and March 31, 2019.

   • Based on your analysis immediately above, do the differences seem material?

   • Assume that you are an equity analyst who is very familiar with IFRS but unfamiliar with Ind AS. Based on the results of your analysis above, would you feel confident in making investment decisions solely using the financial statements prepared using Ind AS?

Chapter **Four**

International Financial Reporting Standards: Part I

Learning Objectives

After reading this chapter, you should be able to

- Discuss the types of differences that exist between International Financial Reporting Standards (IFRS) and U.S. generally accepted accounting principles (GAAP).

- Describe IFRS requirements related to the recognition and measurement of assets, specifically inventories; property, plant, and equipment (PPE); and intangibles.

- Explain major differences between IFRS and U.S. GAAP on the recognition and measurement of assets.

- Analyze the impact that differences in asset recognition and measurement rules have on financial statements.

- Explain how investment property and biological assets differ from PPE and what special rules govern their accounting treatment under IFRS.

- Describe IFRS requirements related to business combinations, goodwill, and noncontrolling interests.

- Describe IFRS requirements for determining effective control and the scope of consolidation.

INTRODUCTION

As discussed in Chapter 3, International Financial Reporting Standards (IFRS) is the financial reporting system overseen by the International Accounting Standards Board (IASB), a multinational, independent standard-setting organization based in London. It is the most widely used reporting framework in the world, mandated in many of the world's largest capital markets and accepted in specific circumstances virtually everywhere else. In U.S. equity markets, foreign companies may use IFRS in lieu of U.S. generally accepted accounting principles (GAAP). Moreover, the U.S. Securities and Exchange Commission (SEC) and the IASB coordinate closely in setting new accounting standards.[1] Because of this coordination, decisions made by the IASB greatly affect the day-to-day work of American accountants. This chapter uses numerical examples to describe and demonstrate the requirements of selected IFRS, particularly those related to the recognition and measurement of assets.

[1] For instance, the SEC and the IASB coordinated closely on recent standards relating to revenue recognition and leases (discussed in Chapter 5).

The label *IFRS* is used in two ways. Most commonly, it is a general term that encompasses all of the authoritative pronouncements issued or adopted by the IASB. These include 41 International Accounting Standards (IAS) enacted by the IASB's predecessor, the International Accounting Standards Committee (IASC), during the period 1973–2001. Some have been withdrawn and many significantly revised. Yet, as a group, the IASs still play a central role in the IFRS reporting system. The label IFRS is also used to refer to specific standards adopted by the IASB after 2001. As of December 2021, the IASB has issued 17 IFRS, labeled *IFRS 1, IFRS 2,* etc. As supplements to these standards, the Standing Interpretations Committee (SIC) and the International Financial Reporting Interpretations Committee (IFRIC) have issued more than 30 interpretations. These interpretations are also included in the general IFRS reporting framework.

Throughout this chapter, in addition to describing specific IFRS, we will highlight differences and similarities between them and U.S. GAAP. For students who are already familiar with American accounting rules, focusing on differences and similarities provides a quick path to a working knowledge of IFRS. In some cases, the differences stem from genuine, unresolved debates about how an accounting system should be designed. Understanding them will deepen students' appreciation of accounting theory and practice.

TYPES OF DIFFERENCES BETWEEN IFRS AND U.S. GAAP

Differences between IFRS and U.S. GAAP can be classified according to the following taxonomy:

- *Definition differences.* Differences in definitions exist even though concepts are similar. Definition differences can lead to recognition or measurement differences.
- *Recognition differences.* Differences in recognition criteria and/or guidance are related to (1) whether an item is recognized or not, (2) how it is recognized (e.g., as a liability or as equity), and/or (3) when it is recognized (timing difference).
- *Measurement differences.* Differences in the *amount* recognized result from either (1) a difference in the method required or (2) a difference in the detailed guidance for applying a similar method.
- *Alternatives.* One set of standards allows a choice between two or more alternative methods; the other set of standards requires one specific method to be used.
- *Lack of requirements or guidance.* IFRS may not cover an issue addressed by U.S. GAAP, and vice versa.
- *Presentation differences.* Differences exist in the presentation of items in the financial statements.
- *Disclosure differences.* Differences in information presented in the notes to financial statements are related to (1) whether a disclosure is required and (2) the manner in which disclosures are required to be made.

In some cases, IFRS are more flexible than U.S. GAAP. For example, several standards covered in this chapter allow firms to choose between two alternative treatments in accounting for a particular item. Also, IFRS traditionally have less bright-line guidance than U.S. GAAP; therefore, more judgment is required in applying them. IFRS have often been portrayed as a principles-based accounting system (broad principles with limited detailed rules), whereas U.S. GAAP is said to be a rules-based system. This issue was covered in Chapter 3. Although these characterizations are still generally valid, in many areas, IFRS are more detailed than U.S. GAAP.

The list above provides an organizing taxonomy for the numerous differences that still remain between IFRS and U.S. GAAP despite several decades of work to align these systems. These differences present a problem for accountants and financial statement readers alike. How does one separate material from immaterial differences and focus on those that are most important? This is a well-known conundrum for accountants. An accounting procedure that is immaterial in one context can be highly material in another, even leading to a spectacular audit failure or investment mistake.

Two important resources to which students of IFRS reporting can refer to better understand material differences for a given company are discussions of *critical accounting policies* by company management and *key audit matters* (KAMs) in the external auditor's audit report. The former are required by International Accounting Standard (IAS) 1 and resemble similar disclosures required by the U.S SEC. The latter are required by International Standard on Auditing (ISA) 701, a widely praised standard that was adopted by the International Auditing and Assurance Standards Board (IAASB) in 2015 and began coming into force in 2016. The goal of both sets of disclosures is to help financial statement readers better understand which reporting and auditing issues are most relevant for a given company. Although neither disclosure focuses specifically on IFRS–U.S. GAAP differences, an IFRS-based accounting policy that differs materially from what would be used in the United States often merits disclosure as a critical policy or a KAM. This is particularly true for differences in the asset recognition and measurement policies discussed below. Most of the examples used in this chapter have been highlighted as critical policies or KAMs in company annual reports.

INVENTORIES

IAS 2, *Inventories,* is an example of an International Accounting Standard that provides more extensive guidance than U.S. GAAP, especially with regard to inventories of service providers and disclosures related to inventories. IAS 2 provides guidance on determining the initial cost of inventories, the cost formulas to be used in allocating the cost of inventories to expense, and the subsequent measurement of inventories on the balance sheet.

The cost of inventories includes costs of purchase, costs of conversion, and other costs:

- *Costs of purchase* include purchase price; import duties and other taxes; and transportation, handling, and other costs directly attributable to acquiring materials, services, and finished products.
- *Costs of conversion* include direct labor and a systematic allocation of variable and fixed production overhead. Fixed overhead should be applied based on a normal level of production.
- *Other costs* are included in the cost of inventories to the extent that they are incurred to bring the inventories to their present location and condition. This can include the cost of designing products for specific customers. Under certain conditions, interest costs are allowed to be included in the cost of inventories for those items that require a substantial period of time to bring them to a salable condition.

Costs that are expressly excluded from the costs of inventories are:

- Abnormal amounts of wasted materials, labor, or other production costs.
- Storage costs, unless they are necessary in the production process prior to a further stage of production.
- Administrative overhead that does not contribute to bringing inventories to their present location and condition.
- Selling costs.

IAS 2 does not allow as much choice with regard to cost formulas as does U.S. GAAP. First-in, first-out (FIFO) and weighted-average cost are acceptable treatments, but last-in, first-out (LIFO) is not. The standard cost method and retail method also are acceptable provided that they approximate cost as defined in IAS 2. The cost of inventories of items that are not ordinarily interchangeable and goods or services produced and segregated for specific projects must be accounted for using the specific identification method. An entity must use the same cost formula for all inventories having a similar nature and use to the entity, even if they are located in different geographical locations. For inventories with a different nature or use, different cost formulas may be justified. U.S. GAAP does not require use of a uniform inventory valuation method for inventories having a similar nature. It is common for U.S. companies to use different methods in different jurisdictions for tax reasons—for example, LIFO in the United States and FIFO or average cost elsewhere.

Lower of Cost or Net Realizable Value

IAS 2 requires inventory to be reported on the balance sheet at the lower of cost or net realizable value. *Net realizable value* is defined as estimated selling price in the ordinary course of business less the estimated costs of completion and the estimated costs necessary to make the sale. This rule typically is applied on an item-by-item basis. However, the standard indicates that it may be appropriate to group similar items of inventory relating to the same product line. Write-downs to net realizable value must be reversed when the selling price increases.

Example: Application of Lower of Cost or Net Realizable Value Rule

Assume that Distributor Company Inc. has the following inventory item on hand at December 31, Year 1:

Historical cost	$1,000.00
Estimated selling price	880.00
Estimated costs to complete and sell	50.00
Net realizable value	830.00
Normal profit margin—15%	124.50
Net realizable value less normal profit margin	$ 705.50

Net realizable value is $830, which is lower than historical cost. In accordance with IFRS, inventory must be written down by $170 ($1,000 − $830). The journal entry at December 31, Year 1, is:

Inventory Loss	$170	
Inventory		$170
To record the write-down on inventory due to decline in net realizable value.		

Assume that at the end of the first quarter in Year 2, replacement cost has increased to $900, the estimated selling price has increased to $980, and the estimated cost to complete and sell remains at $50. The item now has a net realizable value of $930. This is $100 greater than the carrying amount (and $70 less than historical cost). Under IFRS, $100 of the write-down that was made at December 31, Year 1, is reversed through the following journal entry:

Inventory	$100	
Recovery of Inventory Loss (increase in income)		$100
To record a recovery of inventory loss taken in the previous period.		

Prior to 2017, U.S. GAAP required a more complex write-down calculation. Inventory was written down to the lower of cost or market, where market was defined as replacement cost with a ceiling (net realizable value) and a floor (net realizable value less normal profit margin). The U.S. Financial Accounting Standards Board (FASB) abandoned this more complex procedure expressly to harmonize U.S. inventory accounting standards with those of IFRS, mandating the change for public companies beginning in 2017 and private companies beginning in 2018.[2] This is an important recent example of IFRS–U.S. GAAP convergence.

A significant difference that remains, however, is the general prohibition in U.S. GAAP against reversing prior write-downs. Under U.S. GAAP, an inventory write-down is viewed as establishing a new cost basis for the asset. In future periods, the company's application of the lower of cost or net realizable value criterion can only result in a further write-down; inventory can never be written up above the new cost basis. In the example above, the new cost basis after Year 1 is $830. Distributor Company would be prohibited from recognizing the recovery of $100 in the inventory's value in its Year 2 income statement. On the balance sheet, the inventory's carrying value would remain at $830 until the item is sold.

PROPERTY, PLANT, AND EQUIPMENT

IAS 16, *Property, Plant, and Equipment,* provides the primary guidance in accounting for the acquisition and use of property, plant, and equipment (PPE) under IFRS. Although formally adopted in 1993, many of this statement's central provisions have been part of international standards since the 1970s. IAS 16 covers the following aspects of accounting for fixed assets:

1. Recognition of initial costs of property, plant, and equipment.
2. Recognition of subsequent costs.
3. Measurement at initial recognition.
4. Measurement after initial recognition.
5. Depreciation.
6. Derecognition (retirements and disposals).

Impairment of assets, including PPE, is covered by IAS 36, *Impairment of Assets.* Accounting for impairments is discussed later in this chapter.

For students of international accounting differences, IAS 16's most important sections dictate how PPE is measured after initial recognition. IAS 16 allows companies to choose between the historical cost method and a fair value method known as the *revaluation model.* Most companies choose historical cost. For this large majority, the application of IAS 16 will result in PPE carrying amounts and depreciation charges that are generally equivalent to what the companies would report under U.S. GAAP. For companies choosing the revaluation model, however, these amounts may differ dramatically.

Recognition of Initial and Subsequent Costs

Property, plant, and equipment should be initially measured at cost, which includes (1) purchase price, including import duties and taxes; (2) all costs directly attributable to bringing the asset to the location and condition necessary for it to perform as intended; and (3) an

---

[2] The new U.S. rules were not applied to inventory measured using the LIFO or retail inventory methods. The FASB asserted that the costs of migrating to the new system would exceed the benefits in these cases.

estimate of the costs of dismantling and removing the asset and restoring the site on which it is located.

An item of PPE acquired in exchange for a nonmonetary asset or combination of monetary and nonmonetary assets should be initially measured at fair value unless the exchange transaction lacks commercial substance. *Fair value* is defined as the "amount for which an asset could be exchanged between knowledgeable, willing parties in an arm's-length transaction."[3] If the transaction lacks commercial substance or the fair value of the asset acquired and given up cannot be determined, then the cost of the asset acquired is measured as the carrying value of the asset given up. As a result, no gain or loss is recognized.

Example: Dismantling and Removal Costs

Caylor Corporation constructs a powder coating facility at a cost of $3,000,000: $1,000,000 for the building and $2,000,000 for machinery and equipment. Local law requires the company to dismantle and remove the plant assets at the end of their useful life. Caylor estimates that the net cost for removal of the equipment, after deducting salvage value, will be $100,000, and the net cost for dismantling and removing the building will be $400,000. The useful life of the facility is 20 years, and the company uses a discount rate of 10 percent in determining present values.

The initial cost of the machinery and equipment and the building must include the estimated dismantling and removal costs discounted to present value. The present value factor for a discount rate of 10 percent for 20 periods is 0.14864 ($1/1.10^{20}$). The calculations are as follows:

Building

Construction cost	$1,000,000
Present value of dismantling and removal costs ($400,000 × 0.14864)	59,457
Total cost of the building	$1,059,457

Machinery and equipment

Construction cost	$2,000,000
Present value of dismantling and removal costs ($100,000 × 0.14864)	14,864
Total cost of the machinery and equipment	$2,014,864

The journal entry to record the initial cost of the assets would be:

Building	$1,059,457	
Machinery and Equipment	2,014,864	
Cash		$3,000,000
Provision for dismantling and removal (long-term liability)		74,321

Measurement Subsequent to Initial Recognition

The most important difference between IFRS and U.S. GAAP in accounting for PPE relates to the measurement of PPE subsequent to initial recognition. IAS 16 allows two treatments for reporting fixed assets on balance sheets subsequent to their acquisition: the cost model and the revaluation model. Under the cost model, an item of PPE is carried on the balance sheet at cost less accumulated depreciation and any accumulated impairment losses. This is consistent with U.S. GAAP.

[3] IAS 16, paragraph 6.

Under the revaluation model, an item of PPE is carried at a revalued amount, measured as fair value at the date of revaluation less any subsequent accumulated depreciation and any accumulated impairment losses. If an enterprise chooses to follow this measurement model, revaluations must be made often enough that the carrying amount of assets does not differ materially from the assets' fair value. When revaluations are made, an entire class of PPE must be revalued. Revaluation increases are credited directly to the other comprehensive income component of equity as a revaluation surplus. Revaluation decreases are first recognized as a reduction in any related revaluation surplus, and once the surplus is exhausted, additional revaluation decreases are recognized as an expense. The revaluation surplus may be transferred to retained earnings on disposal of the asset. Revalued assets may be presented either (1) at a gross amount less a separately reported accumulated depreciation (both revalued) or (2) at a net amount. Allowing firms the option to revalue fixed assets is one of the most fundamental differences between IFRS and U.S. GAAP. Guidelines for applying this option are presented in more detail in the following paragraphs.

Determination of Fair Value and Frequency of Revaluation

The basis of revaluation is the *fair value* of the asset at the date of revaluation. The definition in IAS 16 indicates that fair value is the amount at which an asset could be exchanged between knowledgeable, willing parties in an arm's-length transaction. The fair value of land and buildings is usually determined through appraisals conducted by professionally qualified valuers. The fair value of plant and equipment is also usually determined through appraisal. In the case of a specialized asset that is not normally sold, fair value may need to be estimated using, for example, a depreciated replacement cost approach.

IAS 16 requires that revalued amounts should not differ materially from fair values at the balance sheet date. The effect of this rule is that once an enterprise has opted for the revaluation model, it has an obligation to keep the valuations up-to-date. Although the IASB avoids mandating annual revaluations, in some circumstances, these will be necessary in order to comply with the standard. In other cases, annual changes in fair value will be insignificant and revaluation may be necessary only every several years.

Selection of Assets to Be Revalued

IAS 16 requires that all assets of the same class be revalued at the same time. Selectivity *within a class* is not permitted, but selection *of a class* is. Different classes of assets described in the standard are as follows: land; land and buildings; machinery; office equipment; furniture and fixtures; motor vehicles; ships; and aircraft.

Detailed disclosures are required for each class of PPE (whether revalued or not). Thus, if a company divides its assets into many classes to minimize the effect of the rule about revaluing a whole class of assets, it will incur the burden of being required to make additional disclosures for each of those classes.

Accumulated Depreciation

Two alternative treatments are described in IAS 16 for the treatment of accumulated depreciation when a class of PPE is revalued:

1. Restate the accumulated depreciation proportionately with the change in the gross carrying amount of the asset so that the carrying amount of the asset after revaluation equals its revalued amount. The standard comments that this method is often used where an asset is revalued by means of an index and is the appropriate method for those companies using current cost accounting.
2. Eliminate the accumulated depreciation against the gross carrying amount of the asset, and restate the net amount to the revalued amount of the asset.

Example: Treatment of Accumulated Depreciation upon Revaluation

Assume that Kiely Company Inc. has buildings that cost $1,000,000, with accumulated depreciation of $600,000 and a carrying amount of $400,000 on December 31, Year 1. On that date, Kiely Company determines that the market value for these buildings is $750,000. Kiely Company wishes to carry buildings on the December 31, Year 1, balance sheet at a revalued amount. Under treatment 1, Kiely Company would restate both the buildings account and accumulated depreciation on buildings such that the ratio of net carrying amount to gross carrying amount is 40 percent ($400,000/$1,000,000) and the net carrying amount is $750,000. To accomplish this, the following journal entry would be made at December 31, Year 1:

Buildings...	$875,000	
Accumulated Depreciation—Buildings.....................		$525,000
Revaluation Surplus......................................		350,000
To revalue buildings and related accumulated depreciation.		

	Original Cost		Revaluation		Total	%
Gross carrying amount............	$1,000,000	+	$875,000	=	$1,875,000	100%
Accumulated depreciation	600,000	+	525,000	=	1,125,000	60
Net carrying amount.............	$ 400,000	+	$350,000	=	$ 750,000	40%

Under treatment 2, accumulated depreciation of $600,000 is first eliminated against the buildings account, and then the buildings account is increased by $350,000 to result in a net carrying amount of $750,000. The necessary journal entries are as follows:

Accumulated Depreciation—Buildings.........................	$600,000	
Buildings..		$600,000
To eliminate accumulated depreciation on buildings to be revalued.		
Buildings...	$350,000	
Revaluation Surplus......................................		$350,000
To revalue buildings.		

As a result of making these two entries, the buildings account has a net carrying amount of $750,000 ($1,000,000 − 600,000 + 350,000). Under both treatments, both assets and equity are increased by a net amount of $350,000.

Treatment of Revaluation Surpluses and Deficits

On the first revaluation after initial recording, the treatment of increases and decreases in carrying amount as a result of revaluation is very straightforward:

- Increases are credited directly to a revaluation surplus in the other comprehensive income component of equity.
- Decreases are charged to the income statement as an expense.

At subsequent revaluations, the following rules apply:

- To the extent that there is a previous revaluation surplus with respect to an asset, a decrease should be charged against it first, and any excess of deficit over that previous surplus should be expensed.

- To the extent that a previous revaluation resulted in a charge to expense, a subsequent upward revaluation first should be recognized as income to the extent of the previous expense and any excess should be credited to other comprehensive income in equity.

Example: Treatment of Revaluation Surplus

Assume that Kiely Company Inc. has elected to measure PPE at revalued amounts. Costs and fair values for Kiely Company's three classes of PPE at December 31, Year 1 and Year 2, are as follows:

	Land	Buildings	Machinery
Cost	$100,000	$500,000	$200,000
Fair value at 12/31/Y1	120,000	450,000	210,000
Fair value at 12/31/Y2	150,000	460,000	185,000

The following journal entries are made at December 31, Year 1, to adjust the carrying amount of the three classes of PPE to fair value:

Land	$20,000	
Revaluation Surplus—Land		$20,000
Loss on Revaluation—Buildings (expense)	$50,000	
Buildings		$50,000
Machinery	$10,000	
Revaluation Surplus—Machinery		$10,000

At December 31, Year 2, the following journal entries are made:

Land	$30,000	
Revaluation Surplus—Land		$30,000
Buildings	$10,000	
Recovery of Loss on Revaluation—Buildings (income)		$10,000
Revaluation Surplus—Machinery	$10,000	
Loss on Revaluation—Machinery (expense)	15,000	
Machinery		$25,000

IAS 16 indicates that the revaluation surplus in equity may be transferred to retained earnings when the surplus is realized. The surplus may be considered to be realized either through use of the asset or upon its sale or disposal. Accordingly, the revaluation surplus in equity may be transferred in one of two ways to retained earnings:

- A lump sum may be transferred at the time the asset is sold or scrapped.
- Within each period, an amount equal to the difference between depreciation on the revalued amount and depreciation on the historical cost of the asset may be transferred to retained earnings.

A third possibility apparently allowed by IAS 16 would be to do nothing with the revaluation surplus. However, this would result in a revaluation surplus being reported in equity related to assets no longer owned by the firm.

Example: *Alternative Accounting Choices for PPE in the Hotel Industry*

The table below profiles two luxury hotel companies that use IAS 16's measurement flexibility to make different choices in accounting for the hotel properties that they own and operate. Hongkong and Shanghai Hotels, Ltd. (HKSH) owns and operates the Peninsula Hotel chain worldwide, including well-known Peninsula Hotel facilities in New York and Chicago. HKSH's 2020 annual report notes:

> *Hotel and other properties held for own use and plant and equipment are stated in the statement of financial position at cost less accumulated depreciation.*

Thus, the company carries its hotel properties in its balance sheet at cost. It depreciates them over useful lives that are established by company management based on factors similar to those used in the United States.

Company	Operations	IAS 16 Choice
Hongkong and Shanghai Hotels, Ltd., headquartered in Hong Kong	Owns the Peninsula Hotel brand. Owns and operates Peninsula Hotels worldwide.	Cost model
Banyan Tree Holdings, Ltd., headquartered in Singapore	Owns and operates hotels in Asia, the Middle East, and Mexico under the Banyan Tree and Angsana brands.	Revaluation model

Banyan Tree Holdings, Ltd. (BTH) is a multinational luxury hotel chain based in Singapore that owns and operates hotels in Asia, the Middle East, and Mexico under the Banyan Tree and Angsana brands. In its 2020 annual report, BTH disclosed that it accounts for its hotels using IAS 16's revaluation method:

> *All items of property, plant and equipment are initially recorded at cost. . . For freehold land and buildings, the Group adopts the revaluation model. Fair value is determined based on appraisal undertaken by professional independent property valuers, using market-based evidence.*

As provided for in IAS 16, BTH applies the revaluation model only to its freehold land and buildings, that is, the hotel properties that it actually owns. It uses the cost model to account for leased hotels, furniture, and equipment. The table below presents the effect that BTH's choice of the revaluation model had on total comprehensive income in 2019 and 2020. In 2019, revaluation gains comprised over 60 percent of total comprehensive income, illustrating their potential importance in communicating information about Banyan Tree's improving economics that year. In 2020, BTH reported a slight revaluation loss, which accentuated the negative effect that the COVID-19 pandemic had on the company's business.

Banyan Tree Holdings Statement of Comprehensive Income for Fiscal 2019 and 2020 (millions of Singapore dollars)	2019	2020
Income statement profit (loss) for the year	2,529	(102,508)
Comprehensive income (loss):		
Revaluation of land and buildings, net of deferred tax	37,161	(550)
Other components of comprehensive income	21,537	(13,654)
Total comprehensive income (loss) for the year	61,227	(116,712)

Depreciation

Depreciation is based on estimated useful lives, taking residual value into account. The depreciation method should reflect the pattern in which the asset's future economic benefits are expected to be consumed; straight-line depreciation will not always be appropriate. IAS 16 requires estimates of useful life, residual value, and the method of depreciation to be reviewed on an annual basis. Changes in depreciation method, residual value, and useful life are treated prospectively as changes in estimates.

When an item of PPE is comprised of significant parts for which different depreciation methods or useful lives are appropriate, each part must be depreciated separately. This is commonly referred to as component depreciation. Components can be physical, such as an aircraft engine, or nonphysical, such as a major inspection. Component depreciation is not commonly used under U.S. GAAP.

Example: Component Depreciation at Air Canada

Air Canada uses IFRS and included the following note in its 2020 annual report:

> *The Corporation allocates the amount initially recognized in respect of an item of property and equipment to its significant components and depreciates separately each component.*

Suppose that on January 1, Year 1, Air Canada acquires a new piece of baggage handling machinery with an estimated useful life of 10 years for $120,000. The machine has an electrical motor that must be replaced every five years and is estimated to cost $10,000 to replace. In addition, by law the machine must be inspected every two years; the inspection cost is $2,000. Air Canada has determined that the straight-line method of depreciation best reflects the pattern in which the asset's future benefits will be consumed. Assuming no residual value, the company would recognize depreciation expense of $13,800 on this machinery in Year 1, determined in the following manner:

Component	Cost	Useful Life	Depreciation
Motor	$ 10,000	5 years	$ 2,000
Inspection	2,000	2 years	1,000
Machine	108,000	10 years	10,800
Total	$120,000		$13,800

Derecognition

Derecognition refers to the removal of an asset or liability from the balance sheet and the accounts. The carrying amount of an item of PPE is derecognized (1) upon disposal or (2) when no future economic benefits are expected from its use or disposal. The gain or loss arising from the derecognition of an item of property, plant, and equipment is included in net income.

Note that an item of PPE should be reclassified as "noncurrent assets held for sale" when the asset's carrying amount is to be recovered by selling the asset rather than by using the asset. IFRS 5, *Noncurrent Assets Held for Sale and Discontinued Operations,* provides guidance with respect to the accounting treatment for noncurrent assets, including PPE, that are held for sale, as well as guidance with respect to the accounting for discontinued operations.

INVESTMENT PROPERTY

As noted in the previous section, Hongkong and Shanghai Hotels, Ltd. (HKSH) accounts for its ownership and management of the Peninsula Hotel chain using the framework established by IAS 16, *Property, Plant, and Equipment.* The company's most famous hotel is the eponymous Peninsula Hotel, a tourist landmark built in 1928 and located on Hong Kong's Kowloon peninsula. The Peninsula Hotel is part of PPE because HKSH both owns the facility and provides the hospitality services that guests receive there. As discussed in the previous section, IAS 16 allows companies to choose between the cost and revaluation models when accounting for PPE. HKSH chooses the cost model for its hotels.

HKSH also owns The Peak, Hong Kong's most popular tourist attraction. The Peak consists of a tram and a shopping, dining, and entertainment complex atop Victoria Peak, known as Peak Tower. HKSH does not operate the retail businesses located within Peak Tower. Instead, it acts as landlord, and these businesses are its rent-paying tenants. The accounting implications of this distinction are important. Whereas the company's hotels are part of its PPE, accountants consider Peak Tower to be an *investment property*. IFRS use a separate reporting framework for such properties.

IAS 40, *Investment Property,* prescribes the accounting treatment for investment properties, which are defined as land and/or buildings held to earn rentals, capital appreciation, or both. Similar to IAS 16, IAS 40 allows companies to measure these assets using either the historical cost or fair value approaches. For companies choosing historical cost, IAS 40 resembles IAS 16 in most respects. However, for companies choosing fair value, the accounting under IAS 40 differs from IAS 16's revaluation model in two important ways. First, changes in fair value are recognized as gains or losses in current income period by period, not as changes to revaluation surplus in comprehensive income. Second, period-by-period updating of fair values is done in lieu of depreciation, eliminating depreciation expenses in the income statement and accumulated depreciation accounts in the balance sheet. If an entity chooses the cost model, it must nevertheless disclose the fair value of its investment property in the footnotes to the financial statements. In contrast to IFRS, U.S. GAAP generally requires use of the cost model for investment property.[4]

PPE and investment property may seem practically indistinguishable to the casual observer. In fact, many luxury hotel complexes around the world are a hybrid of hotel space (PPE, IAS 16) and retail, residential, and office space (investment property, IAS 40). IFRS mandate separate accounting for investment property for two reasons. First, real estate businesses commonly manage their property portfolios using fair value metrics, linking the growth in a portfolio's fair value to performance evaluations, executive bonuses, and so on. Thus, in preparing IFRS financial statements, these businesses often make use of IAS 40's fair value option when it aligns external and internal reporting. Second, the ownership of investment property is more widely distributed among different types of businesses in other countries than it is in the United States. In the United States, real estate investments of the sort covered by IAS 40 are often held in special tax-advantaged entities known as *real estate investment trusts,* or REITs. In other countries, similar tax structures either may not exist or may be more limited in scope. It is relatively more common for foreign industrial companies to have a special division that manages real estate investments as a side business. This is particularly true of corporations that own large amounts of real estate as part of their day-to-day business operations. Readers of non-U.S. financial statements will find IAS 40 being applied in industries such as retail (grocery stores, department stores, restaurant chains, etc.), wholesaling and logistics, hospitality, gaming, and construction. For example, Carrefour, the large French retailer that competes against Walmart in many markets, carries material amounts of investment property on its consolidated balance sheet.

---

[4] In 2011, the FASB proposed mandatory fair value accounting for investment properties held by American real estate investment trusts (Topic 973). The Board withdrew this proposal in the face of industry opposition in 2014. One valid criticism of the proposal was that it differed from IAS 40 to such an extent that it did not contribute to IFRS–U.S. GAAP convergence.

EXHIBIT 4.1
Hong Kong and
Shanghai Hotels, Ltd.
Financial Data for
2017–2020

	Hong Kong and Shanghai Hotels Limited Financial Data for 2017–2020 (HK$ millions)			
	2017	**2018**	**2019**	**2020**
Income statement information:				
Pre-tax profit before fair value increases in investment properties	711	903	612	(1,217)
Increase in fair value of investment properties.	609	523	83	(732)
Pre-tax profit as reported under IFRS	1,320	1,426	695	(1,949)
Balance sheet information, as of December 31:				
Property, plant, and equipment (IAS 16). . .	7,106	8,452	12,314	13,249
Investment properties (IAS 40)	36,249	33,077	33,219	32,407
Other assets.	5,165	7,463	8,146	7,405
Total assets.	48,520	48,992	53,679	53,061

Example: Investment Properties at Hongkong and Shanghai Hotels, Ltd.

Exhibit 4.1 presents financial information pertaining to HKSH's investment properties taken from the company's annual reports for the 2017 to 2020 fiscal years. Although HKSH is primarily known for its Peninsula Hotel chain, investment properties comprised roughly two-thirds of the company's total assets during this time frame. These properties consisted of shopping malls, commercial offices, and apartment complexes. Hotels and other PPE accounted for a much smaller share. Not surprisingly, the annual reports devoted considerable attention to how investment properties are managed and how their values are measured. In its auditor's report, KPMG identified accounting for investment properties to be a key audit matter.

HKSH chooses the fair value option for its investment properties. Under this option, IAS 40 requires the company to revalue investment properties every reporting period and to include the resulting gains or losses in the income statement for that period. As recommended, but not required by IAS 40, HKSH uses licensed third-party appraisers to estimate these values.

Suppose that HKSH were to purchase an investment property for 10 million Hong Kong dollars (HK$) on January 1, Year 1, that increased to an appraised value of 11 million HK$ as of December 31, the end of HKSH's fiscal year. Year 1 journal entries for this property would be as follows:[5]

January 1, Year 1:	Investment property.	$10,000,000	
	Cash		$10,000,000
	To record the purchase investment property.		
December 31, Year 1	Investment property.	$1,000,000	
	Gain on revaluation of investment property (income statement).		$1,000,000
	To record the revaluation gain measured by the property appraiser as of December 31.		

[5] Note that HKSH does not record depreciation on the investment property. Period-by-period fair value remeasurement overrides the need for this step.

Exhibit 4.1 also reports the fair value gains on investment properties that HKSH included in its income statement during 2017–2020. They ranged between 46 percent of pre-tax profits in 2017 and 38 percent of pre-tax losses in 2020. The economic effects of political turmoil in Hong Kong and the COVID-19 pandemic are reflected in the figures from 2019 to 2020. More generally, real estate prices can both rise and fall, sometimes experiencing dramatic year-to-year fluctuations. Exhibit 4.1 illustrates the relatively large influence that fair value gains and losses on investment properties can have on reported profitability under IAS 40.

BIOLOGICAL ASSETS

Weyerhaeuser Company, based in Seattle, Washington, is one of the world's largest owners of timberland and producers of wood products. As of December 31, 2020, the largest asset on its balance sheet was *Timber and timberlands,* valued at $11.8 billion and comprising 72 percent of total assets. Under U.S. GAAP, Weyerhaeuser accounts for this asset class using the cost method. This means that it starts with the historical cost of its forest land and capitalizes expenditures made to plant new trees, called *reforestation costs.* Reforestation is analogous to factory improvements that a manufacturer would capitalize. Weyerhaeuser expenses maintenance costs, such as expenditures for fertilization and pest control.

Many accountants believe that this historical cost approach to timber assets misses an important element: the economic transformation that naturally occurs as the forests grow over time. Under historical cost, this growth will eventually show up in Weyerhaeuser's profits, but only after the trees have been harvested and wood products made from them have been sold as inventory. Accountants who are critical of historical cost in this setting would argue that trees take many years to grow to maturity, and in the meantime, a fair value measurement system would better capture the value transformation that occurs with this growth. Similar arguments can be made with respect to other biological assets, albeit with shorter life cycles, such as a vineyard and its grapes, a dairy farm's cattle herd, and so on.

IAS 41, *Agriculture,* adopts this perspective and therefore differs markedly from U.S. GAAP. It generally requires companies to measure biological assets at fair value (less costs to sell at the point of harvest) period by period, with revaluation gains or losses included in the income statement. The resulting accounting resembles the fair value method for investment property covered in the previous section. However, while IAS 40 makes the fair value method optional for investment property, IAS 41 makes it mandatory for biological assets in all but a few specific cases.[6] The standard also extends fair value measurement to agricultural produce at the point of harvest. Once harvested, the produce enters the company's inventory accounting system as a production input or commodity held for sale to third parties, and IAS 41 no longer applies.

The Finnish company Stora Enso Oyj is one of the world's largest wood products companies and owns or leases substantial tracts of timberland in Scandinavia, South America, and China. Exhibit 4.2 illustrates IAS 41's effects on Stora Enso's financial statements for the 2020 and 2021 fiscal years. *Forest assets* accounted for 35 percent of the company's total assets and were upwardly revalued in both years, adding to income statement profits. In 2020, the revaluation's effect was particularly large, contributing over half of the company's total pre-tax profit that year. Such an effect would be significant to an analyst comparing Stora Enso's profitability with that of an American competitor using the cost method.

---

[6] IAS 41 applies PPE accounting (IAS 16) to bearer plants, such as grapevines, oil palms, and rubber trees. Thus, companies choose between the cost and revaluation models for these plants. The standard makes this exception because once bearer plants grow to maturity, their transformation is largely complete. IAS 41 continues to mandate fair value measurement for the produce of bearer plants, however.

EXHIBIT 4.2
Stora Enso Oyj
Financial Data for
2020–2021

	Stora Enso Oyj Financial Data for 2020–2021 (€ millions)	
	2020	**2021**
Income statement information:		
Pre-tax profit before fair value increases in forest assets	345	1,091
Increase (decrease) in the fair value of forest assets	428	328
Pre-tax profit as reported under IFRS	773	1,419
Balance sheet information as of December 31:		
Property, plant, and equipment (IAS 16)	5,007	5,060
Forest assets (IAS 41)	6,256	6,747
Total assets	17,431	19,026

The following table lists examples of biological assets covered by IAS 41, including their agricultural produce, and examples of end-products made from the produce. By its nature, the standard is used primarily by companies that are active in upstream agricultural production and does not apply to companies that operate exclusively downstream. Thus, Nestlé, the world's largest food company, carries no biological assets on its balance sheet because it purchases its agricultural inputs from upstream suppliers. In contrast, Brazil's JBS, the world's largest producer of beef products, carries large amounts of biological assets on its balance sheet because it is more vertically integrated and controls substantial livestock assets upstream.

Biological Assets	Agricultural Produce	Products That Result from Processing after Harvest
Sheep	Wool	Yarn, carpets
Trees	Felled trees	Lumber
Dairy cattle	Milk	Cheese, yogurt
Cotton plants	Harvested cotton	Clothing
Grapevines*	Grapes	Wine and juice
Oil palms*	Picked fruit	Palm oil
Rubber trees*	Harvested latex	Rubber products

*Subject to special rules for bearer plants.

Fair Value Appraisals and the Relevance-Reliability Trade-Off

IFRS's requirement to apply fair value measurement to biological assets, together with its permission to use fair value for PPE and investment properties, is one of the most fundamental differences between it and U.S. GAAP. Referring back to the reporting concepts introduced in Chapter 3, in effect, the IASB tilted toward *relevance* at the risk of less *reliability* in applying fair value measurement to these asset classes. The central reliability challenges that accountants must overcome are:

- Illiquidity of the markets in which the assets trade, resulting in the need to use valuation modeling in lieu of observed asset prices.
- Competing valuation frameworks and models that lead to different results.
- Subjectivity in estimates of modeling inputs once a particular model is agreed upon.
- Long forecasting horizons, which add to uncertainty of the subjective estimates.
- Management's incentives to exploit modeling choices to improve perceptions of the company's performance and financial health.

Store Enso's valuation of its forest assets provides a good illustration of the challenges faced by its accountants and, by extension, its auditor in applying fair value measurement to long-lived nonfinancial assets. According to the 2021 annual report, the company's modeling is based on forecasts of future market conditions, discount rates, forest growth potential, and wood harvested over one growing cycle. For one of its Nordic forests, one growing cycle reaches between 60 and 100 years. Forecasts extending over such long horizons are extremely complex and sensitive to the inputs used. However, they also may greatly affect the company's profitability under IAS 41. Unsurprisingly, Stora Enso's management devoted considerable attention to this modeling exercise in its discussion of critical accounting policies, while its auditor, PricewaterhouseCoopers Oy of Helsinki, listed it first among key audit matters.

The application of fair value measurement to long-lived assets also presents challenges for investors, creditors, and forensic accountants. The risks have been especially treacherous for investors in agricultural companies in emerging markets. A notorious case was that of China Huishan Dairy. A profile of this company in *The Wall Street Journal* in early 2016 described its vertically integrated supply chain as "grass to glass," meaning that it extended from the cultivation of feed grains for its cattle herds all the way to the distribution of milk products to consumers. The same article described its investment strategy as one that put "every penny that it makes, and more, into farms and cows."[7] Huishan Dairy was one of the Hong Kong Stock Exchange's hottest stocks in 2015. However, the company's stock price plummeted 85 percent in March 2017 when short-sellers released a report critical of its accounting policies, particularly its overvaluation of alfalfa stocks and cattle herds. The company entered bankruptcy proceedings later that year.

IMPAIRMENT OF ASSETS

IAS 36, *Impairment of Assets,* requires impairment testing and recognition of impairment losses for property, plant, and equipment; intangible assets; goodwill; and investments in subsidiaries, associates, and joint ventures. It does not apply to inventory, construction in progress, deferred tax assets, employee benefit assets, or financial assets such as accounts and notes receivable. U.S. GAAP also requires impairment testing of assets. However, several important differences exist between the two sets of standards.

Under IAS 36, an entity must assess annually whether there are any indicators that an asset is impaired. Events that might indicate an asset is impaired are:

- *External events,* such as a decline in market value, an increase in market interest rates, or economic, legal, or technological changes that adversely affect the value of an asset.
- *Internal events,* such as physical damage, obsolescence, idleness of an asset, the restructuring of part of an asset, or the worse-than-expected economic performance of the asset.

If indicators of impairment are present, an entity must estimate the recoverable amount of the asset and compare that amount with the asset's carrying amount (book value).

Definition of Impairment

Under IAS 36, an asset is impaired when its carrying amount exceeds its recoverable amount.

- *Recoverable amount* is the greater of *net selling price* and *value in use.*
- *Net selling price* is the price of an asset in an active market less disposal costs.
- *Value in use* is determined as the present value of future net cash flows expected to arise from continued use of the asset over its remaining useful life and upon disposal. In

---

[7] Scott Deveau and Kevin Crowley, "Exxon Activist Gets major Boost as ISS Backs Three Nominees," Bloomberg, May 14, 2021.

calculating value in use, projections of future cash flows should be based on approved budgets and should cover a maximum of five years (unless a longer period can be justified). The discount rate used to determine present value should reflect current market assessments of the time value of money and the risks specific to the asset under review.

Under U.S. GAAP, impairment exists when an asset's carrying amount exceeds the future cash flows (undiscounted) expected to arise from its continued use and disposal. Net selling price is not involved in the test, and future cash flows are not discounted to their present value. When value in use is the recoverable amount under IAS 36, an impairment is more likely to arise under IFRS (discounted cash flows) than under U.S. GAAP (undiscounted cash flows).

Measurement of Impairment Loss

The measurement of impairment loss under IAS 36 is straightforward. It is the amount by which carrying value exceeds recoverable amount, and it is recognized in income. In the case of PPE carried at a revalued amount, the impairment loss is first taken against revaluation surplus and then to income.

The comparison of carrying value and undiscounted future cash flows under U.S. GAAP is done to determine whether an asset is impaired. The impairment loss is then measured as the amount by which carrying value exceeds *fair value*. Fair value may be determined by reference to quoted market prices in active markets, estimates based on the values of similar assets, or estimates based on the results of valuation techniques. It is unlikely that fair value (U.S. GAAP) and recoverable amount (IFRS) for an asset will be the same, resulting in differences in the amount of impairment loss recognized between the two sets of standards.

Example: Determination and Measurement of Impairment Loss

At December 31, Year 1, Toca Company has specialized equipment with the following characteristics:

Carrying amount	$50,000
Selling price	40,000
Costs of disposal	1,000
Expected future cash flows	55,000
Present value of expected future cash flows	46,000

In applying IAS 36, the asset's recoverable amount would be determined as follows:

Net selling price	$40,000 − 1,000 = $39,000	
Value in use	$46,000	
Recoverable amount (greater of the two)		$46,000

The determination and measurement of impairment loss would be:

Carrying amount	$50,000
Recoverable amount	46,000
Impairment loss	$ 4,000

The following journal entry would be made to reflect the impairment of this asset:

Impairment Loss	$4,000	
Equipment		$4,000
To recognize an impairment loss on equipment.		

Under U.S. GAAP, an impairment test would be carried out as follows:

Carrying value	$50,000
Expected future cash flows (undiscounted)	55,000

Because expected future cash flows exceed the asset's carrying value, no impairment is deemed to exist. The asset would be reported on the December 31, Year 1, balance sheet at $50,000.

Reversal of Impairment Losses

At each balance sheet date, a review should be undertaken to determine if impairment losses have reversed. (Indicators of impairment reversal are provided in IAS 36.) If, subsequent to recognizing an impairment loss, the recoverable amount of an asset is determined to exceed its new carrying amount, the impairment loss should be reversed. However, the loss should be reversed only if there are changes in the estimates used to determine the original impairment loss or there is a change in the basis for determining the recoverable amount (from value in use to net selling price or vice versa). The carrying value of the asset is increased, but not to exceed what it would have been if no impairment loss had been recognized. The reversal of an impairment loss should be recognized in income immediately. U.S. GAAP does not allow the reversal of a previously recognized impairment loss.

Example: *Reversal of Impairment Loss*

Spring Valley Water Company purchased new water filtration equipment at the beginning of Year 1 for $1,000,000. The equipment is expected to have a useful life of 40 years with no residual value. Therefore, annual depreciation is $25,000. By the end of Year 3, Spring Valley concluded that the filtration system was not performing up to expectations. The company determined that the system had a recoverable amount based on net selling price of $740,000. The carrying amount of the asset at the end of Year 3 was $925,000 [$1,000,000 − ($25,000 × 3 years)], so the company recognized an impairment loss of $185,000 in Year 3. Annual depreciation of $20,000 [$740,000/37 years] subsequently was recognized in Years 4 and 5. The carrying amount of the equipment at the end of Year 5 was $700,000 [$740,000 − ($20,000 × 2)]. The summary journal entries to account for this asset in Years 1 through 5 are shown here:

January 1, Year 1		
Equipment	$1,000,000	
Cash		$1,000,000
December 31, Year 1, Year 2, Year 3		
Depreciation Expense	$25,000	
Accumulated Depreciation—Equipment		$25,000
December 31, Year 3		
Impairment Loss	$185,000	
Equipment		$185,000
December 31, Year 4, Year 5		
Depreciation Expense	$20,000	
Accumulated Depreciation—Equipment		$20,000

In January, Year 6, a technician discovered that the filtration equipment had not been properly set up at the time of initial installation. Adjustments to the installation resulted in a significant boost in performance, which led the company to reevaluate whether the equipment was still impaired. New estimates of future cash flows to be generated through continued operation of the equipment resulted in a recoverable amount based on value in use of $900,000, and the company determined that it was appropriate to reverse the impairment loss recognized in Year 3. To determine the amount of impairment loss to reverse, the company calculated what the carrying amount of the equipment would have been if the impairment had never been recognized. Annual depreciation of $25,000 would have been taken for five years, resulting in a carrying amount of $875,000 [$1,000,000 − ($25,000 × 5 years)], which is less than the new recoverable amount of $900,000. With impairment, the carrying amount of the equipment at the end of Year 5 is $700,000. Therefore, early in Year 6, Spring Valley increased the carrying amount of the equipment by $175,000 to write it up to $875,000 and recorded a reversal of impairment loss of the same amount. The reversal of impairment loss results in an increase in income:

January, Year 6		
Equipment	$175,000	
Reversal of Impairment Loss (increase in income)		$175,000

In earlier sections of this chapter, we encountered Hongkong and Shanghai Hotels, Ltd. (HKSH) in our discussion of property, plant, and equipment and investment properties. HKSH accounts for its hotels using the cost method and, as required by IAS 36, tests them for impairment annually. KPMG, the company's auditor, identifies hotel impairment testing as one of two key audit matters in its auditor's note. The other key audit matter is fair value appraisals for investment properties (discussed earlier). In describing this issue, KPMG notes:

> *The valuation of hotel properties is complex and involves a significant degree of judgement and estimation, particularly given the diverse locations of the hotel properties and the particular economic and political circumstances at each location which can affect occupancy rates, revenue per available room and future growth rates.*

In 2020, HKSH's application of IAS 36 led to an impairment charge of 329 million HK$ to reduce the carrying values of two Peninsula Hotel facilities, the Peninsula Manila and the Peninsula Istanbul. In both cases, the hotels' recoverable amounts as of December 31, 2020, were less than their prior carrying values. In the case of the Peninsula Manila, the 2020 annual report attributed the impairment to the Philippine government's COVID-19 quarantine policies and an "uncertain outlook for local tourism." As required by IAS 36, HKSH reevaluates the hotels' carrying values annually, possibly taking additional impairment charges or reversing charges already recorded. The company's 2020 annual report made note of this policy, but stated that, "no provision for or reversal of impairment was required as at 31 December 2019 and 2020."

INTANGIBLE ASSETS

Intangible assets are in many cases a business's most important assets. In 2020, a widely cited study by Ocean Tomo, an intellectual property valuation consultancy, asserted that intangibles account for more than 90 percent of the economic value of the S&P 500 companies. Such lofty estimates are broadly consistent with the findings of academic research, which has documented stock market premiums for companies with superior technology, brands, and human resources policies. In 2021, the list of the world's largest corporations by stock market capitalization included Apple Computer, Alphabet, Facebook, Microsoft, and Tesla. Each possesses vast troves of proprietary technology and is ranked among the world's most valuable brands.

As most accounting students realize, much of the economic value of intangibles does not make it onto corporate balance sheets despite their undeniable importance in the modern economy. U.S. GAAP prohibits the recognition of internally generated intangible assets in all but a few special cases—for instance, for certain types of computer software. Thus, most intangibles on American corporate balance sheets are purchased, either directly from sellers as asset acquisitions or as part of business combinations. In practice, American companies that have not undertaken large-scale merger and acquisition (M&A) activity tend to carry very small levels of intangible assets on their balance sheets. Nike is a good example of this phenomenon. Despite possessing one of the world's most valuable and widely recognized brands and being ranked as one of the best companies to work for in a recent survey by Glassdoor, intangible assets, as recognized and measured by U.S. GAAP, comprised only 1 percent of total assets in the company's 2021 consolidated balance sheet.

IAS 38, *Intangible Assets,* provides the primary guidance on accounting for intangible assets within the IFRS framework. Many of its provisions for both purchased intangibles and those acquired in business combinations are consistent with U.S. GAAP. However, the standard differs fundamentally from American practice on the question of whether to recognize internally generated intangibles. Specifically, IAS 38 requires companies to capitalize many research and development (R&D) expenditures as *development costs* according to specific rules outlined below. This requirement often leads to large differences in how R&D activities are presented in all three of the primary financial statements—the balance sheet, the income statement, and the statement of cash flows.

IAS 38 defines intangible assets as *identifiable,* nonmonetary assets without physical substance that are held for use in the production of goods or services, for rental to others, or for administrative purposes. Examples include patents, brands (generally labeled *trademarks* in American financial statements), copyrights, and various operating rights, such as the right to broadcast programming in a particular frequency of the radio frequency spectrum. Accountants would consider each of these assets to be identifiable because they arise from specific legal rights or are capable of being separately sold or licensed to other parties.[8]

IAS 38 further stipulates that intangibles be *controlled* by the enterprise. One prominent economic resource that generally fails the accountant's control requirement is a company's human capital, or the talent, experience, and workplace capabilities of its employees. Some economists would argue that human capital is an organization's most important resource. However, employees are free to quit their employers, at least in a strictly legal sense, and thus are not controlled within the meaning of IAS 38. For this reason, the standard prohibits the recognition of human capital assets in all but a few special cases.

Purchased Intangibles

The value of a purchased intangible asset is initially measured at its cost, and its useful life is assessed as finite or indefinite. The cost of an intangible asset with a finite useful life is amortized on a systematic basis over the useful life. The residual value is assumed to be zero unless (1) a third party has agreed to purchase the asset at the end of its useful life, or (2) there is an active market for the asset from which a residual value can be estimated.

An intangible asset is deemed to have an indefinite life when there is no foreseeable limit to the period over which it is expected to generate cash flows for the entity. If the useful life of an intangible asset is indefinite, no amortization should be taken until the life is determined to be definite. The distinction made in IAS 38 between intangibles with a finite life

---

[8] For example, brands are often valued using the *royalty relief method.* The starting point for this method is historical evidence of the royalty rates that external parties have been willing to pay for the use of a company's brand. A recent tax case in the United Kingdom revealed that Starbucks assumes that its brand can earn a royalty rate of 6 percent of sales revenue.

and those with an indefinite life and the corresponding accounting treatment are consistent with U.S. GAAP.

Intangibles Acquired in a Business Combination

Under both IAS 38 and U.S. GAAP, identifiable intangibles such as patents, brands, and customer lists acquired in a business combination should be recognized as assets apart from goodwill at their fair values. The acquiring company should recognize these intangibles as assets even if they were not recognized as assets by the acquiree, so long as they are identifiable and controlled and their fair value can be measured reliably. If any of these criteria are not met, the intangible is not recognized as a separate asset but is instead included in goodwill. Similar to purchased intangibles, intangibles acquired in a business combination must be classified as having a finite or an indefinite useful life.

Volkswagen's acquisition of Porsche Automobil Holding SE (Porsche) provides an illustration of the mechanics of intangible asset recognition in a business combination. The acquisition was concluded on August 1, 2012. Exhibit 4.3 lists the valuations that Volkswagen (VW) assigned to Porsche's intangible assets on that date. VW identified three major classes of intangible assets at Porsche: the Porsche brand name, technology, and customer and supplier relationships. Neither the Porsche brand nor the customer and supplier relationships had previously been recorded in Porsche's balance sheet prior to the takeover by VW. Particularly noteworthy is the large fair value assigned to the brand. At €13,823 million, this intangible asset was appraised to be almost four times as valuable as Porsche's PPE, the most valuable tangible asset.

VW classifies brands acquired in business combinations as *indefinitely lived* intangibles, thus, as assets without amortization. As of December 31, 2020, the company's balance sheet carried each of its acquired brands at the fair value assigned to it on its acquisition date. In addition to Porsche, other recorded brands included MAN trucks and Ducati motorcycles. However, just as important is what was *not* recorded. The Interbrand valuation consultancy produces annual rankings of the world's most valuable brands. In 2021, Porsche ranked tenth among global auto brands, a very high ranking given the Porsche unit's size and sales levels, but only third within the VW organization. The Volkswagen brand itself ranked eighth and the group's Audi brand ranked seventh. Neither of these famous brands appears as an asset in VW's balance sheet. In effect, both are homegrown intangibles that fall outside of the recognition framework outlined in the next section.

Internally Generated Intangibles

IAS 38 closely associates the development of homegrown, or internally generated, intangibles with the R&D process. In doing so, it distinguishes between *research,* the search for new knowledge, and *development,* the application of this knowledge to the creation of

EXHIBIT 4.3
Fair Values Assigned to Porsche's Intangible Assets on August 1, 2012 (€ millions)

	IFRS Carrying Amounts Immediately Prior to the Acquisition	Adjustments to Fair Value on the Acquisition Date	Fair Values on the Acquisition Date
Porsche brand name	—	13,823	13,823
Technology	1,489	714	2,203
Customer and dealer relationships	—	691	691
Other identifiable intangibles	386	103	489
for comparison			
Property, plant, and equipment	2,983	565	3,548

commercially viable products and services. The standard requires that all research expenditures be expensed as incurred. Development expenditures too should generally be expensed in a project's early stages, when there is likely to be substantial uncertainty about its technical feasibility or commercial success. The key difference between IAS 38 and U.S. GAAP applies to the project's later stages. Specifically, the standard mandates that development expenditures be capitalized as development cost assets when the enterprise can demonstrate all of the following:

1. The technical feasibility of completing the intangible asset so that it will be available for use or sale.
2. The intention to complete the intangible asset and use or sell it.
3. The ability to use or sell the intangible asset.
4. How the intangible asset will generate probable future economic benefits. Among other things, the enterprise should demonstrate the existence of a market for the output of the intangible asset or, if it is to be used internally, the usefulness of the intangible asset.
5. The availability of adequate technical, financial, and other resources to complete the development and to use or sell the intangible asset.
6. The ability to reliably measure the expenditure attributable to the intangible asset during its development.

The first five of IAS 38's capitalization criteria, taken together, give accountants the requisite level of confidence that they need to treat development expenditures as investment assets with future economic benefits. The sixth criterion serves two purposes. First, it assures that the entity's accounting system reliably tracks costs and attributes them to appropriate projects. Beyond this, it disallows the recognition of internally generated marketing intangibles such as brands, customer lists, mastheads, and publishing titles. IAS 38 asserts that measuring expenditures to create and enhance these intangibles is impossible because they are not distinguishable from the costs of developing the business as a whole. The standard also prohibits the capitalization of expenditures on advertising and corporate training for similar reasons.

If any of the six criteria is not satisfied, then expensing is required. Development costs capitalized as an internally generated intangible can only be treated as having a finite useful life. They must be amortized over the useful life using a method that best reflects the pattern in which the asset's economic benefits are consumed. Declining-balance, units-of-production, and straight-line methods are among the acceptable methods. Amortization begins when the enterprise makes the intangible asset available for sale or use.

In accordance with IAS 23, *Borrowing Costs,* borrowing costs should be included as part of the cost of development activities to the extent that the costs of those activities constitute a "qualifying asset." IAS 23 is discussed in more detail later in this chapter.

Example: Capitalized Development Costs

Szabo Company Inc. incurred costs to develop a specific product for a customer in Year 1 amounting to $300,000. Of that amount, $250,000 was incurred up to the point at which the technical feasibility of the product could be demonstrated and other recognition criteria were met. In Year 2, Szabo Company incurred an additional $300,000 in costs in the development of the product. The product was available for sale on January 2, Year 3, with the first shipment to the customer occurring in mid-February, Year 3. Sales of the product are expected to continue for four years, at which time it is expected that a replacement product will need to be developed. The total number of units expected to be produced over the product's four-year economic life is 2,000,000. The number of units produced in Year 3 is 800,000. Residual value is zero.

In Year 1, $250,000 of development costs is expensed and $50,000 is recognized as an asset. The journal entry is as follows:

Development Expense	$250,000	
Development Costs (intangible asset).	50,000	
Cash, payables, etc.		$300,000
To record development expense and capitalized development costs asset.		

In Year 2, $300,000 of development costs is recognized as an asset, bringing the total asset balance to $350,000:

Development Costs (intangible asset).	$300,000	
Cash, payables, etc.		$300,000
To record capitalized development costs.		

Amortization of the development costs asset begins on January 2, Year 3, when the product becomes available for sale. Szabo Company determines that the units-of-production method best reflects the pattern in which the asset's economic benefits are consumed. Amortization expense for Year 3 is calculated as follows:

Carrying amount of the development costs asset		$350,000
Units produced in Year 3.	800,000	
Total number of units to be produced over economic life	2,000,000	
Percent of total units produced in Year 3.		40%
Amortization expense in Year 3		$140,000

The journal entry to record amortization of the capitalized development costs asset at December 31, Year 3, is as follows:

Amortization Expense	$140,000	
Development Costs (intangible asset)		$140,000
To record annual amortization expense.		

If Szabo Company were unable to estimate with reasonable certainty the number of units to be produced, it would be appropriate to amortize the development costs asset on a straight-line basis over the four-year expected life. In that case, the journal entry to record amortization in Year 3 would be as follows:

Amortization Expense	$87,500	
Development Costs (intangible asset)		$87,500
To record annual amortization expense.		

Examples of Internally Generated Intangible Assets

Development costs consist of (1) all costs directly attributable to development activities and (2) those costs that can be reasonably allocated to such activities, including:

- Personnel costs.
- Materials and services costs.
- Depreciation of property, plant, and equipment.
- Overhead costs, other than general administrative costs.
- Amortization of patents and licenses.

In other words, development costs are similar to costs incurred in producing inventory. Because the costs of some, but not all, development projects will be deferred as assets, it is necessary to accumulate costs for each development project as if it were a separate work in progress.

While the above categories are common to R&D activities at most companies, these activities produce an array of products and services that differ substantially from industry to industry. The following list illustrates the wide range of settings in which IAS 38's development cost capitalization model is applied in practice. Each example is taken from recent annual reports prepared under IFRS:

- Tata Motors (India): Produces cars and trucks and owns Jaguar Land Rover Limited. Tata Motors capitalizes product development costs "incurred on new vehicle platforms, engines, and transmissions."
- Bertelsmann (Germany): Europe's largest media company. Bertelsmann capitalizes software and Web site development costs.
- Minor International (Thailand): A conglomerate that owns The Pizza Company, one of Southeast Asia's largest restaurant chains. Minor International capitalizes a portion of its spending to develop and test new food items for its restaurant menus.
- Sanofi (France): One of the world's largest pharmaceutical companies. Sanofi capitalizes development costs for second-generation improvements of drugs that have already received regulatory approval and for geographic extensions of drugs that have already been approved in a major market.

Sanofi's highly nuanced accounting policy for drug development costs deserves special attention. Pharmaceutical companies must spend vast sums on R&D to remain competitive, but they face great uncertainty regarding the length and ultimate outcome of the complex regulatory approval processes that they must navigate to bring their drugs to market. Because of this uncertainty, very little drug development spending meets IAS 38's capitalization criteria. Sanofi's capitalization policy is standard within the industry. Pharmaceutical companies following IFRS generally capitalize development costs for a particular drug only after obtaining approval in at least one major market.

The Financial Statement Effects of Capitalizing Product Development Costs: The Case of the German Auto Industry

Interbrand's 2021 ranking of the world's top 10 auto brands contained five German entries, the most of any country. In addition to the three Volkswagen brands discussed earlier, the Daimler Group's Mercedes-Benz brand ranked second, and the BMW brand ranked third. In other surveys, German automakers achieve similarly high rankings for innovation and engineering excellence. Indeed, the technological leadership that these companies exercise within the auto industry goes hand in hand with their brands' high valuations.

Technological leadership, in turn, flows from successful R&D. Each of Germany's big three automakers capitalizes substantial amounts of R&D spending and reports the percentage of spending capitalized, termed the *capitalization ratio,* as a key performance indicator in its annual report. Assuming that the capitalization criteria of IAS 38 are consistently applied across the industry, a higher capitalization ratio indicates greater efficiency in transforming R&D spending into intangible assets with probable future economic benefits. Exhibit 4.4 presents data on R&D spending and capitalized development costs for Germany's automakers for the 2020 fiscal year. As shown, Volkswagen spent €13,885 million on R&D and reported the highest capitalization ratio at 46.6 percent.

IAS 38's provisions for capitalizing development costs can dramatically affect an enterprise's reported profitability, assets, and shareholders' equity, as well as the classification of R&D spending within the statement of cash flows. Exhibit 4.4 provides evidence of these effects for Germany's automakers. The figures in this table would provide a starting point for a financial analyst attempting to compare IFRS reporters with competitors that use U.S. GAAP. In the case of the global auto industry, the IFRS reporting camp includes Volkswagen, Daimler, BMW, Toyota, Honda, Nissan, Mazda, Hyundai, and Stellantis (including Dodge, Jeep, and Chrysler). Most of these automakers capitalize substantial amounts of development costs. The U.S. GAAP reporting camp includes Ford, General Motors, and Tesla. Capitalization is negligible for this group.

EXHIBIT 4.4
The Financial Statement Effects of Capitalized Development Costs in the German Auto Industry

	Monetary Amounts Stated in € Millions		
	BMW	Daimler	Volkswagen
R&D expenditure	6,279	8,614	13,885
Less: Capitalized development costs	(2,300)	(2,498)	(6,473)
Capitalization ratio in %	36.6%	29.0%	46.6%
Plus: Amortization of capitalized development costs	1,710	1,925	4,644
R&D expenses as reported under IFRS	5,689	8,041	12,056
Income statement effects in 2020:			
Operating profit as reported under IFRS	4,830	6,160	9,675
Less: Profit attributable to capitalization	(590)	(573)	(1,829)
Operating profit under 100% expensing	4,240	5,587	7,846
Increase (%) in operating profit under IFRS	13.9%	10.3%	23.3%
Balance sheet effects on December 31, 2020:			
Capitalized development costs, net	11,007	13,107	25,534
Percentage of identifiable intangible assets	92.0%	86.4%	57.2%
Equity as reported under IFRS	61,520	128,783	128,783
Less: Equity attributable to capitalization*	(7,724)	(9,198)	(17,918)
Equity under 100% expensing	53,796	119,585	110,864
Increase (%) in equity over 100% expensing	14.4%	7.7%	16.2%
Cash flow statement effects in 2020:			
Net capital expenditure under IFRS	6,063	8,195	17,746
% of which: Capitalized development costs	37.9%	30.5%	36.5%
Operating cash flow under IFRS	13,251	22,332	24,901
Less: Capitalized development costs	(2,300)	(2,498)	(6,473)
Operating cash flow under 100% expensing	10,951	19,834	18,428
Percent increase over 100% expensing	21.0%	12.6%	35.1%

*Cumulative amount capitalized × (1 − 0.29285)

Income statement effects Capitalization delays the expensing of R&D costs and reclassifies them to amortization expenses in future periods. For companies with patterns of increasing R&D spending, the expenses avoided by capitalization in a given period exceed that period's amortization charges. In such cases, capitalization inflates reported profits relative to a full expensing system. Because all of the German auto companies have robust and growing R&D programs, capitalization has inflated their reported profits in recent years, often to a large extent.

Exhibit 4.4 presents the calculations necessary to evaluate the magnitude of this effect for the 2020 fiscal year. Taking Volkswagen as an example, R&D expenditures in 2020 totaled €13,885 million; virtually all of this amount would have been expensed under U.S. GAAP. However, VW capitalized €6,473 million of this amount, increasing reported income under IFRS. Because the company has capitalized R&D spending for many years, it also recorded amortization charges of €4,644 million. The difference between these two numbers, or €1,829 million, is the net amount by which reporting under IFRS inflated pre-tax profits relative to a reporting system requiring 100 percent expensing. IAS 38's capitalization provisions led to a very large increase of 23.3 percent in VW's operating profit in 2020.

Balance sheet effects Capitalization inflates intangible assets by the amount of development costs capitalized less accumulated amortization recorded as of the balance sheet date. The balance of VW's development costs asset, net of amortization, as of December 31, 2020, was €25,534 million. This amounted to 57 percent of VW's net identifiable intangible assets on that date. Intangibles acquired through M&A transactions comprised the remaining 43 percent. These were mainly goodwill and various brands carried without amortization. Development costs accounted for a much larger percentage of the intangible assets at BMW and Daimler because these companies have engaged in fewer M&A transactions.

Capitalization delays expense recognition and thus inflates shareholders' equity. Because R&D expenditures are fully tax deductible in Germany, as they are in most countries, German companies record a deferred tax liability for the timing difference between immediate R&D tax deductions and the delayed expense recognition under IFRS. Capitalization increases shareholders' equity by the net amount of capitalized development costs less the deferred tax liability created by this process. The general formula for estimating the increase in equity caused by capitalization is thus:

$$\text{Capitalized development costs, net} \times (1 - \text{Tax rate})$$

The figures in Exhibit 4.4 estimate the increase in equity traceable to capitalization using Germany's statutory tax rate of 29.825 percent.[9] Daimler's annual report explicitly states that it computes the deferred tax liability for R&D using this rate. The deferred tax liabilities reported by BMW and VW are consistent with having used an equivalent rate as well.

Cash flow statement effects An enterprise's *capital expenditure,* or *capex,* consists of its investments in new PPE as well as in new intangible assets. The decision to begin capitalizing R&D expenditures for a given project simultaneously reclassifies this spending as a capex outflow. On the statement of cash flows, this change moves these expenditures from the operating to the investing sections. Because capex and operating cash flow are two of the financial world's most important metrics, this simple locational shift can heavily influence an analyst's assessment of an enterprise's financial performance and economic value.

[9] In its 2020 annual report, Daimler AG stated in its German statutory tax rate equaled 29.825%. This was a combined rate consisting of the corporate tax rate (körperschaftsteuer) of 15.825% and a trade tax rate (gewerbesteuer) of 14% (p.173). Daimler used this rate to compute deferred tax items. BMW and Volkswagen provided less precise disclosures. However, their tax rates were very close to that of Daimler.

Exhibit 4.4 illustrates that capitalization has large effects on the cash flow data reported by each of the German automakers. Capitalized development costs represent a significant fraction of overall capex for all three, reaching 38 percent for BMW in 2020. Relocating this spending from the operating to the investing categories had a significant effect on the company's reported operating cash flow. BMW capitalized development costs of €2,300 million during 2020. Thus, its reported operating cash flow of €13,251 million would have been only €10,951 million had it been required to expense all R&D spending. Relative to a 100 percent expensing paradigm, which approximates the treatment of this spending under U.S. GAAP, capitalization inflated BMW's operating cash flow by 21 percent. Capitalization bolstered reported operating cash flow at Daimler and Volkswagen by 13 percent and 35 percent, respectively.

Revaluation Model

IAS 38, *Intangible Assets,* allows the use of the revaluation model for intangible assets with finite lives, but only if the intangible has a price that is available on an active market, a condition rarely met in practice. Examples of intangible assets that may be priced on an active market include taxi licenses, fishing licenses, and production quotas. If the company chooses the revaluation method, the asset's fair value should be assessed regularly, typically annually. An increase in fair value of the asset is credited to "revaluation surplus" in equity, except to the extent it reverses a previously recorded decrease reported directly in net income. U.S. GAAP does not provide for the revaluation of intangible assets.

Impairment of Intangible Assets

Even though they are subject to amortization, finite-lived intangible assets also must be tested for impairment whenever changes in events or circumstances indicate an asset's carrying amount may not be recoverable. Goodwill and intangible assets with indefinite lives must be reviewed at least annually for impairment, regardless of the existence of impairment indicators. IAS 36, *Impairment of Assets,* allows reversals of impairment losses on intangible assets under special circumstances. However, reversal of impairment losses on goodwill is prohibited.

BUSINESS COMBINATIONS AND CONSOLIDATED FINANCIAL STATEMENTS

A business combination is the acquisition of one business by another. Companies engage in business combinations, often referred to as mergers and acquisitions, or M&A, to enter new markets, build economies of scale, and gain access to critical resources, such as raw materials or technological know-how. Because the markets and resources that companies wish to tap through M&A are often located in foreign countries, cross-border M&A is a primary vehicle by which multinational corporations (MNCs) expand their business operations. Despite the economic headwinds created by the COVID-19 pandemic, the worldwide value of M&A deals equaled $3.6 trillion in 2020, the seventh consecutive year in which deal values exceeded $3 trillion. More than 60 percent, valued at $2.2 trillion, occurred outside the United States. Approximately one-third transpired between merger partners from different countries.

Businesses can combine their operations in a number of different ways. In many cases, the company being acquired in a business combination is legally dissolved as a separate legal entity. Either the acquired company goes out of existence and is merged into the acquiring company, or both parties to the combination are legally dissolved and a new company is formed to take their place. In yet a third method of combination, one company gains control over another company by acquiring a sufficient number of its voting shares, but the acquired company continues its separate legal existence. In this case, the acquirer becomes the parent company and the acquiree becomes a subsidiary company. Both continue to operate as separate legal entities. However, because the parent controls the subsidiary, accountants worldwide generally require that the subsidiary's financial statements be consolidated with those of the parent. A *group* is defined as a parent together with its various subsidiaries. *Group accounting* is a term commonly used outside the United States to describe the various rules and conventions that accountants use to construct consolidated financial statements from the separate accounts of the group's various members. The group structure is particularly important in multinational reporting because parent companies generally need to maintain legally separate subsidiaries in foreign countries where they have significant operations.

Determination of Control and the Scope of Consolidation

The requirement that parent companies consolidate all of the subsidiaries over which they exercise control is one of the most important principles in accounting. The famous Enron scandal proceeded in large part from a misapplication of this fundamental principle by both Enron and its auditor, Arthur Andersen. In a nutshell, Enron's CFO, together with other members of Enron's senior management team, set up a series of off-balance-sheet *variable interest entities* over which they maintained de facto control. The fact that these entities went unconsolidated for several years allowed the CFO to devise sham transactions between them and Enron that overstated Enron's apparent financial performance and strength. Enron's collapse in December 2001, at the time the largest bankruptcy in U.S. history, shocked the financial community worldwide and spurred it to broaden and tighten consolidation accounting rules, particularly those dealing with control and the scope of consolidation.

IFRS 10 is the primary international standard governing consolidation and its scope. According to this standard, control exists when each of the following conditions is present:

1. The investor has power over the investee.
2. The investor has rights to participate in, or exposure to downside risk from, the variable returns from its involvement with the investee.
3. The investor has the ability to use its power over the investee to affect those returns.

For simplicity, think of variable returns as the varying amounts of profits or cash flows to which the parent company can lay claim by virtue of its investment in a subsidiary. The parent might thus be said to have a *variable economic interest* in the subsidiary's performance. Accounting students may initially find the terms *variable returns* and *variable interest entity* vague and somewhat confusing. Accountants use them precisely because they are overarching concepts that can be applied to the wide variety of indirect or implicit control relationships encountered in practice.

The power over a subsidiary described in IFRS 10's definition of control is generally exercised through ownership of more than 50 percent of its voting shares. However, a variety of legal structures and local business conventions allow companies to gain *effective control* over subsidiaries at lower share ownership thresholds. For instance, Spain's Banco Bilbao Vizcaya Argentaria (BBVA) took effective control of Garanti Bank of Turkey in 2014 with a share ownership stake equal to 39.9 percent. BBVA's control of Garanti Bank is based on an agreement that it struck with the Doğuş Group, one of Turkey's largest industrial conglomerates and Garanti's second largest shareholder. This agreement gives BBVA the power to appoint the chairman of Garanti's board of directors, a majority of the board's members, and Garanti's CEO. Rights to appoint key managers or install a controlling block of board members are two criteria explicitly outlined in IFRS 10 as indicating effective control. Other criteria include:

- The ability to direct the investee to enter into agreements that benefit the investor.
- The ability to direct operating activities of the investee, such as selling and purchasing goods or services.
- The ability to direct investments, such as capital spending or R&D.
- The ability to determine the investee's financial structure.
- The investor's right to obtain direct control of the investee by buying additional voting shares at a later date or in response to certain triggering events.

ASC 810, the primary U.S. accounting standard dealing with control and the scope of consolidation, lays out two separate models, one based on *controlling financial interests* and another for *variable interest entities* (VIEs). Technically, a VIE is an entity for which the amount of equity investment at risk is insufficient to finance its operations. U.S. rules provide that control over a VIE exists when the following conditions are present:

- The direct or indirect ability to make decisions about the entity's activities.
- The obligation to absorb the expected losses of the entity if they occur.
- The right to receive the expected residual returns of the entity if they occur.

The level of ownership is irrelevant in determining control for this type of entity. IFRS 10 has a simpler structure than ASC 810 in that it lays out a single set of rules applicable to all investees. However, both standards are designed to tackle the ambiguities that accountants encounter in determining control and the scope of consolidation. Thus, IFRS and U.S. GAAP are fundamentally aligned in this important area.

The Acquisition Method

Both U.S. GAAP and international standards formerly allowed accountants to choose from among several different structures in accounting for business combinations. Similar flexibility is still found in American tax accounting, where M&A deals are often treated as tax-free *reorganizations,* as opposed to taxable *acquisitions,* if the acquirer issues purchase consideration in the form of stock instead of cash and the acquiree's shareholders maintain a continuing financial interest in the merged entity after the acquisition. However, the issuance of IFRS 3 in 2004 brought international rules largely into line with those now contained in ASC 805. The cornerstone of both IFRS 3 and ASC 805 is the requirement that all combinations be accounted for using the *acquisition method.* This method requires the accountant to designate an *acquirer* and one or more *acquirees* in each combination. Once this determination is made, the accountant records the acquiree's identifiable assets and liabilities in the post-acquisition consolidated balance sheet at their acquisition-date fair values.

The 2015 merger of Lafarge SA of France and Holcim Ltd. of Switzerland illustrates the application of the acquisition method under IFRS. This merger brought together two of the world's largest suppliers of building materials when they were dissolved into the newly created LafargeHolcim Ltd., an industrial behemoth that operated in 90 countries with 115,000 employees. When the deal was originally proposed in 2014, both Lafarge and Holcim described it in press releases and presentations to investors as a $44 billion *merger of equals.* Shareholders of both companies were to exchange their old shares of stock for shares of the new company. In addition, both companies received rights to contribute senior managers and directors to the new company's executive team and board of directors. However, despite this appearance of equality, the acquisition method required the accountants to carefully review the merger's details to identify an acquirer and acquiree. Because Holcim's shareholders ultimately received 57 percent of the new company's shares when the transaction closed on July 9, 2015, the transaction was accounted for as a $22 billion acquisition of Lafarge by Holcim. Thus, the fair values of Lafarge's identifiable assets and liabilities as of that date were folded into Holcim's balance sheet to create the new consolidated balance sheet for LafargeHolcim Ltd.

Goodwill and Noncontrolling Interest

The recognition of goodwill is one of the most important accounting consequences of the acquisition method. Technically, goodwill is measured as the difference between (a) and (b):

a. The consideration transferred by the acquiring firm plus any amount recognized as noncontrolling interest.

b. The fair value of net assets acquired (identifiable assets acquired less liabilities assumed).

When (a) exceeds (b), goodwill is recognized as an asset. When (a) is less than (b), a "bargain purchase" is said to have taken place and the difference between (a) and (b) (sometimes called "negative goodwill") is recognized as a gain in the post-acquisition consolidated income statement. The following table illustrates the computation of goodwill in Holcim's acquisition of Lafarge. Typical of many large acquisitions, goodwill constituted more than half of Lafarge's purchase price.

in millions of Swiss francs	
Fair value of Lafarge SA's assets	35,062
Less: Fair value of Lafarge SA's liabilities	(24,783)
Fair value of Lafarge SA's net assets	10,279
Purchase consideration (primarily the fair value of shares of Lafarge exchanged for newly issued shares of LafargeHolcim on July 9, 2015)	19,483
Plus: Noncontrolling interest	2,407
Less: Fair value of Lafarge SA's net assets	(10,279)
Goodwill	11,611

An acquirer generally gains control of an acquiree by purchasing a majority of its voting shares. Noncontrolling interest (NCI) represents the percentage of the acquiree's shares that the acquirer does not purchase. U.S. GAAP requires that NCI be measured at its fair value on the date of the acquisition, which includes the NCI's share of goodwill. In contrast, IFRS 3 allows noncontrolling interest to be measured at either (1) fair value, or (2) a proportionate share of the fair value of the acquired firm's identifiable net assets, that is, its net assets excluding goodwill. The difference between these methods is important to understand because companies reporting under IFRS commonly choose the proportionate share method, a decision that can result in substantially lower valuations being placed on goodwill in non-U.S. M&A deals. In the above example, Holcim chose the proportionate share method in accounting for its purchase of Lafarge.

Example: Initial Measurement of Goodwill

To illustrate the difference between the two methods, suppose that George Company acquires 90 percent of the outstanding shares of Chris Company by paying $360,000 in cash. The fair value of Chris's identifiable assets is $320,000, and the liabilities assumed by George in this business combination are $40,000. Under IFRS, George may choose between two alternatives to measure the NCI, which in turn will result in different valuations being placed on goodwill. If George chooses to measure the NCI using the proportionate share method, it records goodwill only for its controlling interest in Chris. The fair value of George's controlling interest in Chris's identifiable net assets is 90 percent of

($320,000 − $40,000), or $252,000. Thus, George would record as goodwill the premium that it pays for this controlling interest, which would be $360,000 − $252,000, or $108,000.

Alternative 1: Noncontrolling Interest Measured at Proportionate Share of Acquired Firm's Net Assets

Fair value of Chris's identifiable net assets ($320,000 − $40,000)		$280,000
Noncontrolling interest percentage.		10%
Noncontrolling interest.		$ 28,000
Consideration transferred	$360,000	
Plus: Noncontrolling interest.	28,000	
Subtotal.	$388,000	
Less: Fair value of Chris's identifiable net assets	280,000	
Goodwill	$108,000	

If George instead chooses the fair value method, its accountants must appraise the NCI's fair value on the acquisition date and use this appraisal to estimate the size of the premium that a hypothetical buyer would pay for the remaining 10 percent of Chris that George does not purchase. For simplicity, we will use the fact that George pays $360,000 for 90 percent of Chris to infer that the buyer would be willing to purchase 100 percent of Chris for $360,000 ÷ .9, or $400,000. Under these assumptions, fair value of the NCI would thus be appraised at $40,000. Goodwill attributed to noncontrolling interest would then be $40,000 − $28,000, or $12,000. Overall, George's acquisition of Chris would result in goodwill of $120,000, $108,000 attributed to controlling interest (computed above) and $12,000 to the NCI.

Alternative 2: Noncontrolling Interest Measured at Fair Value

Implied fair value of 100% of Chris Company ($360,000 ÷ 90%).		$400,000
Noncontrolling interest percentage.		10%
Noncontrolling interest.		$ 40,000
Consideration transferred	$360,000	
Plus: Noncontrolling interest.	40,000	
Subtotal.	$400,000	
Less: Fair value of Chris's identifiable net assets	280,000	
Goodwill	$120,000	

A major obstacle in appraising the fair value of noncontrolling interest is the acquirer's tendency to pay a *control premium* in M&A deals. Much of the value that acquirers realize from business combinations lies in gaining control of the acquiree, not in buying 100 percent of the acquiree's shares. In the example above, a control premium would imply that Chris's NCI is probably worth less than our appraisal of $40,000, but how much less would be subject to debate. In practice, accountants use a variety of methods to estimate the NCI's fair value. The most reliable of these would be to base the valuation on prices of NCI shares trading in an active stock market. If the NCI's shares are not publicly traded, more subjective valuation models must be used.

Example: Gain on Bargain Purchase

Assume the same facts as in the previous example, except George acquires 90 percent of Chris for $240,000. Also, assume that noncontrolling interest is measured at the proportionate share of net assets (Alternative 1).

Consideration transferred	$240,000
Plus: Noncontrolling interest	28,000
Subtotal	$268,000
Less: Fair value of Chris's identifiable net assets	280,000
Gain on bargain purchase	$ (12,000)

In this case, George would recognize a gain from a bargain purchase in net income in the year in which the acquisition takes place.

Impairment of Goodwill

Goodwill reflects the acquirer's willingness to pay a premium over the appraised fair value of the acquiree's identifiable net assets. In practice, goodwill is often the largest and most controversial asset recognized in an M&A deal. Companies generally justify large premiums paid for acquirees by pointing to *synergies,* such as their ability to cut costs by closing redundant facilities. However, a large body of academic research, focusing on the post-acquisition financial performance of the M&A partners, asserts that acquirers tend to overpay for acquirees in many situations. This risk of overpayment makes the accountant's ongoing assessment of goodwill a critical source of information to investors and other stakeholders about the acquirer's post-acquisition performance.

Both IFRS and U.S. GAAP require that goodwill be carried as an asset without amortization in post-acquisition balance sheets. In lieu of amortization, accountants must test goodwill for impairment annually. Under IFRS 3, impairment testing of goodwill is performed at the level of the cash-generating unit (CGU). A cash-generating unit is defined as the smallest group of assets that generates cash inflows that are largely independent from the cash inflows of other CGUs. For example, Holcim allocated goodwill recognized in its acquisition of Lafarge to various geographic operating units, with the largest allocations assigned to operations in North America, Algeria, Nigeria, and France.

The impairment test is conducted by comparing the carrying value of the entire CGU, including goodwill attributable to that CGU, with its recoverable amount. The recoverable amount is the higher of the CGU's (1) value in use and (2) fair value less costs to sell. Under U.S. GAAP, impairment of goodwill is tested at the level of the "reporting unit," which can be different (and is typically larger) than a cash-generating unit.

If noncontrolling interest was originally measured at the proportionate share of net assets (Alternative 1), then the carrying value of the entire CGU must be increased by the amount of goodwill attributable to the noncontrolling interest (as if Alternative 2 had been applied). The impairment loss on the CGU is the amount by which the CGU's carrying amount, including goodwill, exceeds its recoverable amount. An impairment loss identified at the CGU level is first applied against goodwill. Once goodwill has been eliminated, any remaining impairment is allocated to the other assets of the CGU on a prorated basis, based on their relative carrying amounts.

Example: Impairment of Goodwill

Continuing with the initial measurement of goodwill in the example presented earlier, at least annually, George Company must conduct an impairment test of the goodwill related to the acquisition of Chris Company. The assets of Chris Company are the smallest group of assets that generate cash inflows that are largely independent of the cash inflows from other assets or groups of assets. Therefore, Chris Company is a separate CGU. The goodwill related to the acquisition of Chris Company will be tested by comparing Chris Company's carrying amount with its recoverable amount. At the end of the year, George Company develops the following estimates for Chris Company:

Fair value	$280,000
Costs to sell	$ 30,000
Present value of future cash flows	$270,000

Alternative 1: Assuming that George Company adopted the proportionate share of acquired firm's net assets approach to measure noncontrolling interest, the impairment loss is determined as follows:

	Chris Co. Net assets	Chris Co. Goodwill	Total
Carrying amount	$280,000	$108,000	$388,000
Unrecognized noncontrolling interest in goodwill		12,000	12,000
Adjusted carrying amount	$280,000	$120,000	$400,000
Determination of recoverable amount:			
Fair value less costs to sell (1)			$250,000
Present value of future cash flows (2)			270,000
Recoverable amount [higher of (1) and (2)]			$270,000
Impairment loss (adjusted carrying amount less recoverable amount)			$130,000

In terms of allocation of impairment loss, $120,000 of the impairment loss is allocated to goodwill. The goodwill impairment is shared between the controlling and noncontrolling interest. Thus, $108,000 (90 percent) is allocated to the parent's investment in Chris Company; the remaining $12,000 (10 percent) is attributable to the noncontrolling interest (but is not recognized because the noncontrolling interest's goodwill is not recognized under this alternative). The remaining $10,000 ($130,000 − $120,000) of impairment loss is allocated to Chris Company's identifiable assets on a pro rata basis.

	Chris Co. Net Assets	Chris Co. Goodwill	Total
Carrying amount	$280,000	$108,000	$388,000
Impairment loss	10,000	108,000	118,000
Carrying amount after impairment loss	$270,000	$ 0	$270,000

Alternative 2: Now assume that George Company had adopted the fair value method to measure noncontrolling interest. The impairment loss is determined in the following manner:

	Chris Co. Net Assets	Chris Co. Goodwill	Total
Carrying amount	$280,000	$120,000	$400,000
Determination of recoverable amount:			
Fair value less costs to sell (1)			$250,000
Present value of future cash flows (2)			270,000
Recoverable amount [higher of (1) and (2)]			$270,000
Impairment loss (carrying amount less recoverable amount)			$130,000

Allocation of impairment loss:

	Chris Co. Net Assets	Chris Co. Goodwill	Total
Carrying amount	$280,000	$120,000	$400,000
Impairment loss	10,000	120,000	130,000
Carrying amount after impairment loss	$270,000	$ 0	$270,000

The Convergence of Goodwill Impairment Testing Rules

Until 2020, goodwill impairment tests under U.S. GAAP consisted of an elaborate two-step process that was more complex than its IFRS counterpart. In the first step, companies appraise the fair value of the reporting unit and compare this estimate with the unit's current book value. Up to this point, U.S. GAAP resembled IFRS in its basic approach. However, if the fair value of the reporting unit was found to be less than its book value, U.S. GAAP diverged from IFRS by requiring a second step. This step required the company to conduct detailed revaluations of the reporting unit's various identifiable assets and liabilities. These revaluations allowed the company to construct a new appraisal of the fair value of goodwill along the lines of the M&A purchase price allocation model.

As discussed earlier in this section, IFRS deal with a shortfall between a CGU's fair and book values by simply assuming that goodwill should be the first asset to be written down. Once goodwill has been eliminated, any shortfall that remains is used to write-down the CGU's other assets on a prorated basis. This approach is called the *one-step method* because it effectively sidesteps the second step formerly required in the United States by using a prespecified formula in lieu of a granular revaluation of all of the unit's identifiable assets and liabilities.

American companies complained for years that the two-step model was overly complex and expensive to execute. In January 2017, after a decade and a half of debates and minor revisions, the FASB finally agreed with this argument and adopted the single-step approach of IFRS. American public companies were allowed to choose this method beginning in 2017 and have been required to do so since January 2020. Because of the importance of goodwill impairment testing to American corporations, the FASB's decision was an important milestone along the road to IFRS–U.S. GAAP convergence.

BORROWING COSTS

IAS 23, *Borrowing Costs,* governs accounting for borrowing costs under IFRS and resembles U.S. GAAP in its general approach. Under both systems, most borrowing costs are recorded as expenses in the periods in which they are incurred. However, both require companies to capitalize borrowing costs that are attributable to the acquisition, construction, or production of qualifying assets, such as PPE and intangible product development costs. The following accounting policy, taken from the 2020 annual report of China National Offshore Oil Company (CNOOC), conforms to this requirement:

> Borrowing costs directly relating to the acquisition, construction or production of a qualifying asset that necessarily takes a substantial period of time to get ready for its intended use or sale are capitalised as part of the cost of the respective assets. All other borrowing costs are expensed in the period in which they are incurred.

During 2020, CNOOC incurred borrowing costs equal to ¥6,037 million Chinese yuan. It directly expensed ¥3,554 million and capitalized the remaining ¥2,483 million, adding this latter amount to *Construction in progress,* an account within the company's PPE:

Interest expense (income statement expense)........................	¥3,554	
Construction in progress (part of PPE)...............................	2,483	
Interest payable or Cash..		¥6,037

Once a particular asset is put into service, CNOOC will begin incurring depreciation charges that include the interest capitalized during the facility's construction.

IAS 23 defines *borrowing costs* as interest and other costs incurred by an enterprise in connection with the borrowing of funds. This definition is broader in scope than the definition of *interest cost* under U.S. GAAP. Borrowing costs in accordance with IAS 23 specifically include foreign exchange gains and losses on foreign currency borrowings to the extent they are regarded as an adjustment to interest costs. An asset that qualifies for borrowing cost capitalization is one that necessarily takes a substantial period to get ready for its intended use or sale. Both IAS 23 and U.S. GAAP exclude inventories that are routinely manufactured or produced in large quantities on a repetitive basis over a short period. However, IAS 23 specifically includes inventories that require a substantial period to bring them to a marketable condition.

The amount to be capitalized is the amount of interest cost that could have been avoided if the expenditure on the qualifying asset had not been made. This is determined by multiplying the weighted-average accumulated expenditures by an appropriate interest rate. The appropriate interest rate, a weighted-average interest rate on borrowings outstanding, is determined similarly under both IAS 23 and U.S. GAAP. If a specific new borrowing can be associated with a qualifying asset, the actual interest rate is used to the extent the weighted-average accumulated expenditures are less than the amount of the specific borrowing. Interest income earned on the temporary investment of a specific new borrowing is offset against the interest cost to determine the net amount of interest to be capitalized. Netting interest income against interest cost is not acceptable under U.S. GAAP. The capitalization of borrowing costs begins when expenditures for the asset are incurred and ceases when substantially all the activities necessary to prepare the asset for sale or use are completed.

Example: Capitalization of Borrowing Costs

On January 1, Year 1, Pinquill Company borrows 30,000,000 euros (€) at an annual interest rate of 8 percent to finance the construction of a new facility in Spain. The facility is expected to cost €30,000,000 and take two years to build. Pinquill temporarily invests the euros borrowed until cash is needed to pay costs. During Year 1, expenditures of €20,000,000 are incurred; the weighted-average expenditures are €12,000,000. Pinquill makes annual interest payments on the loan and will repay the loan in full on December 31, Year 2, by converting U.S. dollars into euros. The U.S. dollar–euro exchange rate was $1.42 on January 1, Year 1, and $1.40 on December 31, Year 1. The change in exchange rate is the result of the difference in interest rates on U.S. dollar and euro borrowings. The following information relates to Year 1:

Capitalizable interest cost (€12,000,000 × 8% = €960,000 × $1.40 exchange rate on 12/31/Y1).......................................	$1,344,000
Income earned on temporary investment of borrowing (€225,000 × $1.40)..	315,000
Exchange rate gain [€12,000,000 × ($1.42 – $1.40)]	240,000

The net interest cost is $1,029,000 ($1,344,000 − $315,000). After deducting the exchange rate gain, the total amount of borrowing cost to be capitalized as part of the cost of the facility is $789,000. Under U.S. GAAP, the amount of interest cost to be capitalized would be $1,344,000.

Summary

1. A large majority of countries use IFRS and those that continue to use their own national standards attempt to align these standards with IFRS. An understanding of IFRS is important for accountants who prepare or audit financial statements in every country in the world.

2. Differences exist between IFRS and U.S. GAAP with respect to recognition, measurement, presentation, disclosure, and choice among alternatives. In some cases, IFRS are more flexible than U.S. GAAP. Several IFRS allow firms to choose between alternative treatments in accounting for a particular item. Also, IFRS generally have less bright-line guidance than U.S. GAAP; therefore, more judgment is required in applying individual IFRS. However, in some cases, IFRS are more detailed than U.S. GAAP.

3. Some of the more important asset recognition and measurement differences between IFRS and U.S. GAAP relate to the following issues: revaluation of PPE; component depreciation; fair value accounting for investment property and biological assets; capitalization of development costs; measurement of impairment losses; and the measurement of goodwill.

4. IAS 2 requires inventory to be reported on the balance sheet at the lower of cost and net realizable value. U.S. GAAP recently adopted this approach. IAS 2 requires that write-downs to net realizable value be reversed when the selling price increases. U.S. GAAP continues to prohibit reversals. Unlike U.S. GAAP, IAS 2 does not allow the use of the last-in, first-out (LIFO) method in determining the cost of inventory.

5. IAS 16 allows PPE to be carried at cost less accumulated depreciation and impairment losses or at a revalued amount less any subsequent accumulated depreciation and impairment losses. Specific guidance is provided for those firms that choose the revaluation option. U.S. GAAP does not permit use of the revaluation model.

6. IAS 16 requires an item of PPE comprised of significant parts for which different useful lives or depreciation methods are appropriate to be split into components for purposes of depreciation. Component depreciation is uncommon in U.S. GAAP.

7. IAS 40 allows fair value accounting for investment property, with revaluation gains and losses included in the income statement. U.S. GAAP does not apply special accounting rules for investment properties.

8. IAS 41 requires fair value accounting for biological assets, with revaluation gains and losses included in the income statement. An exception is made for bearer plants, which are considered part of PPE for accounting purposes.

9. IAS 36 requires impairment testing of PPE; intangibles, including goodwill; and long-term investments. An asset is impaired when its carrying value exceeds its recoverable amount, which is the greater of net selling price and value in use. An impairment loss is the amount by which carrying value exceeds the recoverable amount. If, subsequent to recognizing an impairment loss, the recoverable amount of an asset exceeds its new carrying amount, the impairment loss is reversed and the asset is written back up to the carrying amount that would have existed if the impairment had never been recognized. U.S. GAAP employs a different impairment test, and impairment losses may not be reversed.

10. IFRS 10 provides a comprehensive framework for determining control and the scope of consolidation. Consolidation is required when a parent company exercises effective control over another entity, even if the parent does not own a majority of the entity's shares of voting stock. In many parts of the world, control is exercised through mechanisms other than through stock voting rights.

11. IAS 38 requires development costs to be capitalized as an intangible asset when six specific criteria are met. Development costs can include personnel costs; materials and services; depreciation of PPE; amortization of patents and licenses; and overhead costs, other than general administrative costs. Development costs generally are not capitalized under U.S. GAAP. An exception is certain software costs.

12. Intangible assets (including deferred development costs) are classified as having a finite or indefinite useful life. Finite-lived intangibles are amortized over their useful lives using a straight-line method; indefinite-lived intangibles are reviewed each year to determine if the useful life remains indefinite. If not, the intangible asset is reclassified as having a finite life and amortization begins.

13. Goodwill is measured as the excess of the consideration transferred in a business acquisition by the acquiring firm, plus any noncontrolling interest, over the fair value of net assets acquired. IFRS 3 allows two options in measuring noncontrolling interest, which results in two possible measures of goodwill. U.S. GAAP only allows one method for measuring noncontrolling interest.

14. Indefinite-lived intangibles and goodwill must be reviewed for impairment at least once per year. Finite-lived intangibles are tested for impairment whenever changes in circumstances indicate an asset's carrying amount may not be recoverable. IAS 36 allows the reversal of impairment losses on intangibles when certain conditions are met; however, the reversal of goodwill impairment is not allowed.

15. IAS 23 requires borrowing costs to be capitalized to the extent they are attributable to the acquisition of a qualifying asset; other borrowing costs are expensed immediately. Borrowing costs include interest and other costs, such as foreign exchange gains and losses on foreign currency borrowings, incurred in connection with a borrowing. The amount of borrowing cost to be capitalized is reduced by any interest income earned from the temporary investment of the amount borrowed. U.S. GAAP has a narrower definition of capitalizable interest costs and does not allow the netting of interest income.

Questions

Unless otherwise indicated, questions should be answered based on IFRS.

1. What are the types of differences that exist between IFRS and U.S. GAAP?
2. How do IFRS and U.S. GAAP differ in their approach to allowing reversals of inventory write-downs?
3. How are the estimated costs of removing and dismantling an asset handled upon initial recognition of the asset?
4. What are the two models allowed for measuring PPE at dates subsequent to original acquisition?
5. Which items of PPE may be accounted for under the revaluation model, and how frequently must revaluation occur?
6. How is the revaluation surplus handled under the revaluation model?
7. How is depreciation determined for an item of PPE that is comprised of significant parts, such as an airplane?
8. In what way does the fair value model for investment property differ from the revaluation model for PPE?
9. What types of businesses are likely to own investment property and thus use IAS 40?
10. Where in the food products value chain are biological assets generally located, and which types of businesses are likely to use IAS 41?
11. What are the similarities and differences between the fair value models applied to investment properties and biological assets?
12. How does accounting for bearer plants differ from that for other biological assets?
13. How is an impairment loss on PPE determined and measured under IFRS? How does this differ from U.S. GAAP?

14. When a previously recognized impairment loss is subsequently reversed, what is the maximum amount at which the affected asset may be carried on the balance sheet?

15. What are the three major types of intangible assets, and how does the accounting for them differ?

16. How are internally generated intangibles handled under IFRS? How does this differ from U.S. GAAP?

17. Which intangible assets are subject to annual impairment testing?

18. What is effective control and how is it determined when a parent company does not own a majority of the voting stock of a subsidiary?

19. How is goodwill measured in a business combination with a noncontrolling interest?

20. What is a gain on bargain purchase?

21. What is the process for determining whether goodwill allocated to a specific cash-generating unit is impaired?

22. How does the two-step model formerly used for goodwill impairment testing in the United States differ from the model required by IFRS 3?

23. How are borrowing costs accounted for under IFRS?

24. What are the differences in the amount of borrowing costs that can be capitalized under IFRS and U.S. GAAP?

Exercises and Problems

Unless otherwise indicated, exercises and problems should be solved based on IFRS.

1. A company incurred the following costs related to the production of inventory in the current year:

Cost of materials	$100,000
Cost of direct labor	60,000
Allocation of variable overhead costs	30,000
Allocation of fixed overhead costs (based on normal production levels)	25,000
Storage costs (after production, prior to sale)	2,000
Selling costs	8,000

The cost of materials included abnormal waste of $10,000. What is the cost of inventory in the current year?

a. $190,000

b. $205,000

c. $215,000

d. $217,000

2. A company determined the following values for its inventory as of the end of its fiscal year:

Historical cost	$50,000
Current replacement cost	35,000
Net realizable value	45,000
Net realizable value less a normal profit margin	40,000
Fair value	48,000

What amount should the company report for inventory on its balance sheet?

a. $35,000

b. $40,000

c. $45,000

d. $48,000

3. When an entity chooses the revaluation model as its accounting policy for measuring PPE, which of the following statements is correct?

   a. When an asset is revalued, the entire class of PPE to which that asset belongs must be revalued.

   b. When an asset is revalued, individual assets within a class of PPE to which that asset belongs may be selectively revalued.

   c. Revaluations of PPE must be made at least every three years.

   d. Increases in an asset's carrying value as a result of the first revaluation must be recognized in net income.

4. On January 1, Year 1, an entity acquires a new machine with an estimated useful life of 20 years for $100,000. The machine has an electrical motor that must be replaced every five years at an estimated cost of $20,000. Continued operation of the machine requires an inspection every four years after purchase; the inspection cost is $10,000. The company uses the straight-line method of depreciation. What is the depreciation expense for Year 1?

   a. $5,000

   b. $5,500

   c. $8,000

   d. $10,000

5. An asset is considered to be impaired when its carrying amount is greater than its

   a. Net selling price.

   b. Value in use.

   c. Undiscounted future cash flows.

   d. Recoverable amount.

6. Under IFRS, an entity that acquires an intangible asset may use the revaluation model for subsequent measurement only if

   a. The useful life of the intangible asset can be reliably determined.

   b. An active market exists for the intangible asset.

   c. The cost of the intangible asset can be measured reliably.

   d. The intangible asset has a finite life.

7. Which of the following is a criterion that must be met in order for an item to be recognized as an intangible asset?

   a. The item's fair value can be measured reliably.

   b. The item is part of the entity's activities aimed at gaining new scientific or technical knowledge.

   c. The item is expected to be used in the production or supply of goods or services.

   d. The item is identifiable and lacks physical substance.

8. An entity incurs the following costs in connection with the purchase of a trademark:

Purchase price of the trademark	$80,000
Nonrefundable value added tax paid on the purchase of the trademark	4,000
Training sales department staff on the use of the trademark	2,000
Research expenditures incurred prior to the purchase of the trademark	15,000
Legal fees to register the trademark	8,000
Salaries of personnel who negotiated the purchase of the trademark during the period of negotiation	10,000

Assuming that the trademark meets the criteria for recognition as an intangible asset, at what amount should the trademark be initially measured?

a. $84,000

b. $92,000

c. $104,000

d. $119,000

9. Which of the following best describes the accounting for goodwill subsequent to initial recognition?

a. Goodwill is amortized over its expected useful life, not to exceed 20 years.

b. Goodwill is tested for impairment whenever impairment indicators are present.

c. Goodwill is tested for impairment on an annual basis.

d. Goodwill is revalued using a revaluation model.

10. Pearl Corporation bought Noodle Bowl Limited at the end of the fiscal year. While negotiating the purchase price, Pearl's management team referred to the following three recent appraisals from independent valuation consultants.

	Appraised Value	Appraisal Method
Noodle Bowl brand name	$50 million	Cash flow model based on observed royalty rates
Noodle Bowl workforce	$40 million	Estimate of the replacement cost to recruit and train an equivalent workforce
Favorable lease agreements	$20 million	Cash flow model of the anticipated savings from Noodle Bowl's favorable (below market) contractually guaranteed rental rates for retail space

Required:

Which of the above intangibles is likely to be recorded as a distinct identifiable asset in Pearl Corporation's consolidated financial statement? Which is likely to be recorded as part of goodwill? Explain your reasoning.

11. Saratoga Corporation owns significant amounts of the common stock in three Japanese corporations. The following table describes these investments:

	Percentage of Common Stock Owned by Saratoga	Other Significant Investors
Mishima Corporation	85%	None
Tanizaki Corporation	35%	Mitsui Corporation owns 51% of Tanizaki's common stock
Kawabata Corporation	40%	Softbank owns 20% of Kawabata's common stock

Representation on the boards of directors of Mishima and Tanizaki is proportional to common stock ownership. However, this is not the case at Kawabata. Saratoga has appointed five of Kawabata's eight directors. All eight directors have voting rights. When preparing consolidated financial statements, which of these investments would Saratoga treat as subsidiaries?

    a. Mishima only

    b. Kawabata only

    c. Mishima and Kawabata

    d. All three

12. Changsha Corporation purchased an asset during the fourth quarter of the current fiscal year. It is now the end of the fiscal year, and the asset's fair value exceeds its historical cost. In certain circumstances, IFRS allow or require Changsha to carry the asset at fair value in its year-end balance sheet. In which of the following scenarios might Changsha carry the asset at fair value? (You may select more than one answer.)

    a. The asset is a new home office that Changsha occupied immediately after the purchase.

    b. The asset is a broadcasting license with an indefinite useful life.

    c. The asset is an office park that is being rented to a tenant.

    d. The asset is 100 hectares of young trees that will eventually be turned into wood products.

    e. The asset is a vineyard consisting of mature grapevines.

13. This is a continuation of problem 12. In which of the five scenarios described below might Changsha Corporation record a gain on the asset in its income statement? (You may select more than one.)

    a. The asset is a new home office that Changsha occupied immediately after the purchase.

    b. The asset is a broadcasting license with an indefinite useful life.

    c. The asset is an office park that is being rented to a tenant.

    d. The asset is 100 hectares of young trees that will eventually be turned into wood products.

    e. The asset is a vineyard consisting of mature grapevines.

14. As a result of a downturn in the economy, Optiplex Corporation has excess productive capacity. On January 1, Year 3, Optiplex signed a special order contract to manufacture custom-design generators for a new customer. The customer requested that the generators be ready for pickup by June 15, Year 3, and guaranteed it will take possession of the generators by July 15, Year 3. Optiplex has incurred the following direct costs related to the custom-design generators:

Cost to complete the design of the generators	$ 3,000
Purchase price for materials and parts	80,000
Transportation cost to get materials and parts to manufacturing facility	2,000
Direct labor (10,000 labor hours at $12 per hour)	120,000
Cost to store finished product (from June 15 to June 30)	2,000

Because of the company's inexperience in manufacturing generators of this design, the cost of materials and parts included an abnormal amount of waste totaling $5,000. In addition to direct costs, Optiplex applies variable and fixed overhead to inventory using predetermined rates. The variable overhead rate is $2 per direct labor hour. The fixed overhead rate based on a normal level of production is $6 per direct labor hour. Given the decreased level of production expected in Year 3, Optiplex estimates a fixed overhead application rate of $9 per direct labor hour in Year 3.

Required:
Determine the amount at which the inventory of custom-design generators should be reported on Optiplex Corporation's June 30, Year 3, balance sheet.

15. In the fourth quarter of Year 1, Beech Corporation produced three products (related to different product lines) that it still has in inventory at December 31, the end of its fiscal year. The following table provides information about each product:

Product	Cost	Replacement Cost	Selling Price
101	$130	$140	$160
202	$160	$135	$140
303	$100	$ 90	$ 80

Beech Corporation expects to incur selling costs equal to 5 percent of the selling price on each of the products.

Required:
Determine the amount at which Beech should report its inventory on the December 31, Year 1, balance sheet.

16. This is a continuation of problem 15. At December 31, Year 2, Beech Corporation still had the same three different products in its inventory. The following table provides updated information for the company's products:

Product	Cost	Replacement Cost	Selling Price
101	$130	$180	$190
202	$160	$150	$160
303	$100	$100	$120

Beech Corporation still expects to incur selling costs equal to 5 percent of the selling price.

Required:
a. Determine the amount at which Beech should report its inventory on the December 31, Year 2, balance sheet.
b. How would your answer above differ if Beech used U.S. GAAP rather than IFRS?

17. Steffen-Zweig Company exchanges two used printing presses with a total net book value of $24,000 ($40,000 cost less accumulated depreciation of $16,000) for a new printing press with a fair value of $24,000 and $3,000 in cash. The fair value of the two used printing presses is $27,000. The transaction is deemed to lack commercial substance.

Required:
Determine the amount of gain or loss that would be recognized from this exchange of assets.

18. Stevenson Corporation acquires a one-year-old building at a cost of $500,000 at the beginning of Year 2. The building has an estimated useful life of 50 years. However, based on reliable historical data, the company believes the carpeting will need to be replaced in 5 years, the roof will need to be replaced in 15 years, and the HVAC system will need to be replaced in 10 years. On the date of acquisition, the cost to replace these items would have been carpeting, $10,000; roof, $15,000; and HVAC system, $30,000. Assume no residual value.

Required:
Determine the amount to be recognized as depreciation expense in Year 2 related to this building.

19. Quick Company acquired a piece of equipment in Year 1 at a cost of $100,000. The equipment has a 10-year estimated life, zero salvage value, and is depreciated on a straight-line basis. Technological innovations take place in the industry in which the company operates in Year 4. Quick gathers the following information for this piece of equipment at the end of Year 4:

Expected future undiscounted cash flows from continued use	$59,000
Present value of expected future cash flows from continued use	51,000
Net selling price in the used equipment market	50,000

At the end of Year 6, it is discovered that the technological innovations related to this equipment are not as effective as first expected. Quick estimates the following for this piece of equipment at the end of Year 6:

Expected future undiscounted cash flows from continued use	$50,000
Present value of expected future cash flows from continued use	44,000
Net selling price in the used equipment market	42,000

Required:
   a. Discuss whether Quick Company must conduct an impairment test on this piece of equipment at December 31, Year 4.
   b. Determine the amount at which Quick Company should carry this piece of equipment on its balance sheet at December 31, Year 4; December 31, Year 5; and December 31, Year 6. Prepare any related journal entries.

20. Godfrey Company constructed a new, highly automated chemical plant in Year 1, which began production on January 1, Year 2. The cost to construct the plant was $5,000,000: $1,500,000 for the building and $3,500,000 for machinery and equipment. The useful life of the plant (both building and machinery) is estimated to be 20 years. Local environmental laws require the machinery and equipment to be inspected by engineers after every five years of operation. The inspectors could require Godfrey to overhaul equipment at that time to be able to continue to operate the plant. Godfrey estimates that the costs of the inspection and any required overhaul to take place in five years to be $200,000. Environmental laws also require Godfrey to dismantle and remove the plant assets at the end of their useful life. The company estimates that the net cost, after deducting any salvage value, for removal of the equipment will be $100,000, and the net cost for dismantling and removal of the building, after deducting any salvage value, will be $1,500,000. Godfrey has determined that the straight-line method of depreciation will best reflect the pattern in which the plant's future economic benefits will be received by the company. The company uses the cost model to account for its PPE. The company uses a discount rate of 10 percent in determining present values.

Required:
Determine the cost of the plant assets at January 1, Year 2. Determine the amount of depreciation expense that should be recognized related to the plant assets in Year 2.

21. Jefferson Company acquired equipment on January 2, Year 1, at a cost of $10 million. The equipment has a five-year life, no residual value, and is depreciated on a straight-line basis. On January 2, Year 3, Jefferson Company determines the fair value of the asset (net of any accumulated depreciation) to be $12 million.

Required:

a. Determine the impact the equipment has on Jefferson Company's income in Years 1–5 using (1) IFRS, assuming that the revaluation model is used for measurement subsequent to initial recognition, and (2) U.S. GAAP.

b. Summarize the difference in income, total assets, and total stockholders' equity using the two different sets of accounting rules over the period of Years 1–5.

22. Madison Company acquired a depreciable asset at the beginning of Year 1 at a cost of $12 million. At December 31, Year 1, Madison gathered the following information related to this asset:

Carrying amount (net of accumulated depreciation)	$10 million
Fair value of the asset (net selling price)	$7.5 million
Sum of future cash flows from use of the asset.......................	$10 million
Present value of future cash flows from use of the asset	$8 million
Remaining useful life of the asset	5 years

Required:

a. Determine the impact on Year 2 and Year 3 income from the depreciation and possible impairment of this equipment under (1) IFRS and (2) U.S. GAAP.

b. Determine the difference in income, total assets, and total stockholders' equity for the period of Years 1–6 under the two different sets of accounting rules.

Note: If the asset is determined to be impaired, there would be no adjustment to Year 1 depreciation expense of $2 million.

23. Stratosphere Company acquires its only building on January 1, Year 1, at a cost of $4,000,000. The building has a 20-year life, zero residual value, and is depreciated on a straight-line basis. The company adopts the revaluation model in accounting for buildings. On December 31, Year 2, the fair value of the building is $3,780,000. The company eliminates accumulated depreciation against the building account at the time of revaluation. The company's accounting policy is to reverse a portion of the revaluation surplus account related to increased depreciation expense. On January 2, Year 4, the company sells the building for $3,500,000.

Required:

Determine the amounts to be reflected in the balance sheet related to this building for Years 1–4 in the following table. (Use parentheses to indicate credit amounts.)

Date	Cost	Accumulated Depreciation	Carrying Amount	Revaluation Surplus	Income	Retained Earnings
January 1, Year 1	$4,000,000		$4,000,000			
December 31, Year 1 Balance						
December 31, Year 2 Balance						
December 31, Year 3 Balance						
January 2, Year 4 Balance						

24. QualCore Company began operations on January 1, Year 1, and uses IFRS to prepare its financial statements. QualCore reported net income of $1 million in Year 5 and

had stockholders' equity of $5 million at December 31, Year 5. The company wishes to determine what its Year 5 income and December 31, Year 5, stockholders' equity would be if it had used U.S. GAAP. Relevant information follows:

- QualCore carries property that it uses for its own operations at revalued amounts. This property was last revalued upward by $350,000 on January 1, Year 3. At that time, it had a remaining useful life of 10 years.

- QualCore held no investment properties at the start of Year 5. However, on January 1, it purchased an office facility for $1.2 million and immediately began leasing it to tenants. QualCore accounts for this investment property using the fair value method. An appraiser reported that the facility's fair value was $1.4 million on December 31, Year 5. If QualCore had used the cost method for the facility, it would have computed depreciation using a 20-year useful life with no residual value.

- QualCore capitalized development costs related to a new product in Year 4 in the amount of $800,000. QualCore began selling the new product in January, Year 5, and expects the product to be marketable for a total of five years.

Required:
a. Determine net income for Year 5 if QualCore had used U.S. GAAP.
b. Determine stockholders' equity at December 31, Year 5, if QualCore had used U.S. GAAP.

25. Buch Corporation purchased Machine Z at the beginning of Year 1 at a cost of $100,000. The machine is used in the production of Product X. The machine is expected to have a useful life of 10 years and no residual value. The straight-line method of depreciation is used. Adverse economic conditions develop in Year 3 that result in a significant decline in demand for Product X. At December 31, Year 3, the company develops the following estimates related to Machine Z:

Expected future cash flows.	$75,000
Present value of expected future cash flows.	55,000
Selling price	70,000
Costs of disposal.	7,000

At the end of Year 5, Buch's management determines that there has been a substantial improvement in economic conditions, resulting in a strengthening of demand for Product X. The following estimates related to Machine Z are developed at December 31, Year 5:

Expected future cash flows.	$70,000
Present value of expected future cash flows.	53,000
Selling price	50,000
Costs of disposal.	7,000

Required:
Determine the carrying amounts for Machine Z to be reported on the balance sheet at the end of Years 1–5 and the amounts to be reported in the income statement related to Machine Z for Years 1–5.

26. On January 1, Year 1, Holzer Company hired a general contractor to begin construction of a new office building. Holzer negotiated a $900,000, 5-year, 10 percent loan on January 1, Year 1, to finance construction. Payments made to the general contractor for the building during Year 1 amount to $1,000,000. Payments are made evenly throughout the year. Construction is completed at the end of Year 1, and Holzer moves

in and begins using the building on January 1, Year 2. The building is estimated to have a 40-year life and no residual value. On December 31, Year 3, Holzer Company determines that the market value for the building is $970,000. On December 31, Year 5, the company estimates the market value for the building to be $950,000.

Required:
Use the two alternative methods allowed by IAS 16 with respect to the measurement of PPE subsequent to initial recognition to determine:
a. The carrying amount of the building that would be reported on the balance sheet at the end of Years 1–5.
b. The amounts to be reported in net income related to this building for Years 1–5.

In each case, assume that the building's value in use exceeds its carrying value at the end of each year and therefore impairment is not an issue.

27. During Year 1, Reforce Company conducted research and development on a new product. By March 31, Year 2, the company had determined the new product was technologically feasible, and the company obtained a patent for the product in April, Year 2. The company developed an initial prototype by June 30, Year 2. Also, by June 30, Year 2, the company had developed a business plan, including identification of a ready market for the product, and a commitment of resources to ready the product for market. After completion of the second prototype at the end of September, Year 2, the product was ready for commercial production and marketing. The company has tracked costs associated with the new product as follows:

Market research costs, Year 1	$ 25,000
Research costs, Year 1	100,000
Research costs, 1st quarter, Year 2	70,000
Legal fees to register patent, April, Year 2	25,000
Development costs for initial prototype, 2nd quarter, Year 2	500,000
Testing of initial prototype, June, Year 2	50,000
Management time to develop business plan, 2nd quarter, Year 2	15,000
Cost of revisions and second prototype, 3rd quarter, Year 2	175,000
Legal fees to defend patent, October, Year 2	50,000
Commercial production costs, 4th quarter, Year 2	400,000
Marketing campaign, 4th quarter, Year 2	80,000

Required:
Determine the amount related to this new product that will be reported as intangible assets on the company's December 31, Year 2, balance sheet.

28. In Year 1, in a project to develop Product X, Lincoln Company incurred research and development costs totaling $10 million. Lincoln is able to clearly distinguish the research phase from the development phase of the project. Research-phase costs are $6 million, and development-phase costs are $4 million. All of the IAS 38 criteria have been met for recognition of the development costs as an asset. Product X was brought to market in Year 2 and is expected to be marketable for five years. Total sales of Product X are estimated at more than $100 million.

Required:
a. Determine the impact research and development costs have on Lincoln Company's Year 1 and Year 2 income under (1) IFRS and (2) U.S. GAAP.
b. Summarize the difference in income, total assets, and total stockholders' equity related to Product X over its five-year life under the two different sets of accounting rules.

29. Honda Motor Company converted from U.S. GAAP to IFRS at the beginning of fiscal 2015. At that time, Honda began capitalizing new development costs. It also applied the capitalization rules of IAS 38 retroactively, recognizing development cost assets and amortization expenses as though it had capitalized these costs in earlier periods. Honda's 2017 annual report included the following information on research and development costs incurred during the three fiscal years after the conversion to IFRS:

	2015	2016	2017
Research and development expenditures incurred during the reporting period.........	¥670,331	¥719,810	¥659,918
Amount capitalized...........................	(188,107)	(190,992)	(121,037)
Amortization of capitalized development costs...	123,938	127,684	152,548
Total.......................................	¥606,162	¥656,502	¥691,429

Required:

a. Suppose Honda had not switched to IFRS, but had instead continued to use U.S. GAAP in fiscal 2015. Would its R&D-related expenses have been higher or lower than those that it actually reported in 2015 under IFRS? Explain your reasoning and compute the magnitude of the difference.

b. Suppose Honda had not switched to IFRS, but had instead continued reporting under U.S. GAAP through fiscal 2017. Would its R&D-related expenses have been higher or lower in fiscal 2017 than those that it actually reported? Again, explain your reasoning and compute the magnitude of the difference.

c. Under what circumstances would the decision to capitalize R&D expenditures decrease reported profitability compared with the full expensing system required by U.S. GAAP?

30. The global equities team at your bank is considering investing in Remy Corporation. Remy uses IFRS and capitalizes product development costs when they meet the criteria laid out in IAS 38. You have been assigned to convert several of Remy's financial metrics to a U.S. GAAP basis. To perform your analysis, use the following information, taken from Remy's financial statements for the past three years.

in millions of euros	Year 1	Year 2	Year 3
Research and development expenditures..............	2,500	3,000	3,600
of which: Development costs capitalized...............	1,000	1,240	1,300
from annual income statements:			
Pre-tax profit under IFRS............................	7,400	9,800	9,500
from year-end balance sheets:			
Total assets under IFRS.............................	78,000	80,000	84,000
from annual statements of cash flow:			
Operating cash flow under IFRS	5,000	5,300	4,800

As a starting point, you have reviewed descriptions of Remy's R&D activities and concluded that all R&D expenditures would be expensed as incurred under U.S. GAAP. Your team leader has told you to make the following additional assumptions to simplify your analysis:

- All R&D expenditures occur on the last day of the fiscal year.
- Capitalized development costs have a two-year useful life.

- Products resulting from capitalized development costs are released to the market on the first day of the subsequent fiscal year. For instance, if €100 is capitalized as a development cost asset on December 31, amortization of the development cost asset begins the next day, on January 1 of the following year.
- Apart from capitalizing development costs, all of Remy's other accounting policies conform to U.S. GAAP.

Required:
a. Under the foregoing assumptions, how much pre-tax profit would Remy Corporation have recorded under U.S. GAAP in Year 3?
b. Remy Corporation's fiscal year ends on December 31. Compute the value of total assets under U.S. GAAP as of December 31, Year 3.
c. Compute Remy Corporation's operating cash flow under U.S. GAAP for Year 3.

31. Philosopher Stone Inc. incurred costs of $20,000 to develop an intranet Web site for internal use. The intranet will be used to store information related to company policies, customers, and products. Access to the intranet is password-protected and is restricted to company personnel. As the company's auditor, you have been asked to determine whether Philosopher Stone can capitalize the Web site development costs as an intangible asset or whether the company must expense the costs in the period in which they were incurred. Your research finds that SIC 32, *Intangible Assets-Web Site Costs,* indicates that a Web site developed for internal or external use is an internally generated intangible asset that is subject to the requirements of IAS 38. Specifically, SIC 32 indicates that the recognition criteria in IAS 38 related to development costs must be satisfied. The criterion most in question is whether the company can demonstrate the usefulness of the intranet and how it will generate probable future economic benefits.

Required:
Develop a justification for why Philosopher Stone should, or should not, be allowed to account for the intranet development costs as an intangible asset.

32. Prime Publishing, Inc., purchased 100 percent of the outstanding common stock of Select Media, Inc., on January 1, 2014, for $3,000,000. The following schedule outlines how the purchase price was allocated at the time of acquisition:

Price paid	$3,000,000
Select Media's shareholders' equity	1,400,000
Excess of cost over book value	1,600,000
Attributed to:	
Buildings: 10-year remaining life	80,000
Customer Relationships: 9-year useful life	450,000
Copyrights: Indefinite useful life	470,000
Goodwill	600,000

Select Media is an independent subsidiary of Prime Publishing. It is also classified as a separate cash-generating unit (CGU). As of December 31, 2016, Select Media had earned $500,000 before acquisition adjustments (i.e., before subtracting the extra depreciation on buildings and amortization of customer relationships required by the above purchase price allocations). Select Media pays no dividends to Prime.

Required:
a. What was the book value of the Select Media CGU as of December 31, 2016? Include identifiable intangibles and goodwill in your calculation. Assume that none of the CGU's assets have been impaired since the acquisition.

b. On December 31, 2016, the estimated fair value of the Select Media CGU (based on discounted cash flow analysis) was $2,950,000. Should Prime Publishing take an impairment charge to write-down the value of the CGU's goodwill? If so, what is the value of the charge that Prime Publishing will record?

33. This exercise consists of two parts.

Part 1. Bartholomew Corporation acquired 80 percent of the outstanding shares of Samson Company in Year 1 by paying $5,500,000 in cash. The fair value of Samson's identifiable net assets was $5,000,000 on the acquisition date. Bartholomew uses the proportionate share of the acquired firm's net assets approach to measure noncontrolling interest. Samson is a separate cash-generating unit (CGU).

Required:

Compute the amount of noncontrolling interest and goodwill that Bartholomew Corporation recorded upon acquiring Samson Company.

Part 2. At the end of Year 2, the book value of the Samson CGU had risen to $6,900,000 due to profitable operations. This amount included goodwill assigned to the unit when Bartholomew purchased it the previous year. However, business conditions have recently deteriorated. As part of its year-end impairment review, Bartholomew estimates the following information for Samson:

Amount at which the shares of Samson could be sold	$6,000,000
Costs that would be incurred to sell the shares of Samson	$ 200,000
Present value of future cash flows from continuing to control Samson	$5,750,000

Required:

At what amount should Samson's identifiable net assets and goodwill be reported on Bartholomew's consolidated balance sheet at the end of Year 2? Assume that Bartholomew neither added to Samson's goodwill nor deducted any amounts for impairment charges since the acquisition in Year 1.

34. This exercise consists of two parts.

Part 1. The following table summarizes the assets of the Rocker Division (a separate cash-generating unit) at December 31, Year 5, prior to testing goodwill for impairment. Property, Plant, and Equipment and Other Intangibles are amortized on a straight-line basis over an average useful life of 12 years and 5 years, respectively. Management has estimated the present value of future cash flows from operating the Rocker Division to be $1,560. No fair market value is available.

Required:

Complete the following table to determine the carrying amounts at 12/31/Y5 for the assets of the Rocker Division.

	Goodwill	Property, Plant, and Equipment	Other Intangibles	Total
Carrying amount, 12/31/Y4	$1,000	$1,500	$500	$3,000
Amortization expense, Year 5	0	(125)	(100)	(225)
Subtotal	$1,000	$1,375	$400	$2,775
Impairment loss/recovery				
Carrying amount, 12/31/Y5				

Part 2. Due to favorable changes in export laws, management revises its estimate of the value in use for the Rocker Division at 12/31/Y6 to be $1,930.

Required:
Complete the following table to determine the carrying amounts at 12/31/Y6 for the assets of the Rocker Division.

	Goodwill	Property, Plant, and Equipment	Other Intangibles	Total
Carrying amount, 12/31/Y5......				
Amortization expense, Year 6....				
Subtotal......................				
Impairment loss/recovery.......				
Carrying amount, 12/31/Y6......				

35. Louis Vuitton Moët Hennessy (LVMH), the well-known French luxury goods company, bought from the Bulgari family a controlling 66 percent interest in Bulgari SpA, the Italian jewelry maker. The value of the purchase consideration paid to the Bulgari family at the time of the acquisition was €3,019 million. The fair values of Bulgari's identifiable assets and liabilities on that date were as follows:

€ Millions	Acquisition-Date Fair Values
Current assets	901
Brands	2,365
Other noncurrent assets	64
Current liabilities	319
Noncurrent liabilities	742

The remaining 34 percent interest in Bulgari was 118.6 million common shares of Bulgari SpA that continued to trade publicly on the Milan stock exchange after the acquisition. The price of these shares on the acquisition date was €12.25.

Required:
a. As allowed under IFRS 3, LVMH applied the proportionate share method to account for its acquisition of Bulgari. How much noncontrolling interest and goodwill did LVMH recognize in the Bulgari acquisition?
b. Suppose that LVMH had been an American company reporting under U.S. GAAP. How much noncontrolling interest and goodwill would it have recognized in the Bulgari acquisition in this case?

36. Thurstone Company, a U.S.-based company, borrows 1,500,000 British pounds (£) on January 1, Year 1, at an interest rate of 4 percent to finance the construction of a new office building for its employees in England. Construction is expected to take six months and cost £1,500,000. Thurstone temporarily invests the borrowed British pounds until cash is needed to pay costs. Interest earned in the first quarter of Year 1 is £5,000. During the first quarter of Year 1, expenditures of £500,000 are incurred; the weighted-average expenditures are £300,000. Thurstone will repay the borrowing plus interest on June 30, Year 1, by converting U.S. dollars into British pounds. The U.S. dollar/British pound exchange rate was $2.00 on January 1, Year 1, and $2.10 on March 31, Year 1. The change in exchange rate is the result of the difference in interest rates in the United States and Great Britain.

Required:
Determine the amount of borrowing costs (in U.S. dollars) that Thurstone should include in the cost of the new office building at March 31, Year 1.

37. Indicate whether each of the following describes an accounting treatment that is acceptable under IFRS, U.S. GAAP, both, or neither, by checking the appropriate box.

	Acceptable Under			
	IFRS	U.S. GAAP	Both	Neither
• A company takes out a loan to finance the construction of a building that will be used by the company. The interest on the loan is capitalized as part of the cost of the building.				
• Inventory is reported on the balance sheet using the last-in, first-out (LIFO) cost flow assumption.				
• A company owns 40 percent of a foreign entity's voting stock but consolidates the entity because it controls the entity's operating and financial decisions through other means.				
• A company writes a fixed asset down to its recoverable amount and recognizes an impairment loss in Year 1. In a subsequent year, the recoverable amount is determined to exceed the asset's carrying value, and the previously recognized impairment loss is reversed.				
• A company pays less than the fair value of net assets acquired in the acquisition of another company. The acquirer recognizes the difference as a gain on purchase of another company.				
• A dairy company records a herd of milk cows at fair value based on an independent appraisal.				
• An intangible asset with an active market that was purchased two years ago is carried on the balance sheet at fair value.				
• A company that accounts for inventory using the first-in, first-out (FIFO) method records a write-down of a product line to its net realizable value.				
• A manufacturer capitalizes development costs for an industrial product when certain criteria are met.				
• A hotel contains a shopping arcade filled with independent retailers. The hotel measures the arcade's fair value each accounting period and includes valuation gains and losses in that period's income statement.				

Case 4-1

Jaguar Land Rover PLC

Jaguar Land Rover Automotive PLC (JLR) is a maker of luxury autos based in Coventry, United Kingdom. JLR uses IFRS and has a fiscal year-end of March 31. You have been asked to use your knowledge of IFRS to convert key metrics for the company to a U.S. GAAP basis. For simplicity, you may assume that the only material differences between JLR's as-reported numbers and those it would report under U.S. GAAP are traceable to its policy of capitalizing development costs.

Internally Generated Intangible Assets (from Footnote 2, Accounting Policies)
Research costs are charged to the consolidated income statement in the year in which they are incurred.

Product engineering costs incurred on new vehicle platforms, engines, transmission and new products are recognised as intangible assets—when feasibility has been established, the Group has committed technical, financial and other resources to complete the development and it is probable that the asset will generate future economic benefits.

The costs capitalised include the cost of materials, direct labour and directly attributable overhead expenditure incurred up to the date the asset is available for use.

Interest cost incurred is capitalised up to the date the asset is ready for its intended use, based on borrowings incurred specifically for financing the asset or the weighted average rate of all other borrowings, if no specific borrowings have been incurred for the asset.

Product engineering cost is amortised over a period of between two and ten years.

Capitalised development expenditure is measured at cost less accumulated amortisation and accumulated impairment loss, if any.

Amortisation is not recorded on product engineering in progress until development is complete.

Research and Development (from Footnote 11)

Year ended 31 March	2020 (£ millions)
Total research and development costs incurred..........................	1,847
Research and development expensed..................................	(421)
Development costs capitalized	1,426

Intangible Assets (selections from Footnote 18)

£ millions	Product Development in Progress	Capitalized Product Development
Cost		
Balance at 31 March 2019..............	1,990	6,973
Additions—internally developed	1,426	–
Transfers.............................	(944)	944
Disposals	–	(345)
Balance at 31 March 2020..............	2,472	7,572
Accumulated amortization		
Balance at 31 March 2019..............	–	4,104
Amortization for the year................	–	788
Disposals	–	(345)
Balance at 31 March 2020..............	–	4,547
Net book value at 31 March 2020	2,472	3,025

Required:

1. What percentage of R&D expenditures was capitalized during the fiscal year ending March 31, 2020? How does this percentage compare with the capitalization ratios of the German automakers profiled in Exhibit 4.4?

2. Estimate the average useful life of product development costs by dividing average capitalized product development costs by the amortization expense for fiscal 2019–2020. Compute average capitalized product development costs as simple average balances at the beginning and end of each fiscal year. Does your estimate fall within the range of the useful lives for development costs disclosed in the accounting policy footnote?

3. The following table contains metrics as reported in JLR's three primary financial statements. Convert these metrics to a U.S. GAAP basis. Where necessary assume that JLR's tax rate is 19 percent, the United Kingdom's corporate tax rate during the 2020 fiscal year, as disclosed in Footnote 14, *Taxation*.

	As Reported (IFRS) (£ millions)	U.S. GAAP
Loss before tax	(422)	
Net profit (after tax)	(469)	
Total assets.	24,104	
Shareholders' equity.	6,556	
Operating cash flow	2,314	
Capital expenditures*	2,791	

* Expenditures for both PPE and intangibles.

CASE 4-2

Telco Ltd.

Telco Ltd. is a Danish telecom company that prepares consolidated financial statements in full compliance with IFRS 10. The company has expanded dramatically in Central Asia in recent years by investing in three units: K-Mobe, U-Mobe, and T-Mobe, supplying cellular service to customers in Kazakhstan, Uzbekistan, and Tajikistan, respectively.

Telco's corporate investment policy is to take majority ownership stakes in overseas subsidiaries when possible, but to accept lower levels of ownership when majority ownership is not possible or practical. The investment structures of the three Central Asia units are as follows:

a. Telco owns 45 percent of the voting shares of K-Mobe. The other shares are owned by local institutions: 30 percent are owned by an investment fund connected to the state-owned oil company, and 25 percent are owned by the municipal government of Almaty, Kazakhstan's largest city. The legal documents establishing K-Mobe specify that Telco possesses the right to fill a majority of the seats on K-Mobe's board of directors, as well as to appoint its CEO and CFO. The agreement stipulates that the CEO be a Kazakh national. However, it contains no other restrictions covering whom Telco may appoint or the executives' exercise of power once appointed.

b. Telco also owns 45 percent of the voting shares of U-Mobe. The other shares are owned by local institutions: 30 percent are owned by an investment fund connected to a state-owned mining company, and 25 percent are owned by the municipal government of

Tashkent, Uzbekistan's capital city. The legal documents establishing U-Mobe specify that Telco possesses the right to fill 5 out of 12 seats on U-Mobe's board of directors, as well as to appoint its CEO. Of the 12 seats on U-Mobe's board, only 9 possess voting rights. Tashkent's municipal government has been allocated 3 nonvoting seats as a mechanism to provide the board with expert opinions of key city officials. The agreement contains no restrictions covering whom Telco can appoint or on the CEO's exercise of power in the day-to-day running of the company.

c. Telco owns 55 percent of the voting shares of T-Mobe and possesses the right to fill 7 out of 12 seats on T-Mobe's board of directors, as well as to appoint its CEO. The other 45 percent of the voting shares are owned by Storm Bank, a large local bank that appoints T-Mobe's CFO. The current CFO was a long-time employee of Storm Bank before joining T-Mobe and will return to the bank once her tenure as CFO is completed. T-Mobe relies heavily on short-term loans from Storm that must be rolled over annually. Therefore, the CFO effectively has veto authority over major policy decisions.

For the past year, Storm Bank has opposed an expensive expansion program pushed by Telco and T-Mobe's CEO. Recently, Storm's opposition has become so strident that its five board members have stopped attending board meetings. Local laws require a quorum of nine board members to be present for board decisions to have legal validity. Lacking a quorum, T-Mobe's board is not able to approve strategic decisions, such as the investment plan. Moreover, a quorum is necessary to release sufficient financial information for Telco's external auditors to carry out any audit work in relation to T-Mobe's financial statements. T-Mobe's short-term loans from Storm Bank contain covenants requiring it to provide audited financial statements on a regular basis.

Required:

Decide which of the units, if any, should be consolidated when preparing Telco's annual report. Explain your reasoning in each case.

Chapter **Five**

International Financial Reporting Standards: Part II

Learning Objectives

After reading this chapter, you should be able to

- Describe and apply the requirements of International Financial Reporting Standards (IFRS) related to the financial reporting of current liabilities, provisions, employee benefits, share-based payment, income taxes, revenue, financial instruments, and leases.
- Explain and analyze the effect of major differences between IFRS and U.S. GAAP related to the financial reporting of current liabilities, provisions, employee benefits, share-based payment, income taxes, revenue, financial instruments, and leases.
- Describe the IFRS that deal with disclosure and presentation standards and discuss their various requirements.
- Explain the major differences between IFRS and U.S. GAAP on certain disclosure and presentation issues.

INTRODUCTION

International Financial Reporting Standards (IFRS) issued by the International Accounting Standards Board (IASB) comprise a comprehensive set of standards providing guidance for the preparation and presentation of financial statements. Chapter 4 described and demonstrated the requirements of selected IASB standards, particularly those relating to the recognition and measurement of assets. This chapter continues the study of IFRS by focusing on the recognition and measurement of current liabilities, provisions, employee benefits, share-based payment, income taxes, revenue, financial instruments, and leases.

CURRENT LIABILITIES

International Accounting Standard (IAS) 1, *Presentation of Financial Statements,* requires liabilities to be classified as current or noncurrent. Current liabilities are those liabilities that a company:

1. Expects to settle in its normal operating cycle.
2. Holds primarily for the purpose of trading.

3. Expects to settle within 12 months of the balance sheet date.
4. Does not have the right to defer until 12 months after the balance sheet date.

The classification and accounting for current liabilities under IFRS is very similar to U.S. generally accepted accounting principles (GAAP). Differences relate to the following:

- *Refinanced short-term debt* may be reclassified as long-term debt only if refinancing is completed prior to the balance sheet date. Under U.S. GAAP, a refinancing agreement must be reached, but the refinancing need not be completed by the balance sheet date.
- *Amounts payable on demand due to violation of debt covenants* must be classified as current unless a waiver of at least 12 months is obtained from the lender by the balance sheet date. The waiver must be obtained by the annual report issuance date under U.S. GAAP.
- *Bank overdrafts* are netted against cash if the overdrafts form an integral part of the entity's cash management; otherwise, bank overdrafts are classified as current liabilities. Bank overdrafts are always classified as current liabilities under U.S. GAAP.

Example: Violation of Debt Covenant

On June 30, Year 1, Sprockets Inc. obtains a $100,000 loan from a bank for a manufacturing facility. The loan is due in 24 months and is subject to a number of debt covenants. In December, Year 1, Sprockets distributes too much of its cash on employee bonuses and incurs a debt covenant violation as of December 31, Year 1. As a result of the violation, the loan becomes due within 30 days. Sprockets's CFO asks the bank to waive the violation. On January 5, Year 2, the bank agrees to waive the violation, stipulating that it must be rectified within 90 days. Sprockets issues its financial statements on January 30, Year 2. In this situation, Sprockets would be required to classify the bank loan as a current liability on its December 31, Year 1, balance sheet because it did not obtain a waiver from the bank by the balance sheet date.

Now assume that Sprockets's CFO obtains a waiver from the bank on December 30, Year 1, stipulating that the debt covenant violation must be rectified within 90 days. In this case, although the waiver was obtained before the balance sheet date, Sprockets still would be required to classify the bank loan as a current liability because the waiver is for only 90 days, not for at least 12 months.

PROVISIONS, CONTINGENT LIABILITIES, AND CONTINGENT ASSETS

IAS 37, *Provisions, Contingent Liabilities, and Contingent Assets,* provides guidance for reporting liabilities (and assets) of uncertain timing, amount, or existence. It contains specific rules related to onerous contracts and restructuring costs. By way of examples in IAS 37, Part B, guidance also is provided with regard to issues such as environmental costs and nuclear decommissioning costs.

Contingent Liabilities and Provisions

IAS 37 distinguishes between a contingent liability, which is not recognized on the balance sheet, and a provision, which is. A *provision* is defined as a "liability of uncertain timing or amount." A provision should be recognized when

1. The entity has a *present* obligation (legal or constructive) as a result of a past event.
2. It is *probable* (more likely than not) that an outflow of resources embodying economic events will be required to settle the obligation.
3. A reliable estimate of the obligation can be made.

A *constructive obligation* exists when, through past actions or current statements, a company indicates that it will accept certain responsibilities and, as a result, has created a valid expectation on the part of other parties that it will discharge those responsibilities. For example, an entity has a constructive obligation to restructure when it communicates the details of the restructuring plan to those employees who will be affected by it. Another example of a constructive obligation is where a manufacturer (e.g., Sony) announces that it will honor rebates on its products that have been offered by a retailer going out of business (e.g., Circuit City), even though the manufacturer has no contractual obligation to do so. A constructive obligation is recognized as a provision when it meets the remaining criteria (items 2 and 3 in the previous list). U.S. GAAP does not include the concept of a constructive obligation. Thus, only legal obligations may be accrued when criteria are met.

Contingent liabilities are defined in IAS 37 as one of the following:

- *Possible* obligations that arise from past events and whose existence will be confirmed by the occurrence or nonoccurrence of a future event.
- A *present* obligation that is *not recognized* because (1) it is *not* probable that an outflow of resources will be required to settle the obligation or (2) the amount of the obligation *cannot* be measured with sufficient reliability.

Contingent liabilities are disclosed unless the possibility of an outflow of resources embodying the economic future benefits is *remote.*

The rules for recognition of a provision and disclosure of a contingent liability are generally similar to the U.S. GAAP rules related to contingent liabilities. Under U.S. GAAP, a contingent liability is neither recognized nor disclosed if the likelihood of an outflow of resources is remote; it is disclosed if such an outflow is possible but not probable; and it is recognized on the balance sheet when an outflow of resources is probable. The main difference is that U.S. GAAP requires accrual when it is probable that a loss has occurred, with no guidance as to how the word *probable* should be interpreted. Research suggests that U.S. accountants require the likelihood of occurrence to be in the range of 70 to 90 percent before recognizing a contingent liability.[1] In defining a provision, IAS 37 specifically defines *probable* as "more likely than not," which implies a threshold of just over 50 percent. Thus, in practice, the threshold for recognition of a "liability of uncertain timing or amount" is considerably lower under IFRS than under U.S. GAAP.

IAS 37 establishes guidance for measuring a provision as the *best estimate* of the expenditure required to settle the present obligation at the balance sheet date. The best estimate is the probability-weighted expected value when a range of estimates exists or the midpoint within a range if all estimates are equally likely. Provisions must be discounted to present value. Provisions also must be reviewed at the end of each accounting period and adjusted to reflect the current best estimate. Under U.S. GAAP, contingent liabilities should be recognized at the low end of the range of possible amounts when a range of estimates exists. U.S. GAAP allows discounting of a recognized contingent liability only when the amount of the liability and the timing of payments are fixed or reliably determinable.

Subsequent reduction of a provision can be made only for the expenditures for which the provision was established. For example, if a provision is created for warranties, the provision can be reduced only as warranty costs are incurred. A provision is reversed when it is no longer probable that an outflow of resources will occur.

---

[1] Financial Accounting Standards Board, *The IASC–U.S. Comparison Project: A Report on the Similarities and Differences between IASC Standards and U.S. GAAP,* 2nd ed. (Norwalk, CT: FASB, 1999).

With respect to disclosure of contingent liabilities, IAS 37 allows an enterprise "in extremely rare cases" to omit disclosures that "can be expected to prejudice seriously the position of the enterprise in a dispute with other parties." No such exemption exists under U.S. GAAP.

Example: Provision for Litigation Loss

Former employees of Dreams Unlimited Inc. filed a lawsuit against the company in Year 1 for alleged age discrimination. At December 31, Year 1, external legal counsel provides an opinion that it is 60 percent probable that the company will be found liable, which will result in a total payment to the former employees of between $1,000,000 and $1,500,000, with all amounts in that range being equally likely.

Because it is "more likely than not" that an outflow of resources (cash) will be required as a result of the lawsuit and an amount can be reasonably estimated, Dreams Unlimited should recognize a provision. Because all amounts in the estimated range of loss are equally likely, the amount recognized would be the midpoint of the range, $1,250,000 [($1,000,000 + $1,500,000)/2]. Therefore, Dreams Unlimited would prepare the following journal entry at December 31, Year 1, to recognize a provision:

Litigation Loss	$1,250,000	
Provision for Litigation Loss		$1,250,000

Note that under U.S. GAAP, a provision probably would not be recognized because the likelihood of incurring a loss is only 60 percent. If a provision were recognized under U.S. GAAP, it would be for $1,000,000, the low end of the range.

In Year 2, Dreams Unlimited settles with the former employees, making a total payment of $1,100,000. As a result, the company prepares the following journal entry:

Provision for Litigation Loss	$1,250,000	
Cash		$1,100,000
Reversal of Litigation Loss		150,000

The reversal of litigation loss will result in an increase in income in Year 2.

Onerous Contract

IAS 37 requires the recognition of a provision for the present obligation related to an "onerous contract," that is, a contract in which the unavoidable costs of meeting the obligation of the contract exceed the economic benefits expected to be received from it. However, recognition of a provision for expected future operating losses is not allowed. When an onerous contract exists, a provision should be recognized for the unavoidable costs of the contract, which is the lower of the cost of fulfillment and the penalty that would result from nonfulfillment under the contract. When a contract becomes onerous as a result of an entity's own action, the resulting provision should *not* be recognized until that action has actually occurred.

Example: Onerous Contract

Delicious Chocolate Company (DCC) produces chocolate candies. It has a noncancelable lease on a building in Ridgeway, South Carolina, that it uses for production. The lease expires on March 31, Year 2, and is classified as an operating lease for accounting purposes. The quarterly lease payment is $120,000 and made at the end of each quarter. Assume that at the end of the fourth quarter of Year 1, the company closes its South Carolina facility and moves production to Mexico. The company does not believe it will be possible to sublease the building located in South Carolina.

On December 31, Year 1, DCC makes the lease payment of $120,000 due for the fourth quarter. At that point, it is still contractually obligated to make one more lease payment on March 31, Year 2. However, because it is also closing the facility at the end of December, there is no future economic benefit expected from the lease, and it is now an onerous contract. The unavoidable cost of fulfilling the lease contract for Year 2 of $120,000 should be expensed and recorded as a provision on December 31, Year 1. The journal entry would be:

Noncancelable Lease Expense	$120,000	
Provision for Future Lease Payments		$120,000

Restructuring

A restructuring is a program that is planned and controlled by management and that materially changes either the *scope* of a business undertaken by an entity or the *manner* in which that business is conducted.

Examples of restructurings include:

- The sale or termination of a line of business.
- The closure of business locations in a country or region.
- A change in management structure.
- A fundamental reorganization that has a material effect on the nature and focus of the entity's operations.

A difference exists between IAS 37 and U.S. GAAP with respect to when a provision related to a restructuring plan should be recognized. According to IAS 37, a restructuring provision should be recognized when an entity has a detailed formal plan for the restructuring and has raised a valid expectation in those affected by the plan that it will carry out the restructuring, either by announcing the main features of the plan to those affected by it or by beginning to implement the plan. Also, the cost of the restructuring must be reasonably estimable and the plan must be carried out within a reasonable period of time.

U.S. GAAP does not allow recognition of a restructuring provision until a liability has been incurred. The existence of a restructuring plan and its announcement do not necessarily create a liability. Thus, the recognition of a restructuring provision and related loss may occur at a later date under U.S. GAAP than under IFRS.

Contingent Assets

A contingent asset is a probable asset that arises from past events and whose existence will be confirmed only by the occurrence or nonoccurrence of a future event. Contingent assets should not be recognized, but should be disclosed when the inflow of economic benefits is *probable*. If the realization of income from a contingency is determined to be *virtually certain*, then the related benefit is considered to meet the definition of an asset and recognition is appropriate. IAS 37 allows earlier recognition of a contingent asset (and related gain) than does U.S. GAAP, which generally requires the asset to be realized before it can be recognized.

Exhibit 5.1 provides a summary of the recognition and disclosure guidelines in IAS 37.

EXHIBIT 5.1
IAS 37 Recognition and
Disclosure Guidelines

Contingent Element	Likelihood of Realization	Accounting Treatment
Uncertain liability	Probable (more likely than not)	
	—Reliably measurable	Recognize provision
	—Not reliably measurable	Disclosure
	Not probable	Disclosure
	Remote	No disclosure
Uncertain asset	Virtually certain	Recognize asset
	Probable	Disclosure
	Not probable	No disclosure

Additional Guidance

The IASB document published to accompany IAS 37 (IAS 37, Part B) provides a number of examples to demonstrate the application of the standard's recognition principles. Example 2B, for example, describes a situation involving contaminated land, which gives rise to a constructive obligation.

Example: Contaminated Land Constructive Obligation

Petrocan Company operates in the oil industry and contaminates land at a location in a foreign country. The foreign country does not have environmental legislation that will require the company to clean up the contamination. However, Petrocan has a widely published environmental policy to clean up all contamination that it causes, and the company has a record of honoring this policy.

The company applies the criteria of IAS 37 to determine whether recognition of a provision is appropriate:

1. *Present obligation as a result of a past obligating event:* The past obligating event is the contamination of the land. A present constructive obligation exists because the past conduct of the company creates a valid expectation on the part of those affected by it that the entity will clean up the contamination.

2. *An outflow of resources embodying economic benefits in settlement is probable:* Because the contamination has occurred and the company has a policy of cleaning up all contamination, an outflow of resources to settle the constructive obligation is "more likely than not."

3. *A reliable estimate of the obligation can be made:* The company must determine whether this criterion is met. If so, a provision would be recognized for the best estimate of the costs of cleanup. If not, then disclosures would be made because there is a greater than remote likelihood of an outflow of resources to settle the obligation.

EMPLOYEE BENEFITS

IAS 19, *Employee Benefits,* is a single standard that covers all forms of employee compensation and benefits other than share-based compensation (e.g., stock options), which is covered in IFRS 2. IAS 19 provides guidance with respect to four types of employee benefits:

1. Short-term employee benefits (e.g., compensated absences and bonuses).
2. Post-employment benefits (e.g., pensions, medical benefits, and other post-employment benefits).
3. Other long-term employee benefits (e.g., deferred compensation and disability benefits).
4. Termination benefits (e.g., severance pay and early retirement benefits).

Short-Term Benefits

An employer recognizes an expense and a liability at the time that the employee provides services. The amount recognized is undiscounted.

Compensated Absences

For short-term compensated absences, such as sick pay or vacation pay, an amount is accrued when services are provided only if the compensated absences accumulate over time and can be carried forward to future periods. In the case of nonaccumulating compensated absences, an expense and liability are recognized only when the absence occurs.

Profit-Sharing and Bonus Plans

An expense and a liability are accrued for profit-sharing or bonus plans only if:

- The company has a present legal or constructive obligation to make such payments as a result of past events.
- The amount can be reliably estimated.

Even if a company has no legal obligation to pay a bonus, it can have a constructive obligation to do so if it has no realistic alternative but to pay the bonus.

Post-Employment Benefits

IAS 19 was revised in 2011 and significant changes were made in the treatment of post-employment benefits. Revised IAS 19 became effective in 2013.

IAS 19 distinguishes between defined contribution plans and defined benefit plans. The accounting for a defined contribution plan is simple and straightforward. An employer:

1. Accrues an expense and a liability at the time the employee renders service for the amount the employer is obligated to contribute to the plan.
2. Reduces the liability when contributions are made.

The accounting for a defined post-employment benefit plan is considerably more complicated.

Defined Post-Employment Benefit Plans

Under IFRS, the accounting for both defined benefit pension plans and other defined post-employment benefit plans (such as medical and life insurance benefits) is basically the same and is generally similar to the accounting under U.S. GAAP, but with some differences. The following discussion relates specifically to pensions, but it also is applicable to other post-employment benefits.

The two major issues in accounting for defined benefit pension plans are (1) calculation of the *net defined benefit liability (or asset)* to be reported on the balance sheet and (2) calculation of the *defined benefit cost* to be recognized in income (either net income or other comprehensive income).

Net Defined Benefit Liability (Asset)

The amount recognized on the employer's balance sheet as a *net defined benefit liability (or asset)* is calculated as:

+ Present value of the defined benefit obligation (PVDBO)
− Fair value of plan assets (FVPA)

The PVDBO is based on assumptions related to variables such as employee turnover, life expectancy, and future salary levels. The discount rate used in determining the PVDBO is determined by reference to the yield at the end of the period on high-quality corporate bonds.

When the PVDBO is greater than the FVPA, a *deficit* exists, and the employer reports this amount as a net defined benefit liability on the balance sheet. When the FVPA is greater than the PVDBO, a *surplus* arises, but the amount of the net defined benefit asset recognized is limited to the lower of (1) the surplus, and (2) the asset ceiling, which is the present value of any economic benefits available in the form of refunds from the plan or reductions in future contributions to the plan.

Under U.S. GAAP, the amount recognized on the balance sheet also is equal to the difference between the PVDBO and the FVPA; this is known as the funded status. However, there is no asset ceiling under U.S. GAAP.

Example: Limitation on the Recognition of the Net Defined Benefit Asset

The defined benefit pension plan of Fortsen Company Inc. has the following characteristics at December 31, Year 9:

Present value of defined benefit obligation (PVDBO)	$ 10,000
Fair value of plan assets (FVPA)	(10,800)
Surplus	$ (800)
Asset ceiling (present value of reductions in future contributions)	$ 525

Fortsen recognizes a net defined benefit asset of $525 on its December 31, Year 9, balance sheet and discloses the fact that the asset ceiling reduces the carrying amount of the asset by $275 ($800 − $525). The asset limitation of $275 also is included in *the remeasurements of the net defined benefit liability (asset),* described below. Under U.S. GAAP, Fortsen would report a net defined benefit asset of $800, equal to the difference between the PVDBO and FVPA.

Defined Benefit Cost

The defined benefit cost reported in income is comprised of four components. Three of these components are included in the computation of net income, and the fourth component is included in other comprehensive income. The components of defined benefit cost included in *net income* are:

- Current service cost.
- Past service cost and gains and losses on settlements.
- Net interest on the net defined benefit liability (asset).

Net interest on the net defined benefit liability (asset) (NIDBA) is determined by multiplying the net defined benefit liability (asset) by the same discount rate used to measure PVDBO. As a result, NIDBA is the difference between interest expense (PVDBO × Discount rate) and interest income (FVPA × Discount rate).

Past service cost arises when an employer improves the benefits to be paid to employees in a defined benefit plan. IAS 19 requires all past service costs to be recognized in net income in the period in which the benefit plan is changed, regardless of the status of the employees benefiting from the change.

In comparison, U.S. GAAP requires that the past service cost (referred to as prior service cost) be recognized in other comprehensive income (OCI) and then amortized to net income over time. The past service cost related to retirees is amortized to net income over their remaining expected life, and the past service cost related to active employees is amortized to net income over their expected remaining service period.

Example: Recognition of Past Service Cost

On January 1, Year 7, Eagle Company amends its defined benefit pension plan to increase the amount of benefits to be paid. The benefits vest after five years of service. Eagle has no retirees. At the date of the plan amendment, the increase in the PVDBO attributable to active employees is $18,000. The active employees have an average remaining service life of 12 years.

Under IFRS, Eagle Company recognizes the entire past service cost of $18,000 as an expense to net income in Year 7. Under U.S. GAAP, because all of the employees affected by the plan amendment are active employees, the past service cost of $18,000 would be amortized to net income over the remaining service life of those employees at the rate of $1,500 per year ($18,000/12 years).

Gains and losses on settlements arise when an employer settles a defined benefit plan by making a lump-sum cash payment to employees in exchange for their rights to receive defined future benefits. A pension plan curtailment arises when there is a material reduction in the number of employees covered by a plan (such as when a plant is closed as part of a restructuring) or when the future service by current employees will no longer qualify for pension benefits or will qualify only for reduced benefits. Gains and losses usually arise in conjunction with both plan settlements and curtailments.

IAS 19 treats gains and losses on settlements and curtailments similarly; both are recognized in net income in the period in which the settlement or curtailment takes place or when the related restructuring costs are recognized, if earlier. U.S. GAAP treats gains and losses on plan curtailments and settlements differently, with losses generally being recognized earlier than gains. Under U.S. GAAP, a curtailment gain cannot be recognized until the related employees terminate or the plan has been adopted.

Remeasurements of the net defined benefit liability (asset) are the fourth component of the net defined benefit liability (asset). Remeasurements are recognized in OCI and are never recycled to net income. Remeasurements consist of:

1. Actuarial gains and losses.
2. The difference between the actual return on plan assets in the current period and the interest income component of NIDBA (FVPA × Discount rate).
3. Any change in the effect of the asset ceiling during the period.

Actuarial gains and losses arise when an employer changes the actuarial assumptions used in determining the future benefit obligation or makes adjustments based on differences between past assumptions and past experience. In contrast to IAS 19, which requires actuarial gains and losses to be recognized immediately through OCI with no recycling to net income, U.S. GAAP allows a choice between immediate recognition in OCI or in net income. Actuarial gains and losses recognized in OCI are recycled to net income by adopting either a so-called corridor approach or a systematic method that results in faster recycling.

Other Post-Employment Benefits

IAS 19 does not provide separate guidance for other post-employment benefits. The procedures described earlier for pension plans are equally applicable for other forms of post-employment benefits provided to employees, such as medical benefits and life insurance. In calculating the PVDBO for post-employment medical benefit plans, assumptions also must be made regarding expected changes in the cost of medical services.

U.S. GAAP provides considerably more guidance than IAS 19 with regard to the assumptions to be used and the measurement of the employer's obligation for post-employment medical benefits. As allowed by the IASB's *Framework,* companies using IFRS may refer to the guidance provided in U.S. GAAP to identify an appropriate method for determining the amount of expense to recognize related to post-employment benefits other than pensions.

Other Long-Term Employee Benefits

Other long-term employee benefits include, for example, long-term compensated absences (e.g., sabbatical leaves), long-term disability benefits, bonuses payable 12 months or more after the end of the period, and deferred compensation paid 12 months or more after the end of the period. A liability should be recognized for other long-term employee benefits equal to the difference between (1) the present value of the defined benefit obligation and (2) the fair value of plan assets (if any).

SHARE-BASED PAYMENT

The IASB and the Financial Accounting Standards Board (FASB) have worked closely in developing new standards related to accounting for share-based payments. Concurrent with the IASB's issuance of IFRS 2, the FASB published an exposure draft in March 2004 and subsequently issued a final standard on this topic in December 2004. Although a number of minor differences exist between the two standards, IFRS 2 and U.S. GAAP are substantially similar.

IFRS 2, *Share-Based Payment,* sets out measurement principles and specific requirements for three types of share-based payment transactions:

1. *Equity-settled share-based payment transactions,* in which the entity receives goods or services as consideration for equity instruments of the entity (including stock options granted to employees).
2. *Cash-settled share-based payment transactions,* in which the entity acquires goods or services by incurring liabilities to the supplier of those goods or services for amounts that are based on the price (or value) of the entity's shares or other equity instruments of the entity (e.g., share appreciation rights).
3. *Choice-of-settlement share-based payment transactions,* in which the terms of the arrangement provide either the entity or the supplier of goods or services with a choice of whether the entity settles the transaction in cash or by issuing equity instruments.

IFRS 2 applies to share-based transactions with both employees and nonemployees and requires an entity to recognize all share-based payment transactions in its financial statements; there are no exceptions.

The standard applies a *fair value approach* in accounting for share-based payment transactions. In some situations, these transactions are recognized at the fair value of the goods or services obtained; in other cases, transactions are recognized at the fair value of the equity instrument awarded. The fair value of shares and stock options is based on market prices, if available; otherwise, a generally accepted valuation model should be used. IFRS 2, Part B, contains extensive application guidance with respect to estimating the "fair value of equity instruments granted."

Equity-Settled Share-Based Payment Transactions

Share-based payment transactions entered into by an entity that will be settled by the entity issuing equity shares are accounted for as equity transactions. Typically, a debit is made to either an asset (goods acquired) or an expense (services received), and a credit is made to paid-in capital.

Share-Based Payments to Nonemployees

Entities sometimes will acquire goods or services from external suppliers using shares of the entity's stock as payment. Share-based payments to nonemployees are measured at the fair value of the goods or services received. If the fair value of the goods or services received cannot be reliably determined, then the fair value of the equity instruments is used. If the fair value of the equity instruments is used, the measurement date is the date the entity obtains the goods or services. If the goods or services are received on a number of dates over a period, the fair value at each date should be used.

Under U.S. GAAP, when the transaction is accounted for using the fair value of the equity instruments, the earlier of either the date at which a commitment for performance is reached or when the performance is completed is used as the measurement date for determining the fair value of the equity instruments.

Share-Based Payments to Employees

For share-based payments to employees (including stock options), the transaction should be measured at the fair value of the equity instruments granted because the fair value of the service provided by the employees generally is not reliably measurable. The fair value of stock options must be determined at the date the options are granted (i.e., the grant date).

Stock option plans typically contain vesting conditions that must be met in order for the options to become exercisable. The entity issuing stock options must estimate the number of options that are expected to vest. The product of the number of options expected to vest multiplied by the fair value of those options is the total compensation cost that will be recognized as compensation expense over the vesting period. The estimate of options expected to vest should be revised throughout the vesting period, with corresponding adjustments to compensation expense. As compensation expense is recognized, it is offset by an increase in additional paid-in capital.

Compensation expense associated with stock options that vest on a single date (cliff vesting) is recognized on a straight-line basis over the service period. When stock options vest in installments (graded vesting), the compensation expense associated with each installment (or tranche) must be amortized over that installment's vesting period. U.S. GAAP allows a choice in recognizing compensation cost related to graded-vesting stock options. Entities may choose to amortize compensation cost on an accelerated basis by tranche (similar to IFRS) or on a straight-line basis over the vesting period.

Example: Graded-Vesting Stock Options

Glackin Corporation grants stock options with a fair value of $100,000 to select employees at the beginning of Year 1; 50 percent vest at the end of Year 1 and 50 percent vest at the end of Year 2. Under IFRS, compensation cost associated with the first tranche is fully allocated to expense in Year 1, and compensation cost associated with the second tranche is amortized to expense 50 percent in Year 1 and 50 percent in Year 2. As a result, the amount of compensation expense recognized in Year 1 is $75,000 [$50,000 + (50% × $50,000)], and the amount of compensation expense recognized in Year 2 is $25,000 [50% × $50,000]. The same pattern of compensation expense recognition would be acceptable under U.S. GAAP. Alternatively, U.S. GAAP allows the company to simply amortize the $100,000 compensation cost on a straight-line basis over the two-year vesting period, recognizing compensation expense of $50,000 in each of Year 1 and Year 2.

Modification of Stock Option Plans

Entities that grant stock options sometimes make modifications to the terms and conditions under which equity instruments have been granted. For example, an entity might change the length of the vesting period or change the exercise price, which could change the fair value of the stock options. If an entity modifies the terms and conditions of a stock option, IFRS 2 requires the entity to recognize, at a minimum, the original amount of compensation cost as measured at the grant date. If the fair value of the options is reduced as a result of the modification, then there is no change in the total compensation cost to be recognized. If the modification results in an increase in the fair value of the options, then total compensation cost must be increased by the increase in fair value (the difference between the fair value at the original grant date and the fair value at the modification date). Under U.S. GAAP, when modifications are made to stock options, the fair value of the options at the date of modification determines the total amount of compensation expense to be recognized. Unlike IFRS, there is no minimum amount of compensation cost to recognize.

Cash-Settled Share-Based Payment Transactions

An entity might provide employees with stock appreciation rights in which they are entitled to receive a cash payment when the entity's stock price increases above a predetermined level. Stock appreciation rights are an example of a cash-settled share-based payment transaction. This type of transaction results in the recognition of a liability (because there will be a future outflow of cash) and an expense. The liability (and expense) is measured at the fair value of the share appreciation rights using an option-pricing model. Until the liability is settled, it must be remeasured at each balance sheet date, with the change in fair value reflected in net income. Under U.S. GAAP, certain cash-settled share-based payment transactions are classified as equity; these transactions would be classified as a liability under IFRS.

Choice-of-Settlement Share-Based Payment Transactions

When the terms of a share-based payment transaction allow the *entity to choose* between equity settlement and cash settlement, the entity must treat the transaction as a cash-settled share-based payment transaction only if it has a present obligation to settle in cash; otherwise, the entity treats the transaction as an equity-settled share-based payment transaction.

When the terms of a share-based payment transaction allow the *supplier of goods and services to choose* between equity settlement and cash settlement, the entity has issued a compound financial instrument the fair value of which must be split into separate debt and equity components. The debt component must be remeasured at fair value at each balance sheet date, with the change in fair value reflected in net income. If the supplier of goods and services chooses to receive settlement in cash, the cash payment is applied against only the debt component (i.e., it reduces the liability). The equity component remains in equity. If the supplier chooses to receive settlement in equity, the debt component (liability) is transferred to equity.

Example: Choice-of-Settlement Share-Based Payment Transaction (Supplier Has Choice)

On January 1, Year 1, Leiyu Company issued 100 stock options with an exercise price of $18 each to five employees (500 options in total). The employees can choose to settle the options either (1) in shares of stock ($1 par value) or (2) in cash equal to the intrinsic value of the options on the vesting date. The options vest on December 31, Year 2, after the employees have completed two years of service. Leiyu Company expects that only four of the employees will remain with the company for the next two years and vest in the options. One employee resigns in Year 1, and the company continues to assume an overall forfeiture rate of 20 percent at December 31, Year 1. As expected, four employees vest on

December 31, Year 2, and exercise their stock options. The share prices and fair values of the two settlement alternatives over the vesting period are:

Date	Share Price	Fair Value of Cash-Settlement Alternative	Fair Value of Share-Settlement Alternative
January 1, Year 1	$20	$10.00	$10.00
December 31, Year 1	26	11.00	11.00
December 31, Year 2	30	12.00	12.00

Because Leiyu has granted employees stock options that can be settled either in cash or in shares of stock, this is a compound financial instrument. Because this is a transaction with employees, Leiyu must determine the fair value of the compound financial instrument at the measurement date, taking into account the terms and conditions on which the rights to cash or equity instruments have been granted. To determine the fair value of a compound financial instrument, the company first measures the fair value of the debt component (i.e., the cash-settlement alternative) and then measures the fair value of the equity component (i.e., the equity-settlement alternative), taking into account that the employee must forfeit the right to receive cash in order to receive the shares of stock. The fair value of the compound financial instrument is the sum of the fair values of the two components.

The stand-alone fair value of the cash-settlement alternative at the grant date (January 1, Year 1) is $5,000 (500 options × $10 per option). The stand-alone fair value of the equity-settlement alternative at the grant date also is $5,000 (500 options × $10 per option). IFRS 2 indicates that this type of share-based payment often is structured such that the fair value of the debt component and the fair value of the equity component are the same. In such cases, the fair value of the equity component is zero. Thus, the fair value of the compound financial instrument is $5,000 ($5,000 + $0).

For equity-settled share-based payment transactions, the services received and the equity recognized are measured at the fair value of the equity instrument at grant date. Because the fair value of the equity component in this case is zero, there is no compensation expense recognized related to the equity component. For cash-settled share-based payment transactions, the services received and the liability incurred are initially measured at the fair value of the liability at grant date. The fair value of the liability, adjusted to reflect the number of options expected to vest, is recognized as an expense over the period that the services are rendered. At each reporting date, and ultimately at settlement date, the fair value of the liability is remeasured, with the change in fair value affecting the amount recognized as compensation expense. As a result, the total amount of expense recognized will be the amount paid to settle the liability.

Compensation expense for Year 1 is calculated as follows:

Fair value per option at December 31, Year 1	$11.00
Number of options	500
Subtotal	$5,500
Percentage of options expected to vest	80%
Total compensation expense	$4,400
Vesting period (number of years)	2
Compensation expense, Year 1	$2,200

The journal entry on December 31, Year 1, to recognize Year 1 compensation expense is:

Compensation Expense.	$2,200	
Share-Based Payment Liability.		$2,200

At December 31, Year 2, the fair value of each option is equal to its intrinsic value of $12 ($30 share price − $18 exercise price). The fair value of the liability is $6,000 ($12 × 500 options). The total compensation expense is $4,800 ($6,000 × 80%). The amount to be recognized as compensation expense in Year 2 is $2,600 ($4,800 − 2,200). The journal entry on December 31, Year 2, is:

Compensation Expense.	$2,600	
Share-Based Payment Liability.		$2,600

Accounting for the exercise of the stock options under the two settlement alternatives is as follows:

- *Cash-Settlement Alternative:* If the four employees choose the cash-settlement alternative upon exercise of their stock options, they will receive a total of $4,800, the intrinsic value of the 400 options that they exercise. The journal entry on December 31, Year 2, would be:

Share-Based Payment Liability.	$4,800	
Cash		$4,800

- *Share-Settlement Alternative:* If the four employees choose the share-settlement alterna- tive upon exercise of their stock options, they will receive a total of 400 shares of stock with a fair value of $12,000 in exchange for $7,200 (400 shares × Exercise price of $18 per share). The journal entry on December 31, Year 2, would be:

Cash	$7,200	
Share-Based Payment Liability.	4,800	
Common Stock ($1 par × 400)		$ 400
Additional Paid-In Capital ($29 × 400).		11,600

INCOME TAXES

IAS 12, *Income Taxes,* and U.S. GAAP take a similar approach to accounting for income taxes. Both standards adopt an asset-and-liability approach that recognizes deferred tax assets and liabilities for temporary differences and for operating loss and tax credit carry- forwards. However, differences do exist. The accounting for income taxes is a very complex topic, and only some of the major issues are discussed here.

Tax Laws and Rates

IAS 12 requires that current and deferred taxes be measured on the basis of tax laws and rates that have been enacted or substantively enacted by the balance sheet date. The inter- pretation of *substantively enacted* will vary from country to country. To help make this assessment, the IASB has published guidelines that address the point in time when a tax law change is substantively enacted in many of the jurisdictions that apply IFRS. The IASB's exposure draft (ED) on income taxes clarifies that "substantively enacted" occurs when any future steps in the enactment process cannot change the outcome. The ED notes, for example, that the point of substantive enactment in the United States is when a tax law is passed. U.S. GAAP requires measurement of income taxes using actually enacted tax laws and rates.

To minimize the double taxation of corporate dividends (tax paid by both the company and its shareholders), some countries apply a lower tax rate to profits that are distributed to shareholders than to profits that are retained by the company. Therefore, companies doing business in these countries need to know which tax rate (distributed profits vs undistributed profits) should be applied when measuring the amount of current and deferred taxes. Examples provided in IAS 12 indicate that the tax rate that applies to undistributed profits should be used to measure tax expense.

Example: Undistributed Profits

Multinational Corporation owns a subsidiary in a foreign jurisdiction where income taxes are payable at a higher rate on undistributed profits than on distributed profits. For the year ending December 31, Year 1, the foreign subsidiary's taxable income is $150,000. The foreign subsidiary also has net taxable temporary differences amounting to $50,000 for the year, thus creating the need for a deferred tax liability. The tax rate paid in the foreign country on distributed profits is 40 percent, and the rate on undistributed profits is 50 percent. A tax credit arises when undistributed profits are later distributed. As of the balance sheet date, no distributions of dividends have been proposed or declared. On March 15, Year 2, Multinational's foreign subsidiary distributes dividends of $75,000 from the profit earned in Year 1.

The tax rate on undistributed profits (50 percent) is used to recognize the current and deferred tax liabilities related to earnings of the foreign subsidiary in Year 1:

Current Tax Expense	$75,000	
Taxes Payable ($150,000 × 50%)		$75,000
Deferred Tax Expense	$25,000	
Deferred Tax Liability ($50,000 × 50%)		$25,000

On March 15, Year 2, when the foreign subsidiary distributes a dividend of $75,000, a tax credit receivable from the government of $7,500 [$75,000 × (50% − 40%)] is recognized, with an offsetting reduction in the current tax expense:

Tax Credit Receivable	$7,500	
Current Tax Expense		$7,500

Recognition of Deferred Tax Asset

IAS 12 requires recognition of a deferred tax asset if future realization of a tax benefit is probable, where *probable* is undefined. Under U.S. GAAP, a deferred tax asset must be recognized if its realization is more likely than not. If the word *probable* is interpreted as a probability of occurrence that is greater than the phrase *more likely than not,* then IAS 12 provides a more stringent threshold for the recognition of a deferred tax asset.

Example: Deferred Tax Asset

During the fiscal year ended December 31, Year 1, Janeiro Corporation had a net operating loss of $450,000. Because the company has experienced losses in the last several years, it cannot utilize a net operating loss carryback. However, Janeiro has negotiated several new contracts, and management expects that it is slightly more than 50 percent likely that it will be able to utilize one-third of the net operating loss in future years. The company's effective tax rate is 40 percent.

Depending on the degree of likelihood the company assigns to the word *probable,* it either would not recognize a tax asset, or it would recognize an asset related to the amount of the net operating loss that it expects to be able to use. In the latter case, the deferred tax asset and income tax benefit would be $60,000 ($450,000 × 1/3 × 40%).

Deferred Tax Asset...	$60,000
Income Tax Benefit...	$60,000

Disclosures

IAS 12 requires extensive disclosures to be made with regard to income taxes, including disclosure of the current and deferred components of tax expense. The standard also requires an explanation of the relationship between hypothetical tax expense based on statutory tax rates and reported tax expense based on the effective tax rate using one of two approaches: (1) a numerical reconciliation between tax expense based on the statutory tax rate in the home country and tax expense based on the effective tax rate or (2) a numerical reconciliation between tax expense based on the weighted-average statutory tax rate across jurisdictions in which the company pays taxes and tax expense based on the effective tax rate.

Exhibit 5.2 illustrates these two approaches using portions of the 2018 annual reports of Tesco PLC and Nestlé SA. Tesco PLC uses the first approach, showing that accounting profit multiplied by the UK statutory income tax rate of 20 percent would have resulted in tax expense of £29 million in 2017. However, the actual tax expense was £87 million, resulting in an effective tax rate of 60 percent. Tesco reports numerous significant adjustments to explain this very large difference. The largest and most noteworthy is an adjustment for *Other non-deductible items* of £82 million. This relates to the nondeductible portion of fines levied against the company by the United Kingdom's Financial Conduct Authority for having issued "false or misleading" financial statements in 2014. In 2018, Tesco's effective tax rate reverts to 23.6 percent, much closer to the UK's statutory income tax rate of 19.1 percent that year.

Nestlé SA uses the second approach in reconciling its total tax expense. The reconciliation in this case begins with the amount that would be recognized as tax expense after multiplying the profit earned in each country in which the company operates by the statutory tax rate in that country and then summing across all countries. Nestlé's effective tax rate can be measured by dividing the amount reported as taxes on continuing operations by pre-tax profit on continuing operations (not shown in Exhibit 5.2).

The expected tax expense at the weighted-average applicable tax rate results from applying the domestic statutory tax rates to profits before taxes of each entity in the country it operates. For Nestlé, the weighted-average applicable tax rate varies from one year to another, depending on the relative weight of the profit of each individual entity in the Nestlé Group, as well as changes in the statutory tax rates.

IFRS versus U.S. GAAP

Application of IFRS can create temporary differences unknown under U.S. GAAP. For example, the revaluation of property, plant, and equipment for financial statement purposes (in accordance with IAS 16's revaluation model) with no equivalent adjustment for tax purposes will result in a temporary difference that cannot exist under U.S. GAAP. Other differences between IFRS and U.S. GAAP can create different amounts of temporary differences.

EXHIBIT 5.2
Illustrations of the Two
Methods of Reconciling
Statutory and Effective
Tax Rates

RECONCILIATION OF ACCOUNTING PROFIT TO EFFECTIVE TAX RATE
Tesco PLC
2018 Annual Report

Note 6. Taxation
Reconciliation of effective tax charge

	2018 £m	2017 £m
Profit/(loss) before tax	**1,298**	**145**
Tax credit/(charge) at 19.1% (2017: 20.0%)	(248)	(29)
Effect of:		
Non-qualifying depreciation	(31)	(33)
Other non-deductible items	10	(82)
Unrecognized tax losses	(27)	(48)
Property items taxed on a different basis to accounting entries	25	77
Banking surcharge tax	(19)	(17)
Differences in overseas taxation rates	5	15
Adjustments in respect of prior years	(20)	17
Share of losses of joint ventures and associates	(1)	(21)
Change in tax rate	–	34
Total income tax credit/(charge) for the year	**(306)**	**(87)**
Effective tax rate	**23.6%**	**60.0%**

NESTLÉ
2018 ANNUAL REPORT

Note 13. Taxes Reconciliation of taxes In millions of CHF	2018	2017
Expected tax expense at weighted average applicable tax rate	(2,925)	(3,115)
Tax effect of non-deductible or non-taxable items	(110)	(94)
Prior years' taxes	108	248
Transfers to unrecognized deferred tax assets	(129)	(131)
Transfers from unrecognized deferred tax assets	95	18
Changes in tax rates	(6)	792
Withholding taxes levied on transfers of income	(472)	(491)
Total Taxes	**(3,439)**	**(2,773)**

For example, because of different definitions of impairment, differences in the amount of an impairment loss can exist under the two sets of standards. With no equivalent tax adjustment, the amount of temporary difference related to the impairment loss in a set of IFRS-based financial statements will be different from the amount recognized under U.S. GAAP.

Financial Statement Presentation

Under U.S. GAAP, deferred tax assets and liabilities generally are classified as current or noncurrent based on the classification of the related asset or liability, or for tax losses and credit carryforwards, based on the expected timing of realization. The net deferred tax amount arising from current assets and liabilities is classified as a current asset or liability; the net deferred tax amount arising from noncurrent assets and liabilities is reported as a noncurrent asset or liability. IAS 1, *Presentation of Financial Statements,* stipulates that deferred taxes may *not* be classified as a current asset or current liability, but only as noncurrent.

REVENUE RECOGNITION

IFRS 15, *Revenue from Contracts with Customers,* and its American equivalent, accounting standard codification (ASC) 606, together represent one of the most significant examples of cross-border cooperation in accounting standard-setting. Revenue is arguably the most important number produced by the accounting system. These standards have supplanted a hodgepodge of industry-specific techniques for measuring and recognizing revenue with an overarching framework that will be central to the practice of accounting for years to come. In the United States, in particular, over 200 rules governed revenue recognition prior to ASC 606's enactment. Both standards come into force for fiscal years commencing in 2018. Because they are so closely aligned, we will refer to them interchangeably below.

IFRS 15 requires an entity to apply the following five steps in the recognition of revenue:

1. *Identify the contract with a customer.* A contract is an agreement between the seller and buyer to provide goods and services in exchange for *consideration.* To recognize revenue, the seller must perform according to the terms of the contract. A contract may take the form of a formal written document, an oral agreement, or an implicit understanding between seller and buyer. For a contract to be identifiable, it also must be *probable* that the selling entity will collect the consideration to which the contract entitles it.

2. *Identify the separate performance obligations in the contract.* A performance obligation is defined as "an enforceable promise in a contract with a customer to transfer a good or service to the customer." The entity must evaluate all of the goods and/or services promised in a contract to determine whether there are separate performance obligations.

3. *Determine the transaction price.* If material, the time value of money should be considered in determining the transaction price in a deferred payment contract. When future payments for goods or services are not fixed in amount, consideration is said to be *variable.* In such cases, an expected value should be used to determine the transaction price. It must be highly probable that this statistical approach will not result in a reversal of already recognized revenue in future periods. A common example of variable consideration comes from the pharmaceutical industry. Drug companies often offer rebates to customers, generally large health networks, that increase as those customers buy more of a particular drug. In such cases, the drug company would use a probability-weighted approach to downwardly adjust revenue in periods when the eventual amount of the rebate is uncertain.

4. *Allocate the transaction price to the separate performance obligations.* The transaction price should be allocated to the separate performance obligations in proportion to the stand-alone selling price of each element of the contract. When goods or services are not sold separately, the transaction price must be allocated to the separate performance obligations using a reasonable approach.

5. *Recognize the revenue allocated to each performance obligation when the entity satisfies each performance obligation.* An entity satisfies a performance obligation and recognizes revenue when control of a promised good or service is transferred to the customer. The general principle is that a customer obtains control of a good or service when the customer has the ability to direct the use of, and receive the benefit from, the good or service. For many revenue-generating transactions, transfer of control will occur at a specific point in time, often when the good or service is delivered to the customer. However, transfer of control also can occur over a period of time.

To understand the implications of IFRS 15 and ASC 606, it is useful to consider the revenue recognition conundrum faced by Microsoft Corporation before these standards took effect.

Software sales arrangements often consist of two elements, the software license, which entitles the customer to use the software, and post-sales support, including the right to receive upgrades and patches. The latter element is generally referred to in the software industry as post-contract support services, or PCS. In theory, revenue attributable to the license should be recognized immediately upon purchase, while revenue from PCS should be recognized over the life of the support commitment. Segregating the software's purchase price into license revenue and support revenue requires a determination of the relative value of the two pieces at the time of purchase. Because these elements are recognized over different time frames, the valuations assigned to them have been connected to numerous frauds over the years and are thus subject to close scrutiny. Understating the value of PCS pulls revenue forward. Overstating it creates an unearned revenue "reserve" that can be manipulated to prop up future revenue. Microsoft's annual reports identify the apportionment of software revenue between licenses and PCS as one of its critical accounting policies.

Before ASC 606, U.S. accounting rules required software sellers to defer revenues from software sales if they could not value PCS using vendor-specific objective evidence (VSOE). VSOE was often difficult to obtain for PCS that was not sold separately. This was the case for the implied support commitments bundled with Microsoft's Windows 10 operating system. In its 2017 annual report, Microsoft describes its revenue recognition policy for Windows 10 as follows:

> *Customers purchasing a Windows 10 license will receive unspecified updates and upgrades over the life of their Windows 10 device at no additional cost. As these updates and upgrades will not be sold on a stand-alone basis, we are unable to establish VSOE of fair value. Accordingly, revenue from licenses of Windows 10 is recognized ratably over the estimated life of the related device, which ranges between two to four years.*

In effect, the old rules kept Microsoft from recognizing any upfront revenue from the sales of Windows 10, its most important product. All consideration received from customers for Windows 10 was first recorded on the balance sheet as an unearned revenue liability and subsequently amortized to sales revenue in the income statement on a straight-line schedule. The schedule was tied to the useful life of the particular device on which the software was used. Because of this conservatism, the unearned revenue balance on Microsoft's 2017 balance sheet reached $44.5 billion.

IFRS 15 and ASC 606 apply a best available evidence standard to valuing each element of the sales arrangement. While a stand-alone selling price would be best evidence, in its absence, companies may use other suitable methods, for instance, a cost-plus-margin approach. In Microsoft's case, moving from the old revenue recognition rules to the more flexible rules of ASC 606 completely transformed the company's financials. In a conference call to analysts in early fiscal 2018, Frank Brod, Microsoft's chief accounting officer, disclosed that applying ASC 606 rules to the 2017 accounts would have resulted in a 40 percent reduction in the 2017 unearned revenue balance, from $44.5 billion to $26.7 billion. Whereas Microsoft had previously deferred 100 percent of Windows 10's sales price as unearned revenue, under ASC 606, that figure fell to just 3 percent.[2] Critics of the greater flexibility provided by IFRS 15 and ASC 606 argue that stricter rules are necessary to prevent a recurrence of rampant revenue recognition fraud in the software industry. The debate over this issue illustrates the tension that always exists between relevance and reliability, as discussed in previous chapters.

---

[2] Frank Brod, MFST New Accounting Standards and FY18 Investor Metrics Conference Call, August 3, 2017.

Variable Consideration Example: Sale of Goods with a Right of Return

One of IFRS 15's most important innovations is to shift the accountant's revenue recognition model from the evaluation of the risks and rewards of ownership to the transferral of control. The following example uses a customer's right to return a product to illustrate the difference between these perspectives.

Qwilleran Products Inc. is a manufacturer of lighting fixtures. Qwilleran enters into an agreement with a Mexican company that will import and distribute Qwilleran's products locally. In January, Year 1, the first month of the agreement, Qwilleran ships $2,000,000 of lighting fixtures to the Mexican distributor to cover anticipated demand in Mexico. The distributor has the right to return products to Qwilleran over the subsequent three months if they cannot be sold in Mexico. Qwilleran has extensive experience selling its products in the United States but no experience in Mexico or other foreign countries.

Under old revenue recognition rules (IAS 18 and its U.S. counterparts), Qwilleran would have evaluated whether the risks and rewards of ownership of the goods had been transferred to the buyer. This might not be the case when the buyer has the right to return the products. Depending on the terms of the sales agreement, Qwilleran may have to accept returns of substantial quantities of unsold fixtures in the future. Thus, Qwilleran's accountants might have concluded that delivery to the Mexican distributor did not result in the transfer of all the significant risks of ownership. Such situations were so common under the old rules, particularly when selling industrial products to commercial customers, that accountants sometimes applied a blanket prohibition against recognizing revenue until a product was sold to end consumers. This was known as *sell-through accounting*. Under sell-through accounting, sales revenue was not recorded, nor was inventory removed from the balance sheet, until the sale to an end customer was completed.

Under IFRS 15, Qwilleran's accountants would approach the problem differently. They would note that control has been transferred to the customer. After all, it is the Mexican distributor who controls whether or not to return the inventory. In addition, Step 3 of the standard requires accountants to construct estimates of variable consideration and explicitly incorporate uncertainty in making these forecasts. In this step, the accountants would use best available evidence to forecast the expected value of future returns from the supplier. Note that the *probable* criterion of Step 1 refers to the expected value of variable consideration, not the good's sales price.

Suppose that Qwilleran's accountants estimate that 10 percent of the goods sold to the Mexican retailer will be returned. For expositional purposes, we will assume that Qwilleran earns a 40 percent gross margin on all sales of its products and that the fixtures will be returned undamaged and thus can be resold. Under these assumptions, the value of the inventory sold to the Mexican distributor equals ($2,000,000 × .6) = $1,200,000. Qwilleran will create both a refund liability equal to the consideration that it expects to have to pay back to the distributor and an inventory returns asset equal to the expected returns of fixtures to its inventory. Assuming a 10 percent rate of returns, the resulting journal entry will be:

January 1, Year 1		
Cash (or accounts receivable)	2,000,000	
Sales revenue		1,800,000
Refund liability		200,000
Cost of goods sold	1,080,000	
Inventory returns asset	120,000	
Inventory		1,200,000

Suppose that the Mexican distributor returns 8 percent of the fixtures on March 15. In this case, Qwilleran refunds 8 percent of the sales price, or $(.08 \times \$2,000,000) = \$160,000$, reducing the corresponding refund liability by an equal amount. Assuming a 40 percent gross margin, the value of the inventory returned equals $(.08 \times \$1,200,000) = \$96,000$. If all of the fixtures are in good condition and can be restocked, Qwilleran's journal entry will be:

March 15, Year 1

Refund liability	160,000	
Cash (or receivables)		160,000
Inventory	96,000	
Inventory returns asset		96,000

For illustration purposes, we will assume that no additional returns are received from the distributor before the expiration of the three-month right-of-return window. In other words, the accountants' original forecast was too pessimistic by 2 percent. In this case, Qwilleran will record additional profit of $(\$2,000,000 - \$1,200,000) \times .02 = \$16,000$ when the return period expires. The appropriate journal entries are as follows:

March 31, Year 1

Refund liability	40,000	
Sales revenue		40,000
Cost of goods sold	24,000	
Inventory returns asset		24,000

Bill-and-Hold Sales

An area that has long caused trouble for accountants and will continue to do so under IFRS 15 is bill-and-hold sales. In a bill-and-hold sale, the seller segregates inventory meant for a customer but still maintains physical possession of it. The seller then bills the customer and records the sale as if the physical inventory has been delivered. Under IAS 18, the accounting justification for this practice was that the sales arrangement contained provisions that transferred risks and rewards of ownership to the customer. Under IFRS 15, the justification is that control has been transferred. The following questions help the accountant make this determination.

1. Has the product been separately identified as belonging to the customer?
2. Is the product ready for shipment to the customer?
3. Can the seller use the product or reallocate it to another customer?
4. Is there a substantive business reason for the bill-and-hold arrangement, such as, that the customer's warehouse is full?

While bill-and-hold structures have legitimate business purposes, they have also played a role in high-profile accounting frauds, most notably at Sunbeam. Accountants are particularly concerned that bill-and-hold sales may be used to inappropriately pull sales forward from future periods to the current period—a type of earnings management. This concern will not abate under IFRS 15.

Customer Loyalty Programs

A growing number of entities use customer loyalty programs to provide customers with incentives to buy their goods and services. In many of these programs, "points" are awarded at the time a customer makes a purchase. The question arises as to whether the entity's obligation to provide a free or discounted good or service should be recognized and measured by (1) allocating a portion of the consideration received from the sale transaction or (2) establishing a provision for the estimated future costs of providing the award.

IFRS 15 stipulates that award credits should be treated as a separately identifiable component of the sales transaction in which they are granted. The fair value of the consideration received on the sale must be allocated between the award credits and the other components of the sale. The amount allocated to the award credits is based on their fair value. If the entity supplies the award itself, it recognizes the amount allocated to award credits as revenue when award credits are redeemed and the obligation to provide a free or discounted good or service is fulfilled. The amount of revenue to be recognized is based on the number of award credits that have been redeemed, relative to the total number expected to be redeemed.

Example: *Frequent-Flyer Awards Program*

Redjet Airways, a regional air carrier, has a frequent-flyer program in which customers receive one point for each mile flown on Redjet flights. Frequent-flyer program members can redeem 30,000 points for a free domestic flight, which, on average, would otherwise cost $600. During Year 1, Redjet awarded 1,000,000 points to its customers on flights with total ticket sales of $600,000. Frequent-flyer points expire two years after they are awarded. By the end of Year 1, frequent-flyer program members had redeemed 300,000 points for free tickets. Redjet expects that only 10 percent of points will expire unredeemed. This 10 percent is termed *breakage.* Breakage revenue arises from customers' tendency to overlook their rights to redeem loyalty points, gift card balances, and so on. Estimates of future breakage are important components of accountants' forecasts of variable consideration (Step 3 of IFRS 15) in many consumer sectors. A higher breakage rate generally leads to a higher rate of revenue recognition.[3]

Redjet must allocate the $600,000 collected in ticket sales in Year 1 between flight revenue and frequent-flyer awards (deferred revenue) based on the fair value of the points awarded. The amount to be allocated to the frequent-flyer awards is determined as follows:

Points awarded in Year 1	1,000,000
Percentage expected to be redeemed	× 90%
Points expected to be redeemed	900,000
Points needed for a free flight	÷ 30,000
Expected number of free flights	30
Average value per flight	× $600
Fair value of points awarded	$ 18,000

The journal entry to recognize revenue from ticket sales in Year 1 is as follows:

Cash	$600,000	
Revenue		$582,000
Deferred Revenue		18,000

---

[3] Traditionally, breakage revenue was recognized on unused loyalty points, gift card balances, etc., when the probability of redemption was remote. IFRS 15 requires that breakage revenue be recognized ratably, as the customer exercises his or her rights to receive goods and services under the loyalty program.

During Year 1, 300,000 points were redeemed for 10 free flights, with a value of $6,000. The journal entry to recognize revenue from providing free flights under the awards program is:

Deferred Revenue	$6,000
Revenue	$6,000

FINANCIAL INSTRUMENTS

IFRS guidance for the financial reporting of financial instruments is located in the following three standards:

IAS 32, *Financial Instruments: Presentation*

IFRS 7, *Financial Instruments: Disclosure*

IFRS 9, *Financial Instruments*

IFRS 9, *Financial Instruments,* replaces the recognition and measurement guidance formerly provided by IAS 39. Taken together, these standards cover a wide spectrum of financial assets and liabilities. At one end of the spectrum, one finds relatively straightforward items, such as trade accounts receivable and simple commercial loans; at the other, one finds very complex, specialized financial contracts used by the world's largest financial institutions to hedge interest rate and currency risks. How financial instruments were valued and reported was a central concern during the global financial crisis of 2007–08. The area's complexity and importance to the financial community resulted in a long development window for IFRS 9. The standard itself was rolled out chapter by chapter, between 2009 and 2014. Several of its most important provisions took effect beginning in 2018.

Definitions

IAS 32, *Financial Instruments: Presentation,* defines a *financial instrument* as any contract that gives rise to both a financial asset of one entity and a financial liability or equity instrument of another entity. A *financial asset* is defined as any asset that is:

- Cash.
- A contractual right
  - to receive cash or another financial asset.
  - to exchange financial assets or financial liabilities under potentially favorable conditions.
- An equity instrument of another entity.
- A contract that will or may be settled in the entity's own equity instruments and is not classified as an equity instrument of the entity.

Examples of financial assets include cash, receivables, loans made to other entities, investments in bonds and other debt instruments, and investments in equity instruments of other entities. Investments in equity instruments that are accounted for under the equity method (e.g., associates, joint ventures) or are consolidated (e.g., subsidiaries and variable interest entities) do not fall within the scope of IAS 32 and IFRS 9. Only those investments in equity instruments that result in less than significant influence over the other entity (sometimes labeled as "marketable securities") are accounted for in accordance with IAS 32 and IFRS 9.

IAS 32 defines a *financial liability* as:

- A contractual obligation
  - to deliver cash or another financial asset.
  - to exchange financial assets or financial liabilities under potentially unfavorable conditions.
- A contract that will or may be settled in the entity's own equity instruments.

Examples of financial liabilities include payables, loans from other entities (including banks), issued bonds and other debt instruments, and obligations to deliver the entity's own shares for a fixed amount of cash. *Derivative financial instruments* also are financial assets or financial liabilities.

An *equity* instrument is defined as:

- Any contract that evidences a residual interest in the assets of an entity after deducting all of its liabilities.

In addition to subsidiaries and equity method investees, the following are excluded from the scope of IAS 32 and IFRS 9 and are covered by other standards:

- Insurance contracts.
- An employer's rights and obligations under employee benefit plans.
- Share-based payment programs.
- Transactions in the entity's own equity instruments, such as treasury stock.

Liability or Equity

IAS 32 requires financial instruments to be classified as financial liabilities or equity or both in accordance with the substance of the contractual arrangement and the definitions of financial liability and equity. If an equity instrument contains a contractual obligation that meets the definition of a financial liability, it should be classified as a liability even though its legal form is that of an equity instrument. For example, if an entity issues preferred shares that are redeemable by the shareholder and the entity cannot avoid the payment of cash to shareholders if they redeem their shares, the preferred shares should be accounted for as a liability. Preferred shares that are contingently redeemable based on future events outside the control of either the issuer or the shareholder also would be classified as a financial liability.

Example: Redeemable Preferred Shares

On October 29, Year 1, Griglia Company issued $1,000,000 of 5 percent preferred shares at par value. The preferred shareholders have the right to force the company to redeem the shares at par value if the Federal Reserve Bank interest rate rises above 5 percent. On December 10, Year 3, the Federal Reserve Bank interest rate reaches that level.

Because the future event that triggers redemption of the preferred shares is outside the control of both the company and the shareholders, the 5 percent preferred shares must be classified as a liability under IFRS. The journal entry to record issuance of the shares on October 29, Year 1, is:

Cash	$1,000,000	
Redeemable Preferred Shares Liability		$1,000,000

Under U.S. GAAP, the preferred shares initially would be classified as equity. On December 10, Year 3, when the event triggering redemption occurs, the preferred shares would be reclassified as a liability.

Compound Financial Instruments

If a financial instrument contains both a liability element and an equity element, it is a *compound financial instrument* and should be split into two components that are reported separately. This is referred to as "split accounting." For example, a bond that is convertible into shares of common stock at the option of the bondholder is a compound financial instrument. From the perspective of the issuer, the bond is comprised of two components:

1. A contractual obligation to make cash payments of interest and principal as long as the bond is not converted. This meets the definition of a financial liability.
2. A call option that grants the bondholder the right to convert the bond into a fixed number of common shares. This meets the definition of an equity instrument.

Under split accounting, the initial carrying amounts of the liability and equity components are determined using what can be called the with-and-without method. The fair value of the financial instrument *with* the conversion feature is determined (i.e., the selling price of the instrument). Then the fair value of the financial instrument *without* the conversion feature is determined. This becomes the carrying amount of the financial liability component. The difference between the fair value of the instrument as a whole and the amount separately determined for the liability component is allocated to the equity component. Note that a compound financial instrument is a financial asset for the holder of the instrument.

Example: Convertible Bonds

Sharma Corporation issued $2 million of 4 percent convertible bonds at par value. The bonds have a 5-year life with interest payable annually. Each bond has a face value of $1,000 and is convertible at any time up to maturity into 250 shares of common stock. At the date of issue, the interest rate for similar debt without a conversion feature is 6 percent.

The fair value of the convertible bonds is their selling price of $2 million. The fair value of the liability is calculated using the prevailing interest rate for nonconvertible bonds:

Present value of $2,000,000, n = 5, i = 6%	$2,000,000 × 0.7473 = $1,494,516
Present value of ordinary annuity of	
$80,000, n = 5, i = 6%	$80,000 × 4.2124 = 336,989
Fair value of liability	$1,831,505

The present value of the bond at 6 percent is $1,831,505; this is the fair value of the liability component of the compound financial instrument. The remaining $168,495 from the proceeds of the bond issuance is allocated to the equity component.

Cash	$2,000,000	
Bonds Payable		$1,831,505
Additional Paid-In Capital		168,495

Classification and Measurement of Financial Assets and Financial Liabilities

Financial assets and financial liabilities are initially recognized on the balance sheet at their fair value, which normally will be equal to the amount paid or received. They are subsequently measured according to the rules of the category into which they are classified. IFRS 9 establishes the following three categories for financial assets:

- *Amortized cost:* This category primarily covers trade accounts receivable, simple loans, and bonds held to maturity. Assets in this category will be measured at cost, as opposed to fair value. Thus, placing assets in this category insulates them from the fair value accounting adjustments required in the two categories discussed below. From the entity's perspective, this is often a desirable outcome. The term "amortized" refers to the fact that carrying a debt instrument at cost often requires that it be recorded at a discount or premium to its face value. This discount or premium is amortized over time, generally using the *effective interest rate method.*

For assets to qualify for inclusion in the amortized cost category, they must pass two tests, a business model test and a contractual cash flow test. Under the business model test, the entity's business objective must be to hold the assets in order to collect contractual cash flows. For instance, a division of a bank that makes and holds business loans with a goal of collecting interest on those loans would likely pass this test. Under the contractual cash flow test, the asset must give rise to only interest and principal payments. IFRS 9's amortized cost category is similar to the held-to-maturity category of IAS 39 and equivalent U.S. standards. The difference is that IFRS 9's criteria are designed to be somewhat broader and more flexible. In particular, the relatively general business model test allows amortized cost to be applied in specific cases when a financial asset will not be held to maturity.

- *Financial assets at fair value through other comprehensive income (FVOCI):* This category applies fair value measurement to the financial instruments that fall within it but allows fair value gains and losses to be recorded in comprehensive income rather than in the income statement. It roughly corresponds to the available-for-sale category formerly provided by IAS 39 and equivalent U.S. standards.

  For debt instruments to qualify for inclusion in the FVOCI category, they must pass both business model and contractual cash flow tests, similar to the case for the amortized cost category. The main difference is that FVOCI's business model test allows the entity to engage in larger and more frequent asset sales. It is still the case that the entity's primary business objective must be to hold the instruments in order to collect contractual cash flows.

  IFRS 9 also contains an important provision that allows entities to place equity investments in the FVOCI category if they are not held for trading. Providing an FVOCI option for equity securities differs from U.S. GAAP requirements that took effect in 2018 that require all fair value gains and losses from equity investments to be recorded in the income statement. This provision is an important instance of recent IFRS–U.S. GAAP divergence and is discussed below.

- *Financial assets at fair value through profit or loss (FVPL):* This is IFRS 9's residual category. It includes any financial assets not allocated to the other two categories: assets held for trading, debt instruments not qualifying for amortized cost or FVOCI treatments, equity instruments not included in FVOCI, and derivatives not qualifying for hedge accounting.

A financial liability must be classified as one of the following:

- *Financial liabilities at fair value through profit or loss (FVPL):* This includes financial liabilities that are held for trading, derivatives not designated as part of a hedging relationship, and liabilities that the entity has opted to classify into this category under special rules providing a "fair value option." Examples of liabilities that might be found in this category are interest rate swaps, commodity futures contracts, forward foreign exchange contracts, and contingent consideration promised as part of an M&A transaction.

- *Financial liabilities measured at amortized cost:* This is the default category for most financial liabilities, including accounts payable, notes payable, bonds payable, and deposits from customers.

Example: *Financial Liabilities Measured at Amortized Cost (Bonds Payable)*

On January 1, Year 1, Keane Corp. issued $1,000,000 of 5 percent bonds at face value. The bonds pay interest annually and mature on December 31, Year 2. The company incurred bank and legal fees of $70,000 in conjunction with issuing the bonds.

Under IFRS, the debt issuance costs reduce the fair value of the liability. The fair value of the bonds payable at the date of issuance is $930,000 [$1,000,000 − $70,000]. The entry to initially recognize the liability is:

January 1, Year 1		
Cash	$930,000	
Bonds Payable		$930,000

Subsequent to initial recognition, the bonds payable are measured at amortized cost. The difference between the fair value of the bonds at the date of issuance and their face value is amortized to expense over the life of the bonds using the effective interest rate method. The effective interest rate is 8.9781 percent, calculated as the internal rate of return of the following stream of payments:

January 1, Year 1: Proceeds from debt issuance $930,000

December 31, Year 1: Interest payment [$1,000,000 × 5%] ($50,000)

December 31, Year 2: Interest and principal payment ($1,050,000)

The following journal entries are made over the life of the bonds:

December 31, Year 1		
Interest Expense [$930,000 × 8.9781%]	$83,496	
Cash		$50,000
Bonds Payable		33,496
December 31, Year 2		
Interest Expense [$963,496 × 8.9781%]	$86,504	
Cash		$50,000
Bonds Payable		36,504
Bonds Payable	$1,000,000	
Cash		$1,000,000

Under U.S. GAAP, debt issuance costs are deferred as an asset and amortized on a straight-line basis over the life of the debt. For Keane Corp., total expense in Year 1 and in Year 2 would be determined as follows:

Interest expense [$1,000,000 × 5%]	$50,000
Amortization of debt issuance costs [$70,000/2]	35,000
Total	$85,000

Equity Investments Classified as Financial Assets at Fair Value through Other Comprehensive Income (FVOCI)

Berkshire Hathaway owns one of the world's largest portfolios of marketable equity securities. On December 31, 2021, the portfolio's fair value stood at $351 billion. Because U.S. GAAP requires that marketable equity securities be measured at fair value, this was the portfolio's carrying value in Berkshire's 2021 balance sheet. Had the company instead used acquisition cost accounting, the portfolio's value in the 2021 balance sheet would have been $105 billion, a much lower figure.

Through 2017, both IFRS and U.S. GAAP mandated that companies record fair value fluctuations on most equity investments in other comprehensive income rather than in net income. At companies with large equity portfolios, this exclusion reduced income statement volatility substantially. For instance, Berkshire's holdings of equity securities experienced a fair value gain before tax of $13.9 billion in 2016 but incurred a fair value loss of $8.5 billion the year prior. The ability to shield the income statement from such fluctuations was one of the key provisions of available-for-sale accounting, mandated by IAS 39 and equivalent U.S. rules. Upon sale of the available-for-sale securities, cumulative gains or losses were *recycled* out of OCI into the income statement.

In 2018, U.S. GAAP began to require companies to include fair value gains and losses on equity holdings in the income statement, thus exposing their reported earnings to potentially large volatility. Under IFRS 9, the situation is more complicated. In the case of equity instruments not held for trading, IFRS 9 allows companies to make a one-time irrevocable election at initial recognition to classify the instruments as FVOCI—in other words, to exclude future fair value gains and losses from the income statement. Companies may make this election on a security-by-security basis. In contrast to available-for-sale accounting under IAS 39, cumulative gains and losses are not recycled through the income statement upon disposal.

Example: An Equity Investment Classified as FVOCI

Porfirio S.A. purchases marketable equity securities for $20,000 on October 15, Year 1. At the time of purchase, Porfirio makes an FVOCI election for the investment. On December 31, the end of Porfirio's fourth fiscal quarter and fiscal year, the securities have risen in value to $22,000. Porfirio sells the securities on February 1, Year 2, for $23,000. The company will account for this investment in the following manner:

October 15, Year 1

Marketable equity securities—FVOCI	20,000	
Cash		20,000
To record the securities' purchase.		
December 31, Year 1		
Marketable equity securities—FVOCI	2,000	
Other comprehensive income		2,000
To record the fair value gain in other comprehensive income.		
February 1, Year 2		
Cash	23,000	
Marketable equity securities—FVOCI		22,000
Other comprehensive income		1,000
To record the sale of the securities, including the additional gain allocated to OCI.		

Note that all gains on FVOCI equity securities are recorded in other comprehensive income and never recycled through the income statement upon disposal. Companies may at their discretion transfer these realized gains from accumulated comprehensive income to retained earnings. However, in doing so, they must not pass them through the income statement. As with all equity investments carried at fair value, dividends received on equity securities are recorded as dividend income in the income statement.

Example: A Debt Instrument Classified as FVOCI

Debt securities classified as FVOCI receive a similar accounting treatment to equity securities with one exception. Upon disposal, realized holding gains are recycled through the income statement. Suppose Santiago S.A. purchases 5 percent bonds for $1 million on January 1, Year 1. The bonds mature on December 31, Year 2. Santiago meets the IFRS 9 business model test because it sells its debt securities infrequently. For simplicity, assume that the bonds pay interest once a year on December 31. Interest rates in the economy fall during Year 1, causing the bonds to appreciate. Their fair value is $1.2 million on December 31, Year 1. Rather than hold them to maturity, Santiago sells the bonds for $1.2 million on January 1, Year 2. Santiago closes its books annually. Santiago's Year 1 entries to record the purchase, receipt of the interest payment, and unrealized gain would be as follows:

January 1, Year 1		
Debt securities—FVOCI	1,000,000	
Cash		1,000,000
To record the bonds' purchase.		
December 31, Year 1		
Cash	50,000	
Interest income (I/S)		50,000
To record interest income at 5 percent in the income statement.		
December 31, Year 1		
Debt securities—FVOCI	200,000	
Other comprehensive income		200,000
To record the securities' unrealized holding gain.		

On January 1, Year 2, Santiago records an income statement gain from the sale of the bonds, as depicted in the entry below. Because the gain was originally recorded in OCI, its inclusion in the income statement at sale is termed *recycling*. IFRS 9 mandates recycling of gains on FVOCI debt instruments but prohibits recycling of gains on FVOCI equity instruments.

January 1, Year 2		
Cash	1,200,000	
Other comprehensive income	200,000	
Debt securities—FVOCI		1,200,000
Realized gain on debt securities (I/S)		200,000
To record the sale of FVOCI debt securities at a gain.		

Impairment

IFRS 9's impairment rules apply to financial assets carried at amortized cost (primarily, trade accounts receivable and loans) and debt securities classified as FVOCI. The standard establishes three categories, or *stages,* of impairment adjustments based on the entity's estimate of the deterioration in the asset's credit quality:

Stage 1: Insignificant deterioration: The entity estimates the probability of default over the next 12 months and records a loss provision for this amount. Interest revenue is based on the loan's gross value. Thus, if a $1,000,000 loan with an interest rate of 5 percent has a 2 percent chance of defaulting, its carrying value, net of the allowance for loan losses, is reduced by ($1,000,000 × .02) = $20,000. The resulting net book value is $980,000. Annual interest revenue on the loan is .05 × $1,000,000 = $50,000.

Stage 2: Significant deterioration: The entity estimates the probability of default over the loan's remaining life (a longer horizon than the 12-month window of Stage 1) and records a loss provision for this amount. Interest revenue is still based on the loan's gross value. Thus, if a $1,000,000 loan with an interest rate of 5 percent has a 20 percent chance of defaulting, its carrying value, net of the allowance for loan losses, is reduced by ($1,000,000 × .2) = $200,000. The resulting net book value is $800,000. Annual interest revenue on the loan is still .05 × $1,000,000 = $50,000.

Stage 3: Credit impaired: The entity estimates the probability of default over the loan's remaining life and records a loss provision for this amount. Interest revenue is based on the loan's net value, subtracting the loan loss allowance. Thus, if a $1,000,000 loan with an interest rate of 5 percent has a 50 percent chance of defaulting, its carrying value, net of the allowance for loan losses, is reduced by ($1,000,000 × .5) = $500,000. The resulting net book value is $500,000. Annual interest revenue on the loan is calculated based on the net amount of the loan: .05 × $500,000 = $25,000.

Comparison with U.S. GAAP

In 2016, American accountants published significant changes to impairment rules for accounts receivable and loans that are similar in spirit to the provisions of IFRS 9. Contained in ASC Topic 326 and widely referred to as the CECL (the current expected credit loss) model, the American reforms resembled IFRS 9 in that both sets of rules moved the recognition of credit losses from the *incurred loss approach* to the *expected loss approach.* In a nutshell, IFRS 9 and ASC 326 improved forecasts of future credit losses and more tightly linked credit loss accruals to those forecasts.

The main difference between ASC 326 and IFRS 9 is that the U.S. standard does not distinguish between insignificant and significant deterioration of the loan portfolio. U.S. accountants must always measure credit losses over the lifetime of loan. In the language of IFRS 9, American accountants apply Stage Two treatment to all loans irrespective of their quality.

ASC 326 was scheduled to come into force for large companies in 2020. Due to the Covid-19 pandemic, American regulators delayed mandatory implementation for large companies until 2022 and for smaller companies until 2023.

Derivatives

Derivatives are financial instruments such as options, forwards, futures, and swaps whose values change in response to a change in a specified interest rate, financial instrument price, commodity price, foreign exchange rate, index, credit rating, or other variable. IFRS 9 requires derivatives to be measured at fair value. Whether the change in fair value over time is recognized in net income or deferred in stockholders' equity (i.e., other comprehensive income) depends on whether the derivative is designated as a hedge or not, and if so, what kind of a hedge. If a derivative is not designated as a hedge, the change in fair value must be recognized in net income when the fair value change occurs.

Hedge accounting results in the change in the fair value of the derivative being recognized in net income in the same accounting period in which gains and losses on the underlying hedged item are recognized in net income. Hedge accounting is optional and is permitted only when certain conditions are met. Similar to U.S. GAAP, IFRS 9 identifies three types of hedging relationships: (1) fair value hedge, (2) cash flow hedge, and (3) hedge of a net investment in a foreign operation. We discuss fair value hedges and cash flow hedges in the context of foreign currency risks in Chapter 6 and hedges of a net investment in a foreign operation in Chapter 7.

Sales of Receivables

When an entity sells receivables to a third party, there is a question as to whether the sale is truly a sale of an asset or simply a borrowing secured by the accounts receivable. In the former case, it is appropriate to recognize a sale and derecognize the receivables—that is, remove them from the accounting records. In the latter case, the receivables are not derecognized and the transaction is accounted for as a borrowing. A financial asset may be derecognized when the significant risks and rewards associated with ownership of the asset have been transferred to another entity. In some cases, the seller of receivables retains significant risks, for example, by guaranteeing the collectibility of the receivables through right of recourse, and derecognition of the receivables is not appropriate. Instead, the cash received from the sale of receivables is treated as a loan payable.

A so-called pass-through arrangement exists when an entity retains the right to collect cash flows from a receivable but is obligated to transfer those cash flows to a third party. In this type of arrangement, derecognition is appropriate only if each of the following criteria is met:

1. The entity has no obligation to pay cash to the buyer of the receivables unless it collects equivalent amounts from the receivables.
2. The entity is prohibited by the terms of the transfer contract from selling or pledging the receivables.
3. The entity has an obligation to remit any cash flows it collects on the receivables to the eventual recipient without material delay. In addition, the entity is not entitled to reinvest such cash flows. An exception exists for investments in cash equivalents during the short settlement period from the collection date to the date of remittance to the eventual recipients, as long as interest earned on such investments also is passed to the eventual recipients.

Example: Derecognition of Receivables

Edwards Inc. has receivables from unrelated parties with a face value of $1,000. Edwards transfers these receivables to Main Street Bank for $900, without recourse. The discount reflects the fact that the bank has assumed the credit risk. Edwards will continue to collect the receivables, depositing them in a non-interest-bearing bank account with the cash flows remitted to the bank at the end of each month. Edwards is not allowed to sell or pledge the receivables to anyone else and is under no obligation to repurchase the receivables from Main Street Bank.

This is a pass-through arrangement, and Edwards appears to meet the three criteria required for derecognition: (1) the company is under no obligation to pay any more than it collects, (2) it may not pledge or resell the receivables, and (3) it has agreed to remit the money collected in a timely manner. There is no interest earned on the short-term bank deposits, so there is no question whether Edwards passes on the interest to Main Street Bank. The receivables may be derecognized, as follows:

Cash	$900	
Expense	100	
Accounts Receivable		$1,000

Now assume that Edwards collects the receivables and deposits collections in its interest-bearing bank account. At the end of each month, Edwards remits to Main Street Bank only the amount collected on the receivables; interest earned on the short-term deposits is retained by Edwards. Because Edwards retains the interest on short-term bank deposits, the third pass-through criterion has not been met. Edwards would not be allowed to derecognize the accounts receivable. Instead, the cash received from Main Street Bank would be treated as a secured borrowing.

Cash		$900
Expense		100
Notes Payable		$1,000

LEASES

A lease is a contract that conveys to a lessee the right to use an asset for a period of time in exchange for consideration paid to the asset's owner, or lessor. The lessor retains legal title to the asset. Originally, accounting models treated such contracts as *mutually unexecuted* at signing. The *operating lease model* is based on this idea. Under it, merely signing a lease contract does not obligate the lessee to record a lease liability in its balance sheet for its future lease payments. Instead, the lessee accounts for these payments as rent expenses as they are made, period by period.

The operating lease model has resulted in many abuses. The most significant of these is that it allows companies to acquire usage rights to assets—sometimes a significant portion of the assets used in their operations—without recording either the assets or their corresponding lease obligations in the balance sheet. Companies commonly structure lease agreements to make them eligible for operating lease accounting, thereby avoiding having to recognize lease-related debt in their balance sheets. In this sense, use of the operating lease method is the archetypal form of *off-balance-sheet financing.*

IFRS 16, *Leases,* enacted in 2016, can be viewed as a response to the problems inherent in the operating lease model. It requires lessees to account for virtually all leases using the *finance lease model.* Under this model, signing a lease agreement triggers balance sheet recognition of both a right-of-use asset, generally termed a *leasehold asset* outside the United States, and a corresponding lease liability equal to the present value of future lease payments. The entity then depreciates the right-of-use asset over the lease term. The finance lease model accounts for the lease obligation in a manner similar to a home loan. Lease payments are apportioned between interest expense and a reduction in the lease obligation using the effective interest method to amortize the lease obligation. The leased asset is depreciated in a manner consistent with assets owned by the lessee. Normally, right-of-use assets are depreciated over the shorter of useful life and lease term. If it is reasonably certain that the lessee will obtain ownership of the asset at the end of its lease term, the asset is depreciated over its expected useful life. IAS 36, *Impairment of Assets,* applies to right-of-use assets the same as it does to assets owned by the entity.

IFRS 16 replaces IAS 17, a standard that allowed widespread application of the operating lease method. IFRS 16 was approved in 2016 and takes effect in 2019. In developing the standard, the IASB coordinated closely with the FASB in the United States. On the U.S. side, this collaboration resulted in the issuance of ASC 842, which also comes into force in 2019. While the U.S. standard accomplishes many of the same goals as IFRS 16, the FASB chose to modify the operating lease method rather than eliminate it, introducing a future divergence between IFRS and U.S. GAAP that we will examine later in this section.

Example: Comparing the Finance and Operating Lease Methods

Suppose that Speedy Delivery Service Inc. signs a three-year lease contract for 10 new delivery vans on January 1, Year 1. If Speedy had purchased the vans outright, it would have had to pay $30,000 per vehicle. Each vehicle has an economic useful life of eight years. For simplicity, we will assume that the contract obligates Speedy to make annual lease payments of $60,000 at the end of each year of the lease (i.e., on December 31 of Years 1, 2, and 3). In practice, lease contracts for autos and trucks would normally consist of monthly payments made at the beginning of each month. We will assume that Speedy's borrowing rate is 8 percent. Under this assumption, the present value of the lease payments to which Speedy is committed is $154,626.[4]

Under IAS 17, leases resembling Speedy's are generally accounted for using the operating lease method. This is because the lease term of three years is substantially shorter than the vans' useful economic lives and $154,626 is far less than the vans' fair value when the lease was signed. Under the operating lease method, Speedy would record no right-of-use asset or liability at signing. During the lease term, Speedy would simply recognize the lease payment as a rent expense of $60,000 in each year's income statement.

Under IFRS 16, Speedy will have to account for the lease using the finance lease method. On January 1, Speedy would make the following entry to recognize the lease asset and liability. Both items are set equal to the present value of the lease payments to which Speedy is committed:

January 1, Year 1		
Delivery vans—leasehold	154,626	
Lease obligation—delivery vans		154,626
To record the lease asset and liability upon signing the lease contract.		

The finance lease method requires Speedy to recognize periodic depreciation on the leased asset, normally with the useful life set equal to the length of the lease contract. If Speedy uses a straight-line depreciation policy, the annual depreciation expense would be $154,626 \div 3 = \$51,542$. Assuming that Speedy closes its books annually on December 31, the appropriate annual entry would be identical to the following entry for Year 1:

December 31, Year 1		
Depreciation expense	51,542	
Delivery vans—leasehold (net).		51,542
To record depreciation over the three-year lease term.		

On December 31, Year 1, the finance lease method also requires Speedy to record the lease payment as a combination of interest expense and reduction in the lease obligation. Interest expense is equal to the obligation's opening balance multiplied by the interest rate, or $154,626 \times .08 = \$12,370$. The resulting Year 1 journal entry would be:

December 31, Year 1		
Interest expense	12,370	
Lease obligation—delivery vans.	47,630	
Cash		60,000
To record the Year 1 lease payment, along with interest expense.		

---

[4] Equal to $(60,000/1.08 + 60,000/1.08^2 + 60,000/1.08^3)$.

Subsequent years' entries would be composed of decreasing amounts of interest expense and increasing amounts of principal repayment, each year summing to $60,000. The table below presents a breakdown of interest expense and principal reduction over the term of Speedy's lease. It also presents the balances of the leasehold asset and lease obligation throughout the lease term. The primary effect of finance lease accounting is to reveal the extent to which the lessee has acquired usage rights to right-of-use assets and incurred obligations for future payments. Under the operating lease method of IAS 17, the balance sheet values would be zero.

	Lease Payments			Balance Sheet Accounts	
	Total payments	Interest expense portion	Principal reduction portion	Leasehold asset	Lease obligation
January 1, Year 1				$154,626	$154,626
December 31, Year 1	$60,000	$12,370	$47,630	103,084	106,996
December 31, Year 2	60,000	8,560	51,440	51,542	55,556
December 31, Year 3	60,000	4,444	55,556	0	0

The table below presents the income statement effects of applying the two methods to Speedy's lease. Compared with the operating lease treatment allowed under IAS 17, finance lease treatment mandated by IFRS 16 is more conservative in that it accelerates expense recognition.

Income Statement Effects:	Finance Lease Method (IFRS 16)			Operating Lease Method (IAS 17)
	Depreciation expense	Interest expense	Total	Rent expense
December 31, Year 1	$51,542	$12,370	$ 63,912	$ 60,000
December 31, Year 2	51,542	8,560	60,102	60,000
December 31, Year 3	51,542	4,444	55,986	60,000
Cumulative expense			180,000	180,000

Comparing IFRS 16 to ASC 842

ASC 842 preserves the distinction between operating and finance leases that existed in prior accounting pronouncements. In fact, the standard's classification criteria are virtually identical to that used by U.S. accountants for many years:

1. The lease transfers ownership of the asset to the lessee by the end of the lease term.
2. The lessee has the option to purchase the asset at a price less than fair market value.
3. The lease term is for the major part of the leased asset's economic life.
4. The present value of minimum lease payments at the inception of the lease is equal to substantially all the fair value of the leased asset.
5. The leased asset is of a specialized nature such that only the lessee can use it without major modifications.

Instead of eliminating the operating lease category, ASC 842 achieves an effect similar to that of IFRS 16 by requiring lease assets and liabilities to be recorded for both operating and finance leases. Applying ASC 842's operating lease provisions to Speedy Delivery Service's lease of delivery vans, the journal entry at lease inception would be identical to that required under IFRS 16:

January 1, Year 1

Delivery vans—Operating leasehold. 154,626

    Operating lease obligation—delivery vans 154,626

    To record the lease asset and liability upon signing the lease contract.

The difference lies in the income statement treatment. ASC 842 requires a straight-line expense that spreads total lease payments evenly over the lease term. Because Speedy's lease payment schedule is constant, the journal entry required each year would be equivalent to the following entry for Year 1:

December 31, Year 1

Lease expense 60,000

    Cash 60,000

    To record the Year 1 lease payment along with straight-line lease expense.

The following table compares the resulting differences in lease expense under ASC 842 and IFRS 16 over the term of Speedy's lease:

IFRS 16	ASC 842	Difference
$ 63,912	$ 60,000	$ 3,912
60,102	60,000	102
55,986	60,000	(4,014)
180,000	180,000	0

This table's third column reports the degree to which IFRS accounting is more conservative than U.S. accounting for operating leases. There are balance sheet differences as well. The leasehold asset is reduced by the same amount as the leasehold obligation, resulting in a slower reduction of the leasehold asset relative to a straight-line schedule. In Year 1, the journal entry would be:

January 1, Year 1

Operating lease obligation—delivery vans. 47,630

    Delivery vans—Operating leasehold (net) 47,630

    To record depreciation and principal reduction of the leasehold asset and lease liability.

In addition to the foregoing measurement differences, ASC 842's retention of the operating lease category also introduces presentational differences. IFRS 16 mandates either separate presentation or footnote disclosure of leasehold assets as well as separate reporting of depreciation and interest expenses. In the cash flow statement, the portion of the lease payment allocated to principal reduction is a financing outflow. The portion allocated to interest expense is either an operating or a financing outflow, depending on the entity's election under IAS 7 (discussed at the end of this chapter).

Under ASC 842, the lessee must provide balance sheet or footnote disclosure of operating and finance lease assets and liabilities. In contrast with IFRS, lessees must present the lease expenses as a single operating expense. They should present lease payments as operating cash outflows, unless the payments are necessary to prepare the asset for its intended use, in which case they are classified as investing activities.

DISCLOSURE AND PRESENTATION STANDARDS

Several IFRS deal primarily with disclosure and presentation issues. This section summarizes some of those standards. While briefly introduced here, IFRS 8, *Operating Segments,* is discussed in greater detail in Chapter 9.

Statement of Cash Flows

IAS 7, *Statement of Cash Flows,* reiterates the requirement in IAS 1 that a company must present a statement of cash flows as an integral part of its financial statements. IAS 7 contains the following requirements:

- Cash flows must be classified as being related to operating, investing, or financing activities.
- Cash flow from operations may be presented using the direct method or the indirect method. When using the indirect method, IAS 7 does *not* specify that the reconciliation from income to cash flows must begin with any particular line item (e.g., net income). Thus, an entity could begin the reconciliation with operating income or some other measure of income. When using the direct method, there is no requirement to also present a reconciliation of income to cash from operations.
- Cash flows related to interest, dividends, and income taxes must be reported separately.
- Interest and dividends paid may be classified as operating or financing.
- Interest and dividends received may be classified as operating or investing.
- Income taxes are classified as operating unless they are specifically identified with investing or financing activities.
- Noncash investing and financing transactions are excluded from the statement of cash flows but must be disclosed elsewhere within the financial statements.
- Components of cash and cash equivalents must be disclosed and reconciled with amounts reported on the statement of financial position (balance sheet). However, the total for cash and cash equivalents in the statement of cash flows need not agree with a single line item in the balance sheet.
- IAS 7 makes an explicit distinction between bank borrowings and bank overdrafts. Overdrafts may be classified as a component (i.e., reduction) of cash and cash equivalents, if considered to be an integral part of an enterprise's cash management. Otherwise, bank overdrafts are classified as a financing activity.

Several differences exist between IFRS and U.S. GAAP in the presentation of the statement of cash flows. Under U.S. GAAP:

- Interest paid, interest received, and dividends received are all classified as operating cash flows. Dividends paid are classified as financing cash flows.
- When using the indirect method of presenting operating cash flows, the reconciliation from income to cash flows must begin with net income.
- When using the direct method of presenting operating cash flows, a reconciliation from net income to operating cash flows also must be presented.
- The cash and cash equivalents line item in the statement of cash flows must reconcile with the cash and cash equivalents line in the statement of financial position.

Example: Classification of Interest and Dividends in the Statement of Cash Flows

Star Kissed Corporation (SKC) currently reports under U.S. GAAP but is investigating the effect that the adoption of IFRS might have on its statement of cash flows. For the current year, SKC has interest received of $500, interest paid of $1,250, dividends received of $200, and dividends paid of $2,700. Under U.S. GAAP, the company classifies interest paid, interest received, and dividends received as operating activities, and dividends paid are classified as a financing activity. These items are presented in the company's U.S. GAAP statement of cash flows as follows:

Operating activities:	
Interest paid	$(1,250)
Interest received	500
Dividends received	200
Cash flow from operating activities	$ (550)
Investing activities:	
Nothing reported	$ 0
Financing activities:	
Dividends paid	(2,700)
Cash flow from financing activities	$(2,700)
Net change in cash	$(3,250)

This classification would be acceptable under IFRS. However, the following presentation, among others, also would be acceptable under IAS 7:

Operating activities:	
Nothing reported	$ 0
Investing activities:	
Interest received	$ 500
Dividends received	200
Cash flow from investing activities	$ 700
Financing activities:	
Interest paid	$(1,250)
Dividends paid	(2,700)
Cash flow from financing activities	$(3,950)
Net change in cash	$(3,250)

Events after the Reporting Period

IAS 10, *Events after the Reporting Period,* prescribes when an entity should adjust its financial statements for events occurring after the balance sheet date (referred to in the United States as "subsequent events") and the disclosures to be made related to those events. Events after the reporting period are those events, favorable and unfavorable, that occur between the balance sheet date and the date that the financial statements are *authorized for issuance.* Under U.S. GAAP, the subsequent event period runs through the date that the financial statements are issued (or are available to be issued), which is later than the date they are authorized for issuance.

The two types of after-the-reporting-period events—adjusting events and nonadjusting events—are treated differently, as we discuss next.

Adjusting Events

Events that provide evidence of conditions that existed at the end of the reporting period are referred to as *adjusting events.* These events must be recognized through adjustment of the financial statements. For example, assume a company has recorded an estimated liability of $2 million related to litigation on its December 31, Year 1, balance sheet. On January 20, Year 2, before the board of directors has approved the financial statements for issuance, the judge orders the company to pay $3 million. The liability on the December 31, Year 1, balance sheet should be adjusted upward to $3 million. The judge's decision clarifies the value of the liability that existed at the balance sheet date.

Nonadjusting Events

Events that are indicative of conditions that have arisen after the balance sheet date but before the date the financial statements have been authorized for issuance are referred to as *nonadjusting events.* No adjustments related to these events are made to the financial statements. However, disclosures are required of:

1. The nature of the event.
2. An estimate of the financial effect, or a statement that an estimate cannot be made.

For example, assume inventory carried on the December 31, Year 1, balance sheet at $3 million decreases in net realizable value to $1 million due to a change in the law on February 15, Year 2. The financial statements are approved for issuance on February 20, Year 2. The decline in market value does not relate to the condition of the inventory at the balance sheet date, so no adjustment should be made. If material, the decrease in value should be disclosed in the notes to the financial statements.

IAS 10 specifically states that financial statements should not be adjusted for cash dividends declared after the balance sheet date. The same is true for stock dividends and stock splits.

Accounting Policies, Changes in Accounting Estimates, and Errors

IAS 8, *Accounting Policies, Changes in Accounting Estimates and Errors,* provides guidance with respect to (1) the selection of accounting policies, (2) accounting for changes in accounting policies, (3) dealing with changes in accounting estimates, and (4) the correction of errors.

Selection of Accounting Policies

IAS 8 establishes the following hierarchy of authoritative pronouncements to be followed in selecting accounting policies to apply to a specific transaction or event:

1. IASB Standard or Interpretation that specifically applies to the transaction or event.
2. IASB Standard or Interpretation that deals with similar and related issues.
3. Definitions, recognition criteria, and measurement concepts in the IASB *Framework.*
4. Most recent pronouncements of other standard-setting bodies that use a similar conceptual framework to develop accounting standards.

Changes in Accounting Policy

To ensure comparability of financial statements over time, an entity is required to apply its accounting policies consistently. A change in accounting policy is allowed only if the change:

1. Is required by an IFRS.
2. Results in financial statements that provide more relevant and reliable information.

If practical, the change in accounting policy should be applied retrospectively. The cumulative effect of adopting the new accounting policy is treated as an adjustment to the carrying amounts of the assets and liabilities affected and as an adjustment to the beginning balance in retained earnings. The cumulative effect is *not* included in net income.

Changes in Estimates

A change in estimate due to new developments or new information should be accounted for in the period of the change or in future periods, depending on the periods affected by the change. In other words, the change in estimate should be handled prospectively.

Correction of Errors

Material, prior-period errors should be corrected retrospectively by restating all prior reported accounts (e.g., assets, liabilities, equity) affected by the error and by recording a prior-period adjustment to the beginning balance in retained earnings. When it is impractical to determine the period-specific effects of an error on comparative information for one or more prior periods, the entity restates the opening balances in assets, liabilities, and equity for the earliest period for which retrospective restatement is practicable. This might be the current period. Whereas IFRS provides an exception if it is impractical to restate financial statements for a correction of an error, U.S. GAAP does not provide such an exception but instead requires all material errors to be corrected through restatement.

Related Party Disclosures

Transactions between related parties must be disclosed in the notes to financial statements. Parties are related if one party has the ability to control or exert significant influence over the other party. Related parties can include parent companies, subsidiaries, equity method associates, individual owners, and key management personnel. Similar rules exist in U.S. GAAP.

Earnings per Share

Basic and diluted earnings per share must be reported on the face of the income statement. IAS 33, *Earnings per Share,* provides guidance for calculating earnings per share. U.S. GAAP provides more detailed guidance with respect to the calculation of diluted earnings per share. Application of this guidance would appear to be consistent with IAS 33.

Interim Financial Reporting

IAS 34, *Interim Financial Reporting,* does not mandate which companies should prepare interim statements, how frequently, or how soon after the end of an interim period. The standard defines the minimum content to be included in interim statements by those entities required by their national jurisdiction to present them and identifies the accounting principles that should be applied. With certain exceptions, IAS 34 requires interim periods to be treated as discrete reporting periods. This differs from the position in U.S. GAAP, which treats interim periods as an integral part of the full year. As an example, IAS 34 would require annual bonuses to be recognized as expense in the interim period in which bonuses are paid. Under U.S. GAAP, on the other hand, one-fourth of the expected annual bonus is accrued each quarter.

Noncurrent Assets Held for Sale and Discontinued Operations

Noncurrent assets held for sale must be reported separately on the balance sheet at the lower of (1) carrying value or (2) fair value less costs to sell. Assets held for sale are not depreciated. Similar rules exist in U.S. GAAP.

A discontinued operation is a component of an entity that represents a major line of business or geographical area of operations that either has been disposed of or has been classified as held for sale. The after-tax profit or loss and after-tax gain or loss on disposal must be reported as a single amount on the face of the income statement. Detail of the revenues, expenses, gain or loss on disposal, and income taxes comprising this single amount must be disclosed in the notes or on the face of the income statement. If presented on the face of the income statement, it must be presented in a section identified as discontinued operations. The definition of the type of operation that can be classified as discontinued is somewhat narrower than under U.S. GAAP. In addition, U.S. GAAP requires both pre-tax and after-tax profit or loss to be reported on the income statement. Otherwise, the two sets of standards are substantially similar.

Operating Segments

As part of the short-term convergence project with the FASB, the IASB issued IFRS 8, *Operating Segments,* in 2006 to replace IAS 14, *Segment Reporting.* IFRS 8 adopted the FASB's so-called management approach. Extensive disclosures are required for each separately reportable operating segment. Operating segments are components of a business (1) that generate revenues and expenses, (2) whose operating results are regularly reviewed by the chief operating officer, and (3) for which separate financial information is available. IFRS 8 provides the following guidelines with regard to segment reporting:

- An operating segment is separately reportable if it meets any of three quantitative tests (revenue test, profit or loss test, or asset test). Operating segments can be defined in terms of products and services or on the basis of geography.
- Disclosures required for each operating segment include assets, capital expenditures, liabilities, profit or loss, and the following components of profit or loss: external revenues, intercompany revenues, interest income and expense, depreciation and amortization, equity method income, income tax expense, and noncash expenses. Similar disclosures are required by U.S. GAAP except that liabilities by operating segment need not be reported.
- If the revenue reported by operating segments is less than 75 percent of total revenues, additional operating segments must be reported separately—even if they do not meet any of the three quantitative tests—until at least 75 percent of total revenue is included in reportable segments.
- In addition to disclosures by operating segment, entity-wide disclosures related to products and services, geographic areas, and major customers are required.
- If operating segments are not defined on the basis of products and services, revenue derived from each major product and service must be disclosed, even if the company has only one operating segment.
- Revenues and noncurrent assets must be disclosed for the domestic country and all foreign countries combined. These two items also must be disclosed for each foreign country in which a material amount of revenues or noncurrent assets is located. Materiality is not defined.
- The existence and amount of revenue derived from major customers must be disclosed, along with the identity of the segment generating the revenue. A major customer is defined as one from which 10 percent or more of total revenues are generated.

Summary

1. IAS 1 requires liabilities to be classified as current or noncurrent. The classification and accounting for current liabilities under IFRS is very similar to U.S. GAAP. Differences relate to refinancing short-term debt, amounts payable on demand due to debt covenant violations, and bank overdrafts.

2. IAS 37 defines a provision as a liability of uncertain timing or amount. A provision is recognized when there is a present obligation that can be reliably estimated and for which it is probable (more likely than not) that an outflow of resources will be made. U.S. GAAP has similar requirements but does not provide guidance for the degree of likelihood needed to meet the threshold of being probable.

3. A provision should be recognized for an onerous contract, which is a contract in which the unavoidable costs of fulfilling the contract exceed the benefit expected to be received. A provision should be recognized for a restructuring when an entity has created a constructive obligation—that is, when it has raised a valid expectation in those affected by the plan that it will carry out the restructuring. U.S. GAAP does not allow recognition of a restructuring until a liability has been incurred.

4. Under IAS 19 and U.S. GAAP, the amount reported on the balance sheet related to a defined post-employment benefit plan is equal to the present value of the defined benefit obligation (PVDBO) minus the fair value of plan assets (FVPA). When the FVPA exceeds the PVDBO, IFRS impose a ceiling on the resulting asset. This ceiling is the present value of any economic benefits available in the form of refunds from the plan or reductions in future contributions to the plan.

5. IAS 19 requires the use of the discount rate to compute the expected return on a pension plan's assets. As allowed by U.S. GAAP, U.S. companies generally choose higher rates.

6. IFRS 2 distinguishes between three types of share-based payments. Equity-settled share-based payments are treated as equity transactions; cash-settled and choice-of-settlement share-based payment transactions result in the recognition of a liability. The standard applies a fair value approach to all three types of share-based payment.

7. In a stock option plan that vests in installments, compensation cost associated with each installment is amortized over that installment's vesting period under IFRS. This approach also is acceptable under U.S. GAAP, but a simpler straight-line method also may be used.

8. Similar to U.S. GAAP, IAS 12 uses an asset-and-liability approach that requires recognition of deferred tax assets and liabilities for temporary differences and for operating loss and tax credit carryforwards. A deferred tax asset is recognized only if it is probable that a tax benefit will be realized.

9. With the adoption of IFRS 15 and ASC 606, IFRS and U.S. GAAP have harmonized their revenue recognition standards. Their revenue recognition rules are based on a five-step model with a focus on multiple element sales arrangements. They shift the focus of revenue recognition to the transfer of control rather than the transfer of the risks and rewards of ownership.

10. Changes introduced by IFRS 15 include the upfront recognition of revenue from software licenses, the elimination of sell-through accounting, and a systematic treatment of loyalty programs using the multiple deliverables framework.

11. Entities that use customer loyalty programs to provide customers with incentives to purchase their goods and services must treat the award credits as a separate component of the sale transaction and recognize a portion of the sales price as deferred revenue.

12. The accounting for financial instruments is covered by IAS 32, IFRS 7, and IFRS 9. Financial instruments are contracts that give rise to both a financial asset for one party and either a financial liability or equity for another party.

13. IAS 32 requires financial instruments to be classified as financial liabilities or equity or both in accordance with the substance of the contractual arrangement. If an equity instrument contains a contractual obligation that meets the definition of a financial liability, it should be classified as such. Preferred shares that are redeemable at the option of the shareholders are an example of a financial liability.

14. IFRS 9 establishes three categories of financial assets: amortized cost, fair value through other comprehensive income (FVOCI), and fair value through profit and loss (FVPL). The residual category for financial assets is FVPL. The standard establishes two categories of financial liabilities, FVPL and amortized cost. Amortized cost is the residual category.

15. IFRS 9 allows equity instruments to be classified as FVOCI, with both unrealized and realized gains and losses reported in other comprehensive income. U.S. GAAP requires equity instruments (other than investments in subsidiaries and associates) to be classified as FVPL.

16. IFRS 9 applies a three-stage impairment testing model to assets in the amortized cost category. Stage 1 bases expected credit losses over a 12-month window. Stages 2 and 3

base expected credit losses over the life of the asset. U.S. GAAP bases credit loss measurements on a loan's expected lifetime losses, similar to Stages 2 and 3 under IFRS 9.

17. IFRS 16 and ASC 842 largely eliminate the off-balance-sheet treatment of operating leases. IFRS 16 does this by requiring most leases to be treated as finance leases. ASC 842 retains the operating lease classification but requires balance sheet recognition of the operating lease asset and liability.

18. IFRS 16's requirement to use finance lease accounting for most leases results in the separate presentation of depreciation and interest expenses. U.S. GAAP's retention of the operating lease category results in the presentation of a single expense for these leases.

19. IAS 7 contains requirements for the presentation of the statement of cash flows. Several differences exist between IAS 7 and U.S. GAAP, including the option to present interest and dividends paid as either operating or financing activities and interest and dividends received as either operating or investing activities.

20. IAS 10 prescribes when financial statements should be adjusted for events occurring after the end of the reporting period. The cutoff date for adjusting events is the date financial statements are authorized for issuance. Under U.S. GAAP, the cutoff date is the date financial statements are issued or are available to be issued, which is later than the date the statements are approved.

21. IAS 8 establishes a hierarchy of authoritative pronouncements to be considered in selecting accounting policies. The lowest level in the hierarchy is guidance issued by other standard-setting bodies that use a conceptual framework similar to that of the IASB. This includes standards set by the FASB.

22. Once selected, an entity must use its accounting policies consistently over time. A change in accounting policy is allowed only if (a) the change results in the financial statements providing more relevant and reliable information or (b) the change is required by an IASB pronouncement.

23. Under both IFRS and U.S. GAAP, companies are given wide latitude to define segments as long as they generate revenues and expenses and their results are regularly reviewed by the chief operating officer. At least 75 percent of total revenue must be included in reportable segments.

24. If operating segments are not defined based on products and services, revenue derived from each product and service must be disclosed.

25. Major customers must be identified, along with disclosure of the amount of revenue that they generate. A major customer is one that accounts for more than 10 percent of sales revenue.

Questions

Answer questions based on IFRS unless otherwise indicated.

1. What is a provision, and when must a provision be recognized?
2. What is a contingent liability? What is the financial reporting treatment for contingent liabilities?
3. What is a constructive obligation?
4. What is an onerous contract? How are onerous contracts accounted for?
5. How does a company measure the net pension benefit liability (asset) to report on the balance sheet under IFRS and U.S. GAAP?
6. In accounting for post-employment benefits, when are past service costs and actuarial gains and losses recognized in income?

7. What is the basis for determining compensation cost in an equity-settled share-based payment transaction with nonemployees? With employees?

8. What is the difference in measuring compensation expense associated with stock options that vest on a single date (cliff vesting) and stock options that vest in installments (graded vesting)?

9. How does an entity account for a choice-of-settlement share-based payment transaction?

10. Which income tax rates should be used in accounting for income taxes?

11. What are the rules related to the recognition of a deferred tax asset?

12. What approaches are available for disclosing the relationship between tax expense and accounting profit?

13. How are deferred taxes classified on the balance sheet?

14. What are the five steps that entities take to recognize revenue under IFRS 15?

15. What two performance obligations are generally part of a software sales agreement?

16. What is variable consideration and how is it measured?

17. What is a customer loyalty program, and how is such a program accounted for?

18. What is breakage revenue?

19. What are the three categories of financial assets and which is the residual category?

20. Under what conditions should preferred shares be recognized as a liability on the balance sheet?

21. How are convertible bonds measured initially on the balance sheet?

22. What is the primary difference between how IFRS and U.S. GAAP account for equity investments?

23. Which types of equity investments are excluded from the scope of IFRS 9?

24. What is the primary difference between IFRS 16 and the new U.S. lease accounting standard, ASC 842?

25. How does the classification of interest and dividends in the statement of cash flows differ between IFRS and U.S. GAAP?

26. By what cut-off date should an entity adjust its financial statements for events occurring after the reporting period?

27. What are the guidelines on selecting and changing accounting policies?

28. A cement manufacturer has cement plants around the world and decides to sell one of the plants within the next 12 months. Would this cement plant be classified as a discontinued operation in the current period's financial statements?

29. Segment-level operating results are reviewed by which corporate officer?

30. How much revenue must be generated by a company's reportable segments?

31. How is a major customer defined?

Exercises and Problems

Solve exercises and problems based on IFRS unless otherwise indicated.

1. Halifax Corporation has a December 31 fiscal year-end. As of December 31, Year 1, the company has a debt covenant violation that results in a 10-year note payable to Nova Scotia Bank becoming due on March 1, Year 2. Halifax will be required to classify the 10-year note payable as a current liability unless it obtains a waiver from the bank:

   a. Prior to issuance of its Year 1 financial statements, which gives the company until January 1, Year 3, to rectify the debt covenant violation.

   b. Prior to December 31, Year 1, which gives the company until January 1, Year 3, to rectify the debt covenant violation.

   c. Prior to issuance of its Year 1 financial statements, which gives the company until June 30, Year 2, to rectify the debt covenant violation.

   d. Prior to December 31, Year 1, which gives the company until June 30, Year 2, to rectify the debt covenant violation.

2. Bull Arm Company has the following items at December 31, Year 1:

   • $200,000, 5 percent note payable, due March 15, Year 2. The company has reached an agreement with the bank to refinance the note for two years, but the refinancing has not yet been completed.

   • $1,000,000, 4 percent bonds payable, due December 31, Year 5. The company has violated an agreement with the bondholders to maintain a minimum balance in retained earnings, which causes the bonds to come due on January 31, Year 2.

   • $50,000 overdraft on a bank account. Overdrafts are a normal part of the company's cash management plan.

Required:

Related to these items, what amount should Bull Arm Company report as current liabilities on its December 31, Year 1, balance sheet?

   a. $50,000

   b. $250,000

   c. $1,050,000

   d. $1,200,000

3. Melbourne Inc. is involved in a tax dispute with the national tax authority. Melbourne's legal counsel indicates that there is a 70 percent likelihood that the company will lose this dispute and estimates that the amount the company will have to pay is between $500,000 and $700,000, with all amounts in that range being equally likely. What amount, if any, should Melbourne recognize as a provision related to this tax dispute?

   a. $0

   b. $500,000

   c. $600,000

   d. $700,000

4. Which of the following is *not* a criterion that must be met before an entity recognizes a provision related to a restructuring program?

   a. The entity has a detailed formal plan for the restructuring.

   b. The entity has begun implementation of the restructuring.

   c. The restructuring plan indicates that the restructuring will be carried out in a reasonable period of time.

   d. The cost of the restructuring is reasonably estimable.

5. Past service cost related to nonvested employees should be recognized as expense

   a. In the period the cost is incurred.

   b. Over the nonvested employees' remaining vesting period.

   c. Over the nonvested employees' estimated remaining working life.

   d. Over the nonvested employees' estimated life expectancy.

6. When stock options are granted to employees, what is the basis for determining the amount of compensation cost that will be recognized as expense?

   a. The fair value of the service provided by the employees receiving the options at the grant date.

    b. The fair value of the stock options at the exercise date.

    c. The fair value of the stock options at the grant date.

    d. There is no recognition of expense related to stock options.

7. Which of the following types of share-based payment (SBP) transactions always result in the recognition of a liability?

    a. Equity-settled SBP transactions with employees.

    b. Equity-settled SBP transactions with nonemployees.

    c. Cash-settled SBP transactions with employees.

    d. Choice-of-settlement SBP transactions in which the entity chooses the form of settlement.

8. Sandoval Company operates in a country in which distributed profits are taxed at 25 percent and undistributed profits are taxed at 30 percent. In Year 1, Sandoval generated pre-tax profit of $100,000 and paid $20,000 in dividends from its Year 1 earnings. In Year 2, Sandoval generated pre-tax profit of $120,000 and paid dividends of $40,000 from its Year 1 earnings. What amounts should Sandoval recognize as current tax expense in Years 1 and 2, respectively?

    a. $29,000 and $34,000

    b. $30,000 and $34,000

    c. $25,000 and $30,000

    d. $30,000 and $36,000

9. Which of the following is a criterion that must be met to recognize revenue from the sale of goods?

    a. The receipt of consideration to which the entity is entitled under the contract must be probable.

    b. The goods must have been delivered into the customer's physical possession.

    c. All of the contract's performance obligations must have been satisfied.

    d. It is highly probable that the buyer will pay the consideration promptly.

10. Manometer Company sells accounts receivable of $10,000 to Eck Bank for $9,000 in cash. The sale does not qualify for derecognition of a financial asset. As a result, Manometer's balance sheet will be different in which of the following ways?

    a. $1,000 more in assets than under derecognition.

    b. $9,000 more in assets than under derecognition.

    c. $9,000 more in liabilities than under derecognition.

    d. $10,000 less in equity than under derecognition.

11. Siam Financial Corp. (SFC) actively trades bonds but chooses not to hedge any of its open positions. At the beginning of the year, SFC purchased 50 million baht of Thai government bonds paying 4 percent per annum. The year-end fair market value of the bonds was 51 million baht. How much did the bonds contribute to SFC's pre-tax income during the year?

    a. Nothing, because bonds are always carried at cost.

    b. 1 million baht

    c. 2 million baht

    d. 3 million baht

12. A $3 million loan paying annual interest at a 5 percent rate has been classified as Stage 3 by the lender. Expected credit losses over the next 12 months are $80,000. However,

expected credit losses over the life of the loan are $1 million. How much net interest income is the lender permitted to record in its income statement in the current year?

a. No interest income because the loan is impaired.

b. $150,000

c. $146,000

d. $100,000

13. Monterrey Properties enters into a three-year lease for an automobile to be used by its CEO. The agreement obligates the company to make lease payments of $600 at the end of every month of the lease term. Title to the auto does not transfer at the end of the lease. The contract does not contain a bargain purchase option. If purchased outright, the auto would cost $40,000. Its useful economic life would be six years. What expense will Monterrey Properties record in the first month of the lease under IFRS 16? Assume that the company's borrowing rate is 6 percent.

a. No upfront lease expense.

b. $547.85

c. $600.00

d. $648.46

14. An entity must adjust its financial statement for an event that occurs after the end of the reporting period if:

a. The event occurs before the financial statements have been approved for issuance and provides evidence of conditions that existed at the end of the reporting period.

b. The event occurs before the financial statements have been issued and changes the value of an asset that existed at the end of the reporting period.

c. The event occurs before the financial statements have been audited and changes the value of a liability that existed at the end of the reporting period.

d. The event occurs within 15 days of the end of the reporting period and changes the level of ownership in another entity from a noncontrolling to a controlling interest.

15. In selecting an accounting policy for a transaction, which of the following is the first level within the hierarchy of guidance that should be considered?

a. The most recent pronouncements of other standard-setting bodies to the extent they do not conflict with IFRS or the IASB *Framework*.

b. An IASB Standard or Interpretation that specifically relates to the transaction.

c. The definitions, recognition criteria, and measurement concepts in the IASB *Framework*.

d. An IASB Standard or Interpretation that deals with similar and related issues.

16. An entity can justify a change in accounting policy if

a. The charge will result in a reliable and more relevant presentation of the financial statements.

b. The entity encounters new transactions that are substantively different from existing or previous transactions.

c. The entity previously accounted for similar, though immaterial, transactions under an unacceptable accounting method.

d. An alternative accounting policy gives rise to a material change in current year net income.

17. In Year 1, Better Sleep Company began to receive complaints from physicians that patients were experiencing unexpected side effects from the company's sleep apnea drug.

The company took the drug off the market near the end of Year 1. During Year 2, the company was sued by 1,000 customers who had a severe allergic reaction to the company's drug and required hospitalization. At the end of Year 2, the company's attorneys estimated a 60 percent chance the company would need to make payments in the range of $1,000–$5,000 to settle each claim, with all amounts in that range being equally likely. At the end of Year 3, while none of the cases had been resolved, the company's attorneys now estimated an 80 percent probability the company would be required to make payments in the range of $2,000–$7,000 to settle each claim. In Year 4, 400 claims were settled at a total cost of $1.2 million. Based on this experience, the company believes 30 percent of the remaining cases will be settled for $3,000 each, 50 percent will be settled for $5,000, and 20 percent will be settled for $10,000.

Required:
Prepare journal entries for Years 1–4 related to this litigation.

18. On June 1, Year 1, Charley Horse Company entered into a contract with Good Feed Company to purchase 1,000 bales of organic hay on January 30, Year 2, at a price of $30 per bale. The hay will be grown especially for Charley Horse and is needed to feed the company's herd of bison. On December 1, Year 1, Charley Horse sells its herd of bison. As a result, the company no longer has a need for the organic hay that will be delivered on January 30, Year 2, and the company does not believe it will be able to sell the hay to a third party. Charley Horse is able to cancel the contract with Good Feed for a cancellation fee of $20,000.

Required:
Determine what accounting entries, if any, Charley Horse Company should make on December 31, Year 1, related to the contract to purchase 1,000 bales of hay on January 30, Year 2.

19. The board of directors of Chestnut Inc. approved a restructuring plan on November 1, Year 1. On December 1, Year 1, Chestnut publicly announced its plan to close a manufacturing division in New Jersey and move it to China and the company's New Jersey employees were notified that their jobs would be eliminated. Also on December 1, Year 1, to ensure an orderly transition, management promised a termination bonus of $10,000 to any employee who remains with the company until his or her position is terminated in the fourth quarter of Year 2. Chestnut estimates it will pay termination bonuses to 120 employees at the end of Year 2, for a total of $1,200,000. The present value of the estimated termination bonus is $1,000,000.

Required:
Determine the provision that should be recognized for Chestnut's restructuring plan. Identify the dates on which journal entries should be made and the amounts to be recorded.

20. The Kissel Trucking Company Inc. has a defined benefit pension plan for its employees. At December 31, Year 1, the following information is available regarding Kissel's plan:

Fair value of plan assets	$30,000,000
Present value of defined benefit obligation	38,000,000
Service costs	4,000,000
Interest costs	1,200,000
Actuarial gains	150,000
Past service costs	375,000

Required:
Determine the amount that Kissel will report on the balance sheet as of December 31, Year 1, for this pension plan under IFRS.

21. On January 1, Year 1, the Hoverman Corporation made amendments to its defined benefit pension plan, resulting in $150,000 of past service costs. The plan has 100 active employees with an average expected remaining working life of 10 years. There currently are no retirees under the plan.

Required:
Determine the amount of past service costs to be amortized in Year 1 and subsequent years under (a) IFRS and (b) U.S. GAAP.

22. The Baton Rouge Company compiled the following information for the current year related to its defined benefit pension plan:

Present value of defined benefit obligation, beginning of year	$1,000,000
Fair value of plan assets, beginning of year	800,000
Service cost, current year	50,000
Actuarial gain, current year	8,000
Actual return on plan assets, current year	55,000
Effective yield on high-quality corporate bonds, current year	5%

Required:
Determine the amount of defined benefit cost for the current year to be reported in (a) net income and (b) other comprehensive income.

23. White River Company has a defined benefit pension plan in which the fair value of plan assets (FVPA) exceeds the present value of defined benefit obligations (PVDBO). The following information is available at December 31, Year 1 (amounts in millions):

PVDBO	$3,200
FVPA	3,700

Because the FVPA exceeds the PVDBO, White River will be able to reduce future contributions to the plan for several years. The present value of reductions in future contributions is $100 million.

Required:
Determine the amount at which White River Company will report a defined pension benefit asset on its December 31, Year 1, balance sheet under (a) IFRS and (b) U.S. GAAP.

24. On January 2, Year 1, Argy Company's board of directors granted 12,000 stock options to a select group of senior employees. The requisite service period is three years, with one-third of the options vesting at the end of each calendar year (graded vesting). An option-pricing model was used to calculate a fair value of $5 for each option on the grant date. The company assumes all 12,000 options will vest (i.e., there will be no forfeitures).

Required:
Determine the amount to be recognized as compensation expense in Year 1, Year 2, and Year 3 under (a) IFRS and (b) U.S. GAAP. Prepare the necessary journal entries.

25. SC Masterpiece Inc. granted 1,000 stock options to certain sales employees on January 1, Year 1. The options vest at the end of three years (cliff vesting) but are conditional upon selling 20,000 cases of barbecue sauce over the three-year service period.

The grant-date fair value of each option is $30. No forfeitures are expected to occur. The company is expensing the cost of the options on a straight-line basis over the three-year period at $10,000 per year (1,000 options × $30 ÷ 3 = $10,000).

On January 1, Year 2, the company's management believes the original sales target of 20,000 units will not be met because only 5,000 cases were sold in Year 1. Management modifies the sales target for the options to vest to 15,000 units, which it believes is reasonably achievable. The fair value of each option at January 1, Year 2, is $28.

Required:

Determine the amount to be recognized as compensation expense in Year 1, Year 2, and Year 3 under (a) IFRS and (b) U.S. GAAP. Prepare the necessary journal entries.

26. Belmond Manufacturing Inc., a U.S.-based company, operates in three countries in addition to the United States. The following table reports the company's pre-tax income and the applicable tax rate in these countries for the year ended December 31, Year 1. Belmond does not have any temporary tax differences, but it does have two permanent differences: (1) nontaxable municipal bond interest of $70,000 in the United States and (2) nondeductible expenses of $30,000 in the United States.

Country	Pre-Tax Income	Applicable Tax Rate
United States...............................	$1,450,000	21%
Country One................................	1,000,000	30
Country Two................................	400,000	20
Country Three	310,000	15
Total.......................................	$3,160,000	
Permanent differences.....................	40,000	
Book income	$3,200,000	

Required:

Prepare the numerical reconciliation between tax expense and accounting profit that would appear in Belmond's income tax note in the Year 1 financial statements. Show two different ways in which this reconciliation may be presented.

27. Ultima Company offers its customers discounts to purchase goods and take title before they actually need the goods. The company offers to hold the goods for the customers until they request delivery. This relieves the customers from making room in their warehouses for merchandise not yet needed. The goods are on hand, ready for delivery to the buyer, and not available for an alternative use. Ultima Company pays the cost of storage and insurance prior to shipment. Customers are billed at the time of sale and are given the normal credit period (90 days) to pay.

Required:

Determine whether Ultima Company should recognize revenue from the sale of goods at the time title passes to the customer or whether it should defer revenue recognition until the goods are delivered to the customer.

28. The Miller-Porter Company sells powder coating equipment at a sales price of $50,000 per unit. The sales price includes delivery, installation, and initial testing of the equipment, as well as a monthly service call for one year in which a technician checks to make sure that the equipment is working properly and makes adjustments as needed. After the first year, customers are given the opportunity to enter into an extended service agreement; Miller-Porter prices these extended service agreements to earn an

expected gross profit of 50 percent. Given the wages paid to technicians and the time required to make a service call, the company estimates that the cost of providing each monthly service call is $200.

Required:

Develop a revenue recognition policy consistent with IAS 18 for The Miller-Porter Company for its sales of powder coating equipment.

29. Phil's Sandwich Company sells sandwiches at several locations in the northeastern part of the country. Phil's customers receive a card on their first visit that allows them to receive one free sandwich for every eight sandwiches purchased in a three-month period. Customers must redeem their cards in the month after the three-month period is completed. Each time a customer purchases a sandwich, his or her card is stamped. Past experience shows that only 50 percent of customers accumulate enough stamps within a three-month period to qualify for a free sandwich, and only 80 percent of those customers actually redeem their card to receive a free sandwich. In the first quarter of the current year, Phil's sold 12,000 sandwiches at an average price of $7.00. Phil's only accepts payment in cash.

Required:

Prepare the summary journal entry Phil's Sandwich Company should make to recognize revenue from the sale of sandwiches for the first quarter of the current year.

30. La Panaderia del Sol (LPS), a Mexican bakery, sold a gift card to a customer for 1,000 pesos on December 1, Year 1. At the time of the sale, LPS debited cash and credited an unearned revenue liability. The card has no fees or expiration date. LPS has reliable historical evidence that breakage rates on such cards will be 10 percent of the sales price. The customer redeemed the card during the month of December for food items with menu prices totaling 540 pesos. LPS closes its fiscal year on December 31.

Required:

How much revenue did LPS record for the customer's purchases using the card during December? Compute the value of the unearned revenue liability connected to the card as of December 31, Year 1.

31. KLB Inc. makes satellite phones for the military that incorporate complex software. The company's most recent annual report included the following statement about its revenue recognition policy:

> *Amounts allocated to the delivered hardware and the related essential software are recognized at the time of sale. Amounts allocated to the software upgrade rights are deferred and recognized on a straight-line basis over the 24-month estimated life of the related hardware.*

At the end of the first quarter of the current fiscal year, KLB released SatCom X, a new satellite phone. KLB has decided that the fair value of the "software upgrade rights" for the SatCom X amounts to 25 percent of its sales price. Assume that the military purchased $160 thousand of SatCom X units in the first quarter, $608 thousand in the second quarter, and $512 thousand in both the third and fourth quarters.

Part A. How much sales revenue for the SatCom X did KLB recognize in the second quarter? For simplicity, assume that military rules require all purchases of the phone to occur at the end of the last day of each quarter.

Part B. How much sales revenue did KLB recognize for the SatCom X in the fourth quarter?

Part C. By how much did sales of the SatCom X increase the balance of the unearned revenue account as of the end of the year?

32. Huang Industries, Ltd. (HIL) is based in Singapore and manufactures tools used in Asian auto factories. Shanghai Automotive Industry Corporation (SAIC) purchased $60 million worth of tools from HIL in a single order that was delivered on June 30, the last day of HIL's second fiscal quarter. SAIC may return any portion of the order within three months of delivery for a full refund. HIL's experience with product returns suggests that products that are returned are generally in good enough condition to be restored to inventory and sold at a later date.

    SAIC is a long-term customer that aggressively takes advantage of product return rights but is consistent in its behavior. HIL's accountants estimate that 10 percent of the products shipped to SAIC will eventually be returned.

    Part A. Assume that HIL's gross margin percentage is always 30 percent.

    Required:
    How much pre-tax profit should HIL recognize on the sale in the second fiscal quarter?

    Part B. Assume SAIC returned 9 percent of the shipment on September 12. It did not return any additional product before the right of return expired.

    Required:
    Compute the effect of the sale on HIL's pre-tax income in the third fiscal quarter. Your answer should include the effect of the product return on September 12 as well as the expiry of the right of return on September 30.

33. Ontario Trust Corporation (OTC) purchased 5,000 shares of Lilly Company for $25 per share on November 1, Year 1. As allowed under IFRS 9, OTC chose to classify its investment in Lilly's equity as FVOCI at the time of purchase. Lilly paid a dividend of $1.10 per share on December 1. The year-end market price of Lilly's stock was $28. OTC subsequently sold all 5,000 shares for $27.

    Required:
    Prepare the journal entries required under IFRS as well as those that would be required under U.S. GAAP. Comment on how the investment in Lilly affected OTC's pre-tax income in Years 1 and 2, as well as how income would differ if OTC were a U.S. company.

34. Manitoba Insurance Ltd. (MIL) purchased $10 million of bonds on January 1, Year 1. The bonds were to mature at the end of Year 2 and pay interest equal to 5 percent of their face value at the end of each year they are outstanding. MIL's operations pass IFRS 9's business model test for the FVOCI category. Therefore, MIL categorized the bonds as FVOCI at the time of purchase. MIL received the first interest payment on schedule on December 31, Year 1. As of that date, the bonds' fair value had risen to $11 million due to an economywide drop in interest rates. MIL sold the bonds for $11 million the following day, on January 1, Year 2.

    Required:
    Prepare the journal entries required under IFRS for MIL's investment in the 5 percent bonds. For simplicity, assume that MIL closes its books annually on December 31. Also, prepare an alternative set of journal entries assuming that MIL had categorized the bonds as FVPL instead of FVOCI. Comment on how the investment in the 5 percent bonds affected MIL's pre-tax income in Years 1 and 2, as well as how income would have differed had MIL classified the bonds as FVPL.

35. On January 1, Year 1, Spectrum Fabricators Inc. issues $20 million of convertible bonds at par value. The bonds have a stated annual interest rate of 6 percent, pay interest annually, and come due December 31, Year 5. The bonds are convertible at any time after issuance at the rate of 10 shares of common stock for each $1,000 of the face

value of the convertible bonds. Issuance costs total $100,000. The current market interest rate for nonconvertible bonds is 8 percent.

Required:
Prepare the journal entries to record the issuance of the convertible bonds (round to the nearest dollar). Determine the amount of expense related to the convertible bonds that the company should recognize each year (round to the nearest dollar). [Note: You will need to calculate the effective interest rate on the bonds to determine interest expense. One way to do this is to solve for the internal rate of return (IRR) of the cash flows using Excel.]

36. The Midwest Bank Corporation (MBC) made a five-year $10 million loan to Mattress Mart. The loan carries an annual interest rate of 6 percent. MBC accounts for the loan using the amortized cost method. As of the end of the fiscal year, MBC's statistical credit model estimates the expected value of net credit loss on the loan over the next 12 months to be $100,000. However, the model assigns a comparatively higher probability default over the loan's life. The expected credit loss over this longer time frame is $1.2 million.

Required:
Compute the loan's book value, net of the allowance for credit loss, and interest income recognized on the loan under each of the following scenarios:
a. The loan to Mattress Mart is classified as Stage One.
b. The loan to Mattress Mart is classified as Stage Two.
c. The loan to Mattress Mart is classified as Stage Three.

37. On December 1, Year 1, Traylor Company sells $100,000 of short-term trade receivables to Main Street Bank for $98,000 in cash by guaranteeing to buy back the first $15,000 of defaulted receivables. Traylor's historic rate of noncollection on receivables is 5 percent. Traylor notifies the customers affected that they should make payment on their accounts directly to Main Street Bank.

Required:
Determine whether the sale of receivables by Traylor Company qualifies for derecognition.

38. Bridget's Bakery Inc. enters into a new operating lease for a 10-year term at a monthly rental of $2,500. To induce Bridget's Bakery into the lease, the lessor agreed to provide free rent for the first three months.

Required:
Determine the amount of lease expense, if any, that Bridget's Bakery would recognize in the first month of the lease.

39. On January 1, Year 1, Autonomous Systems Ltd. (ASL) signed a contract to lease computer equipment from Lenovo for three years. The lease agreement requires ASL to pay $30,000 at the end of each year of the lease. The company's borrowing rate is 6 percent. Under U.S. GAAP, the lease would be classified as operating. However, ASL is based in Singapore and will account for the lease using IFRS 16.

Required:
a. Compute the value of the lease liability that ASL will record under IFRS 16 on January 1, Year 1.
b. In each year of the lease, ASL will record depreciation expense on the leasehold asset and interest expense on the lease obligation. Compute the amount of the two expenses in the lease's first year.
c. ASL is partially backed by a U.S. venture capital fund that would like to know how the lease would be accounted for under U.S. GAAP. How much expense would ASL

recognize for the lease if it were a U.S. company and how does this amount differ from the total lease expense recognized under IFRS?

d. How will the lease affect operating cash flow and how would it affect operating cash flow under U.S. GAAP? Assume that ASL classifies interest paid as a financing flow in its statement of cash flows.

40. The Campolino Company has a defined benefit postretirement health-care plan for its employees. To fund the plan, Campolino makes an annual cash contribution to a health-care benefit fund on December 31 of each year. At the beginning of Year 5, Campolino amended the plan to provide additional benefits to all employees. Assume that the health-care benefit fund pays benefits to employees on December 31 of each year.

The following facts apply to the plan for the year ended December 31, Year 5:

Present value of defined benefit obligation (PVDBO) on January 1	$650,000
Plan assets at fair value (FVPA) on January 1	420,000
Service cost	46,000
Past service cost	16,000
Actual return on plan assets	28,000
Employer cash contribution to postretirement benefit fund	50,000
Benefit paid by postretirement benefit fund	42,000
Discount rate	5%
Plan assets at fair value (FVPA) on December 31	$456,000

Required:
Use the following template to determine the postretirement defined benefit cost to be recognized in (a) net income and (b) other comprehensive income (OCI) for the year ended December 31, Year 5, and the postretirement defined benefit liability (asset) at December 31, Year 5, to be reported by Campolino Company under IFRS. Prepare a summary journal entry to reflect the recognition of these amounts.

(Amounts in parentheses represent credits.)

	Campolino Company General Ledger				Benefit Fund General Ledger	
	Defined benefit cost recognized in net income	Defined benefit cost recognized in OCI	Cash	Defined benefit asset (liability)	PVDBO	FVPA
Balance at January 1				$(230,000)	$(650,000)	$420,000
Service cost						
Interest expense						
Interest income						
Net interest						
Excess of actual return on plan assets over interest income						
Past service costs						
Actuarial loss						
Contributions						
Benefits paid						
Balance at December 31						$456,000

41. This problem consists of two parts.

Part A. On January 1, Year 1, Stone Company issued 100 stock options with an exercise price of $38 each to 10 employees (1,000 options in total). The employees can choose to settle the options either (a) in shares of stock ($1 par value) or (b) in cash equal to the intrinsic value of the options on the vesting date. The options vest on December 31, Year 3, after the employees have completed three years of service. Stone Company expects that only seven employees will remain with the company for three years and vest in the options. Two employees resign in Year 1, and the company continues to assume an overall forfeiture rate of 30 percent at December 31, Year 1. In Year 2, one more employee resigns. As expected, seven employees vest on December 31, Year 3, and exercise their stock options.

The following represents the share price and fair value at the relevant dates:

Date	Share Price	Fair Value of Cash Alternative	Fair Value of Stock Alternative
January 1, Year 1	$43	$6.00	$6.00
December 31, Year 1, Year 2	45	8.00	8.00
December 31, Year 3	47	9.00	9.00

Required:
Determine the fair value of the stock options at the grant date and the amount to be recognized as compensation expense in Year 1, Year 2, and Year 3. Prepare journal entries assuming that the vested employees choose (a) the cash alternative and (b) the stock alternative.

Part B. Now assume that if the employees choose to settle the stock options in shares of stock, the employees receive a 10 percent discount on the exercise price (i.e., the exercise price would be $34.20). As a result, the fair value of the share alternative on the grant date is $8.80.

Required:
Determine the fair value of the stock options at the grant date and the amount to be recognized as compensation expense in Year 1.

42. Indicate whether each of the following describes an accounting treatment that is acceptable under IFRS, U.S. GAAP, both, or neither by checking the appropriate box.

	Acceptable Under			
	IFRS	**U.S. GAAP**	**Both**	**Neither**
• Bank overdrafts are netted against cash rather than being recognized as a liability when overdrafts are a normal part of cash management.				
• Uncertain legal obligations, but not constructive obligations, contingent upon a future event are recognized as liabilities when certain criteria are met.				
• A defined benefit pension liability is measured as the excess of the present value of the defined benefit obligation (PVDBO) over the fair value of plan assets (FVPA).				
• Actuarial gains and losses in a defined benefit pension plan are amortized to net income over a period of time.				
• The compensation cost associated with graded-vesting stock options is amortized to expense on a straight-line basis over the vesting period.				
• The minimum amount recognized as compensation expense on a stock option plan is the compensation cost as measured at the grant date, even if a subsequent modification to the plan decreases the total compensation cost.				
• Deferred taxes are classified as current or noncurrent based on the classification of the related asset or liability.				
• A payment on a two-year operating lease is recorded in the operating section of the statement of cash flows.				
• Breakage revenue is recorded on a gift card liability.				
• Fair value gains from holding marketable equity securities are recorded in other comprehensive income (OCI).				

Case 5-1

Accounting for BP PLC's Deepwater Horizon Oil Spill

On April 20, 2010, an explosion at BP PLC's Macondo well in the Gulf of Mexico caused the largest oil spill and one of the worst environmental disasters in U.S. history. Because the incident occurred at the Deepwater Horizon drilling rig, this incident is often referred to as the *Deepwater Horizon* spill. Approximately 4.9 million barrels of oil were released, threatening the marine environment of the Gulf of Mexico as well as the environment and communities of the Gulf Coast region of the United States. In addition, 11 workers died and 17 were injured in the explosion. While BP bore primary legal responsibility for the spill, Transocean Corporation (the drilling rig operator) and Halliburton Company (the construction contractor) were also held partially responsible.

The spill's financial costs to BP were enormous but also highly uncertain in the years that followed. Initially, the company incurred large costs to respond to the explosion and contain the spill. As time passed, the disaster set in motion a complex set of investigations and court cases that resulted in numerous fines and damage awards. In addition, BP made expensive commitments to support various environmental initiatives in the Gulf Coast region.

BP—formerly named British Petroleum and headquartered in London—reports under IFRS and accounted for many of the spill's costs using IAS 37, *Provisions, Contingent Liabilities, and Contingent Assets.* As noted earlier in this chapter, IAS 37 requires accrual of contingent liabilities when they are probable and can be reliably estimated. From the 2010 fiscal year onward, the company disclosed among its significant judgments and estimates those required to account for the spill under IAS 37. Through 2014, KPMG, BP's auditor, included warnings of the uncertainties presented by these contingent liabilities in its auditor's reports. The following passage taken from KPMG's audit opinion in the 2014 annual report expresses these concerns:

> *In forming our opinion on the group financial statements we have considered the adequacy of the disclosure in Note 2 to the financial statements concerning the provisions, future expenditures which cannot be reliably estimated and other contingent liabilities related to the claims, penalties and litigation arising from the Gulf of Mexico oil spill. The total amount that will ultimately be paid by BP in relation to all obligations arising from this significant event is subject to significant uncertainty and the ultimate exposure and cost to BP is dependent on many factors, including but not limited to, the determinations of the Courts and Regulatory authorities in the US. Significant uncertainty exists in relation to the amount of claims that will become payable by BP and the amount of fines that will be levied on BP (including any ultimate determination of BP's culpability based on negligence, gross negligence or willful misconduct). The outcome of litigation and the cost of the longer term environmental consequences of the oil spill are also subject to significant uncertainty. For these reasons it is not possible to estimate reliably the ultimate cost to BP. Our opinion is not qualified in respect of these matters.*

The following table reports the costs recognized by BP through 2014 across four categories. The first—spill response—summarizes the amounts spent directly responding to the explosion and spill. The other three categories are costs initially recorded as contingent liabilities—environmental, litigation and claims, and Clean Water Act penalties. As of December 31, 2014, expenses recognized in the four categories had totaled $47.8 billion.

(in $ millions)	2010	2011	2012	2013	2014	Total 2010–14
Spill response	$13,628	671	118	(113)	–	14,304
Environmental	1,004	1,184	801	42	192	3,223
Litigation and claims	15,123	3,430	5,164	1,926	1,137	26,780
Clean Water Act penalties	3,510	–	–	–	–	3,510
Total	33,265	5,285	6,083	1,855	1,329	47,817
Cumulative Total	33,265	38,550	44,633	46,488	47,817	

The following are summaries of the main spill-related contingent liabilities disclosed in BP's 2014 annual report:

Environmental–As of December 31, 2014, provisions in the Environmental category included the following significant items:

- A commitment to fund the Gulf of Mexico Research Initiative (GoMRI). This was originally a $500 million commitment, of which $279 million had yet to be paid out as of December 31, 2014. The GoMRI is a 10-year environmental research program to study the impact of the spill's long-range environmental impacts. Grants were made to a variety of research institutes, including those affiliated with Louisiana State University, the University of South Florida, Mississippi State University, and the National Institutes of Health.

- A framework agreement between BP, the federal government, and five Gulf Coast states to fund restoration projects in the Gulf Coast region. As of December 31, 2014, $798 million remained of commitments to fund "assessment costs and early restoration projects." However, BP's disclosure for this commitment notes that cost of later restoration projects has not been accrued, or even estimated:

Until the size, location and duration of the impact is assessed, it is not possible to estimate reliably either the amounts or timing of the remaining natural resource damages claims other than the assessment and early restoration costs noted above, therefore no additional amounts have been provided for these items.

Litigation and claims–The litigation and claims provision includes estimates of payments to 1) individuals and businesses for property damage, lost profits, and the impairment of earning capacity, and 2) state and local governments for removal costs, property damages, lost tax revenue, and increased public services. Through 2014, this cost category was by far the largest, containing $26.8 billion of recognized costs. This amount was more than half of total recognized costs and approximately 80 percent of costs recorded in the three contingent liability categories.

Despite the large accruals already made for this category, BP noted that no reliable estimate could be made for future costs and warned that the liability could go much higher. Chief among the lingering uncertainties was the simple fact that many claims had not yet been received, and for those that had been received, many still had not been fully evaluated. The company summarized this uncertainty with the following observation:

There is very little data to build up a track record of claims determinations under the policies and protocols that are now being applied. We therefore cannot estimate future trends of the number and proportion of claims that will be determined to be eligible, nor can we estimate the value of such claims. A provision for such business economic loss claims will be established when these uncertainties are resolved and a reliable estimate can be made of the liability.

As of December 31, 2014, BP had accrued a balance sheet liability for this category of $9.9 billion. However, the company noted:

> *The total cost is likely to be significantly higher than the amount recognized to date of $9.9 billion because the current estimate does not reflect business economic loss claims not yet received, or received but not yet processed, or processed but not yet paid.*

Clean Water Act Penalties—Soon after the spill, BP recorded a contingent liability of $3,510 million for estimated future penalties under Section 311 of the Clean Water Act. It made no subsequent adjustments to this accrual throughout the lengthy court trial that later ensued. A key issue in the trial was whether BP's actions in connection with its operation of the Deepwater Horizon well amounted to *gross negligence* and *willful misconduct*. In September 2014, the U.S. District Court for the District of Eastern Louisiana ruled that BP had acted with gross negligence and willful misconduct. As of the end of 2014, BP was appealing this finding in higher courts. If its appeal were to be unsuccessful, the Clean Water Act penalty could rise to as high as $13.7 billion.

The previous table indicates that BP did not make any adjustment to its balance sheet accrual of $3,510 million in response to the district court's ruling. It did not raise the accrual because it claimed that the ultimate amount of the penalty for gross negligence and willful misconduct could not be reliably measured. Given this new uncertainty, one might reasonably ask the technical accounting question, "Why maintain any accrual at all, given that it is subject to so much uncertainty?" BP answered this question, citing a specific provision of IAS 37:

> *Under IFRS, a provision is reversed when it is no longer probable that an outflow of resources will be required to settle the obligation. With regard to the Clean Water Act penalty obligation, it continues to be probable that there will be an outflow of resources and therefore, in the absence of the ability to identify the best estimate of the liability, the previously recognized provision of $3,510 million has been maintained.*

Required:

1. How did the spill-related costs recognized by BP in its financial statements through 2014 differ from a statistical estimate of the total expected costs that the company's senior management might have prepared and used internally over the same time frame?

2. For each category of contingent liability—environmental, litigation and claims, and Clean Water Act penalties—BP asserts that it is not possible to reliably estimate the full extent of the company's ultimate economic exposure. Identify a specific reason for this uncertainty for each category.

3. Why did BP maintain the $3,510 million provision for the penalty it will have to pay under the U.S. Clean Water Act after the district court's finding of gross negligence and willful misconduct called this amount into question?

4. In 2015 and 2016, BP recognized additional spill-related costs of $18.6 billion, bringing the total cumulative costs recognized across the four categories to over $66 billion. Based on the above information, make an informed guess about how these newly recognized costs were distributed across the four cost categories. How might accounting recognition and disclosure of contingent liabilities be improved to enable readers to formulate better estimates?

Chapter **Six**

Foreign Currency Transactions and Hedging Foreign Exchange Risk

Learning Objectives

After reading this chapter, you should be able to

- Provide an overview of the foreign exchange market.
- Explain how fluctuations in exchange rates give rise to foreign exchange risk.
- Demonstrate the accounting for foreign currency transactions.
- Describe how foreign currency forward contracts and foreign currency options can be used to hedge foreign exchange risk.
- Describe the concepts of cash flow hedges, fair value hedges, and hedge accounting.
- Demonstrate the accounting for forward contracts and options used as cash flow hedges and fair value hedges to hedge foreign currency assets and liabilities, foreign currency firm commitments, and forecasted foreign currency transactions.

INTRODUCTION

International trade (imports and exports) constitutes a significant and growing portion of the world economy. According to the World Trade Organization, more than $17.5 trillion worth of merchandise was exported (and imported) in 2020.[1] Growth in trade has been phenomenal. At the height of the market, from 1990 to 2001, global exports increased by 75 percent, while global gross domestic product increased by only 27 percent.

Apple Inc. is a well-known U.S. multinational corporation that designs, manufactures, and markets smartphones, personal computers, tablets, wearable and accessories, and sells a variety of related services. During 2021 the company's domestic (Americas) and international net sales accounted for 42 and 58 percent of total net sales, respectively (per Apple's Form 10-K for the fiscal year ended September 25, 2021, submitted to the Securities and Exchange Commission). In addition to large corporations like Apple, small businesses also

---

[1] World Trade Organization, *World Trade Statistical Review 2021,* Table A.6, Leading Exporters and Importers in World Merchandise Trade, 2020 (www.wto.org).

are significantly involved in exporting. Companies with fewer than 500 workers comprise 97 percent of U.S. exporters. The total number of companies involved in trade has grown substantially over the years. From 1987 to 1999, the number of U.S. companies making export sales rose by 233 percent, to a total of 231,420 companies.[2] The number of U.S. companies engaged in export according to U.S. Census Bureau reached 270,290 in 2020, of which 263,054 are small and medium exporters (with fewer than 500 employees).[3]

Collections from export sales or payments for imports are not always made in a company's domestic-currency; they may be made in a foreign currency depending on the negotiated terms of the transaction. As the exchange rate for the foreign currency fluctuates, so does the domestic currency value of these export sales and import purchases. Companies often find it necessary to engage in some form of hedging activity to reduce losses arising from fluctuating exchange rates. For example, at the end of September 2021, Apple "uses derivative instruments, such as foreign currency forward and option contracts, to hedge certain exposures to fluctuations in foreign currency exchange rates."[4] At September 25, 2021, the company reported outstanding derivatives instruments to protect gross margins from foreign currency exchange rates fluctuations equal to $76,475 million, up from $57,410 in 2020.

This chapter covers accounting issues related to foreign currency transactions and foreign currency hedging activities. To provide background for subsequent discussion of the accounting issues, we begin with a description of foreign exchange markets. We then discuss the accounting for import and export transactions, followed by coverage of various types of hedging techniques. The discussion concentrates on forward contracts and options because these are the most popular types of hedging instruments. Understanding how to account for these items is important for any company engaged in international transactions. In the chapter we illustrate these concepts using the example of a firm exporting goods and services. Then, in Appendix A, we illustrate the accounting for an importer. Finally, Appendix B covers foreign currency borrowing and loans.

FOREIGN EXCHANGE MARKETS

Each country uses its own currency as the unit of value for the purchase and sale of goods and services. The currency used in the United States is the U.S. dollar, the currency used in Japan is the Japanese yen, and so on. If a U.S. citizen travels to Japan and wishes to purchase local goods, Japanese merchants require payment to be made in Japanese yen. To make the purchase, a U.S. citizen has to purchase yen using U.S. dollars. The price at which the foreign currency can be acquired is known as the *foreign exchange rate*. A variety of factors determine the exchange rate between two currencies; unfortunately for those engaged in international business, the exchange rate fluctuates.[5] In some cases, changes in the exchange rate can be quite large and unexpected.

---

[2] U.S. Department of Commerce, International Trade Administration, "Small and Medium-Sized Enterprises Play an Important Role," *Export America,* September 2001, pp. 26–29.

[3] U.S. Census Bureau, "Preliminary Profile of U.S. Exporting Companies, 2020" November 4, 2021. www.census.gov.

[4] Apple Inc., 2021 Form 10-K, p. 16.

[5] Several theories attempt to explain exchange rate fluctuations, but with little success, at least in the short run. A discussion of exchange rate determination can be found in any international finance textbook. An understanding of the causes of exchange rate changes is not necessary for an understanding of the concepts underlying the accounting for changes in exchange rates.

Exchange Rate Mechanisms

During the period 1945–1973, countries fixed the par value of their currency in terms of the U.S. dollar, and the value of the U.S. dollar was fixed in terms of gold. Countries agreed to maintain the value of their currency within 1 percent of the par value. If the exchange rate for a particular currency began to move outside of this 1 percent range, the country's central bank was required to intervene by buying or selling its currency in the foreign exchange market. Due to the law of supply and demand, the purchase of currency by a central bank would cause the price of the currency to stop falling, and the sale of currency would cause the price to stop rising.

The integrity of the system hinged on the ability of the U.S. dollar to maintain its value in terms of gold and the ability of foreign countries to convert their U.S. dollar holdings into gold at the fixed rate of $35 per ounce. As the United States began to incur balance-of-payment deficits in the 1960s, a glut of U.S. dollars arose worldwide, and foreign countries began converting their U.S. dollars into gold. This resulted in a decline in the U.S. government's gold reserve from a high of $24.6 billion in 1949 to a low of $10.2 billion in 1971. In the latter year, the United States suspended the convertibility of the U.S. dollar into gold, signaling the beginning of the end for the fixed exchange rate system. In March 1973, most currencies were allowed to float in value.

Today, several different currency arrangements exist. The following are some of the more important ones and the countries they affect:

1. *Independent float.* The value of the currency is allowed to fluctuate freely according to market forces, with little or no intervention from the central bank. Countries using this arrangement include Australia, Brazil, Canada, Japan, Mexico, Sweden, Switzerland, and the United States.
2. *Pegged to another currency.* The value of the currency is fixed (pegged) in terms of a particular foreign currency, and the central bank intervenes as necessary to maintain the fixed value. For example, several countries (Hong Kong, Panama, Jordan, and Saudi Arabia, among others) peg their currency to the U.S. dollar.
3. *Euro area.* In 1998, the countries comprising the European Monetary System adopted a common currency called the euro and established the European Central Bank.[6] Until 2002, local currencies such as the German mark and the French franc continued to exist but were fixed in value in terms of the euro. On January 1, 2002, local currencies disappeared and the euro became the currency in 12 European countries. Nowadays, 19 countries are members of the "euro area," with Slovenia joining in 2007, Cyprus and Malta in 2008, Slovakia in 2009, Estonia in 2011, Latvia in 2014, and Lithuania in 2015. The value of the euro floats against other currencies such as the U.S. dollar.

Foreign Exchange Rates

Exchange rates between the U.S. dollar and most foreign currencies are published daily in major U.S. newspapers. Current and past exchange rates are readily obtainable from a variety of Web sites, such as OANDA.com and X-rates.com. U.S. dollar exchange rates at various dates for selected foreign currencies are presented in Exhibit 6.1. These are interbank rates, or wholesale prices, that banks charge one another when exchanging currencies. Prices charged when selling foreign currency to retail customers such as companies engaged in international business are higher, and prices offered to buy foreign currency from retail customers are lower. The difference between the buying and selling rates is the spread through which banks and other foreign exchange brokers earn a profit on foreign exchange trades.

[6] Most long-term members of the European Union (EU) are euro-zone countries. The major exception is the United Kingdom, which decided not to participate. Switzerland is another important European country that is not part of the euro zone because it is not a member of the EU.

EXHIBIT 6.1
Foreign Exchange
Rates: Foreign
Currency per 1.00 USD
(Indirect Quotes) and
U.S. Dollar per Foreign
Currency (Direct
Quotes) on Nov. 6,
2021

U.S. Dollar	1.00 USD	inv. 1.00 USD
Euro	0.861226	1.161135
British pound	0.759076	1.317390
Indian rupee	64.620787	0.015475
Australian dollar	1.300371	0.769011
Canadian dollar	1.270689	0.786975
Singapore dollar	1.361575	0.734443
Swiss franc	0.997412	1.002595
Malaysian ringgit	4.232923	0.236243
Japanese yen	113.723971	0.008793
Chinese yuan renminbi	6.632831	0.150765

EXHIBIT 6.2
Percent Change in the
Last 24 Hours on
Nov. 6, 2021

EUR/USD	−0.03309%
USD/JPY	−0.24393%
GBP/USD	+0.78070%
USD/CHF	−0.21665%
USD/CAD	−0.34224%
EUR/JPY	−0.27695%
AUD/USD	+0.54950%
CNY/USD	+0.06173%

Exhibit 6.1 reflects two exchange rates. One is the U.S. dollar price for one unit of foreign currency. These are known as *direct quotes*. The direct quote for the UK pound on Nov 6, 2021, was $1.317390; in other words, one British pound could be purchased for $1.317390. The other is the number of foreign currency units that can be purchased with one U.S. dollar. These are known as *indirect quotes*. Indirect quotes are simply the inverse of direct quotes. If one British pound costs $1.317390, then $1.00 can purchase only 0.759076 (1/1.317390) British pounds; the indirect quote would be 0.759076.

The percentage changes reported in Exhibit 6.2 demonstrate the great variability that exists in exchange rate changes in terms of both magnitude and direction; exchange rates fluctuate constantly.

Fluctuating exchange rates introduce considerable uncertainty with respect to the cash flows associated with foreign currency transactions. Assume that a U.S. exporter sells parts to an Australian customer on August 6, 2021, with payment of 100,000 Australian dollars (AUD) to be received on November 6, 2021. On August 6, 2021, the U.S. dollar equivalent value of the sale is $79,314 (AUD 100,000 × $0.79314, 1 USD=1.2608 AUD). On November 6, 2021, the U.S. exporter receives AUD 100,000 from the customer and sells them at the spot exchange rate of $0.769011, receiving $76,901. This amount is $2,413 less than what would have been received on August 6, 2021, when the parts were sold. The important point to understand is that, because of fluctuating exchange rates, on August 6, when the sale is made, the U.S. exporter does not know how many U.S. dollars it will receive on November 6 as a result of the sale.

Spot and Forward Rates

Foreign currency trades can be executed on a *spot* or *forward* basis. The *spot rate* is the price at which a foreign currency can be purchased or sold today. In contrast, the *forward rate* is the price today at which foreign currency can be purchased or sold sometime in the future. Because many international business transactions take some time to be completed, the ability to lock in a price today at which foreign currency can be purchased or sold at some future date has definite advantages.

The *Wall Street Journal* publishes forward rates quoted by New York banks for several major currencies (e.g., the Canadian dollar, Japanese yen, Swiss franc, and British pound) on a daily basis. This is only a partial listing of possible forward contracts. A firm and its bank can tailor forward contracts in other currencies and for other time periods to meet the needs of the firm. There is no up-front cost to enter into a forward contract.

The forward rate can exceed the spot rate on a given date, in which case the foreign currency is said to be selling at a *premium* in the forward market, or the forward rate can be less than the spot rate, in which case it is said to be selling at a *discount.* Currencies sell at a premium or a discount because of differences in interest rates between two countries. When the interest rate in the foreign country exceeds the interest rate domestically, the foreign currency sells at a discount in the forward market. Conversely, if the foreign interest rate is less than the domestic rate, the foreign currency sells at a premium.[7] Forward rates are said to be unbiased predictors of the future spot rate.

The spot rate for the Australian dollar on November 6, 2021, was $0.769011, indicating that one Australian dollar could have been sold on that date for $0.769011. On the same day, the one-month forward rate was $0.768817. The Australian dollar was selling at a discount in the one-month forward market. By entering into a forward contract on November 6, it was possible to guarantee that the Australian dollar could be sold one month later at a price of $0.768817 per dollar, regardless of what the spot rate turned out to be on that date. Entering into the forward contract to sell AUD would have been beneficial if the spot rate in one month turned out to be lower than $0.768817. However, such a forward contract would have been detrimental if the future spot rate turned out to be higher than $0.768817. In either case, the forward contract must be honored and Australian dollars must be sold at $0.768817.

Option Contracts

To provide companies more flexibility than exists with a forward contract, a market for *foreign currency options* has developed. A foreign currency option gives the holder of the option *the right but not the obligation* to trade foreign currency in the future. A *put option* refers to the sale of foreign currency by the holder of the option; a *call option* refers to the purchase of foreign currency by the holder of the option. The *strike price* is the exchange rate at which the option will be executed if the holder of the option decides to exercise the option. The strike price is similar to a forward rate. There are generally several strike prices to choose from at any particular time. Most foreign currency options are purchased directly from a bank in the so-called over-the-counter market, but they also may be purchased on the Philadelphia Stock Exchange (PHLX), the London International Financial Futures Exchange (LIFFE), and the Chicago Mercantile Exchange (CME).

Unlike forward contracts, where banks earn their profit through the spread between buying and selling rates, options must actually be purchased by paying an *option premium.* The option premium is a function of two components: intrinsic value and time value. The *intrinsic value* of an option is equal to the gain that could be realized by exercising the option immediately. For example, if the spot rate for a foreign currency is $1.00, a call option (to purchase foreign currency) with a strike price of $0.97 has an intrinsic value of $0.03, whereas a put option (to sell foreign currency) with a strike price of $1.00 or less has an intrinsic value of zero. An option with a positive intrinsic value is said to be "in the money."

The *time value* of an option relates to the fact that the spot rate can change over time and cause the option to become in the money. Even though a 90-day call option with a strike price of $1.00 has zero intrinsic value when the spot rate is $1.00, it will still have a positive

[7] This relationship is based on the theory of interest rate parity, which indicates that the difference in national interest rates should be equal to but opposite in sign to the forward rate discount or premium. This topic is covered in detail in international finance textbooks.

time value because there is a chance that the spot rate could increase over the next 90 days and bring the option into the money.

The value of a foreign currency option can be determined by applying an adaptation of the Black-Scholes option-pricing formula. This formula is discussed in detail in international finance textbooks. In very general terms, the value of an option is a function of the difference between the current spot rate and the strike price, the difference between domestic and foreign interest rates, the length of time to expiration, and the potential volatility of changes in the spot rate. In this book, we provide the premium originally paid for a foreign currency option and its subsequent fair value up to the date of expiration derived from applying the pricing formula.

FOREIGN CURRENCY TRANSACTIONS

Export sales and import purchases are international transactions. When two parties from different countries enter into a transaction, they must decide which of the two countries' currencies to use to settle the transaction. For example, if a U.S. computer manufacturer sells to a customer in Japan, the parties must decide whether the transaction will be denominated (i.e., whether payment will be made) in U.S. dollars or Japanese yen. In some cases, a third country's currency might be used to denominate the transaction.

Assume that a U.S. exporter (Eximco) sells goods to a Spanish customer with payment to be made in euros. In this situation, Eximco has entered into a foreign currency transaction. It must restate the euro amount that actually will be received into U.S. dollars to account for this transaction. This is because Eximco keeps its books and prepares financial statements in U.S. dollars. Although the Spanish importer has entered into an international transaction, it does not have a foreign currency transaction (payment will be made in its home currency) and no restatement is necessary.

Assume that, as is customary in its industry, Eximco does not require immediate payment and allows its Spanish customer three months to pay for its purchases. By doing this, Eximco runs the risk that from the date the sale is made until the date of payment, the euro might decrease in value (depreciate) against the U.S. dollar and the actual number of U.S. dollars generated from the sale will be less than expected. In this situation, Eximco is said to have an *exposure to foreign exchange risk*. Specifically, Eximco has a *transaction exposure*.

Transaction exposure can be summarized as follows:

- *Export sale.* A transaction exposure exists when the exporter allows the buyer to pay in a foreign currency and also allows the buyer to pay sometime after the sale has been made. The exporter is exposed to the risk that the foreign currency might decrease in value between the date of sale and the date of payment, thereby decreasing the amount of domestic currency (U.S. dollars for Eximco) into which the foreign currency can be converted.

- *Import purchase.* A transaction exposure exists when the importer is required to pay in foreign currency and is allowed to pay sometime after the purchase has been made. The importer is exposed to the risk that the foreign currency might increase in price (appreciate) between the date of purchase and the date of payment, thereby increasing the amount of domestic currency that has to be paid for the imported goods.

Accounting Issue

The major issue in accounting for foreign currency transactions is how to deal with the change in the domestic-currency value of the sales revenue and account receivable resulting from the export when the foreign currency changes in value. The corollary issue is how to deal with the change in the domestic-currency value of the foreign currency account payable and goods being acquired in an import purchase.

Assume that Eximco sells goods to a Spanish customer at a price of 1 million euros (€) when the spot exchange rate is $1.50 per euro. If payment were received at the date of sale,

Eximco could have converted €1,000,000 into $1,500,000, and this amount clearly would be the amount at which the sales revenue would be recognized. Instead, Eximco allows the Spanish customer three months to pay for its purchase. At the end of three months, the euro exchange rate to USD is $1.48, and Eximco is able to convert the €1,000,000 received on that date into only $1,480,000. How should Eximco account for this $20,000 change in value?

Accounting Alternatives

Conceptually, there are two methods of accounting for changes in the value of a foreign currency transaction: the one-transaction perspective and the two-transaction perspective. The *one-transaction perspective* assumes that an export sale is not complete until the foreign currency receivable has been collected and converted into U.S. dollars. Any change in the U.S. dollar value of the foreign currency will be accounted for as an adjustment to Accounts Receivable and to Sales. Under this perspective, Eximco would ultimately report Sales at $1,480,000 and an increase in the Cash account of the same amount. This approach can be criticized because it hides the fact that the company could have received $1,500,000 if the Spanish customer had been required to pay at the date of sale. The company incurs a $20,000 loss because of the depreciation in the euro, but that loss is buried in an adjustment to Sales. This approach is not acceptable under either International Financial Reporting Standards (IFRS) or U.S. GAAP.

Instead, both International Accounting Standard (IAS) 21, *The Effects of Changes in Foreign Exchange Rates,* and FASB ASC 830, *Foreign Currency Matters,* require companies to use a *two-transaction perspective* in accounting for foreign currency transactions. This perspective treats the export sale and the subsequent collection of cash as two separate transactions. Because management has made two decisions—(1) to make the export sale, and (2) to extend credit in foreign currency to the customer—the income effect from each of these decisions should be reported separately.

Under the two-transaction perspective, Eximco records the U.S. dollar value of the sale at the date the sale occurs. At that point, the sale has been completed; there are no subsequent adjustments to the Sales account. Any difference between the number of U.S. dollars that could have been received at the date of sale and the number of U.S. dollars actually received at the date of payment due to fluctuations in the exchange rate is a result of the decision to extend foreign currency credit to the customer. This difference is treated as a Foreign Exchange Gain or Loss that is reported separately from Sales in the income statement. Using the two-transaction perspective to account for its export sale to Spain, Eximco would make the following journal entries:

Date of Sale:	Accounts Receivable (€)	1,500,000	
	Sales		1,500,000
	To record the sale and euro receivable at the spot rate of $1.50.		
Date of Payment:	Foreign Exchange Loss	20,000	
	Accounts Receivable (€)		20,000
	To adjust the U.S. dollar value of the euro receivable to the new spot rate of $1.48 and record a foreign exchange loss resulting from the depreciation in the euro.		
	Cash	1,480,000	
	Accounts Receivable (€)		1,480,000
	To record the receipt of €1,000,000 and conversion into U.S. dollars at the spot rate of $1.48.		

Sales are reported in income at the amount that would have been received if the customer had not been given three months to pay the €1,000,000, that is, $1,500,000. A separate Foreign Exchange Loss of $20,000 is reported in income to indicate that because of the decision to extend foreign currency credit to the Spanish customer and because the euro decreased in value, fewer U.S. dollars are actually received.[8]

Note that Eximco keeps its Account Receivable (foreign currency €) account separate from its USD receivables. Companies engaged in international trade need to keep separate payable and receivable accounts in each of the currencies in which they have transactions. Each foreign currency receivable and payable should have a separate account number in the company's chart of accounts.

We can summarize the relationship between fluctuations in exchange rates and foreign exchange gains and losses as follows:

		Foreign Currency (FC)	
Transaction	Type of Exposure	Appreciates	Depreciates
Export sale	Asset (A/R)	Gain	Loss
Import purchase	Liability (A/P)	Loss	Gain

A foreign currency receivable arising from an export sale creates an *asset exposure* to foreign exchange risk. If the foreign currency appreciates, the foreign currency asset increases in terms of domestic-currency value and a foreign exchange gain arises; depreciation of the foreign currency causes a foreign exchange loss. A foreign currency payable arising from an import purchase creates a *liability exposure* to foreign exchange risk. If the foreign currency appreciates, the foreign currency liability increases in domestic-currency value and a foreign exchange loss results; depreciation of the currency results in a foreign exchange gain.

Balance Sheet Date before Date of Payment

What should be done accounting-wise when the balance sheet date (end of period) falls between the date of sale and the date of payment? For example, assume that Eximco shipped goods to its Spanish customer on December 1, Year 1, with payment to be received on March 1, Year 2. Assume that at December 1 the spot rate for euros is $1.50, but by December 31 the euro has appreciated to $1.51. On December 31, Year 1, when the books are closed, is any adjustment needed to account for the fact that the foreign currency receivable has changed in U.S. dollar value since December 1?

The general consensus worldwide is that a foreign currency receivable or foreign currency payable should be revalued at the balance sheet date to account for the change in exchange rates. Under the two-transaction perspective, this means that a foreign exchange gain or loss arises at the balance sheet date. The next question, then, is: What should be done with these foreign exchange gains and losses that have not yet been realized in cash? Should they be included in net income?

The two approaches to accounting for unrealized foreign exchange gains and losses are the deferral approach and the accrual approach. Under the *deferral approach,* unrealized foreign exchange gains and losses are deferred on the balance sheet until cash is actually paid or received. When cash is paid or received, a *realized* foreign exchange gain or loss is then included in income. This approach is not acceptable under either IFRS or U.S. GAAP.

IAS 21 (as well as FASB ASC 830) requires companies to use the *accrual approach* to account for unrealized foreign exchange gains and losses. Under this approach, a firm

---

[8] Note that the foreign exchange loss results because the customer is allowed to pay in euros and is given three months to pay. If the transaction were denominated in U.S. dollars, no loss would result. There would also be no loss if the euros had been received at the date the sale was made.

reports unrealized foreign exchange gains and losses in net income in the period in which the exchange rate changes. Thus, any change in the exchange rate from the date of sale to the balance sheet date results in a foreign exchange gain or loss to be reported in income in that period. Any change in the exchange rate from the balance sheet date to the date of payment results in a second foreign exchange gain or loss that is reported in the second accounting period. The journal entries Eximco would make under the accrual approach are as follows:

12/1/Y1	Accounts Receivable (€)	1,500,000	
	Sales		1,500,000
	To record the sale and euro receivable at the spot rate of $1.50.		
12/31/Y1	Accounts Receivable (€)	10,000	
	Foreign Exchange Gain		10,000
	To adjust the value of the euro receivable to the new spot rate of $1.51 and record a foreign exchange gain resulting from the appreciation in the euro since December 10.		
3/1/Y2	Foreign Exchange Loss	30,000	
	Accounts Receivable (€)		30,000
	To adjust the value of the euro receivable to the new spot rate of $1.48 and record a foreign exchange loss resulting from the depreciation in the euro since December 31.		
	Cash	1,480,000	
	Accounts Receivable (€)		1,480,000
	To record the receipt of €1,000,000 and conversion at the spot rate of $1.48.		

The net impact on income in Year 1 includes Sales of $1,500,000 and a Foreign Exchange Gain of $10,000; in Year 2, a Foreign Exchange Loss of $30,000 is recorded. This results in a net increase in Retained Earnings of $1,480,000 that is balanced by an equal increase in Cash.[9]

One criticism of the accrual approach is that it leads to a *violation of conservatism* when the firm recognizes an unrealized foreign exchange gain at the balance sheet date. In fact, this is one of only two situations in U.S. GAAP (the other relates to trading marketable securities reported at market value) where it is acceptable to recognize an unrealized gain in income. Historically, several European Union (EU) countries (such as Germany and Austria) more strictly adhered to the concept of conservatism. In those countries, if at the balance sheet date the exchange rate had changed such that an unrealized gain had arisen, the change in exchange rate would be ignored and the foreign currency account receivable or payable would continue to be carried on the balance sheet at the exchange rate that existed at the date of the transaction. In contrast, if the exchange rate had changed to cause a foreign exchange loss, the account receivable would be revalued and an unrealized loss would be recorded and reported in income. This is a classic application of conservatism, where unrealized gain and loss are treated differently. With the introduction of the requirement to

[9] Note that the journal entries recorded at March 1, Year 2, could have been combined into the following single entry:

3/1/Y2	Foreign Exchange Loss	30,000	
	Cash	1,480,000	
	Accounts Receivable (€)		1,510,000

use IFRS, this conservative practice is no longer used by EU-based companies in preparing consolidated financial statements.

All foreign currency assets and liabilities carried on a company's books must be restated at the balance sheet date using the spot rate at the balance sheet date. In addition to foreign currency payables and receivables arising from import and export transactions, companies also might have other transactions denominated in a foreign currency, such as dividends receivable from foreign subsidiaries, loans payable to foreign lenders, lease payments receivable from foreign customers, and so on, that must be restated at the balance sheet date. Each of these foreign-currency-denominated assets and liabilities is exposed to foreign exchange risk; therefore, fluctuations in the exchange rate will result in foreign exchange gains and losses.

Many U.S. companies report foreign exchange gains and losses on the income statement in a line item often titled "Other Income (Expense)." Other incidental gains and losses such as gains and losses on sales of assets would be included in this line item as well. Companies must disclose the magnitude of foreign exchange gains and losses if material. For example, the UK subsidiary of Tata Motors (TM), Jaguar Land Rover (JLR), has historically sold more than 80 percent of its cars outside the UK, and most of the foreign sales are invoiced in U.S. dollars. Following the Brexit in late June 2016, the UK pound fell from nearly $1.50 to $1.27. The company appears to have sold its U.S. dollars account receivable with a spot rate of about $1.50 to the pound, and the forward rate sale was very close to the same amount. The company was receiving about 20 percent less pounds per U.S. dollar after the Brexit. This created an estimated exchange loss of about $500 million.

HEDGING FOREIGN EXCHANGE RISK

In the preceding example, Eximco has an asset exposure (account receivable) in euros when it sells goods to the Spanish customer and allows the customer three months to pay for its purchase. If the euro changes in value over the following three months, Eximco incurs a foreign exchange gain/loss. For many companies, the uncertainty of not knowing exactly how much domestic currency will be received on this export sale is of great concern. To avoid this uncertainty, companies often use foreign currency derivatives to hedge against the effect of unfavorable changes in the value of foreign currencies.[10] The two most common derivatives used to hedge foreign exchange risk are foreign currency forward and foreign currency option contracts. Through a forward contract, Eximco can lock in the price at which it will have to sell the euros it receives in three months. Through an option contract, Eximco establishes a price at which it will be able, but is not required, to sell the euros it receives in three months. If Eximco enters into a forward contract or purchases an option contract on the date the sale is made, the derivative is being used as a *hedge of a recognized foreign-currency-denominated asset* (the euro account receivable).

Companies engaged in foreign currency activities often enter into hedging arrangements as soon as a noncancelable sales order is received or a noncancelable purchase order is placed. A noncancelable order that specifies the foreign currency price and date of delivery is known as a *foreign currency firm commitment.* Assume that, on April 1, Eximco accepts an order to sell parts to a customer in Thailand at a price of 20 million Thai baht. The parts will be delivered and payment will be received on May 15. On April 1, before the sale has been made, Eximco enters into a forward contract to sell 20 million Thai baht on May 15. In this case, Eximco is using a foreign currency derivative as a *hedge of an unrecognized foreign currency firm commitment.*

---

[10] A derivative is a financial instrument whose value changes in response to the change in a specified interest rate, security price, commodity price, index of prices or rates, or other variable. The value of a foreign currency derivative changes in response to changes in foreign exchange rates.

Some companies have foreign currency transactions that occur on a regular basis and can be reliably forecast. For example, Eximco regularly purchases components from a supplier in Singapore, making payment in Singapore dollars. Even if Eximco has no contract to make future purchases, it has an exposure to foreign currency risk if it plans to continue making purchases from the Singapore supplier. Assume that, on October 1, Eximco forecasts that it will make a purchase from the Singapore supplier in one month. To hedge against a possible increase in the price of the Singapore dollar, Eximco acquires a call option on October 1 to purchase Singapore dollars in one month. The foreign currency option represents a *hedge of a forecasted foreign-currency-denominated transaction.*

ACCOUNTING FOR DERIVATIVES

In the development of a core set of standards for global use, the International Organization of Securities Commissions (IOSCO) required the International Accounting Standards Board (IASB) to include a standard on the recognition and measurement of financial instruments, off-balance-sheet items, and hedging activities. In 1988, the IASB embarked on a joint project with the Canadian Institute of Chartered Accountants to develop a comprehensive standard in this area. Due to the critical response to an early Exposure Draft, the project was subsequently divided into two parts and IAS 32, *Financial Instruments: Disclosure and Presentation,* was issued in 1995. Work continued on the recognition and measurement dimensions of the project, with a discussion paper published in 1997. Comments on the discussion paper raised numerous issues that caused the IASB to conclude that developing a final standard in the near term was not possible. Therefore, to provide users of IFRS with some guidance in this area, an interim statement, IAS 39, *Financial Statements: Recognition and Measurement,* was issued in 1999.

The IASB continued to work on an integrated standard on financial instruments, with IFRS 9 to replace IAS 39 entirely.[11] Finally in July 2014, with an effective date for annual periods beginning on or after January 1, 2018, the Board issued the complete version of IFRS 9, *Financial Instruments,* which replaces IAS 39 requirements for classification, measurement, impairment, hedge accounting, and derecognition. The following are the general principles with respect to the accounting for derivatives:

1. All derivatives should be reported on the balance sheet as assets and liabilities.
2. Recognize derivatives at fair value (off-balance-sheet treatment is not acceptable).
3. Recognize gains and losses resulting from speculation directly in income.
4. "Hedge accounting" is acceptable for those derivatives used for hedging purposes provided the hedging relationship is clearly defined, measurable, and actually effective. For these transactions, report gains and losses differently, depending on the type of hedge, whether it is classified as fair value or cash flow hedge.

Hedge accounting is described in more detail later in this chapter.

IFRS 9 (as well as FASB ASC 815 and 830) provides guidance for hedges of the following sources of foreign exchange risk:

1. Recognized foreign-currency-denominated assets and liabilities.
2. Unrecognized foreign currency firm commitments.

---

[11] The project was divided into three main phases. As the Board completes each phase, it issues chapters in IFRS 9 that replace the corresponding requirements in IAS 39. In November 2009, the IASB issued the chapters of IFRS 9 relating to the classification and measurement of financial assets. In October 2010, the Board added the requirements related to the classification and measurement of financial liabilities to IFRS 9. In November 2013, the board added a Hedge Accounting chapter.

3. Forecast foreign-currency-denominated transactions.
4. Net investments in foreign operations.

Different accounting requirements apply to each of these different types of foreign currency hedges. This chapter demonstrates the accounting for the first three types of hedges. Hedges of net investments in foreign operations are covered in Chapter 7.

Although an entity should apply IFRS 9 for annual periods beginning on or after January 1, 2018, early adoption is permitted (IFRS 9.7.1.1).

Fundamental Requirement of Derivatives Accounting

In accounting for derivative financial instruments, the fundamental requirement is that all derivatives must be carried on the balance sheet at their fair value. Derivatives are reported on the balance sheet as assets when they have a positive fair value and as liabilities when they have a negative fair value.

The first issue in accounting for derivatives is the determination of fair value. The fair value of derivatives can change over time, causing adjustments to be made to the carrying values of the assets and liabilities. The second issue in accounting for derivatives is the treatment of the unrealized gains and losses that arise from these adjustments.

Determining the Fair Value of Derivatives

The *fair value of a foreign currency forward contract* is determined by reference to changes in the forward rate over the life of the contract, discounted to the present value. Three pieces of information are needed to determine the fair value of a forward contract at any time:

1. The forward rate at the date the forward contract was entered into.
2. The current forward rate for a contract that matures on the same date as the forward contract entered into.
3. A discount rate—typically, the company's incremental borrowing rate.

Assume that Interco enters into a forward contract on November 1 to sell 1 million South African rand on May 1 at a forward rate of $0.15 per rand, or a total of $150,000. There is no cost to Interco to enter into the forward contract, and the forward contract has no value on November 1. On December 31, when Interco closes its books to prepare financial statements, the forward rate to sell South African rand on May 1 has changed to $0.147. On that date, a forward contract for the delivery of 1 million South African rand could be negotiated that would result in a cash inflow on May 1 of only $147,000. This represents a favorable change in the value of Interco's forward contract of $3,000 ($150,000 − $147,000). The fair value of the forward contract on December 31 is the present value of the favorable change of $3,000 that would happen on May 1. Assuming that the company's incremental borrowing rate is 12 percent per year, the fair value of the forward contract must be discounted at the rate of 1 percent per month for four months (from the current date of December 31 to the settlement date of May 1). The fair value of the forward contract at December 31 is $2,883 ($3,000 × 0.96098).[12]

The manner in which the *fair value of a foreign currency option* is determined depends on whether the option is traded on an exchange or has been acquired in the over-the-counter market. The fair value of an exchange-traded foreign currency option is its current market price quoted on the exchange. For over-the-counter options, fair value can be determined by obtaining a price quote from an option dealer (such as a bank). If dealer price quotes are unavailable, the company can estimate the value of an option using the modified Black-Scholes option-pricing model (briefly mentioned earlier in this chapter). Regardless of who

[12] The present value factor for four months at 1 percent per month is calculated as 1/1.01⁴, or 0.96098.

does the calculation, principles similar to those in the Black-Scholes pricing model will be used in determining the fair value of the option.

Accounting for Changes in the Fair Value of Derivatives

Changes in the fair value of derivatives must be included in comprehensive income. *Comprehensive income* is defined as all changes in equity from nonowner sources and consists of two components: net income and other comprehensive income. *Other comprehensive income* consists of unrealized income items that accounting standards require to be deferred in stockholders' equity, such as gains and losses on available-for-sale marketable securities. Other comprehensive income is accumulated and reported as a separate line in the stockholders' equity section of the balance sheet. The account title *Accumulated Other Comprehensive Income* is used in this chapter to describe this stockholders' equity line item.

Gains and losses arising from changes in the fair value of derivatives are recognized initially either (1) on the income statement as a part of net income or (2) on the balance sheet as a component of other comprehensive income. Recognition treatment partly depends on whether the derivative is used for hedging purposes or for speculation.[13] For speculative derivatives, the change in the fair value of the derivative (the unrealized gain or loss) is recognized immediately in net income.[14] The accounting for changes in the fair value of derivatives used for hedging depends on the nature of the foreign exchange risk being hedged and whether the derivative qualifies for hedge accounting.

HEDGE ACCOUNTING

Companies enter into hedging contracts to minimize the adverse effect that changes in exchange rates have on cash flows and net income. As such, companies account for hedges in such a way that the gain or loss from the hedge is recognized in net income in the same period as the loss or gain on the risk being hedged. This approach is known as *hedge accounting*. Hedge accounting for foreign currency derivatives may be used only if three conditions are satisfied (ASC 815-10 and 815-20, *Derivatives and Hedging;* and IFRS 9):

1. The derivative is used to hedge either a fair value exposure or cash flow exposure to foreign exchange risk (nature of the hedge risk).
2. The derivative is highly effective in offsetting changes in the fair value or cash flows related to the hedged item (hedge effectiveness).
3. The derivative is properly documented as a hedge (hedge documentation).

   Each of these conditions is discussed in turn.

Nature of the Hedged Risk

A *fair value exposure* exists if changes in exchange rates can affect the fair value of an asset or liability reported on the balance sheet. To qualify for hedge accounting, the fair value risk must have the potential to affect net income if it is not hedged. For example, there is

---

[13] Companies can acquire derivative financial instruments as investments for speculative purposes. For example, assume the three-month forward rate for Swiss francs is $1.03, and a speculator believes the Swiss franc spot rate in three months will be $1.00. In that case, the speculator would enter into a three-month forward contract to sell Swiss francs. At the future date, the speculator purchases francs at the spot rate of $1.00 and sells them at the contracted forward rate of $1.03, reaping a gain of $0.03 per franc. Of course, such an investment might just as easily generate a loss if the spot rate does not move in the expected direction.

[14] In the next section, we will see that the change in fair value of a derivative designated as the fair value hedge of a foreign-currency-denominated asset or liability also is recognized immediately in net income.

a fair value risk associated with a foreign currency account receivable. If the foreign currency depreciates, the receivable must be written down, with an offsetting loss recognized in net income. A hedge of a firm commitment (for example, a hedge of the exchange rate risk related to an unrecognized contractual commitment by an Italian Airlines to purchase fuel—in U.S. dollars—at a future date) is a hedge of an exposure to a change in fair value (IFRS 9 B6.5.3).

A *cash flow exposure* exists if changes in exchange rates can affect the amount of cash flow to be realized from a transaction, with changes in cash flow reflected in net income. A cash flow exposure exists for (1) recognized foreign currency assets and liabilities, (2) foreign currency firm commitments, and (3) forecasted foreign currency transactions. The purpose of a cash flow hedge is to defer the gain or loss on the hedging instrument to a period or periods in which the hedged expected future cash flows affect profit or loss.

Derivatives for which companies wish to use hedge accounting must be designated as either a *fair value hedge* or a *cash flow hedge.* For hedges of recognized foreign currency assets and liabilities and hedges of foreign currency firm commitments, companies must choose between the two types of designation. Hedges of forecasted foreign currency transactions can qualify only as cash flow hedges. Accounting procedures differ for the two types of hedges. In general, gains and losses on fair value hedges are recognized immediately in net income, whereas gains and losses on cash flow hedges are included in other comprehensive income.[15] Exhibit 6.3 shows the disclosures related to hedge accounting from Nestlé's 2020 Annual Report.

Hedge Effectiveness

For hedge accounting to be used initially, the hedge must be expected to be highly effective in generating gains and losses that will offset losses and gains on the item being hedged. The hedge actually must be effective in generating offsetting gains and losses for hedge accounting to continue to be applied. Previously, IAS 39 involved the calculation of bright lines (80 to 125 percent) to assess the effectiveness of hedging. IFRS 9 replaces this approach with a quantitative approach that depends on the circumstances and can change when the circumstances change.

At inception, a foreign currency derivative can be considered an effective hedge if the critical terms of the hedging instrument match those of the hedged item. Critical terms include the currency type, currency amount, and settlement date. For example, a forward contract to purchase 1 million Japanese yen in 30 days would be an effective hedge of a liability of 1 million Japanese yen that is payable in 30 days. Assessing hedge effectiveness on an ongoing basis can be accomplished using a cumulative dollar offset method.

A hedging contract qualifies for hedge accounting if it meets all of the effectiveness requirements:

1. There is an economic relationship between the eligible hedged item and the hedging instrument;

2. The effect of credit risk does not dominate the value changes that result from that economic relationship;

> Example (IFRS 9 B6.4.8): An example of credit risk dominating a hedging relationship is when an entity hedges an exposure to commodity price risk using an uncollateralised

---

[15] Many companies choose not to designate derivatives used to hedge recognized foreign currency assets and liabilities as hedges per se. In that case, the derivative is accounted for in exactly the same manner as if it had been designated as a fair value hedge; gains and losses are recognized immediately. As a result, designating a hedge of a recognized foreign currency asset/liability as a fair value hedge is of no importance.

EXHIBIT 6.3   Nestlé's 2020 Annual Report Disclosures on Foreign Currency Hedges

Source: Nestlé 2020 Financial Statement, p. 131.

12.2d Derivative assets and liabilities and hedge accounting

Derivative financial instruments

The Group's derivatives mainly consist of currency forwards, options and swaps; commodity futures and options and interest rate swaps. Derivatives are mainly used to manage exposures to foreign exchange, interest rate and commodity price risk as described in section 12.2c Market risk. Derivatives are initially recognized at fair value. They are subsequently remeasured at fair value on a regular basis and at each reporting date as a minimum, with all their gains and losses, realized and unrealized, recognized in the income statement unless they are in a qualifying hedging relationship.

Hedge accounting

The Group designates and documents the use of certain derivatives and other financial assets or financial liabilities as hedging instruments against changes in fair values of recognized assets and liabilities (fair value hedges) and highly probable forecast transactions (cash flow hedges). The effectiveness of such hedges is assessed at inception and verified at regular intervals and at least on a quarterly basis to ensure that an economic relationship exists between the hedged item and hedging instrument. The Group excludes from the designation of the hedging relationship the hedging cost element. Subsequently, this cost element impacts the income statement at the same time as the underlying hedged item. For the designation of hedging relationships on commodities, the Group applies the component hedging model when the hedged item is separately identifiable and measurable in the contract to purchase the materials.

Fair value hedges

The Group uses fair value hedges to mitigate foreign currency and interest rate risks of its recognised assets and liabilities, being mostly financial dept. Changes in fair values of hedging instruments designated as fair value hedges and the adjustments for the risks being hedged in the carrying amounts of the underlying transactions are recognised in the income statement.

Cash flow hedges

The Group uses cash flow hedges to mitigate a particular risk associated with a recognised asset or liability or highly probable forecast transactions, such as anticipated future export sales, purchases of equipment and goods, as well as the variability of expected interest payments and receipts. The effective part of the changes in fair value of hedging instruments is recognised in other comprehensive income, while any ineffective part is recognised immediately in the income statement. When the hedged item results in the recognition of a non-financial asset or liability, including acquired businesses, the gains or losses previously recognised in other comprehensive income are included in the measurement of the cost of the asset or of the liability. Otherwise the gains or losses previously recognised in other comprehensive income are removed and recognised in the income statement at the same time as the hedged transaction.

Undesignated derivatives

Derivatives which are not designated in a hedging relationship are classified as undesignated derivatives. They are acquired in the frame of approved risk management policies.

---

derivative. If the counterparty to that derivative[16] experiences a severe deterioration in its credit standing, the effect of the changes in the counterparty's credit standing might outweigh the effect of changes in the commodity price on the fair value of the hedging instrument, whereas changes in the value of the hedged item depend largely on the commodity price changes.

3. The hedge ratio of the hedging relationship is the same as that resulting from the quantity of the hedged item that the entity actually hedges and the quantity of the hedging

[16] The IFRS website requires registration to access. Much of the content can be viewed through the free basic membership.

instrument that the entity actually uses to hedge that quantity of hedged item. However, that designation shall not reflect an imbalance between the weightings of the hedged item and the hedging instrument that would create hedge ineffectiveness (irrespective of whether recognised or not) that could result in an accounting outcome that would be inconsistent with the purpose of hedge accounting (IFRS 9.6.4.1).

> Example (IFRS 9 B6.4.9): The hedge ratio of the hedging relationship must be the same as that resulting from the quantity of the hedged item that the entity actually hedges and the quantity of the hedging instrument that the entity actually uses to hedge that quantity of hedged item. Hence, if an entity hedges less than 100 per cent of the exposure on an item, such as 85 per cent, it shall designate the hedging relationship using a hedge ratio that is the same as that resulting from 85 per cent of the exposure and the quantity of the hedging instrument that the entity actually uses to hedge those 85 per cent.

Hedge Documentation

For hedge accounting to be applied, the hedging relationship must be formally documented at the inception of the hedge, that is, on the date a foreign currency forward contract is entered into or a foreign currency option is acquired. The hedging company must prepare a document that identifies the hedged item, the hedging instrument, the nature of the risk being hedged, how the hedging instrument's effectiveness will be assessed, and the risk management objective and strategy for undertaking the hedge.

Statement of Cash Flows

How should cash flows arising from hedging instruments be classified in statements of cash flows?

Cash flows arising from hedging instruments are classified as operating, investing, or financing activities, on the basis of the classification of the cash flows arising from the hedged item. While the terminology in IAS 7 has not been updated to reflect IFRS 9, the classification of cash flows arising from hedging instruments in the statement of cash flows should be consistent with the classification of these instruments as hedging instruments under IFRS 9 (IFRS 9 G.2).

HEDGING COMBINATIONS

The specific entries required to account for a foreign currency hedging relationship are determined by a combination of the following factors:

1. The type of item being hedged:
   a. Foreign-currency-denominated asset/liability,
   b. Foreign currency firm commitment, or
   c. Forecasted foreign currency transaction.

2. The nature of the item being hedged:
   a. Existing (or future) asset, or
   b. Existing (or future) liability.

3. The type of hedging instrument being used:
   a. Forward contract,
   b. Option contract,

    c. Swap, or
    d. Futures.

4. The nature of the hedged risk (following IFRS 9):
    a. Fair value hedge,
    b. Cash flow hedge, or
    c. Hedge of a net investment in a foreign operation.

We do not have enough space in this chapter to show the accounting treatment for over 20 different hedging combinations. However, it is important to see the differences in accounting for at least three different types of items being hedged: (1) foreign-currency-denominated assets and liabilities, (2) firm commitments, and (3) forecasted transactions. To simplify, we illustrate the accounting for hedging using the example of an exporting firm that has an existing or future foreign currency asset and that uses forward and option contracts to hedge currency risk. We also show the accounting for both fair value and cash flow hedges. In Appendix A to the chapter we illustrate the accounting for hedging for an importing firm. Chapter 7 covers the hedge of a net investment in a foreign operation.

HEDGES OF FOREIGN-CURRENCY-DENOMINATED ASSETS AND LIABILITIES

Hedges of foreign-currency-denominated assets and liabilities, such as accounts receivable and accounts payable, can qualify as either *cash flow hedges* or *fair value hedges.* To qualify as a cash flow hedge, the hedging instrument must completely offset the variability in the cash flows associated with the foreign currency receivable or payable. If the hedging instrument does not qualify as a cash flow hedge, or if the company elects not to designate the hedging instrument as a cash flow hedge, then the hedge is designated as a fair value hedge. The following lists summarize the basic accounting for the two types of hedges.

Cash Flow Hedge

At each balance sheet date:

1. The hedged asset or liability is adjusted to fair value according to changes in the spot exchange rate, and a foreign exchange gain or loss is recognized in net income.
2. An amount equal to the foreign exchange gain or loss recognized in net income is then transferred to accumulated other comprehensive income (AOCI), to offset any gain or loss on the hedged asset or liability.
3. The derivative hedging instrument is adjusted to fair value (resulting in an asset or liability reported on the balance sheet), with the counterpart recognized as a change in AOCI.
4. An additional amount is removed from AOCI and recognized in net income to reflect *(a)* the current period's amortization of the original discount or premium on the forward contract (if a forward contract is the hedging instrument) or *(b)* the change in the *time value* of the option (if an option is the hedging instrument).

Fair Value Hedge

At each balance sheet date:

1. The hedged asset or liability is adjusted to fair value according to changes in the spot exchange rate, and a foreign exchange gain or loss is recognized in net income.

2. The derivative hedging instrument is adjusted to fair value (resulting in an asset or liability reported on the balance sheet), with the counterpart recognized as a gain or loss in net income.

FORWARD CONTRACT USED TO HEDGE A RECOGNIZED FOREIGN-CURRENCY-DENOMINATED ASSET

We now return to the Eximco example in which the company has a foreign currency account receivable to show the accounting for a hedge of a recognized foreign-currency-denominated asset. In the preceding example, Eximco has an asset exposure in euros when it sells goods to the Spanish customer and allows the customer three months to pay €1,000,000 for its purchase. To hedge its exposure to a decline in the U.S. dollar value of the euro, Eximco decides to enter into a forward contract.

Assume that on December 1, Year 1, the three-month forward rate for euros is $1.485 and Eximco signs a contract with First National Bank to deliver €1,000,000 in three months in exchange for $1,485,000. No cash changes hands on December 1. Given that the spot rate on December 1 is $1.50, the euro is selling at a discount in the three-month forward market (the forward rate is less than the spot rate). Because the euro is selling at a discount of $0.015 per euro, Eximco receives $15,000 less than if payment had been received at the date the goods were delivered ($1,485,000 vs $1,500,000). This $15,000 reduction in cash flow can be seen as an expense; it is the cost of extending foreign currency credit to the foreign customer.[17] Conceptually, this expense is similar to the transaction loss that arises on the export sale. It exists only because the transaction is denominated in a foreign currency. The major difference is that Eximco knows the exact amount of the discount expense at the date of sale, whereas, if the receivable is left unhedged, Eximco will not know whether there will be a transaction loss (or gain) nor the size until three months pass.

Given that the future spot rate turns out to be only $1.48, selling euros at a forward rate of $1.485 is obviously better than leaving the euro receivable unhedged—Eximco will receive $5,000 more as a result of the hedge. This can be viewed as a gain resulting from the use of the forward contract. Unlike the discount expense, the exact size of this gain is not known until three months pass.

Eximco must account for its foreign currency transaction and the related forward contract simultaneously but separately. The process can be better understood by referring to the steps involving the three parties—Eximco, the Spanish customer, and First National Bank—shown in Exhibit 6.4.

Because the settlement date, currency type, and currency amount of the forward contract match the corresponding terms of the account receivable, the hedge is expected to be highly effective. If Eximco properly designates the forward contract as a hedge of its euro account receivable position, hedge accounting may be applied. In particular, because it completely offsets the variability in the cash flows related to the accounting receivable, the forward contract may be designated as a cash flow hedge. Otherwise, Eximco may elect to account for this forward contract as a fair value hedge.

Eximco determines the fair value of the forward contract by referring to the change in the forward rate for a contract maturing on March 1, Year 2. The relevant exchange rates,

---

[17] This should not be confused with the cost associated with normal credit risk; that is, the risk that the customer will not pay for its purchase. That is a separate issue unrelated to the currency in which the transaction is denominated.

EXHIBIT 6.4
Hedge of a Foreign
Currency Account
Receivable with a
Forward Contract

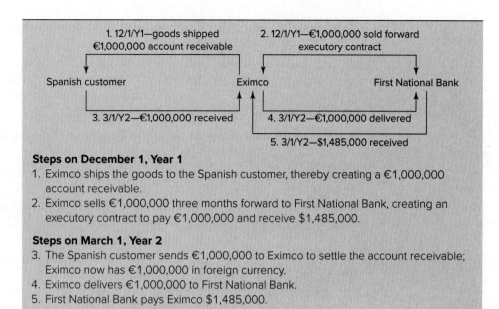

Steps on December 1, Year 1
1. Eximco ships the goods to the Spanish customer, thereby creating a €1,000,000 account receivable.
2. Eximco sells €1,000,000 three months forward to First National Bank, creating an executory contract to pay €1,000,000 and receive $1,485,000.

Steps on March 1, Year 2
3. The Spanish customer sends €1,000,000 to Eximco to settle the account receivable; Eximco now has €1,000,000 in foreign currency.
4. Eximco delivers €1,000,000 to First National Bank.
5. First National Bank pays Eximco $1,485,000.

U.S. dollar value of the euro receivable, and fair value of the forward contract are determined as follows:

		Account Receivable (€)			Forward Contract	
Date	Spot Rate	U.S. Dollar Value	Change in U.S. Dollar Value	Forward Rate to 3/1/Y2	Fair Value	Change in Fair Value
12/1/Y1	$1.50	$1,500,000	—	$1.485	$0	—
12/31/Y1	1.51	1,510,000	+$10,000	1.496	(10,783)*	−$10,783
3/1/Y2	1.48	1,480,000	−$30,000	1.480	5,000†	+$15,783

* $1,485,000 − $1,496,000 = $(11,000) × 0.9803 = $(10,783), where 0.9803 is the present value factor for two months at an annual interest rate of 12 percent (1 percent per month) calculated as $1/1.01^2$.
† $1,485,000 − $1,480,000 = $5,000.

Eximco does not pay anything to enter into the forward contract at December 1, Year 1, because the forward contract is an executory contract. The forward contract has a fair value of zero on that date. At December 31, Year 1, the forward rate for a contract to deliver euros on March 1, Year 2, is $1.496. That means that on December 31, Year 1, Eximco could enter a forward contract to sell €1,000,000 on March 1, Year 2, for $1,496,000. But, because Eximco is committed to sell €1,000,000 for $1,485,000, the nominal value of the forward contract is equal to the difference, negative $11,000. The fair value of the forward contract is the present value at December 31, Year 1, of this amount. Assuming that Eximco has an incremental borrowing rate of 12 percent per year (1 percent per month), and discounting for two months (from 12/31/Y1 to 3/1/Y2), the fair value of the forward contract at December 31, Year 1, is negative $10,783 (a liability). On March 1, Year 2, the forward rate to sell euros on that date is equal to the spot rate—$1.48. At that rate, €1,000,000 could be sold for $1,480,000. Because Eximco has a contract to sell euros for $1,485,000, the fair value of the forward contract on March 1, Year 2, is $5,000 (an asset). This represents an increase in fair value from December 31, Year 1, of $15,783. The original discount on the forward contract is determined by the difference in the euro spot rate and three-month forward rate on December 1, Year 1: ($1.485 − $1.50) × €1,000,000 = $15,000.

Forward Contract Designated as Cash Flow Hedge

Assume that Eximco designates this forward contract as a *cash flow hedge* of a foreign-currency-denominated asset. In this case, the original forward discount or premium is allocated to net income over the life of the forward contract using an effective interest method. The company would prepare the following journal entries to account for the foreign currency transaction and the related forward contract:

Year 1 Journal Entries—Forward Contract Designated as a Cash Flow Hedge

12/1/Y1	Accounts Receivable (€)	$1,500,000	
	Sales		$1,500,000
	To record the sale and €1,000,000 account receivable at the spot rate of $1.50 (Step 1 in Exhibit 6.4).		

There is no formal entry for the forward contract, as it is an executory contract (no cash changes hands) and has a fair value of zero (Step 2 in Exhibit 6.4).

A memorandum would be prepared designating the forward contract as a hedge of the risk of changes in the cash flow to be received on the foreign currency account receivable resulting from changes in the U.S. dollar—euro exchange rate. Missing this documentation, the hedge cannot be designated and accounted for as a cash flow hedge.

12/31/Y1	Accounts Receivable (€)	$10,000	
	Foreign Exchange Gain		$10,000
	To adjust the value of the euro receivable to the new spot rate of $1.51 and record a foreign exchange gain resulting from the appreciation of the euro since December 1.		
	Loss on Forward Contract	$10,000	
	Accumulated Other Comprehensive Income (AOCI) . . .		$10,000
	To record a loss on forward contract to offset the foreign exchange gain on account receivable with a corresponding credit to AOCI.		
	Accumulated Other Comprehensive Income (AOCI)	$10,783	
	Forward Contract[18]		$10,783
	To record the forward contract as a liability at its fair value of $10,783 with a corresponding debit to AOCI.		
	Discount Expense	$ 5,017	
	Accumulated Other Comprehensive Income (AOCI) . . .		$5,017
	To allocate the forward contract discount to net income over the life of the contract using the effective interest method with a corresponding credit to AOCI.		

The first entry on 12/31/Y1 ensures that the foreign-currency-denominated asset is reported on the balance sheet at its current U.S. dollar value of $1,510,000 and that its change in U.S. dollar value is reflected as a $10,000 gain in income. The second entry achieves the objective of hedge accounting by transferring $10,000 to AOCI as a loss on

[18] "Forward Contract" is a generic account title. In practice, the balance sheet line item in which forward contract assets and liabilities are recognized will differ across companies. Chevron Corporation, for example, indicates that the fair values of forward contracts are reported on the Consolidated Balance Sheet as "Accounts and notes receivable, net" or "Accrued liabilities," with gains and losses reported in "Other income" (2009 Form 10-K, Note 10: Financial and Derivative Instruments).

forward contract. As a result of this entry, the loss on forward contract of $10,000 and the foreign exchange gain on the account receivable of $10,000 exactly offset one another, and the net impact on income is zero–this is the essence of hedge accounting. The forward contract should be reported on the balance sheet as a liability. Thus, the third entry makes a credit of $10,783 to Forward Contract. Under cash flow hedge accounting, the change in the fair value of the forward contract, which has gone from $0 to $(10,783), is not recognized immediately in income, but is instead deferred in stockholders' equity. Thus, the debit of $10,783 in the third entry is made to AOCI. As a result of the second and third entries, the forward contract is reported on the balance sheet as a liability at its fair value of $(10,783); a loss on forward contract is recognized in the amount of $10,000 to offset the foreign exchange gain; and AOCI has a negative (debit) balance of $783. The second and third entries could be combined into one entry as follows:

Loss on Forward Contract	10,000	
Accumulated Other Comprehensive Income (AOCI)	783	
Forward Contract		10,783

The negative balance in AOCI of $783 can be understood as that portion of the loss on the forward contract (decrease in fair value of the forward contract) that is not recognized in net income, but instead is deferred in stockholders' equity. Under cash flow hedge accounting, a loss on the hedging instrument (forward contract) is recognized only to the extent that it offsets a gain on the item being hedged (account receivable).

The last entry uses the effective interest method to allocate a portion of the $15,000 forward contract discount as an expense to net income. The company calculates the implicit interest rate associated with the forward contract by considering the fact that the forward contract will generate cash flow of $1,485,000 from a foreign currency asset with an initial value of $1,500,000. Because the discount of $15,000 accrues over a three-month period, the effective interest rate is calculated as $1 - \sqrt[3]{\$1,485,000 / \$1,500,000} = 0.003345$. The amount of discount to be allocated to net income for the month of December, Year 1, is $1,500,000 × 0.3345% = $5,017. A debit of $5,017 is made to Discount Expense in the last journal entry on 12/31/Y1. By making the credit in this journal entry to AOCI, the theoretically correct amounts are reported in net income and on the balance sheet, and the balance sheet remains in balance, as is shown next.

The impact on Year 1 net income is as follows:

Sales		$1,500,000
Foreign Exchange Gain	$ 10,000	
Loss on Forward Contract	(10,000)	
Net gain (loss)		0
Discount Expense		(5,017)
Impact on net income		$1,494,983

The effect on the December 31, Year 1, balance sheet is as follows:

Assets		Liabilities and Stockholders' Equity	
Accounts receivable (€)	$1,510,000	Forward contract	$ 10,783
		Retained earnings	1,494,983
		AOCI	4,234
			$1,510,000

Year 2 Journal Entries—Forward Contract Designated as Cash Flow Hedge

3/1/Y2	Foreign Exchange Loss	$30,000	
	Accounts Receivable (€)		$30,000
	To adjust the value of the euro receivable to the new spot rate of $1.48 and record a foreign exchange loss resulting from the depreciation of the euro since December 31.		
	Accumulated Other Comprehensive Income (AOCI)	$30,000	
	Gain on Forward Contract		$30,000
	To record a gain on forward contract to offset the foreign exchange loss on account receivable with a corresponding debit to AOCI.		
	Forward Contract	$15,783	
	Accumulated Other Comprehensive Income (AOCI)		$15,783
	To adjust the carrying value of the forward contract to its current fair value of $5,000 with a corresponding credit to AOCI.		
	Discount Expense	$9,983	
	Accumulated Other Comprehensive Income (AOCI)		$9,983
	To allocate the remaining forward contract discount to net income ($15,000 − $5,017 = $9,983) with a corresponding credit to AOCI.		

As a result of these entries, the balance in AOCI is zero: $4,234 − $30,000 + $15,783 + $9,983 = $0.

Foreign Currency (€)	$1,480,000	
Accounts Receivable (€)		$1,480,000
To record receipt of €1,000,000 from the Spanish customer as an asset (Foreign Currency) at the spot rate of $1.48 (Step 3 in Exhibit 6.4).		
Cash	$1,485,000	
Foreign Currency (€)		$1,480,000
Forward Contract		5,000
To record settlement of the forward contract, that is, record receipt of $1,485,000 in exchange for delivery of €1,000,000, and remove the forward contract from the accounts (Steps 4 and 5 in Exhibit 6.4).		

The impact on Year 2 net income is:

Foreign Exchange Loss	$(30,000)	
Gain on Forward Contract	30,000	
Net gain (loss)		0
Discount Expense		(9,983)
Impact on net income		$(9,983)

The net effect on the balance sheet over the two years is an increase in cash of $1,485,000 with a corresponding increase in retained earnings of $1,485,000 ($1,494,983 − $9,983). The cumulative Discount Expense of $15,000 reflects the cost of extending credit to the Spanish customer.

The net benefit from having entered into the forward contract is $5,000. Eximco has a cash inflow of $1,485,000 rather than the $1,480,000 that would have been received without a forward contract. This "gain" is reflected in net income as the difference between the net Gain on Forward Contract and the cumulative Discount Expense ($20,000 − $15,000 = $5,000) recognized over the two periods.

Effective Interest versus Straight-Line Methods

Use of the effective interest method results in allocation of the forward contract discount of $5,017 at the end of the first month and $9,983 at the end of the next two months. Straight-line allocation on a monthly basis of the $15,000 discount would result in a reasonable approximation of these amounts:

$$12/31/Y1 \ldots\ldots\ldots \quad \$15,000 \times \frac{1}{3} = \$5,000$$

$$3/1/Y2 \ldots\ldots\ldots \quad \$15,000 \times \frac{2}{3} = \$10,000$$

Determining the effective interest rate is complex, and no conceptual insights are gained by its use. For the remainder of this chapter, we use straight-line allocation of forward contract discounts and premiums, as is allowed by the FASB. The important thing to keep in mind in this example is that, with a cash flow hedge, an expense equal to the original forward contract discount ($15,000 in this example) is recognized in net income over the life of the contract.

What if the forward rate on December 1, Year 1, had been $1.506 (i.e., the euro was selling at a premium in the forward market)? In that case, Eximco would receive $6,000 more through the forward sale of euros ($1,506,000) than if the euros had been received and converted into dollars at the date of sale ($1,500,000). The forward contract premium would be allocated, following straight-line allocation, as an increase in net income at the rate of $2,000 per month: $2,000 at 12/31/Y1 and $4,000 at 3/1/Y2.

Forward Contract Designated as Fair Value Hedge

Assume that Eximco decides not to designate the forward contract as a cash flow hedge, but instead elects to treat it as a fair value hedge. In that case, the gain or loss on the forward contract is taken directly to net income and there is no separate amortization of the original discount on the forward contract.

Year 1 Journal Entries—Forward Contract Designated as a Fair Value Hedge

12/1/Y1	Accounts Receivable (€)	$1,500,000	
	Sales		$1,500,000
	To record the sale and €1,000,000 account receivable at the spot rate of $1.50 (Step 1 in Exhibit 6.4).		

There is no formal entry for the forward contract (Step 2 in Exhibit 6.4). A memorandum would be prepared designating the forward contract as a hedge of the risk of changes in the fair value of the foreign currency account receivable resulting from changes in the U.S. dollar—euro exchange rate.

12/31/Y1	Accounts Receivable (€)	$10,000	
	Foreign Exchange Gain		$10,000
	To adjust the value of the euro receivable to the new spot rate of $1.51 and record a foreign exchange gain resulting from the appreciation of the euro since December 1.		
	Loss on Forward Contract	$10,783	
	Forward Contract		$10,783
	To record the forward contract as a liability at its fair value of $10,783 and record a forward contract loss for the change in the fair value of the forward contract since December 1.		

The impact on Year 1 net income is:

Sales		$1,500,000
Foreign Exchange Gain	$ 10,000	
Loss on Forward Contract	(10,783)	
Net gain (loss)		(783)
Impact on net income		$1,499,217

The effect on the December 31, Year 1, balance sheet is:

Assets		Liabilities and Stockholders' Equity	
Accounts receivable (€)	$1,510,000	Forward contract	$ 10,783
		Retained earnings	1,499,217
			$1,510,000

Year 2 Journal Entries—Forward Contract Designated as a Fair Value Hedge

3/1/Y2	Foreign Exchange Loss	$30,000	
	Accounts Receivable (€)		$ 30,000
	To adjust the value of the euro receivable to the new spot rate of $1.48 and record a foreign exchange loss resulting from the depreciation of the euro since December 31.		
	Forward Contract	$15,783	
	Gain on Forward Contract		$ 15,783
	To adjust the carrying value of the forward contract to its current fair value of $5,000 and record a forward contract gain for the change in the fair value since December 31.		
	Foreign Currency (€)	$1,480,000	
	Accounts Receivable (€)		$1,480,000
	To record receipt of €1,000,000 from the Spanish customer as an asset at the spot rate of $1.48 (Step 3 in Exhibit 6.4).		
	Cash	$1,485,000	
	Foreign Currency (€)		$1,480,000
	Forward Contract		5,000
	To record settlement of the forward contract, that is, record receipt of $1,485,000 in exchange for delivery of €1,000,000 and remove the forward contract from the accounts (Steps 4 and 5 in Exhibit 6.4).		

EXHIBIT 6.5

Microsoft Company
Annual Report
2020

Financial Instruments—Derivatives (p. 55)

Derivative instruments are recognized as either assets or liabilities and measured at fair value. The accounting for changes in the fair value of a derivative depends on the intended use of the derivative and the resulting designation. For derivative instruments designated as fair value hedges, gains and losses are recognized in other income (expense), net with offsetting gains and losses on the hedged items. Gains and losses representing hedge components excluded from the assessment of effectiveness are recognized in other income (expense), net. For derivative instruments designated as cash flow hedges, gains and losses are initially reported as a component of other comprehensive income and subsequently recognized in earnings with the corresponding hedged item. Gains and losses representing hedge components excluded from the assessment of effectiveness are recognized in earnings. For derivative instruments that are not designated as hedges, gains and losses from changes in fair values are primarily recognized in other income (expense), net.

The impact on Year 2 net income is as follows:

Foreign Exchange Loss	$(30,000)
Gain on Forward Contract	15,783
Impact on Net Income	$(14,217)

The net effect on the balance sheet for the two years is an increase in cash of $1,485,000 with a corresponding increase in retained earnings of $1,485,000.

Under fair value hedge accounting, the original forward contract discount is not amortized systematically over the life of the contract. Instead, it is recognized in income as the difference between the Foreign Exchange Gain (Loss) on the account receivable and the Gain (Loss) on the Forward Contract, that is, $(783) in Year 1 and $(14,217) in Year 2. The net impact on net income over the two years is $(15,000), which reflects the cost of extending credit to the Spanish customer. The net Gain on Forward Contract of $5,000 ($10,783 loss in Year 1 and $15,783 gain in Year 2) reflects the net benefit—that is, the increase in cash inflow—from Eximco's decision to hedge the euro receivable.

If the forward contract is not designated as a hedging instrument, the accounting is the same as for a fair value hedge of a foreign-currency-denominated asset or liability: changes in the fair value of the forward contract are immediately recognized in net income. Exhibit 6.5 provides an excerpt from Microsoft Company annual report describing the accounting for forward contracts used as hedges of foreign-currency-denominated assets and liabilities that demonstrate this point.

FOREIGN CURRENCY OPTION USED TO HEDGE A RECOGNIZED FOREIGN-CURRENCY-DENOMINATED ASSET

As an alternative to a forward contract, Eximco could hedge its exposure to foreign exchange risk arising from the euro account receivable by purchasing a foreign currency put option. A put option would give Eximco the right (but not the obligation) to sell €1,000,000 on March 1, Year 2, at a predetermined strike price. Assume that on December 1, Year 1,

Eximco purchases an over-the-counter option from its bank with a strike price of $1.50 when the spot rate is $1.50 and pays a premium of $0.009 per euro.[19] Thus, the purchase price for the option is $9,000 (€1,000,000 × $0.009).

Because the strike price and spot rate are the same, there is no intrinsic value associated with this option. The premium is based solely on time value; that is, it is possible that the euro will depreciate and the spot rate on March 1, Year 2, will be less than $1.50, in which case the option will be in the money. If the spot rate for euros on March 1, Year 2, is less than the strike price of $1.50, Eximco will exercise its option and sell its €1,000,000 at the strike price of $1.50. If the spot rate for euros in three months is greater than the strike price of $1.50, Eximco will not exercise its option and instead will sell euros at the higher spot rate. By purchasing this option, Eximco is guaranteed a minimum cash flow of $1,491,000 ($1,500,000 from exercising the option less the $9,000 cost of the option) from the export sale. There is no limit to the maximum number of U.S. dollars that could be received.

As is true for other derivative financial instruments, foreign currency options must be reported on the balance sheet at fair value. The fair value of a foreign currency option at the balance sheet date is determined by reference to the premium quoted by banks on that date for an option with a similar expiration date. Banks (and other sellers of options) determine the current premium by incorporating relevant variables at the balance sheet date into the modified Black-Scholes option-pricing model. Changes in value for the euro account receivable and the foreign currency option are summarized as follows:

		Account Receivable (€)		Option Premium for 3/1/Y2	Foreign Currency Option	
Date	Spot Rate	U.S. Dollar Value	Change in U.S. Dollar Value		Fair Value	Change in Fair Value
12/1/Y1	$1.50	$1,500,000	—	$0.009	$9,000	—
12/31/Y1	1.51	1,510,000	+$10,000	0.006	6,000	−$3,000
3/1/Y2	1.48	1,480,000	−$30,000	0.020	20,000	+$14,000

Option Designated as Cash Flow Hedge

Assume that Eximco designates the foreign currency option as a *cash flow hedge* of a foreign-currency-denominated asset. In this case, the change in the option's time value is recognized immediately in net income, and then offset through a corresponding entry in AOCI. The company prepares the following journal entries to account for the foreign currency transaction and the related foreign currency option:

Year 1 Journal Entries—Option Designated as a Cash Flow Hedge

12/1/Y1	Accounts Receivable (€)	$1,500,000	
	Sales		$1,500,000
	To record the sale and €1,000,000 account receivable at the spot rate of $1.50.		
	Foreign Currency Option	$9,000	
	Cash		$ 9,000
	To record the purchase of the foreign currency option as an asset at its fair value of $9,000.		

[19] The price of the option (the premium) was determined by the seller of the option through the use of a variation of the Black-Scholes option-pricing formula.

12/31/Y1	Accounts Receivable (€)	$10,000	
	Foreign Exchange Gain........................		$10,000
	To adjust the value of the euro receivable to the new spot rate of $1.51 and record a foreign exchange gain resulting from the appreciation of the euro since December 1.		
	Loss on Foreign Currency Option	$10,000	
	Accumulated Other Comprehensive Income (AOCI)................................		$10,000
	To record a loss on foreign currency option to off-set the foreign exchange gain on the euro account receivable with a corresponding credit to AOCI.		
	Accumulated Other Comprehensive Income (AOCI)	$3,000	
	Foreign Currency Option		$ 3,000
	To adjust the fair value of the option from $9,000 to $6,000 with a corresponding debit to AOCI.		
	Option Expense....................................	$3,000	
	Accumulated Other Comprehensive Income (AOCI)................................		$ 3,000
	To recognize the change in the time value of the option as a decrease in net income with a corresponding credit to AOCI.		

The impact on Year 1 net income is as follows:

Sales		$1,500,000
Foreign Exchange Gain....................................	$10,000	
Loss on Foreign Currency Option	(10,000)	
Net gain (loss)		0
Option Expense..		(3,000)
Impact on net income....................................		$1,497,000

The effect on the December 31, Year 1, balance sheet is:

Assets		Liabilities and Stockholders' Equity	
Cash	$ (9,000)	Retained earnings.......	$1,497,000
Accounts receivable (€).........	1,510,000	AOCI	10,000
Foreign currency option	6,000		$1,507,000
	$1,507,000		

At March 1, Year 2, the option has increased in fair value by $14,000–time value decreases by $6,000, and intrinsic value increases by $20,000. The accounting entries made in Year 2 are as follows:

Year 2 Journal Entries—Option Designated as a Cash Flow Hedge

3/1/Y2	Foreign Exchange Loss	$30,000	
	Accounts Receivable (€).........................		$30,000
	To adjust the value of the euro receivable to the new spot rate of $0.98 and record a foreign exchange loss resulting from the depreciation of the euro since December 31.		

Account	Debit	Credit
Accumulated Other Comprehensive Income (AOCI)	$30,000	
Gain on Foreign Currency Option		$30,000
To record a gain on foreign currency option to offset the foreign exchange gain on account receivable with a corresponding debit to AOCI.		
Foreign Currency Option	$14,000	
Accumulated Other Comprehensive Income (AOCI)		$14,000
To adjust the fair value of the option from $6,000 to $20,000 with a corresponding credit to AOCI.		
Option Expense	$6,000	
Accumulated Other Comprehensive Income (AOCI)		$6,000
To recognize the change in the time value of the option as a decrease in net income with a corresponding credit to AOCI.		
Foreign Currency (€)	$1,480,000	
Accounts Receivable (€)		$1,480,000
To record receipt of €1,000,000 from the Spanish customer as an asset at the spot rate of $1.48.		
Cash	$1,500,000	
Foreign Currency (€)		$1,480,000
Foreign Currency Option		20,000
To record exercise of the option, that is, record receipt of $1,500,000 in exchange for delivery of €1,000,000, and remove the foreign currency option from the accounts.		

The impact on Year 2 net income is as follows:

Foreign Exchange Loss	$(30,000)
Gain on Foreign Currency Option	30,000
Net gain (loss)	0
Option Expense	(6,000)
Impact on net income	$(6,000)

Over the two accounting periods, Eximco would report Sales of $1,500,000 and a cumulative Option Expense of $9,000. The net effect on the balance sheet is an increase in cash of $1,491,000 ($1,500,000 − $9,000) with a corresponding increase in retained earnings of $1,491,000 ($1,497,000 − $6,000).

The net benefit from having acquired the option is $11,000. Eximco has a net cash inflow of $1,491,000 rather than only $1,480,000 if the option had not been purchased. This "gain" is reflected in net income as the net Gain on Foreign Currency Option less the cumulative Option Expense ($20,000 − $9,000 = $11,000) recognized over the two accounting periods.

Spot Rate Exceeds Strike Price

If the spot rate at March 1, Year 2, had been greater than the strike price of $1.50, Eximco would allow its option to expire unexercised and instead sell its foreign currency (€) at the spot rate. The fair value of the foreign currency option on March 1, Year 2, would be $0. The journal entries for Year 1 to reflect this scenario would be the same as above. The option would be reported as an asset on the December 31, Year 1, balance sheet at $6,000, and the euro receivable would have a carrying value of $1,510,000. The entries on March 1, Year 2, assuming a spot rate on that date of $1.505 (rather than $1.48), would be as follows:

3/1/Y2	Foreign Exchange Loss	$5,000	
	Accounts Receivable (€)		$5,000
	To adjust the value of the euro receivable to the new spot rate of $1.505 and record a foreign exchange loss resulting from the depreciation of the euro since December 31.		
	Loss on Foreign Currency Option	$6,000	
	Foreign Currency Option		$6,000
	To adjust the fair value of the option from $6,000 to $0 and record a loss on foreign currency option for the change in fair value since December 31.		
	Accumulated Other Comprehensive Income (AOCI)	$5,000	
	Gain on Foreign Currency Option		$5,000
	To record a gain on foreign currency option to offset the foreign exchange loss on account receivable with a corresponding debit to AOCI.		
	Foreign Currency (€)	$1,505,000	
	Accounts Receivable (€)		$1,505,000
	To record receipt of €1,000,000 from the Spanish customer as an asset at the spot rate of $1.505.		
	Cash	$1,505,000	
	Foreign Currency (€)		$1,505,000
	To record the sale of €1,000,000 at the spot rate of $1.505.		

The preceding entries result in a credit balance in AOCI of $5,000. The following entry must be made to close AOCI and recognize a corresponding increase in net income.

Accumulated Other Comprehensive Income (AOCI)	$5,000	
Adjustment to Net Income		$5,000
To close the balance in AOCI as an adjustment to net income.		

As a result of the last entry, net income related to this hedged transaction is a total of $1,496,000 ($1,500,000 Sales − $9,000 Option Expense + $5,000 Adjustment to Net Income), which is exactly equal to the net increase in cash ($1,505,000 − $9,000). In practice, companies might use a variety of account titles for the adjustment to net income that results from closing AOCI.

Option Designated as Fair Value Hedge

If Eximco had decided to designate the foreign currency option as a fair value hedge, the gain or loss on the option would have been taken directly to net income and there would have been no separate recognition of the change in the time value of the option. The net gain (loss) recognized in Year 1 and Year 2 would be different from the amounts recognized under the cash flow hedge, but over the two-year period, the same amount of net income would be recognized. The accounting method (fair value hedge or cash flow hedge) has no impact on cash flows or on the net amount of income recognized.

HEDGES OF UNRECOGNIZED FOREIGN CURRENCY FIRM COMMITMENTS

In the examples thus far, Eximco does not enter into a hedge of its export sale until the sale is actually made. Assume now that on December 1, Year 1, Eximco receives and accepts an order from a Spanish customer to deliver goods on March 1, Year 2, at a price of €1,000,000. Assume further that under the terms of the sales agreement, Eximco will ship the goods to the Spanish customer on March 1, Year 2, and will receive immediate payment on delivery. In other words, Eximco will not allow the Spanish customer time to pay. Although Eximco will not make the sale until March 1, Year 2, it has a firm commitment to make the sale and receive €1,000,000 in three months. This creates a euro asset exposure to foreign exchange risk as of December 1, Year 1. On that date, Eximco wants to hedge against an adverse change in the value of the euro over the next three months. This is known as a hedge of a foreign currency firm commitment. In the following example, we will only cover the accounting of a fair value hedge for firm commitments.

Under fair value hedge accounting, (1) the gain or loss on the hedging instrument is recognized currently in net income and (2) the gain or loss (i.e., the change in fair value) on the firm commitment attributable to the hedged risk is also recognized currently in net income. This accounting treatment requires (1) measuring the fair value of the firm commitment, (2) recognizing the change in fair value in net income, and (3) reporting the firm commitment on the balance sheet as an asset or liability. This raises the conceptual question of how the fair value of the firm commitment should be measured. Two possibilities are (1) through reference to changes in the spot exchange rate or (2) through reference to changes in the forward rate. These two approaches are shown in the examples that follow.

Forward Contract Used as Fair Value Hedge of a Firm Commitment

To hedge its firm commitment exposure to a decline in the U.S. dollar value of the euro, Eximco decides to enter into a forward contract on December 1, Year 1. Assume that on December 1, Year 1, the three-month forward rate for euros is $1.485 and Eximco signs a contract with New Manhattan Bank to deliver €1,000,000 in three months in exchange for $1,485,000. No cash changes hands on December 1, Year 1. Eximco elects to measure the fair value of the firm commitment through changes in the forward rate. As the fair value of the forward contract is also measured using changes in the forward rate, the gains and losses on the firm commitment and forward contract exactly offset. The fair value of the forward contract and firm commitment are determined as follows:

Date	Forward Rate to 3/1/Y2	Forward Contract		Firm Commitment	
		Fair Value	Change in Fair Value	Fair Value	Change in Fair Value
12/1/Y1	$1.485	$0	—	$0	—
12/31/Y1	1.496	(10,783)*	−$10,783	10,783*	+$10,783
3/1/Y2	1.48 (spot)	5,000†	+$15,783	(5,000)†	−$15,783

*($1,485,000 − $1,496,000) = $(11,000) × 0.9803 = $(10,783), where 0.9803 is the present value factor for two months at an annual interest rate of 12 percent (1 percent per month) calculated as 1/1/Y2 . The amount is the same as the fair value of the forward contract, but with opposite sign. In this case the firm commitment is an asset with a value of $10,783.
†($1,485,000 − $1,480,000) = $5,000. The amount is the same as the fair value of the forward contract, but with opposite sign. In this case the firm commitment is a liability with a value of $(5,000).

Eximco pays nothing to enter into the forward contract at December 1, Year 1. Both the forward contract and the firm commitment have a fair value of zero on that date.

At December 31, Year 1, the forward rate for a contract to deliver euros on March 1, Year 2, is $1.496. A forward contract could be entered into on December 31, Year 1, to sell €1,000,000 for $1,496,000 on March 1, Year 2. Because Eximco is committed to sell €1,000,000 for $1,485,000, the value of the forward contract is negative $11,000; present value is negative $10,783 (a liability). The fair value of the firm commitment is also measured through reference to changes in the forward rate. As a result, the fair value of the firm commitment is equal in amount but of opposite sign to the fair value of the forward contract. At December 31, Year 1, the firm commitment is an asset of $10,783.

On March 1, Year 2, the forward rate to sell euros on that date is the spot rate–$1.48. At that rate, €1,000,000 could be sold for $1,480,000. Because Eximco has a contract to sell euros for $1,485,000, the fair value of the forward contract on March 1, Year 2, is $5,000 (an asset). The firm commitment has a value of negative $5,000 (a liability). The journal entries to account for the forward contract fair value hedge of a foreign currency firm commitment are as follows:

Year 1 Journal Entries—Forward Contract Fair Value Hedge of Firm Commitment

12/1/Y1	There is no entry to record either the sales agreement or the forward contract, as both are executory contracts. A memorandum would be prepared designating the forward contract as a hedge of the risk of changes in the fair value of the firm commitment resulting from changes in the U.S. dollar–euro forward exchange rate.		
12/31/Y1	Loss on Forward Contract...................................	$10,783	
	Forward Contract		$10,783
	To record the forward contract as a liability at its fair value of $(10,783) and record a forward contract loss for the change in the fair value of the forward contract since December 1.		
	Firm Commitment	$10,783	
	Gain on Firm Commitment		$10,783
	To record the firm commitment as an asset at its fair value of $10,783 and record a firm commitment gain for the change in the fair value of the firm commitment since December 1.		

Consistent with the objective of hedge accounting, the gain on the firm commitment offsets the loss on the forward contract and the impact on Year 1 net income is zero. The Forward Contract is reported as a liability and the Firm Commitment is reported as an asset on the 12/31/Y1 balance sheet. This achieves the objective of making sure that derivatives are recognized on the balance sheet and at the same time ensures that there is no impact on net income.

Year 2 Journal Entries—Forward Contract Fair Value Hedge of Firm Commitment

3/1/Y2	Forward Contract	$15,783	
	Gain on Forward Contract.......................		$15,783
	To adjust the fair value of the forward contract from $(10,783) to $5,000 and record a forward contract gain for the change in fair value since December 31.		
	Loss on Firm Commitment.............................	$15,783	
	Firm Commitment		$15,783
	To adjust the fair value of the firm commitment from $10,783 to $(5,000) and record a firm commitment loss for the change in fair value since December 31.		

Foreign Currency (€)	$1,480,000
Sales.....................................	$1,480,000
To record the sale and the receipt of €1,000,000 as an asset at the spot rate of $1.48.	
Cash	$1,485,000
Foreign Currency (€)	$1,480,000
Forward Contract	5,000
To record settlement of the forward contract (receipt of $1,485,000 in exchange for delivery of €1,000,000), and remove the forward contract from the accounts.	
Firm Commitment	$5,000
Adjustment to Net Income	$5,000
To close the firm commitment as an adjustment to net income.	

Once again, the gain on forward contract and the loss on firm commitment offset. As a result of the last entry, the export sale increases Year 2 net income by $1,485,000 ($1,480,000 in Sales plus a $5,000 Adjustment to Net Income). This is exactly equal to the amount of cash received. In practice, companies might use a variety of account titles for the adjustment to net income that results from closing the firm commitment account.

The net Gain on Forward Contract of $5,000 ($10,783 loss in Year 1 plus $15,783 gain in Year 2) measures the net benefit to the company from hedging its firm commitment. Without the forward contract, Eximco would have sold the €1,000,000 received on March 1, Year 2, at the spot rate of $1.48, generating cash flow of $1,480,000. Through the forward contract, Eximco is able to sell the euros for $1,485,000, a net gain of $5,000.

Option Used as Fair Value Hedge of Firm Commitment

Now assume that to hedge its exposure to a decline in the U.S. dollar value of the foreign currency firm commitment, Eximco purchases a put option to sell €1,000,000 on March 1, Year 2, at a strike price of $1.50. The premium for such an option on December 1, Year 1, is $0.009 per euro. With this option, Eximco is guaranteed a minimum cash flow from the export sale of $1,491,000 ($1,500,000 from option exercise less $9,000 cost of the option).

Eximco elects to measure the fair value of the firm commitment through reference to changes in the U.S. dollar–euro spot rate. In this case, the fair value of the firm commitment must be discounted to its present value. The fair value and changes in fair value for the firm commitment and foreign currency option are summarized as follows:

		Foreign Currency Option			Firm Commitment	
Date	Option Premium for 3/1/Y2	Fair Value	Change in Fair Value	Spot Rate	Fair Value	Change in Fair Value
12/1/Y1	$0.009	$9,000	—	$1.50	—	—
12/31/Y1	0.006	6,000	−$3,000	1.51	$9,803*	+$ 9,803
3/1/Y2	0.020	20,000	+$14,000	1.48	(20,000)†	−$29,803

*$1,510,000 - $1,500,000 = $10,000 × 0.9803 = $9,803, where 0.9803 is the present value factor for two months at an annual interest rate of 12 percent (1 percent per month) calculated as $1/1.01^2$.
†$1,480,000 - $1,500,000 = $(20,000).

At December 1, Year 1, given the spot rate of $1.50, the firm commitment to receive €1,000,000 in three months would generate a cash flow of $1,500,000. At December 31, Year 1, the cash flow that could be generated from the firm commitment increases by

$10,000 to $1,510,000. The fair value of the firm commitment at December 31, Year 1, is the present value of $10,000 discounted at 1 percent per month for two months. The fair value of the firm commitment on March 1, Year 2, is determined through reference to the change in the spot rate from December 1, Year 1, to March 1, Year 2. Because the spot rate declines by $0.02 over that period, the firm commitment to receive €1,000,000 has a fair value of negative $20,000 on March 1, Year 2. The journal entries to account for the foreign currency option and related foreign currency firm commitment are as follows:

Year 1 Journal Entries—Option Fair Value Hedge of Firm Commitment

12/1/Y1	Foreign Currency Option	$9,000	
	Cash		$9,000
	To record the purchase of the foreign currency option as an asset.		

There is no entry to record the sales agreement, as it is an executory contract. A memorandum would be prepared designating the option as a hedge of the risk of changes in the fair value of the firm commitment resulting from changes in the spot exchange rate.

12/31/Y1	Firm Commitment	$9,803	
	Gain on Firm Commitment		$9,803
	To record the firm commitment as an asset at its fair value of $9,803 and record a firm commitment gain for the change in the fair value of the firm commitment since December 1.		
	Loss on Foreign Currency Option	$3,000	
	Foreign Currency Option		$3,000
	To adjust the fair value of the option from $9,000 to $6,000 and record the change in the value of the option as a loss.		

The impact on Year 1 net income is as follows:

Gain on Firm Commitment	$ 9,803
Loss on Foreign Currency Option	(3,000)
Impact on net income	$ 6,803

The effect on the December 31, Year 1, balance sheet is as follows:

Assets		Liabilities and Stockholders' Equity	
Cash	$(9,000)	Retained earnings	$6,803
Foreign currency option	6,000		
Firm commitment	9,803		
	$ 6,803		

Year 2 Journal Entries—Option Fair Value Hedge of Firm Commitment

3/1/Y2	Loss on Firm Commitment	$29,803	
	Firm Commitment		$29,803
	To adjust the fair value of the firm commitment from $9,803 to $(20,000) and record a firm commitment loss for the change in fair value since December 31.		

Foreign Currency Option.............................	$14,000	
Gain on Foreign Currency Option................		$14,000
To adjust the fair value of the foreign currency option from $6,000 to $20,000 and record a gain on foreign currency option for the change in fair value since December 31.		
Foreign Currency (€)	$1,480,000	
Sales..		$1,480,000
To record the sale and the receipt of €1,000,000 as an asset at the spot rate of $1.48.		
Cash	$1,500,000	
Foreign Currency (€)		$1,480,000
Foreign Currency Option		20,000
To record exercise of the foreign currency option (receipt of $1,500,000 in exchange for delivery of €1,000,000) and remove the foreign currency option from the accounts.		
Firm Commitment	$20,000	
Adjustment to Net Income		$20,000
To close the firm commitment as an adjustment to net income.		

The impact on Year 2 net income is as follows:

Sales	$1,480,000
Loss on Firm Commitment...................	(29,803)
Gain on Foreign Currency Option	14,000
Adjustment to Net Income...................	20,000
Impact on net income	$1,484,197

The net increase in net income over the two accounting periods is $1,491,000 ($6,803 in Year 1 plus $1,484,197 in Year 2), which is exactly equal to the net cash flow realized on the export sale ($1,500,000 from exercising the option less $9,000 to purchase the option). The net gain on option of $11,000 (loss of $3,000 in Year 1 plus gain of $14,000 in Year 2) reflects the net benefit from having entered into the hedge. Without the option, Eximco would have sold the €1,000,000 received on March 1, Year 2, at the spot rate of $1.48 for $1,480,000.

HEDGE OF FORECASTED FOREIGN-CURRENCY-DENOMINATED TRANSACTION

Cash flow hedge accounting is used for foreign currency derivatives that hedge the cash flow risk associated with a forecasted foreign currency transaction. For hedge accounting to apply, as we already mentioned, the forecasted transaction must be probable (likely to occur), the hedge must be highly effective in offsetting fluctuations in the cash flow associated with the foreign currency risk, and the hedging relationship must be properly documented.

The accounting for a hedge of a forecasted transaction differs from the accounting for a hedge of a foreign currency firm commitment in two ways:

1. Unlike the accounting for a firm commitment, there is no recognition of the forecasted transaction or gains and losses on the forecasted transaction.

2. The hedging instrument (forward contract or option) is reported at fair value, but because there is no gain or loss on the forecasted transaction to offset against, changes in the fair value of the hedging instrument are not reported as gains and losses in net income. Instead they are reported in other comprehensive income. On the projected date of the forecasted transaction, the cumulative change in the fair value of the hedging instrument is transferred from other comprehensive income (balance sheet) to net income (income statement).

Option Designated as a Cash Flow Hedge of a Forecasted Transaction

To illustrate the accounting for a hedge of a forecasted foreign currency transaction, assume that Eximco has a long-term relationship with its Spanish customer and can reliably forecast that the customer will require delivery of goods costing €1,000,000 in March of Year 2, when the spot rate is $0.98. Confident that it will receive €1,000,000 on March 1, Year 2, Eximco hedges its forecasted foreign currency transaction by purchasing a €1,000,000 put option on December 1, Year 1. The facts are essentially the same as for the option hedge of a firm commitment, except that Eximco does not receive a sales order from the Spanish customer until late February, Year 2.

The option, which expires on March 1, Year 2, has a strike price of $1.50 and a premium of $0.009 per euro. The fair value of the option at relevant dates is as follows:

| Date | Option Premium for 3/1/Y2 | Foreign Currency Option | | | | |
		Fair Value	Change in Fair Value	Intrinsic Value	Time Value	Change in Time Value
12/1/Y1	$0.009	$9,000	—	$0	$9,000	—
12/31/Y1	0.006	6,000	−$3,000	0	6,000	−$3,000
3/1/Y2	0.020	20,000	−$14,000	20,000	0	−$6,000

Year 1 Journal Entries—Option Hedge of a Forecasted Transaction

12/1/Y1	Foreign Currency Option.	$9,000	
	Cash		$9,000
	To record the purchase of the foreign currency option as an asset.		

There is no entry to record the forecasted sale. A memorandum would be prepared designating the foreign currency option as a hedge of the risk of changes in the cash flows related to the forecasted sale.

12/31/Y1	Option Expense.	$3,000	
	Foreign Currency Option		$3,000
	To adjust the carrying value of the option to its fair value and recognize the change in the time value of the option as an expense.		

The impact on Year 1 net income is as follows:

| Option Expense. . . . . . | $(3,000) |
| Impact on net income . . . . . . | $(3,000) |

A Foreign Currency Option of $6,000 is reported as an asset on the December 31, Year 1, balance sheet. Cash decreases by $9,000, and retained earnings decrease by $3,000.

Year 2 Journal Entries—Option Hedge of a Forecasted Transaction

3/1/Y2	Foreign Currency Option................................	$14,000	
	Option Expense...	6,000	
	Accumulated Other Comprehensive Income (AOCI)		$20,000
	To adjust the carrying value of the option to its fair value and recognize the change in the time value of the option as an expense, with a corresponding credit to AOCI.		
	Foreign Currency (€)	$1,480,000	
	Sales...		$1,480,000
	To record the sale and the receipt of €1,000,000 as an asset at the spot rate of $0.98.		
	Cash	$1,500,000	
	Foreign Currency (€)		$1,480,000
	Foreign Currency Option		20,000
	To record exercise of the foreign currency option (receipt of $1,000,000 in exchange for delivery of €1,000,000), and remove the foreign currency option from the accounts.		
	Accumulated Other Comprehensive Income (AOCI)	$20,000	
	Adjustment to Net Income		$20,000
	To close AOCI as an adjustment to net income.		

The impact on Year 2 net income is as follows:

Sales	$1,480,000
Option Expense.............................	(6,000)
Adjustment to Net Income..................	20,000
Impact on net income	$1,494,000

Over the two-year period, net income increases by $1,491,000 ($1,494,000 in Year 2 minus $3,000 in Year 1), equal to the net cash inflow realized from the export sale.

USE OF HEDGING INSTRUMENTS

There probably are as many different corporate strategies regarding hedging foreign exchange risk as there are companies exposed to that risk. Some companies simply require hedges of all foreign currency transactions. Others require the use of a forward contract hedge when the forward rate results in a greater cash inflow or smaller cash outflow than with the spot rate. Still other companies have proportional hedging policies that require hedging on some predetermined percentage (e.g., 50, 60, or 70 percent) of transaction exposure.

It is quite common for companies to use foreign currency derivatives to hedge the exposure to foreign exchange risk arising from forecasted foreign currency transactions. Exhibit 6.6 presents information provided by two U.S.-based companies with respect to hedging forecasted transactions. International Business Machines Corporation (IBM) uses forward contracts to hedge transactions that are anticipated to take place in no longer than four years. In contrast, Boeing Company uses both forward contracts and options to hedge

EXHIBIT 6.6
Hedges of Forecasted
Foreign Currency
Transactions

INTERNATIONAL BUSINESS MACHINES CORPORATION
Annual Report
2020

Excerpt from Note T. Derivative Financial Instruments
Anticipated Royalties and Cost Transactions
The company's operations generate significant nonfunctional currency, third-party vendor payments and intercompany payments for royalties and goods and services among the company's non-U.S. subsidiaries and with the company. In anticipation of these foreign currency cash flows and in view of the volatility of the currency markets, the company selectively employs foreign exchange forward contracts to manage its currency risk. These forward contracts are accounted for as cash flow hedges. The maximum length of time over which the company has hedged its exposure to the variability in future cash flows is four years. At December 31, 2020 and 2019, the total notional amount of forward contracts designated as cash flow hedges of forecasted royalty and cost transactions was $8.0 billion and $9.7 billion, respectively. At December 31, 2020 and 2019, the weighted-average remaining maturity of these instruments was approximately 0.7 years and 0.8 years, respectively. At December 31, 2020 and 2019, in connection with cash flow hedges of anticipated royalties and cost transactions, the company recorded net losses of $192 million and net gains of $145 million (before taxes), respectively, in AOCI. The company estimates that $285 million (before taxes) of deferred net losses on derivatives in AOCI at December 31, 2020, will be reclassified to net income within the next 12 months, providing an offsetting economic impact against the underlying anticipated transactions.

THE BOEING COMPANY
Annual Report
2020

Excerpt from Note 19—Derivative Financial Instruments
Cash Flow Hedges
Our cash flow hedges include foreign currency forward contracts, commodity swaps, and commodity purchase contracts. *We use foreign currency forward contracts to manage currency risk associated with certain transactions, specifically forecasted sales and purchases made in foreign currencies. Our foreign currency contracts hedge forecasted transactions through 2025.* We use commodity derivatives, such as fixed-price purchase commitments and swaps to hedge against potentially unfavorable price changes for items used in production. Our commodity contracts hedge forecasted transactions through 2029.

Derivative Instruments Not Receiving Hedge Accounting Treatment
[. . .] We also hold certain foreign currency forward contracts and commodity swaps which do not qualify for hedge accounting treatment.

Author's note: Emphasis added.

---

transactions principally occurring up to five years in the future, with certain contracts hedging transactions up to the year 2029. Some derivative arrangements of Boeing Company do not receive hedge accounting treatment because they don't qualify.

The notes to financial statements of multinational companies also indicate the magnitude of foreign exchange risk and the importance of hedging contracts. Exhibit 6.7 presents information extracted from Abbott Laboratories 2020 Annual Report. At December 31, 2020, Abbott had $8.1 billion in foreign currency forward contracts related to anticipated foreign currency transactions and $11.0 billion in forward contracts used to hedge foreign-currency-denominated payables and receivables. To better appreciate the significance of these amounts, consider that Abbott had assets of $72.5 billion, sales of $34.6 billion, and net earnings of $4.5 billion in 2020.

EXHIBIT 6.7

ABBOTT LABORATORIES
Annual Report
2020

Notes to Consolidated Financial Statements

Note 12—Financial Instruments, Derivatives, and Fair Value Measures

Certain Abbott foreign subsidiaries enter into foreign currency forward exchange contracts to manage exposures to changes in foreign exchange rates primarily for anticipated intercompany purchases by those subsidiaries whose functional currencies are not the U.S. dollar. These contracts, with notional amounts totaling $8.1 billion at December 31, 2020, and $6.8 billion at December 31, 2019, are designated as cash flow hedges of the variability of the cash flows due to changes in foreign exchange rates and are recorded at fair value. Accumulated gains and losses as of December 31, 2020 will be included in Cost of products sold at the time the products are sold, generally through the next 12 to 18 months.

Abbott enters into foreign currency forward exchange contracts to manage currency exposures for foreign-currency-denominated third-party trade payables and receivables, and for intercompany loans and trade accounts payable where the receivable or payable is denominated in a currency other than the functional currency of the entity. For intercompany loans, the contracts require Abbott to sell or buy foreign currencies, primarily European currencies, in exchange for primarily U.S. dollars and other European currencies. For intercompany and trade payables and receivables, the currency exposures are primarily the U.S. dollar and European currencies. At December 31, 2020 and 2019, Abbott held gross notional amounts of $11.0 billion and $9.1 billion, respectively, of such foreign currency forward exchange contracts.

Summary

1. There are a variety of exchange rate mechanisms in use around the world. Most national currencies are allowed to fluctuate in value against other currencies over time.

2. Exposure to foreign exchange risk exists when a payment to be made or received is denominated in terms of a foreign currency. Change in value of the foreign currency will result in a foreign exchange gain or loss on a foreign currency receivable/payable.

3. Foreign exchange gains and losses on foreign currency balances are recorded in income in the period in which an exchange rate change occurs; this is a two-transaction perspective, accrual approach. Foreign currency balances must be revalued to their current domestic-currency equivalent using current exchange rates whenever financial statements are prepared. This approach violates the conservatism principle when unrealized foreign exchange gains are recognized as income.

4. Exposure to foreign exchange risk can be eliminated through hedging. Hedging involves establishing a price today at which a foreign currency to be received (or paid) in the future can be sold (or purchased) at the future date.

5. The two most popular instruments for hedging foreign exchange risk are foreign currency forward and foreign currency option contracts. A forward contract is a binding agreement to exchange currencies at a predetermined exchange rate. An option contract gives the buyer the right, but not the obligation, to exchange currencies at a predetermined exchange rate.

6. Derivative financial instruments must be reported on the balance sheet at their fair value. Hedge accounting is appropriate if the derivative is (*a*) used to hedge an exposure to foreign exchange risk, (*b*) highly effective in offsetting changes in the fair value or cash flows related to the hedged item, and (*c*) properly documented as a hedge. Under hedge

accounting, gains and losses on the hedging instrument are reported in net income in the same period as gains and losses on the item being hedged.

7. Accounting standards provide guidance for hedges of (*a*) recognized foreign-currency-denominated assets and liabilities, (*b*) unrecognized foreign currency firm commitments, and (*c*) forecasted foreign-currency-denominated transactions. Cash flow hedge accounting can be used for all three types of hedges; fair value hedge accounting can be used only for (*a*) recognized foreign-currency-denominated assets and liabilities and (*b*) unrecognized foreign currency firm commitments.

Appendix A to Chapter 6

Illustration of the Accounting for Foreign Currency Transactions and Hedging Activities by an Importer

This appendix illustrates the accounting used by an importing company that buys goods and services from outside the country and has account payable balances denominated in foreign currency (vs account receivable balances denominated in foreign currency, as in the body of the chapter). In the discussion that follows, we illustrate the accounting for the following types of hedges:

1. Forward contract cash flow hedge of a recognized foreign currency liability.
2. Forward contract fair value hedge of a recognized foreign currency liability.
3. Option contract cash flow hedge of a recognized foreign currency liability.
4. Forward contract fair value hedge of a foreign currency firm commitment.
5. Option contract fair value hedge of a foreign currency firm commitment.
6. Option contract cash flow hedge of a forecasted foreign currency transaction.

Basic Facts

Telectro Company is a U.S. company that produces electronic switches for the telecommunications industry. Telectro regularly imports component parts from a supplier located in Guadalajara, Mexico, with payments made in Mexican pesos (Mex$). The following spot exchange rates, forward exchange rates, and call option premiums for Mexican pesos exist during the period August to October.

	US$ per Mexican Peso		
Date	Spot Rate	Forward Rate to October 31	Call Option Premium for October 31 (strike price $0.080)
August 1	$0.080	$0.085	$0.0052
September 30	0.086	0.088	0.0095
October 31	0.091	0.091	0.0110

1. Forward Contract Cash Flow Hedge of a Recognized Foreign Currency Liability

On August 1, Telectro imports parts from its Mexican supplier at a price of Mex$1,000,000. The parts are received on August 1, but are not paid for until October 31. In addition, on August 1, Telectro enters into a forward contract to purchase Mex$1,000,000 on October 31.

The forward contract is appropriately designated as a *cash flow hedge* of the Mexican peso liability exposure. Telectro's incremental borrowing rate is 12 percent per annum (1 percent per month), and the company uses a straight-line method on a monthly basis for allocating forward discounts and premiums.

Journal Entries and Impact on the September 30 and October 31 Trial Balances

8/1	Parts Inventory...	$80,000
	Accounts Payable (Mex$)	$80,000
	To record the purchase of parts and a Mexican peso account payable at the spot rate of $0.080.	

There is no formal entry for the forward contract. A memorandum would be prepared designating the forward contract as a hedge of the risk of changes in the cash flow to be paid on the foreign currency payable resulting from changes in the U.S. dollar–Mexican peso exchange rate.

9/30	Foreign Exchange Loss	$6,000
	Accounts Payable (Mex$)	$6,000
	To adjust the value of the peso payable to the new spot rate of $0.086 and record a foreign exchange loss resulting from the appreciation of the peso since August 1.	
	Accumulated Other Comprehensive Income (AOCI)	$6,000
	Gain on Forward Contract.................................	$6,000
	To record a gain on forward contract to offset the foreign exchange loss on account payable with a corresponding debit to AOCI.	
	Forward Contract	$2,970
	Accumulated Other Comprehensive Income (AOCI)............	$2,970
	To record the forward contract as an asset at its fair value of $2,970 with a corresponding credit to AOCI.	

The fair value of the forward contract is determined by reference to the change in the forward rate for a contract that settles on October 31: ($0.088 − $0.085) × Mex$1,000,000 = $3,000. The present value of $3,000 discounted for one month (from October 31 to September 30) at an interest rate of 12 percent per year (1 percent per month) is calculated as follows: $3,000 × 0.9901 = $2,970.

Premium Expense..		$3,333
Accumulated Other Comprehensive Income (AOCI).................		$3,333
To allocate the forward contract premium to income over the life of the contract using a straight-line method on a monthly basis ($5,000 × $\frac{2}{3}$ = $3,333).		

The original premium on the forward contract is determined by the difference in the Mexican peso spot rate and the three-month forward rate on August 1: ($0.085 − $0.080) × *Mex*$1,000,000 = $5,000.

Trial Balance—September 30	Debit	Credit
Parts Inventory...	$80,000	
Accounts Payable (Mex$)		$86,000
Forward Contract (asset)	2,970	
AOCI		303
Foreign Exchange Loss	6,000	
Gain on Forward Contract............................		6,000
Premium Expense.....................................	3,333	
	$92,303	$92,303

10/31	Foreign Exchange Loss	$5,000	
	Accounts Payable (Mex$)		$5,000
	To adjust the value of the peso payable to the new spot rate of $0.091 and record a foreign exchange loss resulting from the appreciation of the peso since September 30.		
	Accumulated Other Comprehensive Income (AOCI)	$5,000	
	Gain on Forward Contract......................................		$5,000
	To record a gain on forward contract to offset the foreign exchange loss on account payable with a corresponding debit to AOCI.		
	Forward Contract	$3,030	
	Accumulated Other Comprehensive Income (AOCI)..........		$3,030
	To adjust the carrying value of the forward contract to its current fair value of $6,000 with a corresponding credit to AOCI.		

The current fair value of the forward contract is determined by reference to the difference in the spot rate on October 31 and the original forward rate: ($0.091 − $0.085) × Mex$1,000,000 = $6,000. The forward contract adjustment on October 31 is calculated as the difference in the current fair value and the carrying value at September 30: $6,000 − $2,970 = $3,030.

	Premium Expense..	$1,667	
	Accumulated Other Comprehensive Income (AOCI)................		$1,667
	To allocate the forward contract premium to income over the life of the contract using a straight-line method on a monthly basis ($5,000 × $\frac{1}{3}$ = $1,667).		
	Foreign Currency (Mex$)...	$91,000	
	Cash		$85,000
	Forward Contract		6,000
	To record settlement of the forward contract: record payment of $85,000 in exchange for Mex$1,000,000, record the receipt of Mex$1,000,000 as an asset at the spot rate of $0.091, and remove the forward contract from the accounts.		
	Accounts Payable (Mex$)	$91,000	
	Foreign Currency (Mex$).......................................		$91,000
	To record remittance of Mex$1,000,000 to the Mexican supplier.		

Trial Balance—October 31	Debit	Credit
Cash		$85,000
Parts Inventory..................................	$80,000	
Retained Earnings, 9/30	3,333	
Foreign Exchange Loss	5,000	
Gain on Forward Contract.......................		5,000
Premium Expense...............................	1,667	
	$90,000	$90,000

2. Forward Contract Fair Value Hedge of a Recognized Foreign Currency Liability

The facts are the same as in (1), with the exception that Telectro designates the forward contract as a *fair value hedge* of the Mexican peso liability exposure.

Journal Entries and Impact on the September 30 and October 31 Trial Balances

8/1	Parts Inventory..	$80,000	
	Accounts Payable (Mex$)		$80,000
	To record the purchase of parts and a Mexican peso account payable at the spot rate of $0.080.		

There is no formal entry for the forward contract. A memorandum would be prepared designating the forward contract as a hedge of the risk of changes in the cash flow to be paid on the foreign currency payable resulting from changes in the U.S. dollar–Mexican peso exchange rate.

9/30	Foreign Exchange Loss	$6,000	
	Accounts Payable (Mex$)		$6,000
	To adjust the value of the peso payable to the new spot rate of $0.086 and record a foreign exchange loss resulting from the appreciation of the peso since August 1.		
	Forward Contract	$2,970	
	Gain on Forward Contract		$2,970
	To record the forward contract as an asset at its fair value of $2,970 and record a forward contract gain for the change in the fair value of the forward contract since August 1.		

Trial Balance—September 30	Debit	Credit
Parts Inventory..................................	$80,000	
Accounts Payable (Mex$)		$86,000
Forward Contract (asset)	2,970	
Foreign Exchange Loss	6,000	
Gain on Forward Contract..........................		2,970
	$88,970	$88,970

10/31	Foreign Exchange Loss	$5,000	
	Accounts Payable (Mex$)		$5,000
	To adjust the value of the peso payable to the new spot rate of $0.091 and record a foreign exchange loss resulting from the appreciation of the peso since September 30.		
	Forward Contract	$3,030	
	Gain on Forward Contract		$3,030
	To adjust the carrying value of the forward contract to its current fair value of $6,000 and record a forward contract gain for the change in fair value since September 30.		
	Foreign Currency (Mex$)	$91,000	
	Cash		$85,000
	Forward Contract		6,000
	To record settlement of the forward contract: record payment of $85,000 in exchange for Mex$1,000,000, record the receipt of Mex$1,000,000 as an asset at the spot rate of $0.091, and remove the forward contract from the accounts.		
	Accounts Payable (Mex$)	$91,000	
	Foreign Currency (Mex$).		$91,000
	To record remittance of Mex$1,000,000 to the Mexican supplier.		

Trial Balance—October 31	Debit	Credit
Cash		$85,000
Parts Inventory.	$80,000	
Retained Earnings, 9/30	3,030	
Foreign Exchange Loss	5,000	
Gain on Forward Contract.		3,030
	$88,030	$88,030

3. Option Contract Cash Flow Hedge of a Recognized Foreign Currency Liability

On August 1, Telectro imports parts from its Mexican supplier at a price of Mex$1,000,000. The parts are received on August 1 but are not paid for until October 31. In addition, on August 1, Telectro purchases a three-month call option on Mex$1,000,000 with a strike price of $0.080. The option is appropriately designated as a *cash flow hedge* of the Mexican peso liability exposure.

The following schedule summarizes the changes in the components of the fair value of the Mexican peso call option with a strike price of $0.080:

Date	Spot Rate	Option Premium	Fair Value	Change in Fair Value	Intrinsic Value	Time Value	Change in Time Value
8/1	$0.080	$0.0052	$ 5,200	—	$0	$5,200[a]	—
9/30	0.086	0.0095	9,500	+$4,300	6,000[b]	3,500[b]	−$1,700
10/31	0.091	0.0110	11,000	+$1,500	11,000	0[c]	−$3,500

[a] Because the strike price and spot rate are the same, the option has no intrinsic value. Fair value is attributable solely to the time value of the option.
[b] With a spot rate of $0.086 and a strike price of $0.080, the option has an intrinsic value of $6,000. The remaining $3,500 of fair value is attributable to the time value.
[c] The time value of the option at maturity is zero.

Journal Entries and Impact on the September 30 and October 31 Trial Balances

8/1	Parts Inventory..		$80,000	
	Accounts Payable (Mex$)			$80,000
	To record the purchase of parts and a Mexican peso account payable at the spot rate of $0.080.			
	Foreign Currency Option.....................................		$5,200	
	Cash			$5,200
	To record the purchase of a foreign currency option as an asset.			
9/30	Foreign Exchange Loss		$6,000	
	Accounts Payable (Mex$)			$6,000
	To adjust the value of the peso payable to the new spot rate of $0.086 and record a foreign exchange loss resulting from the appreciation of the peso since August 1.			
	Foreign Currency Option.....................................		$4,300	
	Accumulated Other Comprehensive Income (AOCI).........			$4,300
	To adjust the fair value of the option from $5,200 to $9,500 with a corresponding credit to AOCI.			
	Accumulated Other Comprehensive Income (AOCI)		$6,000	
	Gain on Foreign Currency Option........................			$6,000
	To record a gain on foreign currency option to offset the foreign exchange loss on account payable with a corresponding debit to AOCI.			
	Option Expense...		$1,700	
	Accumulated Other Comprehensive Income (AOCI).........			$1,700
	To recognize the change in the time value of the foreign currency option as an expense with a corresponding credit to AOCI.			

Trial Balance—September 30	Debit	Credit
Parts Inventory......................................	$80,000	
Accounts Payable (Mex$)		$86,000
Foreign Currency Option (asset)	9,500	
Cash		5,200
Foreign Exchange Loss	6,000	
Gain on Foreign Currency Option		6,000
Option Expense.....................................	1,700	
	$97,200	$97,200

10/31	Foreign Exchange Loss		$5,000	
	Accounts Payable (Mex$)			$5,000
	To adjust the value of the peso payable to the new spot rate of $0.091 and record a foreign exchange loss resulting from the appreciation of the peso since September 30.			
	Foreign Currency Option.....................................		$1,500	
	Accumulated Other Comprehensive Income (AOCI).......			$1,500
	To adjust the carrying value of the foreign currency option to its current fair value of $11,000 with a corresponding credit to AOCI.			

	Debit	Credit
Accumulated Other Comprehensive Income (AOCI)	$5,000	
Gain on Foreign Currency Option		$5,000
To record a gain on foreign currency option to offset the foreign exchange loss on account payable with a corresponding debit to AOCI.		
Option Expense	$3,500	
Accumulated Other Comprehensive Income (AOCI)		$3,500
To recognize the change in the time value of the foreign currency option as an expense with a corresponding credit to AOCI.		
Foreign Currency (Mex$)	$91,000	
Cash		$80,000
Foreign Currency Option		11,000
To record exercise of the foreign currency option: record payment of $80,000 in exchange for Mex$1,000,000, record the receipt of Mex$1,000,000 as an asset at the spot rate of $0.091, and remove the option from the accounts.		
Accounts Payable (Mex$)	$91,000	
Foreign Currency (Mex$)		$91,000
To record remittance of Mex$1,000,000 to the Mexican supplier.		

Trial Balance—October 31	Debit	Credit
Cash ($5,200 credit + $80,000 credit)		$85,200
Parts Inventory	$80,000	
Retained Earnings, 9/30	1,700	
Foreign Exchange Loss	5,000	
Gain on Foreign Currency Option		5,000
Option Expense	3,500	
	$90,200	$90,200

4. Forward Contract Fair Value Hedge of a Foreign Currency Firm Commitment

On August 1, Telectro orders parts from its Mexican supplier at a price of Mex$1,000,000. The parts are received and paid for on October 31. On August 1, Telectro enters into a forward contract to purchase Mex$1,000,000 on October 31. The forward contract is designated as a *fair value hedge* of the Mexican peso firm commitment. The fair value of the firm commitment is determined through reference to changes in the forward exchange rate.

Journal Entries and Impact on the September 30 and October 31 Trial Balances

Date		Debit	Credit
8/1	There is no formal entry for the forward contract or the purchase order. A memorandum would be prepared designating the forward contract as a fair value hedge of the foreign currency firm commitment.		
9/30	Forward Contract	$2,970	
	Gain on Forward Contract		$2,970
	To record the forward contract as an asset at its fair value of $2,970 and record a forward contract gain for the change in the fair value of the forward contract since August 1.		

	Debit	Credit
Loss on Firm Commitment...	$2,970	
Firm Commitment.......................................		$2,970
To record the firm commitment as a liability at its fair value of $2,970 based on changes in the forward rate and record a firm commitment loss for the change in fair value since August 1.		

Trial Balance—September 30	Debit	Credit
Forward Contract (asset)	$2,970	
Firm Commitment (liability)...........................		$2,970
Gain on Forward Contract...........................		2,970
Loss on Firm Commitment...........................	2,970	
	$5,940	$5,940

		Debit	Credit
10/31	Forward Contract	$3,030	
	Gain on Forward Contract............................		$3,030
	To adjust the carrying value of the forward contract to its current fair value of $6,000 and record a forward contract gain for the change in fair value since September 30.		
	Loss on Firm Commitment....................................	$3,030	
	Firm Commitment.....................................		$3,030
	To adjust the value of the firm commitment to $6,000 based on changes in the forward rate and record a firm commitment loss for the change in fair value since September 30.		
	Foreign Currency (pesos)	$91,000	
	Cash		$85,000
	Forward Contract		6,000
	To record settlement of the forward contract: record payment of $85,000 in exchange for Mex$1,000,000, record the receipt of Mex$1,000,000 as an asset at the spot rate of $0.091, and remove the forward contract from the accounts.		
	Parts Inventory...	$91,000	
	Foreign Currency (Mex$)...............................		$91,000
	To record the purchase of parts through the payment of Mex$1,000,000 to the Mexican supplier.		
	Firm Commitment	$6,000	
	Adjustment to Net Income		$6,000
	To close the firm commitment account as an adjustment to net income.		

Note that the final entry to close the Firm Commitment as an Adjustment to Net Income will be made only in the period in which the Parts Inventory affects net income through Cost of Goods Sold. The Firm Commitment remains on the books as a liability until that time.

Trial Balance—October 31	Debit	Credit
Cash		$85,000
Parts Inventory (Cost of Goods Sold).................	$91,000	
Gain on Forward Contract...........................		3,030
Loss on Firm Commitment...........................	3,030	
Adjustment to Net Income...........................		6,000
	$94,030	$94,030

5. Option Contract Fair Value Hedge of a Foreign Currency Firm Commitment

On August 1, Telectro orders parts from its Mexican supplier at a price of Mex$1,000,000. The parts are received and paid for on October 31. On August 1, Telectro purchases a three-month call option on Mex$1,000,000 with a strike price of $0.080. The option is appropriately designated as a *fair value hedge* of the Mexican peso firm commitment. The fair value of the firm commitment is determined through reference to changes in the spot exchange rate.

Journal Entries and Impact on the September 30 and October 31 Trial Balances

8/1	Foreign Currency Option...	$5,200	
	Cash		$5,200
	To record the purchase of a foreign currency option as an asset.		
9/30	Foreign Currency Option...	$4,300	
	Gain on Foreign Currency Option.........................		$4,300
	To adjust the fair value of the option from $5,200 to $9,500 and record an option gain for the change in fair value since August 1.		
	Loss on Firm Commitment......................................	$5,940	
	Firm Commitment...		$5,940
	To record the firm commitment as a liability at its fair value of $5,940 based on changes in the spot rate and record a firm commitment loss for the change in fair value since August 1.		

The fair value of the firm commitment is determined through reference to changes in the spot rate from August 1 to September 30: ($0.080 − $0.086) × Mex$1,000,000 = $(6,000). This amount must be discounted for one month at 12 percent per annum (1 percent per month): $(6,000) × 0.9901 = $(5,941).

Trial Balance—September 30	Debit	Credit
Cash		$ 5,200
Foreign Currency Option (asset)	$ 9,500	
Firm Commitment (liability)........................		5,941
Gain on Foreign Currency Option		4,300
Loss on Firm Commitment.........................	5,941	
	$15,441	$15,441

10/31	Foreign Currency Option..	$1,500	
	Gain on Foreign Currency Option........................		$1,500
	To adjust the fair value of the option from $9,500 to $11,000 and record an option gain for the change in fair value since September 30.		
	Loss on Firm Commitment......................................	$5,060	
	Firm Commitment...		$5,060
	To adjust the fair value of the firm commitment from $5,940 to $11,000 and record a firm commitment loss for the change in fair value since September 30.		

The fair value of the firm commitment is determined through reference to changes in the spot rate from August 1 to October 31: ($0.080 − $0.091) × Mex$1,000,000 = $(11,000).

	Debit	Credit
Foreign Currency (Mex$)...	$91,000	
Cash		$80,000
Foreign Currency Option		11,000
To record exercise of the foreign currency option; record payment of $80,000 in exchange for Mex$1,000,000, record the receipt of Mex$1,000,000 as an asset at the spot rate of $0.091, and remove the option from the accounts.		
Parts Inventory..	$91,000	
Foreign Currency (Mex$).................................		$91,000
To record the purchase of parts through the payment of Mex$1,000,000 to the Mexican supplier.		
Firm Commitment	$11,000	
Adjustment to Net Income		$11,000
To close the firm commitment account as an adjustment to net income.		

Note that the final entry to close the Firm Commitment as an Adjustment to Net Income will be made only in the period in which the Parts Inventory affects net income through Cost of Goods Sold. The Firm Commitment remains on the books as a liability until that point in time.

Trial Balance—October 31	Debit	Credit
Cash ($5,200 credit + $80,000 credit)...............		$85,200
Parts Inventory (Cost of Goods Sold).................	$91,000	
Retained Earnings, 9/30	1,640	
Gain on Foreign Currency Option		1,500
Loss on Firm Commitment...........................	5,060	
Adjustment to Net Income...........................		11,000
	$97,700	$97,700

6. Option Contract Cash Flow Hedge of a Forecasted Foreign Currency Transaction

Telectro anticipates that it will import component parts from its Mexican supplier in the near future. On August 1, Telectro purchases a three-month call option on Mex$1,000,000 with a strike price of $0.080. The option is appropriately designated as a *cash flow hedge* of a forecasted Mexican peso transaction. Parts costing Mex$1,000,000 are received and paid for on October 31. The table at the beginning of the appendix details the exchange rate information.

Journal Entries and Impact on the September 30 and October 31 Trial Balances

		Debit	Credit
8/1	Foreign Currency Option..	$5,200	
	Cash		$5,200
	To record the purchase of a foreign currency option as an asset.		
9/30	Foreign Currency Option..	$4,300	
	Accumulated Other Comprehensive Income (AOCI)..........		$4,300
	To adjust the fair value of the option from $5,200 to $9,500 with a corresponding adjustment to AOCI.		

	Debit	Credit
Option Expense.	$1,700	
Accumulated Other Comprehensive Income (AOCI).		$1,700
To recognize the change in the time value of the foreign currency option as an expense with a corresponding credit to AOCI.		

Trial Balance—September 30	Debit	Credit
Cash		$ 5,200
Foreign Currency Option (asset)	$ 9,500	
Accumulated Other Comprehensive Income		6,000
Option Expense.	1,700	
	$11,200	$11,200

		Debit	Credit
10/31	Foreign Currency Option.	$1,500	
	Accumulated Other Comprehensive Income (AOCI).		$1,500
	To adjust the fair value of the option from $9,500 to $11,000 with a corresponding adjustment to AOCI.		
	Option Expense.	$3,500	
	Accumulated Other Comprehensive Income (AOCI).		$3,500
	To recognize the change in the time value of the foreign currency option as an expense with a corresponding credit to AOCI.		
	Foreign Currency (Mex$).	$91,000	
	Cash		$80,000
	Foreign Currency Option		11,000
	To record exercise of the foreign currency option: record payment of $80,000 in exchange for Mex$1,000,000, record the receipt of Mex$1,000,000 as an asset at the spot rate of $0.091, and remove the option from the accounts.		
	Parts Inventory.	$91,000	
	Foreign Currency (Mex$).		$91,000
	To record the purchase of parts through the payment of Mex$1,000,000 to the Mexican supplier.		
	Accumulated Other Comprehensive Income (AOCI)	$11,000	
	Adjustment to Net Income		$11,000
	To close AOCI as an adjustment to net income.		

Note that the final entry to close AOCI as an Adjustment to Net Income is made at the date that the forecasted transaction was expected to occur, regardless of when the Parts Inventory affects net income.

Trial Balance—October 31	Debit	Credit
Cash ($5,200 credit + $80,000 credit).		$85,200
Parts Inventory (Cost of Goods Sold).	$91,000	
Retained Earnings, 9/30	1,700	
Loss on Foreign Currency Option	3,500	
Adjustment to Net Income.		11,000
	$96,200	$96,200

Appendix B to Chapter 6

Foreign Currency Borrowing

In addition to the receivables and payables that arise from import and export activities, companies often must account for foreign currency borrowings, another type of foreign currency transaction. Companies borrow foreign currency from foreign lenders either to finance foreign operations or perhaps to take advantage of more favorable interest rates. Accounting for a foreign currency borrowing is complicated by the fact that both the principal and interest are denominated in foreign currency and both create an exposure to foreign exchange risk.

To demonstrate the accounting for foreign currency debt, assume that on July 1, Year 1, Mapleleaf International (a company based in Canada) borrowed 1 billion Japanese yen (¥) on a one-year note at a per annum interest rate of 5 percent. Interest is payable and the note comes due on July 1, Year 2. The following exchange rates apply:

Date	Canadian Dollars (C$) per Japanese Yen (¥) Spot Rate
July 1, Year 1	C$0.00921
December 31, Year 1	0.00932
July 1, Year 2	0.00937

On July 1, Year 1, Mapleleaf borrows ¥1,000,000,000 and converts it into C$9,210,000 in the spot market. Over the life of the note, Mapleleaf must record accrued interest expense at year-end and interest payments on the anniversary date of July 1. In addition, the Japanese yen note payable must be revalued at year-end, with foreign exchange gains and losses reported in income. The journal entries to account for this foreign currency borrowing are as follows:

July 1, Year 1	Cash	9,210,000	
	Note Payable (¥)		9,210,000
	To record the yen note payable at the spot rate of C$0.00921 and the conversion of ¥1,000,000,000 into Canadian dollars.		
December 31, Year 1	Interest Expense	233,000	
	Accrued Interest Payable (¥)		233,000
	To accrue interest for the period July 1– December 31, Year 2: (¥1,000,000,000 × 5% × $\frac{1}{2}$ year = ¥25,000,000 × C$0.00932 = C$233,000).		
	Foreign Exchange Loss	110,000	
	Note Payable (¥)		110,000
	To revalue the yen note payable at the spot rate of C$0.00932 and record a foreign exchange loss of C$110,000 (¥1,000,000,000 × [C$0.00932 − C$0.00921]).		
July 1, Year 2	Interest Expense	234,250	
	Accrued Interest Payable (¥)	233,000	

Foreign Exchange Loss	1,250	
Cash		468,500

To record the interest payment of ¥50,000,000 acquired at the spot rate of C$0.00937 for C$468,500; interest expense for the period January 1–July 1, Year 2 (¥25,000,000 × C$0.00937); and a foreign exchange loss on the yen accrued interest payable (¥25,000,000 × [C$0.00937 − C$0.00932]).

Foreign Exchange Loss	50,000	
Note Payable (¥)		50,000

To revalue the yen note payable at the spot rate of C$0.00937 and record a foreign exchange loss of C$50,000 (¥1,000,000,000 × [C$0.00937 − C$0.00932]).

Note Payable (¥)	9,370,000	
Cash		9,370,000

To record repayment of the ¥1,000,000,000 note through purchase of yen at the spot rate of C$0.00937.

Foreign Currency Loan

Rather than borrowing foreign currency, companies may at times lend foreign currency to related parties, thus creating the opposite situation. The accounting in this case involves keeping track of a note receivable and interest receivable, both of which are denominated in foreign currency. Fluctuations in the U.S. dollar value of the principal and interest will generally give rise to foreign exchange gains and losses, which are included in income. Under U.S. GAAP, an exception arises when the foreign currency loan is being made on a long-term basis to a foreign branch, subsidiary, or equity method affiliate. Foreign exchange gains and losses on "intercompany foreign currency transactions that are of a long-term investment nature (i.e., settlement is not planned or anticipated in the foreseeable future)" are reported in other comprehensive income until the loan is repaid. Only the foreign exchange gains and losses related to the interest receivable are recorded currently in net income.

Questions

1. What is the concept underlying the two-transaction perspective in accounting for foreign currency transactions?

2. A company makes an export sale denominated in a foreign currency and allows the customer one month to pay. Under the two-transaction perspective, accrual approach, how does the company account for fluctuations in the exchange rate for the foreign currency?

3. What factors create a foreign exchange gain on a foreign currency transaction? What factors create a foreign exchange loss?

4. What does the word *hedging* mean? Why do companies hedge foreign exchange risk?

5. How does a foreign currency option differ from a foreign currency forward contract?

6. How does the timing differ for hedges of the following?
   a. Foreign-currency-denominated assets and liabilities.
   b. Foreign currency firm commitments.
   c. Forecasted foreign currency transactions.

7. Why might a company prefer a foreign currency option rather than a forward contract in hedging a foreign currency firm commitment? Why might a company prefer a forward contract over an option in hedging a foreign currency asset or liability?

8. How are foreign currency derivatives such as forward contracts and options reported on the balance sheet?

9. How is the fair value of a foreign currency forward contract determined? How is the fair value of an option determined?

10. What is hedge accounting?

11. What conditions must be met to apply hedge accounting to a foreign currency option used to hedge a forecasted foreign currency transaction?

12. What are the differences in accounting for a forward contract used as (*a*) a cash flow hedge and (*b*) a fair value hedge of a foreign-currency-denominated asset or liability?

13. What are the differences in accounting for a forward contract used as a fair value hedge of (*a*) a foreign-currency-denominated asset or liability and (*b*) a foreign currency firm commitment?

14. What are the differences in accounting for a forward contract used as a cash flow hedge of (*a*) a foreign-currency-denominated asset or liability and (*b*) a forecasted foreign currency transaction?

15. How are changes in the fair value of an option accounted for in a cash flow hedge? In a fair value hedge?

16. In what way is the accounting for a foreign currency borrowing more complicated than the accounting for a foreign currency account payable?

17. What happened in the United Kingdom in June 2016 and why is the event important for the accounting topics covered in this chapter?

Exercises and Problems

1. Which of the following combinations correctly describes the relationship between foreign currency transactions, exchange rate changes, and foreign exchange gains and losses?

	Type of Transaction	Foreign Currency	Foreign Exchange Gain or Loss
a.	Export sale	Appreciates	Loss
b.	Import purchase	Appreciates	Gain
c.	Import purchase	Depreciates	Gain
d.	Export sale	Depreciates	Gain

2. Gracie Corporation had a Japanese yen receivable resulting from exports to Japan and a Brazilian real payable resulting from imports from Brazil. Gracie recorded foreign exchange gains related to both its yen receivable and real payable. Did the foreign currencies increase or decrease in dollar value from the date of the transaction to the settlement date?

	Yen	Real
a.	Increase	Increase
b.	Decrease	Decrease
c.	Decrease	Increase
d.	Increase	Decrease

3. On December 1, Year 1, Tackett Company (a U.S.-based company) entered into a three-month forward contract to purchase 1 million Mexican pesos on March 1, Year 2. The following U.S. dollar–peso exchange rates apply:

Date	Spot Rate	Forward Rate (to March 1, Year 2)
December 1, Year 1	$0.088	$0.084
December 31, Year 1	0.080	0.074
March 1, Year 2	0.076	

Tackett's incremental borrowing rate is 12 percent. The present value factor for two months at an annual interest rate of 12 percent (1 percent per month) is 0.9803.

Which of the following correctly describes the manner in which Tackett Company will report the forward contract on its December 31, Year 1, balance sheet?

a. As an asset in the amount of $3,921.20.

b. As an asset in the amount of $7,842.40.

c. As a liability in the amount of $13,724.20.

d. As a liability in the amount of $9,803.00.

Use the following information for Exercises 4 and 5: Reiter Corp. (a U.S.-based company) sold parts to an Israeli customer on December 1, Year 1, with payment of 100,000 Israeli shekels to be received on March 31, Year 2. The following exchange rates apply:

Date	Spot Rate	Forward Rate (to March 31, Year 2)
December 1, Year 1	$0.24	$0.23
December 31, Year 1	0.22	0.20
March 31, Year 2	0.25	

Reiter's incremental borrowing rate is 12 percent. The present value factor for three months at an annual interest rate of 12 percent (1 percent per month) is 0.9706.

4. Assuming no forward contract was entered into, how much foreign exchange gain or loss should Reiter report on its Year 1 income statement with regard to this transaction?

a. A $5,000 gain.

b. A $3,000 gain.

c. A $2,000 loss.

d. A $1,000 loss.

5. Assuming a forward contract to sell 100,000 Israeli shekels was entered into on December 1, Year 1, as a fair value hedge of a foreign currency receivable, what would be the net impact on net income in Year 1 resulting from a fluctuation in the value of the shekel?

a. No impact on net income.

b. A $58.80 decrease in net income.

c. A $2,000 decrease in income.

d. A $911.80 increase in income.

Use the following information for Exercises 6 through 8: On September 1, Year 1, Keefer Company received an order to sell a machine to a customer in Canada at a price of

100,000 Canadian dollars. The machine was shipped and payment was received on March 1, Year 2. On September 1, Year 1, Keefer Company purchased a put option giving it the right to sell 100,000 Canadian dollars on March 1, Year 2, at a price of $75,000. Keefer Company properly designates the option as a fair value hedge of the Canadian-dollar firm commitment. The option cost $1,700 and had a fair value of $2,800 on December 31, Year 1. The fair value of the firm commitment is measured through reference to changes in the spot rate. The following spot exchange rates apply:

Date	U.S. Dollar per Canadian Dollar
September 1, Year 1..........	$0.75
December 31, Year 1.........	0.73
March 1, Year 2.............	0.71

Keefer Company's incremental borrowing rate is 12 percent. The present value factor for two months at an annual interest rate of 12 percent (1 percent per month) is 0.9803.

6. What was the net impact on Keefer Company's Year 1 income as a result of this fair value hedge of a firm commitment?
   a. $0.
   b. An $860.60 decrease in income.
   c. A $1,100.00 increase in income.
   d. A $1,960.60 increase in income.

7. What was the net impact on Keefer Company's Year 2 income as a result of this fair value hedge of a firm commitment?
   a. $0.
   b. An $839.40 decrease in income.
   c. A $74,160.60 increase in income.
   d. A $76,200.00 increase in income.

8. What was the net increase or decrease in cash flow from having purchased the foreign currency option to hedge this exposure to foreign exchange risk?
   a. $0.
   b. A $1,000 increase in cash flow.
   c. A $1,700 decrease in cash flow.
   d. A $2,300 increase in cash flow.

Use the following information for Problems 9 and 10: On November 1, Year 1, Black Lion Company forecasts the purchase of raw materials from an Argentinian supplier on February 1, Year 2, at a price of 200,000 Argentinian pesos. On November 1, Year 1, Black Lion pays $1,200 for a three-month call option on 200,000 Argentinian pesos with a strike price of $0.35 per peso. The option is properly designated as a cash flow hedge of a forecasted foreign currency transaction. On December 31, Year 1, the option has a fair value of $900. The following spot exchange rates apply:

Date	U.S. Dollar per Argentinian Peso
November 1, Year 1...........	$0.35
December 31, Year 1..........	0.30
February 1, Year 2	0.36

9. What is the net impact on Black Lion Company's Year 1 net income as a result of this hedge of a forecasted foreign currency purchase?

   a. $0.

   b. A $200 increase in net income.

   c. A $300 decrease in net income.

   d. An $800 decrease in net income.

10. What is the net impact on Black Lion Company's Year 2 net income as a result of this hedge of a forecasted foreign currency purchase? Assume that the raw materials are consumed and become a part of cost of goods sold in Year 2.

    a. A $70,000 decrease in net income.

    b. A $70,900 decrease in net income.

    c. A $71,100 decrease in net income.

    d. A $72,900 decrease in net income.

11. Garden Grove Corporation made a sale to a foreign customer on September 15, Year 1, for 100,000 foreign currency units (FCU). Payment was received on October 15, Year 1. The following exchange rates apply:

Date	U.S. Dollar per FCU
September 15, Year 1	$0.40
September 30, Year 1	0.42
October 15, Year 1	0.37

Required:

Prepare all journal entries for Garden Grove Corporation in connection with this sale, assuming that the company closes its books on September 30 to prepare interim financial statements.

12. On December 1, Year 1, El Primero Company purchases inventory from a foreign supplier for 40,000 coronas. Payment will be made in 90 days after El Primero has sold this merchandise. Sales are made rather quickly, and El Primero pays this entire obligation on February 15, Year 2. The following exchange rates for 1 corona apply:

Date	U.S. Dollar per Corona
December 1, Year 1	$0.87
December 31, Year 1	0.82
February 15, Year 2	0.91

Required:

Prepare all journal entries for El Primero in connection with the purchase and payment.

13. On September 30, Year 1, the Lester Company negotiated a two-year loan of 1,000,000 markkas from a foreign bank at an interest rate of 2 percent per annum. Interest payments are made annually on September 30, and the principal will be repaid on September 30, Year 3. Lester Company prepares U.S. dollar financial statements and

has a December 31 year-end. Prepare all journal entries related to this foreign currency borrowing, assuming the following exchange rates for 1 markka:

Date	U.S. Dollars per Markka
September 30, Year 1	$0.20
December 31, Year 1.	0.21
September 30, Year 2	0.23
December 31, Year 2.	0.24
September 30, Year 3	0.27

Required:
Prepare all journal entries for the Lester Company in connection with the foreign currency borrowing. What is the effective annual cost of borrowing in dollars in Year 1, Year 2, and Year 3?

14. The Budvar Company sells parts to a foreign customer on December 1, Year 1, with payment of 20,000 crowns to be received on March 1, Year 2. Budvar enters into a forward contract on December 1, Year 1, to sell 20,000 crowns on March 1, Year 2. Relevant exchange rates for the crown on various dates are as follows:

Date	Spot Rate	Forward Rate (to March 1, Year 2)
December 1, Year 1	$1.00	$1.04
December 31, Year 1.	1.05	1.10
March 1, Year 2	1.12	

Budvar's incremental borrowing rate is 12 percent. The present value factor for two months at an annual interest rate of 12 percent (1 percent per month) is 0.9803. Budvar must close its books and prepare financial statements at December 31.

Required:
a. Assuming that Budvar designates the forward contract as a cash flow hedge of a foreign currency receivable, prepare journal entries for these transactions in U.S. dollars. What is the impact on Year 1 net income? What is the impact on Year 2 net income? What is the impact on net income over the two accounting periods?

b. Assuming that Budvar designates the forward contract as a fair value hedge of a foreign currency receivable, prepare journal entries for these transactions in U.S. dollars. What is the impact on Year 1 net income? What is the impact on Year 2 net income? What is the impact on net income over the two accounting periods?

15. The same facts apply as in Exercise 14 except that Budvar Company purchases parts from a foreign supplier on December 1, Year 1, with payment of 20,000 crowns to be made on March 1, Year 2. On December 1, Year 1, Budvar enters into a forward contract to purchase 20,000 crowns on March 1, Year 2. The parts purchased on December 1, Year 1, become a part of the cost of goods sold on March 15, Year 2.

Required:
a. Assuming that Budvar designates the forward contract as a cash flow hedge of a foreign currency payable, prepare journal entries for these transactions in U.S. dollars. What is the impact on Year 1 net income? What is the impact on Year 2 net income? What is the impact on net income over the two accounting periods?

b. Assuming that Budvar designates the forward contract as a fair value hedge of a foreign currency payable, prepare journal entries for these transactions in U.S. dollars. What is the impact on Year 1 net income? What is the impact on Year 2 net income? What is the impact on net income over the two accounting periods?

16. On November 1, Year 1, Alexandria Company sold merchandise to a foreign customer for 100,000 francs with payment to be received on April 30, Year 2. At the date of sale, Alexandria Company entered into a six-month forward contract to sell 100,000 francs. The forward contract is properly designated as a cash flow hedge of a foreign currency receivable. Relevant exchange rates for the franc are:

Date	Spot Rate	Forward Rate (to April 30, Year 2)
November 1, Year 1	$0.23	$0.22
December 31, Year 1	0.20	0.18
April 30, Year 2	0.19	

Alexandria Company's incremental borrowing rate is 12 percent. The present value factor for four months at an annual interest rate of 12 percent (1 percent per month) is 0.9610.

Required:
Prepare all journal entries, including December 31 adjusting entries, to record the sale and forward contract. What is the impact on net income in Year 1? What is the impact on net income in Year 2?

17. Artco Inc. engages in various transactions with companies in the country of Santrica. On November 30, Year 1, Artco sold artwork at a price of 400,000 ricas to a Santrican customer, with payment to be received on January 31, Year 2. In addition, on November 30, Year 1, Artco purchased art supplies from a Santrican supplier at a price of 300,000 ricas; payment will be made on January 31, Year 2. The art supplies are consumed by the end of November, Year 1. To hedge its net exposure in ricas, Artco entered into a two-month forward contract on November 30, Year 1, wherein Artco will deliver 100,000 ricas to the foreign currency broker in exchange for U.S dollars at the agreed-on forward rate. Artco properly designates its forward contract as a fair value hedge of a foreign currency receivable. The following rates for the rica apply:

Date	Spot Rate	Forward Rate (to January 31, Year 2)
November 30, Year 1	$0.13	$0.12
December 31, Year 1	0.10	0.08
January 31, Year 2	0.09	

Artco Inc.'s incremental borrowing rate is 12 percent. The present value factor for one month at an annual interest rate of 12 percent (1 percent per month) is 0.9901.

Required:
Prepare all journal entries, including December 31 adjusting entries, to record these transactions and the forward contract. What is the impact on net income in Year 1? What is the impact on net income in Year 2?

18. On October 1, Year 1, Butterworth Company entered into a forward contract to sell 100,000 rupees in four months (on January 31, Year 2). Relevant exchange rates for the rupee are as follows:

Date	Spot Rate	Forward Rate (to January 31, Year 2)
October 1, Year 1	$0.069	$0.065
December 31, Year 1	0.071	0.074
January 31, Year 2	0.072	

Butterworth Company's incremental borrowing rate is 12 percent. The present value factor for one month at an annual interest rate of 12 percent (1 percent per month) is 0.9901. Butterworth must close its books and prepare financial statements on December 31.

Required:

a. Prepare journal entries assuming the forward contract was entered into as a fair value hedge of a 100,000-rupee receivable arising from a sale made on October 1, Year 1. Include entries for both the sale and the forward contract.

b. Prepare journal entries assuming the forward contract was entered into as a fair value hedge of a firm commitment related to a 100,000-rupee sale that will be made on January 31, Year 2. Include entries for both the firm commitment and the forward contract. The fair value of the firm commitment is measured through reference to changes in the forward rate.

19. On August 1, Year 1, Huntington Corporation placed an order to purchase merchandise from a foreign supplier at a price of 100,000 dinars. The merchandise is received and paid for on October 31, Year 1, and is fully consumed by December 31, Year 1. On August 1, Huntington entered into a forward contract to purchase 100,000 dinars in three months at the agreed-on forward rate. The forward contract is properly designated as a fair value hedge of a foreign currency firm commitment. The fair value of the firm commitment is measured through reference to changes in the forward rate. Relevant exchange rates for the dinar are as follows:

Date	Spot Rate	Forward Rate (to October 31, Year 1)
August 1	$1.300	$1.310
September 30	1.305	1.325
October 31	1.320	

Huntington's incremental borrowing rate is 12 percent. The present value factor for one month at an annual interest rate of 12 percent (1 percent per month) is 0.9901. Huntington Corporation must close its books and prepare its third-quarter financial statements on September 30, Year 1.

Required:

Prepare journal entries for the forward contract and firm commitment. What is the impact on net income in Year 1? What is the net cash outflow on the purchase of merchandise from the foreign customer?

20. On June 1, Year 1, Tsanumis Corporation (a U.S.-based manufacturing firm) received an order to sell goods to a foreign customer at a price of 1 million euros. The goods

will be shipped and payment will be received in three months on September 1, Year 1. On June 1, Tsanumis Corporation purchased an option to sell 1 million euros in three months at a strike price of $1.00. The option is properly designated as a fair value hedge of a foreign currency firm commitment. The fair value of the firm commitment is measured through reference to changes in the spot rate. Relevant exchange rates and option premiums for the euro during Year 1 are as follows:

Date	Spot Rate	Call Option Premium for September 1, Year 1 (strike price $1.00)
June 1	$1.00	$0.010
June 30	0.99	0.015
September 1	0.97	

Tsanumis Corporation's incremental borrowing rate is 12 percent. The present value factor for two months at an annual interest rate of 12 percent (1 percent per month) is 0.9803. Tsanumis Corporation must close its books and prepare its second-quarter financial statements on June 30.

Required:
Prepare journal entries for the foreign currency option and firm commitment. What is the impact on Year 1 net income? What is the net cash inflow resulting from the sale of goods to the foreign customer?

21. The Zermatt Company ordered parts from a foreign supplier on November 20 at a price of 100,000 francs when the spot rate was $0.80 per peso. Delivery and payment were scheduled for December 20. On November 20, Zermatt acquired a call option on 100,000 francs at a strike price of $0.80, paying a premium of $0.008 per franc. The option is designated as a fair value hedge of a foreign currency firm commitment. The fair value of the firm commitment is measured through reference to changes in the spot rate. The parts are delivered and paid for according to schedule. Zermatt does not close its books until December 31.

Required:
a. Assuming a spot rate of $0.83 per franc on December 20, prepare all journal entries to account for the option and firm commitment.
b. Assuming a spot rate of $0.78 per franc on December 20, prepare all journal entries to account for the option and firm commitment.

22. Given its experience, Garnier Corporation expects that it will sell goods to a foreign customer at a price of 1 million lire on March 15, Year 2. To hedge this forecasted transaction, a three-month put option to sell 1 million lire is acquired on December 15, Year 1. Garnier selects a strike price of $0.15 per lire, paying a premium of $0.005 per unit, when the spot rate is $0.15. The spot rate decreases to $0.14 at December 31, Year 1, causing the fair value of the option to increase to $12,000. By March 15, Year 2, when the goods are delivered and payment is received from the customer, the spot rate has fallen to $0.13, resulting in a fair value for the option of $20,000.

Required:
Prepare all journal entries for the option hedge of a forecasted transaction and for the export sale, assuming that December 31 is Garnier Corporation's year-end. What is the overall impact on net income over the two accounting periods? What is the net cash inflow from this export sale?

Case 6-1

Zorba Company

Zorba Company, a U.S.-based importer of specialty olive oil, placed an order with a foreign supplier for 500 cases of olive oil at a price of 100 crowns per case. The total purchase price is 50,000 crowns. Relevant exchange rates are as follows:

Date	Spot Rate	Forward Rate (to January 31, Year 2)	Call Option Premium for January 31, Year 2 (strike price $1.00)
December 1, Year 1	$1.00	$1.08	$0.04
December 31, Year 1	1.10	1.17	0.12
January 31, Year 2	1.15	1.15	0.15

Zorba Company has an incremental borrowing rate of 12 percent (1 percent per month) and closes the books and prepares financial statements on December 31.

Required

1. Assume the olive oil was received on December 1, Year 1, and payment was made on January 31, Year 2. There was no attempt to hedge the exposure to foreign exchange risk. Prepare journal entries to account for this import purchase.

2. Assume the olive oil was received on December 1, Year 1, and payment was made on January 31, Year 2. On December 1, Zorba Company entered into a two-month forward contract to purchase 50,000 crowns. The forward contract is properly designated as a fair value hedge of a foreign currency payable. Prepare journal entries to account for the import purchase and foreign currency forward contract.

3. The olive oil was ordered on December 1, Year 1. It was received and paid for on January 31, Year 2. On December 1, Zorba Company entered into a two-month forward contract to purchase 50,000 crowns. The forward contract is properly designated as a fair value hedge of a foreign currency firm commitment. The fair value of the firm commitment is measured through reference to changes in the forward rate. Prepare journal entries to account for the foreign currency forward contract, firm commitment, and import purchase.

4. The olive oil was received on December 1, Year 1, and payment was made on January 31, Year 2. On December 1, Zorba Company purchased a two-month call option for 50,000 crowns. The option was properly designated as a cash flow hedge of a foreign currency payable. Prepare journal entries to account for the import purchase and foreign currency option.

5. The olive oil was ordered on December 1, Year 1. It was received and paid for on January 31, Year 2. On December 1, Zorba Company purchased a two-month call option for 50,000 crowns. The option was properly designated as a fair value hedge of a foreign currency firm commitment. The fair value of the firm commitment is measured through reference to changes in the spot rate. Prepare journal entries to account for the foreign currency option, firm commitment, and import purchase.

Case 6-2

Portofino Company

Portofino Company made purchases on account from three foreign suppliers on December 15, 2021, with payment made on January 15, 2022. Information related to these purchases is as follows:

Supplier	Location	Invoice Price
Beija Flor Ltda.	São Paulo, Brazil	65,000 Brazilian reals
Yepez A. SA	Buenos Aires, Argentina	250,000 Argentine pesos
Mariposa SA de CV	Guadalajara, Mexico	400,000 Mexican pesos

Portofino Company's fiscal year ends December 31.

Required

1. Use historical exchange rate information available on the internet at www.x-rates.com to find interbank exchange rates between the U.S. dollar and each foreign currency for the period December 15, 2021, to January 15, 2022.
2. Determine the foreign exchange gains and losses that Portofino would have recognized in net income in 2021 and 2022 and the overall foreign exchange gain or loss for each transaction. Determine for which transaction it would have been most important for Portofino to hedge its foreign exchange risk.
3. Portofino could have acquired a one-month call option on December 15, 2021, to hedge the foreign exchange risk associated with each of the three import purchases. In each case, the option would have had an exercise price equal to the spot rate at December 15, 2021, and would have cost $50. Determine for which hedges, if any, Portofino would have recognized a net gain on the foreign currency option.

Case 6-3

2020 Brexit–Jaguar Land Rover

In a referendum on June 23, 2016, the UK electorate voted to leave the European Union (EU). On March 29, 2017, the British government invoked Article 50 of the Treaty on the EU. The UK left the EU at the end of January 31, 2020.

Required

Read, summarize, and explain what happened to the UK subsidiary of Tata Motors (TM), Jaguar Land Rover (JLR) right after the June 2016 Brexit vote. How could JLR have hedged the foreign exchange risk and avoided foreign exchange losses?

For reference, see the following article: *https://www.reuters.com/article/us-britain-eu-jaguarlandrover-exclusive/exclusive-jaguar-land-rover-could-face-1-billion-pound-brexit-hit-sources-idUSKCN0Z71SJ.*

Case 6-4

Better Food Corporation

Better Food Corporation (BFC) regularly purchases nutritional supplements from a supplier in Japan with the invoice price denominated in Japanese yen. BFC has experienced several foreign exchange losses in the past year due to increases in the U.S. dollar price of the Japanese currency. As a result, BFC's CEO, Harvey Carlisle, has asked you to investigate the possibility of using derivative financial instruments—specifically, foreign currency forward contracts and foreign currency options—to hedge the company's exposure to foreign exchange risk.

Required

Draft a memo to CEO Carlisle comparing the advantages and disadvantages of using forward contracts and options to hedge foreign exchange risk. Make a recommendation for which type of hedging instrument you believe the company should employ, and provide your justification for this recommendation.

Chapter **Seven**

Translation of Foreign Currency Financial Statements

Learning Objectives

After reading this chapter, you should be able to

- Describe the conceptual issues involved in translating foreign currency financial statements.
- Explain balance sheet exposure and how it differs from transaction exposure.
- Describe the concepts underlying the current rate and temporal methods of translation.
- Apply the current rate and temporal methods of translation and compare the results.
- Describe the requirements of applicable International Financial Reporting Standards (IFRS) and U.S. generally accepted accounting principles (GAAP).
- Discuss hedging of balance sheet exposure.

INTRODUCTION

In today's global business environment, many companies have operations in foreign countries. In its 2021 Form 10-K, Ford Motor Company provided a list of subsidiaries located in some 15 different countries around the world, none of which uses the U.S. dollar as its national currency. The German automaker Volkswagen AG reports having production subsidiaries in more than 30 countries other than Germany. Twenty of these countries use a currency other than the euro, which is Volkswagen's financial reporting currency. Many operations located in foreign countries keep their accounting records and prepare financial statements in the local currency using local accounting principles. To prepare consolidated financial statements, parent companies must restate their foreign subsidiaries' financial statements in terms of the parent company's generally accepted accounting principles (GAAP) and then translate the statements into the parent company's reporting currency. The diversity in national accounting standards and the problems associated with that diversity (such as the GAAP reconciliation for consolidation purposes) are discussed in Chapter 2.

This chapter focuses on the *translation* of foreign currency financial statements into the parent company's reporting currency for the purpose of preparing consolidated financial statements. We begin by examining the conceptual issues related to translation and then describe the manner in which these issues have been addressed by the International Accounting Standards Board (IASB) and by the Financial Accounting Standards Board (FASB) in the United States. We then illustrate application of the two methods prescribed by those standard-setters and compare the results from applying the two different methods. We also discuss hedging the net investment in foreign operations to avoid the adverse impact the translation of foreign currency financial statements can have on the consolidated accounts. The appendix to this chapter demonstrates the process for translating foreign currency financial statements when the foreign subsidiary is located in a hyperinflationary country.

TWO CONCEPTUAL ISSUES

In translating foreign currency financial statements into the parent company's reporting currency, two questions must be addressed:

1. What is the appropriate exchange rate to be used in translating each financial statement item?
2. How should the translation adjustment that inherently arises from the translation process be reflected in the consolidated financial statements?

We introduce these issues and the basic concepts underlying the translation of financial statements using the following example.

Example

Parentco, a U.S.-based company, establishes a wholly owned subsidiary, Foreignco, in Foreign Country on January 1 by investing US$600 when the exchange rate between the U.S. dollar and the foreign currency (FC) is FC1 = US$1.00. The equity investment of US$600 is physically converted into FC600. In addition, Foreignco borrows FC400 from local banks on January 2. Foreignco purchases inventory that costs FC900 and maintains FC100 in cash. Foreignco's opening balance sheet appears as follows:

		FOREIGNCO		
		Opening Balance Sheet		
Cash	FC 100	Liabilities.......................	FC 400	
Inventory......................	900	Common stock	600	
Total..........................	FC1,000	Total..........................	FC1,000	

To prepare a consolidated balance sheet in US$ at the date of acquisition, all FC balances on Foreignco's balance sheet are translated at the exchange rate of US$1.00 per FC1. There is no other exchange rate that possibly could be used on that date. A partial consolidation worksheet at the date of acquisition would appear as follows:

Consolidation Worksheet at Date of Acquisition for Parentco and Its Subsidiary Foreignco

	Parentco US$	Foreignco FC	Exchange Rate	US$	Eliminations Dr.	Cr.	Consolidated Balance Sheet US$
Investment	600	—				(1) 600*	0
Cash....................	(600)	100	$1.00	100			(500)
Inventory	xx	900	$1.00	900			900
Total	xxx	1,000		1,000			400
Liabilities	xx	400	$1.00	400			400
Common stock...........	xx	600	$1.00	600	(1) 600		0
Total	xxx	1,000		1,000			400

* The elimination entry eliminates Parentco's Investment in Subsidiary account against Foreignco's Common Stock account.

By translating each FC balance on Foreignco's balance sheet at the same exchange rate (US$1.00), Foreignco's US$ translated balance sheet reflects an equal amount of total assets and total liabilities and equity.

Three Months Later

During the period January 1 to March 31, Foreignco engages in no transactions. However, during that period the FC appreciates in value against the U.S. dollar such that the exchange rate at March 31 is US$1.20 per FC1.

In preparing the March 31 interim consolidated financial statements, Parentco now must choose between the current exchange rate of US$1.20 and the past (historical) exchange rate of US$1.00 to translate Foreignco's balance sheet into U.S. dollars. Foreignco's stockholders' equity must be translated at the historical rate of US$1.00 so that Parentco's Investment account can be eliminated against the subsidiary's common stock in the consolidation worksheet. Two approaches exist for translating the subsidiary's assets and liabilities:

1. All assets and liabilities are translated at the *current exchange rate* (the spot exchange rate on the balance sheet date).
2. Some assets and liabilities are translated at the current exchange rate, and other assets and liabilities are translated at *historical exchange rates* (the exchange rates that existed when the assets and liabilities were acquired or incurred).

All Assets and Liabilities Are Translated at the Current Exchange Rate

If the first approach is adopted, in which all assets and liabilities are translated at the current exchange rate, the consolidation worksheet on March 31 would appear as follows:

Consolidation Worksheet Three Months after Date of Acquisition for Parentco and Its Subsidiary Foreignco

	Parentco US$	Foreignco FC	Exchange Rate	US$	Change in US$ Value Since January 1	Eliminations Dr.	Cr.	Consolidated Balance Sheet US$
Investment	600	—					(1) 600	0
Cash	(600)	100	$1.20	120	+20			(480)
Inventory	xx	900	$1.20	1,080	+180			1,080
Total	xxx	1,000		1,200	+200			600
Liabilities	xx	400	$1.20	480	+80			480
Common stock	xx	600	$ 1.00	600	0	(1) 600		0
Subtotal	xxx	1,000		1,080	+80			480
Translation adjustment				120	**+120**			120
Total				1,200	+200			600

By translating all assets at the higher current exchange rate, assets are written up in terms of their U.S. dollar value by US$200 (from US$400 to US$600). Liabilities are also written up by US$80 (from US$400 to US$480). To keep the U.S.-dollar translated balance sheet in balance, a *positive* (credit) translation adjustment of US$120 must be recorded. As a result, total assets on the consolidated balance sheet at March 31 are US$120 greater than on January 1, as are consolidated total liabilities and stockholders' equity.

Translating foreign currency balances at the current exchange rate is similar to revaluing foreign currency receivables and payables at the balance sheet date. The translation adjustment is analogous to the *net* foreign exchange gain or loss caused by a change in the exchange rate:

$20 gain on cash + $180 gain on inventory − $80 loss on liabilities = $120 net gain

The net foreign exchange gain (positive translation adjustment) is *unrealized,* that is, it does not result in a cash inflow of US$120 for Parentco. However, the gain can be *realized* by Parentco selling Foreignco at the book value of its net assets (FC600) and converting the proceeds into U.S. dollars at the current exchange rate (FC600 × $1.20 = US$720). In that case, Parentco would realize a gain from the sale of its investment in Foreignco that would be due solely to the appreciation in value of the foreign currency:

Proceeds from the sale	$720
Original investment.	600
Realized gain	$120

The translation adjustment reflects the *change in the U.S. dollar value of the net investment* in Foreignco if the subsidiary were to be sold. In addition, a *positive* translation adjustment signals that the appreciation of the foreign currency will result in an increase in the U.S. dollar value of future foreign currency dividends to be paid by Foreignco to its parent. For example, a dividend of FC10 distributed on March 31 can be converted into US$12, whereas the same amount of foreign currency dividend would have been worth only US$10 at the beginning of the year.

Monetary Assets and Liabilities Are Translated at the Current Exchange Rate

Now assume that only monetary assets (cash and receivables) and monetary liabilities (most liabilities) are translated at the current exchange rate. The worksheet to translate Foreignco's financial statements into U.S. dollars on March 31 appears as follows:

Consolidation Worksheet Three Months after Date of Acquisition for Parentco and Its Subsidiary Foreignco

	Parentco US$	Foreignco FC	Exchange Rate	US$	Change in US$ Value Since January 1	Eliminations Dr.	Cr.	Consolidated Balance Sheet US$
Investment	600	—					(1) 600	0
Cash	(600)	100	**$1.20**	120	+20			(480)
Inventory.	xx	900	$ 1.00	900	0			900
Total.	xxx	1,000		1,020	+20			420
Liabilities.	xx	400	**$1.20**	480	**+80**			480
Common stock	xx	600	$ 1.00	600	0	(1) 600		0
Subtotal.	xxx	1,000		1,080	+80			480
Translation adjustment				(60)	**−60**			(60)
Total.				1,020	+20			420

Using this approach, cash is written up by US$20 and liabilities are written up by US$80. To keep the balance sheet in balance, a *negative* (debit) translation adjustment of US$60 must be recorded. As a result, both total assets and total liabilities and stockholders' equity on the March 31 consolidated balance sheet are US$20 greater than on January 1.

The translation adjustment is analogous to the *net* foreign exchange gain or loss caused by a change in the exchange rate:

$$\$20 \text{ gain on cash} - \$80 \text{ loss on liabilities} = \$60 \text{ net loss}$$

This net foreign exchange loss (negative translation adjustment) also is *unrealized.* However, the loss can be *realized* through the following process:

1. The subsidiary uses its cash (FC100) to pay its liabilities to the extent possible.
2. The parent sends enough U.S. dollars to the subsidiary to pay its remaining liabilities (FC300). At January 1, the parent would have sent US$300 to pay FC300 of liabilities (at the $1.00/FC1 exchange rate). At March 31, the parent must send US$360 to pay FC300 of liabilities (at the $1.20/FC1 exchange rate). It takes US$60 (US$360 − US$300) more on March 31 than on January 1 to pay Foreignco's liabilities solely because of the change in exchange rate. A foreign exchange loss (negative translation adjustment) of US$60 arises on the net monetary liability position because the foreign currency has appreciated from January 1 to March 31.

Note that under this translation approach, the *negative* translation adjustment does not reflect the change in the U.S.-dollar value of the net investment in Foreignco. Moreover, the *negative* translation adjustment is not consistent with the change in the U.S.-dollar value of future foreign currency dividends. As the foreign currency appreciates, the U.S.-dollar value of foreign currency dividends received from Foreignco increases.

Balance Sheet Exposure

As exchange rates change, those assets and liabilities translated at the *current* exchange rate change in value from balance sheet to balance sheet in terms of the parent company's reporting currency (e.g., U.S. dollar). These items are *exposed* to translation adjustment. Balance sheet items translated at *historical* exchange rates do not change in parent currency value from one balance sheet to the next. These items are *not* exposed to translation adjustment. Exposure to translation adjustment is referred to as balance sheet, translation, or accounting exposure. *Balance sheet exposure* can be contrasted with the *transaction exposure* discussed in Chapter 6 that arises when a company has foreign currency receivables and payables as follows:

> Transaction exposure gives rise to foreign exchange gains and losses that are ultimately realized in cash; translation adjustments that arise from balance sheet exposure do not directly result in cash inflows or outflows.

Each item translated at the current exchange rate is exposed to translation adjustment. In effect, a separate translation adjustment exists for each of these exposed items. However, positive translation adjustments on assets when the foreign currency appreciates are offset by negative translation adjustments on liabilities. If total exposed assets are equal to total exposed liabilities throughout the year, the translation adjustments (although perhaps significant on an individual basis) net to a zero balance. The *net* translation adjustment needed to keep the consolidated balance sheet in balance is based solely on the *net* asset or *net* liability exposure.

A foreign operation will have a *net asset balance sheet exposure* when assets translated at the current exchange rate are greater in amount than liabilities translated at the current exchange rate. A *net liability balance sheet exposure* exists when liabilities translated at the current exchange rate are greater than assets translated at the current exchange rate. The relationship between exchange rate fluctuations, balance sheet exposure, and translation adjustments can be summarized as follows:

Balance Sheet Exposure	Foreign Currency (FC)	
	Appreciates	**Depreciates**
Net asset	Positive translation adjustment	Negative translation adjustment
Net liability	Negative translation adjustment	Positive translation adjustment

Exactly how the translation adjustment should be reported in the consolidated financial statements is a matter of some debate. The major question is whether the translation adjustment should be treated as a *translation gain or loss reported in net income* or an *unrealized gain or loss reported as a component of other comprehensive income* (i.e., deferred in stockholders' equity). This issue is considered in this chapter in more detail after first examining different methods of translation.

TRANSLATION METHODS

Two methods of translating foreign currency financial statements are currently used worldwide: (1) the temporal method and (2) the current rate method. Although neither the FASB nor the IASB specifically uses these names in their authoritative guidance, *temporal method* and *current rate method* provide a useful shorthand for describing the procedures required.

Temporal Method

The basic objective underlying the *temporal method* of translation is to produce a set of parent currency translated financial statements as if the foreign subsidiary had actually used the parent currency in conducting its operations. For example, Land carried on the books of a foreign subsidiary should be translated such that it is reported on the consolidated balance sheet at the amount of parent currency that would have been spent if the parent had sent parent currency to the subsidiary to purchase the land. Assume that a piece of land in Japan costs 12,000,000 Japanese yen (¥) and is acquired at a time when one yen costs 0.012 New Zealand dollars (NZ$). A New Zealand parent company would send NZ$144,000 (¥12 million × NZ$0.012) to its Japanese subsidiary to acquire the land. This is the land's historical cost in parent currency terms.

Consistent with the temporal method's underlying objective, assets and liabilities reported on the foreign operation's balance sheet at historical cost are translated at historical exchange rates to yield an equivalent historical cost in parent currency terms. Conversely, assets and liabilities reported on the foreign operation's balance sheet at a current (or future) value are translated at the current exchange rate to yield an equivalent current value in parent currency terms. (As is true under any translation method, stockholders' equity accounts are translated at historical exchange rates.) Application of these rules maintains the underlying valuation method (historical cost or current value) used by the foreign subsidiary in accounting for its assets and liabilities.

Cash, receivables, and most liabilities are carried at current or future values under the traditional historical cost model of accounting. These balance sheet accounts are translated at the current exchange rate under the temporal method. Both IFRS and U.S. GAAP require inventory to be carried on the balance sheet at the lower of cost or net realizable value. The temporal method requires inventory to be translated at historical exchange rates when it is carried at cost and at the current exchange rate when it is carried at net realizable value. Marketable securities are carried at fair value under both IFRS and U.S. GAAP, and therefore they are also translated at the current exchange rate.

The temporal method generates either a net asset or a net liability balance sheet exposure depending on whether assets translated at the current exchange rate are greater than or less than liabilities translated at the current exchange rate. This can be generalized as follows:

Cash + Marketable securities + Receivables + Inventory (when carried at net realizable value) > Liabilities → Net asset exposure

Cash + Marketable securities + Receivables + Inventory (when carried at net realizable value) < Liabilities → Net liability exposure

Because liabilities (current plus long-term) usually are greater than assets translated at current exchange rates, *a net liability balance sheet exposure generally exists when the temporal method is used.*

Under the temporal method, income statement items are translated at exchange rates that exist when the revenue (or gain) is generated or the expense (or loss) is incurred. For most items, an assumption can be made that revenues and expenses are incurred evenly throughout the accounting period and an average-for-the-period exchange rate can be used for translation. However, some expenses—such as cost of goods sold; depreciation of property, plant, and equipment; and amortization of intangibles—are related to assets carried at historical cost. Because these assets are translated at historical exchange rates, the expenses related to them must be translated at historical exchange rates as well. Also, gains and losses that occur on a specific date are translated at the exchange rate on that date (a historical rate).

The major difference between the translation adjustment resulting from the use of the temporal method and a foreign exchange gain or loss on a foreign currency transaction is that the translation adjustment is not necessarily realized through inflows or outflows of cash. The translation adjustment *could be realized* as a gain or loss only if (1) the foreign subsidiary collects all its receivables in cash and then uses its cash to pay off liabilities to the extent possible, and (2) *if there is a net asset balance sheet exposure,* the excess of cash over liabilities is remitted to the parent, where it is converted into parent currency, or *if there is a net liability balance sheet exposure,* the parent sends parent currency to its foreign subsidiary which is converted into foreign currency to pay the remaining liabilities.

Current Rate Method

The fundamental concept underlying the *current rate method* is that a parent's entire investment in a foreign operation is exposed to foreign exchange risk, and translation of the foreign operation's financial statements should reflect this risk. To measure the net investment's exposure to foreign exchange risk:

- All assets and liabilities of the foreign operation are translated using the *current exchange rate.*
- Stockholders' equity accounts are translated at *historical exchange rates.*

The balance sheet exposure measured by the current rate method is equal to the foreign operation's net asset position (total assets minus total liabilities).

Total assets > Total liabilities → Net asset exposure

A positive translation adjustment results when the foreign currency appreciates, and a negative translation adjustment results when the foreign currency depreciates (assuming that assets exceed liabilities). The translation adjustment arising when the current rate method is used also is unrealized. It can become a realized gain or loss if the foreign operation is sold (for its book value) and the foreign currency proceeds from the sale are converted into parent currency.

Under the current rate method, income statement items are translated using the exchange rate in effect at the date of accounting recognition. In most cases, an assumption is made that the revenue or expense is incurred evenly throughout the year, and an average-for-the-period exchange rate is used. Unlike under the temporal method, cost of goods sold; depreciation of property, plant, and equipment; and amortization of intangibles also are translated at the average exchange rate. However, when an income item, such as a gain or loss on the sale of an asset, occurs at a specific point in time, the exchange rate at that date should be used for translation.

The example presented earlier in this chapter in which all of Foreignco's assets and liabilities are translated at the current exchange rate demonstrates the current rate method. Foreignco has a net asset exposure that, because of the appreciation in the foreign currency, results in a positive translation adjustment.

The current rate method and the temporal method are the two methods required to be used under IAS 21, *The Effects of Changes in Foreign Exchange Rates,* and FASB ASC 830, *Foreign Currency Matters.* A summary of the appropriate exchange rate for selected financial statement items under these two methods is presented in Exhibit 7.1.

Translation of Retained Earnings

Stockholders' equity items are translated at historical exchange rates under both the temporal and current rate methods. This creates somewhat of a problem in translating retained earnings, which is a composite of many previous transactions: revenues, expenses, gains, losses, and declared dividends occurring over the life of the company. At the end of the first year of operations, foreign currency (FC) retained earnings are translated as follows:

$$
\begin{array}{ll}
\text{Net income in FC} & \text{[Translated per method} \\
& \text{used to translate income} \\
& \text{statement items]} \qquad = \quad \text{Net income in PC} \\
\underline{-\text{ Dividends in FC}} \quad \times \text{ Historical exchange rate} \quad = \underline{-\text{ Dividends in PC}} \\
\text{Ending R/E in FC} \qquad \text{when declared} \qquad\qquad \underline{\text{Ending R/E in PC}}
\end{array}
$$

The ending parent currency retained earnings in Year 1 become the beginning parent currency retained earnings for Year 2, and the translated retained earnings in Year 2 (and subsequent years) are then determined as follows:

$$
\begin{array}{ll}
\text{Beginning R/E in FC} & \text{(from last year's translation)} = \quad \text{Beginning R/E in PC} \\
+\text{ Net income in FC} & \text{[Translated per method} \\
& \text{used to translate income} \\
& \text{statement items]} \qquad = + \text{ Net income in FC} \\
-\text{ Dividends in FC} & \times \text{ Historical exchange rate} \quad = \underline{-\text{ Dividends in PC}} \\
& \text{when declared} \\
\underline{\text{Ending R/E in PC}} & \qquad\qquad\qquad\qquad \underline{\text{Ending R/E in PC}}
\end{array}
$$

The same approach is used for translating retained earnings under both the current rate and the temporal methods. The only difference is that translation of the current period's net income is done differently under the two methods.

EXHIBIT 7.1
Exchange Rates Used
under the Current
Rate Method and the
Temporal Method for
Selected Financial
Statement Items

Balance Sheet		
	Exchange Rate Used under the Current Rate Method	Exchange Rate Used under the Temporal Method
Assets		
Cash and receivables	Current	Current
Marketable securities	Current	Current*
Inventory at net realizable value	Current	Current
Inventory at cost	Current	Historical
Prepaid expenses	Current	Historical
Property, plant, and equipment	Current	Historical
Intangible assets	Current	Historical
Liabilities		
Current liabilities	Current	Current
Deferred income	Current	Historical
Long-term debt	Current	Current
Stockholders' Equity		
Capital stock	Historical	Historical
Additional paid-in capital	Historical	Historical
Retained earnings	Historical	Historical
Dividends	Historical	Historical

Income Statement		
	Exchange Rate Used under the Current Rate Method	Exchange Rate Used under the Temporal Method
Revenues	Average	Average
Most expenses	Average	Average
Cost of goods sold	Average	Historical
Depreciation of property, plant, and equipment	Average	Historical
Amortization of intangibles	Average	Historical

* Marketable debt securities classified as hold-to-maturity are carried at cost and therefore are translated at the historical exchange rate under the temporal method.

Complicating Aspects of the Temporal Method

Under the temporal method, it is necessary to keep a record of the exchange rates that exist when inventory; prepaid expenses; property, plant, and equipment; and intangible assets are acquired because these assets, carried at historical cost, are translated at historical exchange rates. Keeping track of the historical rates for these assets is not necessary under the current rate method. Translating these assets at historical rates makes application of the temporal method more complicated than the current rate method.

Calculation of Cost of Goods Sold (COGS)

Under the *current rate method,* cost of goods sold (COGS) in foreign currency (FC) is simply translated into the parent currency (PC) using the average-for-the-period exchange rate (ER):

$$\text{COGS in FC} \times \text{Average ER} = \text{COGS in PC}$$

Under the *temporal method,* COGS must be decomposed into beginning inventory, purchases, and ending inventory, and each component of COGS must then be translated at its appropriate historical rate. For example, if beginning inventory (FIFO basis) in Year 2 was acquired evenly throughout the fourth quarter of Year 1, then the average exchange rate in the fourth quarter of Year 1 will be used to translate beginning inventory. Likewise, the fourth-quarter (4thQ) Year 2 exchange rate will be used to translate Year 2 ending inventory. If purchases were made evenly throughout Year 2, then the average Year 2 exchange rate will be used to translate purchases:

Beginning inventory in FC	× Historical ER (e.g., 4thQ Year 1) =	Beginning inventory in PC
+ Purchases in FC	× Average ER, Year 2	=	+ Purchases in PC
− Ending inventory in FC	× Historical ER (e.g., 4thQ Year 2) =	− Ending inventory in PC
COGS in FC			COGS in PC

There is no single exchange rate that can be used to directly translate COGS in FC into COGS in PC.

Application of the Lower of Cost or Net Realizable Value Rule

Under the *current rate method,* the ending inventory reported on the foreign currency balance sheet is translated at the current exchange rate regardless of whether it is carried at cost or at a lower net realizable value. Application of the *temporal method* requires the foreign currency cost and foreign currency net realizable value of the inventory to be translated into parent currency at appropriate exchange rates, and the *lower of the parent currency cost or parent currency net realizable value* is reported on the consolidated balance sheet. As a result of this procedure, under the temporal method, it is possible for inventory to be carried at cost on the foreign currency balance sheet and at net realizable value on the parent currency consolidated balance sheet, and vice versa.

Property, Plant, and Equipment, Depreciation, and Accumulated Depreciation

Under the *temporal method,* items of property, plant, and equipment (PPE) acquired at different times must be translated at different (historical) exchange rates. The same is true for depreciation of PPE and accumulated depreciation related to PPE.

For example, assume that a company purchases a piece of equipment on January 1, Year 1, for FC1,000 when the exchange rate is $1.00 per FC1. Another item of equipment is purchased on January 1, Year 2, for FC4,000 when the exchange rate is $1.20 per FC1. Both pieces of equipment have a five-year useful life. Under the temporal method, the amount at which equipment would be reported on the consolidated balance sheet on December 31, Year 2, when the exchange rate is $1.50 per FC1, would be:

$$FC1{,}000 \times \$1.00 = \$1{,}000$$
$$FC4{,}000 \times \$1.20 = \$4{,}800$$
$$\overline{FC5{,}000} \qquad \overline{\$5{,}800}$$

Depreciation expense for Year 2 under the temporal method would be calculated as follows:

$$
\begin{array}{rcl}
\text{FC} \quad 200 \times \$1.00 &=& \$ \ \ 200 \\
\text{FC} \quad 800 \times \$1.20 &=& \underline{\$ \ \ 960} \\
\overline{\text{FC}1,000} & & \underline{\underline{\$1,160}}
\end{array}
$$

Accumulated depreciation at December 31, Year 2, under the temporal method would be calculated as follows:

$$
\begin{array}{rcl}
\text{FC} \quad 400 \times \$1.00 &=& \$ \ \ 400 \\
\text{FC} \quad 800 \times \$1.20 &=& \underline{\$ \ \ 960} \\
\overline{\text{FC}1,200} & & \underline{\underline{\$1,360}}
\end{array}
$$

Similar procedures apply for intangible assets as well.

Under the *current rate method,* equipment would be reported on the December 31, Year 2, balance sheet at FC5,000 × $1.50 = $7,500. Depreciation expense would be translated at the average Year 2 exchange rate of $1.40: FC1,000 × $1.40 = $1,400, and accumulated depreciation would be FC1,200 × $1.50 = $1,800.

In this example, the foreign subsidiary has only two items of PPE that require translation. For subsidiaries that own hundreds and thousands of PPE assets, the temporal method can require substantial additional work as compared to the current rate method.

DISPOSITION OF TRANSLATION ADJUSTMENT

The first issue related to the translation of foreign currency financial statements is selection of the appropriate method. The second issue in financial statement translation relates to *where the resulting translation adjustment should be reported in the consolidated financial statements.* There are two prevailing schools of thought with regard to this issue:

1. *Translation gain or loss in net income.* Under this treatment, the translation adjustment is considered to be a gain or loss analogous to the gains and losses that arise from foreign currency transactions and should be reported in net income in the period in which the fluctuation in exchange rate occurs. As a result of the closing process, translation gains and losses are included in retained earnings.

   The first of two conceptual problems with treating translation adjustments as gains/ losses in net income is that the gain or loss is unrealized; that is, there is no accompanying cash inflow or outflow. The second problem is that the gain or loss may not be consistent with economic reality. For example, the depreciation of a foreign currency may have a *positive* impact on the foreign operation's export sales and income, but the particular translation method used may nonetheless give rise to a translation *loss.*

2. *Cumulative translation adjustment in stockholders' equity (other comprehensive income).* The alternative to reporting the translation adjustment as a gain or loss in net income is to include it as a component of other comprehensive income, which is closed to the balance sheet line item *accumulated other comprehensive income.* In effect, this treatment defers the unrealized gain or loss in stockholders' equity until it is realized in some way, and at that point the cumulative translation adjustment is transferred to net income. As a balance sheet account, the cumulative translation adjustment reported as a part of accumulated other comprehensive income (AOCI) is not closed at the end of the accounting period and will fluctuate in amount over time.

   The two major translation methods and the two possible treatments for the translation adjustment give rise to four possible combinations as shown in Exhibit 7.2.

EXHIBIT 7.2
Translation
Combinations

	Translation Combinations	
Combination	**Translation Method**	**Disposition of Translation Adjustment**
A	Temporal	Gain or loss in net income
B	Temporal	Deferred in stockholders' equity (other comprehensive income)
C	Current rate	Gain or loss in net income
D	Current rate	Deferred in stockholders' equity (other comprehensive income)

U.S. GAAP

Prior to 1975, there were no authoritative rules in the United States as to which translation method to use or where the translation adjustment should be reported in the consolidated financial statements. Different companies used different combinations, creating a lack of comparability across companies. In 1975, to eliminate this noncomparability, the FASB issued SFAS 8, *Accounting for the Translation of Foreign Currency Transactions and Foreign Currency Financial Statements.* SFAS 8 mandated use of the temporal method with translation gains/losses reported in income by all companies for all foreign operations (in effect, Combination A shown in Exhibit 7.2).

U.S. multinational companies were strongly opposed to SFAS 8. Specifically, they considered reporting translation gains and losses in income to be inappropriate given that the gains and losses are unrealized. Moreover, because currency fluctuations often reverse themselves in subsequent quarters, artificial volatility in quarterly earnings resulted.

After releasing two Exposure Drafts proposing new translation rules, the FASB finally issued SFAS 52, *Foreign Currency Translation,* in 1981. This resulted in a complete overhaul of U.S. GAAP with regard to foreign currency translation. SFAS 52 was approved by a narrow four-to-three vote of the FASB, indicating how contentious the issue of foreign currency translation has been. The guidance provided in SFAS 52 was incorporated into FASB ASC 830, *Foreign Currency Matters,* in 2009.

FASB ASC 830

Implicit in the *temporal method* is the assumption that foreign subsidiaries of U.S. multinational corporations have very close ties to their parent company and would actually carry out their day-to-day operations and keep their books in the U.S. dollar if they could. To reflect the integrated nature of the foreign subsidiary with its U.S. parent, the translation process should create a set of U.S.-dollar translated financial statements as if the dollar had actually been used by the foreign subsidiary. This is described as the *U.S.-dollar perspective* to translation, and is consistent with the temporal method.

Subsequently, the FASB recognized that, whereas some foreign entities are closely integrated with their parent and do in fact conduct much of their business in U.S. dollars, other foreign entities are relatively self-contained and integrated with the local economy and primarily use a foreign currency in their daily operations. For the first type of entity, the FASB determined that the U.S.-dollar perspective still applies.

For the second, relatively independent type of entity, a *local-currency perspective* to translation is applicable. For this type of entity, the FASB determined that a different translation methodology is appropriate; namely, the *current rate method* should be used for translation, and translation adjustments should be reported as a separate component in other comprehensive income (Combination D in Exhibit 7.2).

Functional Currency

To determine whether a specific foreign operation is (1) integrated with its parent or (2) self-contained and integrated with the local economy, the FASB developed the concept of the functional currency. The *functional currency* is the primary currency of the foreign entity's operating environment. It can be either the parent's currency (the US$ for U.S. companies) or a foreign currency (generally the local currency). The functional currency orientation results in the following rule:

Functional Currency	Translation Method	Translation Adjustment
U.S. dollar	Temporal method	Recognized as gain (loss) in net income
Foreign currency	Current rate method	Deferred in stockholders' equity (accumulated other comprehensive income)

When a foreign operation is sold or otherwise disposed of, the cumulative translation adjustment related to it that has been deferred in accumulated other comprehensive income is transferred to net income as a realized gain or loss.

In addition to introducing the concept of the functional currency, the FASB also introduced some new terminology. The *reporting currency* is the currency in which the entity prepares its financial statements. For U.S.-based corporations, this is the U.S. dollar. If a foreign operation's functional currency is the U.S. dollar, foreign currency balances must be *remeasured* into U.S. dollars using the temporal method, with translation adjustments reported as *remeasurement gains and losses* in net income. When a foreign currency is the functional currency, foreign currency balances are *translated* using the current rate method and a *cumulative translation adjustment* is reported on the balance sheet.

FASB ASC 830-10-55-5 provides a list of indicators to guide parent company management in its determination of a foreign entity's functional currency (see Exhibit 7.3). However, no guidance is provided as to how these indicators are to be weighted in determining the functional currency. Leaving the decision about identifying the functional currency up to management allows some leeway in this process.

Different companies approach the selection of functional currency in different ways. For some companies, the functional currency is intuitively obvious. Other companies use an analytical model. For example, one company indicated that it took the six criteria and developed a matrix, considered the dollar amount and related percentages in developing a point scheme, and then gave equal weight to each criterion in determining the functional currency.[1]

Research has shown that the weighting schemes used by U.S. multinationals for determining the functional currency might be biased toward selection of the foreign currency as the functional currency.[2] This would be rational behavior for multinationals given that, when the foreign currency is the functional currency, the translation adjustment does not affect net income.

Highly Inflationary Economies

For those foreign entities located in a *highly inflationary economy,* U.S. GAAP mandates use of the *temporal method* with *translation gains/losses reported in net income.* A country is defined as a highly inflationary economy if its cumulative three-year inflation exceeds

[1] Jerry L. Arnold and William W. Holder, *Impact of Statement 52 on Decisions, Financial Reports and Attitudes* (Morristown, NJ: Financial Executives Research Foundation, 1986), p. 89.

[2] Timothy S. Doupnik and Thomas G. Evans, "Functional Currency as a Strategy to Smooth Income," *Advances in International Accounting,* Vol. 2, 1988, pp. 171–182.

EXHIBIT 7.3
U.S. GAAP Indicators
for Determining the
Functional Currency

	Indication That the Functional Currency Is the:	
Indicator	**Foreign Currency (FC)**	**Parent's Currency**
Cash flow	Primarily in FC and does not affect parent's cash flows	Directly impacts parent's cash flows on a current basis
Sales price	Not affected on short-term basis by changes in exchange rates	Affected on short-term basis by changes in exchange rates
Sales market	Active local sales market	Sales market mostly in parent's country or sales denominated in parent's currency
Expenses	Primarily local costs	Primarily costs for components obtained from parent's country
Financing	Primarily denominated in FC, and FC cash flows are adequate to service obligations	Primarily obtained from parent or denominated in parent currency, or FC cash flows not adequate to service obligations
Intercompany transaction	Low volume of intercompany transactions; no extensive interrelationships with parent's operations	High volume of intercompany transactions and extensive interrelationships with parent's operations

100 percent. With compounding, this equates to an average of approximately 26 percent per year for three years in a row. Countries that have met this definition in the past include Argentina, Brazil, Israel, Mexico, Turkey, Venezuela, and Zimbabwe. In any given year, a country might or might not be classified as highly inflationary in accordance with U.S. GAAP, depending on its most recent three-year experience with inflation.

One reason for this rule is to avoid a "disappearing plant problem" that exists when the current rate method is used in a country with high inflation. Remember that under the current rate method, all assets (including property, plant, and equipment) are translated at the current exchange rate. To see the problem this creates in a highly inflationary economy, consider a hypothetical example in which the Brazilian subsidiary of a U.S. parent purchased land at the end of 1984 for 10,000,000 cruzeiros (CR$) when the exchange rate was $0.001 per CR$1. Under the *current rate method,* Land would be reported in the parent's consolidated balance sheet at $10,000.

	Historical Cost		Current Exchange Rate		Consolidated Balance Sheet
1984	CR$10,000,000	×	$0.001	=	$10,000

In 1985, Brazil experienced roughly 200 percent inflation. Accordingly, with the forces of purchasing power parity at work, the cruzeiro plummeted against the U.S. dollar to a value of $0.00025 at the end of 1985. Under the current rate method, Land now would be reported in the parent's consolidated balance sheet at $2,500 and a negative translation adjustment of $7,500 would result.

	Historical Cost		Current Exchange Rate		Consolidated Balance Sheet
1985	CR$10,000,000	×	$0.00025	=	$2,500

Using the current rate method, land has lost 75 percent of its U.S.-dollar value in one year, and land is not even a depreciable asset!

High rates of inflation continued in Brazil, reaching the high point of roughly 1,800 percent in 1993. As a result of applying the current rate method, the land, which was originally reported on the 1984 consolidated balance sheet at $10,000, would have been carried on the 1993 balance sheet at less than $1.00.

In an Exposure Draft preceding the issuance of current authoritative guidance, the FASB proposed requiring companies with operations in highly inflationary countries to first *restate* the historical costs for inflation and then *translate* using the current exchange rate. For example, with 200 percent inflation in 1985, the land would have been written up to CR$40,000,000 and then translated at the current exchange rate of $0.00025. This would have produced a translated amount of $10,000, the same as in 1984.

Companies objected to making inflation adjustments, however, because of a lack of reliable inflation indexes in many countries. The FASB backed off from requiring the restate/ translate approach. Instead, current U.S. GAAP requires that the temporal method be used in highly inflationary countries. In our example, Land would be translated at the historical rate of $0.001 at each balance sheet date and carried at $10,000, thus avoiding the disappearing plant problem.

INTERNATIONAL FINANCIAL REPORTING STANDARDS

IAS 21, *The Effects of Changes in Foreign Exchange Rates,* contains guidance for the translation of foreign currency financial statements. To determine the appropriate translation method, IAS 21 originally required foreign subsidiaries to be classified as either (1) foreign operations that are integral to the operations of the reporting enterprise or (2) foreign entities. As part of a comprehensive improvements project, IAS 21 was revised in 2003, adopting the functional currency approach developed more than 20 years earlier by the FASB. The revised standard defines *functional currency* as the currency of the primary economic environment in which a subsidiary operates. It can be either (a) the same as the currency in which the parent presents its financial statements or (b) a different, foreign currency. IAS 21 provides a list of factors that should be considered in determining the functional currency (shown in Exhibit 7.4). Unlike U.S. GAAP, IAS 21 provides a hierarchy of primary and secondary factors to be considered in determining the functional currency of a foreign subsidiary. In addition, there are several differences in the factors to be considered under IFRS standards and U.S. GAAP. As a result of these differences, it is possible that a foreign subsidiary could be viewed as having one functional currency under IFRS standards but a different functional currency under U.S. GAAP.

For a foreign subsidiary that has a functional currency different from the reporting currency of the parent, IAS 21 requires the financial statements to be translated using the current rate method, with the resulting translation adjustment reported as a separate component of stockholders' equity. Upon disposal of a foreign subsidiary, the cumulative translation adjustment related to that particular foreign subsidiary is transferred to net income in the same period in which the gain or loss on disposal is recognized. For a foreign subsidiary whose functional currency is the same as the parent's reporting currency, the financial statements are translated using the temporal method, with the resulting translation adjustment reported currently as a gain or loss in net income. The same combinations are required under U.S. GAAP.

For foreign subsidiaries whose functional currency is the currency of a hyperinflationary economy, IAS 21 requires the parent first to restate the foreign financial statements for inflation using rules in IAS 29, *Financial Reporting in Hyperinflationary Economies,* and then translate the statements into parent company currency using the current exchange rate. All balance sheet accounts, including stockholders' equity, and all income statement accounts

EXHIBIT 7.4
IAS 21: Functional Currency Indicators

Factors Considered in Determining the Functional Currency

In accordance with IAS 21, *The Effects of Changes in Foreign Exchange Rates,* the following factors should be considered first in determining an entity's functional currency:

1. The currency that primarily influences sales prices for goods and services
2. The currency of the country whose competitive forces and regulations primarily determine sales prices.
3. The currency that primarily affects the cost of providing goods and services.
   If the primary factors listed above are mixed and the functional currency is not obvious, the following secondary factors must be considered:
4. The currency in which funds from financing activities are received.
5. The currency in which receipts from operating activities are retained.
6. Whether the activities of the foreign entity are an extension of the parent's or are carried out with significant autonomy.
7. Whether transactions with the parent are a large or a small proportion of the foreign entity's activities.
8. Whether cash flows generated by the foreign entity directly affect the cash flow of the parent and are available to be remitted to the parent.
9. Whether operating cash flows generated by the foreign entity are sufficient to service its debt or whether the foreign entity will need funds from the parent to service its debt.

are translated at the current exchange rate. This approach is substantively different from U.S. GAAP, which requires use of the temporal method in translating the financial statements of a foreign subsidiary operating in a highly inflationary economy. IAS 29 provides no specific definition for hyperinflation but suggests that one characteristic, among several, is a cumulative three-year inflation rate approaching or exceeding 100 percent. We demonstrate the process of restating foreign currency financial statements for inflation and then translating into parent company currency in the Appendix to this chapter.

THE TRANSLATION PROCESS ILLUSTRATED

To provide a basis for demonstrating the translation procedures prescribed by both IFRS and U.S. GAAP, assume that Multico (a U.S.-based company) forms a wholly owned subsidiary in Italy (Italco) on December 31, Year 0. On that date, Multico invests $1,350,000 in exchange for all of the subsidiary's capital stock. Given the exchange rate of €1.00 = $1.35, the initial capital investment is €1,000,000, of which €600,000 is immediately invested in inventory and the remainder is held in cash. Thus, Italco begins operations on January 1, Year 1, with stockholders' equity (net assets) of €1,000,000 and net monetary assets of €400,000. Italco's beginning balance sheet on January 1, Year 1, is shown in Exhibit 7.5.

During Year 1, Italco purchases property and equipment, acquires a patent, and makes additional purchases of inventory, primarily on account. A five-year loan is negotiated to help

EXHIBIT 7.5
Italco's Balance Sheet, January 1, Year 1

		ITALCO		
		Beginning Balance Sheet		
		January 1, Year 1		
Assets	**€**	**Liabilities and Equity**		**€**
Cash................	400,000	Capital stock		1,000,000
Inventory..............	600,000			1,000,000
	1,000,000			

EXHIBIT 7.6
Italco's Financial
Statements, Year 1

Income Statement
Year 1

	€
Sales	8,000,000
Cost of goods sold	6,000,000
Gross profit	2,000,000
Selling and administrative expenses	500,000
Depreciation expense	200,000
Amortization expense	20,000
Interest expense	180,000
Income before income taxes	1,100,000
Income taxes	275,000
Net income	825,000

Statement of Retained Earnings
Year 1

	€
Retained earnings, 1/1/Y1	0
Net income, Y1	825,000
Less: Dividends, 12/1/Y1	(325,000)
Retained earnings, 12/31/Y1	500,000

Balance Sheet
December 31, Year 1

Assets	€	Liabilities and Equity	€
Cash	550,000	Accounts payable	330,000
Accounts receivable	600,000	Total current liabilities	330,000
Inventory*	800,000	Long-term debt	2,000,000
Total current assets	1,950,000	Total liabilities	2,330,000
Property and equipment	2,000,000	Capital stock	1,000,000
Less: Accumulated		Retained earnings	500,000
depreciation	(200,000)	Total	3,830,000
Patents, net	80,000		
Total assets	3,830,000		

* Inventory is carried at first-in, first-out (FIFO) cost; ending inventory was acquired evenly throughout the month of December.

finance the purchase of equipment. Sales are made, primarily on account, and expenses are incurred. Income after taxes of €825,000 is generated, with dividends of €325,000 declared on December 1, Year 1. Financial statements for Year 1 (in euros) appear in Exhibit 7.6.

To properly translate the euro financial statements into U.S. dollars, we must gather exchange rates between the euro and the U.S. dollar at various times. Relevant exchange rates are as follows:

January 1, Year 1	$1.35
Rate when property and equipment were acquired and long-term debt was incurred, January 15, Year 1	1.33
Rate when patent was acquired, February 1, Year 1	1.32
Average Year 1	1.30
Rate when dividends were declared, December 1, Year 1	1.27
Average for the month of December	1.26
December 31, Year 1	1.25

As can be seen, the euro steadily declined in value against the U.S. dollar during the year.

TRANSLATION OF FINANCIAL STATEMENTS: CURRENT RATE METHOD

The first step in translating foreign currency financial statements is the determination of the functional currency. Continuing with our example, and assuming that the euro is the functional currency, Italco's income statement and statement of retained earnings would be translated into U.S. dollars using the current rate method, as shown in Exhibit 7.7.

All revenues and expenses are translated at the exchange rate in effect at the date of accounting recognition. The weighted-average exchange rate for Year 1 is used because each revenue and expense in this illustration would have been recognized evenly throughout the year. However, when an income account, such as a gain or loss, occurs at a specific time, the exchange rate as of that date is applied. Depreciation and amortization expense are also translated at the average rate for the year. These expenses accrue evenly throughout the year even though the journal entry may have been delayed until year-end for convenience.

The translated amount of net income for Year 1 is transferred from the income statement to the statement of retained earnings. Dividends are translated at the exchange rate that exists on the date of declaration.

Translation of the Balance Sheet

Italco's translated balance sheet is shown in Exhibit 7.8. All assets and liabilities are translated at the current exchange rate. Capital stock is translated at the exchange rate that

EXHIBIT 7.7
Translation of Income Statement and Statement of Retained Earnings: Current Rate Method

Income Statement Year 1			
	€	Translation Rate*	US$
Sales	8,000,000	$1.30 (A)	10,400,000
Cost of goods sold	6,000,000	1.30 (A)	7,800,000
Gross profit.	2,000,000		2,600,000
Selling and administrative expenses.	500,000	1.30 (A)	650,000
Depreciation expense	200,000	1.30 (A)	260,000
Amortization expense	20,000	1.30 (A)	26,000
Interest expense	180,000	1.30 (A)	234,000
Income before income taxes	1,100,000		1,430,000
Income taxes	275,000	1.30 (A)	357,500
Net income.	825,000		1,072,500

Statement of Retained Earnings Year 1			
	€	Translation Rate*	US$
Retained earnings, 1/1/Y1.	0		0
Net income, Year 1	825,000	From income statement	1,072,500
Less: Dividends, 12/1/Y1.	(325,000)	$1.27 (H)	(412,750)
Retained earnings, 12/31/Y1	500,000		659,750

* Indicates the exchange rate used and whether the rate is the current rate (C), the average rate (A), or a historical rate (H).

EXHIBIT 7.8
Translation of Balance
Sheet: Current Rate
Method

Balance Sheet December 31, Year 1			
Assets	**€**	**Translation Rate***	**US$**
Cash	550,000	$1.25 (C)	687,500
Accounts receivable	600,000	1.25 (C)	750,000
Inventory	800,000	1.25 (C)	1,000,000
Total current assets	1,950,000		2,437,500
Property and equipment	2,000,000	1.25 (C)	2,500,000
Less: Accumulated depreciation	(200,000)	1.25 (C)	(250,000)
Patents, net	80,000	1.25 (C)	100,000
Total assets	3,830,000		4,787,500
Liabilities and Equity			
Accounts payable	330,000	$1.25 (C)	412,500
Total current liabilities	330,000		412,500
Long-term debt	2,000,000	1.25 (C)	2,500,000
Total liabilities	2,330,000		2,912,500
Capital stock	1,000,000	1.35 (H)	1,350,000
Retained earnings	500,000	From statement of retained earnings	659,750
Cumulative translation adjustment . . .	—	To balance	(134,750)
Total equity	1,500,000		1,875,000
	3,830,000		4,787,500

* Indicates the exchange rate used and whether the rate is the current rate (C), the average rate (A), or a historical rate (H).

existed when the capital stock was originally issued. Retained earnings at December 31, Year 1, is brought down from the statement of retained earnings. Application of these procedures results in total assets of $4,787,500 and total liabilities and equities of $4,922,250. The balance sheet is brought back into balance by creating a negative translation adjustment of $134,750, which is treated as a decrease in stockholders' equity.

Note that the translation adjustment for Year 1 is a *negative* $134,750 (debit balance). The sign of the translation adjustment (positive or negative) is a function of two factors: (1) the nature of the balance sheet exposure (asset or liability) and (2) the direction of change in the exchange rate (appreciation or depreciation). In this illustration, Italco has a *net asset exposure* (total assets translated at the current exchange rate are greater than total liabilities translated at the current exchange rate), and the euro has *depreciated,* creating a *negative translation adjustment.*

The translation adjustment can be derived as a balancing figure that brings the balance sheet back into balance. The translation adjustment also can be calculated by considering the impact of exchange rate changes on the beginning balance and subsequent changes in the net asset position. The following steps are applied:

1. The net asset balance of the subsidiary at the beginning of the year is translated at the exchange rate in effect on that date.

2. Individual increases and decreases in the net asset balance during the year are translated at the rates in effect when those increases and decreases occur. Only a few events actually change net assets (e.g., net income, dividends, stock issuance, and the acquisition of treasury stock). Transactions such as the acquisition of equipment or the payment of a liability have no effect on total net assets.

3. The translated beginning net asset balance (*a*) and the translated value of the individual changes (*b*) are then combined to arrive at the relative value of the net assets being held prior to the impact of any exchange rate fluctuations.

4. The ending net asset balance is then translated at the current exchange rate to determine the reported value after all exchange rate changes have occurred.

5. The translated value of the net assets prior to any rate changes (*c*) is compared with the ending translated value (*d*). The difference is the result of exchange rate changes during the period. If (*c*) is greater than (*d*), then a negative (debit) translation adjustment arises. If (*d*) is greater than (*c*), a positive (credit) translation adjustment results.

Computation of Translation Adjustment

According to the process just described, determination of the translation adjustment to be reported for Italco in this example is calculated as follows:

	€		Translation Rate		US$
Net asset balance, 1/1/Y1	1,000,000	×	$1.35	=	1,350,000
Change in net assets:					
Net income, Year 1	825,000	×	1.30	=	1,072,500
Dividends, 12/1/Y1	(325,000)	×	1.27	=	(412,750)
Net asset balance, 12/31/Y1	1,500,000				2,009,750
Net asset balance, 12/31/Y1, at current exchange rate	1,500,000	×	1.25	=	1,875,000
Translation adjustment, Year 1 (negative)					134,750

Since this subsidiary began operations at the beginning of the current year, $134,750 is the amount of cumulative translation adjustment reported on the consolidated balance sheet. The translation adjustment is reported as a separate component of equity only until the foreign operation is sold or liquidated. In the period in which a sale or liquidation occurs, the cumulative translation adjustment related to the particular foreign subsidiary must be removed from equity and reported as part of the gain or loss on the sale of the investment.

REMEASUREMENT OF FINANCIAL STATEMENTS: TEMPORAL METHOD

Now assume that a careful examination of the functional currency indicators leads Multico's management to conclude that Italco's functional currency is the U.S. dollar. In that case, the euro financial statements will be remeasured into U.S. dollars using the temporal method and the remeasurement gain or loss will be reported in income. To ensure that the remeasurement gain or loss is reported in income, it is easier to remeasure the balance sheet first (as shown in Exhibit 7.9).

According to the procedures outlined in Exhibit 7.1, under the temporal method, cash, receivables, and liabilities are remeasured into U.S. dollars using the current exchange rate ($1.25 in our example). Inventory, carried at first-in, first-out (FIFO) cost; property and equipment; patents; and the capital stock account are remeasured at historical rates. These procedures result in total assets of $4,945,100 and liabilities and capital stock of $4,262,500. In order for the balance sheet to balance, retained earnings must be $682,600. The accuracy of this amount is verified in the section "Computation of Remeasurement Gain."

EXHIBIT 7.9
Translation of Balance
Sheet: Temporal
Method

Balance Sheet December 31, Year 1			
Assets	**€**	**Translation Rate***	**US$**
Cash	550,000	$1.25 (C)	687,500
Accounts receivable.	600,000	1.25 (C)	750,000
Inventory.	800,000	1.26 (H)	1,008,000
Total current assets.	1,950,000		2,445,500
Property and equipment	2,000,000	1.33 (H)	2,660,000
Less: Accumulated depreciation	(200,000)	1.33 (H)	(266,000)
Patents, net.	80,000	1.32 (H)	105,600
Total assets	3,830,000		4,945,100
Liabilities and Equity			
Accounts payable.	330,000	$1.25 (C)	412,500
Total current liabilities.	330,000		412,500
Long-term debt	2,000,000	1.25 (C)	2,500,000
Total liabilities.	2,330,000		2,912,500
Capital stock	1,000,000	1.35 (H)	1,350,000
Retained earnings.	500,000	To balance	682,600
Total equity.	1,500,000		2,032,600
	3,830,000		4,945,100

* Indicates the exchange rate used and whether the rate is the current rate (C), the average rate (A), or a historical rate (H).

Remeasurement of Income Statement

The remeasurement of Italco's income statement and statement of retained earnings is demonstrated in Exhibit 7.10. Revenues and expenses incurred evenly throughout the year (sales, selling and administrative expenses, interest expense, and income taxes) are remeasured at the average exchange rate. Expenses related to assets remeasured at historical exchange rates (depreciation expense and amortization expense) are themselves remeasured at relevant historical rates.

Cost of goods sold is remeasured at historical exchange rates using the following procedure. Beginning inventory was acquired on January 1 and is remeasured at the exchange rate from that date ($1.35). Purchases were made evenly throughout the year and are therefore remeasured at the average rate for the year ($1.30). Ending inventory (at FIFO cost) was purchased evenly throughout the month of December, and the average exchange rate for that month ($1.26) is used to remeasure that component of cost of goods sold. These procedures result in cost of goods sold of $7,862,000, calculated as follows:

	€		**Translation Rate**		**US$**
Beginning inventory	600,000	×	$1.35	=	810,000
Plus: Purchases	6,200,000	×	$1.30	=	8,060,000
Less: Ending inventory	(800,000)	×	$1.26	=	(1,008,000)
Cost of goods sold	6,000,000				7,862,000

EXHIBIT 7.10
Translation of Income
Statement and
Statement of Retained
Earnings: Temporal
Method

Income Statement
Year 1

	€	Translation Rate*	US$
Sales	8,000,000	$1.30 (A)	10,400,000
Cost of goods sold	6,000,000	Calculation (see below)	7,862,000
Gross profit.	2,000,000		2,538,000
Selling and administrative expenses.	500,000	1.30 (A)	650,000
Depreciation expense	200,000	1.33 (H)	266,000
Amortization expense	20,000	1.32 (H)	26,400
Interest expense	180,000	1.30 (A)	234,000
Income before income taxes	1,100,000		1,361,600
Income taxes	(275,000)	1.30 (A)	(357,500)
Remeasurement gain	—	To balance	91,250
Net income.	825,000		1,095,350

Statement of Retained Earnings Year 1

	€	Translation Rate*	US$
Retained earnings, 1/1/Y1.	0		0
Net income, Year 1	825,000	From income statement	1,095,350
Less: Dividends, 12/1/Y1.	(325,000)	1.27 (H)	(412,750)
Retained earnings, 12/31/Y1	500,000		682,600

* Indicates the exchange rate used and whether the rate is the current rate (C), the average rate (A), or a historical rate (H).

The ending balance in retained earnings on the balance sheet and in the statement of retained earnings must reconcile with one another. Given that dividends are remeasured into a U.S.-dollar equivalent of $412,750 and the ending balance in retained earnings on the balance sheet is $682,600, net income must be $1,095,350.

In order for the amount of income reported in the statement of retained earnings and the income statement to reconcile with one another, a remeasurement gain of $91,250 is required in the calculation of income. Without this remeasurement gain, the income statement, statement of retained earnings, and balance sheet will not be consistent with one another.

The remeasurement gain can be calculated by considering the impact of exchange rate changes on the subsidiary's balance sheet exposure. Under the temporal method, Italco's balance sheet exposure is defined by its net monetary asset or net monetary liability position. Italco began Year 1 with net monetary assets (cash) of €400,000. During the year, however, expenditures of cash and the incurrence of liabilities caused monetary liabilities (Accounts payable + Long-term debt = €2,330,000) to exceed monetary assets (Cash + Accounts receivable = €1,150,000). A net monetary liability position of €1,180,000 exists at December 31, Year 1. The remeasurement gain is computed by translating the beginning net monetary asset position and subsequent changes in monetary items at appropriate exchange rates and then comparing this with the U.S.-dollar value of net monetary liabilities at year-end based on the current exchange rate.

Computation of Remeasurement Gain

	€	Translation Rate		US$
Net monetary assets, 1/1/Y1	400,000 ×	$1.35	=	540,000
Increase in monetary items:				
Sales, Year 1	8,000,000 ×	1.30	=	10,400,000
Decrease in monetary items:				
Purchases of inventory, Year 1	(6,200,000) ×	1.30	=	(8,060,000)
Selling and administrative expenses, Year 1	(500,000) ×	1.30	=	(650,000)
Payment of interest, Year 1	(180,000) ×	1.30	=	(234,000)
Income taxes, Year 1	(275,000) ×	1.30	=	(357,500)
Purchase of property and equipment, 1/15/Y1	(2,000,000) ×	1.33	=	(2,660,000)
Acquisition of patent, 2/1/Y1	(100,000) ×	1.32	=	(132,000)
Dividends, 12/1/Y1.	(325,000) ×	1.27	=	(412,750)
Net monetary liabilities, 12/31/Y1	(1,180,000) ×		=	(1,566,250)
Net monetary liabilities, 12/31/Y1, at the current exchange rate.	(1,180,000) ×	1.25	=	(1,475,000)
Remeasurement gain				(91,250)

If Italco had maintained its net monetary asset position (cash) of €400,000 for the entire year, a remeasurement loss of $40,000 would have resulted. (The euro amount held in cash was worth $540,000 [€400,000 × $1.35] at the beginning of the year and $500,000 [€400,0000 × $1.25] at year-end.) However, the net monetary asset position is not maintained. Indeed, a net monetary liability position arises. The *depreciation* of the foreign currency coupled with an increase in *net monetary liabilities* generates a *remeasurement gain* for the year.

NONLOCAL CURRENCY BALANCES

An additional issue relates to how nonlocal currency balances in the foreign currency financial statements of foreign operations are reported in the consolidated financial statements. For example, if any of the accounts of the Italian subsidiary Italco were denominated in a currency other than the euro, those balances would first have to be restated into euros in accordance with the rules discussed in Chapter 6. Both the foreign currency balance and any related foreign exchange gain or loss would then be translated (or remeasured) into U.S. dollars. For example, assume that Italco borrows 100,000 Swiss francs on January 1, Year 1, and has a 100,000 Swiss franc note payable throughout Year 1. Exchange rates in Year 1 between the Swiss franc (CHF) and the euro (€) and between the euro and the U.S. dollar ($) are as follows:

	€ per CHF	$ per €
January 1, Year 1	€0.80	$1.35
Average for Year 1	€0.82	$1.30
December 31, Year 1	€0.85	$1.25

On December 31, Year 1, Italco remeasures the CHF 100,000 note payable into CHF using the current exchange rate as follows: CHF100,000 × €0.85 = €85,000. Italco also recognizes a foreign exchange loss of €5,000 [CHF 100,000 × (€0.85 − €0.80)] on the Swiss franc note payable due to the appreciation of the Swiss franc against the euro. To consolidate Italco's Swiss franc financial statements with those of its parent, the note payable remeasured in euros is then translated into U.S. dollars using the current exchange rate (C) and the related foreign exchange loss in euros is translated into U.S. dollars using the average exchange rate (A) as follows:

Note payable......................	€85,000 × $1.25 (C) = $106,250
Foreign exchange loss............	€5,000 × $1.30 (A) = $6,500

A note payable of $106,250 will be reported on the consolidated balance sheet, and a loss of $6,500 will be reflected in the measurement of consolidated net income.

COMPARISON OF THE RESULTS FROM APPLYING THE TWO DIFFERENT TRANSLATION METHODS

The use of different translation methods can have a significant impact on a parent company's consolidated financial statements. Continuing with our example, the chart below shows differences for Italco in several key items under the two different translation methods:

	Translation Method		
Item	Current Rate	Temporal	Difference
Net income.........................	$1,072,500	$1,095,350	+2.1%
Total assets.........................	$4,787,500	$4,945,100	+3.3%
Total equity.........................	$1,875,000	$2,032,600	+8.4%
Return on ending equity	57.2%	53.9%	−5.8%

If the temporal method is applied, net income is 2.1 percent greater, total assets are 3.3 percent greater, and total equity is 8.4 percent greater than if the current rate method is applied. Because of the larger amount of equity under the temporal method, return on ending equity (net income/total equity) is only 53.9 percent as opposed to 57.2 percent using the current rate method.

It should be noted that the temporal method does not always result in larger net income (and a greater amount of equity) than the current rate method. For example, if Italco had maintained its net monetary asset position throughout the year, a remeasurement loss would have been computed under the temporal method, leading to lower income than under the current rate method. Moreover, if the euro had appreciated during Year 1, the current rate method would have resulted in higher net income.

The important point is that selection of translation method can have a significant impact on the amounts reported by a parent company in its consolidated financial statements. Different functional currencies selected by different companies in the same industry could have a significant impact on the comparability of financial statements within that industry.

In addition to differences in amounts reported in the consolidated financial statements, the results of the Italco illustration can be used to demonstrate several conceptual differences between the two translation methods.

Underlying Valuation Method

Using the temporal method, Italco's property and equipment was remeasured as follows:

Property and equipment	€2,000,000	×	$1.33 H	=	$2,660,000

By multiplying the historical cost in euros by the historical exchange rate, $2,660,000 represents the U.S.-dollar equivalent historical cost of this asset. It is the amount of U.S. dollars that the parent company would have had to pay to acquire assets having a cost of €2,000,000 when the exchange rate was $1.33 per euro.

In contrast, property and equipment was translated under the current rate method as follows:

Property and equipment	€2,000,000	×	$1.25 C	=	$2,500,000

The $2,500,000 amount is not readily interpretable. It does not represent the U.S.-dollar equivalent historical cost of the asset; that amount is $2,660,000. It also does not represent the U.S.-dollar equivalent fair value of the asset, because €2,000,000 is not the fair value of the asset in Italy. The $2,500,000 amount is simply the product of multiplying two numbers together!

Underlying Relationships

The following table reports the values for selected financial ratios calculated from the original foreign currency financial statements and from the U.S.-dollar translated statements using the two different translation methods.

		US$	
Ratio	€	Current Rate	Temporal
Current ratio (Current assets/Current liabilities)	5.91	5.91	5.93
Debt/equity ratio (Total liabilities/Total equity)	1.55	1.55	1.43
Gross profit ratio (Gross profit/Sales)	25.0%	25.0%	24.4%
Return on equity (Net income/Total equity)	55.0%	57.2%	53.9%

The temporal method distorts all of the ratios as measured in the foreign currency. The subsidiary appears to be more liquid, less highly leveraged, and less profitable than it does in euro terms.

The current rate method maintains the first three ratios, but return on equity is distorted. This distortion occurs because income was translated at the average-for-the-period exchange rate, whereas total equity was translated at the current exchange rate. In fact, any ratio that combines balance sheet and income statement figures, such as turnover ratios, will be distorted because of the use of the average rate for income and the current rate for assets and liabilities.

Conceptually, when the current rate method is employed, income statement items could be translated either at exchange rates in effect when sales are made and expenses are incurred (approximated by the average rate) or at the current exchange rate at the balance sheet date. IFRS and U.S. GAAP require the average exchange rate to be used. In this illustration, if revenues and expenses had been translated at the current exchange rate, net income would have been $1,031,250 (€825,000 × $1.25), and the return on equity would have been 55.0 percent ($1,031,250/$1,875,000), exactly the amount reflected in the euro financial statements.

HEDGING BALANCE SHEET EXPOSURE

When a foreign operation is determined to have the parent's reporting currency as its functional currency or is located in a highly inflationary economy, remeasurement gains and losses will be included in the measurement of consolidated net income. Management of multinational companies might wish to avoid reporting remeasurement losses in net income because of the perceived negative impact this has on the company's stock price or the adverse effect on incentive compensation. Likewise, when the foreign operation has a foreign currency as its functional currency, management might wish to avoid reporting negative translation adjustments in stockholders' equity because of the adverse impact on ratios such as the debt-to-equity ratio.

Translation adjustments and remeasurement gains/losses are a function of two factors: (1) changes in the exchange rate and (2) balance sheet exposure. While individual companies have no influence over exchange rates, there are several techniques that parent companies can use to hedge the balance sheet exposures of their foreign operations. Each of these techniques involves creating an equilibrium between foreign currency assets and foreign currency liability balances that are translated at current exchange rates.

Balance sheet exposure can be hedged through the use of a derivative financial instrument such as a forward contract or a foreign currency option, or through the use of a nonderivative hedging instrument such as a foreign currency borrowing. To illustrate, assume that Italco's functional currency is the euro; this creates a *net asset balance sheet exposure*. Multico believes that the euro will lose value against the U.S. dollar over the course of the next year, thereby generating a negative translation adjustment that will reduce consolidated stockholders' equity. Multico can hedge this balance sheet exposure by borrowing euros for a period of time, thus creating an offsetting euro liability exposure. As the euro depreciates, a foreign exchange gain will arise on the euro liability that offsets the negative translation adjustment arising from the translation of Italco's financial statements.

As an alternative to the euro borrowing, Multico might have acquired a euro call option to hedge its balance sheet exposure. As the euro depreciates, the fair value of the call option should increase, resulting in a gain. Both IFRS and U.S. GAAP provide that the gain or loss on a hedging instrument that is designated and effective as a *hedge of the net investment in a foreign operation* should be reported in the same manner as the translation adjustment being hedged. Thus, the foreign exchange gain on the euro borrowing or the gain on the foreign currency option would be included in other comprehensive income along with the negative translation adjustment arising from the translation of Italco's financial statements. This is an exception to the general rule that foreign currency gains and losses are taken directly to net income. However, in the event that the gain on the hedging instrument is greater than the translation adjustment being hedged, the excess must be taken to net income. Exhibit 7.11 contains disclosures made by International Business Machines Corporation (IBM) in its 2020 annual report with respect to hedging net investments in foreign operations. IBM uses a combination of foreign currency-denominated debt, swaps, and forward contracts to hedge its long-term investments in foreign subsidiaries, with the total amount of such instruments being $7.2 billion at the end of 2020.

The paradox of hedging a balance sheet exposure is that in the process of avoiding an unrealized translation adjustment, realized foreign exchange gains and losses can result. Consider Multico's foreign currency borrowing to hedge a euro exposure. At initiation of the loan, Multico will convert the borrowed euros into U.S. dollars at the spot exchange rate. When the liability matures, Multico will purchase euros at the spot rate prevailing at that date to repay the loan. The change in exchange rate over the life of the loan will generate a realized gain or loss. If the euro depreciates as expected, the result will be a realized foreign exchange gain that will offset the negative translation adjustment in other comprehensive income. Although the net effect on other comprehensive income is zero, there is a net increase in cash as a

EXHIBIT 7.11
IBM's Disclosure
Related to Hedging Net
Investments in Foreign
Subsidiaries

INTERNATIONAL BUSINESS MACHINES CORPORATION
Annual Report
2020

Excerpt from Note T. Derivative Financial Instruments

Foreign Exchange Risk

Long-Term Investments in Foreign Subsidiaries (Net Investment)

A large portion of the company's foreign currency denominated debt portfolio is designated as a hedge of net investment in foreign subsidiaries to reduce the volatility in stockholders' equity caused by changes in foreign currency exchange rates in the functional currency of major foreign subsidiaries with respect to the U.S. dollar. The company also uses cross-currency swaps and foreign exchange forward contracts for this risk management purpose. At December 31, 2020 and 2019, the total notional amount of derivative instruments designated as net investment hedges was $7.2 billion and $7.9 billion, respectively. At December 31, 2020 and 2019, the weighted-average remaining maturity of these instruments was approximately 0.3 years and 0.1 years, respectively.

result of the hedge. If the euro unexpectedly appreciates, a realized foreign exchange loss will occur. This will be offset by a positive translation adjustment in other comprehensive income, but a net decrease in cash will arise. While a hedge of a net investment in a foreign operation eliminates the possibility of reporting a negative translation adjustment in other comprehensive income, the result can be realized gains and losses that affect cash flow.

Exhibit 7.12 presents an excerpt from the notes to the consolidated financial statements in Nokia Corporation's 2020 annual report. Nokia prepares its financial statements in accordance with IFRS, and the excerpt describes Nokia's compliance with IAS 39 with respect to hedging of net investments. The first full paragraph in Exhibit 7.12 indicates that Nokia uses forward contracts and options to hedge its balance sheet exposures. Changes in the fair value

EXHIBIT 7.12
Nokia's Disclosure
Related to Hedging Net
Investments in Foreign
Subsidiaries

NOKIA CORPORATION
Annual Report
2020

Excerpt from Note 2. Significant Accounting Policies

Hedges of net investments in foreign operations

The Group applies hedge accounting for its foreign currency hedging of selected net investments.

The Group only designates the spot element of the foreign exchange forward contract as the hedging instrument. Currency options, or option strategies, may also be used for net investment hedging, in which case the intrinsic value of the option is designated as the hedging instrument.

For qualifying foreign exchange forwards, foreign exchange options, and option strategies, the change in fair value that reflects the change in spot exchange rates is recognized in translation differences within consolidated shareholders' equity. The changes in the forward element of foreign exchange forwards as well as the changes in the time value of options (collectively known as the "cost of hedging") is recognized in cost of hedging reserve in other comprehensive income. The cost of hedging at the date of designation of the foreign exchange forward or option contract as a hedging instrument is amortized to financial income and expenses in the consolidated income statement over the duration of the contract. Hence, in each reporting period, the change in fair value of forward element of the foreign exchange forward contract or the time value of the option contract is recorded in cost of hedging reserve, while the amortization amount is reclassified from cost of hedging reserve to profit or loss.

Accumulated changes in fair value from qualifying hedges are derecognized from translation differences within consolidated shareholders' equity on the disposal of all or part of a foreign subsidiary by sale, liquidation, repayment of share capital or abandonment. The cumulative amount or proportionate share of changes in the fair value of qualifying hedges deferred in translation differences is recognized as income or expense on disposal.

of forward contracts attributable to changes in the spot rate, and changes in the intrinsic value of options are deferred in stockholders' equity (as "translation differences"). Nokia also discloses in Note 2 that, upon disposal of a subsidiary, the accumulated amount deferred as translation differences in stockholders' equity related to that subsidiary is recognized as income or expense in net income. It should be noted that the procedures followed by Nokia in accordance with IAS 39 are consistent with the guidance provided under U.S. GAAP.

DISCLOSURES RELATED TO TRANSLATION

Accounting standards require an analysis of the change in the cumulative translation adjustment account to be presented in the financial statements or notes thereto. Many U.S. companies comply with this requirement by providing information on the current year's translation adjustment in their statement of comprehensive income and including a column titled "Accumulated Other Comprehensive Income" (AOCI) in their statement of changes in equity. Exhibit 7.13 demonstrates this method of disclosure as used by McDonald's Corporation. In 2020, McDonald's has three items that affect AOCI, including one labeled *Foreign currency translation adjustments.* McDonald's 2020 Consolidated Statement of Comprehensive Income reported a negative foreign currency translation adjustment in 2018

EXHIBIT 7.13

MCDONALD'S CORPORATION
Annual Report
2020

Excerpt from Consolidated Statement of Comprehensive Income

	Years ended December 31		
In millions	2020	2019	2018
Other comprehensive income (loss), net of tax			
Foreign currency translation adjustments:			
Gain (loss) recognized in accumulated other comprehensive income (AOCI), including net investment hedges......................	$46.0	$127.5	$(453.6)
Reclassification of (gain) loss to net income	17.1	46.8	—
Foreign currency translation adjustments—net of tax benefit (expense) of $204.8, $(55.4) and $(90.7).......................	$63.1	$174.3	$(453.6)

Excerpt from Consolidated Statement of Shareholders' Equity

	Accumulated other comprehensive income (loss)		
In millions, except per share data	Pensions	Cash flow hedges	Foreign currency translation
Balance at December 31, 2017...............................	$(190.2)	$ (16.5)	$(1,971.7)
Other comprehensive income (loss), net of tax.................	(26.4)	48.9	(453.6)
Balance at December 31, 2018...............................	(216.6)	32.4	(2,425.3)
Other comprehensive income (loss), net of tax.................	(27.1)	(20.4)	174.3
Balance at December 31, 2019...............................	(243.7)	12.0	(2,251.0)
Other comprehensive income (loss), net of tax.................	(43.9)	(123.3)	63.1
Balance at December 31, 2020...............................	$(287.6)	$(111.3)	$(2,187.9)

of $453.6 million, and positive foreign currency translation adjustments in 2019 and 2020 of $127.5 million, and $46.0 million, respectively. From the negative sign of the 2018 translation adjustment, we can infer that the currencies in which McDonald's foreign subsidiaries operate, on average, depreciated against the U.S. dollar. In contrast, from the positive signs of the 2019 and 2020 translation adjustments, we can infer that the currencies in which McDonald's foreign subsidiaries operate, on average, increased in value against the U.S. dollar in those years. From the size of the translation adjustments, we can infer that the rate of foreign currency appreciation was considerably higher in 2019 than in 2020. Note that in 2019 and 2020, the company reported reclassifying $46.8 million and $17.1 million, respectively, of cumulative translation adjustment to net income as a loss. This was related to the disposal of one or more foreign operations. In effect, the cumulative negative translation adjustment related to those foreign operations that had been deferred in AOCI was recognized as a loss in net income in those years. McDonald's Consolidated Statement of Shareholders' Equity reports the balances in the cumulative foreign currency translation account that, although not shown, are included on the Consolidated Balance Sheet within the shareholders' equity line item labeled *Accumulated other comprehensive income.* McDonald's had a negative cumulative translation adjustment of $2,187.9 million included in AOCI at the end of 2020.

IAS 21 also requires companies to provide information related to cumulative translation adjustments (referred to as "translation reserves" in IFRS). Exhibit 7.14 presents an excerpt

EXHIBIT 7.14

ERICSSON AB
Annual Report
2020

Excerpt from Note E1. Equity
Other reserves

SEK million	2020			
	Translation reserves	Cash flow hedge reserve	Revaluation of borrowings	Total other reserves
Opening balance	2,967	−230	−445	2,292
Other comprehensive income				
Items that will not be reclassified to profit or loss				
Revaluation of borrowings due to change in credit risk.	—	—	99	99
Tax on items that will not be reclassified to profit or loss.	—	—	−20	−20
Items that have been or may be reclassified to profit or loss				
Cash flow hedges.				
Gains/losses arising during the period. . . .	—	136	—	136
Reclassification to profit and loss.	—	281	—	281
Translation reserves				
Changes in translation reserves.	−5,434	—	—	−5,434
Reclassification to profit and loss.	124	—	—	124
Share of other comprehensive income of JV and associated companies.	−81	—	—	−81
Tax on items that have been or may be reclassified to profit or loss	—	−86	—	−86
Other comprehensive income, net of tax	−5,391	331	79	−4,981
Closing balance	**−2,424**	**101**	**−366**	**−2,689**

from Sweden–based Ericsson AB's financial statement note related to shareholders' equity. Ericsson refers to accumulated other comprehensive income as "Other reserves," which is comprised of three components, including Translation reserves. Exhibit 7.14 shows that Ericsson had a cumulative translation adjustment with a negative "opening balance" of SEK 2,967 million on January 1, 2020. In 2020, the company recorded a negative translation adjustment of SEK 5,434 million from the consolidation of foreign subsidiaries and transferred SEK 124 million of translation reserve to profit and loss (net income) related to the disposal of foreign subsidiaries during the year. In addition, Ericsson recognized a negative translation adjustment of SEK 81 million related to the consolidation of foreign joint ventures (JV) and foreign associated companies accounted for under the equity method. These changes resulted in a negative cumulative translation adjustment of SEK 2,424 million at the end of 2020. Note that, consistent with IFRS standards, Ericsson splits other reserve items into those that will never be recognized in profit or loss and those items that have been or may be reclassified to profit or loss.

Although there is no specific requirement to do so, many companies include a description of translation procedures followed in the "summary of significant accounting policies" in the notes to the financial statements. The following excerpt from IBM's 2020 annual report illustrates this type of disclosure:

Translation of Non-U.S. Currency Amounts

Assets and liabilities of non-U.S. subsidiaries that have a local functional currency are translated to U.S. dollars at year-end exchange rates. Translation adjustments are recorded in OCI. Income and expense items are translated at weighted-average rates of exchange prevailing during the year.

Inventories, property, plant, and equipment—net, and other nonmonetary assets and liabilities of non-U.S. subsidiaries and branches that operate in U.S. dollars are translated at the approximate exchange rates prevailing when the company acquired the assets or liabilities. All other assets and liabilities denominated in a currency other than U.S. dollars are translated at year-end exchange rates with the transaction gain or loss recognized in other (income) and expense. Income and expense items are translated at the weighted-average rates of exchange prevailing during the year. These translation gains and losses are included in net income for the period in which exchange rates change.[3]

Summary

1. The two major issues related to the translation of foreign currency financial statements concern (*a*) which method should be used, and (*b*) where the resulting translation adjustment should be reported in the consolidated financial statements.

2. Translation methods differ on the basis of which accounts are translated at the current exchange rate and which are translated at historical rates. Accounts translated at the current exchange rate are exposed to translation adjustment. Different translation methods give rise to different concepts of balance sheet exposure and translation adjustments of differing sign and magnitude.

3. Under the current rate method, all assets and liabilities are translated at the current exchange rate, giving rise to a net asset balance sheet exposure. Appreciation in the foreign currency will result in a positive translation adjustment. Depreciation in the foreign currency will result in a negative translation adjustment. By translating assets carried at historical cost at the current exchange rate, the current rate method maintains relationships that exist among account balances in the foreign currency financial statements but distorts the underlying valuation method used by the foreign operation.

[3] IBM Corporation, 2020 Annual Report, Note A. Significant Accounting Policies, p. 82.

4. Under the temporal method, assets carried at current or future value (cash, marketable securities, receivables) and liabilities are translated (remeasured) at the current exchange rate. Assets carried at historical cost and stockholders' equity are translated (remeasured) at historical exchange rates. When liabilities are greater than the sum of cash, marketable securities, and receivables, a net liability balance sheet exposure exists. Appreciation in the foreign currency will result in a negative translation adjustment (remeasurement loss). Depreciation in the foreign currency will result in a positive translation adjustment (remeasurement gain). By translating (remeasuring) assets carried at historical cost at historical exchange rates, the temporal method maintains the underlying valuation method used by the foreign operation but distorts relationships that exist among account balances in the foreign currency financial statements.

5. The appropriate combination of translation method and disposition of translation adjustment is determined under both IFRS and U.S. GAAP by identifying the functional currency of a foreign operation. The financial statements of foreign operations whose functional currency is different from the parent's reporting currency are translated using the current rate method, with the translation adjustment included in stockholders' equity. The financial statements of foreign operations whose functional currency is the same as the parent's reporting currency are translated using the temporal method, with the resulting translation gain or loss reported currently in net income.

6. The only substantive difference in translation rules between IFRS and U.S. GAAP relates to foreign operations that report in the currency of a hyperinflationary economy. IAS 21 requires the parent first to restate the foreign financial statements for inflation using rules in IAS 29 and then to translate the statements into parent-company currency using the current rate method. FASB ASC 830 requires the financial statements of foreign operations that report in the currency of a highly inflationary economy to be translated using the temporal method, as if the U.S. dollar were the functional currency. A country is considered highly inflationary if its cumulative three-year inflation rate exceeds 100 percent.

7. Some companies hedge their balance sheet exposures to avoid reporting remeasurement losses in income and/or negative translation adjustments in stockholders' equity. Foreign exchange gains and losses on foreign currency borrowings or foreign currency derivatives employed to hedge translation-based exposure (under the current rate method) are treated as part of the cumulative translation adjustment in stockholders' equity. Foreign exchange gains and losses on balance sheet hedges used to hedge remeasurement-based exposure (under the temporal method) are offset against remeasurement gains and losses on the income statement.

Appendix to Chapter 7

Translation of Foreign Currency Financial Statements in Hyperinflationary Economies

If a parent company has a foreign operation located in a hyperinflationary economy, IAS 21, *The Effects of Changes in Foreign Exchange Rates,* requires application of IAS 29, *Financial Reporting in Hyperinflationary Economies,* to restate the foreign operation's financial statements to a general purchasing power-adjusted historical cost (GPP) basis. Each and every line item in the GPP financial statements, including revenues, expenses, and stockholders' equity, is then translated into the parent company's reporting currency using the *current* exchange rate. This approach is referred to as the *restate/translate method.*

In contrast, U.S. GAAP requires a foreign operation located in a highly inflationary economy to be treated as a U.S. dollar functional currency operation. The *temporal method* must be used for translation purposes, and the foreign currency financial statements are not restated for inflation.

The procedures required by IAS 29 for the restatement of financial statements prior to translation are summarized as follows:

Balance Sheet

• Nonmonetary assets and nonmonetary liabilities are restated for changes in the GPP of the monetary unit. Nonmonetary assets are those assets whose fair value can change over time, including inventory, financial instruments, intangibles, and property, plant, and equipment. Nonmonetary liabilities are those liabilities for which the amount to be repaid is not fixed in monetary amount, such as obligations under warranties. Most nonmonetary items are carried at historical cost. In these cases, the GPP restated cost is determined by applying to the historical cost the change in *general price index* from the date of acquisition to the balance sheet date. Some nonmonetary items are carried at revalued amounts, for example, property, plant, and equipment revalued according to the allowed alternative treatment in IAS 16, *Property, Plant, and Equipment.* These items are restated for inflation using the change in general price index from the date of the most recent revaluation.

• Monetary assets and monetary liabilities are *not* restated for inflation because they are already expressed in terms of the monetary unit current at the balance sheet date. Monetary assets are those assets whose fair value does not change over time, such as cash and accounts and notes receivable. Monetary liabilities are those obligations for which the amount to be repaid is fixed in amount, such as accounts, notes, and bonds payable.

• All components of stockholders' equity are restated by applying the change in the general price index from the beginning of the period or the date of contribution, if later, to the balance sheet date.

Income Statement

• All income statement items are restated for inflation by applying the change in the general price index from the dates when the items were originally recorded to the balance sheet date.

• The gain or loss on net monetary position (*net purchasing power gain or loss*) is included in net income.

IAS 29 requires use of a *general price index* to restate financial statement balances and inclusion of a *purchasing power gain or loss* in net income. These concepts are discussed next.

GENERAL PRICE INDEX

When the prices of goods and services in an economy increase in general, we say that inflation has occurred. Economists often measure inflation by determining the current price for a representative "basket" of goods and services and then comparing the current price with the price for the same basket of goods and services at an earlier time. For example, if a basket of goods and services costs $100 on January 1, Year 1, and the same basket costs $120 on December 31, Year 1, then inflation in Year 1 is 20 percent [($120 - $100)/$100].

Economists convert the purchase price for a common basket of goods and services into a *general price index*. Continuing with the example above, the general price index (GPI) on January 1, Year 1, is 100 and the GPI on December 31, Year 1, is 120. The rate of inflation rate is measured by the change in the GPI ([(120 − 100)/100] = 20%), which reflects the decrease in the purchasing power of the currency. In our example, it takes $120 at the end of Year 1 to purchase as much as $100 could purchase at the beginning of Year 1. Thus, the dollar has lost 20 percent of its purchasing power during Year 1.

PURCHASING POWER GAINS AND LOSSES

Holding monetary assets (such as cash and receivables) during a period of inflation results in a purchasing power loss. On the other hand, holding monetary liabilities (such as accounts and notes payable) during a period of inflation results in a purchasing power gain. Further explanation of purchasing power gains and losses is provided below.

Purchasing Power Loss

Assume that you had $100 on January 1, Year 1. On that date, you could have purchased 100 percent of a general basket of goods and services. If you hold $100 throughout Year 1, on December 31, Year 1, when the GPI is 120, you now can purchase only 83.3 percent ($100/$120) of a general basket of goods and services. Thus, you would have incurred a loss in purchasing power by holding cash during the year. The difference between (a) the $120 you would need on December 31, Year 1, to purchase 100 percent of a basket of goods and services and (b) the $100 in cash that you actually have results in a purchasing power loss of $20. This can be computed by multiplying the amount of cash held at the beginning of the year by the inflation rate of 20 percent ($100 × 20% = $20). Holding receivables during a period of inflation also results in losses in purchasing power.

Purchasing Power Gain

Now assume that you expect to receive $100 on December 31, Year 1. When that cash is received, and the GPI is 120, you will be able to purchase 83.3 percent ($100/$120) of a general basket of goods and services. Instead, if you were to borrow $100 on January 1, Year 1, you could purchase 100 percent of a general basket of goods and services on that date and then repay the borrowing with the $100 in cash you receive on December 31. Thus, borrowing cash during a period of inflation results in a gain in purchasing power. The difference between (a) the $100 in cash that you actually spent on January 1, Year 1, to purchase 100 percent of a basket of goods and services, and (b) the $120 in cash you would need on December 31, Year 1, to purchase the same basket of goods and services results in a purchasing power gain of $20. This can be computed by multiplying the amount of debt held at the beginning of the year by the inflation rate of 20 percent ($100 × 20% = $20). Holding other types of payables during a period of inflation also results in gains in purchasing power.

Historical cost accounting ignores the fact that purchasing power gains and losses exist during a period of inflation. On the other hand, during hyperinflation, IAS 29 requires purchasing power gains on monetary liabilities and purchasing power losses on monetary assets to be combined. A net purchasing power gain or loss is then included in the determination of net income. The net purchasing power gain or loss is determined by netting monetary liabilities against monetary assets to determine an entity's *net monetary position*. Thus, the net purchasing power gain or loss also is referred to as the *gain or loss on net monetary position*. A *net* purchasing power gain will result when an entity maintains monetary liabilities in excess of monetary assets during inflation, and a *net* purchasing power loss will result when the opposite situation exists.

HYPERINFLATIONARY ECONOMY TRANSLATION EXAMPLE

To demonstrate the translation of foreign currency financial statements in a hyperinflationary economy, assume that Sean Regan Company formed a subsidiary in a foreign country

EXHIBIT A7.1

SEAN REGAN COMPANY
YEAR 1 FINANCIAL STATEMENTS
Foreign Subsidiary
Income Statement
Year 1

(in FC)

Rent revenue	1,000
Interest expense	(250)
Net income	750

Foreign Subsidiary
Balance Sheets
Year 1

(in FC)	January 1	December 31
Cash	1,000	1,750
Land	9,000	9,000
Total	10,000	10,750
Note payable (5%)	5,000	5,000
Capital stock	5,000	5,000
Retained earnings	0	750
Total	10,000	10,750

on January 1, Year 1, through a combination of debt and equity financing. The foreign subsidiary acquired land on January 1, Year 1, which it rents to a local farmer. The foreign subsidiary's financial statements for its first year of operations, in foreign currency units (FC), are presented in Exhibit A7.1.

Rent revenue and interest expense were realized in cash during the year. Thus, the balance in the Cash account at December 31, Year 1 (FC 1,750) is equal to the beginning balance in cash (FC 1,000) plus net income for the year (FC 750).

The foreign country experienced significant inflation in Year 1, especially in the second half of the year. The general price index (GPI) during Year 1 was:

January 1, Year 1	100
Average, Year 1	125
December 31, Year 1	200

The rate of inflation in Year 1 was 100 percent ([200 − 100]/100), and the foreign country clearly meets the definition of a hyperinflationary economy.

As a result of the high rate of inflation in the foreign country, the FC weakened substantially during the year relative to other currencies. Relevant exchange rates between Sean Regan's parent company currency (PC) and the FC during Year 1 were:

	PC per FC
January 1, Year 1	1.00
Average, Year 1	0.80
December 31, Year 1	0.50

EXHIBIT A7.2

SEAN REGAN COMPANY
Foreign Subsidiary in Hyperinflationary Economy—Application of IFRS Standards

	FC	Restatement Factor		Inflation-Adjusted (Restated) FC	Exchange Rate	PC
Year 1						
Rent revenue	1,000	× 200/125	=	1,600	× 0.50	800
Interest expense	(250)	× 200/125	=	(400)	× 0.50	(200)
Subtotal	750			1,200		600
Purchasing power gain (loss)			=	3,550	× 0.50	1,775
Net income			=	4,750		2,375
December 31, Year 1						
Cash	1,750	× 200/200	=	1,750	× 0.50	875
Land	9,000	× 200/100	=	18,000	× 0.50	9,000
Total	10,750			19,750		9,875
Note payable	5,000	× 200/200	=	5,000	× 0.50	2,500
Capital stock	5,000	× 200/200	=	10,000	× 0.50	5,000
Retained earnings	750	From I/S		4,750	× 0.50	2,375
Total	10,750			19,750		9,875

IFRS Restate/Translate Approach

Assuming that Sean Regan Company prepares its consolidated financial statements in accordance with IFRS standards, the foreign subsidiary's FC financial statements would be (1) restated for local inflation and then (2) translated into PC using the current exchange rate, as shown in Exhibit A7.2.

Other than retained earnings, all financial statement items are restated to the GPI of 200 at December 31, Year 1. This is the numerator in the restatement factor shown in Exhibit A7.2.

Restatement of Income Statement

Rent revenue and Interest expense occurred evenly throughout the year when the average GPI was 125. Therefore, the appropriate restatement factor for these items is 200/125. A purchasing power gain or loss must be included in the calculation of net income. The net purchasing power gain of FC 3,550 can be computed as follows:

Gain from holding note payable	FC 5,000 × (200 − 100)/100 =	FC5,000
Loss from holding beginning balance in cash	(1,000) × (200 − 100)/100 =	(1,000)
Loss from increase in cash during the year	(750) × (200 − 125)/125 =	(450)
Net purchasing power gain (loss)		FC3,550

Holding a note payable of FC 5,000 during a period of 100 percent inflation gives rise to a purchasing power gain of FC 5,000 on that monetary liability. Holding the beginning cash balance of FC 1,000 for the entire year generates a purchasing power loss of FC 1,000. The increase in cash of FC 750 which occurred evenly throughout the year resulted in a purchasing power loss of FC 450.

Alternatively, the net purchasing power gain can be calculated by focusing on the foreign subsidiary's net monetary liability position, as follows:

	Actual	Restatement Factor	Restated
Net monetary liabilities, 1/1/Y1	FC (4,000) ×	200/100 =	FC (8,000)
Plus: Increase in monetary assets, Year 1	750 ×	200/125 =	1,200
Net monetary liabilities, 12/31/Y1	FC (3,250)		(6,800)
Net monetary liabilities, 12/31/Y1 (Actual)			(3,250)
Purchasing power gain			FC (3,550)

The foreign subsidiary had a net monetary liability position of FC 4,000 on January 1 (Note payable 5,000 less Cash 1,000), an increase in monetary assets (Cash) during Year 1, and an actual net monetary liability position of FC 3,250 on December 31 (Note payable 5,000 less Cash 1,750). The net monetary liability position coupled with an increase in the GPI in Year 1 resulted in a purchasing power gain for the year.

Restatement of Balance Sheet

Monetary assets and liabilities already are stated in terms of December 31, Year 1, purchasing power. Therefore, the restatement factor for Cash and Note payable is 200/200. In effect, these accounts are not restated. Land and Capital stock are restated from the GPI of 100 that existed at the beginning of the year (when the Land was acquired and the Capital stock was contributed) to the GPI of 200 at year-end; the restatement factor for these accounts is 200/100. Retained earnings are not directly restated. The restated FC amount of Retained earnings is equal to the FC amount of Net income (4,750).

Once the FC financial statements are restated for inflation, each inflation-adjusted (restated) FC amount is translated into PC using the exchange rate at December 31, Year 1. Note that all inflation-adjusted (restated) FC amounts, including shareholders' equity accounts, are translated at the current exchange rate, and therefore no translation adjustment is needed.

U.S. GAAP Approach

Now assume that Sean Regan Company wishes to comply with U.S. GAAP in preparing its consolidated financial statements. In that case, the foreign subsidiary's FC financial statements would be translated into PC using the temporal method, as required by FASB ASC Topic 830, *Foreign Currency Matters,* without first adjusting for inflation. The resulting translation gain or loss is reported in net income. Application of U.S. GAAP is shown in Exhibit A7.3.

The translation gain of FC 1,775 can be determined as follows:

	FC	Translation Rate	PC
Net monetary liabilities, 1/1/Y1	(4,000) ×	1.00 H =	(4,000)
Rent revenue, Year 1	1,000 ×	0.80 A =	800
Interest expense, Year 1	(250) ×	0.80 A =	(200)
Net monetary liabilities, 12/31/Y1	(3,250)		(3,400)
Net monetary liabilities, 12/31/Y1, at the current exchange rate..................	(3,250) ×	0.50 C =	(1,625)
Remeasurement gain..........................			(1,775)

EXHIBIT A7.3

SEAN REGAN COMPANY
Foreign Subsidiary in Hyperinflationary Economy—Application of U.S. GAAP

	FC	Exchange Rate	PC
Year 1			
Rent revenue	1,000	× 0.80 A	= 800
Interest expense	(250)	× 0.80 A	= (200)
Subtotal	750		600
Translation gain			1,775
Net income			2,375
December 31, Year 1			
Cash	1,750	× 0.50 C	= 875
Land	9,000	× 1.00 H	= 9,000
Total	10,750		9,875
Note payable	5,000	× 0.50 C	= 2,500
Capital stock	5,000	× 1.00 H	= 5,000
Retained earnings	750	From I/S	2,375
Total	10,750		9,875

Where: C = current exchange rate; A = average-for-the-year exchange rate; H = historical exchange rate

The foreign subsidiary had a net monetary liability position of FC 4,000 on January 1 (Note payable 5,000 less Cash 1,000), and a net monetary liability position of FC 3,250 on December 31 (Note payable 5,000 less Cash 1,750). The net monetary liability position coupled with a depreciating FC in Year 1 resulted in a remeasurement gain for the year.

Application of the temporal method as required by U.S. GAAP in this situation results in exactly the same PC amounts as were obtained under the restate/translate approach required by IFRS standards. The equivalence of results under the two approaches exists because of the exact one-to-one inverse relationship between the change in the GPI in the foreign country and the change in the PC value of the FC, as predicted by the theory of purchasing power parity. The GPI doubled during Year 1 and the FC lost half its purchasing power, which caused the FC to lose exactly one-half its value in PC terms. To the extent that this one-to-one inverse relationship does not hold in the real world, and it rarely does, the two different methodologies for translating the foreign currency financial statements of subsidiaries located in hyperinflationary countries will generate different translated amounts. For example, if the December 31, Year 1, exchange rate had dropped to only PC 0.60 per FC (rather than PC 0.50 per FC), then translated net income would have been PC 2,050 under U.S. GAAP and PC 2,850 under IFRS standards.

Identification of High Inflation Countries

U.S. GAAP requires that a country be considered highly inflationary when its cumulative inflation rate for the three years preceding the beginning of the current year exceeds 100 percent. However, even if the three-year cumulative inflation rate is less than 100 percent, FASB ASC 830 indicates that historical inflation rate trends and other pertinent economic factors should be taken into account in determining whether the country should be considered highly inflationary.

In contrast to U.S. GAAP, IFRS standards do not establish an absolute definition for hyperinflation, leaving this determination to individual companies. Instead, IAS 29 provides the following list of characteristics that could indicate that a country is hyperinflationary:

1. The general population keeps its wealth in nonmonetary assets or in a stable foreign currency; receipts of local currency are immediately invested to maintain purchasing power.
2. The general population thinks about prices in terms of a stable currency, and prices may actually be quoted in that currency.
3. Prices for credit sales and purchases include an amount to compensate for the expected loss in purchasing power during the credit period.
4. Interest rates, wages, and prices are linked to a price index.
5. The cumulative inflation rate over a three-year period is 100 percent or higher.

Neither the FASB nor the IASB identifies which specific countries a company should treat as hyperinflationary. The International Practices Task Force (IPTF) of the Center for Audit Quality (CAQ) monitors the inflationary status of countries in order to assist companies in complying with U.S. GAAP. In November 2020, the IPTF identified these seven countries as having a three-year cumulative inflation rate exceeding 100 percent: Argentina, Iran, Lebanon, South Sudan, Sudan, Venezuela, and Zimbabwe.[1] The IPTF determined that the rate of inflation in Venezuela for 2020 was more than 3,000 percent, with a three-year cumulative inflation rate exceeding 380,000 percent! In contrast, Argentina had a 2020 inflation rate of 36 percent, and a three-year cumulative rate of 209 percent.

Sodexo SA is a French food services company that uses IFRS standards to prepare its financial statements. Exhibit A7.4 provides an excerpt from Sodexo's 2020 Universal Registration Statement (annual report) in which the company discloses its use of the IFRS "restate/translate" approach with respect to the financial statements of foreign subsidiaries in countries with hyperinflationary economies. Sodexo indicates that, in preparing its 2019 and 2020 financial statements, Argentina was determined to be hyperinflationary, but that the impact of hyperinflation on the company's consolidated financial statements was not material in either year.

EXHIBIT A7.4

SODEXO SA
Universal Registration Statement
2020

Excerpt from Note 3. Main Changes in Scope of Consolidation
Foreign Currency Translation
Financial Statements Denominated in Foreign Currencies
(ii) Countries with hyperinflationary economies

Non-monetary assets and liabilities in hyperinflationary countries, as well as the income statement, are adjusted to reflect the changes in the general pricing power of the functional currency in accordance with IAS 29. Moreover, subsidiaries financial statements in hyperinflationary countries are translated at the closing rate of the period in accordance with IAS 21.

Since July 1, 2018, Argentina has been classified as a country with a hyperinflationary economy. However, the impacts of hyperinflation in that country were not material at Group level during Fiscal 2019 and Fiscal 2020.

---

[1] Center for Audit Quality, International Practices Task Force, *Document for Discussion: Monitoring Inflation in Certain Countries,* November 6, 2021, available at **www.thecaq.org** (accessed January 21, 2022).

Questions

1. What are the two major conceptual issues that must be resolved in translating foreign currency financial statements?
2. What factors create a balance sheet (or translation) exposure to foreign exchange risk? How does balance sheet exposure compare with transaction exposure?
3. What is the concept underlying the current rate method of translation? What is the concept underlying the temporal method of translation? How does balance sheet exposure differ under these two methods?
4. What are the major procedural differences in applying the current rate and temporal methods of translation?
5. How does a parent company determine the appropriate method for translating the financial statements of a foreign subsidiary?
6. What are the major differences between IFRS and U.S. GAAP in the translation of foreign currency financial statements?
7. What does the term *functional currency* mean? How is the functional currency determined under IFRS and under U.S. GAAP?
8. Which translation method does U.S. GAAP require for operations in highly inflationary countries? What is the rationale for mandating use of this method?
9. Why might a company want to hedge its balance sheet exposure? What is the paradox associated with hedging balance sheet exposure?
10. How are gains and losses on foreign currency borrowings used to hedge the net investment in a foreign subsidiary reported in the consolidated financial statements?

The following questions relate to the Appendix *to this chapter:*

11. What procedures do IFRS standards require when translating the foreign currency financial statements of a foreign operation located in a hyperinflationary economy?
12. Which balance sheet accounts give rise to purchasing power gains, and which accounts give rise to purchasing power losses?

Exercises and Problems

1. Which one of the following items normally is translated the same way under both the current rate and temporal methods of translation?
   a. Inventory.
   b. Equipment.
   c. Sales revenue.
   d. Depreciation expense.

2. Which one of the following items is remeasured using the current exchange rate under the temporal method?
   a. Accounts payable.
   b. Dividends declared.
   c. Additional paid-in capital.
   d. Amortization expense.

3. In translating the financial statements of a foreign subsidiary into the parent's reporting currency under the current rate method, which of the following statements is true?
   a. Expenses are translated using a combination of current and historical exchange rates.
   b. Intangible assets are translated at the historical exchange rates in effect on the date the assets are purchased.
   c. The translation adjustment is a function of the foreign subsidiary's net assets.
   d. The translation adjustment is a function of the relative amount of monetary assets and monetary liabilities held by the foreign subsidiary.

4. A foreign subsidiary of Wampoa Ltd. has one asset (inventory) and no liabilities. The subsidiary operates with a significant degree of autonomy from Wampoa and primarily uses the local currency (the won) in carrying out its transactions. Since the date the inventory was acquired, the won has decreased in value in relation to Wampoa's reporting currency. In translating the foreign subsidiary's won financial statements into the parent's reporting currency, which of the following is true under IFRS?

   a. A translation gain must be reported in net income.

   b. A positive translation adjustment must be reported in stockholders' equity.

   c. A negative translation adjustment must be reported in stockholders' equity.

   d. A translation loss must be reported in net income.

5. Which of the following best explains how a translation loss arises when the temporal method of translation is used to translate the foreign currency financial statements of a foreign subsidiary?

   a. The foreign subsidiary has more monetary assets than monetary liabilities, and the foreign currency appreciates in value.

   b. The foreign subsidiary has more monetary liabilities than monetary assets, and the foreign currency depreciates in value.

   c. The foreign subsidiary has more monetary assets than monetary liabilities, and the foreign currency depreciates in value.

   d. The foreign subsidiary has more total assets than total liabilities, and the foreign currency appreciates in value.

6. In the translated financial statements, which method of translation maintains the underlying valuation methods used in the foreign currency financial statements?

   a. Current rate method; income statement translated at average exchange rate for the year.

   b. Current rate method; income statement translated at exchange rate at the balance sheet date.

   c. Temporal method.

   d. Monetary/nonmonetary method.

7. In accordance with U.S. generally accepted accounting principles (GAAP), which translation combination would be appropriate for a foreign operation whose functional currency is the U.S. dollar?

Method	Treatment of Translation Adjustment
a. Temporal	Separate component of stockholders' equity
b. Temporal	Gain or loss in income statement
c. Current rate	Separate component of stockholders' equity
d. Current rate	Gain or loss in income statement

8. In accordance with International Financial Reporting Standards (IFRS), which translation combination would be appropriate for a foreign operation whose functional currency is the currency of the host country (foreign currency)?

Method	Treatment of Translation Adjustment
a. Temporal	Separate component of stockholders' equity
b. Temporal	Gain or loss in income statement
c. Current rate	Separate component of stockholders' equity
d. Current rate	Gain or loss in income statement

9. The functional currency of Garland Inc.'s Japanese subsidiary is the Japanese yen. Garland borrowed Japanese yen as a partial hedge of its investment in the subsidiary. How should the transaction gain on the foreign currency borrowing be reported in Garland's consolidated financial statements in accordance with IFRS?

   a. The transaction gain is reported as an adjustment to interest expense in the income statement.

   b. The transaction gain is reported as an extraordinary item in the income statement.

   c. The transaction gain is offset against the negative translation adjustment related to the Japanese subsidiary in the stockholders' equity section of the balance sheet.

   d. The transaction gain is offset against the negative translation adjustment related to the Japanese subsidiary on the income statement.

10. Selected balance sheet accounts of a foreign subsidiary of the Pacter Company have been translated into parent currency (F) as follows:

	Translated at	
	Current Rates	**Historical Rates**
Accounts receivable	F 100,000	F 120,000
Marketable securities, at cost	200,000	240,000
Prepaid insurance	120,000	130,000
Goodwill	250,000	300,000
	F 670,000	F 790,000

   Required:

   a. Assuming that the foreign subsidiary is determined to have the foreign currency as its functional currency in accordance with IAS 21, determine the total amount that should be included in Pacter's consolidated balance sheet for the assets listed in accordance with IFRS.

   b. Assuming that the foreign subsidiary is determined to have Pacter's reporting currency as its functional currency in accordance with IAS 21, determine the total amount that should be included in Pacter's consolidated balance sheet for the assets listed in accordance with IFRS.

11. The Year 1 financial statements of the Chinese subsidiary of Auswold Limited (an Australian-based company) revealed the following:

	Chinese Yuan (CNY)
Beginning inventory	750,000
Purchases	1,500,000
Ending inventory	450,000
Cost of goods sold	1,800,000

Australian dollar (AUD) exchange rates for 1 CNY are as follows:

January 1, Year 1	AUD 0.229
Average, Year 1	0.217
December 31, Year 1	0.204

The beginning inventory was acquired in the last quarter of the previous year, when the exchange rate was AUD 0.230 = CNY 1; ending inventory was acquired in the last quarter of the current year, when the exchange rate was AUD 0.210 = CNY 1.

Required:

a. Assuming that the current rate method is the appropriate method of translation, determine the amounts at which the Chinese subsidiary's ending inventory and cost of goods sold should be included in Auswold's Year 1 consolidated financial statements.

b. Assuming that the temporal method is the appropriate method of translation, determine the amounts at which the Chinese subsidiary's ending inventory and cost of goods sold should be included in Auswold's Year 1 consolidated financial statements.

12. Simga Company's Turkish subsidiary reported the following amounts in Turkish lira (TL) on its December 31, Year 4, balance sheet:

Equipment	TL 100,000,000,000
Accumulated depreciation (straight-line)	32,000,000,000

Additional information related to the equipment is as follows:

Date	Amount Purchased	Useful Life	US$/TL Exchange Rate
1/1/Y1	TL 60,000,000,000	10 years	$0.0000070 = TL 1
1/1/Y3	TL 40,000,000,000	10 years	$0.0000020 = TL 1

U.S.-dollar exchange rates for the Turkish lira for Year 4 are as follows:

January 1, Year 4	$0.0000010
December 31, Year 4	0.0000006

Required:

a. Assume that Turkey is a highly inflationary economy. Determine the amounts at which the Turkish subsidiary's equipment and accumulated depreciation should be carried on Simga Company's December 31, Year 4, consolidated balance sheet in accordance with U.S. GAAP. Determine the net carrying amount for equipment.

b. Now assume that Turkey is not a highly inflationary economy and that the Turkish subsidiary primarily uses Turkish lira in conducting its operations. Determine the amounts at which the Turkish subsidiary's equipment and accumulated depreciation should be carried on Simga Company's December 31, Year 4, consolidated balance sheet in accordance with U.S. GAAP. Determine the net carrying amount for equipment.

13. Spindleruv s.r.o. (a Czech company) invests 2,000,000 euros in a foreign subsidiary on January 1, Year 1. The subsidiary commences operations on that date and generates net income of 100,000 euros during its first year of operations. No dividends are sent to the parent this year. Spindleruv uses IFRS in preparing its financial statements. Relevant exchange rates between Spindleruv's reporting currency, Czech koruna (CZK), and the euro are as follows:

January 1, Year 1	CZK 25.0 per 1 euro
Average, Year 1	CZK 25.5 per 1 euro
December 31, Year 1	CZK 27.0 per 1 euro

Required:

Determine the amount of translation adjustment that Spindleruv will report on its December 31, Year 1, balance sheet related to this foreign subsidiary assuming that the euro is the foreign subsidiary's functional currency.

14. Zesto Company (a U.S. company) establishes a subsidiary in Mexico on January 1, Year 1. The subsidiary begins the year with 1,000,000 Mexican pesos (MXN) in cash and no other assets or liabilities. It immediately uses MXN 600,000 to acquire equipment. Inventory costing MXN 300,000 is acquired evenly throughout the year and sold for MXN 500,000 cash. A dividend of MXN 100,000 is paid to the parent on October 1, Year 1. Depreciation on the equipment for the year is MXN 60,000. Currency exchange rates between the U.S. dollar ($) and MXN for Year 1 are as follows:

January 1	$0.090
October 1	.0.080
December 31	.0.078
Average for the year	.0.085

Required:

Determine the amount of remeasurement loss under the temporal method to be recognized in the Year 1 consolidated income statement.

15. Tornado Corporation (a U.S.-based company) acquired 100 percent of a Canadian company for 16 million Canadian dollars on December 20, Year 1. At the date of acquisition, the exchange rate was US$0.75 per Canadian dollar. The acquisition price is attributable to the following assets and liabilities denominated in Canadian dollars:

Cash	1,000,000
Inventory	5,000,000
Fixed assets	13,000,000
Notes payable	(3,000,000)

Tornado Corporation prepares consolidated financial statements on December 31, Year 1. By that date, the Canadian dollar appreciated to US$0.78. Because of the year-end holidays, no transactions took place between the date of acquisition and the end of the year. Property, plant, and equipment is depreciated using a units-of-production method, so no depreciation is required from December 20 to December 31. The Canadian subsidiary has no revenues and no expenses from December 20 to December 31, and its book value is unchanged from December 20 to December 31.

Required:

a. Determine the translation adjustment to be reported on Tornado's December 31, Year 1, consolidated balance sheet, assuming that the Canadian dollar is the Canadian subsidiary's functional currency. What is the economic relevance of this translation adjustment?

b. Determine the remeasurement gain or loss to be reported in Tornado's Year 1 consolidated income, assuming that the U.S. dollar is the functional currency. What is the economic relevance of this remeasurement gain or loss?

16. Gramado Company was created as a wholly owned subsidiary of Porto Alegre Corporation (a U.S.-based company) on January 1, Year 1. On that date, Porto Alegre invested $42,000 in Gramado's capital stock. Given the exchange rate on that date of

$0.84 per cruzeiro, the initial investment of $42,000 was converted into 50,000 cruzeiros (Cz). Other than the capital investment on January 1, there were no transactions involving stockholders' equity in Year 1. Gramado's cruzeiro-denominated financial statements for Year 2 are as follows:

Income Statement
Year 2

	Cz
Sales	540,000
Cost of goods sold	(310,000)
Gross profit	230,000
Operating expenses	(108,000)
Income before tax	122,000
Income taxes	(40,000)
Net income	82,000

Statement of Retained Earnings
Year 2

	Cz
Retained earnings, 1/1/Y2	154,000
Net income	82,000
Dividends (paid on 12/1/Y2)	(20,000)
Retained earnings, 12/31/Y2	216,000

Balance Sheet
December 31, Year 2

	Cz
Cash	50,000
Receivables	100,000
Inventory	72,000
Plant and equipment (net)	300,000
Less: Accumulated depreciation	(70,000)
Total assets	452,000
Liabilities	186,000
Capital stock	50,000
Retained earnings, 12/31/Y2	216,000
Total liabilities and stockholders' equity	452,000

The cruzeiro is the primary currency that Gramado uses in its day-to-day operations. The cruzeiro has steadily fallen in value against the dollar since Porto Alegre made the investment in Gramado on January 1, Year 1. Relevant U.S. dollar ($) exchange rates for the cruzeiro for Years 1 and 2 are as follows:

January 1, Year 1	$0.84
Average for Year 1	0.80
December 31, Year 1	0.75
Average for Year 2	0.72
December 1, Year 2	0.71
December 31, Year 2	0.70

Required:

a. Translate Gramado Company's Year 2 financial statements into U.S. dollars.

b. Compute the translation adjustment for Year 1 and for Year 2 and reconcile these amounts to the cumulative translation adjustment reported on the translated balance sheet at December 31, Year 2.

17. Brookhurst Company (a U.S.-based company) established a subsidiary in South Africa on January 1, Year 1, by investing 300,000 South African rand (ZAR) when the exchange rate was US$0.09/ZAR 1. On that date, the foreign subsidiary borrowed ZAR 500,000 from local banks on a 10-year note to finance the acquisition of plant and equipment. The subsidiary's opening balance sheet (in ZAR) was as follows:

Balance Sheet
January 1, Year 1

Cash	300,000	Long-term debt	500,000
Plant and equipment	500,000	Capital stock	300,000
Total	800,000	Total	800,000

During Year 1, the foreign subsidiary generated sales of ZAR 1,000,000 and net income of ZAR 110,000. Dividends in the amount of ZAR 20,000 were paid to the parent on June 1 and December 1. Inventory was acquired evenly throughout the year, with ending inventory acquired on November 15, Year 1. The subsidiary's ZAR financial statements for the year ended December 31, Year 1, are as follows:

Income Statement
Year 1

	ZAR
Sales	1,000,000
Cost of goods sold	(600,000)
Gross profit	400,000
Depreciation expense	(50,000)
Other operating expenses	(150,000)
Income before tax	200,000
Income taxes	(90,000)
Net income	110,000

Statement of Retained Earnings
Year 1

	ZAR
Retained earnings, 1/1/Y1	0
Net income	110,000
Dividends.....................................	(40,000)
Retained earnings, 12/31/Y1	70,000

Balance Sheet
December 31, Year 1

	ZAR
Cash	80,000
Receivables	150,000
Inventory	270,000
Plant and equipment (net)	450,000
Total assets	950,000
Accounts payable	80,000
Long-term debt	500,000
Common stock	300,000
Retained earnings, 12/31/Y1	70,000
Total liabilities and stockholders' equity	950,000

Relevant exchange rates for Year 1 are as follows (US$ per ZAR):

January 1, Year 1	$ 0.090
June 1, Year 1	0.095
Average for Year 1	0.096
November 15, Year 1	0.100
December 1, Year 1	0.105
December 31, Year 1	0.110

Required:

a. Translate the South African subsidiary's financial statements into U.S. dollars, assuming that the South African rand is the functional currency. Compute the translation adjustment by considering the impact of exchange rate changes on the subsidiary's net assets.

b. Translate (remeasure) the South African subsidiary's financial statements into U.S. dollars, assuming that the U.S. dollar is the functional currency. Compute the translation adjustment (remeasurement gain or loss) by considering the impact of exchange rate changes on the subsidiary's net monetary asset or liability position.

18. San Clemente Corporation, whose reporting currency is the mark (M), establishes a foreign subsidiary, whose reporting currency is the peseta (P). On January 1, Year 1, San Clemente contributes Cash of P20,000 to the foreign subsidiary in exchange for Common Stock, and the subsidiary purchases Land for P30,000 by negotiating a 10-year Note Payable of P30,000. On February 1, Year 1, the subsidiary purchases Equipment for P12,000. Sales, Salary Expense, and Other Operating Expenses are incurred evenly throughout Year 1. The foreign subsidiary declares Dividends of P10,000 on December 1, Year 1. Relevant exchange rates for Year 1 are as follows (Mark per Peseta):

January 1	M 0.71
February 1	0.69
Weighted average	0.66
December 1	0.65
December 31	0.63

On December 31, Year 1, the subsidiary reports the following trial balance (in pesetas):

	Debits	Credits
Cash	6,000	
Accounts receivable	10,000	
Equipment	12,000	
Accumulated depreciation		3,000
Land	30,000	
Accounts payable		2,000
Note payable		30,000
Common stock		20,000
Dividends (declared 12/1/Y1)	10,000	
Sales		40,000
Salary expense	15,000	
Depreciation expense	3,000	
Other operating expenses	9,000	
Total	95,000	95,000

Required:

a. Assume that the foreign subsidiary's functional currency is the peseta (P). Prepare a trial balance for it in marks (M) so that Year 1 consolidated financial statements can be prepared. Show the calculation of translation adjustment for Year 1. Ignore income taxes.

b. Assume that the foreign subsidiary's functional currency is the mark (M). Prepare a trial balance for it in marks (M) so that Year 1 consolidated financial statements can be prepared. Show the calculation of remeasurement gain (loss) for Year 1. Ignore income taxes.

19. Access the most recent annual report for a U.S.-based multinational company with which you are familiar to complete the requirements of this exercise.

Required:

a. Determine whether the company's foreign operations have a predominant functional currency.

b. If possible, determine the amount of remeasurement gain or loss, if any, reported in net income in each of the three most recent years.

c. Determine the amount of translation adjustment, if any, reported in other comprehensive income in each of the three most recent years. Explain the sign (positive or negative) of the translation adjustment in each of the three most recent years.

d. Determine whether the company hedges net investments in foreign operations. If so, determine the type(s) of hedging instrument(s) used.

20. To complete the requirements of this exercise, access the 2020 annual reports for ExxonMobil Corporation and Chevron Corporation.

Required:

a. Determine whether each company's foreign operations have a predominant functional currency. Discuss the implication this has for the comparability of financial statements between the two companies.

b. Determine the amount of translation adjustment, if any, reported in other comprehensive income in each of the three most recent years. Explain the sign (positive or negative) of the translation adjustment in each of the three most recent years. Compare the relative magnitude of the translation adjustments between the two companies.

c. Determine whether each company hedges the net investment in foreign operations. If so, determine the type(s) of hedging instrument(s) used.

d. Prepare a brief report comparing and contrasting the foreign currency translation and foreign currency hedging policies of these two companies.

The following exercises and problems relate to the Appendix *to this chapter:*

21. Cari Company borrows 5,000,000 Argentinian pesos (ARS) on January 1, Year 1, at an annual interest rate of 60 percent by signing a two-year note payable. During Year 1, the Argentinian inflation index changed from 100 at January 1 to 155 at December 31.

Required:
Related to the note payable, determine the following amounts for Cari Company for Year 1:
a. Purchasing power gain.
b. Nominal interest expense (note payable multiplied by annual interest rate).
c. Real interest expense (nominal interest expense less purchasing power gain).
d. Real (inflation-adjusted) rate of interest paid.

22. Doner Company Inc. established a foreign subsidiary on January 1, Year 1. The subsidiary's financial statements in foreign currency (FC) for the year ended December 31, Year 1, appear as follows:

Balance Sheets	January 1, Year 1	December 31, Year 1
Cash and receivables	FC 20,000	FC 85,000
Property and equipment, net	50,000	45,000
Total	FC 70,000	FC130,000
Payables	FC 15,000	FC 15,000
Contributed capital	55,000	55,000
Retained earnings	—	60,000
Total	FC 70,000	FC130,000

Income Statement	Year 1
Revenues	FC 100,000
Depreciation	(5,000)
Other expenses	(35,000)
Net income	FC 60,000

Revenues and expenses occur evenly throughout the year. Revenues and other expenses are realized in cash during the year.

General price indexes (GPI) and parent currency (PC) per FC exchange rates for Year 1 are as follows:

Date	General Price Index	Exchange Rate (per FC)
January 1, Year 1	100	PC 100
Average for Year 1	160	PC 70
December 31, Year 1	240	PC 40

Required:
a. Translate the foreign subsidiary's Year 1 foreign currency (FC) financial statements into parent currency (PC) using IFRS.
b. Remeasure the foreign subsidiary's Year 1 foreign currency (FC) financial statements into parent currency (PC) using U.S. GAAP.

Case 7-1

Columbia Corporation

Columbia Corporation, a U.S.-based company, acquired a 100 percent interest in Swoboda Company in Lodz, Poland, on January 1, Year 1, when the exchange rate for the Polish zloty (PLN) was $0.25. The financial statements of Swoboda as of December 31, Year 2, two years later, are as follows:

BALANCE SHEET
December 31, Year 2

Assets

Cash	PLN 1,000,000
Accounts receivable (net)	1,650,000
Inventory	4,250,000
Equipment	12,500,000
Less: Accumulated depreciation	(4,250,000)
Building	36,000,000
Less: Accumulated depreciation	(15,150,000)
Land	3,000,000
Total assets	PLN 39,000,000

Liabilities and Stockholders' Equity

Accounts payable	PLN 1,250,000
Long-term debt	25,000,000
Common stock	2,500,000
Additional paid-in capital	7,500,000
Retained earnings	2,750,000
Total liabilities and stockholders' equity	PLN 39,000,000

STATEMENT OF INCOME AND RETAINED EARNINGS
For the Year Ending December 31, Year 2

Sales	PLN 12,500,000
Cost of goods sold	(6,000,000)
Depreciation expense—equipment	(1,250,000)
Depreciation expense—building	(900,000)
Research and development expense	(600,000)
Other expenses (including taxes)	(500,000)
Net income	PLN 3,250,000
Plus: Retained earnings, 1/1/Y2	250,000
Less: Dividends, Year 2	(750,000)
Retained earnings, 12/31/Y2	PLN 2,750,000

Additional information:

- The January 1, Year 2, beginning inventory of PLN 3,000,000 was acquired on December 15, Year 1, when the exchange rate was $0.215. Purchases of inventory during Year 2 were acquired uniformly throughout the year. The December 31, Year 2, ending inventory of PLN 4,250,000 was acquired evenly throughout the fourth quarter of Year 2 when the exchange rate was $0.16.

- All fixed assets were on the books when the subsidiary was acquired except for PLN 2,500,000 of equipment, which was acquired on January 3, Year 2, when the exchange rate was $0.18, and PLN 6,000,000 in buildings, which were acquired on August 5, Year 2, when the exchange rate was $0.17. Equipment is depreciated on a straight-line basis over 10 years. Buildings are depreciated on a straight-line basis over 40 years. A full year's depreciation is taken in the year of acquisition.

- Dividends were declared and paid on December 15, Year 2, when the exchange rate was $0.155.

- Other exchange rates for Year 2 are:

January 1	$0.200
Average for the year	0.175
December 31	0.150

Required:

1. Translate Swoboda's financial statements into U.S. dollars in accordance with U.S. GAAP at December 31, Year 2, using the following scenarios.

   a. Assume the Polish zloty is the functional currency. The December 31, Year 1, retained earnings amount that appeared in Swoboda's translated financial statements was $56,250. The December 31, Year 1, cumulative translation adjustment that appeared in Swoboda's translated balance sheet was negative $506,250.

   b. Assume the U.S. dollar is the functional currency. The December 31, Year 1, retained earnings amount that appeared in Swoboda's remeasured financial statements was $882,500.

   c. Assume the same scenario described in (b) except Swoboda has no long-term debt. Instead, Swoboda has common stock of PLN 10,000,000 and additional paid-in capital of PLN 25,000,000. The December 31, Year 1, retained earnings amount that appeared in Swoboda's remeasured financial statements was negative $367,500.

2. Explain why the sign of the translation adjustments in (1a), (1b), and (1c) is positive or negative.

Case 7-2

Palmerstown Company

Palmerstown Company established a subsidiary in a foreign country on January 1, Year 1, by investing 8,000,000 pounds when the exchange rate was $1.00/pound. Palmerstown negotiated a bank loan of 4,000,000 pounds on January 5, Year 1, and purchased plant and equipment in the amount of 10,000,000 pounds on January 8, Year 1. Plant and equipment is depreciated on a straight-line basis over a 10-year useful life. The first purchase of inventory in the amount of 1,000,000 pounds was made on January 10, Year 1. Additional inventory of 12,000,000 pounds was acquired at three points in time during the year at an average exchange rate of $0.86/pound. Inventory on hand at year-end was acquired when the exchange rate was $0.83/pound. The first-in, first-out (FIFO) method is used to determine cost of goods sold. Additional exchange rates for the pound during Year 1 are as follows:

January 1–31, Year 1	$1.00
Average for Year 1	0.90
December 31, Year 1	0.80

The foreign subsidiary's income statement for Year 1 and balance sheet at December 31, Year 1, are as follows:

INCOME STATEMENT
For the Year Ended December 31, Year 1

	Pounds (in thousands)
Sales	15,000
Cost of goods sold	9,000
Gross profit	6,000
Selling and administrative expenses	3,000
Depreciation expense	1,000
Income before tax	2,000
Income taxes	600
Net income	1,400
Retained earnings, 1/1/Y1	0
Retained earnings, 12/31/Y1	1,400

BALANCE SHEET
At December 31, Year 1

	Pounds (in thousands)
Cash	2,400
Inventory	4,000
Property, plant, and equipment	10,000
Less: Accumulated depreciation	(1,000)
Total assets	15,400
Current liabilities	2,000
Long-term debt	4,000
Contributed capital	8,000
Retained earnings	1,400
Total liabilities and stockholders' equity	15,400

As the controller for Palmerstown Company, you have evaluated the characteristics of the foreign subsidiary to determine that the pound is the subsidiary's functional currency.

Required:

1. Use an electronic spreadsheet to translate the foreign subsidiary's financial statements into U.S. dollars at December 31, Year 1, in accordance with U.S. GAAP. Insert a row in the spreadsheet after retained earnings and before total liabilities and stockholders' equity for the cumulative translation adjustment. Calculate the translation adjustment separately to verify the amount obtained as a balancing figure in the translation worksheet.

2. Use an electronic spreadsheet to remeasure the foreign subsidiary's financial statements into U.S. dollars at December 31, Year 1, assuming that the U.S. dollar is the subsidiary's functional currency. Insert a row in the spreadsheet after depreciation expense and before income before taxes for the remeasurement gain (loss).

3. Prepare a report for the chief executive officer of Palmerstown Company summarizing the differences that will be reported in the Year 1 consolidated financial statements because the pound, rather than the U.S. dollar, is the foreign subsidiary's functional currency. In your report, discuss the relationship between the current ratio, the debt-to-equity ratio, and the profit margin calculated from the foreign currency financial statements and from the translated U.S.-dollar financial statements. Also, include a discussion of the meaning of the translated U.S.-dollar amounts for inventory and for property, plant, and equipment.

Chapter **Eight**

International Taxation

Learning Objectives

After reading this chapter, you should be able to:

- Describe differences in corporate income tax and withholding tax regimes across countries.
- Explain how overlapping tax jurisdictions cause double taxation.
- Describe some of the benefits provided by tax treaties.
- Demonstrate how the participation exemption system and rules related to controlled foreign corporations, Subpart F income, and foreign tax credit baskets affect U.S. taxation of foreign source income.
- Show how foreign tax credits reduce the incidence of double taxation.
- Explain and demonstrate procedures for translating foreign currency amounts for tax purposes.

INTRODUCTION

Taxes paid to governments are one of the most significant costs incurred by business enterprises. Taxes reduce net profits as well as cash flow. Well-managed companies attempt to minimize the taxes they pay while making sure they are in compliance with applicable tax laws. For a multinational corporation (MNC) that pays taxes in more than one country, the objective is to minimize taxes worldwide. The achievement of this objective requires expertise in the tax law of each foreign country in which the corporation operates. Knowledge of how the domestic country taxes the profits earned in foreign countries is also of great importance.

MNCs make a number of very important decisions in which taxation is an important variable. For example, tax issues are important in deciding (1) where to locate a foreign operation, (2) what legal form the operation should take, and (3) how the operation will be financed.

Investment Location Decision

The decision to make a foreign investment is based on forecasts of *after-tax* profit and cash flows. Because effective tax rates vary across countries, after-tax returns from competing investment locations vary. The decision of whether to place an operation in either Spain or Portugal, for example, could be affected by differences in the tax systems in those two countries.

Legal Form of Operation

A foreign operation of an MNC is organized legally either as a branch of the MNC or as a subsidiary, in which case the operation is incorporated in the foreign country. Some countries tax foreign branch income differently from foreign subsidiary income. The different tax treatment for branches and subsidiaries could result in one legal form being preferable to the other because of the impact on profits and cash flows.

Method of Financing

MNCs can finance their foreign operations by making capital contributions (equity) or through loans (debt). Cash flows generated by a foreign operation can be repatriated back to the MNC by making either dividend payments (on equity financing) or interest payments (on debt financing). Countries often impose a special (withholding) tax on dividend and interest payments made to foreigners. Withholding tax rates within a country can differ by type of payment. When this is the case, the MNC may wish to use more of one type of financing than the other because of the positive impact on cash flows back to the MNC.

For these reasons, it is important for the management of an MNC to develop an expertise in international taxation. It is impossible (and unnecessary) for every manager of an MNC to become a true expert in international taxation. However, all managers should be familiar with the major issues in international taxation so that they know when it might be necessary to call on the experts to help make a decision.

It is not possible in this book to cover all aspects of international taxation in depth; that would require years of study and many more pages of reading than can be included here. However, there are certain issues with which international accountants and managers of MNCs should be familiar to make sure that corporate goals are being achieved. The objective of this chapter is to examine the major issues of international taxation without getting bogged down in the minutiae for which tax laws are well known. We will concentrate on taxes on income and distributions of income, ignoring other taxes such as Social Security and payroll taxes, sales and value-added taxes, and excise taxes. Although this chapter concentrates on the taxation of corporate profits, the appendix describes certain features of individual income taxation relevant for expatriates working overseas.

TYPES OF TAXES AND TAX RATES

Corporations are subject to many different types of taxes, including property taxes, payroll taxes, and excise taxes. While it is important for managers of MNCs to be knowledgeable about these taxes, we focus on taxes on profit. The two major types of taxes imposed on profits earned by companies engaged in international business are (1) corporate income taxes and (2) withholding taxes.

Income Taxes

Most, but not all, national governments impose a direct tax on business income. Exhibit 8.1 shows that national corporate income tax rates vary substantially across countries. The corporate income tax rate in most countries is between 15 and 35 percent. Differences in corporate tax rates across countries provide MNCs with a tax-planning opportunity as they decide where to locate foreign operations. In making this decision, MNCs must be careful to consider both national and local taxes in their analysis. In some countries, local governments impose a separate tax on business income in addition to the tax levied by the national government. For example, the national tax rate in Switzerland is 8.5 percent, but individual cantons levy an additional corporate income tax that results in an effective tax rate from 12 to 24 percent depending on the canton in which the company is located. Corporate income tax rates imposed by individual states in the United States vary from 0 percent (e.g., South Dakota) to as high as 11.5 percent (New Jersey).

In a few countries, corporate income taxes can vary according to the size of the company, the type of activity in which a company is engaged, or the nationality of the

EXHIBIT 8.1

International Corporate Tax Rates, 2021

Source: KPMG, Corporate Tax Rates Table, available at home.kpmg/xx/en/home.xhtml (accessed January 21, 2022).

Country	Effective Tax Rate (%)	Country	Effective Tax Rate (%)
Argentina	25	Italy	24
Australia	30	Japan	30.62[d]
Austria	25	Korea (South)	25
Belgium	25	Malaysia	24
Brazil	34[a]	Mexico	30
Canada	26.5[b]	Netherlands	25
Chile	27	New Zealand	28
China	25	Russia	20
Czech Republic	19	Singapore	17
Denmark	22	Spain	25
France	26.5	Sweden	20.6
Germany	30[c]	Switzerland	14.93[e]
Greece	24	Taiwan	20
Hong Kong	16.5	Thailand	20
Hungary	9	Turkey	20
India	30	United Kingdom	19
Indonesia	22	United States	21[f]
Ireland	12.5	Venezuela	34
Israel	23	Global Average	23.65

[a] The effective tax rate on corporate profits in Brazil is the sum of a 15 percent basic rate, a 10 percent surtax on income that exceeds BRL 240,000 per year, plus a social contribution on net profits of 9 percent.

[b] The Canadian effective tax rate is comprised of a federal corporate income tax rate of 15 percent plus a provincial corporate income tax rate, which varies by province. Depending on the province, the combined general corporate income tax rates ranges from 25 to 31 percent.

[c] This is an approximate rate consisting of a 15 percent federal corporate income tax, an 0.825 percent solidarity tax, and an additional trade tax, which varies by locality.

[d] The effective tax rate in Japan varies by locality. The rate presented relates to a company located in Tokyo.

[e] The Swiss federal corporate income tax rate is 8.5 percent. Individual cantons levy an additional corporate income tax. The rate presented is the average of the corporate income tax rates across Swiss cantons.

[f] The U.S. federal corporate income tax rate is 21 percent. In addition, many U.S. states assess a state corporate income tax, ranging from 0 to 11.5 percent. KPMG estimates 27 percent as the approximate average effective tax rate (federal plus state) across U.S. states.

company's owners. For example, in Chile, the corporate income tax rate is reduced from 27 to 25 percent for small- and medium-sized entities; in China, the income tax rate is reduced to 15 percent for high and new technology companies; in Malaysia, a special 3 percent rate applies to corporations involved in specific qualified business activity; and in India, foreign companies are taxed at a 10 percent higher rate than domestic companies.

In making foreign investment decisions, MNCs often engage in a capital budgeting process in which the future cash flows to be generated by the foreign investment are forecasted, discounted to their present value, and then compared with the amount to be invested to determine a net present value. Taxes paid to the foreign government will have a negative impact on future cash flows and might affect the location decision. For example, assume that a Japanese musical instrument manufacturer is deciding whether to locate a new factory in Hungary or in Switzerland. Although the national tax rate in Hungary is slightly higher than in Switzerland, the effective tax rate in some parts of Switzerland would be higher than in Hungary because of the high local (cantonal) taxes that would have to be paid.

Of course, the amount of taxes paid to a government is not determined solely by the corporate tax rate. The manner in which taxable income is calculated also will greatly affect a company's tax liability. Just as tax rates vary from country to country, so does the way in which taxable income is calculated. Expenses that can be deducted for tax purposes can vary greatly from country to country. For example, in the United States, only the first $1 million of the chief executive officer's salary is tax deductible. Most other countries do not have a similar rule.

The United States allows companies to use the last-in, first-out (LIFO) method for inventory valuation and accelerated depreciation methods for fixed assets in determining taxable income, whereas Brazil does not. All else being equal, a company with increasing inventory prices that is replacing or expanding its fixed assets will have smaller taxable income in the United States than in Brazil.

Changes in Corporate Income Tax Rates

Corporate income tax rates around the world have not remained constant. For the most part, there has been a continuing international trend to reduce corporate tax rates. The United States appears to have led the way in 1986 when the corporate tax rate was reduced from 46 to 34 percent (it was subsequently raised to 35 percent in 1994). The United Kingdom quickly followed suit by reducing its rate from 50 to 35 percent, and Canada reduced its rate as well, from 34 to 29 percent. This follow-the-leader effect can be explained by the fact that countries compete against one another in attracting foreign investment and/or want to make sure their companies are internationally competitive. The average corporate income tax rate across countries declined from approximately 40 percent in 1980 to only about 24 percent in 2021.

In 2017, at an average of 40 percent across individual states, the United States had the highest effective corporate income tax rate (federal plus state income tax) among the countries listed in Exhibit 8.1. In late December 2017, the United States lowered its federal corporate income tax rate from 35 to 21 percent, effective for tax years beginning in 2018. This change was part of the "Tax Cuts and Jobs Act," which made the most extensive change to U.S. tax law in three decades. As a result, the average effective corporate income tax rate (federal plus state) across U.S. states is 27 percent, which is only a few percentage points above the global average reported in Exhibit 8.1. (Note that a company doing business in the United States prepares a U.S. federal income tax return using the U.S. federal corporate income tax rate of 21 percent. In addition, in most states, the company prepares a separate state income tax return using that state's corporate income tax rate.)

Tax Holidays

One way to compete for foreign investment is to offer a so-called *tax holiday,* which is a government incentive program that provides a temporary reduction or elimination of corporate income tax. In Malaysia, for example, foreign corporations that qualify for "pioneer status" receive an exemption from income tax on 70 percent of annual profit for five years. Corporations that undertake a project involving the manufacture of specialized machinery and equipment receive a 100 percent exemption for up to 10 years. In Indonesia, the Ministry of Finance can provide a 100 percent tax holiday for 5 to 20 years depending on the investment amount. The criteria for an investment to be eligible for the tax holiday include that it be export-oriented, that it employs a large number of people, or that its product contains a large proportion of local content.

Countries in other parts of the world also use tax holidays in an attempt to attract specific types of investment. For example, Romania offers taxpayers that exclusively perform innovation and R&D activities exemption from corporate income tax for the first 10 years of activity. In Zimbabwe, an operator of a tourist facility in a tourist development zone pays zero corporate income tax for the first five years of operation.

Tax Havens

There are a number of tax jurisdictions with abnormally low corporate income tax rates (or no corporate income tax at all) that companies and individuals have found useful in minimizing their worldwide income taxes. These tax jurisdictions, known as *tax havens,* include the Bahamas, Jersey, and Vanuatu, which have no corporate income tax, and Ireland, which has a corporate income tax rate of 12.5 percent. A list of countries identified as tax havens

EXHIBIT 8.2

Tax Havens

Source: Oxfam International,
"Blacklist or Whitewash: What
a Real EU List of Tax Havens
Should Look Like," Oxfam
Briefing Note, November 2017,
available at https://www
.oxfam.org (accessed January
21, 2022).

Atlantic Ocean
Bermuda, Faroe Islands, Greenland
Caribbean
Anguilla, Antigua and Barbuda, Aruba, Bahamas, British Virgin Islands, Cayman Islands, Curacao, Trinidad and Tobago, U.S. Virgin Islands
East Asia
Hong Kong, Singapore, Taiwan
Europe
Albania, Bosnia and Herzegovina, Gibraltar, Ireland, Jersey, Luxembourg, Macedonia, Malta, Montenegro, Netherlands, Serbia, Switzerland
Indian Ocean
Mauritius
Middle East
Bahrain, Oman, United Arab Emirates
Pacific Ocean
Cook Islands, Guam, Marshall Islands, Nauru, New Caledonia, Niue, Palau, Vanuatu

by the global non-profit group Oxfam is provided in Exhibit 8.2. Many of the jurisdictions listed are small island nations located in the Atlantic, Caribbean, or Pacific. In addition, a significant number of tax havens are located in Europe.

A company involved in international business might find it beneficial to establish an operation in a tax haven to avoid paying taxes in one or more countries in which the company operates. For example, assume a Brazilian company manufactures a product for $70 per unit that it exports to a customer in Mexico at a sales price of $100 per unit. The $30 of profit earned on each unit is subject to the Brazilian corporate tax rate of 34 percent. The Brazilian manufacturer could take advantage of the fact that there is no corporate income tax in the Bahamas by establishing a sales subsidiary there that it uses as a conduit for export sales. The Brazilian parent company would then sell the product to its Bahamian sales subsidiary at a price of, say, $80 per unit, and the Bahamian sales subsidiary would turn around and sell the product to the customer in Mexico at $100 per unit. In this way, only $10 of the total profit is earned in Brazil and subject to Brazilian income tax; $20 of the $30 total profit is recorded in the Bahamas and is therefore not taxed at all.

There is considerable indirect evidence that multinational companies from the United States and other countries shift income to tax haven countries. A study conducted by the Congressional Research Service for members of the United States Congress in 2015 estimated that 50.1 percent ($611 million) of profits earned by U.S. companies overseas were located in just seven tax haven countries.[1] The Netherlands and Ireland combined were the locations for 24.1 percent of all income earned overseas by U.S. companies. The extent to which the Netherlands, in particular, is used as a tax haven can be inferred from the fact that, in 2013, foreign direct investment into the Netherlands and the United States was $4.3 billion and $2.8 billion, respectively, even though the U.S. economy is 24 times larger than the economy of the Netherlands.

A study published in 2016 indicated that 376 of the Fortune 500 companies had at least one subsidiary in a tax haven country, with the most popular location being the Netherlands.[2]

[1] Mark P. Keightley and Jeffry M. Stupak, "Corporate Tax Base Erosion and Profit Shifting (BEPS): An Examination of the Data," Congressional Research Service, April 30, 2015, available at https://sgp.fas .org/crs/misc/R44013.pdf (accessed January 21, 2022).

[2] Richard Phillips, Matt Gardner, Kayla Kitson, Alexandria Robins, and Michelle Surka, "Offshore Shell Games 2016: The Use of Offshore Tax Havens by Fortune 500 Companies," Citizens for Tax Justice, October 4, 2016, available at https://ctj.org (accessed January 21, 2022).

Anecdotally, Pfizer Inc., the world's largest pharmaceutical company, had 181 subsidiaries in tax havens, and Goldman Sachs & Co. LLC had 987 tax haven subsidiaries with 537 in the Cayman Islands alone. From disclosures provided in annual reports, the authors of this study were able to calculate the foreign tax rate paid by about 50 U.S. companies on their foreign income. For 28 of these companies, the average tax rate paid overseas was less than 10 percent, which the authors claim is evidence of the use of tax havens. For example, Oracle paid an average foreign tax rate of 3.8 percent, whereas Nike paid an average of 1.4 percent tax on its foreign earnings.

Withholding Taxes

When a foreign citizen who invests in the shares of a U.S. company receives a dividend payment, theoretically he or she should file a tax return with the U.S. Internal Revenue Service and pay taxes on the dividend income. If the foreign investor does not file this tax return, the U.S. government has no recourse for collecting the tax. To avoid this possibility, the United States (like most other countries) will require the payer of the dividend (the U.S. company) to withhold some amount of taxes from the dividend payment and remit that amount to the U.S. government. This type of tax is referred to as a *withholding tax.* The withholding tax rate on dividends in the United States is 30 percent.

To see how the withholding tax works, assume that International Business Machines Corporation (IBM), a U.S.-based company, pays a $100 dividend to a stockholder in Brazil. Under U.S. withholding tax rules, IBM would withhold $30 from the payment (which is sent to the U.S. Internal Revenue Service) and the Brazilian stockholder would be issued a check in the amount of $70.

Withholding taxes also are imposed on payments made to foreign parent companies or foreign affiliated companies. There are three types of payments typically subject to withholding tax: dividends, interest, and royalties. Withholding tax rates vary across countries, and in some countries, withholding rates vary by type of payment or recipient. Exhibit 8.3 provides withholding rates generally applicable in selected countries. In many cases, the rate listed will be different for some subset of activity. For example, although the U.S. withholding rate on interest payments is generally 30 percent, interest on bank deposits and on certain registered debt instruments (bonds) is tax exempt (0 percent tax). In addition, many of the rates listed in Exhibit 8.3 vary with tax treaties (discussed later in this chapter).

Tax-Planning Strategy

Differences in withholding rates on different types of payments in some countries provide an opportunity to reduce taxes (increase cash flow) by altering the method of financing a foreign operation. For example, a Chinese company planning to establish a manufacturing facility in France would prefer that future cash payments received from the French subsidiary be in the form of interest rather than dividends because of the lower withholding tax rate (0 percent on interest vs 26.5 percent on dividends). This objective could be achieved by the Chinese parent using a combination of loan and equity investment in financing the French subsidiary. For example, rather than the Chinese parent investing €10 million in equity to establish the French operation, €5 million could be contributed in equity and the other €5 million lent to the French operation by the Chinese parent. Interest on the loan, which is a cash payment to the Chinese parent, would be exempt from French withholding tax, whereas any dividends paid on the capital contribution would be taxed at 26.5 percent.

Several countries have a lower rate of withholding tax on interest than on dividends. In addition, interest payments are generally tax deductible, whereas dividend payments are not. Thus, there is often an incentive for companies to finance their foreign operations with as much debt and as little equity capital as possible. This is known as *thin capitalization,* and several countries have set limits as to how thinly capitalized a company may be.

EXHIBIT 8.3
Nontreaty Withholding
Rates in Selected
Countries, 2021

Country	Dividends	Interest	Royalties
Australia	30%	10%	30%
Austria	27.5	27.5	20
Brazil	0	15	15
Canada	25	25	25
Chile	35	35	30
China	10	10	10
France	26.5	0	26.5
Germany	25	0	15
Hong Kong	0	0	4.95
Hungary	0	0	0
India	20	20	10
Indonesia	20	20	20
Italy	26	26	22.5
Japan	20	20	20
Malaysia	0	15	10
Mexico	10	35	35
New Zealand	0	15	15
Philippines	15	20	30
Russia	15	20	20
Singapore	0	15	10
South Korea	20	20	20
Spain	19	19	24
Sweden	30	0	0
Switzerland	35	0	0
Taiwan	21	20	20
Thailand	10	15	15
United Kingdom	0	20	20
United States	30	30	30

Source: Deloitte, Withholding Tax Rates 2021, available at https://www2.deloitte.com/global/en/pages/tax/articles/global-tax-rates.xhtml (accessed January 21, 2022).
Note: These rates generally apply to payments made to foreign parents. In some countries, the general rate can be higher or lower depending on various conditions. As examples:

- Brazil generally taxes interest and royalties at 15 percent unless payment is made to a recipient in a "low-tax" country (as defined by the Brazilian government) and then the rate is 25 percent.
- Spain reduces withholding tax on interest to 0 percent and on royalties to 19 percent if the recipient is a resident of the European Union.
- In South Korea, the general rate on interest payments of 20 percent is reduced to 14 percent for interest on bonds.

For example, in France, interest paid to a foreign parent will not be tax deductible for the amount of the loan that exceeds 150 percent of equity capital. In other words, the ratio of debt to equity may not exceed 150 percent for tax purposes. If equity capital is €1 million, any interest paid on loans exceeding €1.5 million will not be tax deductible. Similarly, in Mexico, subsidiaries of foreign parents run the risk of having some interest declared nondeductible when the debt-to-equity ratio exceeds 3 to 1.

Value-Added Tax

Many countries generate a significant amount of revenue through the use of a national *value-added tax* (VAT). Standard VAT rates in the European Union, for example, range from a low of 17 percent (Luxembourg) to a high of 27 percent (Hungary).[3] Value-added taxes are used in lieu of a sales tax and are generally incorporated into the price of a product or service. This type of tax is levied on the value added at each stage in the production or

[3] VATLive, 2017 European Union EU VAT Rates, available at https://www.avalara.com/vatlive/en/vat-rates/european-vat-rates.html (accessed January 21, 2022).

distribution of a product or service. For example, if a Swedish forest products company sells lumber that it has harvested to a Swedish wholesaler at a price of €100,000, it will pay a VAT to the Swedish government of €25,000 (€100,000 × 25%). When the Swedish wholesaler, in turn, sells the lumber to its customers for €160,000, the wholesaler will pay a VAT of €15,000 (25% × €60,000 value added at the wholesale stage). The VAT concept is commonly used in countries other than the European Union, including Australia, Canada, China, Mexico, Nigeria, Russia, Saudi Arabia, South Africa, and Turkey, among others.

Value-added taxes as well as other indirect taxes (such as sales and payroll taxes) need to be considered in determining the total rate of taxation to be paid in a country. A study conducted by the World Bank and PricewaterhouseCoopers in 2018 determined the total tax rate paid on business income in 190 countries.[4] The study was based on a simulated case study company in its second year of operations with 60 employees and sales equal to 1,050 times per capita income. Total taxes included federal and local income taxes; VAT and other forms of sales tax; and workers' compensation, Social Security, and other mandatory contributions on behalf of employees. Total tax rates ranged from 8.5 percent (Vanuatu) to 216.5 percent (Comoros). Total tax rates in selected other countries were:

Brazil	68.4%	Hong Kong	22.9%	New Zealand	34.5%
Canada	20.9%	India	55.3%	Poland	40.5%
Chile	33.0%	Italy	48.0%	Saudi Arabia	15.7%
China	67.3%	Japan	47.4%	Switzerland	28.8%
France	62.2%	Mexico	52.1%	United Kingdom	30.7%
Germany	48.9%	Namibia	20.7%	United States	43.8%

TAX JURISDICTION

One of the most important issues in international taxation is determining which country has the right to tax which income. In many cases, two countries will assert the right to tax the same income, resulting in the problem of *double taxation*. For example, consider a Brazilian investor earning dividends from an investment in Microsoft Corporation common stock. The United States might want to tax this dividend because it was earned in the United States, and Brazil might want to tax the dividend because it was earned by a resident of Brazil. This section discusses general concepts used internationally in determining tax jurisdiction. Subsequent sections examine mechanisms used for providing relief from double taxation.

Worldwide versus Territorial Approach

One tax jurisdiction issue is related to the taxation of income earned overseas, known as *foreign source income*. There are two general approaches taken on this issue:

1. *Worldwide approach.* Under this approach, all income of a resident of a country or a company incorporated in a country is taxed by that country regardless of where the income is earned. In other words, foreign source income is taxed by the country of residence. For example, under a worldwide approach, Canada could impose a tax on dividend income earned by a Canadian company from its subsidiary in Hong Kong, even though that income was earned outside of Canada.

2. *Territorial approach.* Under this approach, only the income earned within the borders of the country (*domestic source income*) is taxed. For example, the dividend income earned by a resident of Botswana from investments in South African stocks will not be taxed in

---

[4] World Bank and PricewaterhouseCoopers, *Paying Taxes 2018,* available at https://www.doingbusiness .org/en/reports/thematic-reports/paying-taxes (accessed January 21, 2022).

Botswana. Only a few countries follow a strict territorial approach to taxation, including the Dominican Republic, Gabon, and Jordan.

Some countries have adopted a hybrid approach to tax jurisdiction by taxing some types of foreign income but not others. For example, income earned by a foreign branch might be taxed by the parent company's home country but income earned by a foreign subsidiary of the parent company might be exempt from home-country taxation. This is referred to as a *participation exemption* system. A majority (29 of 35) of OECD member countries exempt some or all foreign subsidiary income earned in some or all foreign countries.[5] For example:

- Australia and New Zealand exempt 100 percent of foreign subsidiary income from all countries, whereas Germany and Japan exempt only 95 percent of foreign subsidiary income from all countries.
- Greece exempts 100 percent of income earned by foreign subsidiaries in the European Union, whereas Finland exempts 100 percent of income earned in EU countries and in non-EU countries with whom Finland has a tax treaty.
- Luxembourg exempts 100 percent of income earned in countries with an effective corporate income tax rate of at least 10.5 percent, and Turkey exempts 100 percent of income earned by foreign subsidiaries located in countries with an effective corporate tax rate of at least 15 percent.

United States Participation Exemption System

Prior to 2018, the United States employed a worldwide approach to corporate income taxation. Foreign branch income was taxed in the United States currently and foreign subsidiary income was subject to U.S. tax when dividends from that income were repatriated to the U.S. parent company.

To make U.S. corporations more competitive internationally, in addition to lowering the corporate tax rate to 21 percent, the Tax Cuts and Jobs Act (TCJA) of 2017 moved the United States away from a worldwide system to a *participation exemption* (partial territorial) system of taxation. Beginning in 2018, dividends received from foreign subsidiaries generally are no longer subject to U.S. corporate income taxation.[6] More specifically, a U.S. parent company is entitled to a 100 percent dividends received deduction (DRD) for dividends it receives from any 10-percent-or-greater-owned foreign corporation. Income earned by a foreign branch of a U.S. corporation continues to be subject to U.S. income taxation in the year in which it is earned.

Source, Citizenship, and Residence

Regardless of the approach used in determining the scope of taxation, a second issue related to jurisdiction is the basis for taxation. Countries generally use source, citizenship, residence, or some combination of the three for determining jurisdictional authority.

Source of Income

In general, almost all countries assert the jurisdictional authority to tax income where it is earned—in effect, at its source—regardless of the residence or citizenship of the recipient. An example would be the United States taxing dividends paid by Microsoft Corporation to a stockholder in Brazil because the dividend income was earned in the United States.

[5] Tax Foundation, "Designing a Territorial Tax System: A Review of OECD Systems," July 2017, available at https://taxfoundation.org/territorial-tax-system-oecd-review/ (accessed January 21, 2022).

[6] An exception exists when the foreign subsidiary is located in a tax haven country and generates Subpart F income. This issue is discussed later in this chapter in the section titled "Controlled Foreign Corporations."

Citizenship

Under the citizenship basis of taxation, citizens are taxed by their country of citizenship regardless of where they reside or the source of the income being taxed. The United States is unusual among countries in that it taxes on the basis of citizenship. Thus, a U.S. citizen who lives and works overseas will be subject to U.S. income tax on his or her worldwide income regardless of where the citizen earns that income or resides.

Residence

Under the residence approach, residents of a country are taxed by the country in which they reside regardless of their citizenship or where the income is earned. For example, assume a citizen of Singapore resides permanently in the United States and earns dividends from an investment in the shares of a company in the United Kingdom. Taxing on the basis of residence, this individual will be subject to taxation on his or her foreign source income in the United States, even though he or she is a citizen of Singapore.

The United States is one country that taxes on the basis of residence. For tax purposes, a U.S. resident is any person who is a permanent resident of the United States, as evidenced by either holding a permanent resident permit issued by the U.S. Citizenship and Immigration Services (the "green card" test) or being physically present in the United States for 183 or more days in a year (physical presence test). Note that because the United States levies taxes using a worldwide approach, the worldwide income of an individual holding a U.S. permanent resident card is subject to U.S. taxation *even if he or she is not actually living in the United States.*

Companies created or organized in the United States are considered to be U.S. residents for tax purposes. A foreign branch of a U.S. corporation also is considered to be a U.S. resident and thus is subject to U.S. income taxation. However, the foreign *subsidiary* of a U.S. parent company is not considered to be a U.S. resident and, since 2018, foreign subsidiary income generally is not taxed in the United States.

Double Taxation

The combination of either a worldwide or participation exemption approach to taxation and the various bases for taxation can lead to overlapping tax jurisdictions that, in turn, lead to double or even triple taxation. For example, a German citizen residing in Chile with investment income in Austria might be expected to pay taxes on the investment income to Germany (on the basis of citizenship), Chile (on the basis of residence), and Austria (on the basis of source).

The same is true for corporate taxpayers with foreign source income. The most common overlap of jurisdictions for corporations is the situation in which the home-country taxes on the basis of residence and the country in which the foreign branch or subsidiary is located taxes on the basis of source. Without some relief, this could result in a tremendous tax burden for the parent company. For example, income earned by the Japanese branch of an Australian company would be taxed at the effective Japanese corporate income tax rate of 31 percent and at the rate of 30 percent in Australia, for an aggregate tax rate of 61 percent. The Australian parent has only 39 percent of the profit after income taxes. At that rate, there is a disincentive to establish operations overseas. Without any relief from double taxation, all investment by the Australian company probably would remain at home in Australia, where income would be taxed only at the rate of 30 percent.

An important goal of most national tax systems is neutrality; that is, the tax system should remain in the background, and business, investment, and consumption decisions should be made for nontax reasons. In an international context, there are three standards for neutrality, one of which is *capital-export neutrality.* A tax system meets this standard if a taxpayer's decision whether to invest at home or overseas is not affected by taxation.

Double taxation from overlapping tax jurisdictions precludes a tax system from achieving capital-export neutrality; all investment will remain at home. To achieve capital-export neutrality, most countries have one or more mechanisms for eliminating the problem of double taxation.

Relief from Double Taxation

Double taxation of income earned by foreign operations generally arises because the country where the foreign operation is located taxes the income at its source and the parent company's home-country taxes worldwide income on the basis of residence. To relieve the double taxation, the question is, Which country should give up its right to tax the income? The international norm is that source should take precedence over residence in determining tax jurisdiction. In that case, it is up to the parent company's home country to eliminate the double taxation.

This can be accomplished in several ways. One way would be to exempt some or all foreign source income from taxation by adopting a participation exemption or territorial approach to corporate income taxation. A second approach to provide relief from double taxation would be to allow the parent company to deduct the taxes paid to the foreign government in calculating its taxable income. A third mechanism would be to provide the parent company with a credit for taxes paid to the foreign government. This is known as a *foreign tax credit,* which results in a direct reduction in the amount of tax that otherwise would be owed. As a point of reference, the specific U.S. rules related to foreign tax credits and deductions are described later in this chapter in the section titled "Foreign Tax Credits."

TAX TREATIES

Tax treaties are bilateral agreements between two countries regarding how companies and individuals from one country will be taxed when earning income in the other country. Tax treaties are designed to facilitate international trade and investment by reducing tax barriers to the international flow of goods and services.

As noted in the previous section, a major problem in international trade and investment is double taxation where tax jurisdictions overlap. For example, both Australia and the United Kingdom might claim tax jurisdiction over dividends earned by an Australian citizen from investments in U.K. stocks. Treaties reduce the possibility of double taxation through the clarification of tax jurisdiction. Treaties also provide for the possibility of reduced taxes through a reduction in withholding tax rates. Generally, treaties require the exchange of information between countries to help in enforcing their domestic tax provisions.

Model Tax Treaties

OECD Model

Most income tax treaties signed by the major industrial countries are based on a model treaty developed by the Organization for Economic Cooperation and Development (OECD). An important article in the OECD model treaty indicates that business profits may be taxed by a treaty partner country only if they are attributable to a *permanent establishment* in that country. A permanent establishment can include an office, branch, factory, construction site, mine, well, or quarry. Facilities used for storage, display, or the delivery and maintenance of goods solely for processing by another enterprise do not constitute permanent establishments. If there is no permanent establishment, then income—which otherwise would be taxable in the country in which the income is earned if there were no tax treaty—is not taxable in that country.

One of the most important benefits afforded by tax treaties is the reduction in withholding tax rates. The OECD model treaty recommends withholding rates of:

- 5 percent for direct investment dividends (paid by a subsidiary to its parent).
- 15 percent for portfolio dividends (paid to individuals).
- 10 percent for interest.
- 0 percent for royalties.

Although the OECD model might be the starting point for negotiation, countries with more outbound investment than inbound investment often try to reduce the host country's right to tax, most conspicuously seeking zero withholding on interest. A very specific deviation from the model treaty is where countries that import most of their movies and TV programming seek higher withholding rates on film royalties than on other copyright royalties.

United Nations Model

The OECD model assumes that countries are economic equals. The United Nations (UN) model treaty, designed to be used between developed and developing countries, assumes an imbalance. The UN model recognizes that the host country (often a developing country) should have more taxing rights when profit repatriation essentially is a one-way street (from the developing to the developed country).

U.S. Tax Treaties

The United States also has a model treaty it uses as the basis for negotiating bilateral tax agreements. The U.S. model exempts interest and royalties from withholding tax and establishes 15 percent as the maximum withholding rate on dividends. Withholding rates from selected U.S. tax treaties are shown in Exhibit 8.4. As that exhibit shows, neither the U.S. model nor the OECD's recommendations regarding withholding rates are always followed. U.S. tax treaties reduce the withholding rate on dividends paid to a parent company to somewhere between 5 and 20 percent; interest paid to a parent to between 0 and 15 percent; and royalties paid on patents to between 0 and 15 percent.

EXHIBIT 8.4
Selected U.S. Tax Treaty Withholding Tax Rates

Source: U.S. Internal Revenue Service, Tax Treaty Tables, Table 1, available at www.irs .gov/pub/irs-utl/Tax_Treaty _Table_1_2019_Feb.pdf (accessed January 21, 2022).

Country	Dividend Paid to Parent	Interest Paid to Parent	Royalties on Patents
Nontreaty	30%	30%	30%
Australia	5	10	5
Canada	5	0	0
China	10	10	10
France	5	0	0
Germany	5	0	0
Hungary	5	0	0
India	15	15	15
Indonesia	10	10	10
Japan	5	10	0
Mexico	5	15	10
New Zealand	5	10	5
Philippines	20	15	15
Russia	5	0	0
South Korea	10	12	15
Spain	10	15	10
Thailand	10	15	15
United Kingdom	5	0	0
Venezuela	5	10	10

The United States has treaties with more than 50 countries, including all 27 members of the European Union; Australia and New Zealand; Ukraine and Russia; Egypt and Israel; Mexico and Canada; and India, Korea, Japan, and China. As of 2021, except for Venezuela, the United States did not have a tax treaty with any country in South America. This includes Argentina, Chile, and also Brazil, which is one of the top 10 locations for U.S. foreign direct investment.

One explanation for why there is no treaty between the United States and Brazil is that there is very little Brazilian investment in the United States. The reduction in withholding taxes that would result from a tax treaty would mostly benefit U.S. individuals and companies who are receiving interest and dividends from their Brazilian investments, but there would be little benefit for taxpayers in Brazil. The Brazilian government is not interested in entering into a treaty with the United States that would reduce the withholding taxes collected on payments made to U.S. investors without much reciprocal benefit to Brazilians.

There is also very little Polish investment in the United States. However, Poland differs from Brazil in that Poland is interested in attracting new U.S. investment. The United States/Poland tax treaty allows Poland to better compete with other countries in attracting U.S. investment.

Understanding the potential benefits to be derived from a tax treaty is very important when deciding where to locate a foreign investment. For example, of $100 of dividends paid by a subsidiary in Japan, $95 would be received by its U.S. parent (after paying a 5 percent withholding tax under the United States/Japan tax treaty). Because there is no treaty between the United States and Taiwan, for $100 of dividends paid by a subsidiary in Taiwan, only $80 would land in the United States (after paying a 20 percent Taiwanese withholding tax). All else being equal, a U.S.-based investor would prefer to establish a subsidiary in Japan rather than in Taiwan to reduce the amount of withholding taxes paid on dividends.

Treaty Shopping

Treaty shopping describes a process in which a resident of Country A uses a corporation in Country B to get the benefit of Country B's tax treaty with Country C. As an example, assume that a Brazilian taxpayer has investments in U.S. company shares. Because the United States has no treaty with Brazil, dividend payments made to the Brazilian investor by U.S. companies are taxed by the U.S. government at the withholding rate of 30 percent. As demonstrated here, the Brazilian investor receives only 70 percent of the dividend:

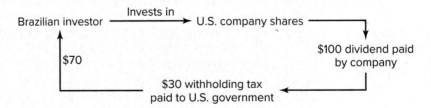

Until 1987, the Netherlands Antilles, located off the coast of South America, had a treaty with the United States that reduced the withholding rate on dividends to 10 percent. Returning to our example, the Brazilian taxpayer could use this treaty to its advantage by establishing a wholly owned holding company in the Netherlands Antilles that in turn makes investments in U.S. company shares. Dividends paid by the U.S. companies to the Netherlands Antilles (NA) stockholder would then be taxed at the treaty rate of 10 percent, and income earned by the NA holding company would not be taxed in the Netherlands Antilles. Dividends paid by the NA holding company to the Brazilian investor from its income—in effect, the dividends received from the U.S. companies—would not be subject to NA withholding tax. In this way, the Brazilian investor would be able to keep 20 percent more of the gross dividend than if the investment had been made directly from Brazil. This is demonstrated as follows:

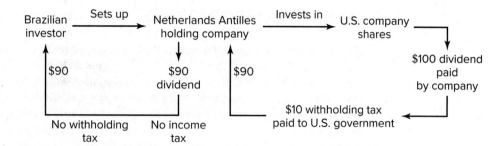

In this situation, there is no incentive for Brazil to negotiate a treaty with the United States.

Since the 1980s, U.S. treaty negotiations have insisted that a "limitation of benefits" provision be included in U.S. tax treaties. A typical treaty might provide that certain treaty benefits (such as reduced withholding rates) are not available if 50 percent or more of a corporation's stock is held by third-party taxpayers (unless the stock is publicly traded). The insertion of such a limitation into the United States/Netherlands Antilles treaty would preclude the Brazilian investor from enjoying the reduced withholding rate on dividends paid by the U.S. companies.

In addition to entering into new treaties, the United States has attempted to renegotiate its existing tax treaties with tax haven countries to include a limitation-of-benefits provision. In some cases, negotiations have failed and the existing treaty has been canceled. This is true in the Netherlands Antilles case. The United States terminated its double taxation treaty with the Netherlands Antilles in 1987. (The Netherlands Antilles itself was dissolved as a self-governing part of the Kingdom of the Netherlands in 2010.)

OECD BASE EROSION AND PROFIT SHIFTING ACTION PLAN

Tax planning by multinational entities to artificially shift profits to no- or low-tax jurisdictions (tax havens) where there is little or no real economic activity is referred to as *base erosion and profit shifting* (BEPS). In 2013, the OECD developed a 15-item BEPS action plan to help nations close the gaps in tax laws that allow MNCs to artificially, but legally, reduce their taxes. The action plan covers issues such as designing effective controlled foreign corporation (CFC) rules, limiting base erosion via interest deductions, mandatory disclosure of aggressive tax planning by MNCs, and the design of domestic rules to prevent tax treaty abuse. More than 100 countries and jurisdictions have expressed interest in the OECD's work in this area, and the goal is that most, if not all, of them will adopt the BEPS action items over time.

Action item 15 of the OECD's plan resulted in the development of an innovative multilateral convention that would allow jurisdictions to quickly improve their existing network of bilateral tax treaties to reduce opportunities for tax avoidance by MNCs. By May 2020, more than 90 countries and jurisdictions had signed this multilateral convention agreeing to modify the more than 1,600 bilateral tax treaties between them.[7] The agreement was signed by a number of tax haven countries, including Hong Kong, Ireland, Luxembourg,

---

[7] OECD, *Multilateral Convention to Implement Tax Treaty Related Measures to Prevent Base Erosion and Profit Shifting: Information Brochure,* May 2020, available at https://www.oecd.org (accessed March 1, 2022).

and Switzerland. However, the United States is not a signatory to the agreement because its bilateral tax treaties already contain provisions to prevent treaty abuse.

CONTROLLED FOREIGN CORPORATIONS

To crack down on the use of tax havens (base erosion and profit shifting) by U.S. companies seeking to avoid paying U.S. taxes, the U.S. Congress created *controlled foreign corporation* (CFC) rules in 1962.[8] A CFC is any foreign corporation in which U.S. shareholders hold more than 50 percent of the combined voting power or fair market value of the stock. Only those U.S. taxpayers (corporations, citizens, or tax residents) directly or indirectly owning 10 percent or more of the stock are considered U.S. shareholders in determining whether the 50 percent threshold is met. *All* majority-owned foreign subsidiaries of U.S.-based companies are CFCs.

As noted earlier in this chapter, the United States generally exempts from U.S. taxation income earned by a foreign subsidiary (CFC) of a U.S. corporation. However, there is no exemption for so-called *Subpart F income* earned by a CFC. Instead, Subpart F income is taxed currently by the United States, similar to foreign branch income. Subpart F of the U.S. Internal Revenue Code lists the income that will be treated in this fashion.

Subpart F Income

Conceptually, Subpart F income is income that is easily movable to a low-tax jurisdiction. There are four types of Subpart F income:

1. Income derived from insurance of U.S. risks.
2. Income from countries engaged in international boycotts.
3. Certain illegal payments.
4. Foreign base company income.

Foreign base company income is the most important category of Subpart F income and includes the following:

1. *Passive income* such as interest, dividends, royalties, rents, and capital gains from sales of assets. An example would be dividends received by a CFC from holding shares of stock in affiliated companies.
2. *Sales income,* where the CFC makes sales outside of its country of incorporation. For example, the U.S. parent manufactures a product that it sells to its CFC in Hong Kong, which in turn sells the product to customers in Japan. Sales to customers outside of Hong Kong generate Subpart F income.
3. *Service income,* where the CFC performs services out of its country of incorporation.

Determination of the Amount of CFC Income Currently Taxable

The amount of a CFC's income currently taxable in the United States depends on the percentage of income generated from Subpart F activities, as indicated here:

1. If Subpart F income is *less than 5 percent* of the CFC's total income, then none of the CFC's income will be taxed currently.

---

[8] Other countries—including Australia, Denmark, France, Italy, Sweden, the United Kingdom, and Venezuela—have similar anti–tax haven rules. For example, France uses a territorial approach to taxation and as a result does not tax profit earned by its companies outside of France. However, under French controlled foreign corporation rules, income earned by a French company outside of France may become subject to French taxation if the effective tax rate paid in the foreign country is 40 percent lower than the tax that would have been paid in France. See Ernst & Young, *Worldwide Corporate Tax Guide 2020,* available at https://www.ey.com (accessed March 1, 2022).

2. If Subpart F income is *between 5 percent and 70 percent* of the CFC's total income, then that percentage of the CFC's income which is Subpart F income will be taxed currently.

3. If Subpart F income is *greater than 70 percent* of the CFC's total income, then 100 percent of the CFC's income will be taxed currently.

Safe Harbor Rule

If the foreign tax rate is greater than 90 percent of the U.S. corporate income tax rate, then none of the CFC's income is considered to be Subpart F income. With the current U.S. tax rate of 21 percent, U.S. MNCs need not be concerned with the CFC rules for those foreign operations located in countries with an effective tax rate of 18.9 percent or higher. These countries are not considered to be tax havens for Subpart F purposes. A country's effective tax rate is a combination of the corporate income tax rate and the withholding tax rate applicable to dividends.

FOREIGN TAX CREDITS

Foreign branch income and foreign subsidiary (CFC) Subpart F income must be included in U.S. federal taxable income in the year earned. In determining the net U.S. income tax liability on these sources of taxable foreign income, U.S. companies are allowed to either (1) deduct *all* foreign taxes paid on the related foreign income or (2) take a credit for foreign *income* taxes paid on the foreign income. Income taxes that are creditable include withholding taxes on dividends, as discussed earlier, but sales, excise, and other types of taxes not based on income are not creditable. Unless creditable taxes other than income taxes are substantial, it is more advantageous for a company to take the foreign tax credit rather than a tax deduction.

Example: Deduction for Foreign Taxes Paid versus Foreign Tax Credit

Assume ASD Company's foreign branch earns income before income taxes of $100,000. Income taxes paid to the foreign government are $15,000 (15 percent). Sales and other taxes paid to the foreign government are $10,000. ASD Company must include the $100,000 of foreign branch income in its U.S. federal income tax return in calculating U.S. taxable income. The options of taking a deduction or tax credit are as follows:

ASD Company's U.S. Federal Income Tax Return		
	Deduction	**Credit**
Foreign source income	$100,000	$100,000
Deduction for all foreign taxes paid	−25,000	0
U.S. taxable income	$ 75,000	$100,000
U.S. income tax before credit (21%)	$ 15,750	$ 21,000
Foreign tax credit (for income taxes paid)	0	−15,000
Net U.S. tax liability	$ 15,750	$ 6,000

Note that ASD's foreign branch earns its income in a foreign currency that must be translated into U.S. dollars for tax purposes. Foreign currency translation for tax purposes is discussed later in this chapter in the section titled "Translation of Foreign Operation Income."

The foreign tax credit provides a dollar-for-dollar reduction in tax liability; that is, for every dollar of income tax ASD pays to the foreign government, ASD is allowed a $1 reduction in the amount of income taxes to be paid to the U.S. government. In this example, the foreign tax credit results in considerably less net U.S. federal income tax liability than the deduction for foreign taxes paid. In the case of foreign branch income, the credit allowed is known as a *direct foreign tax credit* because ASD is given a credit for the taxes it paid directly to the foreign government.

Prior to 2018, foreign subsidiary income was taxed by the U.S. federal government when dividends were paid by the foreign subsidiary to the U.S. parent. At that time, dividend income paid from foreign sources was included in the calculation of U.S. taxable income and an *indirect foreign tax credit* was allowed for the foreign taxes actually paid by the foreign subsidiary but deemed to have been paid by the U.S parent. By exempting dividends received from foreign subsidiaries from U.S. federal income taxation beginning in 2018, the Tax Cuts and Jobs Act of 2017 also eliminated the indirect foreign tax credit.

Calculation of Foreign Tax Credit

The rules governing the calculation of the direct foreign tax credit (FTC) in the United States are rather complex. In general, the FTC allowed is equal to the lower of (1) the actual taxes paid to the foreign government, or (2) the amount of taxes that would have been paid if the income had been earned in the United States.

This latter amount, in many cases, can be calculated by multiplying the amount of foreign source taxable income (e.g., foreign branch income) by the U.S. corporate income tax rate. This is known as the *overall FTC limitation* because the United States will not allow a foreign tax credit greater than the amount of taxes that would have been paid in the United States. To allow an FTC greater than the amount of taxes that would have been paid in the United States would require the U.S. government to refund U.S. companies for higher taxes paid in foreign countries. More formally, the overall FTC limitation is calculated as follows:

$$\text{Overall FTC limitation} = \frac{\text{Foreign source taxable income}}{\text{Worldwide taxable income}} \times \text{U.S. taxes before FTC}$$

The overall FTC limitation must be calculated separately for foreign branch income and for CFC Subpart F income. This is explained in more detail later in this chapter, in the section titled "FTC Baskets."

Example: Calculation of Foreign Tax Credit for Branches

Assume that two different U.S.-based companies have foreign branches. Alpha Company has a branch in Country A, and Zeta Company has a branch in Country Z. The amount of income before tax earned by each foreign branch and the amount of income tax paid to the local government is as follows:

	Alpha Company Branch in A	Zeta Company Branch in Z
Income before taxes.....	$100,000	$100,000
Income tax paid.........	$ 11,000 (11%)	$ 23,000 (23%)

Both Alpha and Zeta will report $100,000 of foreign branch income on their U.S. federal income tax return, and each will determine a U.S. federal income tax liability before FTC of $21,000 ($100,000 × 21%). For both companies, $21,000 is the amount of tax that would have been paid to the U.S. government if the foreign branch income had been earned in the United States. The overall FTC limitation is $21,000 for each company.

Alpha compares the income tax of $11,000 paid to the government of Country A with the limitation of $21,000 and will be allowed an FTC of $11,000, the lesser of the two. Zeta compares actual taxes of $23,000 paid to the government of Country Z with the limitation of $21,000 and will be allowed an FTC of $21,000, the lesser of the two. The U.S. federal income tax return related to foreign branch income for Alpha and Zeta reflects the following:

U.S. Federal Income Tax Return		
	Alpha	**Zeta**
U.S. taxable income	$100,000	$100,000
U.S. tax before FTC (21%)	$ 21,000	$ 21,000
FTC	11,000	21,000
Net U.S. tax liability	$ 10,000	$ 0

Alpha has a net U.S. federal income tax liability after foreign tax credit on its foreign branch income of $10,000, an additional 10 percent over what has already been paid in Country A (which is 11 percent). The United States requires Alpha to pay an effective tax rate of at least 21 percent (the U.S. corporate income tax rate) on all of its income, both U.S. source and foreign source.

Zeta has no U.S. tax liability after foreign tax credit on its foreign branch income. Zeta has already paid more than the U.S. federal income tax rate in Country Z, so no additional taxes will be paid in the United States. Instead, the $2,000 difference between the $23,000 in foreign taxes paid and the foreign tax credit of $21,000 allowed in the United States becomes an *excess foreign tax credit.*

Excess Foreign Tax Credits

Excess foreign tax credits may be used to offset additional taxes paid to the United States on foreign source income in years in which foreign tax rates are lower than the U.S. tax rate. An excess FTC may be:

1. Carried back 1 year. The company applies for a refund of additional taxes paid to the United States government on foreign source income in the previous year.
2. Carried forward 10 years. The company reduces future U.S. federal income tax liability in the event that additional U.S. income taxes must be paid on foreign source income in any of the next 10 years.

In effect, the excess FTC can be used only if, in the previous year or in the next 10 years, *the average foreign tax rate paid by the company is less than the U.S. federal income tax rate.*

Example: Calculation of Excess Foreign Tax Credit (One Branch, Multiple Years)

Assume Zeta's foreign branch in Country Z had $50,000 of pre-tax income in Year 1, $70,000 in Year 2, and $100,000 in Year 3. Assume the effective corporate income tax rate in Country Z in Year 1 was 20 percent. In Year 2, Country Z increased its corporate income tax rate to 23 percent. The U.S. income tax rate in each year is 21 percent. Zeta's U.S. federal income tax return would reflect the following:

	Year 1	Year 2	Year 3
Foreign source income	$50,000	$70,000	$100,000
Foreign taxes paid	$10,000 20%	$16,100 23%	$ 23,000 23%
U.S. tax before FTC.	$10,500 21%	$14,700 21%	$ 21,000 21%
FTC allowed in the United States. . . .	10,000	14,700	21,000
Net U.S. tax liability	$ 500	$ 0	$ 0
Excess FTC.	$ 0	$ 1,400	$ 2,000

In Year 2, Zeta has an excess foreign tax credit of $1,400 ($16,100 foreign taxes paid less $14,700 FTC allowed in the United States). In that year, Zeta will file for a refund of $500 for the additional taxes paid on foreign source income in Year 1 and will have an excess FTC to carry forward in the amount of $900. Zeta is unable to use its FTC carryforward in Year 3 because its effective foreign tax rate exceeds the U.S. income tax rate. If Zeta is not able to use its excess FTC carryforward of $900 in any of the next 10 years, the carryforward will be lost.

Example: Calculation of Foreign Tax Credit (One Company, Multiple Branches)

Let us return to the example of two branches located in countries A and Z, but now assume that both foreign branches belong to Alpha Company. In this case, Alpha has total foreign source income in Year 3 of $200,000, and the actual amount of taxes paid to foreign governments is $34,000 ([$100,000 × 11% in Country A] + [$100,000 × 23% in Country Z]). Alpha determines the amount of FTC allowed by the United States and its net U.S. federal income tax liability on foreign source income as follows:

U.S. Tax Return	
	Alpha Company
U.S. taxable income	$200,000
U.S. tax before FTC (21%)	$ 42,000
FTC allowed*	34,000
Net U.S. tax liability	$ 8,000

* Calculation of FTC allowed:

Actual tax paid	=		= $34,000
Overall FTC limitation	=	Foreign source income × U.S. tax rate	
	=	$200,000 × 21%	= $42,000
Lesser amount	=		$34,000

In the earlier example involving Alpha Company and Zeta Company, Alpha had an additional U.S. federal income tax liability on its foreign branch income of $10,000 and Zeta had an excess FTC related to its foreign branch of $2,000. In this example, when both foreign branches belong to Alpha Company, the otherwise excess FTC from the branch in Country Z partially offsets the additional taxes on the branch income earned in Country A, and a net U.S. federal income tax liability of $8,000 remains.

FTC Baskets

Initially in the United States, all foreign source income was combined to determine a single FTC limitation and a single amount of FTC allowed. In 2004, the American Jobs Creation Act required foreign source taxable income to be classified into two categories (referred to as "baskets"): (1) a *general income* basket and (2) a *passive income* basket, with an FTC computed separately for each basket of foreign income. More recently, the TCJA of 2017 created an additional FTC basket for foreign branch income. As a result of this change, CFC Subpart F income must be allocated to either a general income basket or a passive income basket, while foreign branch income must be allocated to a foreign branch income basket. Companies are not allowed to net FTCs across baskets. In other words, the excess FTC from one basket cannot be used to reduce additional U.S. taxes owed on other baskets. The excess FTC for one basket can be carried back and carried forward to offset additional U.S. taxes paid on only that basket of income.

Returning to the example involving Alpha Company, assume that the branch in Country A makes passive investments in stocks and bonds and the branch in Country Z is a manufacturing operation. Under current U.S. tax rules, the income from both branches would be placed in the foreign branch income FTC basket. Therefore, total branch income is $200,000, the FTC limitation and FTC allowed is $34,000, and the net U.S. federal income tax liability on branch income is $8,000.

Now assume that the entity in Country A is incorporated as a subsidiary, and the operation in Country Z is a branch. The Country A subsidiary earns foreign base company-passive income, and Country A has a tax rate that is less than 90 percent of the U.S. federal corporate income tax rate. Therefore, the subsidiary in Country A generates Subpart F income, which must be allocated to the passive income FTC basket. Alpha Company has an additional U.S. tax liability of $10,000 on the passive income earned in Country A. Country Z branch income is placed in a separate foreign branch income FTC basket, and Alpha Company has an excess FTC of $2,000 related to its branch income. Alpha is not allowed to use the excess FTC of $2,000 from the foreign branch basket to offset the additional tax of $10,000 from the passive income basket. The foreign branch basket excess FTC of $2,000 can be carried back and forward only to offset additional taxes owed on foreign branch income.

U.S. TAX TREATMENT OF FOREIGN OPERATION INCOME

Determining the appropriate amount of U.S. taxable income from foreign operations requires consideration of the following factors:

1. Legal form of the foreign operation (branch or corporation).
2. Percentage level of ownership (CFC or not).
3. Effective foreign tax rate ("tax haven" or not).
4. Nature of the foreign source income (Subpart F income or not) (appropriate FTC basket).

Exhibit 8.5 provides a flowchart with general guidelines for determining the amount of foreign source income to be included on the U.S. tax return, the FTC allowed, and the net U.S. tax liability on income generated by foreign operations. Use of the flowchart for determining a company's U.S. tax liability on its foreign source income is demonstrated through the following example.

Example: U.S. Taxation of Foreign Income

Assume that MNC Company (a U.S. taxpayer) has four operations located in four different foreign countries. Information for each foreign entity's country location, legal form, percentage owned, nature of activity, before-tax income, income tax rate and withholding tax rate in the host country, and dividend paid to MNC is summarized as follows:

Foreign Entity	A	B	C	D
Country	Costa Rica	Zimbabwe	Uzbekistan	Cayman Is.
Legal form	Branch	Corporation	Corporation	Corporation
MNC's ownership	100%	80%	100%	100%
Activity	Manufacturing	Mining	Sales	Investment
Before-tax income	$100,000	$100,000	$100,000	$100,000
Income tax rate	30%	25%	7.5%	0%
After-tax income	$ 70,000	$ 75,000	$ 92,500	$100,000
Gross dividend paid to MNC	$ 0	$ 20,000	$ 92,500	$ 0
Withholding tax rate	n/a	10%	10%	n/a
Net dividend received by MNC	$ 0	$ 18,000	$ 83,250	$ 0

EXHIBIT 8.5
Flowchart for
Determining U.S.
Taxation of Foreign
Operations

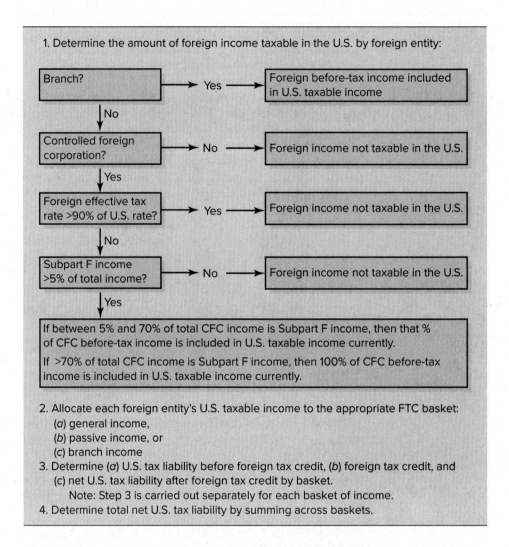

1. Determine the amount of foreign income taxable in the U.S. by foreign entity:

Branch? → Yes → Foreign before-tax income included in U.S. taxable income

↓ No

Controlled foreign corporation? → No → Foreign income not taxable in the U.S.

↓ Yes

Foreign effective tax rate >90% of U.S. rate? → Yes → Foreign income not taxable in the U.S.

↓ No

Subpart F income >5% of total income? → No → Foreign income not taxable in the U.S.

↓ Yes

If between 5% and 70% of total CFC income is Subpart F income, then that % of CFC before-tax income is included in U.S. taxable income currently.

If >70% of total CFC income is Subpart F income, then 100% of CFC before-tax income is included in U.S. taxable income currently.

2. Allocate each foreign entity's U.S. taxable income to the appropriate FTC basket:
   (*a*) general income,
   (*b*) passive income, or
   (*c*) branch income
3. Determine (*a*) U.S. tax liability before foreign tax credit, (*b*) foreign tax credit, and
   (*c*) net U.S. tax liability after foreign tax credit by basket.
      Note: Step 3 is carried out separately for each basket of income.
4. Determine total net U.S. tax liability by summing across baskets.

Determination of the Amount of Foreign Source Income Taxable in the United States

The amount of income from each foreign entity that will be taxable in the United States is either $0 or equal to the entity's before-tax income. Applying the flowchart in Exhibit 8.5, the first step is to determine whether the foreign entity is a branch or a corporation. In this example, the Costa Rican operation is organized as a branch, so its before-tax income of $100,000 will be included in MNC's U.S. taxable income. Each of the other foreign entities is legally incorporated in the country in which it resides.

The next step is to determine whether the foreign corporations are controlled foreign corporations (CFC) and therefore subject to testing for Subpart F income. Because MNC owns more than 50 percent of each foreign corporation, the answer to this question in each case is yes.

The following step determines whether any of the foreign countries meets the U.S. tax law definition of a tax haven. The effective tax rate (income tax plus withholding tax) must be calculated and compared with 90 percent of the U.S. tax rate of 21 percent, or 18.9 percent. The effective tax rate in each country is determined by adding the income tax rate plus the withholding tax rate applied to after-tax income:

Zimbabwe..............	25% + 10% (1 − 25%) = 32.5%	> 18.9%	Not a tax haven
Uzbekistan.............	7.5% + 10% (1 − 7.5%) = 16.75%	< 18.9%	Tax haven
Cayman Is.	0%	< 18.9%	Tax haven

Neither Uzbekistan nor the Cayman Islands meets the safe harbor test and thus both countries would be considered tax havens for purposes of Subpart F rules. Because Zimbabwe is not a tax haven, none of the income earned by the Zimbabwean CFC is subject to U.S. taxation.

The next step is to determine whether the CFCs in Uzbekistan and the Cayman Islands had any Subpart F income. In general, Subpart F income is income that can be easily moved from one tax jurisdiction to another. The Uzbeki subsidiary imports finished goods from MNC and then sells them throughout the Central Asian region; only 15 percent of its sales are made to customers in Uzbekistan. Thus, 85 percent of the Uzbeki CFC's income meets the definition of Subpart F income (foreign base company sales income). As a result, 100 percent of the Uzbeki subsidiary's before-tax income ($100,000) must be included in MNC's U.S. taxable income.

The Cayman Islands subsidiary generates its income from passive investments, which is foreign base company passive income under Subpart F. Because the Cayman CFC generates all of its income through investments, 100 percent of its before-tax income ($100,000) is taxable in the United States.

Determination of Foreign Tax Credits, U.S. Tax Liability, and Excess Foreign Tax Credits, by Basket

To determine MNC's foreign tax credit, foreign taxes (both income tax and withholding tax) paid on the income taxable in the United States must be determined. For the Costa Rican branch, this amount is $30,000 ($100,000 × 30%). Total taxes paid to Uzbekistan by the Uzbeki subsidiary are $16,750 ($7,500 of income tax plus $9,250 of dividend withholding tax). For the Cayman Islands subsidiary, foreign tax paid is $0.

The amount of income taxable in the United States next must be allocated to the appropriate FTC basket according to each foreign entity's activity. The income generated by the Costa Rican branch is allocated to a *branch income* FTC basket; the taxable income from Uzbekistan is allocated to the *general income* FTC basket, and the Cayman Islands subsidiary's income is placed in a *passive income* FTC basket. The foreign tax credit, U.S. income tax liability, and excess FTC for each basket of income can now be calculated as follows:

	Branch Income	General Income	Passive Income
U.S. taxable income	$100,000	$100,000	$100,000
U.S. income tax before FTC (21%)	$ 21,000	$ 21,000	$ 21,000
Less: FTC			
(a) Taxes paid to foreign government	$ 30,000	$ 16,750	$ 0
(b) Overall FTC limitation	$ 21,000	$ 21,000	$ 21,000
FTC allowed—lesser of (a) and (b)	21,000	16,750	$ 0
U.S. tax liability.	$ 0	$ 4,250	$ 21,000
Excess FTC.	$ 9,000	$ 0	$ 0

MNC Company has a total U.S. tax liability on its foreign source income of $25,250 ($4,250 on general income plus $21,000 on passive income) and an excess foreign tax credit on its branch income of $9,000.

Note that prior to the TCJA taking effect in 2018, MNC would have included the dividend received from its Zimbabwean subsidiary in taxable income. Under the TCJA's participation exemption approach to taxing foreign operation income, this is no longer the case. It also should be noted that lowering the U.S. corporate income tax rate in 2018 from

35 to 21 percent has resulted in far fewer countries meeting the definition of tax haven for determining Subpart F income. Until 2017, the safe harbor effective foreign tax rate was 31.5 percent (90 of 35 percent); since 2018, the safe harbor rate has been only 18.9 percent.

U.S. TAX REFORM: OTHER INTERNATIONAL TAX PROVISIONS

The TCJA, passed in December 2017, made the most extensive changes to the international tax provisions in U.S. tax law since 1986. Generally speaking, the objectives of the new provisions were to: (1) make U.S. corporations more competitive internationally, and (2) prevent erosion of the U.S. tax base. Arguably, the most significant change to international taxation was the adoption of a participation exemption (partial territorial) system of taxation in which most foreign subsidiary income is exempt from U.S. taxation. Other major international tax provisions of the new law are:

1. Deemed repatriation of accumulated foreign earnings.
2. Taxation of global intangible low-taxed income.
3. Imposition of a base erosion anti-abuse tax.

Deemed Repatriation of Accumulated Foreign Earnings

Prior to 2018, U.S. companies had an incentive *not* to repatriate income earned by foreign subsidiaries because dividends received from low-tax countries resulted in an additional U.S. income tax being paid. Some observers estimate that, from 1986 to 2017, U.S. corporations stockpiled an accumulated $3.1 trillion in earnings overseas.[9]

The TCJA required U.S. corporations to include in their 2017 U.S. tax return any foreign subsidiary income earned from 1987 through 2017 that had not previously been taxed in the United States. In other words, accumulated retained earnings of foreign subsidiaries generated from 1987 to 2017 was deemed to have been repatriated to the United States at the end of 2017, when dividends received from foreign subsidiaries were still subject to U.S. taxation.

Although the U.S. corporate income tax rate in 2017 was 35 percent, the deemed repatriated earnings were taxed at greatly reduced rates: 15.5 percent for retained earnings held in cash or cash equivalents, and 8 percent for retained earnings that had been reinvested in noncash assets (such as property, plant, and equipment). The TCJA allowed U.S. corporations to pay the tax in installments, over eight years.

A foreign tax credit was allowed to reduce the U.S. parent company's U.S. tax liability on the deemed repatriated dividend. As a result, additional U.S. tax was owed on the accumulated foreign earnings only if the average foreign effective tax rate was less than 15.5 percent (for retained earnings held as cash) or less than 8 percent (for retained earnings invested in noncash assets).

Example: Tax on Accumulated Foreign Earnings

Assume that over the period 1987–2017, the foreign subsidiaries of Multiminion Corporation (a U.S. taxpayer) generated an aggregate before-tax income of $10,000,000, upon which they paid $1,200,000 in corporate income taxes (average effective tax rate of 12 percent). Over the years, the foreign subsidiaries repatriated $2,000,000 of before-tax income to Multiminion, which the company properly included in its U.S. tax returns. The $8,000,000 of accumulated earnings not repatriated to the United States was held in cash and cash equivalents by the foreign subsidiaries.

[9] Lynlley Browning, "IRS Issues Tax Rate Guidance for Stockpiled Foreign Income," *Bloomberg,* December 29, 2017, available at https://www.bloomberg.com/news/articles/2017-12-29/irs-issues -guidance-on-tax-rates-for-stockpiled-foreign-income (accessed January 25, 2022).

In accordance with the TCJA, Multiminion included in its 2017 U.S. taxable income a deemed repatriation of earnings from its foreign subsidiaries in the amount of $8,000,000. These earnings were subject to a one-time tax of 15.5 percent, resulting in a tax of $1,240,000 ($8,000,000 × 15.5%) before subtracting any FTC. Multiminion was allowed an FTC for the $960,000 ($8,000,000 × 12%) in foreign taxes actually paid on the accumulated foreign earnings. As a result, Multiminion incurred a net U.S. tax liability of $280,000 ($1,240,000 − $960,000) on the deemed repatriation of accumulated foreign earnings.

If the foreign accumulated earnings had been invested in noncash assets (such as property, plant, and equipment), an 8 percent tax rate would have been applied. In this case, Multiminion would not have paid any tax to the United States on the accumulated foreign earnings because the tax before FTC of $640,000 ($8,000,000 × 8%) would have been more than offset by the FTC of $960,000.

The deemed repatriation of foreign earnings tax reached a significant amount for some companies. For example, in their fiscal year 2018 Form 10-K, The Procter & Gamble Company reported a repatriation tax liability of $2.9 billion, Cisco Systems, Inc. indicated it had a transition tax payable of $8.1 billion, and Apple Inc. disclosed a deemed repatriation tax payable of $33.6 billion. Each of these companies also disclosed that it would pay the deemed repatriation tax in installments over several years.

Global Intangible Low-Taxed Income

The TCJA introduced several new provisions intended to prevent the erosion of the U.S. tax base. Recall that *base erosion* refers to the process through which multinational companies artificially shift profits to low- or no-tax locations where there is little or no economic activity. The first of these provisions is described here.

Beginning in 2018, a U.S. corporation must include in taxable income its "global intangible low-taxed income" (GILTI), which is the income earned by CFCs exceeding a specified return on all CFCs' tangible assets. The amount of GILTI to be included in U.S. taxable income is based upon two concepts: (1) tested income, and (2) a specified return. *Tested income* is the aggregate amount of foreign subsidiary income across countries, less certain deductions. Thus, GILTI can exist regardless of whether the CFC derives income from intangible assets or not. The *specified return* is equal to 10 percent of CFCs' aggregate "qualified business asset investments" (QBAI), which generally is equal to the book value of tangible depreciable assets. If the CFCs' aggregate tested income exceeds the specified return, the excess amount is the amount of GILTI.

U.S. corporations may deduct 50 percent of the amount of GILTI included in taxable income, which effectively reduces the tax on GILTI to 10.5 percent (50 of the 21 percent U.S. corporate tax rate). The tax on GILTI can be further reduced by 80 percent of the foreign tax credit on the CFCs' amount of GILTI. Thus, U.S. corporations whose CFCs earn income in jurisdictions with a very low average foreign tax rate will be most affected by the GILTI tax.

GILTI is allocated to its own FTC basket, separate from the other FTC baskets described earlier in this chapter. If the FTC allowed exceeds the amount of tax owed on GILTI, an excess FTC arises. Unlike other FTCs, the excess FTC related to GILTI may not be carried back or carried forward.

Once it has been included in the U.S. parent's taxable income, GILTI can be repatriated to the U.S. parent company without incurring any further U.S. income tax.

Example: *Computation and Taxation of GILTI*

In the most recent calendar year, Bogey Golf Corporation's foreign subsidiaries had aggregate property, plant, and equipment (tangible depreciable assets, or QBAI) of $20,000,000 and generated aggregate before-tax income of $5,000,000. In that year, the company was required to include $1,500,000 of GILTI in its U.S. taxable income, calculated as follows:

Tested income	$5,000,000
Less: Specified return	
QBAI × Specified rate of return ($20,000,000 × 10%)	2,000,000
Excess (gross amount of GILTI)	$3,000,000
Less: 50% reduction	1,500,000
GILTI included in U.S parent's taxable income	$1,500,000

Bogey's foreign subsidiaries paid an average corporate income tax of 16 percent. Thus, the amount of foreign tax actually paid on the amount of GILTI included in Bogey's taxable income was $240,000 ($1,500,000 × 16%). Bogey is allowed an FTC related to the GILTI of $192,000 (80% × $240,000 foreign tax paid on GILTI). As a result, the company's net U.S. tax liability related to its GILTI is determined as follows:

GILTI	$1,500,000
U.S. corporate income tax rate	× 21%
U.S. tax liability before FTC	$ 315,000
Less: FTC allowed	192,000
Net U.S. tax liability	$ 123,000

Base Erosion Anti-Abuse Tax

The second notable provision to combat base erosion in the TCJA is the imposition of a "base erosion anti-abuse tax" (BEAT). The BEAT is a new tax that is intended to apply to companies that significantly reduce their U.S. tax liability by making payments to foreign affiliates (foreign parent, foreign subsidiary, or foreign branch).

The BEAT only applies to U.S. corporations that (1) are part of a group with average revenue of at least $500 million over the previous three years and (2) have *base erosion payments* exceeding 3 percent of the company's total deductible expenses. Base erosion payments include most payments made to a foreign affiliate, such as royalties and management fees, but exclude payments for cost of goods sold.

Whether BEAT is owed is determined by comparing (a) the company's tax liability when base erosion payments are deducted (actual taxable income) against (b) 10 percent of the company's income when base erosion payments are *not* deducted (modified taxable income). If the 10 percent amount is larger, then the BEAT is owed. The amount of BEAT is the difference between (a) and (b).

Example: Calculation of BEAT

In the most recent calendar year, Giganta Corporation (a U.S. taxpayer) generated revenues of $800 million in the United States and incurred tax-deductible expenses of $700 million, resulting in U.S. source taxable income of $100 million. Expenses included royalty and management fee payments made to foreign affiliates in the amount of $200 million. Because Giganta's revenues exceeded $500 million and its base erosion payments ($200 million) were greater than 3 percent of total expenses ($200 million/$700 million = 28.6%), Giganta is subject to a possible BEAT.

Giganta's regular U.S. tax liability is $21 million ($100 million × 21%). To determine whether BEAT is owed, this amount is compared with modified taxable income of

$300 million ($800 million − $500 million) multiplied by 10 percent: $300 million × 10% = $30 million. Because $30 million is greater than $21 million, Giganta must pay a BEAT of $9 million. As a result, Giganta's total U.S. tax liability is $30 million ($21 million + $9 million).

Note that BEAT is based on a U.S. corporation's U.S. source income and its *payments to foreign affiliates*. BEAT is *not* based on the U.S. corporation's foreign source income.

TRANSLATION OF FOREIGN OPERATION INCOME

In the examples presented thus far in this chapter, the income earned by foreign operations and the foreign taxes paid have been stated in terms of the parent company's domestic currency. In reality, foreign operations generate income and pay taxes in the local, foreign currency. The parent company's tax liability, however, is determined in terms of the domestic currency, for example, U.S. dollars for U.S. companies. The foreign currency income generated by a foreign operation, as well as the foreign currency taxes paid, must be translated into the parent company's currency for purposes of home country taxation. This section demonstrates procedures used in the United States for translating foreign currency income for U.S. tax purposes. Although we focus on U.S. tax rules, similar procedures are followed in other countries.

As is true for financial reporting, the appropriate translation procedures for determining U.S. taxable income depend on the *functional currency* of the foreign operation. The functional currency is the currency in which the foreign operation primarily conducts business and can be either a foreign currency or the U.S. dollar. For operations located in highly inflationary countries (cumulative three-year inflation exceeding 100 percent), the U.S. dollar must be used as the functional currency. Moreover, a U.S. company with a foreign branch or foreign subsidiary that primarily operates in a foreign currency can elect to use the U.S. dollar as the functional currency for tax purposes if it so chooses.

A foreign operation that has the U.S. dollar as its functional currency keeps its books in U.S. dollars. Any transactions that take place in a foreign currency are translated into U.S. dollars at the date of the transaction. Income of the foreign operation is directly calculated in U.S. dollars, so there is no need for currency translation at the end of the year.

For those foreign branches and subsidiaries that have a foreign currency as their functional currency, accounting records are kept and income is determined in the foreign currency and must be translated into U.S. dollars for U.S. tax purposes.

Translation of Foreign Currency Income

To determine U.S. taxable income, foreign operation net income taxable in the United States is translated into U.S. dollars using the average exchange rate for the year. Foreign operation net income is then grossed up by adding taxes paid to the foreign government translated at the exchange rate at the date of payment. When foreign operation income is repatriated to the home country and foreign currency is actually converted into U.S. dollars, any difference between the exchange rate used to originally translate the foreign income and the exchange rate at the date of repatriation creates a taxable foreign exchange gain or loss. The foreign tax credit is determined by translating foreign taxes at the exchange rate at the date of payment. The following example demonstrates these procedures.

Example: *Translation of Foreign Branch Income*

Sabin Company (a U.S.-based taxpayer) establishes a branch in Thailand in January of Year 1 when the exchange rate is US$0.04 per Thai baht (THB). During Year 1, the Thai branch generates THB 5,000,000 of pre-tax income. On October 15, Year 1, THB 1,000,000 is repatriated to Sabin Company and converted into U.S. dollars. The effective income tax rate in Thailand is 20 percent. Taxes were paid in Thailand on the Thai branch income on December 31, Year 1. Relevant exchange rates for Year 1 are as follows:

	US$/THB
January 1	$0.040
October 15.	$0.032
December 31.	$0.030
Average for the year.	$0.035

The amount of foreign branch income Sabin Company reports on its Year 1 U.S. tax return is determined as follows:

Pretax income	THB 5,000,000				
Taxes paid (20%)	THB 1,000,000				
Net income × Average exchange rate	THB 4,000,000	×	$0.035	=	$140,000
Taxes paid × Actual exchange rate	THB 1,000,000	×	$0.030	=	30,000
Gain (loss) on October 15 repatriation.	THB 1,000,000	×	($0.032 − $0.035)	=	(3,000)
U.S. taxable income					$167,000

The foreign tax credit (FTC) allowed by the United States is determined by comparing the actual tax paid to the Thai government (translated into US$) and the overall FTC limitation based on the U.S. tax rate of 21 percent:

(a) Foreign taxes paid (in US$) (THB 1,000,000 × $0.030)	$30,000
(b) Overall FTC limitation ($167,000 × 21%).	$35,070
FTC allowed—lesser of (a) and (b)	$30,000

The U.S. tax return includes the following:

U.S. taxable income (above)	$167,000
U.S. tax before FTC (21%)	$ 35,070
FTC allowed (above).	30,000
Net U.S. tax liability.	$ 5,070

Foreign Currency Transactions

U.S. taxpayers often engage in transactions denominated in foreign currency, such as export sales, import purchases, and foreign currency borrowings. In general, gains or losses arising from fluctuations in exchange rates between the date of the transaction and its settlement will be taxable only when realized—in effect, at the settlement date. For tax purposes, gains and losses on forward contracts and options used to hedge foreign currency transactions and firm commitments are integrated with the underlying item being hedged. For example, if a foreign currency receivable is hedged by a forward contract that guarantees that the foreign currency can be sold for $1,000, taxable revenue of $1,000 is reported when the receivable is collected. Any gains and losses on the foreign currency receivable and forward contract recorded for financial reporting purposes are not recognized for tax purposes.

Summary

1. Taxes are a significant cost of doing business. Taxes often are an important factor to consider in making decisions related to foreign operations. Although tax returns will be prepared by tax experts, managers of multinational corporations (MNCs) should be familiar with the major issues of international taxation.

2. Most countries have a national corporate income tax rate that varies between 15 and 35 percent. Countries with no or very low corporate taxation are known as tax havens. MNCs often attempt to use operations in tax haven countries to minimize their worldwide tax burden.

3. Withholding taxes are imposed on payments made to foreigners, especially in the form of dividends, interest, and royalties. Withholding rates vary across countries and often vary by type of payment within one country. Differences in withholding rates provide tax-planning opportunities for the location or nature of a foreign operation.

4. Countries can exert tax jurisdiction using a worldwide approach, a territorial approach, or a hybrid (participation exemption) approach. The basis for taxation can be source of income, residence of the taxpayer, and/or citizenship of the taxpayer. The existence of overlapping tax jurisdictions and bases leads to double taxation.

5. Tax treaties between two countries govern the way in which individuals and companies residing or doing business in the partner country are taxed by that country. A significant feature of most tax treaties is a reduction in withholding tax rates. The U.S. model treaty reduces withholding taxes to 0 percent on interest and royalties and 15 percent on dividends. However, these guidelines often are not followed.

6. Some countries provide relief from double taxation through foreign tax credits (FTCs). FTCs reduce the tax liability on income in one country based on the taxes already paid on that income in another country. In general, the tax credit allowed by the home country is limited to the amount of taxes that would have been paid if the income had been earned in the home country.

7. The excess of taxes paid to a foreign country over the FTC allowed by the home country is an excess FTC. In the United States, an excess FTC may be carried back 1 year and carried forward 10 years. U.S. tax law requires companies to allocate foreign source income to three foreign tax credit baskets—branch income, general income, and passive income. Excess FTCs may be applied only within the basket to which they relate.

8. Income earned by a foreign branch is taxable in the United States, whereas income earned by a foreign subsidiary generally is not taxable in the United States. However, the exemption of foreign subsidiary income from U.S. taxation does not apply to so-called Subpart F income earned by a controlled foreign corporation (CFC). Income earned by a CFC that can be moved easily from one country to another (Subpart F income) is taxed in the United States currently.

9. In 2017, the Tax Cuts and Jobs Act introduced several new international tax provisions into U.S. tax law. In addition to moving the United States to a participation exemption system with respect to the taxation of foreign operation income, the new law also (a) levied a one-time tax on accumulated foreign earnings, (b) requires the inclusion of "global intangible low-taxed income" in U.S. taxable income, and (c) imposes a "base erosion anti-abuse" tax on payments made to foreign affiliates.

10. Foreign operation net income is translated into U.S. dollars for U.S. tax purposes using the average exchange rate for the year and then grossed up by adding taxes paid to the foreign government translated at the exchange rate at the date of payment. When foreign operation income is repatriated to the home country, any difference in the exchange rate used to originally translate the income and the exchange rate at the date of repatriation creates a taxable foreign exchange gain or loss.

Appendix to Chapter 8

U.S. Taxation of Expatriates

This chapter has concentrated on international corporate tax issues. This appendix examines several issues related to U.S. taxation of expatriates—individuals who live and work overseas.

The United States is unusual in that it taxes its citizens on their worldwide income regardless of whether they are actually living in the United States. To make U.S. businesses more competitive by making it less expensive to use U.S. employees overseas, the U.S. Congress provides tax advantages for U.S. citizens who work abroad. These advantages are (1) a foreign earned income exclusion and (2) a foreign housing cost exclusion.

FOREIGN EARNED INCOME EXCLUSION

The following items of foreign earned income must be reported as income by a U.S. taxpayer:

- Wages, salaries, and professional fees.
- Overseas allowance (cash payment made by an employer to compensate for the "inconvenience" of living overseas).
- Housing allowance (cash payment made by an employer or fair market value of housing provided by an employer).
- Automobile allowance (cash allowance or fair market value).
- Cost of living allowance.
- Education allowance.
- Home leave.
- Rest and relaxation airfare.
- Tax reimbursement allowance (reimbursement for additional taxes paid to a foreign government that exceed what would have been paid in the home country).

If certain criteria are met, a U.S. taxpayer may exclude $108,700 (in 2021) of foreign earned income from U.S. taxable income. An exclusion is allowed even if the earned income is not taxed by the foreign country (or is taxed at a lower rate than in the United States). The amount of the exclusion increases each year by the rate of inflation.

In addition, a U.S. taxpayer receives a direct foreign tax credit for foreign taxes paid on the amount of foreign earned income exceeding the amount of the exclusion. As a result, a U.S. taxpayer working in a foreign country that has a higher tax rate than the United States will pay no additional U.S. tax on their foreign earned income.

The real benefit of the foreign earned income exclusion arises when a U.S. taxpayer is working in a foreign country with no individual income tax or an individual tax rate less than in the United States. For example, in 2021, a U.S. taxpayer working in Saudi Arabia (which has no individual income tax) would have paid no income tax at all on the first $108,700 of foreign earned income. Income over that amount would have been taxed in the United States at normal rates.

The foreign earned income exclusion is available only to U.S. taxpayers who

1. Have their tax home in a foreign country, and
2. Meet either (a) a bona fide residence test or (b) a physical presence test.

Tax Home

An individual's *tax home* is the place where they are permanently or indefinitely engaged to work as an employee or as a self-employed individual. An individual's tax home cannot be a foreign country if their abode is in the United States. *Abode* is variously defined as "home," "residence," "domicile," or "place of dwelling." It relates to where one lives rather than where one works. For your tax home to be in a foreign country, your abode must also be outside of the United States.

As an example, assume that your company transfers you to work in London for 18 months. Your home in New York is rented out, and your automobile is placed in storage. In London, you purchase an automobile, and you and your spouse get British driving licenses. All members of your family get a local library card and join the local golf club. You open bank accounts at the local bank. In this case, both your abode and your tax home are in London.

Bona Fide Residence Test

A *bona fide residence* is not necessarily the same as a domicile. A domicile is a permanent home. For example, you could have your domicile in New York and a bona fide residence in London even if you intend to eventually return to New York. Going to work in London does not necessarily mean that you have established a bona fide residence there. But if you go to London to work for an indefinite or extended period and you set up permanent quarters there for you and your family, you probably have established a bona fide residence in a foreign country, even though you intend to return to the United States at some point.

To establish a bona fide residence, you must reside in a foreign country for an uninterrupted period that includes an entire tax year. You may leave for brief trips to the United States or other foreign countries, but you must always return to the bona fide residence at the end of a trip.

The Internal Revenue Service (IRS) will determine whether you meet the bona fide residence test, given information you report in Form 2555, Foreign Earned Income.

Physical Presence Test

More objective than the bona fide residence test is the *physical presence* test. You meet this test if you are physically present in a foreign country or countries for 330 full days during a consecutive 12-month period. Days spent in transit to the foreign country do not count; only days in which you are in a foreign country for 24 hours count. Time spent in international waters or airspace also does not count.

The minimum time requirement can be waived if you must leave a foreign country due to war, civil unrest, or similar adverse conditions. Each year, the IRS publishes a list of countries that meet these conditions.

FOREIGN HOUSING COST EXCLUSION

For those U.S. taxpayers meeting the two conditions necessary for the foreign earned income exclusion, a foreign housing cost exclusion also is available. Up to a limit, a U.S. taxpayer may exclude from taxable income foreign housing costs paid out of employer-provided amounts (such as salary) that exceed a base amount. The base amount is 16 percent of the foreign earned income exclusion, which amounted to $17,392 ($108,700 × 16%) in 2021. The general limit to the amount of the housing cost exclusion is 30 percent of the foreign earned income exclusion, which was $32,610 ($108,700 × 30%) in 2021. Thus, for example, an individual working in Salzburg, Austria, in 2021 who incurred $36,000 in housing costs could exclude $15,218 ($32,610 − $17,392) from U.S. taxable income that year.

Housing expenses eligible for the foreign housing exclusion include rent, utilities, personal property insurance, fees to obtain a lease, rental of furniture, and residential parking. Expenses not eligible for the foreign housing exclusion/deduction include the cost of purchasing a house or apartment, mortgage interest, property taxes, the cost of purchasing furniture, pay television, wages of housekeepers and gardeners, and any costs that are lavish and extravagant. The housing cost exclusion limit is higher in high-cost cities around the world. For example, the limit in 2021 for Hong Kong was $114,300, the limit for Beijing was $69,000, and the limit for Shanghai was $57,001.

The amount taken as a foreign housing cost exclusion reduces the amount of foreign earned income that is available for the foreign earned income exclusion. As a result, the housing cost exclusion provides no additional tax benefit for an individual whose foreign income is equal to or smaller than the foreign earned income exclusion. Only those individuals whose foreign income is greater than the foreign earned income exclusion will benefit from the foreign housing cost exclusion. For example, a U.S. taxpayer living in Salzburg, Austria, in 2021, with foreign earned income of $150,000 and qualifying foreign housing costs of $36,000 would have taken a housing cost exclusion of $15,218. This would have reduced the amount of income eligible for the foreign earned income exclusion to $134,782 ($150,000 − $15,218). Nonetheless, the taxpayer would have been able to take the maximum foreign earned income exclusion allowed in 2021, which was $108,700. As a result, this individual would have excluded a total of $123,918 ($108,700 + $15,218) in determining 2021 U.S. taxable income.

Questions

1. How can a country's tax system affect the manner in which an operation in that country is financed by a foreign investor?
2. Why might the effective tax rate paid on income earned within a country be different from that country's national corporate income tax rate?
3. What is a tax haven? How might a company use a tax haven to reduce income taxes?
4. What is the difference between the worldwide and territorial approaches to taxation?
5. What are the different ways in which income earned in one country becomes subject to double taxation?
6. What are the mechanisms used by countries to provide relief from double taxation?
7. What is a tax treaty? What is one of the most important benefits provided by most tax treaties?
8. What is treaty shopping?
9. What is base erosion and profit shifting (BEPS)?
10. What is the purpose of the OECD's base erosion and profit shifting action plan?
11. Under what circumstances is it advantageous to take a deduction rather than a credit for taxes paid in a foreign country?
12. How are foreign branch income and foreign subsidiary income taxed differently by the United States?
13. Under U.S. tax law, what is a controlled foreign corporation (CFC)? What is Subpart F income?
14. Under what circumstances will the income earned by a foreign subsidiary of a U.S. taxpayer be taxed as if it had been earned by a foreign branch?
15. What is the maximum amount of foreign tax credit that a U.S. company is allowed to take with respect to the income earned by a foreign operation?
16. What are excess foreign tax credits? How are they created and how can U.S. companies use them?
17. How does the foreign tax credit basket system used in the United States affect the excess foreign tax credits generated by a U.S.-based company?
18. What are the four factors that determine the manner in which income earned by a foreign operation of a U.S. taxpayer will be taxed by the U.S. government?

19. What are the major international tax provisions in the Tax Cuts and Jobs Act that became effective in the United States in 2018?

20. What procedures are used to translate the foreign currency income of a foreign operation into U.S. dollars for U.S. tax purposes?

    The following questions relate to the Appendix *to this chapter:*

21. For an individual taxpayer in the United States, what benefit is provided by the foreign earned income exclusion?

22. How does an individual taxpayer in the United States qualify for the foreign earned income exclusion?

23. For an individual taxpayer in the United States, what benefit is provided by the foreign housing cost exclusion?

Exercises and Problems

1. In deciding whether to establish a foreign operation, which factor(s) might a multinational corporation (MNC) consider?
   a. After-tax returns from competing investment locations.
   b. The tax treatments of branches versus subsidiaries.
   c. Withholding rates on dividend and interest payments.
   d. All of the above.

2. Why might a company involved in international business find it beneficial to establish an operation in a tax haven?
   a. The OECD recommends the use of tax havens for corporate income tax avoidance.
   b. Tax havens never tax corporate income.
   c. Tax havens are jurisdictions that tend to have abnormally low corporate income tax rates.
   d. Tax havens' banking systems are less secretive.

3. Which of the following items might provide an MNC with a tax-planning opportunity as it decides where to locate a foreign operation?
   a. Differences in corporate tax rates across countries.
   b. Differences in local tax rates across countries.
   c. Whether a country offers a tax holiday.
   d. All of the above.

4. Why might companies have an incentive to finance their foreign operations with as much debt as possible?
   a. Interest payments are generally tax deductible.
   b. Withholding rates are lower for dividends.
   c. Withholding rates are lower for interest.
   d. Both (a) and (c).

5. Kerry is a U.S. citizen residing in Portugal. Kerry receives some investment income from Spain. Why might Kerry be expected to pay taxes on the investment income to the United States?
   a. The United States taxes its citizens on their worldwide income.
   b. The United States taxes its citizens on the basis of residency.
   c. Portugal requires all of its residents to pay taxes to the United States.
   d. None of the above.

6. Patak Corporation is a U.S. company with a branch in China. Income earned by the Chinese branch is taxed in both China, at the corporate income tax rate of 25 percent, and the United States, at the rate of 21 percent. What is this an example of?

   a. Capital-export neutrality.

   b. Double taxation.

   c. A tax treaty.

   d. Taxation on the basis of consumption.

7. What are the methods used by the United States to reduce the double taxation of income earned by foreign operations of U.S. companies?

   a. Exempting some foreign source income and allowing a deduction for all foreign taxes paid.

   b. Allowing a deduction for all foreign taxes paid and providing a foreign tax credit for foreign income taxes paid.

   c. Exempting some foreign source income and providing a foreign tax credit for foreign income taxes paid.

   d. Exempting some foreign source income, allowing a deduction for all foreign taxes paid, and providing a foreign tax credit for foreign income taxes paid.

8. Jordan Inc., a U.S. company, is required to translate into U.S. dollars the foreign currency income generated by its foreign branch. To determine U.S. taxable income, what must Jordan use to translate the net income of its foreign branch into U.S. dollars?

   a. The exchange rate at the end of the year.

   b. The average exchange rate for the year.

   c. The exchange rate at the beginning of the year.

   d. The previous year's ending exchange rate.

9. Mondrake, Inc., has total worldwide income of $500,000. Mondrake's Polish branch has foreign source income of $200,000 and paid taxes of $38,000 to the Polish government. The U.S. corporate tax rate is 21 percent. What is Mondrake's overall foreign tax credit limitation?

   a. $38,000.

   b. $42,000.

   c. $70,000.

   d. $105,000.

   Use the following information for Exercises 10 through 12: Information for Year 1, Year 2, and Year 3 for the Alpinian branch of Rawl Corporation is presented in the following table. The corporate tax rate in the Alpinian Republic in Year 1 was 11 percent. In Year 2, the Alpinian Republic increased its corporate income tax rate to 15 percent. In Year 3, the Alpinian Republic increased its corporate tax rate to 22 percent. The U.S. corporate tax rate in each year is 21 percent.

	Year 1	Year 2	Year 3
Foreign source income	$75,000	$100,000	$100,000
Foreign taxes paid	8,250	15,000	22,000
U.S. tax before FTC............	15,750	21,000	21,000

10. For Year 1, Year 2, and Year 3, what is the foreign tax credit allowed in the United States?
    a. $8,250, $15,000, and $21,000.
    b. $8,250, $15,000, and $22,000.
    c. $15,750, $21,000, and $22,000.
    d. $15,750, $15,000, and $21,000.

11. For Year 3, what is the net U.S. tax liability?
    a. $0.
    b. $1,000.
    c. $6,000.
    d. $21,000.

12. In Year 3, how much excess foreign tax credit can Rawl carry back?
    a. $7,500.
    b. $6,000.
    c. $1,000.
    d. $0.

13. King Street Bakery, Inc., a U.S. company, has a branch located in Cabo Marco and another in the Windswept Islands. The before-tax income earned by the Cabo Marco branch is $100,000, and the before-tax income generated by the Windswept Islands branch is $200,000. The corporate tax rates in Cabo Marco, the Windswept Islands, and the United States are 16, 10, and 21 percent, respectively.

    Required:
    Determine King Street Bakery's (a) U.S. foreign tax credit and (b) net U.S. tax liability related to these foreign sources of income.

14. Boston Beanery, a U.S.-based company, establishes a branch in Great Britain in January of Year 1, when the exchange rate is US$1.30 per British pound (£). During Year 1, the British branch generates £5,000,000 of pre-tax income. On October 15, Year 1, £2,000,000 is repatriated to Boston Beanery and converted into U.S. dollars. Assume the effective income tax rate in Great Britain is 19 percent. Taxes were paid in Great Britain on December 31, Year 1. Relevant exchange rates for Year 1 are provided here (US$ per £):

January 1	1.30
Average	1.40
October 15	1.45
December 31	1.50

    Assume a U.S. tax rate of 21 percent.

    Required:
    Determine the amount of U.S. taxable income, U.S. foreign tax credit, and net U.S. tax liability related to the British branch (all in U.S. dollars).

15. Mama Corporation (a U.S. taxpayer) has a wholly owned sales subsidiary in the Bahamas (Bahamamama Ltd.) that purchases finished goods from its U.S. parent and sells those goods to customers throughout the Caribbean Basin. In the most recent year, Bahamamama generated income of $100,000. There are no income or withholding taxes in the Bahamas.

Required:

a. Determine the amount of income taxable in the United States assuming that Bahamamama makes 20 percent of its sales in the Bahamas and 80 percent in other countries.

b. Determine the amount of income taxable in the United States assuming that Bahamamama makes 40 percent of its sales in the Bahamas and 60 percent in other countries.

16. Lionais Company has a foreign branch that earns income before income taxes of 500,000 currency units (CU). Income taxes paid to the foreign government are CU 150,000 (30 percent). Sales and other taxes paid to the foreign government are CU 50,000. Lionais Company must include the CU 500,000 of foreign branch income in determining its home-country taxable income. In determining its taxable income, Lionais can choose between taking a deduction for all foreign taxes paid or a credit only for foreign income taxes paid. The corporate income tax rate in Lionais's home country is 40 percent.

Required:

Determine whether Lionais would be better off taking a deduction or a credit for foreign taxes paid.

17. Avioco Limited has two branches located in Hong Kong and Australia, each of which manufactures goods primarily for export to countries in the Asia-Pacific region. The corporate income tax rate in Avioco's home country is 20 percent. The amount of income before taxes and the actual tax paid (stated in terms of Avioco's home currency) are as follows:

	Hong Kong Branch	Australia Branch
Income before taxes.........	100,000	100,000
Actual tax paid.............	16,500 (16.5%)	30,000 (30%)

Required:

Determine the amount of foreign tax credit Avioco will be allowed to take in determining its home-country income tax liability.

18. Garcia Company is in the process of deciding where to establish a European manufacturing operation: Germany, Italy, or Spain. Garcia's home country does not have a tax treaty with any of these countries. Regardless of location, the operation is expected to generate pre-tax income of 1 million euros annually. The operation will distribute 100 percent of its after-tax income to Garcia Company as a dividend each year.

Required:

a. Using the information on effective income tax rates and withholding tax rates provided in Exhibits 8.1 and 8.3, determine the net amount of dividend that Garcia would receive annually from an investment in each of these three countries.

b. If maximizing after-tax dividends is the sole criterion, in which of the three countries should Garcia locate its European operation?

19. Fullerton Company (a U.S. taxpayer) has wholly owned subsidiaries located in Hungary and Hong Kong. The Hungarian operation purchases electric generators manufactured by Fullerton and sells them throughout Eastern Europe; 90 percent of sales are made outside of Hungary. The Hungarian subsidiary generated pre-tax income of $200,000 in the current year. The Hong Kong subsidiary is an investment company that makes

investments in world financial markets; 100 percent of its income is generated from passive investments. The Hong Kong subsidiary generated pre-tax income of $100,000 in the current year. Both subsidiaries distribute 100 percent of income to Fullerton Company as a dividend each year. Corporate income tax rates and withholding rates are provided in Exhibits 8.1 and 8.3.

Required:

a. Explain why the income earned by the subsidiaries in Hungary and Hong Kong should be included in Fullerton's U.S. taxable income.

b. Determine the amount of foreign tax credit allowed by the United States in the current year and the amount of excess foreign tax credit, if any.

20. Streep Company (a U.S.-based company) has branches in three countries: X, Y, and Z. All three branches sell goods and services in their host country. Income tax rates on branch profits in these three countries over the most recent three-year period are as follows:

Country	Year 1	Year 2	Year 3
X..............	36%	36%	26%
Y..............	11	11	11
Z..............	28	16	16

None of these countries imposes a withholding tax on branch profits distributed to a foreign parent company. The U.S. corporate income tax rate over this three-year period was 21 percent.

Pre-tax income earned by each branch over the most recent three-year period is as follows:

	Year 1	Year 2	Year 3
Branch X	$100,000	$100,000	$100,000
Branch Y	150,000	150,000	150,000
Branch Z.	200,000	200,000	200,000

Required:

a. Determine the amount of foreign source income Streep will include in its U.S. tax return in each of the three years.

b. Determine the amount of foreign tax credit Streep will be allowed to take in determining its U.S. tax liability in each of the three years.

c. Determine the amount of excess foreign tax credit, if any, Streep will have in each of the three years.

d. Determine Streep's net U.S. tax liability in each of the three years.

21. Heraklion Company (a U.S.-based company) is considering making an equity investment in an Australian manufacturing operation. The total amount of capital, in Australian dollars (A$), that Heraklion would need to invest is A$1,000,000. Heraklion has three alternatives for financing this investment:

- 100 percent equity.
- 80 percent equity and 20 percent long-term loan from Heraklion (5 percent interest rate).
- 50 percent equity and 50 percent long-term loan from Heraklion (5 percent interest rate).

Heraklion estimates that the Australian operation will generate A\$200,000 of income before interest and taxes in its first year of operations. The operation will pay 100 percent of its net income to Heraklion as a dividend each year.

Required:

a. Assume there is no tax treaty between the United States and Australia. Using the information on Australian tax rates found in Exhibits 8.1 and 8.3, determine the total amount of taxes that will be paid in Australia under each of the three financing alternatives. Which alternative results in the least amount of taxes being paid in Australia?

b. The United States/Australia tax treaty provides reduced withholding tax rates on certain payments made to a foreign parent company. Using the information on Australian tax rates found in Exhibits 8.1 and 8.4, determine the total amount of taxes that will be paid in Australia under each of the three financing alternatives. Which alternative results in the least amount of taxes being paid in Australia?

22. The corporate income tax rates in two countries, A and B, are 40 and 25 percent, respectively. Additionally, both countries impose a 30 percent withholding tax on dividends paid to foreign investors. However, a bilateral tax treaty between Country A and Country B reduces the withholding tax to 10 percent if the dividend is paid to an investor that owns more than 50 percent of the paying company's stock (parent). Both countries use a worldwide approach to taxation but allow taxpayers to take a foreign tax credit for total taxes (income tax plus withholding tax) paid on foreign earned income. The credit is limited to the amount of tax that would have been paid in the domestic country on that income. Both countries use the same currency, so foreign currency translation is not required.

Part 1.

Alpha Company is headquartered in Country A and has a wholly owned subsidiary in Country B. In the current year, Alpha's foreign subsidiary generated before-tax income of 100,000 and remitted 100 percent of its net income to the parent company as a dividend.

Required:

a. Determine the amount of taxes paid in Country A.

b. Determine the amount of taxes paid in Country B.

Part 2.

Beta Company is headquartered in Country B and has a wholly owned subsidiary in Country A. In the current year, Beta's foreign subsidiary generated before-tax income of 100,000 and remitted 100 percent of its net income to the parent company as a dividend.

Required:

a. Determine the amount of taxes paid in Country A.

b. Determine the amount of taxes paid in Country B.

23. Caragua Corporation (a U.S. taxpayer) has several foreign subsidiaries that generated aggregate before-tax income of \$42,000,000 in the current year, upon which they paid corporate income tax at an average rate of 15 percent. Caragua's foreign subsidiaries had an aggregate amount of property, plant, and equipment of \$280,000,000.

Required:

a. Determine the amount of global intangible low-taxed income (GILTI) Caragua was required to report in its U.S. taxable income in the current year.

b. Determine the amount of U.S. tax liability related to GILTI in the current year.

24. Fina Corporation is a U.S.-based taxpayer that provides logistics services to companies in the food products industry. Fina is wholly owned by a company headquartered in Asia. Fina's U.S. taxable income for the current year is calculated as follows (amounts are in millions of U.S. dollars):

Revenues	$600
Expenses:	(80)
Salaries	(400)
Royalties	(80)
Interest	(40)
Taxable income	$ 80

Salaries are paid to U.S. employees in 100 locations around the country. Royalties and interest are paid by Fina to its parent company in Asia. Fina has generated more than $500 million in revenues in each of its 10 years of operation.

Required:

Determine the amount of base erosion anti-abuse tax (BEAT), if any, that Fina Corporation owes in the current year.

25. Hitech Corporation (a U.S.-based company) has a branch located in Singapore that generated income before tax of 1,000,000 Singaporean dollars (SGD) in the current year. The foreign branch paid income taxes to Singapore at the rate of 17 percent evenly throughout the year and remitted after-tax profits of SGD 200,000 to Hitech on October 1. Singapore does not impose a withholding tax on the repatriation of branch profits. The following exchange rates for the current year apply:

	US$ per SGD
January 1	$0.745
Average for the year	0.750
October 1	0.758
December 31	0.760

Required:

Determine the following related to the income earned by Hitech's branch in Singapore:

a. The amount of U.S. taxable income in U.S. dollars.

b. The amount of foreign tax credit allowed in the United States.

c. The amount of net U.S. tax liability.

26. Rigo Corporation has a branch in Spain that sells products manufactured at Rigo's factory in Arden, North Carolina. In the current year, Rigo's Spanish branch earned €10 million before tax, upon which it paid tax to the Spanish government at an effective tax rate of 25 percent. Spanish taxes were paid at the end of the year. The Spanish branch made cash distributions to Rigo Corporation on July 1 and December 31 in the amount of €1 million each. Relevant exchange rates for the current year are as follows:

January 1	€1 = $1.12
July 1	€1 = $1.14
Average	€1 = $1.15
December 31	€1 = $1.18

Required:
a. Determine the amount of Spanish branch profit in U.S. dollars that Rigo Corporation must include in its U.S. taxable income.
b. Determine the amount of available U.S. foreign tax credit in U.S. dollars related to the Spanish branch profit.

The following exercises and problems relate to the Appendix *to this chapter:*

27. Which of the following items is *not* a tax benefit available to U.S. taxpayers working abroad?
a. Foreign earned income exclusion.
b. Foreign tax credit.
c. Dividend income exclusion.
d. Foreign housing cost exclusion.

28. The exchange rate between the U.S. dollar (US$) and the Hong Kong dollar (HK$) remained constant at HK$8.00 = US$1.00 throughout 2021. J. Vander (a U.S. citizen) lives and works in Hong Kong. In 2021, Vander earned income in Hong Kong of HK$1,600,000 and paid taxes to the local government at the rate of 15 percent. Vander qualifies for the foreign earned income exclusion.

Required:
a. Determine the amount of foreign earned income Vander included in the calculation of U.S. taxable income for the year 2021.
b. Determine the amount of foreign tax credit Vander was allowed to take in determining U.S. tax liability for the year 2021.
c. Assuming Vander has a marginal U.S. income tax rate of 28 percent, determine the amount of U.S. income taxes Vander paid on foreign earned income in the year 2021.

29. The exchange rate between the U.S. dollar (US$) and the euro (€) remained constant at €1.00 = US$1.10 throughout 2021. L. Straeten (a U.S. citizen) lives and works in Belgium. In 2021, Straeten earned income in Belgium of €200,000 and paid taxes to the local government at the rate of 50 percent. Straeten qualifies for the foreign earned income exclusion.

Required:
a. Determine the amount of foreign earned income Straeten included in the calculation of U.S. taxable income for the year 2021.
b. Determine the amount of foreign tax credit Straeten was allowed to take in determining U.S. tax liability for the year 2021.
c. Assuming Straeten has a marginal U.S. income tax rate of 28 percent, determine the amount of U.S. income taxes Straeten paid on foreign earned income in the year 2021.

Case 8-1

Worldwide United Corporation

Worldwide United Corporation (WUC), a U.S. taxpayer, manufactures and sells products through a network of foreign branches and wholly owned foreign subsidiaries. Relevant information for these entities for the current fiscal year appears in the following table:

Entity	Country	Legal Form	Activity	Income Before Tax	Income Tax Rate	Dividend Withholding Tax Rate	Net Dividend Received by Parent
A	Bahrain	Branch	Sales	$ 1,000,000	0%	0%	$ 1,000,000
B	Bermuda	Corporation	Sales	8,000,000	0	0	8,000,000
C	Hong Kong	Corporation	Manufacturing	10,000,000	16.5	0	8,350,000
D	Hungary	Corporation	Sales	10,000,000	9	0	9,100,000
E	Ireland	Corporation	Investment	2,000,000	12.5	0	1,750,000
F	Malaysia	Branch	Manufacturing	10,000,000	24	0	7,600,000
G	Mexico	Corporation	Manufacturing	5,000,000	30	10	3,3250,000
H	Switzerland	Corporation	Service	500,000	14.93	35	269,750

Additional Information:

1. Entities C, F, and G manufacture products that are sold in their home countries as well as to related entities within the WUC group.

2. Entity A purchases finished products from Entity F and then sells them throughout the Middle East. Only 5 percent of A's income is generated from sales to customers in Bahrain; 95 percent of A's income is from sales to foreign customers.

3. Entity B purchases finished products from Entity G and sells them throughout North and South America. Only 1 percent of B's income is from sales to customers in Bermuda; 99 percent of B's income is from sales to foreign customers.

4. Entity D purchases finished products from Entity C and then sells them throughout Europe. Only 40 percent of D's income is generated from sales to customers in Hungary; 60 percent of D's income is from sales to foreign customers.

5. Entity E makes passive investments in stocks and bonds in European financial markets. All of E's income is derived from dividends and interest.

6. Entity H provides accounting and other management services to WUC's other foreign operations. All of H's income is derived from providing services to related companies within the WUC group.

Required:

1. Determine the amount of U.S. taxable income for each entity (A, B, C, D, E, F, G, and H).

2. Calculate the foreign tax credit allowed in the United States, first by foreign tax credit basket and then in total.

3. Determine the net U.S. tax liability on foreign source income.

4. Determine any excess foreign tax credits and identify by basket.

Chapter Nine

International Transfer Pricing

Learning Objectives

After reading this chapter, you should be able to:

- Describe the importance of transfer pricing in achieving goal congruence in decentralized organizations.
- Explain how the objectives of performance evaluation and cost minimization can conflict in determining international transfer prices.
- Show how discretionary transfer pricing can be used to achieve specific cost minimization objectives.
- Describe governments' reaction to the use of discretionary transfer pricing by multinational companies.
- Discuss the transfer pricing methods used in sales of tangible property.
- Explain how advance pricing agreements can be used to create certainty in transfer pricing.
- Describe worldwide efforts to enforce transfer pricing regulations.

INTRODUCTION

Transfer pricing refers to the determination of the price at which transactions between related parties will be carried out. Transfers can be from a subsidiary to its parent (upstream), from the parent to a subsidiary (downstream), or from one subsidiary to another of the same parent. Transfers between related parties are also known as *intercompany transactions*. Intercompany transactions represent a significant portion of international trade. In 2020, intercompany transactions comprised 42.6 percent of U.S. total goods trade: $1,119 billion (48 percent) of the $2,336 billion in U.S. imports, and $484 billion (34 percent) of the $1,425 billion in U.S. exports.[1] As shown in Exhibit 9.1, there are many types of intercompany transactions and each transaction type has a price associated with it. The basic question that must be addressed is, At what price should intercompany transfers be made? This chapter focuses on international transfers, that is, intercompany transactions that cross national borders.

Two factors heavily influence the manner in which international transfer prices are determined. The first is the objective that headquarters management wishes to achieve through

---

[1] U.S. Department of Commerce, "U.S. Goods Trade: Imports and Exports by Related Parties, 2020," *U.S. Census Bureau News,* September 2, 2021, p. 1, available at https://www.census.gov/foreign-trade /Press-Release/related_party/rp20.pdf (accessed February 15, 2022).

EXHIBIT 9.1
Types of Intercompany Transactions and Their Associated Prices

Transaction	Price
Sale of tangible property (e.g., raw materials, finished goods, equipment, buildings)	Sales price
Use of tangible property (leases) (e.g., land, buildings)	Rental or lease payment
Use of intangible property (e.g., patents, trademarks, copyrights)	Royalty, licensing fee
Intercompany services (e.g., research and development, management assistance)	Service charge, management fee
Intercompany loans	Interest rate

its transfer pricing practices. One possible objective relates to management control and performance evaluation. Another objective relates to the minimization of one or more types of costs. These two types of objectives often conflict.

The second factor affecting international transfer pricing is the law governing the manner in which intercompany transactions that cross borders may be priced. These laws have been established in most countries to make sure that multinational corporations (MNCs) are not able to avoid paying their fair share of taxes, import duties, and so on by virtue of the fact that they operate in multiple jurisdictions. In establishing international transfer prices, MNCs often must walk a fine line between achieving corporate objectives and complying with applicable rules and regulations. In a recent survey, 78 percent of companies identified tax risk as the most critical issue driving transfer pricing policies, and 80 percent indicated having experienced government challenges to their transfer pricing in the prior three years.[2]

We begin this chapter with a discussion of management accounting theory with respect to transfer pricing. We then describe various objectives that MNCs might wish to achieve through discretionary transfer pricing. Much of this chapter focuses on government response to MNCs' discretionary transfer pricing practices, emphasizing the transfer pricing regulations in the United States.

DECENTRALIZATION AND GOAL CONGRUENCE

Business enterprises often are organized by *division*. A division may be a profit center, responsible for revenues and operating expenses, or an investment center, responsible also for assets. In a company organized by division, top managers delegate or decentralize authority and responsibility to division managers. *Decentralization* has several advantages. Local managers are able to make decisions quickly, and tend to be more motivated that if they are asked to simply follow orders from top managers. Top managers, on the other hand, can focus on companywide, strategic issues.

However, decentralization is not without its potential disadvantages. The most important pitfall is that local managers who have been granted decision-making authority may make decisions that are in their self-interest but detrimental to the company as a whole. The corporate accounting and control system should be designed in such a way that it provides incentives for local managers to make decisions that are consistent with corporate goals. This is known as *goal congruence*. The system used for evaluating the performance of decentralized managers is an important component in achieving goal congruence.

[2] Ernst & Young, *2021 Transfer Pricing and International Tax Survey,* p. 3, available at https://www.ey.com/en_be/tax/how-leaning-into-transfer-pricing-transformation-helps-manage-tax-risk (accessed February 15, 2022).

The price at which an intercompany transfer is made determines the level of revenue generated by the seller, becomes a cost for the buyer, and therefore affects the operating profit and performance measurement of both related parties. Appropriate transfer prices can ensure that each division or subsidiary's profit accurately reflects its contribution to overall company profits, thus providing a basis for efficient allocation of resources. To achieve this, transfer prices should motivate local managers to make decisions that enhance corporate performance, while at the same time providing a basis for measuring, evaluating, and rewarding local manager performance in a way that managers perceive as fair.[3] If this does not happen (i.e., if goal congruence is not achieved), then the potential benefits of decentralization can be lost.

Even in a purely domestic context, determining a transfer pricing policy is a complex matter for multidivision organizations, which often try to achieve several objectives through such policies. For example, they may try to use transfer pricing to ensure that it is consistent with the criteria used for performance evaluation, to motivate divisional managers, to achieve goal congruence, and to help manage cash flows. For MNCs, there are additional factors that influence international transfer pricing policy.

TRANSFER PRICING METHODS

The methods used in setting transfer prices in an international context are essentially the same as those used in a purely domestic context. The following three methods are commonly used:

1. *Cost-based transfer price.* The transfer price is based on the cost to produce a good or service. Cost can be determined as variable production cost, variable plus fixed production cost, or full cost, based on either actual or budgeted amounts (standard costs). The transfer price often includes a profit margin for the seller (a "cost-plus" price). Cost-based systems are simple to use, but there are at least two problems associated with them. The first problem relates to the issue of which measure of cost to use. The other problem is that inefficiencies in one unit may be transferred to other units, as there is no incentive for selling divisions to control costs. The use of standard, rather than actual, costs alleviates this problem.

2. *Market-based transfer price.* The transfer price charged a related party is either based on the price that would be charged to an unrelated customer or determined by reference to sales of similar products or services by other companies to unrelated parties. Market-based systems avoid transferring the inefficiencies of one division or subsidiary to others, which is a problem associated with cost-based systems. They help ensure divisional autonomy and provide a good basis for evaluating subsidiary performance. However, market-based pricing systems also have problems. The efficient working of a market-based system depends on the existence of competitive markets and dependable market quotations. For certain items, such as unfinished products, there may not be any buyers outside the organization and hence no external market price.

3. *Negotiated price.* The transfer price is the result of negotiation between buyer and seller and may be unrelated to either cost or market value. A negotiated pricing system can be useful, as it allows subsidiary managers the freedom to bargain with one another, thereby preserving the autonomy of subsidiary managers. However, for this system to work efficiently, it is important that there are external markets for the items being transferred so that the negotiating parties can have objective information as the basis for negotiation.

[3] Robert G. Eccles, *The Transfer Pricing Problem: A Theory for Practice* (Lexington, MA: Lexington Books, 1985), p. 8.

One disadvantage of negotiated pricing is that negotiation can take a long time, particularly if the process deteriorates and the parties involved become more interested in winning arguments than in considering the issues from the corporate perspective. Another disadvantage is that the price agreed on, and therefore a manager's measure of performance, may be more a function of a manager's ability to negotiate than of his or her ability to control costs and generate profit.

Management accounting theory suggests that different pricing methods are appropriate in different situations. Market-based transfer prices lead to optimal decisions when (1) the market for the product is perfectly competitive, (2) interdependencies between the related parties are minimal, and (3) there is no advantage or disadvantage to buying and selling the product internally rather than externally.[4] Prices based on full cost can approximate market-based prices when the determination of market price is not feasible. Prices that have been negotiated by buyer and seller rather than being mandated by upper management have the advantage of allowing the related parties to maintain their decentralized authority.

A 1990 survey of *Fortune* 500 companies in the United States found that 41 percent of respondent companies relied on cost-based methods in determining international transfer prices, 46 percent used market-based methods, and 13 percent allowed transfer prices to be determined through negotiation.[5] The most widely used approach was full production cost plus a markup. Slightly less than half of the respondents reported using more than one method to determine transfer prices.

OBJECTIVES OF INTERNATIONAL TRANSFER PRICING

Broadly speaking, there are two possible objectives to consider in determining the appropriate price at which an intercompany transfer that crosses national borders should be made: (1) performance evaluation and (2) cost minimization.

Performance Evaluation

To fairly evaluate the performance of both parties to an intercompany transaction, the transfer should be made at a price acceptable to both parties. An acceptable price could be determined by reference to outside market prices (e.g., the price that would be paid to an outside supplier for a component part), or it could be determined by allowing the two parties to the transaction to negotiate a price. Policies for establishing prices for domestic transfers generally should be based on objectives that generate reasonable measures for evaluating performance; otherwise, dysfunctional manager behavior can occur and goal congruence will not exist. For example, forcing the manager of one operating unit to purchase parts from a related operating unit at a price that exceeds the external market price will probably result in an unhappy manager. As a result of the additional cost, the unit's profit will be less than it otherwise would be, perhaps less than budgeted, and the manager's salary increase and annual bonus may be adversely affected. In addition, as upper management makes corporate resource allocation decisions, fewer resources may be allocated to this unit because of its lower reported profitability.

Assume that Alpha Company (a manufacturer) and Beta Company (a retailer) are both subsidiaries of Parent Company, located in the United States. Alpha produces DVD players at a cost of $100 each and sells them both to Beta and to unrelated customers. Beta purchases DVD players from Alpha and from unrelated suppliers and sells them for $160 each. The total gross profit earned by both producer and retailer is $60 per DVD player.

[4] Charles T. Horngren, Srikant M. Datar, George Foster, Madhav Ragan, and Christopher Ittner, *Cost Accounting: A Managerial Emphasis,* 13th ed. (Upper Saddle River, NJ: Prentice Hall, 2009), p. 776.

[5] Roger Y. W. Tang, "Transfer Pricing in the 1990s," *Management Accounting,* February 1992, pp. 22–26.

Alpha Company can sell DVD players to unrelated customers for $127.50 per unit, and Beta Company can purchase DVD players from unrelated suppliers at $132.50. The manager of Alpha should be happy selling DVD players to Beta for $127.50 per unit or more, and the manager of Beta should be happy purchasing DVD players from Alpha for $132.50 per unit or less. A transfer price somewhere between $127.50 and $132.50 per unit would be acceptable to both managers, as well as to Parent Company. Assuming that a transfer price of $130.00 per unit is agreed on by the managers of Alpha and Beta, the impact on income for Alpha Company, Beta Company, and Parent Company (after eliminating the intercompany transaction) is as follows:

	Alpha	Beta	Parent
Sales	$130.00	$160.00	$160.00
Cost of goods sold	100.00	130.00	100.00
Gross profit.	$ 30.00	$ 30.00	$ 60.00
Income tax effect.	6.30 (21%)	6.30 (21%)	12.60
After-tax profit	$ 23.70	$ 23.70	$ 47.40

Now assume that Alpha Company is located in Taiwan and Beta Company is located in the United States. Because the income tax rate in Taiwan is only 17 percent, compared with a U.S. income tax rate of 21 percent, Parent Company would like as much of the $60.00 gross profit to be earned by Alpha as possible. Rather than allowing the two managers to negotiate a price based on external market values, assume that Parent Company intervenes and establishes a "discretionary" transfer price of $150.00 per unit.[6] Given this price, the impact of the intercompany transaction on income for the three companies is as follows:

	Alpha	Beta	Parent
Sales.	$150.00	$160.00	$160.00
Cost of goods sold	100.00	150.00	100.00
Gross profit.	$ 50.00	$ 10.00	$ 60.00
Income tax effect	8.50 (17%)	2.10 (21%)	10.60
After-tax profit.	$ 41.50	$ 7.90	$ 49.40

The chief executive officer of Parent Company is pleased with this result, because consolidated income for Parent Company increases by $2.00 per unit, as will cash flow when Alpha Company and Beta Company remit their after-tax profits to Parent Company as dividends. The president of Alpha Company is also happy with this transfer price. As is true for all managers in the organization, a portion of the president's compensation is linked to profit, and this use of discretionary transfer pricing will result in a nice bonus for her at year-end. However, the president of Beta Company is less than pleased with this situation. His profit is less than if he were allowed to purchase from unrelated suppliers. He doubts he will receive a bonus for the year, and he is beginning to think about seeking employment

---

[6] The price is "discretionary" in the sense that it is not based on market value, cost, or negotiation, but has been determined at Parent's discretion to reduce income taxes.

elsewhere. Moreover, Beta Company's profit clearly is understated, which could lead top managers to make erroneous decisions with respect to Beta.

Cost Minimization

When intercompany transactions cross national borders, differences between countries might lead an MNC to attempt to achieve certain cost-minimization objectives through the use of discretionary transfer prices mandated by headquarters.

The most well-known use of discretionary transfer pricing is to minimize worldwide income taxes by recording profits in lower-tax countries. As illustrated in the preceding example, this objective can be achieved by establishing an arbitrarily high price when transferring to a higher-tax country. Conversely, this objective is also met by selling at a low price when transferring to a lower-tax country.

Conflicting Objectives

There is an inherent conflict between the performance evaluation and cost-minimization objectives of transfer pricing. To minimize costs, top managers must *dictate* a discretionary transfer price. By definition, this is not a price that has been negotiated by the two managers who are party to the transaction, nor is it necessarily based on external market prices or production costs. The benefits of decentralization can evaporate when headquarters managers assume responsibility for determining transfer prices.

One way that companies deal with this conflict is through *dual pricing.* The official records for tax and financial reporting are based on the cost-minimizing transfer prices. When it comes time to evaluate performance, however, the actual records are adjusted to reflect prices acceptable to both parties to the transaction, factoring out the effect of discretionary transfer prices. Actual transfers are invoiced so as to minimize costs, but evaluation of performance is based on simulated prices.

Other Cost-Minimization Objectives

In addition to the objective of minimizing worldwide income taxes, a number of other objectives can be achieved through the use of discretionary transfer prices for international transactions.

Avoidance of Withholding Taxes

A parent company might want to avoid receiving cash payments from its foreign subsidiaries in the form of dividends, interest, and royalties on which withholding taxes will be paid to the foreign government. Instead, cash can be transferred in the form of the sales price for goods and services provided to the foreign subsidiary by its parent or other affiliates. There is no withholding tax on payments for purchases of goods and services. The higher the price charged the foreign subsidiary, the more cash can be extracted from the foreign country without incurring withholding tax. For example, assume that the European subsidiary of Ansel Corporation purchases finished goods from its foreign parent at a price of €100 per unit; sells those goods in the local market at a price of €130 per unit; and remits 100 percent of its profit to the parent company, upon which it pays a 30 percent dividend withholding tax. Ignoring income taxes, the total cash flow received by Ansel Corporation from its European subsidiary is €121 per unit: €100 from the sale of finished goods and €21 (€30 −[€30 × 30%]) in the form of dividends after withholding tax. If Ansel Corporation were to raise the selling price to its European subsidiary to €120 per unit, the total cash flow it would receive would increase to €127 per unit: €120 in the form of the transfer price plus €7 (€10 −[€10 × 30%]) in net dividends. Raising the transfer price even further to €130 per unit results in cash flow to Ansel Corporation of €130 per unit.

Selling goods and services to a foreign subsidiary (downstream sale) at a higher price reduces the amount of profit earned by the foreign subsidiary that will be subject to a dividend withholding tax. Sales of goods and services by the foreign subsidiary to its parent (upstream sale) at a lower price will achieve the same objective.

Minimization of Import Duties (Tariffs)

Countries generally assess tariffs on the value (based on invoice prices) of goods being imported into the country. These are known as ad valorem import duties. One way to reduce ad valorem import duties is to transfer goods to a foreign operation at lower prices.

Circumvention of Profit Repatriation Restrictions

Some countries restrict the amount of profit that can be paid as a dividend to a foreign parent company. This is known as a profit repatriation restriction. A company might be restricted to paying a dividend equal to or less than a certain percentage of annual profit or a certain percentage of capital contributed to the company by its parent. When such restrictions exist, the parent can get around the restriction and remove "profit" indirectly by setting high transfer prices on goods and services provided to the foreign operation by the parent and other affiliates. This strategy is consistent with the objective of avoiding withholding taxes.

Protection of Cash Flows from Currency Devaluation

In many cases, some amount of the net cash flow generated by a subsidiary in a foreign country will be moved out of that country, if for no other reason than to distribute it as a dividend to stockholders of the parent company. As the foreign currency devalues, the parent currency value of any foreign currency cash decreases. For operations located in countries whose currency is prone to devaluation, the parent may want to accelerate the removal of cash from that country before more devaluation occurs. One method for moving more cash out of a country is to set high transfer prices for goods and services provided to the foreign operation by the parent and other related companies.

Improvement of the Foreign Operation's Competitive Position

MNCs also are able to use international transfer pricing to maintain competitiveness in international markets and to penetrate new foreign markets. To penetrate a new market, a parent company might establish a sales subsidiary in a foreign country. To capture market share, the foreign operation must compete aggressively on price, providing its customers with significant discounts. To ensure that the new operation is profitable, while at the same time expecting it to compete on price, the parent company can sell finished goods to its foreign sales subsidiary at low prices. In effect, the parent company absorbs the discount.

The parent company might want to improve the credit status of a foreign operation so that it can obtain local financing at lower interest rates. This generally involves improving the balance sheet by increasing assets and retained earnings. This objective can be achieved by setting low transfer prices for inbound goods to the foreign operation and high transfer prices for outbound goods from the foreign operation, thereby improving profit and cash flow.

Exhibit 9.2 summarizes the transfer price (high or low) needed to achieve various cost-minimization objectives. High transfer prices can be used to (1) minimize worldwide income taxes when transferring to a higher-tax country, (2) reduce withholding taxes (downstream sales), (3) circumvent repatriation restrictions, and (4) protect foreign currency cash from devaluation. However, low transfer prices are necessary to (1) minimize worldwide income taxes when transferring to a lower-tax country, (2) reduce withholding taxes (upstream sales), (3) minimize import duties, and (4) improve the competitive position of a foreign operation.

EXHIBIT 9.2
Cost-Minimization
Objectives and Transfer
Prices

Objective	Transfer Pricing Rule
Minimize income taxes	
Transferring to a country with higher tax rate	High price
Transferring to a country with lower tax rate	Low price
Minimize withholding taxes	
Downstream transfer	High price
Upstream transfer	Low price
Minimize import duties	Low price
Protect foreign cash flows from currency devaluation	High price
Avoid repatriation restrictions	High price
Improve competitive position of foreign operation	Low price

It should be noted that these different cost-minimization objectives might conflict with one another. For example, charging a higher transfer price to a foreign affiliate to reduce the amount of withholding taxes paid to the foreign government will result in a higher amount of import duties paid to the foreign government. Companies can employ linear programming techniques to determine the optimum transfer price when two or more cost-minimization objectives exist. Electronic spreadsheets also can be used to conduct sensitivity analysis, examining the impact of different transfer prices on consolidated profit and cash flows.

Interaction of Transfer Pricing Method and Objectives

In a study published in 2004, Professors Chan and Lo hypothesized that MNCs would prefer either a cost-based or a market-based transfer pricing method, depending on the importance of specific environmental variables that affect transfer pricing:[7]

1. Cost-based methods of determining transfer prices are preferred when the following variables are important:

   - Differences in income tax rates.
   - Minimization of import duties.
   - Foreign exchange controls and risks.
   - Restrictions on profit repatriation.
   - Risk of expropriation and nationalization.

2. Market-based methods of determining transfer prices are preferred when the following variables are important:

   - Interests of local partners.
   - Good relationship with local government.

Chan and Lo tested these hypotheses by conducting interviews with managers of MNCs (U.S., Japanese, and European) with operations in China. They found support for their hypotheses related to foreign exchange controls and risks, interests of local partners, and relationship with the local government. Local partners find market-based methods to be more fair and objective, and these methods also are easier to defend in disputes with the government. Cost-based methods afford more flexibility in circumventing foreign exchange controls. The other environmental variables (including differences in income tax rates and repatriation restrictions) were not important in deciding upon a transfer pricing method.

---

[7] K. Hung Chan and Agnes W. Y. Lo, "The Influence of Managerial Perception of Environmental Variables on the Choice of International Transfer-Pricing Methods," *International Journal of Accounting* 39, Issue 1 (2004), pp. 93–110.

GOVERNMENT REACTIONS

National tax authorities are aware of the potential for MNCs to use discretionary transfer pricing to avoid paying income taxes, import duties, and so on. Most countries have guidelines regarding what will be considered an acceptable transfer price for tax purposes. Across countries, these guidelines can conflict, creating the possibility of double taxation when a price accepted by one country is disallowed by another.

OECD Guidelines

The Organization for Economic Cooperation and Development (OECD) developed transfer pricing guidelines in 1979 that have been supplemented or amended several times since then. The basic rule is that transfers must be made at *arm's-length prices,* that is, prices that would be charged between independent parties in the same circumstances. The guidelines also acknowledge the need for companies to document the arm's-length nature of their transfer prices. The idea is that, by adopting the OECD guidelines, member countries will thereby avoid conflicts. The OECD rules are only a model and do not have the force of law in any country. However, most developed countries have transfer pricing rules generally based on OECD guidelines with some variations. The next section of this chapter discusses the specific transfer pricing rules adopted in the United States, which are broadly consistent with OECD guidelines. Although the rules we discuss are specific to the United States, similar rules can be found in many other countries.

OECD Country-by-Country Reporting

The OECD's Base Erosion and Profit Shifting (BEPS) project was introduced in the previous chapter. In addition to creating a multilateral tax convention to combat treaty shopping (Action 15), the BEPS project includes Action 13, "Transfer Pricing Documentation and Country-by-Country Reporting," which provides a template for country-by-country (CbC) reporting by multinational enterprises (MNEs). CbC reporting is intended to provide tax authorities with information that can be used to identify situations in which companies have the capability of shifting profit to a low- or no-tax jurisdiction. This will assist tax authorities in targeting their audits and building cases against MNEs involved in profit shifting.

Action 13 requires an MNE to annually file a CbC Report with its home taxing authority that discloses, for each jurisdiction in which it conducts business, its amount of revenue, before-tax profit, income tax paid, number of employees, capital, and tangible assets. In addition, each entity within a jurisdiction must be described separately, with an indication of its business activities. By early 2021, a total of 83 countries had implemented CbC Reporting requirements, including European Union nations, Canada, Mexico, the United States, China, Japan, and Russia.[8]

U.S. TRANSFER PRICING RULES

Understanding U.S. transfer pricing rules is important for both U.S. and non-U.S. business enterprises and tax practitioners for two reasons. First, most MNCs either are headquartered in or have significant business activities in the United States. Second, the transfer pricing reforms that took place in the United States in the 1990s have influenced changes in transfer pricing regulation in many other countries.

---

[8] KPMG, "BEPS Action 13: Country Implementation Summary," March 12, 2021, available at https://home.kpmg/us/en/home/insights/2016/09/tnf-beps-action-13-latest-country-implementation.html (accessed March 1, 2022).

Section 482 of the U.S. Internal Revenue Code gives the Internal Revenue Service (IRS) the authority to audit international transfer prices and adjust a company's tax liability if the price is deemed to be inappropriate. The IRS may audit and adjust transfer prices between companies controlled directly or indirectly by the same taxpayer. Thus, Section 482 applies to both upstream and downstream transfers between a U.S. parent and its foreign subsidiary, between a foreign parent and its U.S. subsidiary, or between the U.S. subsidiary and foreign subsidiary of the same parent. The IRS, of course, is primarily concerned that a proper amount of income is being recorded and taxed in the United States.

Similar to the OECD guidelines, Section 482 requires transactions between commonly controlled entities to be carried out at arm's-length prices. Arm's-length prices are prices that would be agreed to by unrelated parties for the same or similar transactions under similar conditions. Because same or similar transactions with unrelated parties often do not exist, determination of an arm's-length price generally will involve reference to comparable transactions under comparable circumstances.

The U.S. Treasury Regulations supplementing Section 482 establish more specific guidelines for determining an arm's-length price. In general, a "best-method rule" requires taxpayers to use the transfer pricing method that under the facts and circumstances provides the most reliable measure of an arm's-length price. There is no hierarchy in application of methods, and no method always will be considered more reliable than others. In determining which method provides the most reliable measure of an arm's-length price, the two primary factors to be considered are (1) the degree of comparability between the intercompany transaction and any comparable uncontrolled transactions, and (2) the quality of the data and assumptions used in the analysis. Determining the degree of comparability between an intercompany transaction and an uncontrolled transaction involves a comparison of the five factors listed in Exhibit 9.3. Each of these factors must be considered in determining the degree of comparability between an intercompany transaction and an uncontrolled transaction and the extent to which adjustments must be made to establish an arm's-length price.

Treasury Regulations establish guidelines for determining an arm's-length price for various kinds of intercompany transactions, including sales of tangible property, licensing of intangible property, intercompany loans, and intercompany services. Because it is the most common type of international intercompany transaction, we focus on regulations related to the sale of tangible property; however, we also describe regulations related to licensing of intangible assets, intercompany loans, and intercompany services.

Sale of Tangible Property

Treasury Regulations require the use of one of five specified methods to determine the arm's-length price in a sale of tangible property (inventory and fixed assets):

1. Comparable uncontrolled price method.
2. Resale price method.
3. Cost-plus method.
4. Comparable profits method.
5. Profit split method.

If none of these methods is determined to be appropriate, companies are allowed to use an unspecified method, provided its use can be justified.

Comparable Uncontrolled Price Method

The *comparable uncontrolled price method* is generally considered to provide the most reliable measure of an arm's-length price when a comparable uncontrolled transaction exists.

EXHIBIT 9.3

Factors to Be Considered in Determining the Comparability of an Intercompany Transaction and an Uncontrolled Transaction

Source: U.S. Treasury Regulations, Sec. 1.482-1(d).

1. Functions performed by the various parties in the two transactions, including
   - Research and development.
   - Product design and engineering.
   - Manufacturing, production, and process engineering.
   - Product fabrication, extraction, and assembly.
   - Purchasing and materials management.
   - Marketing and distribution functions, including inventory management, warranty administration, and advertising activities.
   - Transportation and warehousing.
   - Managerial, legal, accounting and finance, credit and collection, training, and personnel management services.
2. Contractual terms that could affect the results of the two transactions, including
   - The form of consideration charged or paid.
   - Sales or purchase volume.
   - The scope and terms of warranties provided.
   - Rights to updates, revisions, and modifications.
   - The duration of relevant license, contract, or other agreement, and termination and negotiation rights.
   - Collateral transactions or ongoing business relationships between the buyer and seller, including arrangements for the provision of ancillary or subsidiary services.
   - Extension of credit and payment terms.
3. Risks that could affect the prices that would be charged or paid, or the profit that would be earned, in the two transactions, including
   - Market risks.
   - Risks associated with the success or failure of research and development activities.
   - Financial risks, including fluctuations in foreign currency rates of exchange and interest rates.
   - Credit and collection risk.
   - Product liability risk.
   - General business risks related to the ownership of property, plant, and equipment.
4. Economic conditions that could affect the price or profit earned in the two transactions, such as
   - The similarity of geographic markets.
   - The relative size of each market, and the extent of the overall economic development in each market.
   - The level of the market (e.g., wholesale, retail).
   - The relevant market shares for the products, properties, or services transferred or provided.
   - The location-specific costs of the factors of production and distribution.
   - The extent of competition in each market with regard to the property or services under review.
   - The economic condition of the particular industry, including whether the market is in contraction or expansion.
   - The alternatives realistically available to the buyer and seller.
5. Property or services transferred in the transactions, including any intangibles that are embedded in tangible property or services being transferred.

Assume that a U.S.-based parent company (Parentco) makes sales of tangible property to a foreign subsidiary (Subco). Under this method, the price for tax purposes is determined by reference to sales by Parentco of the same or similar product to unrelated customers, or purchases by Subco of the same or similar product from unrelated suppliers. Also, sales of the same product between two unrelated parties could be used to determine the transfer price.

To determine whether the comparable uncontrolled price method results in the most reliable measure of arm's-length price, a company must consider each of the factors listed in Exhibit 9.3. Section 1.482-3 of the Treasury Regulations indicates specific factors that may be particularly relevant in determining whether an uncontrolled transaction is comparable:

1. Quality of the product.
2. Contractual terms.
3. Level of the market.
4. Geographic market in which the transaction takes place.
5. Date of the transaction.
6. Intangible property associated with the sale.
7. Foreign currency risks.
8. Alternatives realistically available to the buyer and seller.

If the uncontrolled transaction is not exactly comparable, some adjustment to the uncontrolled price is permitted in order to make the transactions more comparable. For example, assume that Sorensen Company, a U.S. manufacturer, sells the same product to both controlled and uncontrolled distributors in Mexico. The price to uncontrolled distributors is $40 per unit. Sorensen affixes its trademark to the products sold to its Mexican subsidiary but not to the products sold to the uncontrolled distributor. The trademark is considered to add approximately $10 of value to the product. The transactions are not strictly comparable because the products sold to the controlled and uncontrolled parties are different (one has a trademark and the other does not). Adjusting the uncontrolled price of $40 by $10 would result in a more comparable price, and $50 would be an acceptable transfer price under the comparable uncontrolled price method. If the value of the trademark could not be reasonably determined, the comparable uncontrolled price method might not result in the most reliable arm's-length price in this scenario.

Resale Price Method

The *resale price method* determines the transfer price by subtracting an appropriate gross profit from the price at which the controlled buyer resells the tangible property. In order to use this method, a company must know *the final selling price to uncontrolled parties* and be able to determine *an appropriate gross profit for the reseller.* An appropriate gross profit is determined by reference to the gross profit margin earned in comparable uncontrolled transactions. For example, assume that Odom Company manufactures and sells automobile batteries to its Canadian affiliate, which in turn sells the batteries to local retailers at a resale price of $50 per unit. Other Canadian distributors of automobile batteries earn an average gross profit margin of 25 percent on similar sales. Applying the resale price method, Odom Company would establish an arm's-length price of $37.50 per unit for its sale of batteries to its Canadian affiliate (resale price of $50 less an appropriate gross profit of $12.50 [25 percent] to be earned by the Canadian affiliate).

In determining an appropriate gross profit, the degree of comparability between the sale made by the Canadian affiliate and sales made by uncontrolled Canadian distributors need not be as great as under the comparable uncontrolled price method. The decisive factor is the similarity of functions performed by the affiliate and uncontrolled distributors in making sales. For example, if the functions performed by the Canadian affiliate in selling batteries are similar to the functions performed by Canadian distributors of automobile parts in general, the company could use the gross profit earned by uncontrolled sellers of automobile parts in Canada in determining an acceptable transfer price. Other important factors affecting comparability might include the following:

- Inventory levels and turnover rates.
- Contractual terms (e.g., warranties, sales volume, credit terms, transport terms).
- Sales, marketing, and advertising programs and services, including promotional programs and rebates.
- Level of the market (e.g., wholesale, retail).

The resale price method is typically used when the buyer/reseller is merely a distributor of finished goods—a so-called sales subsidiary. The method is acceptable only when the buyer/reseller does not add a substantial amount of value to the product. The resale price method is not feasible in cases where the reseller adds substantial value to the goods or where the goods become part of a larger product, because there is no "final selling price to uncontrolled parties" for the goods that were transferred. Continuing with our example, if Odom Company's Canadian affiliate operates an auto assembly plant and places the batteries purchased from Odom in automobiles that are then sold for $20,000 per unit, the company cannot use the resale price method for determining an appropriate transfer price for the batteries.

Cost-Plus Method

The *cost-plus method* is most appropriate when there are no comparable uncontrolled sales and the related buyer does more than simply distribute the goods it purchases. Whereas the resale price method subtracts an appropriate gross profit from the resale price to establish the transfer price, the cost-plus method adds an appropriate gross profit to the cost of producing a product to establish an arm's-length price. This method is normally used in cases involving manufacturing, assembly, or other production of goods that are sold to related parties. Once again, the appropriate gross profit markup is determined by reference to comparable uncontrolled transactions. Physical similarity between the products transferred is not as important in determining comparability under this method as it is under the comparable uncontrolled price method. Factors to be included in determining whether an uncontrolled transaction is comparable include similarity of functions performed, risks borne, and contractual terms. Factors that may be particularly relevant in determining comparability under this method include the following:

- Complexity of the manufacturing or assembly process.
- Manufacturing, production, and process engineering.
- Procurement, purchasing, and inventory control activities.
- Testing functions.

To illustrate use of the cost-plus method, assume that Pruitt Company has a subsidiary in Taiwan that acquires materials locally to produce an electronic component. The component, which costs $4 per unit to produce, is sold only to Pruitt Company. Because the Taiwanese subsidiary does not sell this component to other, unrelated parties, the comparable uncontrolled price method is not applicable. Pruitt Company combines the electronic component imported from Taiwan with other parts to assemble electronic switches that are sold in the United States. Because Pruitt does not simply resell the electronic components in the United States, the resale price method also is not applicable. Therefore, Pruitt must look for a comparable transaction between unrelated parties in Taiwan to determine whether the cost-plus method can be used. Assume that an otherwise comparable company in Taiwan manufactures similar electronic components from its inventory of materials and sells them to unrelated buyers at an average gross profit markup on cost of 25 percent. In this case, application of the cost-plus method results in a transfer price of $5 ($4 + [$4 × 25%]) for the electronic component that Pruitt purchases from its Taiwanese subsidiary.

Now assume that Pruitt's Taiwanese subsidiary manufactures electronic components using materials provided by Pruitt on a consignment basis. To apply the cost-plus method, Pruitt would have to make a downward adjustment to the otherwise comparable gross profit markup of 25 percent, because the inventory risk assumed by the manufacturer in the comparable transaction justifies a higher gross profit markup than is appropriate for Pruitt's foreign subsidiary. If Pruitt cannot reasonably ascertain the effect of inventory procurement and handling on gross profit, the cost-plus method might not result in a reliable transfer price.

Comparable Profits Method

The *comparable profits method* is based on the assumption that similarly situated taxpayers will tend to earn similar returns over a given period.[9] Under this method, one of the two parties in a related transaction is chosen for examination. An arm's-length price is determined by referring to an objective measure of profitability earned by uncontrolled taxpayers on comparable, uncontrolled sales. Profit indicators that might be considered in applying this method include the ratio of operating income to operating assets, the ratio of gross profit to operating expenses, or the ratio of operating profit to sales. If the transfer price used results in ratios for the party being examined that are in line with those ratios for similar businesses, then the transfer price will not be challenged.

To demonstrate the comparable profits method, assume that Glassco, a U.S. manufacturer, distributes its products in a foreign country through its foreign sales subsidiary, Vidroco. Assume that Vidroco has sales of $1,000,000 and operating expenses (other than cost of goods sold) of $200,000. Over the past several years, comparable distributors in the foreign country have earned operating profits equal to 5 percent of sales. Under the comparable profits method, a transfer price that provides Vidroco an operating profit equal to 5 percent of sales would be considered arm's length. An acceptable operating profit for Vidroco is $50,000 ($1,000,000 × 5%). To achieve this amount of operating profit, cost of goods sold must be $750,000 ($1,000,000 − $200,000 − $50,000); this is the amount that Glassco would be allowed to charge as a transfer price for its sales to Vidroco. This example demonstrates use of the ratio of operating profit to sales as the profit-level indicator under the comparable profits method. The Treasury Regulations also specifically mention use of the ratio of operating profit to operating assets and the ratio of gross profit to operating expenses as acceptable profit-level indicators in applying this method.

Profit Split Method

The *profit split method* assumes that the buyer and seller are one economic unit.[10] The total profit earned by the economic unit from sales to uncontrolled parties is allocated to the members of the economic unit based on their relative contributions in earning the profit. The relative value of each party's contribution in earning the profit is based on the functions performed, the risks assumed, and the resources employed in the business activity that generates the profit. There are in fact two versions of the profit split method: (1) the comparable profit split method and (2) the residual profit split method.

Under the *comparable profit split method,* the profit split between two related parties is determined through reference to the operating profit earned by each party in a comparable

---

[9] The comparable profits method is described in Treasury Regulations, Sec. 1.482-5.

[10] The profit split method is described in Treasury Regulations, Sec. 1.482-6.

uncontrolled transaction. Each of the factors listed in Exhibit 9.3 must be considered in determining the degree of comparability between the intercompany transaction and the comparable uncontrolled transaction. The degree of similarity in the contractual terms between the controlled and comparable uncontrolled transaction is especially critical in determining whether this is the "best method."

When controlled parties possess intangible assets that allow them to generate profits in excess of what is earned in otherwise comparable uncontrolled transactions, the *residual profit split method* should be used. Under this method, the combined profit is allocated to each of the controlled parties following a two-step process. In the first step, profit is allocated to each party to provide a market return for its routine contributions to the relevant business activity. This step will not allocate all of the combined profit earned by the controlled parties, because it will not include a return for the intangible assets that they possess. In the second step, the residual profit attributable to intangibles is allocated to each of the controlled parties on the basis of the relative value of intangibles that each contributes to the relevant business activity. The reliability of this method hinges on the ability to measure the value of the intangibles reliably.

The transfer pricing methods allowed for tangible property transfers under U.S. regulations also are used in other countries. In a survey of 877 MNCs located in 25 different countries, Ernst & Young found the cost-plus method to be most commonly used (30 percent), followed by the comparable uncontrolled price method (27 percent), and the comparable profits method (23 percent). The resale price method (12 percent) and profit split method (3 percent) were not often used. Some MNCs indicated using other methods (6 percent).[11]

Licenses of Intangible Property

Treasury Regulations, Section 1.482-4, list six categories of intangible property. The first five categories of intangible include: patents, copyrights, trademarks, franchises, and methods. The sixth category includes any item that derives its value from its intellectual content or other intangible attribute, rather than from its physical properties.

Four methods are available for determining the arm's-length consideration for the license of intangible property:

- Comparable uncontrolled transaction method.
- Comparable profits method.
- Profit split method.
- Unspecified methods.

The comparable profits method and profit split method are the same methods as those available for establishing the transfer price on tangible property. The comparable uncontrolled transaction method is similar in concept to the comparable uncontrolled price method available for tangible property.

Comparable Uncontrolled Transaction (CUT) Method

The *comparable uncontrolled transaction (CUT) method* determines whether or not the amount a company charges a related party for the use of intangible property is an arm's-length price by referring to the amount it charges an unrelated party for the use of the intangible. Treasury Regulations indicate that if an uncontrolled transaction involves the license of the same intangible under the same (or substantially the same) circumstances as the controlled transaction, the results derived from applying the CUT method will generally be the most reliable measure of an arm's-length price.

---

[11] Ernst & Young, *2010 Global Transfer Pricing Survey,* p. 13, available at https://ub.unibas.ch/digi/a125 /sachdok/2011/BAU_1_005682903_2010.pdf (accessed September 16, 2022).

The controlled and uncontrolled transactions are substantially the same if there are only minor differences that have a measurable effect on the amount charged for use of the intangible. If an uncontrolled transaction that is substantially the same does not exist, an uncontrolled transaction that involves the transfer of a comparable intangible under comparable circumstances may be used in applying the CUT method.

In evaluating the comparability of an uncontrolled transaction, factors such as the terms of the transaction, the stage of development of the intangible, and the uniqueness of the intangible should be considered. Furthermore, differences in economic conditions also can affect comparability and therefore the appropriateness of the CUT method. For example, if a U.S. pharmaceutical company licenses a patented drug to an uncontrolled manufacturer in Country A and licenses the same drug under the same contractual terms to its subsidiary in Country B, the two transactions are not comparable if the potential market for the drug is higher in Country B because of a higher incidence of the disease the drug is intended to combat.

Comparable Profits Method

To demonstrate the comparable profits method for intangible assets, assume that Frameco (a U.S. taxpayer) develops a new material for eyeglass frames, for which it receives an international patent. Frameco licenses the patent to Taico, its wholly owned subsidiary in Taiwan. Taico uses the new material to manufacture eyeglass frames and sells them to eyeglass retailers for distribution in the United States. Assume that Taico has operating assets of $30 million, sales of $40 million, pays a royalty on the licensed patent to Frameco of $2 million (5 percent of sales), and generates operating profit of $6 million. Assume further that Frameco's tax return is under audit, and the U.S. Internal Revenue Service (IRS) must determine whether the 5 percent royalty rate represents an arm's-length price.

The IRS determines that the comparable profits method will provide the best measure of an arm's-length price and selects Taico as the tested party because it engages in relatively routine manufacturing activities (whereas Frameco engages in a variety of more complex activities). In addition, the IRS determines that the ratio of operating profit to operating assets is the most appropriate profitability measure for applying the comparable profits method. The IRS samples uncontrolled foreign manufacturers of eyeglass frames and determines the average ratio of operating profit to operating assets is 15 percent. Applying this percentage to Taico's operating assets results in a comparable operating profit of $4.5 million ($30 million in operating assets × 15%). Therefore, the IRS adjusts the royalty that Taico pays to Frameco by $1.5 million (from $2 million to $3.5 million), which is the difference between Taico's reported profit of $6 million and the comparable operating profit of $4.5 million. Frameco's U.S. taxable income increases by $1.5 million.

Profit Split Method

Treasury Regulations provide the following example to demonstrate application of the residual profit split method to licensing intangibles. P, a U.S.-based company, manufactures and sells products for police use in the United States. P develops and obtains a patent for a bulletproof material, Nulon, for use in its protective clothing and headgear. P licenses its European subsidiary, S, to manufacture and sell Nulon in Europe. S has adapted P's products for military use and sells to European governments under brand names that S has developed and owns. S's revenues from the sale of Nulon in Year 1 are $500, and S's direct operating expenses (excluding royalties) are $300. The royalty the IRS will allow P to charge S for the license to produce Nulon is determined as follows:

1. The IRS determines that the operating assets used by S in producing Nulon are worth $200. From an examination of profit margins earned by other European companies performing similar functions, it determines that 10 percent is a fair market return on S's

operating assets. Of S's operating profit of $200 (sales of $500 less direct operating expenses of $300), the IRS determines that $20 ($200 × 10%) is attributable to S's operating assets. The remaining $180 is attributable to intangibles. In the second step, the IRS determines how much of this $180 is attributable to P's intangibles and how much is attributable to S's intangibles. The amount attributable to P's intangibles is the amount the IRS will allow P to charge S for the license to produce Nulon.

2. The IRS establishes that the market values of P and S's intangibles cannot be reliably determined. Therefore, it estimates the relative values of the intangibles from Year 1 expenditures on research, development, and marketing. P's research and development expenditures relate to P's worldwide activities, so the IRS allocates these expenditures to worldwide sales. By comparing these expenditures in Year 1 with worldwide sales in Year 1, the IRS determines that the contribution to worldwide gross profit made by P's intangibles is 20 percent of sales. In contrast, S's research, development, and marketing expenditures pertain to European sales, and the IRS determines that the contribution that S's intangibles make to S's gross profit is equal to 40 percent of sales. Thus, of the portion of S's gross profit that is not attributable to a return on S's operating assets, one-third (20%/60%) is attributable to P's intangibles and two-thirds is attributable to S's intangibles (40%/60%). Under the residual profit split method, P will charge S a license fee of $60 ($180 × $\frac{1}{3}$) in Year 1.

Intercompany Loans

When one member of a controlled group makes a loan to another member of the group, Section 482 of the U.S. Internal Revenue Code requires an arm's-length rate of interest to be charged on the loan. In determining an arm's-length interest rate, all relevant factors should be considered, including the principal and duration of the loan, the security involved, the credit standing of the borrower, and the interest rate prevailing for comparable loans between unrelated parties.

A safe harbor rule exists when the loan is denominated in U.S. dollars and the lender is not regularly engaged in the business of making loans to unrelated persons. Such would be the case, for example, if a U.S. manufacturing firm made a U.S.-dollar loan to its foreign subsidiary. In this situation, the stated interest rate is considered to be at arm's length if it is at a rate not less than the applicable federal rate (AFR) and not greater than 130 percent of the AFR. The AFR is based on the average interest rate on obligations of the federal government with similar maturity dates. The AFR is recomputed each month. Assuming an AFR of 4 percent on one-year obligations, the U.S. manufacturing firm could charge an interest rate anywhere from 4 to 5.2 percent on a one-year U.S.-dollar loan to its foreign subsidiary without having to worry about a transfer pricing adjustment being made by the IRS.

Intercompany Services

When one member of a controlled group provides a service to another member of the group, the purchaser must pay an arm's-length price to the service provider. If the services provided are incidental to the business activities of the service provider, the arm's-length price is equal to the direct and indirect costs incurred in connection with providing the service. There is no need to include a profit component in the price in this case. However, if the service provided is an "integral part" of the business function of the service provider, the price charged must include profit equal to what would be earned on similar services provided to an unrelated party. For example, assume that engineers employed by Brandlin Company travel to the Czech Republic to provide technical assistance to the company's Czech subsidiary in setting up a production facility. Brandlin must charge the foreign subsidiary a fee for this service equal to the direct and indirect costs incurred. Direct costs include the cost of the engineers' travel to the Czech Republic and their salaries while on the assignment. Indirect costs might include a portion of Brandlin's overhead costs allocated to the engineering department. If Brandlin is in the business of providing this type of service to unrelated parties, it must also include an appropriate amount of profit in the technical assistance fee it charges its Czech subsidiary.

No fee is required to be charged to a related party if the service performed on its behalf merely duplicates an activity the related party has performed itself. For example, assume that engineers employed by Brandlin's Czech subsidiary design the layout of the production facility themselves, and their plan is simply reviewed by Brandlin's U.S. engineers. In this case, the U.S. parent company need not charge the foreign subsidiary a fee for performing the review.

Arm's-Length Range

The IRS acknowledges that application of a specific transfer pricing method could result in a number of transfer prices, thereby creating an "arm's-length range" of prices. A company will not be subject to IRS adjustment so long as its transfer price falls within this range. For example, assume that Harrell Company determines the comparable uncontrolled price method to be the "best method" for purchases of Product X from its wholly owned Chinese subsidiary. Four comparable uncontrolled transactions are identified with prices of $9.50, $9.75, $10.00, and $10.50. Harrell Company can purchase Product X from its Chinese subsidiary at a price anywhere from $9.50 to $10.50 without the risk of an adjustment being made by the IRS. The company may wish to choose that price within the arm's-length range (either the highest price or the lowest price) that would allow it to achieve one or more cost-minimization objectives.

Correlative Relief

Determination of an arm's-length transfer price acceptable to the IRS is very important. If the IRS adjusts a transfer price in the United States, there is no guarantee that the foreign government at the other end of the transaction will reciprocate by providing a correlative adjustment. If the foreign government does not provide correlative relief, the total tax liability for the MNC increases. For example, assume that Usco Inc. manufactures a product for $10 per unit that is sold to its affiliate in Oman (Omanco) for $12 per unit. The Omani affiliate sells the product at $20 per unit in the local market. Assuming a U.S. tax rate of 21 percent and an Omani tax rate of 15 percent, the worldwide income tax paid on this sale would be $1.62 per unit, calculated as follows:

	Usco	Omanco
Sales	$ 12	$ 20
Cost of sales	10	12
Taxable income	$ 2	$ 8
Tax liability	$0.42 (21%)	$1.20 (15%)

Assume further that Usco is unable to justify its transfer price of $12 through use of one of the acceptable transfer pricing methods, and the IRS adjusts the price to $15. This results in U.S. taxable income of $5 per unit. If the Omani government refuses to allow Omanco to adjust its cost of sales to $15 per unit, the worldwide income tax paid on this sale would be $2.25 per unit, determined as follows:

	Usco	Omanco
Sales	$ 15	$ 20
Cost of sales	10	12
Taxable income	$ 5	$ 8
Tax liability	$1.05 (21%)	$1.20 (15%)

Article 9 of the U.S. Model Income Tax Treaty requires that, when the tax authority in one country makes an adjustment to a company's transfer price, the tax authority in the other country will provide correlative relief if it agrees with the adjustment. If the other country does not agree with the adjustment, the competent authorities of the two countries are required to attempt to reach a compromise. If no compromise can be reached, the company will find itself in the situation described in the example above. In the absence of a tax treaty (such as in the case of the United States and Oman), there is no compulsion for the other country to provide a correlative adjustment.

When confronted with either an IRS-initiated transfer pricing adjustment or a foreign government-initiated adjustment, a U.S. taxpayer may request assistance from the U.S. Competent Authority through its Advance Pricing and Mutual Agreement (APMA) Program to obtain correlative relief. In 2015, the APMA process resolved 193 cases, with full correlative relief obtained in only 3.2 percent of them.[12] In 7.2 percent of cases, the APMA process resulted in the withdrawal of the adjustment by the initiating tax authority. Partial correlative relief and partial withdrawal was obtained in 75.3 percent of cases. The APMA process is not speedy; it took an average of 32.1 months to reach a case resolution in 2015.

Penalties

In addition to possessing the power to adjust transfer prices, the IRS has the authority to impose penalties on companies that significantly underpay taxes as a result of inappropriate transfer pricing. A penalty equal to 20 percent of the underpayment in taxes may be levied for a substantial valuation misstatement. The penalty increases to 40 percent of the underpayment on a gross valuation misstatement. A substantial valuation misstatement exists when the transfer price is 200 percent or more (50 percent or less) of the price determined under Section 482 to be the correct price. A gross valuation misstatement arises when the price is 400 percent or more (25 percent or less) than the correct price.

For example, assume Tomlington Company transfers a product to a foreign affiliate for $10 and the IRS determines the correct price should have been $50. The adjustment results in an increase in U.S. tax liability of $1,000,000. Because the original transfer price was less than 25 percent of the correct price ($50 × 25% = $12.50), the IRS levies a penalty of $400,000 (40% of $1,000,000). Tomlington Company will pay the IRS a total of $1,400,000 as a result of its gross valuation misstatement.

Contemporaneous Documentation

Taxpayers must create documentation that justifies the transfer pricing method selected as the most reliable measure of arm's-length price, and they must be able to provide that documentation to the IRS within 30 days of its being requested. It has become standard practice for IRS auditors to request a taxpayer's contemporaneous documentation at the beginning of an audit involving intercompany transactions.

The documentation needed to justify the transfer pricing method chosen must include:

1. An overview of the taxpayer's business, including an analysis of economic and legal factors that affect transfer pricing.
2. A description of the taxpayer's organizational structure, including an organizational chart, covering all related parties engaged in potentially relevant transactions.
3. Any documentation specifically required by the transfer pricing regulations.

---

[12] U.S. Internal Revenue Service, *Competent Authority Statistics,* April 27, 2016, pp. 2–3, available at https://www.irs.gov/businesses/corporations/annual-competent-authority-statistics (accessed March 10, 2022).

4. A description of the selected pricing method and an explanation of why that method was selected.

5. A description of alternative methods that were considered and an explanation of why they were not selected.

6. A description of the controlled transactions, including the terms of sale, and any internal data used to analyze those transactions.

7. A description of the comparable uncontrolled transactions or parties that were used with the transfer pricing method, how comparability was evaluated, and what comparability adjustments were made, if any.

8. An explanation of the economic analysis and projections relied upon in applying the selected transfer pricing method.

A report published by PricewaterhouseCoopers (PwC) in 2016 indicates that the preparation of documentation to demonstrate compliance with transfer pricing rules is an important and growing problem for MNCs. That report indicates that most countries now have documentation rules that require companies to provide evidence of how their transfer pricing policies comply with the arm's-length standard. In addition, many countries have implemented penalties to enforce compliance with the documentation rules. PwC suggests that a significant difficulty for multinational companies in avoiding costly penalties is dealing with the differences in transfer pricing documentation rules that exist across countries.[13]

Reporting Requirements

To determine whether intercompany transactions meet the arm's-length price requirement, the IRS often must request substantial information from the company whose transfer pricing is being examined. Historically, the IRS has found it extremely difficult to obtain such information when the transaction involves a transfer from a foreign parent company to its U.S. subsidiary. The information might be held by the foreign parent, which is beyond the jurisdiction of the IRS.

To reduce this problem, U.S. tax law now requires substantial reporting and record keeping of any U.S. company that (*a*) has at least one foreign shareholder with a 25 percent interest in the company and (*b*) engages in transactions with that shareholder. Accounting and other records must be physically maintained in the United States by a U.S. company meeting this definition. In addition, Form 5472 must be filed each year for each related party with whom the company had transactions during the year. Failure to keep appropriate records results in a $10,000 fine, and a fine of $10,000 is assessed for each failure to file a Form 5472. If the company does not resolve the problem within 90 days of notification by the IRS, the fine doubles and increases by $10,000 for every 30 days' delay after that. For example, a U.S. subsidiary of a foreign parent that neglects to file Form 5472 would owe the IRS $50,000 in penalties 180 days after being notified of its deficiency.

Country-by-Country Reporting

In June 2016, the U.S. Treasury Department released final regulations that require annual CbC reports to be filed by U.S. companies along with their annual income tax return. The regulations are based on the template developed by the OECD, and they must be followed by the ultimate parent entity (UPE) of an MNE group that has annual revenue of $850 million or more. More specifically, the UPE must file a new form—Form 8975—with the IRS that provides information for each of its "constituent entities," that is, for each foreign subsidiary. Part 1 of Form 8975 requires UPEs to report the following information for each

[13] PricewaterhouseCoopers, *International Transfer Pricing 2015/16,* p. iv, available at https://www.pwc.com/gx/en/services/tax/publications/international-transfer-pricing.html (accessed July 1, 2021).

jurisdiction in which it operates: unrelated party revenues, related party revenues, total revenues, profit or loss before income tax, income tax paid on cash basis, income tax accrued for the current year, stated capital, accumulated earnings, number of employees, and tangible assets other than cash and cash equivalents. Part 2 of Form 8975 requires disclosure of the tax jurisdiction and main business activities of each constituent entity.

Consistent with the OECD's goal of increasing transparency, the CbC reports filed by U.S. parent entities with the IRS are shared with tax authorities in dozens of other jurisdictions, including Australia, Mexico, Portugal, and South Africa.

ADVANCE PRICING AGREEMENTS

To introduce some certainty into the transfer pricing issue, the United States originated and actively promotes the use of advance pricing agreements (APAs). An APA is an agreement between a company and the IRS to apply an agreed-on transfer pricing method to specified transactions. The IRS agrees not to seek any transfer pricing adjustments for transactions covered by the APA if the company uses the agreed-on method. A unilateral APA is an agreement between a taxpayer and the IRS establishing an approved transfer pricing method for U.S. tax purposes. Whenever possible, the IRS will also negotiate the terms of the APA with foreign tax authorities to create a bilateral APA, which is an agreement between the IRS and one or more foreign tax authorities that the transfer pricing method is correct.

The APA process consists of five phases: (1) application; (2) due diligence; (3) analysis; (4) discussion and agreement; and (5) drafting, review, and execution. The request for an APA involves the company proposing a particular transfer pricing method to be used in specific transactions. Generally, one of the methods required to be followed by Treasury Regulations will be requested, but another method can be requested if none of the methods specified in the regulations is applicable or practical. In considering the request for an APA, the IRS is likely to require the following information as part of the application:

1. An explanation of the proposed methodology.
2. A description of the company and its related party's business operations.
3. An analysis of the company's competitors.
4. Data on the industry showing pricing practices and rates of return on comparable transactions between unrelated parties.

For most taxpayers, the APA application is a substantial document filling several binders.[14]

The clear advantage to negotiating an APA is the assurance that the prices determined using the agreed-on transfer pricing method will not be challenged by the IRS. Disadvantages of the APA are that it can be very time-consuming to negotiate and involves disclosing a great deal of information to the IRS. The IRS indicates that new unilateral agreements take an average of 36.2 months to negotiate, and bilateral agreements take even longer (50.8 months).[15] Although thousands of companies engage in transactions that cross U.S. borders, by the end of 2020, only 2,067 APAs had been executed since the program's inception in 1991, almost 30 years earlier.

The first completed APA was for sales between Apple Computer Inc. and its Australian subsidiary. In 1992, Japan's largest consumer electronics firm, Matsushita (known for its

---

[14] U.S. Internal Revenue Service, "Announcement and Report Concerning Advance Pricing Agreements," *Internal Revenue Bulletin: 2012–16,* April 2, 2012, p. 5.

[15] U.S. Internal Revenue Service, "Announcement and Report Concerning Advance Pricing Agreements," March 23, 2021, p. 12, available at https://www.irs.gov/pub/irs-drop/a-21-06.pdf (accessed March 1, 2022).

Panasonic and Technics brands), announced that after two years of negotiation, it had entered into an APA with both the IRS and the Japanese National Tax Administration.[16] Companies in the computer and electronics product manufacturing industry have been heavy users of APAs.

Foreign companies with U.S. operations are as likely to request an APA as U.S. companies with foreign operations. Of a total of 127 APAs that were executed in 2020, 61 percent were between a U.S. subsidiary and its foreign parent.[17]

Most APAs cover transactions that involve a number of business functions and risks. For example, manufacturing firms typically conduct research and development, design and engineer products, manufacture products, market and distribute products, and provide after-sales services. Risks include market risks, financial risks, credit risks, product liability risks, and general business risks. The IRS indicates that, in the APA evaluation process, substantial time and effort is spent in understanding how functions and risks are allocated among the companies that are party to the covered transactions.[18] To facilitate this evaluation, the company must provide a functional analysis as part of the APA application. The functional analysis identifies the economic activities performed, the assets employed, the costs incurred, and the risks assumed by each of the related parties. The purpose is to determine the relative value being added by each function and therefore by each related party. The IRS uses the economic theory that higher risks demand higher returns and that different functions have different opportunity costs in making its evaluation. Each IRS APA team generally includes an economist to help with this analysis.

Sales of tangible property are the type of intercompany transaction most frequently covered by an APA, and the comparable profits method is the transfer pricing method most commonly applied.[19] This is because reliable public data on comparable business activities of uncontrolled companies may be more readily available than potential comparable uncontrolled price data, ruling out the CUP method. In addition, because the comparable profits method relies on operating profit margin rather than gross profit margin (as do the resale price and cost-plus methods), the comparable profits method is not as dependent on exact comparables being available. Companies that perform different functions may have very different gross profit margins, but earn similar levels of operating profit. The comparable profits method also tends to be less sensitive than other methods to differences in accounting practices, such as whether expenses are classified as cost of goods sold or as operating expenses.

A relatively large number of countries have developed their own APA programs, including Canada, in 1993; France and the United Kingdom, in 1999; and the Netherlands, in 2002. Other countries in which APAs are available include, but are not limited to, Australia, Brazil, China, Germany, Japan, Korea, Mexico, Taiwan, and Venezuela.

ENFORCEMENT OF TRANSFER PRICING REGULATIONS

The United States has made periodic attempts over the years to make sure that MNCs doing business in the United States pay their fair share of taxes. Enforcement has concentrated on foreign companies with U.S. subsidiaries, but U.S. companies with foreign

[16] "Big Japan Concern Reaches an Accord on Paying U.S. Tax," *New York Times,* November 11, 1992, p. A1.

[17] U.S. Internal Revenue Service, "Announcement and Report Concerning Advance Pricing Agreements," March 23, 2021, p. 8.

[18] U.S. Internal Revenue Service, "Announcement and Report Concerning Advance Pricing Agreements," March 23, 2021, p. 9.

[19] U.S. Internal Revenue Service, "Announcement and Report Concerning Advance Pricing Agreements," March 23, 2021, pp. 8 and 9.

operations also have been targeted. Anecdotal evidence suggests that foreign companies are using discretionary transfer pricing to waft profits out of the United States and back to their home country. In one case cited in a *Newsweek* article, a foreign manufacturer was found to sell TV sets to its U.S. subsidiary for $250 each, but it charged an unrelated U.S. company only $150.[20] In two additional cases, a foreign company was found to charge its U.S. distributor $13 apiece for razor blades, and a U.S. manufacturer sold bulldozers to its foreign parent for only $551 apiece.[21] As a result, foreign companies doing business in the United States are able to pay little or no U.S. income tax. For example, the IRS concluded that Yamaha Motor U.S.A. paid only $5,272 in U.S. corporate income tax over a four-year period, whereas arm's-length prices would have resulted in taxable income of $500 million and U.S. corporate income tax of $127 million.[22]

In two of its biggest victories in the 1980s, the IRS was able to make the case that Toyota and Nissan had overcharged their U.S. subsidiaries for products imported into the United States. Nissan paid $1.85 billion and Toyota paid $850 million to the U.S. government as a result of adjustments made by the IRS. In both cases, however, the competent authorities in the United States and Japan agreed on the adjustments, and the Japanese government paid appropriate refunds to the companies. In effect, tax revenues previously collected by the Japanese tax authority were transferred to the IRS. Japanese companies are not the only ones found to violate transfer pricing regulations. In a well-publicized case, Coca-Cola Japan was found by the Japanese tax authority to have overpaid royalties to its parent by about $360 million. In another case, the IRS proposed an adjustment to Texaco's taxable income of some $140 million.

In 1994, the IRS was armed with the ability to impose penalties (discussed earlier) for misstating taxable income through the use of non-arm's-length transfer prices. The administration hoped that the threat of additional penalties would provide an incentive for companies to comply with the regulations.

The transfer pricing saga continues. In 2008, the U.S. General Accounting Office released a report indicating that a majority of large corporations paid no U.S. income tax for the period 1998–2005.[23] During that period, 66 to 72 percent of foreign-controlled corporations and 61 to 69 percent of U.S.-controlled corporations paid no federal income tax. As a result, Congress has put renewed pressure on the IRS to enhance its enforcement of transfer pricing regulations. Ernst & Young reported that the IRS hired 2,000 additional employees in 2009–2010 to deal with international issues.[24]

In January 2017, the IRS Large Business and International (LB&I) Division announced 13 compliance areas in which it would focus its enforcement efforts. Two of these compliance campaigns, "Related Party Transactions" and "Inbound Distributor," relate to the enforcement of transfer pricing regulations. As part of the Inbound Distributor Campaign (which has since been retired), the IRS developed a comprehensive training program to aid IRS revenue agents in their examination of taxpayers related to the issue of transfer pricing.[25]

Although enforcement of IRC Section 482 has received increased attention by the IRS, its track record in winning court cases on this issue is poor at best. A notable exception occurred in November 2020, when the Tax Court decided for the IRS and against

[20] "The Corporate Shell Game," *Newsweek,* April 15, 1991, pp. 48–49.

[21] "Legislators Prepare to Crack Down on Transfer Pricing," *Accounting Today,* July 13–26, 1998, pp. 10, 13.

[22] "The Corporate Shell Game," *Newsweek,* April 15, 1991, pp. 48–49.

[23] U.S. General Accounting Office, *Comparison of the Reported Tax Liabilities of Foreign- and U.S.-Controlled Corporations, 1998–2005,* July 2008, p. 23.

[24] Ernst & Young, *2010 Global Transfer Pricing Survey,* 2011, p. 5.

[25] U.S. Internal Revenue Service, "Large Business and International Retired Campaigns," available at https://www.irs.gov/businesses/corporations/lbi-retired-campaigns (accessed February 15, 2022).

The Coca-Cola Company in a transfer pricing case. The IRS claimed that Coca-Cola undercharged its foreign operations for the use of the company's intangible assets (trademarks, logos, secret formulas, and so on). As a result, foreign affiliates earned above arm's-length amounts of profits and Coca-Cola earned profit that was below an arm's-length amount. Coca-Cola used a fixed profit margin approach in pricing the use of its intangible assets, and the IRS argued that this was not the "best method" for this type of transaction. Instead, the IRS argued that the Comparable Profits Method was the best method, and the Tax Court agreed with this argument, ruling that Coca-Cola's taxable income should be increased by $9 billion.

Worldwide Enforcement

Over the last several years, most major countries have strengthened their transfer pricing rules, often through documentation requirements and penalties, and have stepped up enforcement. One reason for the increased challenge to taxpayers on their transfer prices is that tax authorities view transfer pricing as a "soft target."[26] Because of the difficulty involved in proving that their transfer price is acceptable, companies might prefer to simply pay the additional tax rather than engage in a lengthy, complicated dispute. The risks associated with local tax authorities scrutinizing a company's transfer prices include:

- Increased local tax liability.
- Potential double taxation.
- Penalties for underpayment of tax.
- Uncertainty with regard to the company's worldwide tax burden.
- Problems in relationships with local tax authorities.

As evidence of the extent to which tax authorities investigate MNCs' transfer pricing policies, a survey conducted by Ernst & Young in 2010 discovered that more than two-thirds of MNC respondents had experienced a transfer pricing audit somewhere in the world since 2006.[27] More than one-fourth of completed audits resulted in an adjustment being made by a tax authority, and penalties were imposed in almost 20 percent of those cases.

Worldwide, there are certain types of transfers and certain industries that are more at risk for examination by tax authorities. For example, imports are more likely to be scrutinized than exports, partly for political reasons. Exports help the balance of trade; imports do not, and they compete with the local workforce. In addition, royalties paid for the use of intangible assets such as brand names, management service fees, research and development conducted for related parties, and interest on intercompany loans are all high on tax authorities' radar screen for examination. Intercompany services are the type of transaction most likely to be audited. Historically, the industry most at risk for a transfer pricing adjustment is pharmaceuticals.

There are a number of red flags that can cause a tax authority to examine a company's transfer prices. The most important of these is if the company is less profitable than the tax authority believes it should be. For example, a domestic company with a foreign parent that makes losses year after year is likely to fall under scrutiny, especially if its competitors are profitable. Price changes and royalty rate changes are another red flag. Companies that have developed a poor relationship with the tax authority are also more likely to be scrutinized. A reputation for aggressive tax planning is one way to develop a poor relationship with the local tax authority.

---

[26] PricewaterhouseCoopers, *International Transfer Pricing 2015/16*, p. 3, available at www.pwc.com.

[27] Ernst & Young, *2010 Global Transfer Pricing Survey*, 2011, p. 3, available at www.pwc.com.

Summary

1. Two factors heavily influence the manner in which international transfer prices are determined: (1) corporate objectives and (2) national tax laws.

2. The objective of establishing transfer prices to enhance performance evaluation and the objective of minimizing one or more types of cost through discretionary transfer pricing often conflict.

3. Cost-minimization objectives that can be achieved through discretionary transfer pricing include minimization of worldwide income tax, minimization of import duties, circumvention of repatriation restrictions, and improvement of the competitive position of foreign subsidiaries.

4. National tax authorities have guidelines regarding what will be considered an acceptable transfer price for tax purposes. These guidelines often rely on the concept of an arm's-length price.

5. Section 482 of the U.S. tax law gives the IRS the power to audit and adjust taxpayers' international transfer prices if they are not found to be in compliance with Treasury Department regulations. The IRS also may impose a penalty of up to 40 percent of the underpayment in the case of a gross valuation misstatement.

6. Treasury Regulations require the use of one of five specified methods to determine the arm's-length price in a sale of tangible property. The best-method rule requires taxpayers to use the method that under the facts and circumstances provides the most reliable measure of an arm's-length price. The comparable uncontrolled price method is generally considered to provide the most reliable measure of an arm's-length price when a comparable uncontrolled transaction exists.

7. Application of a particular transfer pricing method can result in an arm's-length range of prices. Companies can try to achieve cost-minimization objectives by selecting prices at the extremes of the relevant range.

8. Advance pricing agreements (APAs) are agreements between a company and a national tax authority on what is an acceptable transfer pricing method. So long as the agreed-on method is used, the company's transfer prices will not be adjusted.

9. Countries have been stepping up their enforcement of transfer pricing regulations. Transfer pricing is the most important international tax issue faced by MNCs internationally. The U.S. government is especially concerned with foreign MNCs not paying their fair share of taxes in the United States.

Questions

1. What are the various types of intercompany transactions for which a transfer price must be determined?

2. What are possible cost-minimization objectives that a multinational company might wish to achieve through transfer pricing?

3. What is the performance evaluation objective of transfer pricing?

4. Why is there often a conflict between the performance evaluation and cost-minimization objectives of transfer pricing?

5. How can transfer pricing be used to reduce the amount of withholding taxes paid to a government on dividends remitted to a foreign stockholder?

6. According to U.S. tax regulations, what are the five methods to determine the arm's-length price in a sale of tangible property? How does the best-method rule affect the selection of a transfer pricing method?

7. What is the arm's-length range of transfer pricing, and how does it affect the selection of a transfer pricing method?
8. Under what conditions would a company apply for a correlative adjustment from a foreign tax authority? What effect do tax treaties have on this process?
9. What is an advance pricing agreement?
10. What are the costs and benefits associated with entering into an advance pricing agreement?

Exercises and Problems

1. Which of the following objectives is *not* achieved through the use of lower transfer prices?
   a. Improving the competitive position of a foreign operation.
   b. Minimizing import duties.
   c. Protecting foreign currency cash flows from currency devaluation.
   d. Minimizing income taxes when transferring to a lower-tax country.

2. Which of the following methods does U.S. tax law always require to be used in pricing intercompany transfers of tangible property?
   a. Comparable uncontrolled price method.
   b. Comparable profits method.
   c. Cost-plus method.
   d. Best method.

3. Which international organization has developed transfer pricing guidelines that are used as the basis for transfer pricing laws in several countries?
   a. World Bank.
   b. Organization for Economic Cooperation and Development.
   c. United Nations.
   d. International Accounting Standards Board.

4. Which one of the following types of intercompany transactions is most likely to be audited?
   a. Sales of tangible property.
   b. Licenses of intangible property.
   c. Intercompany loans.
   d. Intercompany services.

5. Which of the following is *not* a method commonly used for establishing transfer prices?
   a. Cost-based transfer price.
   b. Negotiated price.
   c. Market-based transfer price.
   d. Industrywide transfer price.

6. Market-based transfer prices lead to optimal decisions in which of the following situations?
   a. When interdependencies between the related parties are minimal.
   b. When there is no advantage or disadvantage to buying and selling the product internally rather than externally.
   c. When the market for the product is perfectly competitive.
   d. All of the above.

7. U.S. Treasury Regulations require the use of one of five specified methods to determine the arm's-length price in a sale of tangible property. Which of the following is not one of those methods?

    a. Cost-plus method.

    b. Market-based method.

    c. Profit split method.

    d. Resale price method.

8. The greatest number of advance pricing agreements have been negotiated with the IRS for which type of intercompany transaction?

    a. Sales of tangible property.

    b. Licenses of intangible property.

    c. Intercompany loans.

    d. Intercompany services.

9. The IRS has the authority to impose penalties on companies that significantly under-pay taxes as a result of inappropriate transfer pricing. Acme Company, a U.S. taxpayer, transfers a product to a foreign affiliate at $15 per unit, and the IRS determines the correct price should have been $65 per unit. The adjustment results in an increase in U.S. tax liability of $1,250,000. Due to this change in price, what amount of penalty for underpayment of taxes will Acme Company pay?

    a. $0.

    b. $125,000.

    c. $250,000.

    d. $500,000.

Use the following information for Exercises 10 through 12: Babcock Company manu-factures fast-baking ovens in the United States at a production cost of $500 per unit and sells them to uncontrolled distributors in the United States and a wholly owned sales subsidiary in Canada. Babcock's U.S. distributors sell the ovens to restaurants at a price of $1,000, and its Canadian subsidiary sells the ovens at a price of $1,100. Other distributors of ovens to restaurants in Canada normally earn a gross profit equal to 25 percent of selling price. Babcock's main competitor in the United States sells fast-baking ovens at an average 50 percent markup on cost. Babcock's Canadian sales subsidiary incurs operating costs, other than cost of goods sold, that average $250 per oven sold. The average operating profit margin earned by Canadian distributors of fast-baking ovens is 5 percent.

10. Which of the following would be an acceptable transfer price under the resale price method?

    a. $700.

    b. $750.

    c. $795.

    d. $825.

11. Which of the following would be an acceptable transfer price under the cost-plus method?

    a. $700.

    b. $750.

    c. $795.

    d. $825.

12. Which of the following would be an acceptable transfer price under the comparable profits method?
    a. $700.
    b. $750.
    c. $795.
    d. $825.

13. Lahdekorpi OY, a Finnish corporation, owns 100 percent of Three-O Company, a subsidiary incorporated in the United States.

    Required:
    Given the limited information provided, determine the best transfer pricing method and the appropriate transfer price in each of the following situations:
    a. Lahdekorpi manufactures tablecloths at a cost of $20 each and sells them to unrelated distributors in Canada for $30 each. Lahdekorpi sells the same tablecloths to Three-O Company, which then sells them to retail customers in the United States.
    b. Three-O Company manufactures men's flannel shirts at a cost of $10 each and sells them to Lahdekorpi, which sells the shirts in Finland at a retail price of $30 each. Lahdekorpi adds no significant value to the shirts. Finnish retailers of men's clothing normally earn a gross profit equal to 40 percent of sales price.
    c. Lahdekorpi manufacturers wooden puzzles at a cost of $2 each and sells them to Three-O Company for distribution in the United States. Other Finnish puzzle manufacturers sell their product to unrelated customers and normally earn a gross profit equal to 50 percent of the production cost.

14. Superior Brakes Corporation manufactures truck brakes at its plant in Mansfield, Ohio, at a cost of $10 per unit. Superior sells its brakes directly to U.S. truck makers at a price of $15 per unit. It also sells its brakes to a wholly owned sales subsidiary in Brazil that, in turn, sells the brakes to Brazilian truck makers at a price of $16 per unit. Transportation cost from Ohio to Brazil is $0.20 per unit. Superior's sole competitor in Brazil is Bomfreio SA, which manufactures truck brakes at a cost of $12 per unit and sells them directly to truck makers at a price of $16 per unit. There are no substantive differences between the brakes manufactured by Superior and Bomfreio.

    Required:
    Given the information provided, discuss the issues related to using (a) the comparable uncontrolled price method, (b) the resale price method, and (c) the cost-plus method to determine an acceptable transfer price for the sale of truck brakes from Superior Brakes Corporation to its Brazilian subsidiary.

15. Banff Limited (a Canadian company) imports die-cast parts from its Taiwanese subsidiary that are used in the production of children's toys. Per unit, part 169 costs the Taiwanese subsidiary C$10.00 to produce and C$2.00 to ship to Banff Limited. Banff uses part 169 to produce a toy airplane that it sells to local toy stores for C$52.00 per unit. The following tax rates apply:

Taiwanese income tax	17%
Canadian income tax	26.5%
Canadian import duty	20% of invoice price

Required:

a. Determine the total amount of income taxes and import duties paid to the Canadian and Taiwanese governments if part 169 is sold to Banff Limited at a price of C$20.00 per unit.

b. Determine the total amount of income taxes and import duties paid to the Canadian and Taiwanese governments if part 169 is sold to Banff Limited at a price of C$30.00 per unit.

c. Explain why the results obtained in parts (a) and (b) differ.

16. Smith-Jones Company, a U.S.-based corporation, owns 100 percent of Joal SA, located in Guadalajara, Mexico. Joal manufactures premium leather handbags at a cost of 500 Mexican pesos each. Joal sells its handbags to Smith-Jones, which sells them under Joal's brand name in its retail stores in the United States. Joal also sells handbags to an uncontrolled wholesaler in the United States. Joal invoices all sales to U.S. customers in U.S. dollars. Because the customer is not allowed to use Joal's brand name, it affixes its own label to the handbags and sells them to retailers at a markup on cost of 30 percent. Other U.S. retailers import premium leather handbags from uncontrolled suppliers in Italy, making payment in euros, and sell them to generate gross profit margins equal to 25 percent of selling price. Imported Italian leather handbags are of similar quality to those produced by Joal. Bolsa SA also produces handbags in Mexico and sells them directly to Mexican retailers, earning a gross profit equal to 60 percent of production cost. However, Bolsa's handbags are of lesser quality than Joal's due to the use of a less complex manufacturing process, and the two companies' handbags do not compete directly.

Required:

a. Given the facts presented, discuss the various factors that affect the reliability of (1) the comparable uncontrolled price method, (2) the resale price method, and (3) the cost-plus method.

b. Select the method from those listed in (a) that you believe is best, and describe any adjustment that might be necessary to develop a more reliable transfer price.

17. Raval Company, based in Sydney, Australia, has a wholly owned subsidiary in Singapore. The Singaporean subsidiary manufactures bicycles at a cost equal to A$20 per bicycle, which it sells to Raval at an FOB shipping point price of A$100 each. Raval pays shipping costs of A$10 per bicycle and an import duty of 10 percent on the A$100 invoice price. Raval sells the bicycles in Australia for A$200 each. The Australian tax authority discovers that Raval's Singaporean subsidiary also sells its bicycles to uncontrolled Australian customers at a price of A$80 each. Accordingly, the Australian tax authority makes a transfer pricing adjustment to Raval's tax return, which decreases Raval's cost of goods sold by A$20 per bicycle. An offsetting adjustment (refund) is made for the import duty previously paid. The effective income tax rate in Singapore is 17 percent, and Raval's effective income tax rate in Australia is 30 percent.

Required:

a. Determine the total amount of income taxes and import duty paid on each bicycle (in Australian dollars) under each of the following situations:

1. Before the Australian tax authority makes a transfer pricing adjustment.

2. After the Australian tax authority makes a transfer pricing adjustment (assume the tax authority in Singapore provides a correlative adjustment).

3. After the Australian tax authority makes a transfer pricing adjustment (assume the tax authority in Singapore does not provide a correlative adjustment).

b. Discuss Raval Company management's decision to allow its Singaporean subsidiary to charge a higher price to Raval than to uncontrolled customers in Australia.

c. Assess the likelihood that the Singaporean tax authority will provide a correlative adjustment to Raval Company.

18. ABC Company has subsidiaries in Countries X, Y, and Z. Each subsidiary manufactures one product at a cost of $10 per unit that it sells to both of the other subsidiaries. Each buyer then distributes the product in its local market at a price of $15 per unit. The following information applies:

	Country X	Country Y	Country Z
Income tax rate	20%	30%	40%
Import duty...........	20%	10%	0%

Import duties are levied on the invoice price and are deductible for income tax purposes.

Required:

Formulate a transfer pricing strategy for each of the six intercompany sales between the three subsidiaries, X, Y, and Z, that would minimize the amount of income taxes and import duties paid by ABC Company.

19. Vlado Corporation (a U.S.-based company) has a wholly owned subsidiary in Moldova that manufactures insulated wire at a cost of $3 per meter. Vlado imports the insulated wire and sells it to U.S. retailers at a price of $12 per meter. The following information applies:

	United States	Moldova
Income tax rate	21%	12%
Import duty rate	20%	—
Withholding tax rate on dividends	—	6%

Import duties are levied on the invoice price and are deductible for income tax purposes. The Moldovan subsidiary must repatriate 100 percent of after-tax income to Vlado each year. Vlado has determined an arm's-length range of reliable transfer prices to be $5.00–$6.00.

Required:

a. Determine the transfer price within the arm's-length range that would maximize Vlado's after-tax cash flow from the sale of insulated wire in the United States.

b. Now assume that the withholding tax rate on dividends is 0 percent. Determine the transfer price within the arm's-length range that would maximize Vlado's after-tax cash flow from the sale of insulated wire in the United States.

20. Ranger Company, a U.S. taxpayer, manufactures and sells medical products for animals. Ranger holds the patent on Z-meal, which it sells to horse ranchers in the United States. Ranger Company licenses its Bolivian subsidiary, Yery SA, to manufacture and sell Z-meal in South America. Through extensive product development and marketing, Yery has developed a South American llama market for Z-meal, which it sells under the brand name Llameal. Yery's sales of Llameal in Year 1 were $800,000, and its

operating expenses related to these sales, excluding royalties, were $600,000. The IRS has determined the following:

Value of Yery's operating assets used in the production of Z-meal.............	$300,000
Fair market return on operating assets..	20%
Percentage of Ranger's worldwide sales attributable to its intangibles.........	10%
Percentage of Yery's sales attributable to its intangibles......................	15%

Required:

Determine the amount that Ranger would charge as a license fee to Yery in Year 1 under the residual profit split method.

Case 9-1

Litchfield Corporation

Litchfield Corporation is a U.S.-based manufacturer of fashion accessories that produces umbrellas in its plant in Roanoke, Virginia, and sells directly to retailers in the United States. As chief financial officer, you are responsible for all of the company's finance, accounting, and tax-related issues.

S. Litchfield, chief executive officer (CEO) and majority shareholder, has informed you of a plan to begin exporting to the Caribbean region, where a substantial market for Litchfield umbrellas appears to exit. Rather than selling directly to umbrella retailers in the Caribbean, the plan is to establish a wholly owned sales subsidiary in the Bahamas that would purchase umbrellas from its U.S. parent and then distribute them throughout the Caribbean. Yesterday, you received the following memo from CEO Litchfield.

Memorandum

SUBJECT: Export Sales Prices

It has come to my attention that the corporate income tax rate in the Bahamas is zero, as compared to the much higher rate we pay here in the United States. Since our average production cost is $15.00 per unit and the price we expect to sell our umbrellas to Caribbean retailers is $25.00 per unit, why don't we plan to sell to our Bahamian subsidiary at $15.00 per unit? That way we make no profit here in the United States and $10.00 of profit in the Bahamas, where we would pay no income tax. We have plans to invest in a factory in the Bahamas in the next few years anyway, so we can keep the profit we earn over there for that purpose. What do you think?

Required:

Draft a memo responding to CEO Litchfield's question by explaining U.S. income tax regulations related to the export sales described in the above memorandum. Include a discussion of any significant risks associated with the proposal. Make a recommendation with respect to how the price for these sales might be determined.

Case 9-2

International Lamp Company

International Lamp Company (ILC), a U.S. taxpayer, manufactures crystal chandeliers at its wholly owed subsidiary in Poland (Polampa) at a production cost of $185 per chandelier. Polampa chandeliers are sold to two customers in the United States—Lighting Supermart (an ILC wholly owned subsidiary) and Home Store (an unaffiliated customer). Polampa and Lighting Supermart are related parties and transactions between them fall under Section 482 of the U.S. Internal Revenue Code.

The cost to transport the chandeliers to the United States is $15 per unit and is paid by Polampa. Other Polish manufacturers of crystal chandeliers sell to customers in the United States at a markup on total cost (production plus transportation cost) of 40 percent. Polampa sells chandeliers to Home Store at a landed price of $320 per unit (Polampa pays transportation costs). Home Store pays applicable U.S. import duties of 2 percent on its purchases of chandeliers. Lighting Supermart also pays import duties on its purchases from Polampa. Consistent with industry practice, Home Store places a 50 percent markup on the total cost of a chandelier and sells them at a retail price of $489.60 per unit. Lighting Supermart sells Polampa chandeliers at a retail price of $459.00 per unit.

Polampa is a Polish taxpayer, and Lighting Supermart is a U.S. taxpayer. Assume the following tax rates apply:

Polish corporate income tax rate	19%
Polish withholding tax rate on dividends	19%
U.S. corporate income tax rate	21%
U.S. ad valorem import duty	2%

Required:

1. Determine three possible prices for the sale of crystal chandeliers from Polampa to Lighting Supermart that comply with U.S. tax regulations under (*a*) the comparable uncontrolled price method, (*b*) the resale price method, and (*c*) the cost-plus method. Assume that none of the three methods is clearly the best method and that ILC would be able to justify any of the three prices for both U.S. and Polish tax purposes.

2. Assume that Polampa's profits are *not* repatriated back to ILC in the United States as a dividend. Lighting Supermart distributes 100 percent of its income to ILC as a dividend. However, there is a 100 percent exclusion for dividends received from a domestic subsidiary, so ILC will not pay additional taxes on dividends received from Lighting Supermart. Only Lighting Supermart pays taxes on the income it earns. Determine which of the three possible transfer prices calculated in (1) maximizes ILC's consolidated after-tax net income. Show your calculation of consolidated net income for all three transfer prices.

3. Assume that Polampa's profits *are* repatriated back to ILC in the United States as a dividend and that Lighting Supermart's profits are paid to ILC as a dividend. There is a 100 percent exemption from U.S. taxation for dividends received from a foreign subsidiary. Only Polampa pays taxes on the income it earns. Determine which of the three possible transfer prices maximizes net after-tax cash flow to ILC. Show your calculation of net after-tax cash flow for all three transfer prices.

4. Assume the same facts as in (3) except that a United States/Poland income tax treaty reduces withholding taxes on dividends to 5 percent. Determine which of the three possible transfer prices maximizes net cash flow to ILC. Show your calculation of net after-tax cash flow for all three transfer prices.

Chapter Ten

Management Accounting Issues in Multinational Corporations

Learning Objectives

After reading this chapter, you should be able to:

- Demonstrate an understanding of multinational capital budgeting.
- Describe issues involved in designing a management control system for foreign operations.
- Identify issues involved in the design and implementation of an effective performance evaluation system within a multinational corporation.
- Understand different approaches for incorporating exchange rate changes in operational budgeting within a multinational corporation.
- Explain the impact of cultural diversity on strategic accounting issues within a multinational corporation.

INTRODUCTION

Management accounting is that part of an organization's accounting system responsible for providing information to management to assist in formulating and implementing strategy. Strategy formulation is the process of deciding on the goals of the organization and the strategies for attaining those goals. The decisions made in formulating strategy have a long-term focus and include *capital budgeting* decisions, that is, decisions related to making long-term capital investments.

Strategy implementation refers to the process by which managers influence other members of the organization to behave in accordance with the organization's goals. Managerial influence is also known as *management control*. Two very important management control activities are preparing operating budgets and evaluating the performance of decentralized operations. *Operating budgets* are plans for the future expressed in quantitative terms that generally cover one year. Budgets provide a means for communicating management's plans throughout the organization. *Performance evaluation* is the task of ascertaining the extent to which organizational goals have been achieved. Identifying and rewarding good performance is important in achieving strategic goals. Performance is often evaluated by comparing actual results with expected results as summarized in the operating budget.

The accounting function within an organization plays an important role in strategy formulation and implementation through the activities of *capital budgeting, operational budgeting,* and *performance evaluation.* This chapter focuses on issues specifically related to carrying out these activities for foreign investments and foreign operations, including issues related to foreign currency fluctuations and the differences in culture and business environment that exist across countries.

CAPITAL BUDGETING

Multinational companies often need to commit large amounts of resources to overseas projects, with costs and benefits expected over a long period of time. Such projects are known as capital investments. Examples include the purchase of new equipment and the expansion into foreign territories through either greenfield investments or acquisition of existing operations. *Capital budgeting* is the process of identifying, evaluating, and selecting projects that require commitments of large sums of funds and generate benefits stretching well into the future. Sound capital investments are often a result of careful capital budgeting.[1]

The evaluation of foreign investment opportunities involves a more complicated set of economic, political, and strategic considerations than those factors influencing most domestic investment decisions. Although the decision to undertake a particular foreign investment may be determined by a mix of factors, the specific project should be subjected to traditional investment analysis. We first explain the main features of traditional capital budgeting before considering the unique issues that need to be considered in foreign investment analysis.

The capital budgeting process includes three steps: (1) project identification and definition, (2) evaluation and selection, and (3) monitoring and review.[2] The first step is critical, because without a clear definition of a proposed investment project, it is difficult to estimate the associated revenues, expenses, and cash flows, which is an integral part of the second step. The second step involves identifying the cash inflows and outflows expected from a specific project and then using one or more capital budgeting techniques to determine whether the project is acceptable. The third step becomes important during implementation of the project. Monitoring and review may lead management to alter the initial plan in response to changing circumstances.

Capital Budgeting Techniques

There are several techniques often used in evaluating and making capital investment decisions, including payback period, return on investment, net present value, and internal rate of return. Each of these techniques involves forecasting future cash flows to be generated from an investment project and comparing these with the amount initially invested in the project. In the simplest of these techniques, payback period, the amount of the initial investment is divided by the estimated annual after-tax net cash inflow from the investment to calculate the number of years it will take to recoup the initial cash outflow. Many companies, however, use more sophisticated techniques that incorporate the time value of money into the analysis. We demonstrate issues in multinational capital budgeting by focusing on the calculation of net present value.

---

[1] Edward J. Blocher, Kung H. Chen, Gary Cokins, and Thomas W. Lin, *Cost Management: A Strategic Emphasis* (New York: McGraw-Hill, 2005), p. 840.

[2] Edward J. Blocher, Kung H. Chen, Gary Cokins, and Thomas W. Lin, *Cost Management: A Strategic Emphasis* (New York: McGraw-Hill, 2005), p. 841.

Net Present Value

The net present value (NPV) of an investment is the difference between the initial investment and the sum of the present values of all future after-tax net cash inflows from the investment, calculated as follows:

$$\text{Present value of future after-tax net cash flows} - \text{Initial investment}$$
$$= \text{Net present value (NPV)}$$

The amount of NPV can be positive, negative, or zero. A positive NPV means that the investment is expected to provide a rate of return on the initial investment greater than the discount rate used to calculate present values, whereas a negative NPV means that the return provided would be less than the discount rate. If the NPV is zero, the project is expected to provide a rate of return exactly equal to the discount rate. The decision rule is to accept positive (or zero) NPV investment projects. Calculation of NPV requires knowledge of the amount of the initial investment; an estimation of the future cash flows to be derived from the investment, including cash flows to be received upon the investment's liquidation (known as terminal value); and an appropriate discount rate based on the desired rate of return on the investment.

The discount rate used in capital budgeting usually is the firm's cost of capital or some other minimum rate of return. The cost of capital is a composite of the cost of various sources of funds comprising a firm's capital structure. A minimum rate of return is often determined by referring to the strategic plan, the industry average rate of return, or other investment opportunities.

Regardless of the technique used, the quality of the capital budgeting decision rests on the accuracy with which future cash flows can be estimated. Forecasting future income to be generated by a project is often the starting point for determining future cash flows.

Research shows that preference for a particular capital budgeting technique differs across countries. Shields and colleagues found that U.S. firms commonly use discounted cash flow techniques such as net present value, whereas Japanese firms prefer payback period.[3] One explanation for Japanese firms' preference for payback period is that it is consistent with their corporate strategies. Many Japanese firms have adopted a strategy of creating competitive advantage through large investments in technology, and it is necessary to recoup the investment as quickly as possible to reinvest in new technologies. Another reason is that Japanese firms are increasingly competing on the basis of short product life cycles. This requires flexibility, and short payback periods increase flexibility. Japanese firms also recognize that with innovative products in the global market, it is difficult to predict cash flows in the distant future with meaningful accuracy.

Multinational Capital Budgeting

As noted earlier, application of NPV as the technique for evaluating potential capital investment projects requires identification of the following:

1. The amount of initial capital invested.
2. Estimated future cash flows to be derived from the project over time.
3. An appropriate discount rate for determining present values.

[3] M. D. Shields, C. W. Chow, Y. Kato, and Y. Nakagawa, "Management Accounting Practices in the U.S. and Japan: Comparative Survey Findings and Research Implications," *Journal of International Financial Management and Accounting* 3, no. 1 (1991), pp. 61–77.

Calculation of NPV for a foreign investment project is more complex than for a domestic project primarily because of the additional risks that affect future cash flows. Broadly, the various risks facing multinational corporations (MNC) can be described as political risk, economic risk, and financial risk.

Political risk refers to the possibility that political events within a host country may adversely affect cash flows to be derived from an investment in that country. Nationalization or expropriation of assets by the host government with or without compensation to the investor is the most extreme form of political risk. Foreign exchange controls, profit repatriation restrictions, local content laws, changes in tax or labor laws, and requirements for additional local production are additional aspects of political risk. Cross-border transactions also can be affected by special rules and regulations imposed by foreign governments. For example, the European Union (EU) requires companies that export products to the EU to comply with and certify that their products and quality control systems meet International Standardization Organization (ISO) 9000 minimum quality standards.

Economic risk refers to issues concerning the condition of the host country economy. Inflation and the country's balance of payments situation are aspects of economic risk. Inflation affects the cost structure in an economy and the ability of the local population to afford goods and services. High inflation also increases the cost of doing business in a foreign country as managers invest time and resources in devising strategies to cope with rapidly changing prices. Continuous deterioration of the balance of payments situation of a country may lead to devaluation of its currency, which may aggravate the problem of inflation. Currency devaluation, in particular, increases the price of imported goods in the host country.

Financial risk refers to the possibility of loss due to unexpected changes in currency values, interest rates, and other financial circumstances. The degree to which a firm is affected by exchange rate changes is called *foreign exchange risk*. Of the three types of exposure to foreign exchange risk—balance sheet exposure, transaction exposure, and economic exposure—the latter two have a direct impact on cash flows.[4]

Project Perspective versus Parent Company Perspective

The initial consideration in analyzing a potential foreign investment project is whether it should be evaluated on the basis of project cash flows (in local currency) or parent company cash flows (in parent company currency), taking into account the amount, timing, and form of transfers to the parent company. Project cash flows are especially susceptible to economic and political risk, whereas parent company cash flows can be significantly affected by political risk and foreign exchange risk. MNCs usually evaluate foreign investments from both project and parent company viewpoints.

Factors that vary across countries and should be considered in evaluating a potential foreign investment from a *project perspective* include the following:

1. *Taxes.* Income and other taxes, import duties, and tax incentives directly affect cash flows.
2. *Rate of inflation.* Inflation can cause changes in a project's competitive position, cost structure, and cash flows over time.
3. *Political risk.* Host government intervention in the business environment, for example, through the imposition of local content laws or price controls, can alter expected cash flows.

---

[4] Rivera and Milani (2020) indicate that inflation, interest rates, and exchange rates are the three factors that greatly affect budgeting in a multinational corporation. While inflation affects both interest rates and exchange rates, changes in exchange rates are seen as having the most direct effect on the budgeting process. Juan Rivera and Ken Milani, "Managing International Operations in Uncertain Times," *Strategic Finance,* November 1, 2020. For further insights into managing international operations, see Rivera and Milani, "Budgeting for International Operations," *Strategic Finance,* December 1, 2020, and "Strategies for Global Operations," *Strategic Finance,* January 1, 2021.

The following additional factors should be considered in evaluating a foreign investment from the *parent company perspective:*

1. *The form in which cash is remitted to the parent.* Different types of payments—dividends, interest, royalties—may be subject to different withholding tax rates.
2. *Foreign exchange risk.* Changes in the foreign currency exchange rate over the project's life will directly affect the parent currency value of local cash flows.
3. *Political risk.* Foreign exchange and/or profit repatriation restrictions imposed by the host government may limit the amount of cash flow to the parent.

Incorporating these factors into the foreign investment analysis can be accomplished in two ways:

1. The factors are incorporated into estimates of expected future cash flows.
2. The discount rate used to determine the present value of expected future cash flows is adjusted upward to compensate for the risk associated with changes in these various factors—the higher the risk, the higher the discount rate should be.

It makes sense to use a common standard in choosing among competing foreign and domestic projects. Thus, making adjustments to the expected cash flows would seem to be more appropriate than making ad hoc, country-specific adjustments to the discount rate. While adjusting cash flows is preferable, it also is more difficult because it involves forecasting future foreign tax rates, foreign inflation rates, changes in exchange rates, changes in foreign government policy, and so on. Sensitivity analysis, in which factors are varied over a relevant range of possible values, can show how sensitive the investment decision is to a particular factor. Because of the difficulty in adjusting cash flows, many companies appear to adjust the discount rate instead.

Next we illustrate how some of the complexities associated with the evaluation of potential foreign investments can be incorporated into the multinational capital budgeting process.

Illustration: International Wire Company

International Wire Company (IWC), a U.S.-based firm, is considering establishing a facility in Hungary to manufacture wire harnesses locally. IWC is attracted to Hungary because of cheaper costs and substantial tax incentives offered by the local government. However, IWC is concerned about the stability of the political situation in Hungary. IWC has gathered the following information:

Initial investment. The proposed plant will be constructed in Year 0 on a turnkey basis such that IWC incurs its entire cash outflow on December 31, Year 0. The subsidiary will begin operations on January 1, Year 1. The total investment will be 50,000,000 Hungarian forints (F), of which F 24,000,000 is for property, plant, and equipment to be depreciated on a straight-line basis over three years with no salvage value. The remaining F 26,000,000 of initial investment is for working capital.

Financing. The project will be financed as follows:

Forint debt (10%)..		F 15,000,000
Parent loan (10%)	$150,000 × F 100 =	F 15,000,000
Parent equity	$200,000 × F 100 =	F 20,000,000

The subsidiary will obtain a three-year F 15,000,000 loan from a local bank at an interest rate of 10 percent per annum. IWC will lend the subsidiary $150,000 and make an equity investment of $200,000, for a total initial cash outlay of $350,000. The parent loan ($150,000) is denominated and will be repaid in U.S. dollars. Interest of 10 percent on the parent loan is paid at the end of each year (in U.S. dollars).

Inflation and exchange rates. Inflation in Hungary is expected to be 20 percent per year over the next three years. As a result, the forint is expected to depreciate 20 percent per year relative to the U.S. dollar. The January 1, Year 1, exchange rate is 100 forints to the dollar. Forecasted exchange rates over the next three years are as follows:

January 1, Year 1	F 100 per U.S. dollar
December 31, Year 1	F 120 per U.S. dollar
December 31, Year 2	F 144 per U.S. dollar
December 31, Year 3	F 172.8 per U.S. dollar

Earnings. Expected earnings before interest and taxes (EBIT) is comprised of the following:

- Sales—Year 1:
  - Local: 200,000 units; sales price—F 50 per unit
  - Export: 200,000 units; sales price—F 50 per unit

  Local sales in units are expected to increase 10 percent per year. Export sales in units are expected to increase by the rate of devaluation of the Hungarian forint (20 percent per year). The unit price (in forints) for both local and export sales is expected to increase by the rate of Hungarian inflation (20 percent per year).
- Variable costs (other than taxes)—40 percent of sales.
- Fixed costs (other than interest)—consists of depreciation on property, plant, and equipment only. Depreciation is F 8,000,000 each year (F 24,000,000/3 years).

Taxes. The Hungarian national corporate income tax rate is 9 percent, plus most companies are subject to a local corporate income tax rate of 1 percent. Thus, IWC estimates an effective Hungarian corporate income tax rate of 10 percent for the first three years. Hungary does not impose withholding tax on interest or dividends, but would levy a withholding tax of 10 percent on the repatriation of terminal value. The U.S. corporate tax rate is 21 percent. Interest received in the United States from foreign sources is taxed as ordinary income. Dividends received from foreign subsidiaries, repayment of the parent loan, and receipt of terminal value are not taxed in the United States.

Political risk. Recently, Moody's has downgraded Hungary's sovereign credit rating to Ba1, just below investment grade, because of mounting financial-sector funding pressures and the high level of government debt. Analysts have predicted that the political party in government might be changed in the next election. IWC estimates this probability at 40 percent. If this occurs, it is possible that the new government will nationalize selected industries. With a change in government, IWC estimates that the probability that its Hungarian manufacturing facility would be nationalized is 60 percent. If the plant is nationalized, IWC expects that no terminal value will be recovered for the equity. However, the parent loan will still be repaid, and local loans will not be repaid. If the plant is not nationalized, the company will receive its expected terminal value at the end of the third year. Given the timing of future elections, any change in government would take place at the end of the third year.

Terminal value. Cash flow forecasts are made for only three years. At the end of the third year, the operation will be sold to local investors. The terminal value at the end of three years is expected to be equal to (1) the present value of an infinite stream of third-year cash flow from operations if no nationalization occurs and (2) zero if the project is nationalized.

Repatriation restrictions. Because of a shortage of foreign exchange, the Hungarian government allows only 50 percent of after-tax accounting income to be remitted as dividends to foreign parent corporations. This restriction is expected to exist for the foreseeable future. However, foreign exchange is readily available for interest and principal repayments on any foreign currency debt.

Weighted-average cost of capital. IWC's weighted-average cost of capital is 20 percent. In Hungary, investment projects would be expected to earn an after-tax return of 20 percent.

Present value factors. Present value factors at 20 percent are as follows:

Period	Factor
1........	0.833
2........	0.694
3........	0.579

In making the decision whether to invest in Hungary, IWC's chief executive officer has requested that the accounting department conduct an analysis to determine the investment's expected NPV from both (1) a project perspective and (2) a parent company perspective.

Project Perspective

To calculate NPV from a project perspective, IWC begins by calculating cash flow from operations (CFO) in Hungarian forints over the three-year investment horizon using the following formula:

$$CFO = \text{Earnings (after-tax)} + \text{Depreciation}$$

Depreciation is added back to after-tax earnings because it does not represent an annual cash outflow. Remember that sales volume and selling prices fluctuate each year. Export sales and the amount of Hungarian forint interest expense on the parent loan are a function of changes in the exchange rate.

IWC then calculates total annual cash flow (TACF) in Hungarian forints over the three-year investment horizon, where TACF is equal to CFO in Years 1 and 2. In Year 3, TACF is equal to CFO plus terminal value minus repayment of local debt, if the project is not nationalized. If the project is nationalized, Year 3 TACF is equal to CFO only. TACF over the three-year life of the investment is determined as follows:

	Calculation of Total Annual Cash Flow (in forints)		
	Year 1	**Year 2**	**Year 3**
Sales			
Local.............	200,000 u. × F 50 = F 10,000,000	220,000 u. × F 60 = F 13,200,000	242,000 u. × F 72 = F 17,424,000
Export............	200,000 u. × F 50 = 10,000,000	240,000 u. × F 60 = 14,400,000	288,000 u. × F 72 = 20,736,000
Total sales......	20,000,000	27,600,000	38,160,000
Variable costs.......	40% (8,000,000)	40% (11,040,000)	40% (15,264,000)
Depreciation	(8,000,000)	(8,000,000)	(8,000,000)
EBIT................	4,000,000	8,560,000	14,896,000
Interest.............			
Local.............	F 15,000,000 × 10% = (1,500,000)	F 15,000,000 × 10% = (1,500,000)	F 15,000,000 × 10% = (1,500,000)
Parent*..........	$15,000 × 120 = (1,800,000)	$15,000 × 144 = (2,160,000)	$15,000 × 172.8 = (2,592,000)
Earnings before tax	700,000	4,900,000	10,804,000
Taxes..............	10% (70,000)	10% (490,000)	10% (1,080,400)
Earnings after tax....	630,000	4,410,000	9,723,600
Add: Depreciation ...	8,000,000	8,000,000	8,000,000
CFO...............	F 8,630,000	F 12,410,000	F 17,723,600
Terminal value†			88,618,000
Repayment of local debt.................			(15,000,000)
Total annual cash flow (without nationalization)........................	F 8,630,000	F 12,410,000	F 91,341,600
Total annual cash flow (with nationalization)........................	F 8,630,000	F 12,410,000	F 17,723,600

* Annual interest on parent loan is $15,000, which is translated into a larger amount of forints each year due to the expected change in the F per U.S. dollar exchange rate.
† Terminal value is equal to the present value of an infinite stream of Year 3 CFO calculated as: $17,723,600/0.20.

IWC next calculates the net present value of the TACF in Hungarian forints over the three-year investment horizon (1) without nationalization and (2) with nationalization, as follows:

Calculation of Net Present Value (without nationalization)

TACF			PV Factor		Present Value
Year 1	F 8,630,000	×	0.833	=	F 7,188,790
Year 2	12,410,000	×	0.694	=	8,612,540
Year 3	91,341,600	×	0.579	=	52,886,786
					F 68,688,116
Less: Initial investment					(35,000,000)
NPV					F 33,688,116

Calculation of Net Present Value (with nationalization)

TACF			PV Factor		Present Value
Year 1	F 8,630,000	×	0.833	=	F 7,188,790
Year 2	12,410,000	×	0.694	=	8,612,540
Year 3	17,723,600	×	0.579	=	10,261,964
					F 26,063,294
Less: Initial investment					(35,000,000)
NPV					F (8,936,706)

Finally, IWC determines the project's expected value in Hungarian forints given the probability of nationalization:

Calculation of Project Expected Net Present Value

Net Present Value			Probability		Expected NPV
• Without nationalization	F 33,688,116	×	0.76	=	F 25,602,968
• With nationalization	F (8,936,706)	×	0.24*	=	(2,144,809)
Project expected value					F 23,458,159

* The probability of nationalization is determined by multiplying the probability of a change in government by the probability of nationalization if the government changes: 40% × 60% = 24%.

If IWC were to base the investment decision solely on the expected net present value from a project perspective, the positive expected value of F 23,458,159 would result in acceptance of the project.

Parent Company Perspective

To calculate NPV from a parent company perspective, IWC begins by calculating cash flows to parent (CFP) on an after-tax basis in U.S. dollars over the three-year investment horizon, where

CFP = Interest on parent loan in Years 1, 2, and 3 (net of withholding taxes, if any)
       + Dividends in Years 1, 2, and 3 (net of withholding taxes, if any)
       − U.S. taxes on interest in Years 1, 2, and 3
       + Repayment of parent loan in Year 3
       + Terminal value in Year 3 (net of withholding taxes, if any)

Hungary does not impose a withholding tax on dividends, interest, or terminal value, so withholding taxes have no effect on CFP. However, CFP is affected by Hungarian dividend repatriation restrictions (50 percent of accounting earnings) and changes in the exchange rate. In addition, CFP is reduced by the amount of U.S. income tax that must be paid on the interest received from Hungary. CFP in U.S. dollars is determined as follows:

Calculation of Cash Flows to Parent														
				Year 1				**Year 2**						**Year 3**
Foreign exchange rates.......				120				144						172.8
Interest on parent loan........	$150,000	×	10%	=	$15,000			$ 15,000						$ 15,000
Less: U.S. income tax.........			21%		(3,150)			(3,150)						(3,150)
Net interest					$11,850			$ 11,850						$ 11,850
Dividend	F 630,000	×	50%	=	$ 2,625	F 4,410,000	×	50%	=	$ 15,313	F 9,723,600	×	50%	=	$ 28,135
Repayment of parent loan.....														$150,000
Terminal value										F 88,618,000				$512,836
Less: Hungarian withholding tax												10%		(51,284)
														$461,552
Total cash flow to parent					$14,475			$ 27,163						$623,402

Note that in calculating total cash flow to parent, the forint amounts for dividends and terminal value are translated into U.S. dollars using each year's expected exchange rate.

If the project is nationalized in Year 3, terminal value will be zero, but the parent loan still will be repaid. In that case, the total cash flow to parent in Year 3 is only $189,985 ($11,850 + $28,135 + $150,000).

IWC then calculates the net present value of cash flows to the parent over the three-year investment horizon (1) without nationalization and (2) with nationalization, as follows:

Calculation of Net Present Value (without nationalization)					
CFP			**PV Factor**		**Present Value**
Year 1	$14,475	×	0.833	=	$ 12,058
Year 2	27,163	×	0.694	=	18,851
Year 3	651,538	×	0.579	=	377,240
					$ 408,149
Less: Initial investment....					(350,000)
NPV					$ 58,149

Calculation of Net Present Value (with nationalization)					
CFP			**PV Factor**		**Present Value**
Year 1	$14,475	×	0.833	=	$ 12,058
Year 2	27,163	×	0.694	=	18,851
Year 3	189,985	×	0.579	=	110,001
					$ 140,910
Less: Initial investment....					(350,000)
NPV					$(209,090)

Finally, IWC determines the expected value from a parent company perspective given the probability of nationalization:

Calculation of Parent Company Perspective Expected Net Present Value				
Net Present Value		**Probability**		**Expected NPV**
• Without nationalization	$ 58,149	× 0.76	=	$44,193
• With nationalization	$ (209,090)	× 0.24	=	(50,182)
Expected value				$ (5,989)

If IWC were to base the investment decision solely on the expected net present value from a parent company perspective, the negative expected value of $(5,989) would lead to rejection of the project. Evaluation of the potential Hungarian investment from both a project perspective and a parent company perspective leads to conflicting results. IWC's accountants should conduct sensitivity analyses to determine whether the results are particularly sensitive to one or more assumptions that have been made. The result may be sensitive, for example, to the assumption regarding future fluctuations in the exchange rate. Further, the company might want to consider alternative financing arrangements or attempt to obtain government concessions with respect to repatriation of earnings that could increase the likelihood of a positive NPV from a parent company perspective. Ultimately, corporate management will need to decide whether the parent company perspective or the project perspective should dominate the decision process.

MANAGEMENT CONTROL SYSTEMS

The function of ensuring that an organization's strategies are implemented and goals are attained is known as *management control.* Management control systems are tools designed for implementing strategies and monitoring their effectiveness. Accountants play a vital role in the management control process through the development of operating budgets and performance evaluation systems. Operating budgets help express a firm's long-term strategy within shorter time frames, provide a mechanism for monitoring the implementation of strategy within that time frame, and specify criteria for evaluating performance. We discuss issues related to performance evaluation and operating budgets for foreign operations later in this chapter. In this section, we briefly describe other issues related to MNCs' management control systems.

Management Control Issues in MNCs

Management control involves planning what the organization should do to effectively implement strategy, coordinating the activities of several parts of the organization, communicating information to organizational members, evaluating information, deciding what action should be taken, and influencing organizational members to change their behavior consistent with the organization's strategy.[5]

The extent to which decision-making authority is delegated to other members of the organization is an important issue in management control. In the case of MNCs, some level of delegation to foreign subsidiary managers is inevitable because of the need to respond to

---

[5] Robert N. Anthony and Vijay Govindarajan, *Management Control Systems,* 9th ed. (International ed.) (New York: McGraw-Hill, 1998), pp. 6–7.

local conditions and to provide a mechanism for motivating subsidiary managers. However, the issue of delegation is particularly complex for MNCs because of the possibility that geographically dispersed subsidiary managers may work toward parochial ends—which may conflict with the interests of the organization as a whole. Therefore, with delegation of decision-making authority to subsidiary managers, the need arises for effective control systems to ensure that subsidiary managers behave in accordance with organizational goals. Determining the appropriate level of responsibility to delegate to managers of foreign operations and designing the related control system necessary to ensure goal congruence are major issues facing MNCs in implementing strategy. Key factors that influence the design of an effective control system for an MNC include the company's organizational structure and the strategic role assigned to subsidiaries.

Organizational Structures in MNCs

MNCs organize their cross-border activities in different ways depending on the main purpose of such activities. When an MNC focuses on producing products for the parent company market, its organizational structure can be described as *ethnocentric*. Firms operating on an ethnocentric principle assume that their own cultural background—including values, beliefs, language, nonverbal communication, and ways of analyzing problems—is universally applicable. In contrast, some MNCs focus on providing products to the host country market with a unique product strategy for each market. Foreign subsidiaries in this case operate as strategic business units. The structure of such a firm can be described as *polycentric*. Polycentricism implies that the culture of the host country is important and should be adopted. Obviously, this creates the problem of adapting to multiple national cultures within the overall multinational organization. Some firms have a global networked structure, which supports both product line and geographic divisions in order to meet changing market demands. Such a structure can be described as *geocentric*. Those firms that use the principle of geocentricism believe that a synergy of ideas from different countries in which the firm operates should prevail.

An MNC with a geocentric structure organizes its activities as a network of transactions in knowledge, goods, and capital among subsidiaries located in different countries. Focusing on knowledge flows, the firm can identify different roles for subsidiaries. A subsidiary that serves as the source of knowledge for other units, taking a leading role in a particular area, can be described as a *global innovator*. For example, if the Swedish company Ericsson's Italian subsidiary serves as the company's global center for the development of transmission systems, and its Finnish subsidiary holds the leading global role for mobile telephones, they both play the role of a global innovator. In some cases, subsidiaries also take responsibility for creating knowledge in specific areas that other units can use. Such a subsidiary can be described as an *integrated player*. The integrator role is similar to the global innovator role. However, unlike a global innovator, which is self-sufficient in the fulfillment of its own knowledge needs, an integrated player relies on other units within the organization for some of its knowledge needs. Motorola's Chinese subsidiary is an example of an integrated player. In contrast, a unit may engage in little knowledge creation of its own and rely heavily on knowledge inflows from the parent or peer subsidiaries. Such a unit can be described as an *implementer*. Finally, a unit that has almost complete local responsibility for the creation of relevant know-how in the local context can be described as a *local innovator*. In this case, the local knowledge is seen as too specific to be of much competitive use outside of the country in which the local innovator is located. These different subsidiary roles are shown in Exhibit 10.1.

Organizational structure influences the extent to which responsibilities are delegated to individual foreign operations. Where the focus of a subsidiary's activities is on the host country (a polycentric organizational structure), the extent of delegation to the individual

EXHIBIT 10.1
A Knowledge Flow-Based Framework of Generic Subsidiary Roles

Source: Adapted from A. K. Gupta and V. Govindarajan, "Knowledge Flows and the Structure of Control within Multinational Corporations," *Academy of Management Review* 16, no. 4 (1991), pp. 773–75.

Outflow of Knowledge† / Inflow of Knowledge*	Low	High
High	Global innovator	Integrated player
Low	Local innovator	Implementer

* From the rest of the organization to the focal subsidiary.
† From the focal subsidiary to the rest of the organization.

foreign subsidiary would be greater than in a situation in which the focus is on the synergy of activities in different countries (a geocentric organizational structure). The extent of delegation appropriate for a particular foreign subsidiary can also depend on the specific strategic role assigned to it. For example, a foreign subsidiary that plays the role of a local innovator may have a higher level of responsibility compared to one that plays the role of an integrated player because of the lower level of interdependence between a local innovator and its peer units.

Types of Management Control Systems

Two dominant control systems are available for corporate management to control subsidiaries—bureaucratic (output) control systems and cultural (behavioral) control systems.[6] U.S. MNCs tend to exercise tighter output (bureaucratic) control over their foreign subsidiaries (approach 1) than do European firms, which tend to use more behavioral (cultural) control (approach 2). U.S. MNCs tend to monitor subsidiary outputs and rely more heavily upon frequently reported performance data than do European MNCs, which tend to assign more parent company nationals to key positions in foreign subsidiaries and count on a higher level of behavioral control than their U.S. counterparts. A bureaucratic control system makes extensive use of rules, regulations, and procedures that clearly specify subsidiary management's role and authority and set out expected performance in terms of identified targets, such as financial targets. These targets are used as a basis for evaluating performance. In contrast, in a system of cultural control, broad organizational culture plays a crucial role.[7] A cultural control system is more implicit and informal than a bureaucratic control system. Control mechanisms such as budgeting have both bureaucratic and cultural elements. The bureaucratic element of budgeting relates to setting specific targets to achieve, and the cultural element relates to the role budgeting plays in changing the behavior patterns within an organization.

The implications of these two approaches can be described using five categories. First, control in a bureaucratic system (approach 1) tends to measure more quantifiable and objective aspects of a foreign subsidiary and its environment, whereas control in a cultural system (approach 2) tends to measure more qualitative aspects. The former facilitates more centralized comparison against standards and cross-comparison between subsidiaries or between a foreign subsidiary and domestic operations. The latter measures aspects of the subsidiary and its environment that can vary widely from one subsidiary to the next.

[6] B. R. Baliga and A. M. Jaeger, "Multinational Corporations: Control Systems and Delegation Issues," *Journal of International Business,* Fall 1984, pp. 25–40.

[7] *Organizational culture* can be defined as the common beliefs and expectations shared by the organization's members.

Second, control in approach 1 requires more precise plans and budgets to generate suitable standards for comparison. Control in approach 2, on the other hand, requires a higher level of company-wide understanding and agreement about what constitutes appropriate behavior and how such behavior supports the goals of the subsidiary and the parent.

Third, control in approach 1 requires larger central staffs and more centralized information-processing capacity to make the necessary comparisons and generate the necessary feedback. Control in approach 2 requires a larger cadre of capable expatriate managers who are willing to spend long periods of time abroad.

Fourth, control in approach 2, which can be described as decentralized control, requires more decentralization of operating decisions than does control in approach 1; and fifth, control in approach 2, compared to control in approach 1, favors short vertical spans or reporting channels from the foreign subsidiary to responsible positions in the parent. Consequently, control in approach 2 may not transfer well across hierarchical levels of an organization (i.e., there is substantial control loss). Control in approach 1, on the other hand, transfers well across levels of an organization, with little control loss.

An important factor that influences an MNC's decision with regard to the level of control and the extent of delegation is cultural proximity, or the extent to which the host cultural ethos permits adoption of the home (parent company) organizational culture.[8] Those countries that permit easy adoption of the parent company culture would be considered high in cultural proximity. For example, a U.S. MNC might have relatively less difficulty in transmitting its organizational culture to a subsidiary in Australia than to a subsidiary in Indonesia. In this case, the cultural proximity between the United States and Australia would be higher than the cultural proximity between the United States and Indonesia. Cultural proximity becomes crucial in the selection of control systems because the lower the cultural proximity, the higher the familiarization costs. For example, an extra effort would be needed to familiarize the managers of the Indonesian subsidiary with the U.S. corporate culture, incurring additional costs.[9]

MNCs often use some combination of both output and behavioral control, so what has been described is more a difference in pattern, or the relative use of one approach over the other, than a difference in type. The effectiveness of any MNC management control system depends on the quality and cooperation of management at the foreign subsidiary level. The ability and willingness of foreign subsidiary management to comprehend what is involved and accept what is required are crucial to the successful implementation of any management control system. Furthermore, the quality of the mechanisms and processes through which information is collected, processed, and transmitted at the subsidiary level will determine the quality of the performance evaluation of foreign operations.

PERFORMANCE EVALUATION

Performance evaluation is about monitoring an organization's effectiveness in fulfilling its objectives. It is a key management control task. In addition to providing measures that can be used to evaluate management performance, corporate management also expects the performance evaluation system to help assess the profitability of current operations, identify areas that need closer attention, and allocate scarce resources efficiently. Furthermore, the

---

[8] B. R. Baliga and A. M. Jaeger, "Multinational Corporations: Control Systems and Delegation Issues," *Journal of International Business,* Fall 1984, pp. 25–40.

[9] Similarly, the concept of "psychic distance" (the interaction between geographic distance and culture) has been used to explain budget control of foreign subsidiaries. See Lars G. Hassel and Gary M. Cunningham, "Psychic Distance and Budget Control of Foreign Subsidiaries," *Journal of International Accounting Research* 3, no. 2 (2004), pp. 79–93.

performance evaluation and related reward systems are expected to motivate organizational members to behave in a manner consistent with the organization's goals.

Prior studies have shown that no single criterion can be used meaningfully to evaluate the performance of all subsidiaries, as no single criterion is capable of capturing all facets of performance that are of interest to corporate management. It is common for MNCs to use a mixture of measures, financial and nonfinancial, formal and informal, and formula-based and subjective, to evaluate performance. For example, when there is a lower level of perceived environmental uncertainty, firms tend to use a more formula-based type of evaluation, whereas when there is a higher level of environmental uncertainty they tend to use more subjective judgment.[10] The operating environment of a foreign subsidiary is influenced by many factors. Exhibit 10.2 shows the social, political and legal, economic, and technological factors that are likely to influence a firm's operations in a national environment, thus creating a particular level of uncertainty and risk. Performance evaluation measures that attempt to capture these complexities are bound to contain a high degree of subjectivity.

EXHIBIT 10.2   Influences Affecting the Operating Environment of Subsidiaries in Foreign Countries

Source: H. Noerreklit and H. W. Schoenfeld, "Controlling Multinational Companies: An Attempt to Analyse Some Unresolved Issues," *International Journal of Accounting* 35, no. 3 (2000), pp. 415–30.

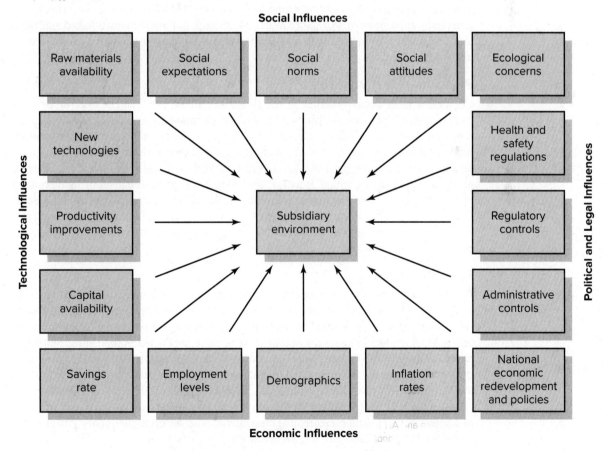

[10] V. Govindarajan, "Appropriateness of Accounting Data in Performance Evaluation: An Empirical Examination of Environmental Uncertainty as an Intervening Variable," *Accounting, Organizations and Society* 9, no. 2 (1984), pp. 125–35.

Performance evaluation is a complex issue even in a purely domestic context. It becomes much more complex in an international context, particularly due to the issues that are unique to foreign operations, such as exchange rate fluctuations, varying rates of inflation in foreign countries, international transfer pricing, and cultural and environmental differences that exist across countries. It is important to ensure that the performance targets set for a foreign subsidiary are in line with overall corporate goals and strategies, and at the same time are appropriate for the local circumstances. In the remainder of this section, we discuss in some detail the issues related to designing and implementing a system for evaluating the performance of foreign operations.

Evaluating the Performance of Foreign Operations

Designing an effective performance evaluation system for foreign operations requires decisions to be made with regard to the following:

1. The type of measure or measures on which performance will be evaluated.
2. The treatment of the foreign operation as a revenue, cost, profit, or investment center.
3. The issue of evaluating the foreign operating unit versus the manager of that unit.
4. The method of measuring profit for those foreign operations evaluated on the basis of profitability.

There are no universally right or wrong decisions with regard to these issues. There is no generically appropriate performance evaluation system, nor are there established guidelines that companies are required to follow. Each company will have a unique system tailored to its strategic objectives.

Performance Measures

Companies must decide whether to use financial criteria, nonfinancial criteria, or some combination of the two to measure and evaluate performance. Considering the diverse environments in which MNCs operate and the interdependencies among units in a multinational context in the current global environment, developing a global business strategy can be a highly complex task. A potential problem for MNCs in this regard is the tendency for headquarters to rely on simple financial control systems, often designed for home-country operations and extended to foreign subsidiaries. Subsidiary managers can be highly sensitive to these systems unless the systems are adapted to the local operating environment.[11] The danger here is that inappropriate performance standards may lead to dysfunctional behavior not in line with corporate goals.

Financial Measures

Financial measures are those measures of performance that are based on accounting information. They include sales growth, cost reduction, profit, and return on investment. Several surveys have asked MNCs which financial measures they use in evaluating the performance of foreign operations. The results of four surveys, three conducted in the United States and one conducted in the United Kingdom, are presented in Exhibit 10.3. In all four surveys, the top three financial measures used in evaluating foreign subsidiary performance (by both the U.S. and UK MNCs) are profit, ROI, and comparison of budgeted and actual profit, although the rank order changes slightly among the four studies. Given the large percentage of companies using each measure, it is clear that MNCs use multiple financial measures in evaluating the performance of foreign operations.

---

[11] L. G. Hassel, "Headquarter Reliance on Accounting Performance Measures in a Multinational Context," *Journal of International Financial Management and Accounting* 3, no. 1 (1991), pp. 17–38.

EXHIBIT 10.3
Financial Measures Used by U.S. and UK MNCs to Evaluate Subsidiary Performance

Sources: [a] H.G. Morsicato, *Currency Translation and Performance Evaluation in Multinationals* (Ann Arbor, MI: UMI Press, 1980);
[b] W. M. Abdallah and D. E. Keller, "Measuring the Multinational's Performance," *Management Accounting,* October 1985, pp. 26-30, 56;
[c] A. Hosseini and Z. Rezaee, "Impact of SFAS No. 52 on Performance Measures of Multinationals," *International Journal of Accounting* 25 (1990), pp. 43-52;
[d] I. S. Demirag, "Assessing Foreign Subsidiary Performance: The Currency Choice of U.K. MNCs," *Journal of International Business Studies,* Summer 1988, pp. 257-75.

| | Ranking | | | |
| | United States | | | United Kingdom |
Financial Measures	**1980[a]**	**1984[b]**	**1990[c]**	**1988[d]**
Profit	1	2	1	3
Return on investment (ROI)	2	3	3	2
Budget compared to actual profits	3	1	2	1

EXHIBIT 10.4
Comparison of Japanese and U.S. Performance Evaluation Measures

Source: J. C. Bailes and T. Assada, "Empirical Differences between Japanese and American Budget and Performance Evaluation Systems," *International Journal of Accounting* 26, no. 2 (1991), p. 137.

Percentage of Times Ranked in Top Three Budget Goals for Divisional Managers		
Measure	**Japan**	**United States**
Sales volume	86.3%	27.9%
Net profit	44.7	35.0
Production cost	40.7	12.4
Return on sales	30.7	30.5
Controllable profit	28.2	51.8
Sales growth	19.4	22.4
Return on investment	3.1	68.4

In contrast, the results of a 1991 survey of U.S. and Japanese MNCs (reported in Exhibit 10.4) indicate that, compared with U.S. MNCs, Japanese MNCs are much more concerned with sales volume and production cost. In addition, Japanese MNCs are not very concerned with ROI, whereas this is the most important measure for the U.S. MNCs responding to the survey. U.S. MNCs are also more concerned with controllable profit than their Japanese counterparts. We discuss the concept of controllable profit more fully later in this chapter.

Nonfinancial Measures
Nonfinancial measures are those measures of performance that are based on information not obtained directly from financial statements. A survey of U.S. MNCs was conducted in 1983 to determine the use of various nonfinancial measures in evaluating the performance of foreign operations. Respondents were asked to indicate the level of importance of each measure on a scale of 1 (very important) to 4 (not important) in evaluating (1) the foreign subsidiary and (2) the manager of the foreign subsidiary. The results are reported in Exhibit 10.5.

Survey participants indicated that market share is the most important nonfinancial measure of performance. Other important measures included relationship with the host country

EXHIBIT 10.5
Importance of
Nonfinancial
Measures in
Evaluating
Performance

Source: F. D. S. Choi and I. J.
Czechowicz, "Assessing Foreign
Subsidiary Performance: A
Multinational Comparison,"
*Management International
Review* 23 (1983), p. 17.

Nonfinancial Measure	Average Importance	
	Subsidiary	Manager
Increasing market share.........................	1.8	1.5
Relationship with host country government...............	2.1	1.8
Quality control........................	2.2	1.9
Productivity improvement........................	2.2	2.1
Cooperation with parent company...................	2.4	2.0
Environmental compliance.................	2.4	2.3
Employee development........................	2.4	2.0
Employee safety........................	2.4	2.2
Labor turnover........................	2.7	2.5
Community service........................	2.9	2.8
Research and development in foreign subsidiary..........	3.1	3.2

Scale 1 = Very important to 4 = Not important

government, quality control, and productivity improvement. Nonfinancial measures such as community service and labor turnover were deemed less important. Overall, the less quantifiable and nonfinancial measures are subjective as compared with their financial counterparts.

In general, the method of evaluation depends largely on the type of subsidiary involved. It is common to use simple and straightforward criteria for evaluating a subsidiary with specific tasks, such as a sales unit. The criteria used to evaluate such affiliates include number of new customers, market share, or a combination of similar measures.

Financial versus Nonfinancial Measures

Prior studies have found national differences with respect to the prominence given to financial and nonfinancial measures in evaluating subsidiary performance. Partial results of a study of U.S. and Japanese management accounting practices that included both types of measures are reported in Exhibit 10.6. It shows that financial measures, albeit different ones, are given primary importance in both Japan and the United States. In Japan, market share is far less important than sales as a performance measure; in the United States, market share is about as important as sales, but both sales and market share are much less important than return on investment (ROI) in evaluating performance. In a separate study, profit-based measures also were given primary importance by European companies.[12]

Another study investigated the evaluation criteria used by MNCs from four countries (Great Britain, Canada, Germany, and Japan) with regard to their operations in the United States. Some of the results are reported in Exhibit 10.7. Although differences exist across the four countries, the MNCs are similar in their ranking of several criteria. Profit margin is the number one criterion for MNCs in three of the four countries (tied with sales growth in Canada), but it ranks fourth in Japan. Sales growth is the number one criterion in Japan and number two in the other three countries (with some ties). Cost reduction is a top-five criterion in each country. Net income ranks in the top five in each country, with the exception of Great Britain. Market share ranks among the top-five criteria only for German MNCs.

[12] Business International Corporation, "Evaluating the Performance of International Operations" (New York: Business International Corporation, 1989), p. 174.

EXHIBIT 10.6 **Comparison of Financial and Nonfinancial Measures in Japan and the United States**

Source: M. D. Shields, C. W. Chow, Y. Kato, and Y. Nakagawa, "Management Accounting Practices in the U.S. and Japan: Comparative Survey Findings and Research Implications," *Journal of International Financial Management and Accounting* 3, no. 1 (1991), p. 68.

	Percentage of Time Considered Important	
Measure	**Japan**	**United States**
Sales	69%	19%
Return on investment	7	75
Market share	12	19

EXHIBIT 10.7 **Ranking of Evaluation Criteria by MNCs with Operations in the United States**

Source: S. C. Borkowski, "International Managerial Performance Evaluation: A Five Country Comparison," *Journal of International Business Studies,* Third Quarter 1999, pp. 533–56.

Criterion	**British**	**Canadian**	**German**	**Japanese**
Profit margin	1	1,2	1	4
Sales growth	2,3,4	1,2	2	1
Cost reduction	2,3,4	3,4	5	5
Net income	12	5	4	3
Goal attainment	5	3,4	8	2
Budget adherence	2,3,4	6	9	9
Return on sales	6	13	13	7
Return on assets	7,8	10	14	13
Technical innovation	7,8	11,12	7	10
Return on investment	9,10	9	11	10
Product innovation	9,10	11,12	6	12
Market share	11	8	3	7
Company standards	13	7	10	5
Residual income	14	14	12	13

A 2002 survey of 167 U.S. chief financial officers conducted by PricewaterhouseCoopers found that top executives at MNCs consider nonfinancial performance measures such as product/service quality and customer satisfaction/loyalty more important than current financial results in creating long-term shareholder value (see Exhibit 10.8). According to the survey, 69 percent of MNCs have attempted to develop a balanced scorecard combining both financial and nonfinancial measures in a comprehensive system to measure performance. While nonfinancial measures are viewed as being most important for long-term shareholder value, financial results are still viewed as a key factor in making ongoing management decisions. The major advantage of profit as a measure of performance is that it embodies all the major business functions from marketing (sales revenue) to production (cost of goods sold) to financing (interest expense).

Responsibility Centers

A company must decide whether a foreign affiliate should be evaluated as a revenue center, a cost center, a profit center, or an investment center. Managers of revenue centers and cost centers tend to have the least amount of responsibility compared to managers of other responsibility centers within a group. They normally have no right to sell existing assets or acquire new assets. Revenue centers are expected to generate revenues from selling

EXHIBIT 10.8 CFOs' Views on Factors Contributing to Long-Term Shareholder Return

Source: PricewaterhouseCoopers, "Non-financial Measures Are Highest-Rated Determinants of Total Shareholder Value, PricewaterhouseCoopers Survey Finds," Management Barometer news release, April 22, 2002.

Measure	Importance*
Product and service quality	89%
Customer satisfaction and loyalty	83
Operating efficiency	75
Current financial results	71
Innovation	62
Employee satisfaction and turnover	47

* Percentage of respondents indicating that a particular measure is important in determining long-term shareholder value.

products, providing services, or engaging in other revenue-generating activities. Treating an operating unit as a revenue center implies that responsibility is assigned only to generating revenues, and not to controlling expenses. Cost centers (e.g., internal service units of an organization, such as accounting, manufacturing, and research and development) are expected to produce as much as possible for a given amount of resources or produce a given amount of output with specified quality at the lowest possible cost. Treating an operating unit as a cost center implies that responsibility is assigned only to cost control and reduction, but not to sales generation.

Evaluation as a profit center implies that profit will be used to determine whether the operating unit is achieving its objectives and that resources will be allocated according to the unit's profit. In effect, the operating unit and its management are being held responsible for generating profit. Profit center managers are given a fixed amount of assets and are ultimately responsible for both costs and revenues.

The responsibilities of an investment center manager include all the responsibilities of a profit center manager plus the responsibility for investment decisions. Return on investment is the most common investment center performance measure. If a foreign operating unit is evaluated as an investment center, the unit and its management are held responsible for generating an adequate ROI. Although identifying appropriate responsibility centers for foreign subsidiaries is a difficult task, it is also important because of the need to match the performance measure chosen to the responsibilities assigned to the responsibility center.

Foreign Operating Unit Treated as a Profit Center

To the extent that foreign management is not directly responsible for all of the foreign operation's activities, treating that operation as a profit center may not be useful for evaluating management's performance. An MNC's transfer pricing policy may not be compatible with the profit center concept. When corporate management dictates the use of certain transfer prices to achieve a specific worldwide cost-minimization objective, the local operation loses control over determination of profit. For example, it would be inappropriate to evaluate an assembly plant in a high-tax country as a profit center when it is required to purchase inputs from foreign affiliates at high prices (dictated by the parent company) in order to minimize worldwide income taxes.

Some foreign operations have strategic importance unrelated to generating profit. For example, a company might invest in a mining operation in a foreign country with the purpose of having a captive source of an important raw material. Since the original reason for making this investment is not to generate profit, perhaps it should not be evaluated on the basis of profitability. Further, if all of the output is sold (transferred) to affiliated companies, and none of the output is sold on the open market, then this operation may have no control over either sales volume or sales price—both of which are dictated by the parent or affiliated customers. For this particular type of operation, performance might be better evaluated on the basis of cost reduction or productivity, rather than profit. Further, if the foreign affiliate is established with the purpose of selling products produced by the parent, perhaps sales volume or market share is a more appropriate performance measure than profit. The important point is that for some foreign operations, it might not be relevant to evaluate performance on the basis of profitability. Dysfunctional behavior can occur, for example, if a parent company decides to shut down an unprofitable component parts manufacturer when the reason it is not profitable is that the parent mandates low transfer prices. Headquarters management must decide which foreign operations should or should not be evaluated as profit centers.

Separating Managerial and Unit Performance

Intertwined with assigning levels of responsibility to foreign operating units is the question of whether the foreign operating unit and the management of that unit should be evaluated using the same performance measure. The performance of a foreign subsidiary is the result of decisions made by various parties, for example, local management, corporate management, and host governments. Local managers make most operating decisions, whereas corporate management makes transfer pricing and funds transfer decisions. Host governments may have specific rules concerning pricing and the use of foreign exchange that affect an operating unit's performance.

It is possible to have good management performance despite poor unit performance and vice versa. To properly reward and keep good managers and not inadvertently reward bad managers, the evaluation system should be able to separate subsidiary from managerial performance. The poor overall performance of the subsidiary may be largely due to circumstances beyond the manager's control—for example, market disruption caused by terrorism—even though the manager performed well under the circumstances.

The main issue here revolves around *uncontrollable items,* that is, items that affect the performance measure over which the local manager has no control or is not permitted to attempt to manage. The concept of *responsibility accounting* suggests that costs, revenues, assets, and liabilities should be traced to the individual manager who is responsible for them. Individual managers should not be held responsible for costs over which they have no control, nor should they be given credit for uncontrollable revenues.

Uncontrollable Items

Uncontrollable items can be classified as those that are controlled by the parent company, the host country government, and other parties. The following is a list of examples of each type:

Items Controlled by the Parent Company

- Sales revenue and cost of goods sold determined by discretionary transfer pricing.
- Allocation of corporate expenses, such as the chief executive officer's salary and research and development costs, to individual operating units.
- Interest expense on financing obtained from the parent (or an affiliated finance subsidiary), which sets the interest rate.

Items Controlled by the Host Government

- Restrictions on foreign exchange spending that affect the supply of imported materials and parts.
- Controls on prices that may be charged for products and services.
- Local content laws that require component parts to be sourced locally, sometimes at noncompetitive prices.

Items Controlled by Others

- Lost production due to labor strikes.
- Lost production due to power outages.
- Losses resulting from war, riots, and terrorism.
- Foreign exchange losses.

Managers normally prefer to be evaluated on the basis of controllable items because such evaluation is perceived as being fair and will make their rewards more predictable. However, costs often cannot be classified as either completely controllable or completely uncontrollable, because they are often influenced by both managerial actions and external factors.

Some companies use a measure of profit other than net profit to evaluate managers' performance. For example, using *earnings before interest and taxes (EBIT)* to measure performance does not hold the local manager responsible for interest and taxes. Likewise, the use of *operating profit* as the performance criterion avoids holding local management responsible for interest, taxes, and incidental gains and losses that are not a part of normal operations.

Business International asked survey participants what kinds of adjustments are made to the measures of profit and assets in measuring return on assets for evaluation purposes. Some of the results are reported in Exhibit 10.9. These results indicate, for example, that a majority of U.S.-based MNCs remove allocated corporate overhead costs from the measure of profit and intercompany receivables from the measure of total assets in calculating return on assets.

In evaluating the foreign operating unit, the decision of whether to adjust the performance measure for uncontrollable items should be based on whether the item in question has any impact on cash flows to be received by the parent from the foreign operation. Generally, only those items controlled by the parent should be removed from the measurement of profit because all other items do affect cash flows. For example, although the local manager should not be fired over lost production due to power outages over which he or she has no control, the cost associated with lost production should be relevant in deciding whether to continue with this particular operation. In contrast, it would be dysfunctional to abandon a particular foreign operation located in a high-tax jurisdiction because of inadequate returns if the parent's discretionary transfer pricing policies contributed to the subpar ROI.

EXHIBIT 10.9
Calculation of Return on Assets for Performance Evaluation

Source: Rosemary Schlank, *Evaluating the Performance of International Operations* (New York: Business International Corp., 1989), p. 31.

	Percentage of MNCs	
	U.S.	European
Items Deducted from Profit		
Depreciation	68%	57%
Share of HQ administration costs	60	36
Foreign exchange gains and losses	48	50
Taxes	46	71
Interest	42	57
Share of corporate R&D	38	64
Items Included in Assets		
External receivables	80	86
Intercompany receivables	33	57
Other current assets	75	79
Fixed assets	82	71
Goodwill	44	14

With regard to the issue of whether management and the unit itself should be evaluated on the same basis, companies tend to use the same performance measurement techniques in evaluating both managers and foreign operating units.

Choice of Currency in Measuring Profit

It appears that most MNCs evaluate performance, at least partially, on some measure of profitability (net income, profit margin, return on investment, etc.). In using profit for performance evaluation, a major issue that companies must address is whether profit should be measured in local currency or parent company currency. If profit is to be measured in parent company currency, the company must select a *method of translation* and decide whether to include the *effects of exchange rate changes.*

Measurement of profit in the local currency is generally considered to be appropriate if the foreign subsidiary is not expected to generate parent currency for payment of dividends to stockholders. This would be true in the case where the operation provides a strategic benefit to the MNC other than an ability to generate parent currency dividends. An example would be a foreign operation that was established specifically to supply affiliated companies with raw materials. Measurement of profit in the parent currency is considered appropriate when the foreign subsidiary is expected to generate parent currency that could be paid as dividends to stockholders. This is true for most foreign subsidiaries.

Foreign Currency Translation

If parent currency is to be used in evaluating performance, the company must translate foreign currency profit into parent currency and decide which translation method to use. For internal purposes, a company need not use the same translation methods that it is required to use for financial reporting. A U.S.-based MNC, for example, need not use U.S. GAAP rules for internal performance evaluation purposes. MNCs should consider which translation method best reflects economic reality for the particular foreign operation being evaluated.

A corollary issue is whether the *translation adjustment* should be included in the measurement of profit. Under both IFRS and U.S. GAAP, the translation adjustment that arises when the *temporal method* is used is included as a *gain or loss in net income,* whereas the translation adjustment under the *current rate method* is *deferred on the balance sheet.* Whether to include the translation adjustment in the measure of profit used for performance evaluation purposes would seem to hinge on two issues:

1. Does the translation adjustment accurately reflect the impact on parent currency cash flows resulting from a change in the exchange rate?
2. Does the foreign operation manager have authority to hedge his or her translation exposure?

If the answer to both questions is yes, then the translation adjustment should be included in the performance evaluation measure regardless of whether it is required by financial reporting rules. If the answer to either question is no, then the translation adjustment may or may not be included in the measure of profit.

OPERATIONAL BUDGETING

Accounting's primary contribution to strategy implementation is through operational budgeting. Whereas long-term budgets are mainly used as a strategy formulation and long-term planning device, annual operational budgets help express a firm's long-term strategy within shorter time frames. Operational budgets provide the mechanisms to translate organizational goals into financial terms, assign responsibilities and scarce resources, and monitor actual performance. Budgeted numbers become targets for managers to achieve.

Many MNCs find it necessary to translate operational budgets of foreign subsidiaries using an appropriate exchange rate. This process is complicated as a result of exchange rate fluctuations.

Choice of Currency in Operational Budgeting

Many MNCs evaluate annual performance by comparing actual operating performance to a budget. The company exerts management control by focusing on the variance between budgeted and actual profit. Budgetary control allows corporate management to trace the variance between budget and actual performance to the manager or the unit responsible. In the case of an MNC, the question arises as to whether the budget should be prepared and actual profit measured in the local currency or the parent currency. If "actual" is compared to "budget" in *local* currency, the overall budget variance will be a function of a sales volume variance and local currency price and quantity variances. If "actual" is compared to "budget" in *parent* currency, both the budget and actual results must be translated into parent currency using appropriate exchange rates. If one exchange rate is used to translate the budget (e.g., beginning-of-period exchange rate) and another exchange rate is used to translate actual results (e.g., end-of-period exchange rate), the total variance between budget and actual will be a function of sales volume variance, local currency price and quantity variances, and *the difference in exchange rates used to translate budgeted profit and actual profit*. This can be seen as follows:

Budgeted profit in local currency	×	Beginning exchange rate	=	Budgeted profit in parent currency
vs				vs
Actual profit in local currency = Total Variance (sales volume variance plus local currency price and quantity variances)	×	Ending exchange rate	=	Actual profit in parent currency = Total Variance (sales volume variance plus local currency price and quantity variances plus exchange rate variance)

If budget is compared to actual in parent currency, the question arises as to whether the manager of a foreign operation should be held responsible for foreign exchange risk, that is, the risk that actual results in parent currency will deviate from the budget due to changes in the exchange rate. This question should be answered by determining whether foreign management has the authority to hedge, and therefore control, foreign exchange risk. If so, then it would make sense to translate the budget and actual results into parent currency and hold management responsible for the exchange rate component of the total budget variance. If not, then perhaps profit measured in local currency rather than parent currency should be used for evaluation because the exchange rate variance is uncontrollable.

MNCs generally centralize their foreign exchange risk management activities and do not allow individual foreign operation managers to hedge their foreign exchange risk. Yet top management often wants to evaluate the performance of operations located in a variety of foreign countries on the basis of a common denominator—the parent currency. The question then arises as to how the local currency budget and actual local currency results can be translated into parent currency without holding foreign management responsible for foreign exchange risk. The answer is fairly obvious: Use the same exchange rate to translate both budgeted profit and actual profit.

Conceptually, there are three possible exchange rates to use in preparing the budget and translating actual results into parent currency:[13]

1. The actual exchange rate at the time the budget is prepared.
2. A projected future exchange rate at the time the budget is prepared.
3. The actual exchange rate at the end of the budget period.

As shown in Exhibit 10.10, these three exchange rates lead to nine possible combinations, only five of which would make sense for evaluation purposes.

The five meaningful combinations of exchange rates differ as follows in the extent to which management is held responsible for fluctuations in exchange rates:

1. *Translate the budget and actual results using the exchange rate that exists at the time the budget is prepared.* Under this combination, the total budget variance is a function of sales volume and local currency (LC) price and quantity variances only. Exchange rates have no effect on evaluation. However, there is little incentive to incorporate anticipated exchange rate changes into operating decisions. This combination is equivalent to evaluating results in local currency.

2. *Translate the budget and actual results using the exchange rate that exists at the end of the budget period.* The comments related to combination 1 apply equally to this combination.

3. *Translate the budget and actual results using a projected ending exchange rate (projected at the time the budget is prepared).* Under this combination, the total budget variance also is a function of sales volume and local currency price and quantity variances only. However, unlike combinations 1 and 2, the use of a projected exchange rate provides managers an incentive to incorporate expected exchange rate changes into their operating plans, but they are not held responsible for actual exchange rate changes. For example, if the local currency is expected to decrease in value during the year, the foreign operation's ability to export should improve, and local managers should attempt to take advantage of this opportunity. On the other hand, the cost of imports will increase, and local managers should search for alternative domestic inputs. (This is discussed more fully later in this chapter in discussing how to incorporate economic exposure into the operating budget process.) Because of its potential for causing local managers to consider the impact that exchange rate changes will have on parent currency profit, this combination is generally favored in the literature.

4. *Translate the budget at the initial exchange rate and translate actual results using the ending exchange rate.* In this case, the total budget variance is a function of sales volume, local currency price and quantity variances, and the change in exchange rate *whether*

EXHIBIT 10.10
Combinations for Translation of Budget and Actual Results

Source: D. R. Lessard and P. Lorange, "Currency Changes and Management Control: Resolving the Centralization/ Decentralization Dilemma," *Accounting Review,* July 1977, pp. 628–37.

	Rate Used to Track Actual Performance Relative to Budget		
Rate Used for Determining Budget	**Actual at TOB**	**Projected at TOB**	**Actual at EOP**
Actual at time of budget (TOB)	1	n/a	4
Projected at time of budget	n/a	3	5
Actual at end of period (EOP)	n/a	n/a	2

[13] The discussion here is based on D. R. Lessard and P. Lorange, "Currency Changes and Management Control: Resolving the Centralization/Decentralization Dilemma," *Accounting Review,* July 1977, pp. 628–37.

anticipated or not. Because local managers bear full responsibility for exchange rate changes, noneconomic hedging may result if they are allowed to hedge. Local managers will want to hedge their exposure even though a natural hedge may exist elsewhere in the MNC's worldwide organization.[14]

5. *Translate the budget at the projected ending exchange rate and translate actual results at the actual ending rate.* In this scenario, the total budget variance is a function of sales volume, local currency price and quantity variances, and the *unanticipated* change in exchange rate. Through this combination of exchange rates, local managers are asked to incorporate projected exchange rate changes into their operating plans. They are then held responsible for the impact that unanticipated exchange rate changes have on actual operating results.

Illustration of the Combinations

To illustrate the five combinations of exchange rates in translating the budget and actual results, consider an example of a U.S.-based MNC with a subsidiary in Foreign Country. Budgeted amounts in foreign currency (FC) are as follows:

	Budget
Sales	FC 100
Cost	90
Profit	FC 10

Assume that the foreign subsidiary's actual results in FC are exactly as budgeted and that exchange rates for the budget period are as follows:

Actual at time of budget preparation	$1.00/FC 1
Projected ending	$0.90/FC 1
Actual at end of period	$0.70/FC 1

The following shows the translation of the budget and actual results into U.S. dollars under each of the five combinations:

	Combination									
	1		**2**		**3**		**4**		**5**	
	Budget	Actual	Budget	Actual	Budget	Actual	Budget	Actual	Budget	Actual
Exchange rate	$1.00	$1.00	$0.70	$0.70	$0.90	$0.90	$1.00	$0.70	$0.90	$0.70
Sales	100	100	70	70	90	90	100	70	90	70
Costs	90	90	63	63	81	81	90	63	81	63
Profit	10	10	7	7	9	9	10	7	9	7
Variance		$ 0		$ 0		$ 0		($ 3)		($ 2)

[14] A natural hedge within the MNC group exists, for example, if a subsidiary in Canada has a €1 million receivable and a subsidiary in Mexico has a €1 million payable, both due on the same date. From the group perspective, neither subsidiary should hedge its individual foreign exchange risk, because the loss (or gain) on the euro payable will be offset by a gain (or loss) on the euro receivable. If local managers are held responsible for exchange rate variances, however, there will be an incentive for both managers (in Canada and in Mexico) to hedge their specific foreign exchange exposure.

Because the foreign subsidiary exactly met its sales volume and cost targets in terms of foreign currency, any U.S.-dollar variances are due solely to the change in the exchange rate. There is no exchange rate variance in combinations 1, 2, and 3, because the same exchange rate is used to translate both the budget and the actual figures. The exchange rate variance in combination 4 is ($3) (unfavorable), which is equal to the change in exchange rate from the beginning to the end of the period (− $0.30) multiplied by the actual amount of FC profit (FC 10). The unfavorable exchange rate variance of ($2) in combination 5 reflects the unanticipated change in the exchange rate [($0.70 − $0.90) × FC 10].

Incorporating Economic Exposure into the Budget Process

There are three types of exposure to foreign exchange risk: transaction exposure, translation (or balance sheet) exposure, and economic exposure. Transaction exposure refers to the risk that changes in exchange rates will have an adverse effect on cash flows related to foreign currency payables and receivables. Translation exposure refers to the risk that through the translation of foreign currency financial statements of its subsidiaries, a change in exchange rates will cause the parent company to report a negative translation adjustment (or remeasurement loss) in its consolidated financial statements. Chapters 6 and 7 cover financial accounting issues related to these two types of exposure to foreign exchange risk.

Economic exposure refers to the risk that changes in exchange rates will have a negative impact on an entity's cash flows. The concept of economic exposure encompasses more than transaction exposure, which is just one aspect. Unlike transaction and translation exposure, economic exposure is not directly measured by the accounting system.

Economic exposure can be explained using the following example. If the value of the British pound were to increase from US$1.50 to US$2.00, customers in the United States would have to pay a higher U.S.-dollar price for purchases denominated in British pounds and may therefore shift to non-British suppliers. An appreciation of the British pound creates economic exposure for British companies; their customers might switch to non-British suppliers. The depreciation of a company's home currency also creates economic exposure through an increase in the home currency price paid for import purchases. The extent of economic exposure for a business enterprise is at least partially a function of its mix of imports and exports.

Transaction and translation exposures are often reduced (or avoided completely) through the use of financial instruments such as foreign currency forward contracts and options. Economic exposure is reduced by making operating and strategic decisions to make the company more competitive in the face of exchange rate changes. Shifting from the use of imported parts to locally produced parts when the home currency is losing value and reducing the local currency price in the short term to shore up export sales when the home currency is increasing in value are examples of actions that a company could take to reduce its economic exposure to exchange rate changes.

Economic exposure also provides opportunities to take advantage of exchange rate changes to increase local currency cash flows. For example, if the U.S. dollar were to decrease in value from $1.00 per euro to $1.20 per euro, U.S.-dollar priced goods would become less expensive in terms of euros. A U.S.-based company could pursue a strategy to increase sales volume and market share in Europe without having to reduce its U.S.-dollar prices. Conversely, the company could pursue a skimming strategy by increasing its U.S.-dollar price such that the euro price (and therefore European demand) after the exchange rate change would remain the same as before. In either case, total U.S.-dollar sales and therefore U.S.-dollar cash flows should increase.

Designing a management control system that allows the parent company to evaluate the performance of its foreign subsidiary managers on their ability to manage economic exposure and at the same time motivates those managers to exploit opportunities afforded by exchange rate changes is not easy. Because economic exposure deals with opportunity costs, its effects are not separately measured by the normal accounting system. Let us consider what can happen if a company does not attempt to incorporate economic exposure into the evaluation system.

Assume U.S.-based Parent Company has two subsidiaries in Foreign Country: Exporter and Importer. Exporter makes export sales to the United States but sources inputs locally, and Importer imports all of its inputs from the United States but makes no export sales. Budgets in FC and US$ (using the initial exchange rate of US$1.00 = FC 1) are as follows:

	Exporter		Importer	
	FC	US$	FC	US$
Sales	100	100	100	100
Costs	90	90	90	90
Profit	10	10	10	10

During the budget period, the US$ appreciates 25 percent against the FC such that the ending exchange rate is US$1.00 = FC 1.25 or US$0.80 = FC 1. Assuming that Parent Company uses the ending exchange rate to track actual performance, actual results in FC and US$ are as follows:

	Exporter		Importer	
	FC	US$	FC	US$
Sales	118	94.4	103	82.4
Costs	101	80.8	99	79.2
Profit	17	13.6	4	3.2

Actual FC sales and FC costs are larger than budgeted for both Exporter and Importer. Because the favorable sales variance is greater than the unfavorable cost variance, Exporter's actual profit exceeds the budget in both FC and US$. Although Importer outperformed the FC sales budget, FC costs rose more rapidly, and Importer's actual profit is less than budgeted in both FC and US$. Given these results, should Exporter's manager, but not Importer's manager, be rewarded? Not necessarily. Incorporating the expected effect of a currency devaluation on FC sales and FC costs paints a different picture.

Exporter

Because Exporter has only export sales, a 25 percent depreciation in the FC should allow Exporter to either (1) generate 25 percent more sales volume (if FC prices are not increased) or (2) increase FC prices by 25 percent to generate higher total FC sales revenue at the same level of sales volume. In either case, Exporter's sales should have been FC 125. Actual sales are only FC 118, or FC 7 less than they would have been if Exporter's manager had fully exploited the opportunity to increase export sales.

Because Exporter sources all inputs locally, the depreciation in the FC should not affect costs. Exporter's manager has not effectively controlled costs; costs are FC 11 (FC 101 − FC 90) higher than they should be.

The appreciation of the U.S. dollar should have allowed Exporter to generate the following amount of FC and US$ profit:

	FC	US$
Sales	125	100
Costs	90	72
Profit	35	28

Actual profit is only $13.60, or $14.40 less than it should have been.

Importer

Because Importer imports all inputs from the United States, a 25 percent appreciation in the U.S. dollar should cause Importer's FC costs to increase by 25 percent, from FC 90 to FC 101.25. Actual costs are only FC 99 because Importer's manager has sourced some inputs locally rather than through imports.

Because all of Importer's sales are made locally, the appreciation in the U.S. dollar should have no effect on FC sales. Nonetheless, Importer's manager was able to outperform the FC sales budget.

The appreciation of the U.S. dollar should have caused Importer to incur the following amount of FC and US$ loss:

	FC	US$
Sales	100.00	80
Costs	101.25	81
Profit (loss)	(1.25)	(1)

Actual profit is $3.20, or $4.20 greater than it should have been.

After incorporating the effects of economic exposure into the analysis, it would appear that only the manager of Importer should be rewarded.

The accounting system does not measure the amount of profit that *should have been* earned, so information provided by that system is not helpful in measuring a manager's effectiveness in coping with economic exposure. The use of translation combinations 3 and 5 outlined earlier, in which projected rates are used to prepare the budget, is a partial solution to this problem. Using projected rates to translate the budget provides an incentive for managers to take operating and strategic actions to minimize negative effects on cash flows caused by changes in exchange rates and to take advantage of positive effects. However, this approach is limited in that projected exchange rates may not become reality. A refinement to this process would be to periodically update the projected ending exchange rate and ask local managers to update their plans as the projection changes. Clearly, this is not an easy process, but any system that forces managers of foreign operations to consider the effect that exchange rate changes have on their operating results should help in reducing the risk associated with those changes.

CULTURE AND MANAGEMENT CONTROL

The success of a performance evaluation system will be determined by its design as well as by its implementation. Important factors for a successful performance evaluation system include: (1) integration with the company's business strategy, (2) measuring factors that actually contribute to the company's success, (3) comparing actual results with the original plan, (4) employee support of the system, and (5) fair and achievable goals.

For MNCs, another factor should be added for the successful implementation of a performance evaluation system: The system must be sensitive to the national cultures to which local managers belong. Indeed, cultural factors should be considered in the entire strategy implementation process. Implementing a corporate strategy that will influence human behavior in the desired manner requires cultural awareness, as a given method of implementation may not produce the desired outcome across all cultures.

Due to cultural differences, MNCs may find that changes are necessary to the manner in which strategies are implemented in different countries. For example, Japanese companies assign responsibility to the group rather than to the individual, and every group member is partially responsible for the group's performance.[15] This notion of group responsibility conflicts with the way standard costs and budgets are used in the United States, in which responsibility is assigned to specific individuals within an organization. This also calls into question the universal acceptability of one of the fundamental assumptions of the Western concept of management control—that the responsibility for specific tasks lies with the individual to whom the task is traceable. Research also has found differences between the United States and Japan in the use of budgets. U.S. managers tend to be more involved in the budgeting process, and budget variances are used as the basis for evaluating performance and determining rewards. Japanese managers, in contrast, tend to view budget variances as providing information that can be used to improve performance.[16]

Local managers' attitudes toward budgets also can be influenced by environmental factors. Researchers have discovered, for example, that compared to managers in the United States, managers in Central American countries view budgets as being less critical.[17] Central American managers are more likely to see budgets as a source of certainty and security and as a means to protect resources amid turbulence, rather than as a performance evaluation and planning tool. The researchers argue that the differing attitudes toward budgets are due partly to the widely varying levels of environmental turbulence in the United States and Central America.

Culture also can affect management style. For example, researchers have found that Mexican executives tend to use an authoritarian leadership style, do not see the need to share information with subordinates, and have little faith in participative management styles. These cultural tendencies have direct implications for the manner in which budgeting is applied within Mexican organizations. In particular, the idea of participative budgeting is not likely to be well received.[18]

Finally, cultural differences also can influence capital budgeting decisions. For example, strong uncertainty avoidance (intolerance of uncertainty) can lead managers to require short payback periods for capital investments, because once the investment is recouped, the level of uncertainty associated with the investment is reduced significantly. This makes projects with shorter payback periods the preferred choice for some managers, even though projects with longer payback periods may produce greater longer-term benefits.

[15] L. Kelley, A. Whatley, and R. Worthley, "Assessing the Effects of Culture on Managerial Attitudes: A Three-Country Test," *Journal of International Business Studies,* Summer 2001, p. 22.

[16] J. C. Bailes and T. Assada, "Empirical Differences between Japanese and American Budget and Performance Evaluation Systems," *International Journal of Accounting* 26, no. 2 (1991).

[17] R. Mandoza, F. Collins, and O. J. Holzmann, "Central American Budgeting Scorecard: Cross Cultural Insights," *Journal of International Accounting, Auditing and Taxation* 6 (1997), pp. 192–209.

[18] L. Kelley, A. Whatley, and R. Worthley, "Assessing the Effects of Culture on Managerial Attitudes: A Three-Country Test," *Journal of International Business Studies,* Summer 2001, p. 22.

Summary

1. The management accounting function within an organization plays an important role in strategy formulation and implementation through the activities of *capital budgeting, operational budgeting,* and *performance evaluation.* Carrying out these activities for foreign investments and foreign operations requires the consideration of issues such as foreign currency fluctuations and differences in the business environment and culture that exist across countries—issues that are not relevant to domestic operations.

2. *Multinational capital budgeting* is complicated by the various risks to which foreign investments are exposed. Forecasted future cash flows are likely to be influenced by factors such as local inflation, changes in exchange rates, and changes in host government policy.

3. Foreign capital investment opportunities can be evaluated from a *project perspective,* focusing on project cash flows in local currency, and/or from a *parent company perspective,* focusing on parent cash flows in parent currency.

4. Determining the appropriate level of responsibility to delegate to managers of foreign operations and designing the related *management control system* are major issues facing MNCs in implementing strategy. Key factors that influence the design of an effective control system for an MNC include the company's organizational structure and the strategic role assigned to foreign subsidiaries.

5. In designing a performance evaluation system for foreign operations, an MNC must decide on *performance evaluation measures.* Although companies often use multiple measures, both financial and nonfinancial, most focus on financial measures of performance, and profit-based measures are most commonly used.

6. Companies must decide whether a foreign operation will be evaluated as an *investment center,* a *profit center,* a *cost center,* or a *revenue center.* Some foreign operations may have a strategic purpose other than profit creation and should therefore be evaluated differently.

7. Companies also must decide *whether the foreign operating unit and the managers of that unit should be evaluated in the same manner,* or whether they should be evaluated separately using different measures of performance. Responsibility accounting suggests that managers should not be held responsible for uncontrollable items. For foreign managers, this would consist of revenues and expenses controlled by the parent company, the host government, and others.

8. For those foreign operations evaluated on the basis of profitability, the company must decide *whether profit will be measured in local or parent currency.* Most companies evaluate the performance of foreign operations in parent currency, which necessitates *translation* from the local currency. These companies must decide whether the local manager will be held responsible for the resulting translation adjustment.

9. Many companies evaluate performance by comparing actual operating results to an operating budget. For foreign operations, the question arises as to *whether the operating budget should be prepared and actual results measured in the local currency or in the parent currency.* If operating budgets and actual results are measured in parent currency, exchange rate variances can be avoided by using the same exchange rate to translate both the budgeted and actual results. Using a projected exchange rate to translate the budget provides an incentive for local managers to factor the effects of expected exchange rate changes into their operating plans.

10. Management control systems must be sensitive to the *national cultures* to which local managers belong. Cultural awareness is needed when implementing a system designed to influence human behavior in a particular manner, because a given method of implementation may not produce the desired outcome across all cultures.

Questions

1. What are the three pieces of information needed to calculate the net present value (NPV) of a potential capital investment, whether domestic or foreign?

2. What makes calculation of NPV for a foreign capital investment project more complex than the calculation of NPV for a domestic capital investment project?

3. How does the evaluation of a potential foreign capital investment differ under the parent company perspective versus under the project perspective?

4. In foreign investment analysis, what are the two methods used to incorporate factors affecting cash flows that vary across countries?

5. How does an ethnocentric organizational structure of an MNC differ from a polycentric organizational structure?

6. What are the main issues that need to be considered in designing and implementing a successful performance evaluation system for a foreign subsidiary?

7. When might it be appropriate to evaluate the performance of a foreign subsidiary in terms of local currency rather than in terms of parent company currency?

8. Why might it be important to separate the evaluation of the performance of a foreign subsidiary from that of its manager?

9. In evaluating the performance of a manager of a foreign subsidiary, what issues are associated with the calculation of profit?

10. How can a local currency operating budget and actual results be translated into parent currency without holding the foreign manager responsible for foreign exchange risk?

11. When actual results are compared to an operating budget, under what conditions might it be appropriate to hold the manager of a foreign subsidiary responsible for an exchange rate variance as part of the total budget variance?

12. What is the advantage of using a projected future exchange rate to translate both the local currency operating budget and actual results into parent currency?

Exercises and Problems

1. A U.S. company is considering an investment project proposal to expand its operations in Germany. As part of the proposed project, the German operation is required to pay an annual royalty of €500,000 to the parent company.

   Required:
   Explain the cash flow implications of the €500,000 payment for the parent company.

2. Foursquare Technology Corp. established foreign operations in Lithuania and Taiwan in the current year. Corporate management has decided to evaluate the foreign operations and their managers on the basis of earnings before tax.

   Required:
   Discuss the issues that Foursquare's corporate management should consider in determining exactly how its foreign operations' earnings before tax will be measured for performance evaluation purposes.

3. All Kiwi Ltd. (a New Zealand-based company) has a wholly owned subsidiary in Malaysia whose manager is being evaluated on the basis of the variance between actual profit and budgeted profit in New Zealand dollars (NZD). Relevant information in Malaysian ringgits (MYR) for the current year is as follows:

	Budget	Actual
Revenues	MYR 12,000,000	MYR 11,000,000
Expenses	9,000,000	9,000,000

Current year actual and projected exchange rates between the NZD and the MYR are as follows:

Actual at time of budget preparation................	NZD 0.312 per MYR 1
Projected ending at time of budget preparation.......	NZD 0.340 per MYR 1
Actual at end of budget period	NZD 0.357 per MYR 1

Required:

a. Calculate the total budget variance for the current year using each of the five combinations of exchange rates for translating budgeted and actual results shown in Exhibit 10.10.

b. Make a recommendation to All Kiwi's corporate management as to which combination in item (a) should be used, assuming that the manager of the Malaysian subsidiary does *not* have the authority to hedge against changes in exchange rates.

c. Make a recommendation to All Kiwi's corporate management as to which combination in item (a) should be used, assuming that the manager of the Malaysian subsidiary has the authority to hedge against unexpected changes in exchange rates.

4. Havel Robotics Company (a U.S.-based firm) exports 25,000 industrial robots per year to its Chinese sales subsidiary under an agreement that covers a five-year period. In China, the robots are sold for the RMB (Chinese currency) equivalent of $50 per unit. The total costs in the United States are direct manufacturing costs and shipping costs, which amount to $35 per unit. Thus, Havel generates a pre-tax profit of $15 on each robot it exports to China. The market for industrial robots in China is stable, and Havel holds the major portion of the market.

In 2020, the Chinese government, adopting a policy of replacing imported robots with local products, invited Havel to open an assembly plant in China. If Havel makes the investment, it will operate the plant for five years and then sell the building and equipment to Chinese investors at net book value (cost less accumulated depreciation) at the time of sale plus the current amount of any working capital. Havel will be allowed to repatriate 100 percent of cash flow from operations (net income plus depreciation) to the United States each year.

Havel's anticipated outlay in 2020 would be $1,500,000 (buildings and equipment, $750,000, and working capital, $750,000). Buildings and equipment will be depreciated over five years on a straight-line basis (no salvage value). At the end of the fifth year, buildings and equipment will have a net book value of $0. However, the $750,000 of initial working capital will be allowed to be repatriated to the United States, and will not be subject to any taxation.

Locally assembled robots will be sold for the RMB equivalent of $50 each. Operating expenses per robot are as follows:

Materials purchased in China (dollar equivalent of RMB cost)	$15
Components imported from U.S. parent......................	8
Variable costs per unit.......................................	$23

The $8 transfer price per unit for components sold by Havel to its Chinese subsidiary consists of $4 of direct costs incurred in the United States and $4 of pre-tax profit to Havel. There are no other operating costs in either China or the United States.

The corporate income tax rates in China and the United States are 25 and 21 percent, respectively.

Havel uses a 15 percent discount rate to evaluate all its investment projects. The present value factor for a single payment in five periods at 15 percent is 0.497. The present value factor for an annuity of payments for five periods at 15 percent is 3.352.

Assume the investment is made at the end of 2020, and all operating cash flows occur at the end of 2021 through 2025. The RMB/U.S. dollar exchange rate is expected to remain constant over the five-year period. If Havel decides not to make the investment in China, it will still be able to export fully assembled robots to its Chinese sales subsidiary for the foreseeable future.

Required:

a. Assuming that Havel uses a parent company perspective in making foreign capital investment decisions, do you recommend that the company make the investment?

b. Havel learns that if it decides not to invest in China, a German company will probably make an investment similar to that being considered by Havel. The German investment would be protected by the Chinese government against imports by other foreign robot manufacturers. Thus, Havel would no longer be able to export robots to its Chinese sales subsidiary. How does this information affect your analysis and recommendation?

5. Imogdi Corporation (a U.S.-based company) has a wholly owned subsidiary in Argentina, whose manager is being evaluated on the basis of the variance between actual profit and budgeted profit in U.S. dollars. Relevant information in Argentine pesos (ARS) for the current year is as follows:

(in ARS)	Budget	Actual
Revenues	40,000,000	50,000,000
Expenses	30,000,000	42,000,000

Current year actual and projected exchange rates between the ARS and the U.S. dollar (USD) are as follows:

Actual at time of budget............................	USD 0.063 per ARS 1
Projected ending at time of budget preparation......	USD 0.058 per ARS 1
Actual at end of budget period	USD 0.056 per ARS 1

Required:

a. Calculate the total budget variance for the current year using each of the five combinations of exchange rates for translating budgeted and actual results shown in Exhibit 10.10.

b. Make a recommendation to Imogdi's corporate management as to which combination in requirement (a) should be used, assuming that the manager of the Argentinian subsidiary does *not* have the authority to hedge against changes in exchange rates.

c. Make a recommendation to Imogdi's corporate management as to which combination in requirement (a) should be used, assuming that the manager of the Argentinian subsidiary has the authority to hedge against unexpected changes in exchange rates.

6. Stratford Industries, Inc., has a foreign operation with the following current year contribution margin income statement (amounts in foreign currency, FC):

Sales revenue	FC 5,750,000
Variable operating costs	(3,450,000)
Contribution margin	2,300,000
Fixed operating costs.	(1,800,000)
Operating profit.	500,000
Interest expense	(200,000)
Profit before tax.	300,000
Income taxes	(60,000)
Net profit.	FC 240,000

Corporate management has decided to evaluate the performance of the manager of the foreign operation on the basis of controllable profit. The following information has been gathered to assist in calculating controllable profit for the current year:

- A national labor strike in the foreign subsidiary's home country caused it to shut down operations for one week, resulting in lost production of 1,000 units. Weekly fixed operating costs are FC 35,000.

- Stratford required the foreign subsidiary to sell 25 percent of its output to an affiliated company in Japan at a price of FC 100 per unit, even though all of the foreign subsidiary's output could have been sold locally at a price of FC 120 per unit.

- The host government requires companies to purchase 20 percent of component parts from local manufacturers. As a result, the foreign subsidiary paid FC 60,000 more for parts in the current year than if it had been allowed to import 100 percent of parts needed.

- Stratford requires the foreign subsidiary to borrow FC from its Swiss subsidiary at an annual interest rate of 10 percent, even though local banks charge 6 percent interest on similar loans.

Required:
Develop an estimate of the amount of controllable profit to be used in evaluating the performance of the manager of Stratford's foreign subsidiary for the current year.

7. Attica SA (a Greek company) has a foreign subsidiary in Morocco, whose manager is evaluated on the basis of profit in euros (EUR). In the current year, the foreign subsidiary was budgeted to generate a profit of 1,000,000 Moroccan dirham (MAD), and actual profit for the year was MAD 1,050,000. Prometheus's corporate management has calculated an unfavorable total budget variance for the foreign subsidiary of EUR 7,650. Current year actual and projected exchange rates are as follows:

Actual exchange rate at time of budget preparation	EUR 0.086 per MAD 1
Projected ending exchange rate at time of budget preparation	EUR 0.090 per MAD 1
Actual exchange rate at end of budget period	EUR 0.093 per MAD 1

Required:
a. Identify the combination of exchange rates (see Exhibit 10.10) used by Attica's corporate management in translating budget and actual amounts that results in the total budget variance of EUR 7,650.

b. Determine the portion of the total budget variance calculated by Attica's corporate management that is caused by a change in the exchange rate between the EUR and the MAD. (There are three possible correct responses to this requirement.)

8. Fitzwater Limited (an Irish company) has a foreign subsidiary in Norway, whose manager is evaluated on the basis of profit in euros (EUR). In the current year, the foreign subsidiary was budgeted to generate a profit of 500,000 Norwegian kroner (NOK), and actual profit for the year was NOK 480,000. Fitzwater's corporate management has calculated an unfavorable total budget variance for the foreign subsidiary of EUR 8,560. Current year actual and projected exchange rates are as follows:

Actual at time of budget preparation................	EUR 0.116 per NOK 1
Projected ending at time of budget preparation.......	EUR 0.105 per NOK 1
Actual at end of budget period	EUR 0.103 per NOK 1

Required:
a. Identify the combination of exchange rates (see Exhibit 10.10) used by Fitzwater's corporate management in translating budgeted and actual amounts that results in the total budget variance of EUR 8,560.

b. Determine the portion of the total budget variance calculated by Fitzwater's corporate management that is caused by a change in the exchange rate between the EUR and the NOK. (There are three possible correct responses to this requirement.)

9. Woodlands Company (a U.S.-based company) has a subsidiary in Mexico that exports all of its production to customers in Asian markets and sources all of its inputs locally. Budgets in Mexican pesos (MXN) and U.S. dollars (USD) using the beginning of period exchange rate of USD 0.08 per MXN 1.00 are as follows:

	MXN	USD
Sales	40,000,000	3,200,000
Costs........	30,000,000	2,400,000
Profit	10,000,000	800,000

During the budget period, the MXN decreased in value by 25 percent against world currencies, such that the end-of-period exchange rate was USD 0.06 per MXN 1.00. Assuming that Woodlands uses the end-of-period exchange rate to track actual performance, actual results in MXN and USD are as follows:

	MXN	USD
Sales	45,000,000	2,700,000
Costs........	35,500,000	2,130,000
Profit	9,500,000	570,000

As a result, there is an unfavorable total budget variance of MXN 500,000 and an unfavorable total budget variance of USD 230,000.

Required:
a. Determine the amount of the USD 230,000 unfavorable total budget variance caused by a change in the USD/MXN exchange rate.

b. Taking economic exposure to foreign exchange risk into consideration, estimate what profit would have been (in both MXN and USD) if the Mexican subsidiary's manager had taken full advantage of the decrease in value of the MXN.

10. Viking Corporation (a U.S.-based company) has a subsidiary in Japan that imports finished products from unrelated suppliers in China and sells all of its purchases to customers in Japan. Cost of goods sold represents 75 percent of total costs. Budgets in Japanese yen (JPY) and U.S. dollars (USD) using the beginning-of-period exchange rate of USD 0.010 per JPY 1.00 are as follows:

	JPY	USD
Sales	300,000,000	3,000,000
Costs	200,000,000	2,000,000
Profit	100,000,000	1,000,000

During the budget period, the JPY decreased in value by 20 percent against world currencies, such that the end-of-period exchange rate was USD 0.008 per JPY 1.00. As a result of the increased cost of imports, the manager of the Japanese subsidiary switched to purchasing some of the goods it sells from Japanese manufacturers. Assuming that Viking uses the end-of-period exchange rate to track actual performance, actual results in JPY and USD are as follows:

	JPY	USD
Sales	310,000,000	2,480,000
Costs	225,000,000	1,800,000
Profit	85,000,000	680,000

As a result, there is an unfavorable total budget variance of JPY 15,000,000 and an unfavorable total budget variance of USD 320,000.

Required:

a. Determine the amount of the USD 320,000 unfavorable total budget variance caused by the change in the USD/JPY exchange rate.

b. Taking economic exposure to foreign exchange risk into consideration, estimate what profit would have been (in both JPY and USD) if the Japanese subsidiary's manager had not taken advantage of the decrease in value of the JPY.

11. Duncan Street Company (DSC), a British company, is considering establishing an operation in the United States to assemble and distribute smart speakers. The initial investment is estimated to be 25,000,000 British pounds (GBP), which is equivalent to 30,000,000 U.S. dollars (USD) at the current exchange rate. Given the current corporate income tax rate in the United States, DSC estimates that total after-tax annual cash flow in each of the three years of the investment's life would be US$10,000,000, US$12,000,000, and US$15,000,000, respectively. However, the U.S. national legislature is considering a reduction in the corporate income tax rate that would go into effect in the second year of the investment's life and would result in the following total annual cash flows: US$10,000,000 in Year 1, US$14,000,000 in Year 2, and US$18,000,000 in Year 3. DSC estimates the probability of the tax rate reduction occurring at 50 percent.

DSC uses a discount rate of 12 percent in evaluating potential capital investments. Present value factors at 12 percent are as follows:

Period	PV Factor
1.......	0.893
2.......	0.797
3.......	0.712

The U.S. operation will distribute 100 percent of its after-tax annual cash flow to DSC as a dividend at the end of each year. The terminal value of the investment at the end of three years is estimated to be US$25,000,000. The U.S. withholding tax on dividends is 5 percent; repatriation of the investment's terminal value will not be subject to U.S. withholding tax. Neither the dividends nor the terminal value received from the U.S. investment will be subject to British income tax.

Exchange rates between the GBP and USD are forecasted as follows:

Year 1	GBP 0.74 = USD 1.00
Year 2	GBP 0.70 = USD 1.00
Year 3	GBP 0.60 = USD 1.00

Required:

a. Determine the expected net present value of the potential U.S. investment from a project perspective.

b. Determine the expected net present value of the potential U.S. investment from a parent company perspective.

Case 10-1

Felix Machine Company

Late in 2021, Felix Machine Company (FMC) management was considering expansion of the company's international business activities. FMC is a U.S.-based manufacturer of compound machines for use in industrial equipment. FMC's worldwide market was supplied from subsidiaries in France, Brazil, and Taiwan, as well as from the United States. The company was particularly successful in Asia, mainly due to the high quality of its products, its technical expertise, and excellent after-sale service. This success led corporate management to consider the feasibility of further expansion of its business in the Asian region.

FMC's Taiwanese subsidiary assembled and distributed machines and had limited manufacturing capability so that it could undertake special adaptations required. The Taiwanese subsidiary had been urging corporate management to expand its manufacturing capacity for several years. However, an alternative scenario appeared more promising. The Indian economy, with its liberalized economic policies, was growing at annual rates much higher than in many other countries. Further, India had considerably lower labor costs and certain government incentives that were not available in Taiwan. Therefore, FMC's corporate management chose to first consider India for its Asian expansion and had a four-year investment project proposal prepared by the chief financial officer's staff.

The proposal involved establishing a wholly owned subsidiary in India that would produce machines for the Indian domestic market as well as for export to other Asian countries. The initial equity investment would be $1.5 million, equivalent to 67.5 million Indian rupees (Rs) at the exchange rate of Rs 45 to the U.S. dollar. (Assume that the Indian rupee is freely convertible, and there are no restrictions on transfers of foreign exchange out of India.) An additional Rs 27 million would be raised by borrowing from a commercial bank in India at an interest rate of 10 percent per annum. The principal amount of the bank loan would be payable in full at the end of the fourth year. The combined capital would be sufficient to purchase plant and equipment of $1.8 million and would cover other initial expenditures, including working capital. The cost of equipment installation would be $15,000, with another $5,000 for testing. No additional working capital would be required during the four-year period. The plant was expected to have a salvage value of Rs 10 million at the end of four years. Straight-line depreciation would be applied to the original cost of the plant.

The firm's overall marginal after-tax cost of capital was about 12 percent. However, because of the higher risks associated with an Indian venture, FMC decided that a 16 percent discount rate would be applied in evaluating the potential project.

Present value factors at 16 percent are as follows:

Period	Factor
1...........	0.862
2...........	0.743
3...........	0.641
4...........	0.552

Sales forecasts (in units) are as follows:

Year	Sales (units) (Domestic)	(Export)
1...........	5,000	10,000
2...........	6,000	12,000
3...........	7,000	14,000
4...........	8,000	16,000

The initial selling price of a machine was to be Rs 4,500 for both Indian domestic sales and export sales in the Asian region, and the selling price in both cases was to increase at an annual rate of 10 percent. The exchange rate between the Indian rupee and the U.S. dollar was expected to vary as follows:

January 1, Year 1	Rs 45 per U.S. dollar
December 31, Year 1...........	Rs 45 per U.S. dollar
December 31, Year 2...........	Rs 43 per U.S. dollar
December 31, Year 3...........	Rs 40 per U.S. dollar
December 31, Year 4...........	Rs 38 per U.S. dollar

The cash expenditure for operating expenses, excluding interest payments, would be Rs 44 million in Year 1. This amount was expected to increase at a rate of 8 percent per year. The Indian subsidiary would be expected to pay a royalty of Rs 20 million to the parent company at the end of each of the four years. In addition, in those years in which the subsidiary generated a profit, it would pay a dividend to FMC equal to 100 percent of net earnings. Through negotiation with the Indian government, the subsidiary would be exempt from Indian corporate income taxes and withholding taxes on payments made to the parent company. Royalties received from the Indian subsidiary would be fully taxable in the United States at the U.S. corporate tax rate of 21 percent. Dividends received from the Indian subsidiary would be exempt from U.S. taxation.

Assuming the project proposal is accepted, FMC expects to be able to sell the Indian subsidiary at the end of the fourth year for its salvage value. FMC also expects to be able to repatriate to the parent the cash balance at the end of Year 4. The cash balance will be equal to the difference between the aggregate amount of cash from operations generated by the subsidiary and the aggregate amount of dividends paid to FMC, after paying back the local bank loan, plus salvage value. The repatriated cash balance will be taxed in the United States at 21 percent only if there is a gain after deducting the cost of the original investment.

Required:

1. Calculate the net present value (NPV) of the proposed investment in India from both a project and a parent company perspective.
2. Recommend to Felix Machine Company's corporate management whether or not to accept the proposal.

Chapter **Eleven**

Auditing and Corporate Governance: An International Perspective

Learning Objectives

After reading this chapter, you should be able to:

- Define corporate governance and discuss the circumstances that have caused it to receive worldwide attention in recent years.
- Describe the corporate governance guidelines at the international level.
- Explain the link between auditing and corporate governance in an international context.
- Examine international diversity in external auditing.
- Explain the meaning of *audit expectation gap*.
- Describe the steps taken toward international harmonization of auditing standards.
- Discuss the ethical issues involved in external auditing at the international level.
- Discuss the issues concerning auditor liability and auditor independence.
- Explain the role of audit committees.
- Examine internal auditing issues in an international context.

INTRODUCTION

The term *corporate governance* relates broadly to the manner in which an organization is governed or managed. Specifically, it encompasses the framework of rules, relationships, systems, and processes designed to exercise authority and control within a company, and it includes the mechanisms by which companies and those in control are held to account. Corporate governance, therefore, facilitates effective, entrepreneurial, and prudent management, which in turn delivers long-term success. Companies usually are financed through equity capital taken from investors. The stock of many such companies is listed on stock exchanges, which exposes them to the public. This brings them under close statutory and regulatory scrutiny, as the interests of shareholders/stakeholders are supreme. In short, corporate governance is about what the board of directors (the board) of a company does and how it sets the values of the company. It refers to the spirit of the statute rather than the letter alone. Thus morality and ethics are also important parts of corporate governance.

By providing information to the market, external reporting, external auditing, and internal auditing provide direct input toward the successful implementation of corporate governance mechanisms in a company. External reporting was discussed in earlier chapters. In this chapter, we focus on the link between auditing (external and internal) and corporate governance, paying special attention to the international dimension. We describe international diversity in external auditing and some issues related to the international harmonization of auditing standards, including the audit expectation gap. We also briefly discuss selected additional issues of international auditing, namely, auditor liability, auditor independence, and the role of audit committees. Further, we examine issues related to internal auditing. Finally, we provide some thoughts on the future direction of international auditing and corporate governance.

CORPORATE GOVERNANCE PRINCIPLES

In recent years and in many countries, numerous reports focusing on corporate governance have been produced.[1] The Organization for Economic Cooperation and Development (OECD) issued *Principles of Corporate Governance* (2004 Edition) to assist member and nonmember governments in their efforts to evaluate and improve the legal, institutional, and regulatory framework for corporate governance, as well as to provide guidance and suggestions for various stakeholders in corporate governance.[2] According to the OECD,

> Corporate governance . . . involves a set of relationships between a company's management, its board, its shareholders, and other stakeholders. Corporate governance also provides the structure through which the objectives of the company are set, and the means of attaining those objectives and monitoring performance are determined. Good corporate governance should provide proper incentives for the board and management to pursue objectives that are in the interests of the company and shareholders and should facilitate effective monitoring. (p. 1)

The OECD principles deal with, among other issues, the rights and fair treatment of various groups of shareholders, the role of various stakeholders, the importance of disclosure and transparency of information, and the responsibility of the board. They clarify the notion that the board of directors has the ultimate responsibility for governing a company, as opposed to being responsible for its day-to-day operations. The OECD principles formed the basis of the corporate governance component of the World Bank/International Monetary Fund's Reports on the Observance of Standards and Codes (ROSC). The OECD gives shareholders strong rights in most of the member countries.[3]

Corporate governance principles in countries have evolved based on their political, economic, and cultural philosophies. For example, the corporate governance models in the United Kingdom and the United States (shareholder-oriented models) are similar, and they differ from the stakeholder-oriented models prevalent in Continental Europe (e.g., France, Germany, Italy, and Spain). The countries with shareholder-oriented models usually have single-tier boards, whereas many countries with stakeholder-oriented models have two-tier boards. The two-tier system consists of a supervisory board of nonexecutive directors and a separate management board of executive directors, and it distinguishes between the monitoring and managerial functions. The supervisory board assumes the monitoring function. This corporate governance model explicitly incorporates representation from many types

[1] The term *corporate governance* first appeared in 1962 in a book by Richard Eells of Columbia University.

[2] See: https://www.oecd.org/corporate/ca/corporategovernanceprinciples/31557724.pdf.

[3] Organization for Economic Cooperation and Development, *OECD Principles of Corporate Governance* (Paris: OECD, 1999), available at www.oecd.org. The OECD member countries are thirty-eight high income countries committed to democracy and market economies. The OECD's members include Australia, Canada, most of the European Union, Japan, Korea, Mexico, Turkey, the United Kingdom, and the United States.

of stakeholders, including employees, suppliers, customers, and local communities, in addition to shareholders. In a country with a socialistic ideology (e.g., France), the corporate governance would be based on the inclusion of all stakeholders and place an especially large weight on issues that are important to trade unions and other employee groups. In a country where the banks have a major financial stake in the organization through collateral credit (e.g., Japan or Germany), corporate governance would give due weight to the banks' view of the best possible strategic course for the organization. In countries with strong traditions of capitalism (e.g., the United States and the United Kingdom), corporate governance has tended to focus on increasing the wealth of shareholders. However, governance reforms in the United States and the United Kingdom have recently tried to incorporate certain elements of the multi-stakeholder governance model in response to increasing societal demands.

The ownership pattern of most U.S. corporations is such that they are widely held, with capital provided by people who are not involved in the day-to-day management of the organization. The large institutional investors (mutual funds, pension funds, and so on) have a significant stake in these organizations and the capital markets are more liquid as equity is the preferred mode of business funding. In the United States, there is separation of ownership and management to the extent that managers have a free hand in running the affairs of the organization. However, the board monitors the performance of the managers and takes appropriate actions to encourage or discourage the strategies attempted by them. Likewise, the primary duty of the independent directors of a company is to provide oversight of all of the board's activities.

In the United States, the board of a company is a single-tier body. For example, Citigroup Inc. has a single-tier board structure, with several committees for managing the governance affairs and for oversight of management, including the Executive Committee, the Audit Committee, the Personnel and Compensation Committee, the Nomination, Governance and Public Affairs Committee, the Risk Management Committee, and the Ethics, Conduct, and Culture Committee. The presence of these committees highlights the critical areas requiring attention. The executive and nonexecutive directors of the company, together, chart the course of the organization.

The corporate governance system in the United States is based on shareholder wealth maximization principles, enunciated in the Sarbanes-Oxley Act of 2002 (SOX), the Securities and Exchange Commission (SEC), and the guidelines of the stock exchanges (e.g., NASDAQ and NYSE). Accordingly, disclosure of information to the market and transparency are considered essential to enhance corporate governance. Also it is assumed that the interests of other stakeholders such as creditors are suitably taken care of by their own shareholders. In addition, court judgments in various states are relevant because U.S. corporations are registered in particular states.

In the United Kingdom, the first version of the UK Code on Corporate Governance was produced in 1992 by the Cadbury Committee. It states, "Corporate governance is the system by which companies are directed and controlled." Boards of directors are responsible for the governance of their companies. The responsibilities of the board include setting the company's strategic aims, providing the leadership to put them into effect, supervising the management of the business, and reporting to shareholders on their stewardship. The board's actions are subject to laws, regulations, and the decisions of shareholders in general meetings. The shareholders' role in governance is to appoint the directors and the auditors and to satisfy themselves that an appropriate governance structure is in place.

The UK CG Code, which has been updated several times, was again updated in 2018. It applies to all companies with a premium listing of equity shares regardless of whether they were incorporated in the United Kingdom or elsewhere, for accounting periods beginning in January 2019. It is part of a framework of legislation, regulation, and best practice standards aimed at delivering high-quality corporate governance with in-built flexibility for companies to adapt their practices to take into account their particular circumstances. The 2018

Code emphasizes that boards must continue to think comprehensively about their overall tasks and the implications of these for the roles of their individual members. While in law a company is primarily accountable to its shareholders and should focus on the relationship between the company and its shareholders, the Code encourages companies to recognize the contribution made by other stakeholders and to confirm the board's interest in listening to their views insofar as they are relevant to the company's overall approach to governance. Specific provisions of the 2018 code added guidance on addressing the growing disparity between executive compensation and that received by ordinary workers. One example would be publishing the ratio between senior executive pay and median worker pay.

The "comply or explain" approach is the trademark of corporate governance in the United Kingdom. It is the foundation of the Code's flexibility. It is strongly supported by both companies and shareholders and as a consequence has been adopted in many other countries. The "comply or explain" approach recognizes that an alternative to following a provision may be justified in particular circumstances if good governance can be achieved by other means. A condition of doing so is that the reasons for it should be explained clearly to shareholders (and other interested parties), who may wish to discuss the position with the company and whose voting intentions may be influenced as a result. In providing an explanation, the company should aim to illustrate how its actual practices are both consistent with the principle to which the particular provision relates and contribute to good governance.

Today it is common for companies in many countries to include in their annual reports a statement about conformity to the applicable corporate governance standards. For example, the 2021 annual report of Rio Tinto, the global mining company with headquarters in London and Melbourne, contains a six-page statement outlining the company's compliance with the UK Corporate Governance Code as well as the governance principles and recommendations of the Australian Stock Exchange.[4] German companies publish an annual *Declaration of Conformity with the German Corporate Governance Code.* Siemens AG included the full text of this declaration in its 2021 annual report. In it, the company stated:

> Siemens AG has complied, and will continue to comply, with all the recommendations of the Government Commission on the German Corporate Governance Code in the version of December 16, 2019 published by the Federal Ministry of Justice and Consumer Protection in the official section of the Federal Gazette (Bundesanzeiger), with the following exceptions. . .[5]

Among these exceptions, Siemens disclosed that the chair of its compensation committee was not an independent director. The company's disclosure here is an example of the comply or explain system that was discussed above. The New York Stock Exchange imposes an even stricter rule on its member companies: that compensation committees be composed solely of independent directors. However, companies violating this rule are not given an explicit comply or explain escape hatch.

AUDITING AND CORPORATE GOVERNANCE

Auditing improves the precision, quality, and reliability of information made available to users of financial statements.[6] The assurance services provided by auditing firms play an important role in ensuring the quality of financial information, help

---

[4] Rio Tinto plc, Annual Report 2021, pp. 205–10.

[5] Siemens AG, "Corporate Governance Statement pursuant to Sections 289f and 315d of the German Commercial Code," Fiscal Report 2021, p.197.

[6] Auditing is "a systematic process of objectively obtaining and evaluating evidence regarding assertions about economic actions and events to ascertain the degree of correspondence between those assertions and established criteria and communicating the results to interested parties." American Accounting Association, *A Statement of Basic Auditing Concepts* (AAA Committee on Basic Auditing Concepts, 1973).

lower the cost of debt offerings, and contribute to greater investor confidence in the information provided. *International auditing* refers to the rules to be applied internationally for the auditing of financial statements and the processes associated with auditing financial statements prepared by multinational corporations (MNCs). With the increasing trend toward globalization of markets and rapid growth in international transactions, the issues associated with providing reliable, high-quality information have become crucial for MNCs in their efforts to succeed in increasingly competitive global markets. The 1997–1998 Asian financial crisis; the subsequent corporate scandals, particularly in the United States, involving large companies such as Enron, WorldCom, and Global Crossing; and the global financial crisis (GFC) of 2007–2008 have further highlighted the importance of assurance services in enhancing corporate governance.

The Sarbanes-Oxley Act (SOX) has been described as the most sweeping corporate legislation since the Securities Acts of 1933 and 1934. Enacted in 2002, SOX was a direct response the accounting scandals that rocked U.S. capital markets in the early 2000s. The act included detailed provisions dealing with corporate governance and auditors' duties that were designed to restore investor confidence in the financial reporting system.[7] Among SOX's many provisions, two of the most significant were:

- the creation of the Public Company Accounting Oversight Board (PCAOB), a body explicitly charged with regulating the auditing industry.
- a requirement that management report on, and auditors assess, the adequacy of the company's internal control system.

Below, we will look at how the SOX reforms were mirrored in measures adopted in other countries.

Another milestone in the history of auditing occurred in June 2017 when the Public Company Accounting Oversight Board (PCAOB) adopted a new auditing standard, *The Auditor's Report on an Audit of Financial Statements When the Auditor Expresses an Unqualified Opinion,* to enhance the relevance and usefulness of the auditor's report. This standard and related amendments required auditors to include in the auditor's report a discussion of the critical audit matters (CAMs), which are any matters arising from the audit of the financial statements communicated, or required to be communicated, to the audit committee. CAMs relate to accounts or disclosures that are material to the financial statements and involve especially challenging, subjective, or complex auditor judgment. The inclusion of a discussion of CAMs in the auditor's report marked a new era in the way auditors communicate with investors.

Further, the standard required the auditor's report to disclose, among other things, the tenure of an auditor, specifically, the year in which the auditor began serving consecutively as the company's auditor. Over many years, auditors have provided a binary "pass/fail" opinion on a company's financial statements. That means, either the financial statements fairly present the company's financial position and results from operations in accordance with applicable accounting standards, or they do not. The new standard retained this pass/fail model of the existing auditor's report, but required the auditors to expand on the various judgments and data that underlay their opinion. This reform to the auditor's report took effect for audits of fiscal years ending on or after June 30, 2019, and substantially improved the informativeness of audit opinions in the United States.

---

[7] A summary of the Sarbanes-Oxley Act is available at https://en.wikipedia.org/wiki/Sarbanes-Oxley_Act.

Rules vs Principles in Auditing

The corporate governance code in the United Kingdom (including the amended version in 2018) resembles those of many countries in that it adopts a principles-based approach. A principle-based approach relies on general guidelines of best practice, and differs from the rules-based approach in the United States, which rigidly defines exact provisions that must be adhered to.

In February 2008, the Financial Reporting Council (FRC) in the United Kingdom published a document, *The Audit Quality Framework,* where it stated that it would assist companies (in evaluating audit proposals), audit committees (in undertaking annual assessments of the effectiveness of external audits), all stakeholders (in evaluating the policies and actions taken by audit firms to ensure that high-quality audits are performed, whether in the United Kingdom or overseas), and regulators (when undertaking and reporting on their monitoring of the audit profession). The *Framework* identifies the following key drivers of audit quality:

1. The culture within an audit firm.
2. The skills and personal qualities of audit partners and staff.
3. The effectiveness of the audit process.
4. The reliability and usefulness of audit reporting.
5. Factors outside the control of auditors affecting audit quality.

Auditing issues concerning both external and internal auditing are directly linked to corporate governance. In a multinational context, the linkages between auditing and corporate governance can be explained in terms of a set of relationships, as depicted in Exhibit 11.1.

External auditing provides assurance to financial statement users that the information contained in those statements is of high quality. Monitoring risks and providing assurance regarding controls are two main internal auditing functions. Monitoring risks involves identifying risks, assessing their potential effect on the organization, determining the strategy to minimize them, and monitoring the possibility for new risks. Companies may find that their precise circumstances are not expressly provided for in the standards. One of the strengths of principles-based standards is the flexibility that they provide companies in the essential tasks of risk monitoring and adaptation.

The preference for a principles-based approach was expressed in a report published in early 2008 by the International Federation of Accountants (IFAC). In it the IFAC identified

EXHIBIT 11.1
International Auditing and Corporate Governance

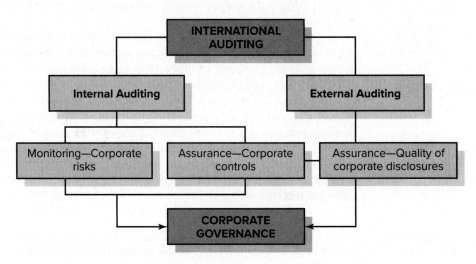

positive areas, areas of concern, and areas for further improvement.[8] With regard to the positive areas, the report stated that there was increased awareness that good corporate governance would count; there were new codes and standard improvements in board structure, risk management, and internal control; and there was more disclosure and transparency in business and financial reporting. The report identified five areas of concern: governance in name but not in spirit; overregulation; the development of a checklist mentality; personal risk and liability for company directors and senior management; and cost-benefit concerns. With regard to the areas for further improvement, IFAC identified behavioral and cultural aspects of governance; the existing rules, many of which were introduced as a response to crises and in need of review; the quality of directors; the relationship of remuneration to performance; and the need to expand the view from compliance governance to business governance.

Professional Accountants' Role

The external auditor's primary concern is whether the financial statements are free of material misstatement. Despite a number of governance and auditing reforms that began with the passage of SOX in 2002, the global investing community continues to be plagued by financial accounting irregularities that cause heavy losses to investors. Three prominent recent cases—the collapse of Carillion plc in the United Kingdom in 2018, of Wirecard in Germany in 2020, and a large fraud at the U.S.-listed Chinese coffee chain Luckin Coffee in 2020—illustrate the global scope and persistent nature of the problem.

Such cases continue to create problems for the accounting profession, particularly in view of the fact that many of these companies had received clean audit reports from large international accounting firms. The question often asked by investors and other interested parties is, "Where was the auditor?" However, this is not new; the same question has been asked on many occasions in the past. For example, following the global financial market crisis that emerged in Asia in 1997 and 1998, the World Bank asked international accounting firms to refuse to give clean audit reports for financial statements that had not been prepared in accordance with internationally acceptable accounting standards. Later, commenting on the causes of the Asian financial crisis, an official of the SEC pointed to (1) the failure of company accounts to show billions of dollars of debt, allowing companies to continue borrowing with no hope of repayment, and (2) the failure of auditing to detect the vulnerabilities.[9]

IFAC guidance on corporate governance addresses risks and organizational accountability. In June 2008, the Professional Accountants in Business (PAIB) Committee of IFAC released a new *International Good Practice Guidance* document entitled, "Evaluating and Improving Governance in Organizations." It includes a framework, a series of fundamental principles, supporting guidance, and references on how applying the principles can contribute to evaluating and improving governance in organizations. Further, the International Auditing and Assurance Standards Board (IAASB) requires the auditors of listed entities to communicate "key audit matters," those areas of the audit that have demanded the most significant auditor attention. Further, the European Union (EU) has introduced a similar requirement as part of the audit reform legislation, which became effective for June 30, 2017, fiscal year-end audits. These requirements are similar but not identical to the PCAOB requirement that audit reports should include a discussion on CAMs. For example, in

[8] IFAC comprises more than 160 professional accounting bodies from throughout the world, representing more than 2.5 million accountants in public practice, education, the public sector, industry, and commerce.

[9] L. Turner, "The 'Best of Breed' Standards: Globalising Accounting Standards Challenges the Profession to Fulfill Its Obligation to Investors," *Financial Times,* March 8, 2001.

Europe, the emphasis is on voluntary internal controls rather than enforcement of controls by statutes because the board structure appears to have inherent checks and balances that prevent the directors from making decisions that may be to their own advantage. Further, in Europe the requirement that the auditor's report should include a statement that no prohibited nonaudit services were provided seems to be unique.

The measures that have been taken around the world by governments, worldwide regulators, IFAC, accountancy organizations, and others to strengthen and improve corporate governance rules, regulations, and audit standards have had an impact on the operations of MNCs. Most MNCs now include a separate section in their annual reports explaining corporate governance issues. For example, the 2021 Annual Report of Volkswagen Group had a 42-page section on corporate governance. The auditors report was 13 pages, more than half devoted to describing key audit matters.

The International Response to Sarbanes-Oxley

As stated above, the Sarbanes-Oxley Act (SOX), enacted in 2002, was the most consequential piece of American securities legislation since the Great Depression. After SOX's passage, the global predominance of U.S. capital markets all but assured that its provisions would be mirrored in legislation enacted around the world. Early responses to SOX occurred in the developed capital markets of Europe and Japan. In fact, Japan's reforms to its Financial Instruments and Exchange Act were passed in 2006 and explicitly labeled as *J-SOX* by Japanese accountants. Eventually, SOX reforms reached emerging market economies as well. For instance, in 2014 India enacted comprehensive SOX-inspired changes to its Companies Act.[10] Here, we will briefly survey several of the act's most important provisions and list some of the effects they engendered in other countries.

Auditing Oversight Boards

As noted above, SOX created the PCAOB and gave it broad powers to regulate the audit industry in the United States. Many countries enacted legislation that created a local statutory body to regulate auditing if one did not already exist. Perhaps the best example is the establishment of the above-mentioned Financial Reporting Council by the United Kingdom in 2006. The FRC resembles the PCAOB in the powers it has been given to regulate audit services in the United Kingdom. The FRC also sets the UK's Corporate Governance and Stewardship Codes. The FRC is scheduled to be replaced by a new regulator, the Audit, Reporting and Governance Authority, in 2023.

Auditor Independence Provisions

At the time of SOX's enactment, most of the accounting world had come to recognize the threat to auditor independence posed by the growing amount of lucrative nonaudit services that audit firms were providing to clients. This threat had certainly been real at Worldcom. From 1999 to 2001, Worldcom paid its auditor Arthur Andersen $14.4 million in audit fees but $50 million for services such as consulting and litigation support.[11] Congressional reformers responded by including in SOX a list of prohibited nonaudit services and by requiring all nonaudit services to be pre-approved by the client's audit committee. Mirroring SOX, many countries enacted similar restrictions, including Australia, China, France, Germany, and Japan.

---

[10] Securities and Exchange Board of India, "Corporate Governance in listed entities - Amendments to Clauses 35B and 49 of the Equity Listing Agreement," April 17, 2014.

[11] Dennis Beresford, Nicholas deB. Katzenback, and C. B. Rogers, Report of Investigation: Special Investigative Committee of the Board of Directors of Worldcom. March 31, 2003, p. 226.

Audit Committee Independence

SOX required that all members of the audit committee of the board of directors be independent directors. It also required the company to disclose whether any member of the committee was a financial expert. Australia, Canada, Hong Kong, and the United Kingdom subsequently introduced similar independence requirements. Meanwhile, France, China, India, and Japan introduced the less stringent requirement that a majority of the audit committee members be independent directors. At a minimum, the EU's 8th Directive mandated that at least one member of the committee be independent.

Most of aforementioned countries also began requiring disclosure of whether a financial expert served on the committee, as did the EU's 8th Directive.

CEO Certification Statement

SOX mandated that the company include a statement by the CEO and another certifying officer, almost always the CFO, of responsibility for establishing and maintaining the company's internal control system. This statement also certifies that the company has disclosed material weaknesses in the internal control system and "any fraud, whether or not material." The annual reports of most countries now contain statements of this nature from senior management. The version mandated by India's Securities and Exchange Board is quite similar to that of the United States. Exhibit 11.2 reproduces the CEO/CFO certification statement from Tata Motors Limited for the 2021 fiscal year.

Auditor's Assessment of the Internal Control System

SOX's most controversial provision was a requirement that the company's external auditor attest to and report on management's assessment of the internal control system. In U.S. financial statements, the results of these assessments are published as formal opinions about whether the company has "maintained, in all material respects, effective control over financial reporting" for the accounting period in question.

EXHIBIT 11.2
Tata Motors Limited CEO/CFO Certification in Respect of Financial Statements and Cash Flow Statement for the Financial Year Ended March 31, 2021

1. The Financial Statements and Cash Flow statement do not contain any materially untrue statement or omit any material fact or contain statements that might be misleading.
2. The Financial Statements and the Cash Flow Statement together present a true and fair view of the affairs of the Company and are in compliance with existing accounting standards, applicable laws and regulations.
3. There are no transactions entered into by the Company during the year ended March 31, 2021, which are fraudulent, illegal, or violative of Company's Code of Conduct.
4. We accept responsibility for establishing and maintaining internal controls for Financial Reporting and we have evaluated the effectiveness of these internal control systems of the Company pertaining to financial reporting. Deficiencies noted, if any, are discussed with the Auditors and Audit Committee, as appropriate, and suitable actions are taken to rectify the same.
5. There have been no significant changes in the above-mentioned internal controls over financial reporting during the relevant period.
6. That there have been no significant changes in the accounting policies during the relevant period.
7. We have not noticed any significant fraud particularly those involving the management or an employee having a significant role in the Company's internal control system over Financial Reporting.

For Tata Motors Limited
Guenter Butschek, Chief Executive Officer & Managing Director
P B Balaji, Chief Financial Officer

Assessments of internal controls by external auditors were initially controversial because of the high costs that they were thought to entail. However, over time the global accounting community came to a consensus that the benefits of these assessments outweighed their costs. Thus, some form of assessment and report is now required in most of the world's major capital markets. In some countries, the auditor refers to its evaluation of the internal control system but does not express a formal opinion as to its effectiveness. For example, Ernst & Young stated in its 2021 audit report for Volkswagen:

> [We] obtain an understanding of internal control relevant to the audit of the consolidated financial statements and of arrangements and measures (systems) relevant to the audit of the group management report in order to design audit procedures that are appropriate in the circumstances, but not for the purpose of expressing an opinion on the effectiveness of these systems.

Japan and India are both examples of countries that require separate reports of the evaluation of internal control evaluation. In Japan, the auditor expresses a formal opinion about management's assessment of the internal control system. While these reports are generally filed separately (in Japanese), Nissan included Ernst & Young's opinion in its 2021 annual report. This opinion closely mirrors that required by SOX in the United States and is reproduced in Exhibit 11.3.

INTERNATIONAL DIVERSITY IN EXTERNAL AUDITING

We concluded the prevision section with a discussion of how the accounting scandals of the early 2000s, together with the Sarbanes-Oxley Act that was passed in reaction to them, set off a wave of governance and auditing reforms around the world. However, the responses of different countries to the growing demand for audit reforms were not uniform. They were preconditioned by fundamental differences in the role auditing plays in different countries. In this section, we will examine various aspects of these differences. These aspects include the purpose of external auditing, the audit environment, the regulation of auditing, and audit reports.

EXHIBIT 11.3
The Internal Control Audit Section of Ernst & Young's Independent Auditor's Report for Nissan, June 28, 2021

AUDITOR'S REPORT

Opinion

Pursuant to Article 193-2, Section 2 of the Financial Instruments and Exchange Act of Japan, we have audited the accompanying Management's Report on Internal Control Over Financial Reporting for the consolidated financial statements as at March 31, 2021 of Nissan Motor Co., Ltd. ("Management's Report").

In our opinion, Management's Report referred to above, which represents that the internal control over financial reporting as at March 31, 2021 of Nissan Motor Co., Ltd. is effective, presents fairly, in all material respects, the result of management's assessment of internal control over financial reporting in accordance with standards for assessment of internal control over financial reporting generally accepted in Japan.

Basis for Opinion

We conducted our internal control audit in accordance with auditing standards on internal control over financial reporting generally accepted in Japan. Our responsibilities under those standards are further described in the *Auditor's Responsibilities for the Audit of Internal Control* section of our report. We are independent of the Group in accordance with the ethical requirements that are relevant to our audit of the financial statements in Japan, and we have fulfilled our other ethical responsibilities in accordance with these requirements. We believe that the audit evidence we have obtained is sufficient and appropriate to provide a basis for our opinion.

Purpose of Auditing

The role of the auditor varies in different countries. For example, in Germany, the role of the statutory auditor is much wider compared to that of his or her counterparts in the United Kingdom and the United States. The UK Companies Act of 2019, which requires that audits of large- and medium-sized companies must be performed by a registered auditor, specifies that the role of the auditor is to report to shareholders whether the financial statements give a true and fair view of the financial position and results of operations of the company and whether the financial reports have been properly prepared in accordance with the provisions of the act (Section 235). In Germany, Section 316 of the German Commercial Code requires that in addition to financial statements, an auditor should examine management reports of large- and medium-sized corporations. The role of the statutory auditor in Germany is legally defined by the Auditors' Regulation and the German Commercial Code. German auditors take a much broader view of the concept of "client" than their counterparts in the United Kingdom and the United States. It is less problematic for German auditors to view the state and thus society as in part constituting the client.[12] country's corporate governance structure is a major factor that determines the purpose of external auditing. In Anglo-Saxon traditions, auditors' primary reporting responsibilities are to the shareholders of companies. However, this is not the case in some other countries, which have different corporate structures. In some European countries, a two-tiered board of directors is required for a public company, in that in addition to the management board, a company is also required to have a supervisory board. In Germany, for example, limited liability companies (public companies and private companies with over 500 employees) are required to appoint a supervisory board (*Aufsichtsrat*) to oversee the management board (*Vorstand*). The management board is composed solely of insiders and is responsible for the company's daily business activity, whereas the supervisory board has general oversight functions and is responsible for safeguarding the company's overall welfare by reviewing management board activities. The supervisory board consists of directors who are representatives of employees, creditors, and shareholder groups. The duties of the supervisory board as set out in the German Commercial Code (Article 225a, 1870 Amendment) are as follows:

- To supervise the management of the corporation in all branches of its administration;
- To ask the management for information, for the purpose of supervision, to have access to the books of account, and to review the cash on hand;
- To audit the income statement, the balance sheet, and the application of profits suggested by the management (Vorstand); and
- To call a general assembly if it is deemed necessary and is in the interest of the corporation.

The German Commercial Code establishes a duty for the supervisory board to conduct audits of the financial statements presented by the management to the shareholders' general meeting. It was envisaged that the supervisory board would perform substantive corporate governance. As accounting valuation issues became increasingly complex, supervisory boards started to use external auditors to fulfill their audit and control duties. This was the beginning of the development of the profession of external auditors in Germany. Historically, the German auditor's primary reporting responsibility has been to the supervisory board and not to shareholders, as in the Anglo-Saxon tradition. The basic function of the statutory auditor in Germany is to assist the supervisory board, and the audit report is normally addressed to the supervisory board, which engages the auditor.

[12] C. R. Baker, A. Mikol, and R. Quick, "Regulation of the Statutory Auditor in the European Union: A Comparative Survey of the United Kingdom, France and Germany," *European Accounting Review* 10, no. 4 (2001), pp. 763–86.

In China, many former state-owned enterprises were restructured to create new economic enterprises that have listed their securities on domestic and foreign stock exchanges. However, these enterprises do not conform to the Anglo-Saxon concept of an accounting entity. Historically, it was common in China for the principal business of a geographical region to be designated as the reporting entity, and made responsible for the education and health care of its citizens as well as employment and production. In the transition to a market economy, the State identified some of these entities as business enterprises. As these entities moved into international markets, they encountered the Anglo-Saxon concept of entity for the first time.[13]

These enterprises still have many related-party transactions with formerly related business units that are now outside the new entity. There are also intercompany transactions involving these units. The auditor's role or responsibilities in defining the boundaries of these entities and reviewing their transactions thus becomes unclear.

In China, some public companies have a supervisory committee, somewhat similar to the German supervisory board. The 2021 annual report of China Eastern Airlines Corporation Ltd., for example, includes a separate report of the supervisory committee, in addition to the auditor's report. The report of the supervisory committee states, among other things, that in 2021 it monitored the procedures of convening the general meetings and Board meetings of the company and their resolutions, and execution of those resolutions, and the supervisory committee is of the view that it has complied with the Company Law, the Securities Law, the rules governing the stock exchanges in Shanghai and Hong Kong, and so on.

Audit Environments

Cultural values in different countries can have an impact on the nature and quality of the audit work undertaken. For example, perceptions of auditors' ethical conduct may be influenced by cultural norms. Similarly, perceptions of auditor independence may vary as a result of underlying cultural and environmental differences across countries. Therefore, culture may be helpful in understanding the differences in auditor behavior patterns in different countries.[14] For example, the concept of an independent auditor is neither historically nor culturally appropriate in Japan, and legal liability suits against Japanese auditors are almost nonexistent.[15] The exercise of legal rights in a court of law is not in accordance with the underlying Japanese belief in the maintenance of harmony in interpersonal and intergroup relationships and the avoidance of open confrontation.[16]

Chinese cultural values—including respect for seniors, the desire to avoid confrontation and to look for agreeable compromises, and the concern for "saving face"—are likely to have implications in the audit judgment area. Further, history also plays a part in shaping the practice of auditing in China. Graham explains the manner in which culture affects auditors steeped in "risk-based audit" concept, which means the statutory limitation on allowances for doubtful accounts. However, the need for obsolescence reserves or written-downs in the Chinese State enterprise system was obviated, as all products were perceived as useful for something, someday. Further, since enterprises were State owned, and State credit was always considered "good," bad debt provisions were unnecessary.[17]

---

[13] L. E. Graham, "Setting a Research Agenda for Auditing Issues in the People's Republic of China," *International Journal of Accounting* 31, no. 1 (1996), p. 29.

[14] J. Soeters and H. Schreuder, "The Interaction between National and Organizational Cultures in Accounting Firms," *Accounting, Organizations and Society* 13, no. 1 (1988), pp. 75–85.

[15] J. McKinnon, "The Accounting Profession in Japan," *Australian Accountant,* July 1983, pp. 406–10.

[16] G. G. Mueller, "Is Accounting Culturally Determined?" Paper presented at the EIASM Workshop on Accounting and Culture, Amsterdam, June 1985.

[17] L. E. Graham, "Setting a Research Agenda for Auditing Issues in the People's Republic of China," *International Journal of Accounting* 31, no. 1 (1996), p. 30.

The various environmental factors affecting auditing issues can be identified in terms of a broad concept often referred to as the accounting infrastructure, which includes producers of information; final users of information; information intermediaries; laws and regulations that govern the production, transmission, and usage of information; and legal entities that monitor and implement the laws and regulations.[18]

In less developed countries, in particular, creditors and investors play a minimal role in the accounting infrastructure, and so accordingly, a less developed auditing profession, compared to that in a developed country, would be expected. Further, the primary source of finance in a country may influence the degree to which the audit profession in that country has evolved. Countries in which the primary source of capital is absentee owners (stockholders) and creditors, such as the United States, the United Kingdom, and Australia, may have a much greater need for audit services and more sophisticated audit procedures compared to those countries in which state-controlled banks or commercial banks are the primary source of capital. In a debt-financing country such as Japan, for example, there may be a much-reduced need for audited information or reliance on public financial information.

Different legal systems are also likely to influence auditing in different countries. For example, a codified Roman law system that exists in countries such as Germany and France may require more reliance on the stated legal objectives of the auditing profession. Countries with a common law system, such as the United Kingdom, Canada, or New Zealand, may allow audit characteristics to develop more freely or rely more on the auditing profession to set a general tone for the profession.[19]

Differences in the environments in which auditing operates can have implications for the transfer of auditing technology among countries. The international diversity in accounting and securities market regulations and practices, economic and political systems, patterns of business ownership, size and complexity of business firms, and stages of economic development affect the nature of the demand for audit services and the complexity of the audit task. Therefore, audit technologies that are cost-beneficial in one national setting can be ineffective, or even dysfunctional, in a different setting.[20]

Further, audit quality is also likely to vary across different audit environments. *Audit quality* can be defined as the probability that an error or irregularity will be detected and reported.[21] The detection probability is affected by the actual work done by auditors to reach their opinion. This in turn is influenced by the level of competence of the auditors (eligibility and qualifications), the requirements regarding the conduct of the audit (quality review and monitoring), and the reporting requirements. The reporting probability is affected by the auditor's independence. High independence implies a high probability of publicly reporting a detected material error or irregularity. We further discuss the issue of auditor independence later in this chapter.

Audit quality is also affected by the nature of the legal liability regime that exists in a country (we also discuss auditor liability later in this chapter). A strong liability regime will provide incentives for auditors to be independent and produce high-quality audits. In some Asian countries, for example, this is an unlikely scenario, because (due to cultural and other reasons) the liability regimes may not be strong and violations of professional conduct may go unpunished. This creates audit markets of uneven quality. In some countries, such as

[18] C. J. Lee, "Accounting Infrastructure and Economic Development," *Journal of Accounting and Public Policy,* Summer 1987, pp. 75–86.

[19] R. A. Wood, "Global Audit Characteristics across Cultures and Environments: An Empirical Examination," *Journal of International Accounting, Auditing, and Taxation* 5, no. 2 (1996), pp. 215–29.

[20] See C. W. Chow and R. N. Hwang, "The Cross-Border Transferability of Audit Technology: An Exploratory Study in the U.S.–Taiwan Context," *Advances in International Accounting* 7 (1994), pp. 217–29.

[21] L. DeAngelo, "Auditor Size and Audit Quality," *Journal of Accounting and Economics* 3 (1981), pp. 183–200.

Indonesia, Malaysia, and Thailand, fraud and irregularities are required to be reported to the board of directors, not in the audit report.[22]

Regulation of Auditors and Audit Firms

The approaches taken to regulate auditing in different countries range from those that leave the task largely in the hands of the profession to those that rely heavily on the government. In Anglo-Saxon countries, mechanisms are put in place to regulate auditors within the framework of professional self-regulation. In the United States, the PCAOB was established in 2002 by the SEC pursuant to SOX, and that act reaffirmed the necessity for the auditor to be independent of management, in fact and appearance, and expanded the auditor's reporting responsibility.

Auditors of SEC-registered companies are required to be members of the PCAOB, which has the authority to (1) establish or adopt auditing standards, quality control standards, and ethical rules in relation to the conduct of audits of public companies and (2) inspect audit firms. However, in the case of audit firms in Canada, Japan, and many European countries, including the United Kingdom, the PCAOB relies on the auditor's home-country regulators.[23]

In the United Kingdom, the word *accountant* is not defined in statute and there is no qualification requirement in order for someone to practice as an accountant. However, most accountants—but not the auditors—choose to qualify under the auspices of one of the professional bodies. The Companies Act of 1985 prescribed a statutory scheme for the regulation of auditors, under which the Department of Trade and Industries (DTI) recognizes certain accountancy bodies for the training and supervision of auditors. It stated that every company should appoint an auditor or auditors (except for most small companies or dormant companies). The Companies Act of 1989, which implemented the European Union's Eighth Directive, introduced stronger statutory arrangements for the regulation of auditors. It restricted qualifications for appointment as a statutory auditor to those who held a recognized professional qualification and were subject to the requirements of a recognized supervisory body. It made specific provision for the independence of company auditors. An officer or employee of a company being audited, for example, should not act as auditor for that company.

Under the regulatory structure for the accounting profession introduced in 1998, an independent body, the Accountancy Foundation, with a nonaccountant board of trustees, was established in 2000. With the establishment of the Foundation, a strong and independent element was introduced into the regulatory framework. This element involved oversight arrangements concerning the regulatory activities undertaken by the principal professional accountancy bodies. The Foundation was funded by the Consultative Committee of Accountancy Bodies (CCAB).

The Foundation[24] and its related bodies[25] were responsible for the nonstatutory independent regulation of the six chartered accountancy bodies of the CCAB. This framework was

[22] M. Favere-Marchesi, "Audit Quality in ASEAN," *International Journal of Accounting* 35, no. 1 (2000), pp. 121–49.

[23] James Feldman, "Give your skills a CAT Scan: Compare where you are with where you want to be by using the AICPA competency self-assessment tool," *Journal of Accountancy,* July 1, 2004.

[24] The documents issued by the Accountancy Foundation and its related bodies are available at www.frc.org.uk.

[25] The structure of the Foundation comprises five limited companies: the Accountancy Foundation Ltd.; The Review Board Ltd. (to monitor the operation of the regulatory system to ensure that it serves the public interest); the Auditing Practices Board Ltd. (to establish and develop auditing standards); the Ethics Standards Board Ltd. (to secure the development of ethical standards for all accountants); and the Investigation and Discipline Board Ltd. (to investigate disciplinary cases of public interest).

developed in light of a growing recognition in the profession of the need for the regulatory arrangements to reflect the wider public interest. The regulatory functions of the Foundation included monitoring the work of accountants and auditors, handling complaints and disciplinary violations, and conducting investigations. The regulatory structure under the Foundation provided an increased level of public oversight regarding statutory auditors, while essentially retaining the self-regulatory nature of the profession.[26] In 2004, the responsibilities of the Accountancy Foundation were taken over by the Financial Reporting Council (FRC). The responsibility for determining who might be recognized as a statutory auditor has been delegated primarily to four CCAB members: the Association of Chartered Corporate Accountants (ACCA), the Institute of Chartered Accountants in England and Wales (ICAEW), the Institute of Chartered Accountants in Ireland (ICAI), and the Institute of Chartered Accountants in Scotland (ICAS). Each of the four recognized professional bodies has its own examinations to assess the technical competence of the entry-level registered auditor (the term used in the United Kingdom for statutory auditor). In order to become a registered auditor in the United Kingdom, the professional accountant must be listed in a register maintained for that purpose by a recognized professional body.

The Auditing Practices Board (APB) was responsible for setting and developing auditing standards in the United Kingdom. The APB, as constituted under the Accountancy Foundation arrangements, continued the work of its predecessor body, which was established in 1991 under the auspices of the CCAB. Failure to abide by the professional standards issued by the APB might be grounds for disciplinary action.

The Companies (Audit, Investigation and Community Enterprises) Act of 2004 provided the Financial Reporting Review Panel with statutory power to require companies, directors, and auditors to provide documents, information, and explanations if it appears that accounts do not comply with relevant reporting requirements.

Under that regime, the FRC became the United Kingdom's unified, independent regulator for corporate reporting and governance. Its functions, which were relevant to auditing, included the following:

- Setting, monitoring, and enforcing auditing standards, statutory oversight, and regulation of auditors.
- Operating an independent investigation and discipline scheme for public interest cases involving professional accountants.
- Overseeing the regulatory activities of the professional accountancy bodies.

The FRC was also responsible for the 2012 Code of Corporate Governance. Similar bodies had been established in Canada, Australia, Japan, France, Germany, and several other countries in the European Union.

The requirements for becoming an auditor may vary in different countries. For example, unlike in the United States, there is no uniform system of examination in the United Kingdom, where four professional bodies conduct their own examinations. On the other hand, in Germany, the examinations for the prospective auditors are set by the Ministry of Economics, and self-regulation of the auditing profession takes place within the strict boundaries of the law. Unlike in the United Kingdom, instead of the professional bodies, quasi-governmental agencies play a major role in the regulatory functions in Germany. The Auditors' Regulation specifies the admission requirements to become a statutory auditor and defines, among other things, the rights and duties of the auditor, the organization of the Chamber of Auditors, or *Wirtschaftsprüferkammer* (WPK), and the disciplinary measures for

[26] Department of Trade and Industry, *A Framework of Independent Regulation for the Accountancy Profession: A Consultation Document* (London: Department of Trade and Industry of Her Majesty's Government, 1998).

breaches of professional duties. The WPK is supervised by the Ministry of Justice. Statutory auditors, including audit corporations, must be members of the WPK, a public law body created in 1961. The WPK also participates in disciplining auditors who violate standards.[27]

In China, the government is heavily involved in the regulation of the auditing profession. China's accounting and auditing profession is sanctioned and regulated by the state. All certified public accounting (CPA) firms, both state owned and privately owned, are under the supervision of the local Audit Bureau, which is itself supervised by the state. The CPA firms must be approved by the state in order to be able to audit foreign-owned or joint venture companies or Chinese companies listed on the stock exchange, as required by law. The state may also intervene in the allocation of audit assignments among CPA firms.

Audit Reports

There are significant differences in the audit reports across different countries and sometimes across different companies within the same country. In this section, we describe some of these differences. Audit reports in company annual reports from different countries show a variety of applicable audit standards and formats. In the United States, SEC-registered U.S. companies such as Boeing, Coca-Cola, and Kellogg mention in their 2021 annual reports that their audit reports were prepared in accordance with the *PCAOB standards,* whereas SEC-registered foreign companies are likely to prepare their audit reports in accordance with the audit standards of their own countries. For example, Nokia Corporation's 2021 annual report mentions that its audit report was prepared in accordance with *good auditing practices in Finland;* BHP's 2021 annual report mentions that its audit report was prepared in accordance with *Australian Auditing Standards, International Standards on Auditing* (UK), and *applicable law;* China Eastern Airlines's 2020 annual report mentions that its audit report was prepared in accordance with *International Standards on Auditing* (ISA); Siemens AG in its 2021 annual report mentions that its audit report was prepared in accordance with *HGB* ("*Handelsgesetzbuch*": German Commercial Code) and *German Generally Accepted Standards for Financial Statement Audits* promulgated by the *Institute of Public Auditors in Germany* (IDW) and additionally in accordance with International Standards on Auditing; Nissan Motor Corporation in their 2021 annual report mentions that the audit report was prepared in accordance with *auditing standards generally accepted in Japan;* and Heineken N.V.'s 2021 annual report mentions that the audit report was prepared in accordance with *Dutch law* and the *Dutch standards of auditing.*

INTERNATIONAL STANDARDS ON AUDITING (ISA) AND GENERALLY ACCEPTED AUDITING STANDARDS (GAAS) IN THE UNITED STATES

International Standards on Auditing (ISAs) are professional standards for the performance of financial audit, and they are issued by the International Federation of Accountants (IFAC) through the International Auditing and Assurance Standards Board (IAASB). In the United States, the Auditing Standards Board (ASB), a division of the American Institute of Certified Public Accountants (AICPA), promulgates generally accepted auditing standards (GAAS) for non-public companies, and the Public Company Accounting Oversight Board (PCAOB) promulgates GAAS for public companies. The PCAOB considers the IAASB standards in developing its own standards, and the quality of audits in the United States is usually judged against GAAS.

---

[27] C. R. Baker, A. Mikol, and R. Quick, "Regulation of the Statutory Auditor in the European Union: A Comparative Survey of the United Kingdom, France and Germany," *European Accounting Review* 10, no. 4 (2001), pp. 763–86.

There are differences between GAAS and ISAs, similar to those between GAAP (rules-based standards) and IFRS (principles-based standards). In other words, U.S. standards are more prescriptive compared to international standards. For example, GAAS require auditors to obtain an engagement letter before they start audit work, whereas there is no such requirement under ISAs; in regard to documentation retention policy, GAAS require the audit work to be retained for seven years, whereas ISAs require the audit work to be retained for at least five years; GAAS provide for reporting on financial statements that are prepared in accordance with fair presentation financial reporting frameworks and compliance financial reporting frameworks, whereas ISAs do not necessarily require fair presentation; GAAS require two categories of professional requirements, unconditional requirements and presumptively mandatory requirements, whereas ISAs require only one category of professional requirements, when such requirements are relevant, except in rare circumstances.

In 2004, the PCAOB commenced a project to clarify and converge GAAS with ISAs. Accordingly, the PCAOB has made several changes to the language of ISAs to be able to use them more easily in the United States. Starting in 2017, the PCAOB also requires companies to name its engagement partner for the audit of its annual financial statements. In June 2017, the PCAOB adopted a new standard (*The Auditor's Report on an Audit of Financial Statements When the Auditor Expresses an Unqualified Opinion*) to enhance the relevance and usefulness of the auditor's report with additional information for investors. The new standard requires auditors to include in the audit report a discussion of the CAMs, which are matters that (a) have been communicated to the audit committee; (b) are related to accounts or disclosures that are material to the financial statements; and (c) have involved especially challenging, subjective, or complex auditor judgment. In other words, CAMs represent the areas in the audit of the financial statements that were most difficult for the auditor, including those matters that involved subjective or complex auditor judgments. A similar requirement was introduced by the IAASB in 2015. That standard (effective for 2016 calendar year-end audits) requires the auditors of listed entities to include key audit matters (KAMs)—those areas of the audit that have demanded the most significant auditor attention—in their reports. The CAMs as required by the PCAOB are similar but not identical to the IAASB's KAMs. The European Union legislation (effective for June 30, 2017, fiscal year-end audits) is similar in some respects to the ISAs, but one unique feature in the EU standards is the requirement that the auditor's report should include a statement that no prohibited nonaudit services have been provided.

As stated earlier in this chapter, under the new PCAOB standard, the auditor's report is also required to disclose, among other things, the tenure of the auditor and the year in which the auditor began serving consecutively as the company's auditor. This standard marks a new era in the way auditors communicate with investors. The new PCAOB auditing standard retains the pass/fail model of the existing auditor's report.

Audit Expectation Gap

The meaning of the term *audit expectation gap* has been defined in several ways, as (a) the difference between what the public and financial statement users believe auditors are responsible for, and what auditors themselves believe to be their responsibilities; (b) the difference between public expectations about the responsibilities and duties of the auditing profession and what the auditing profession actually provides; and (c) the gap between the expectations of society about auditors and the performance of auditors (the "expectation-performance gap"). Following a financial disaster, regulators and standard-setters usually propose changes to current regulations and standards, aimed at bridging the expectation gap. One of the biggest factors contributing to the expectation gap has been the controversy about the auditor's responsibility to detect fraud. Information users require the auditor to act as an investigator and unearth even the most sophisticated fraud events, and they do not agree with the explanation that the auditor is not responsible to detect fraud. The global financial crisis (GFC) triggered the need to revisit the audit report. While narrowing the audit expectation gap was the main objective of previous changes to the audit report (e.g., revised ISA 700), with the GFC the focus was changed to narrowing the information gap—the gap that exists between the information users believe is needed to make informed investment and fiduciary decisions and the information that is available to them through the entity's audited financial statements or other publicly available information.

Further, the gaps related to the audit process and results can be broken down into a number of categories (e.g., normative gap, interpretative gap, information gap, and performance gap). A *normative gap* encompasses both the role of the auditor (meaning the scope of the assurance or other services being engaged) and the responsibilities of the auditor to provide certain levels of assurance over information within that scope. There could be a gap between what market participants believe an audit *should* be versus what an audit actually is *required* to be (by applicable standards, laws, and regulations). An *interpretative gap* arises from different interpretations of stakeholders and market participants regarding what the existing auditing requirements are for auditors or what should be communicated to the user about the audit process or results. An *information gap* is when stakeholders and market participants need or want more information than what is actually available through the audit report about the audit and the results of the audit, the nature and extent of the audit procedures performed, and the quality of the audit. Finally, a *performance gap* can exist between actual auditor performance and the requirements of the standards, the related laws and regulations, or the level of auditor performance expected by users.

Both the information users and the auditors of financial statements need to take the responsibility for bridging any of the above gaps. Users of financial statements must:

- Understand that auditors can provide only reasonable assurance and not absolute assurance and that there are inherent limitations of the audit;
- Recognize that general purpose financial statements are meant for general needs of users and, even if they have been audited in the best way possible, audited financial statements cannot help in all decision-making situations;
- Realize that the auditor's work is relative to circumstances that require the use of judgment, which may be wrong; and
- Accept that although the auditor and management are required to produce financial statements in a way that is easy to understand, users are also expected to have a certain degree of relevant knowledge regarding how to use and interpret financial statements, and financial statements are not for everyone to read and act upon.

Auditors of financial statements, on the other hand, must:

- Understand users' expectations, and arrange workshops or seminars so that users at least feel that they have been heard and are not being ignored due to their lack of knowledge;
- Make audit reports easy to understand for the masses, and avoid as much as possible the use of any technical jargon that could impair an ordinary person's understanding of the information contained in financial statements; and
- Realize that the auditor is already providing less than absolute assurance so he/she must not leave any effort undone to maintain a reasonable level of assurance by complying with the requirements of relevant auditing standards (e.g., engaging in proper planning, gaining an appropriate understanding of the entity to design further audit procedures, maintaining a skeptical attitude, reducing sampling risk to an appropriate level, and so on).

INTERNATIONAL HARMONIZATION OF AUDITING STANDARDS

The audit report is the primary tool auditors use to communicate with financial statement users about the results of the audit function. The globalization of capital markets and the growth of international capital flows have heightened the significance of cross-national understanding of corporate financial reports and the associated audit reports.[28] For MNCs, the ideal situation would be for both the parent company and its foreign subsidiaries to adopt one set of accounting standards, and for the auditors in both cases to use one set of auditing standards in providing their opinion on the financial statements. However, as explained earlier, the audit environments and the mechanisms for audit regulation can vary significantly among different countries, and this could affect the form, content, and quality of the audit report.

International harmonization of auditing standards is important in view of the drive toward international convergence of financial reporting standards. In the international capital markets, harmonization of auditing standards would ensure that the audit process has been consistent across companies, and in particular that one set of high-quality standards has been applied in auditing both the parent and its subsidiary companies. This would enhance the credibility of the information in corporate financial reports and lead to a more efficient and effective allocation of resources in international capital markets. In addition, harmonization of auditing standards would enable audit firms to increase the efficiency and effectiveness of the audit process globally. However, efforts to harmonize auditing standards internationally have met with limited success.

As mentioned earlier, the responsibility for developing international auditing standards rests mainly with the International Federation of Accountants (IFAC) through its International Auditing and Assurance Standards Board (IAASB).[29] As a condition of IFAC membership, a professional accountancy body is obliged to support the work of IFAC by informing its members of every pronouncement developed by IFAC; to work toward implementation, to the extent possible under local circumstances, of those pronouncements; and specifically to incorporate IFAC's International Standards on Auditing (ISAs) into national auditing pronouncements.[30]

The IAASB develops ISAs and International Auditing Practice Statements (IAPSs). These standards and statements outline basic principles and essential procedures for auditors and serve as the benchmark for high-quality auditing standards and statements worldwide. The IAASB also develops quality control standards for firms and engagement teams in the practice areas of audit, assurance, and related services.

IFAC's international regulatory and compliance regime consists of the Forum of Firms (FOF) and the Compliance Committee, with participation from outside the accounting profession. Firms that carry out transnational audit work are eligible for membership in the FOF. Membership obligations include compliance with ISAs and the IFAC Code of Ethics for Professional Accountants and submission to periodic quality control review. The Compliance Committee monitors and encourages compliance with international standards and other measures designed to enhance the reliability of financial information and professional standards around the world.

The International Organization of Securities Commissions (IOSCO) supports IFAC's efforts in this area. IOSCO's Technical and Emerging Markets Committees participate in the discussions that take place between IFAC and the international regulatory community

---

[28] J. S. Gangolly, M. E. Hussein, G. S. Seow, and K. Tam, "Harmonization of the Auditor's Report," *International Journal of Accounting* 37 (2002), pp. 327–46.

[29] The IAASB was formerly known as the International Auditing Practices Committee (IAPC).

[30] Preface to International Standards on Auditing and Related Services.

EXHIBIT 11.4
ISA 700 Illustrative
Audit Report

AUDITOR'S REPORT

(Appropriate Address)

We have audited the accompanying (the reference can be by page numbers) balance sheet of the ABC Company as of December 31, 20x1, and the related statements on income, and cash flows for the year then ended. These financial statements are the responsibility of the company's management. Our responsibility is to express an opinion on these financial statements based on our audit.

We conducted our audit in accordance with International Standards on Auditing (or refer to relevant national standards or practices). Those standards require that we plan and perform the audit to obtain reasonable assurance about whether the financial statements are free of material misstatement. An audit includes examining, on a test basis, evidence supporting the amounts and disclosures in the financial statements. An audit also includes assessing the accounting principles used and significant estimates made by management, as well as evaluating the overall financial statements presentation. We believe that our audit provides a reasonable basis for our opinion.

In our opinion, the financial statements give a true and fair view of (or "present fairly" in all material respects) the financial position of the company as of December 31, 20x1, and of the results of its operations and its cash flows for the year then ended in accordance with International Accounting Standards (or [title of financial reporting framework with reference to the country of origin]*) (and comply with. . . .†)

---

* In some circumstances it also may be necessary to refer to a particular jurisdiction within the country of origin to identify clearly the financial reporting framework used.
† Refer to relevant statutes or law.

---

regarding processes for the development of international auditing standards. IOSCO has recommended that its members endorse ISAs and accept audits of financial statements from other countries audited in accordance with ISAs.

The issuance of ISA 13 in October 1983 by the International Auditing Practices Committee (IAPC) was an important landmark in international efforts to harmonize the audit report. The purpose of ISA 13 was to "provide guidance to auditors on the form and content of the auditor's report issued in connection with the independent audit of the financial statements of any entity" (paragraph 2). ISA 13 has been revised several times.

In an attempt to harmonize audit reports, ISA 700 provides an illustrative audit report as shown in Exhibit 11.4.

In June 2003, IFAC issued an IAPS providing guidance on expressing an audit opinion when the financial statements are asserted by management to have been prepared (1) solely in accordance with IFRS, (2) in accordance with IFRS and a national financial reporting framework, or (3) in accordance with a national financial reporting framework with disclosure of the extent of compliance with IFRS.[31]

In accordance with IAS 1, the IAPC specifies that financial statements should not be described as complying with IFRS unless they comply with all the requirements of each applicable standard and each applicable interpretation of the IFRIC. An unqualified opinion may be expressed only when the auditor is able to conclude that the financial statements give a true and fair view (or are presented fairly, in all material respects) in accordance with the identified financial reporting framework. In all other circumstances, the auditor is required to disclaim an opinion or to issue a qualified or adverse opinion, depending on the circumstances. An opinion paragraph, which indicates that "the financial statements

---

[31] International Federation of Accountants, "Reporting by Auditors on Compliance with International Financial Reporting Standards," International Auditing Practice Statement 1014 (New York: IFAC International Auditing and Assurance Standards Board, June 1, 2003).

give a true and fair view and are in substantial compliance with International Financial Reporting Standards" does not meet the requirements of ISA 700. Further, financial statements claimed to have complied with more than one financial reporting framework must comply with each of the indicated frameworks individually.

There have been efforts at harmonizing auditing standards at the regional level, particularly within the EU. For example, the Fourth Directive of the European Commission requires that the auditor's report should include whether the financial statements present a "true and fair view." The Eighth Directive is aimed at harmonizing the educational and training prerequisites necessary to become a statutory auditor. Many EU member countries, including the United Kingdom (note that this was before Brexit in 2017), modified their company laws and regulations to comply with the provisions of the Eighth Directive. As a result, the UK professional bodies amended their entry requirements to include a rule that new members must have a university degree in any area. In addition, a prospective candidate for membership in one of the professional bodies is also required to undergo a three-year training period under the supervision of a practicing member of that professional body. Lately, the representative body for the accountancy profession in Europe, the Fédération des Experts Comptables Européens (FEE), conducted a survey and found that fundamental requirements to be recognized as a professional accountant and auditor largely have converged across Europe. More recently, FEE has changed its name to "Accountancy Europe" (see https://www.accountancyeurope.eu).

International Adoption of ISAs

Most countries have revised their auditing standards to align them more closely with the ISAs developed by the IAASB. For instance, in the United States, the Accounting Standards Board redrafted its standards to largely converge to ISAs as part of its *Clarity Project,* a process completed in 2019. In the United Kingdom, the Financial Reporting Council (FRC) issued *International Standards on Auditing (UK),* which are based on ISAs issued by the IAASB. In China, the Ministry of Finance has accepted standards drafted by the Chinese Institute of Certified Public Accountants that are mostly converged with ISAs. The situation in most countries resembles these cases. The IFAC website reports that most countries of the world have either *adopted* or *partially adopted* ISAs.

However, underneath this surface convergence, the fundamental differences in countries' auditing practices that we examined earlier in this chapter continue to play an important role. The most important differences are traceable to variations in local cultural and institutions. Another source of difference is pressure on local regulators to ensure that audit standards adequately address local risks. For instance, the UK's FRC responded to the bankruptcy and subsequent accounting scandal at Carillion plc in 2018 by substantially strengthening its version of *ISA 870, Going Concern.* The UK version of this standard, adopted in 2019, mandates that auditors take a more skeptical posture toward management's assertion that its business is a going concern. Many differences between ISAs and national auditing standards are of this nature, arising from specific adjustments that local regulators believe are necessary for their audit environments.

Cross-border Cooperation in U.S. Audit Regulation

Several of the largest accounting scandals of the last decade have involved problems in auditing cross-border operations. The most spectacular example was the collapse of Wirecard AG, the German payment processor that had grown to be one of Germany's most valuable companies before its bankruptcy in 2020. The Wirecard fraud involved transactions between entities in many countries, including German, India, Singapore, Turkey, and the Philippines. Such scandals shine a light on the need for a cross-border framework for auditing and audit regulation.

The U.S. stock exchanges are the world's largest and as such are attractive venues for non-U.S. companies to raise capital and cross-list shares. As a condition of a U.S. listing, however, the PCAOB requires that it be able to inspect the auditors of non-U.S. companies and their overseas operations in the same manner that it inspects those of U.S. companies. These inspections may be carried out in two ways:

- The PCAOB itself may conduct the inspection in coordination with the home country regulator.
- The PCAOB may adopt a cooperative framework with the non-U.S. regulator that allows the PCAOB to rely on inspections performed by that regulator.

For example, in 2016 the PCAOB signed a Statement of Protocol with the Auditor Oversight Body at Germany's Federal Office for Economic Affairs and Export Control. This agreement created a framework for joint inspections and in rare cases inspections in Germany conducted by the PCAOB. In 2018, the two countries augmented this framework with a supplemental Data Protection Agreement.

Criteria that the PCAOB uses in establishing such joint frameworks fall into five broad areas:

1. Adequacy and integrity of the oversight system.
2. Independent operation of the oversight system.
3. Independence of the system's source of funding.
4. Transparency of the system.
5. The system's historical performance.

In addition to Germany, the PCAOB has entered into arrangements to inspect non-U.S. auditors in 49 other jurisdictions. In fact, China is the only country with which the PCAOB has failed to establish a cooperative framework. This stand-off over PCAOB access is been a simmering problem since 2012. It was fueled by a series of frauds involving U.S.-listed Chinese companies, the most high profile of which was the Luckin Coffee scandal. Tensions between Chinese and U.S. regulators over foreign inspections reached a denouement in December 2020, when the U.S. Congress passed the *Holding Foreign Companies Accountable Act* (HFCAA). The HFCAA requires that a foreign registrant be delisted from U.S. exchanges if the PCAOB has been unable to inspect its home country auditor for three consecutive years beginning in 2021. China Eastern Airlines, with American Depositary Shares (ADSs) listed in the New York Stock Exchange, commented on the threat that a possible delisting poses to its investors in the Risk Factors section its 2020 Form 20-F:

> Our ADSs may be delisted under the Holding Foreign Companies Accountable Act if the PCAOB is unable to inspect our auditor who is located in China. The delisting of our ADSs, or the threat of their being delisted, may materially and adversely affect the value of your investment.

When the HFCAA was enacted, approximately 200 U.S.-listed Chinese companies faced possible delisting, representing a combined market capitalization of almost $2 trillion. The economic costs of failing to resolve this dispute over audit inspections are very large. Implicitly, the PCAOB believes that the investor protection benefits of asserting its rights to inspect foreign auditors are worth the cost.

ETHICS AND INTERNATIONAL AUDITING

Globalization of corporations and the accounting profession has raised some questions that are of fundamental importance, among them:

What does the new global profession stand for?

Can the moral standing of the accounting profession be based on a consensus of international morals and values?

Further, accounting does not operate in a static environment and is undergoing change with community and business values. What was local—including business and professional fundamentals and community values—is now global. These values are currently directed to corporate responsibility and social and environmental issues and are communicated in nonmonetary terms. These changes in community values form part of what accounting is. Further, the realm of the accounting profession's jurisdiction does not seem to remain within the boundaries of monetary symbols and financial reporting. These issues are important in judging professional credibility and integrity into the next generation.

The moral standing of the accounting profession is based on trust, which is established by the ethical conduct of its members. This is as important as an asset such as plant and equipment. At an international level, the profession has been directed to ethics education by international organizations such as the IFAC. For example, IFAC membership obligations include compliance with ISAs and the IFAC Code of Ethics for Professional Accountants. The importance of consistency of ethical codes for the various professional bodies operating within individual geographical locations has also been emphasized. At the international level, the Public Interest Oversight Board (PIOB) was formed in early 2005 to oversee the work of IFAC committees, including an ethics standard-setting committee. Audit reports of some companies, for example, those of China Southern Airlines, China Eastern Airlines, Unilever PLC, and Unilever N.V., specifically mention that the auditors need to comply with ethical requirements. Following the consideration and approval by the PIOB, the revised Code of Ethics for Professional Accountants was issued by the APB. The revised code clarifies requirements for all professional accountants and significantly strengthens the independence requirements of auditors.

However, ethical codes may also offer opportunities for "creative accounting." Further, a focus on individual benefits has resulted in corporate failures, and the accounting profession—as stewards of corporate behavior—has been admonished in terms of public trust. When ethical values are falling, people often turn to the government for help, as reflected during the GFC.

The response to crises of the accounting profession in the United States has been to form committees and commissions whose recommendations end up changing little of substance. Those recommendations generally focus on rules of behavior. However, the shift from social norms to rules of behavior may not be the right path, as the focus on norms and culture is important to society.

A More Communitarian View of Professional Ethics

Professionals face their careers constrained by local laws and a set of values that appear to be universally held. Ethical standards are important in professional accounting work, and professional ethics reside in the form of a contract between a professional group and the community within which that professional group operates. Therefore, ethical issues can be local and contextual. Consequently, the notion of a universal or global set of ethical norms that is embedded in IFRS can be challenged, as the notion of an "international community" reflects the aspirations of Anglo-American culture. For example, some of the methods of relationship building that are generally accepted in Chinese society may be considered bribery and corruption in an Anglo-American culture. Considering the above, one might ask whether a more communitarian view of professional ethics needed.

ADDITIONAL INTERNATIONAL AUDITING ISSUES

As a result of the renewed interest in restoring investor confidence internationally, the issues of auditors' liability, auditor independence, and the role of audit committees have figured prominently in discussion and debate. The fact that there is no international agreement on how to deal with any of these issues is of particular interest to MNCs, because they have to operate under different regulatory regimes in different countries.

Auditors' Liability

In general, auditors can be subject to three kinds of liability—civil liability, criminal liability, and professional sanctions. Civil liability arises when auditors break contractual or civil obligations or both, and criminal liability arises when they engage in criminal acts, such as intentionally providing misleading information. Professional sanctions (warnings and exclusions by professional bodies) are imposed when auditors violate the rules of the professional bodies to which they belong.[32]

In terms of civil liability, the auditor may be exposed to litigation initiated by (1) the client company (the other party to the engagement contract) or (2) a third party (a party not involved in the original contract, such as a shareholder). In certain national jurisdictions, auditors are not liable to third parties. This was the case in Germany prior to 1998, but the situation changed as a consequence of a court decision in that year. Statutory auditors in Germany currently are liable to third parties in cases of negligent behavior. In the United Kingdom, under the Companies Act, the auditor reports to the members of the company but enters into a contract with the company as a corporate entity. Accordingly, the auditor's primary duty of care is to the company and its shareholders as a group, not necessarily to individual shareholders. To be liable in negligence, the auditor must owe a "duty of care" to a third-party claimant. It is relatively difficult for individual shareholders to successfully assert claims against statutory auditors under British law.[33]

In China, the concept of legal liability extending beyond the firm to its owners does not appear to exist. This is due to the flexibility in the ownership structure of CPA firms and the lack of a developed legal environment. A unique feature of the ownership structure of Chinese CPA firms is that other entities, such as universities, may also have ownership interests in them. For example, Shanghai University has an ownership interest in Da Hua CPAs, one of the larger CPA firms in China.[34]

Limiting Auditors' Liability

Prompted by the collapse of Arthur Andersen, the UK government conducted a public consultation on whether it should initiate legislation to limit auditors' liability. In its response, one of the Big Four firms pointed out that the risks involved in auditing are uninsurable, unquantifiable, unmanageable, and could at any time destroy the firm or any of its competitors.[35] This should be of concern to MNCs, given that further reduction in the number of global accounting firms could seriously affect MNCs' ability to obtain the necessary professional services at reasonable prices. The remainder of this section describes some of the alternatives available for limiting auditors' liability.

Change the Ownership Structure

Audit firms, particularly in the UK tradition, are often organized as partnerships in which the principle of "joint and several liability" applies. Under this principle, each audit partner of the firm against whom a claim is made for negligence may be held liable for the whole amount of

---

[32] M. Favere-Marchesi, "Audit Quality in ASEAN," *International Journal of Accounting* 35, no. 1 (2000), pp. 121–49.

[33] C. R. Baker, A. Mikol, and R. Quick, "Regulation of the Statutory Auditor in the European Union: A Comparative Survey of the United Kingdom, France and Germany," *European Accounting Review* 10, no. 4 (2001), p. 769.

[34] L. E. Graham, "Setting a Research Agenda for Auditing Issues in the People's Republic of China," *International Journal of Accounting* 31, no. 1 (1996), p. 29.

[35] Andrew Parker, "PwC Steps Up Litigation Fight," *Financial Times,* April 19, 2004, p. 18.

the claim. However, the joint and several liability feature is seen as a weakness of the partnership form of ownership. An effective way to limit auditor liability would be to change the ownership structure of audit firms. Under the U.S. model of limited liability partnerships, "innocent" partners are able to protect their personal wealth from legal action. The Big Four firms are using limited liability partnerships, where permitted by law, to reduce their exposure to litigation. For example, Deloitte & Touche LLP became a limited liability partnership in August 2003.

Under UK law, limited partnerships are effective only if the limited partners are simply passive investors and take no role in the firm's professional work. Consequently, for many audit firms in the United Kingdom, the principle of joint and several liability applies to audit partners, as the firms are organized as partnerships. However, it is possible in the United Kingdom for audits to be carried out by limited liability companies.[36] It was reported recently that of the United Kingdom's top 60 accountancy firms, the majority had turned to limited liability.[37] In 1995, KPMG announced the formation of a new company, KPMG Audit PLC, to audit its top 700 clients worldwide.[38] In Germany also, statutory audits can be performed by audit corporations with limited liability.

Proportionate Liability

Another approach that has been suggested to limit auditors' liability is to apply the concept of proportionate liability, by which the claim against each auditor would be restricted to the proportion of the loss for which he or she was responsible. However, this is not a widely adopted approach. For example, in September 1998, the New Zealand Law Commission declined a proposal by the then Institute of Chartered Accountants of New Zealand (ICANZ) [now, New Zealand Institute of Chartered Accountants (NZICA)] for changing auditors' liability from "joint and several liability" to "proportionate liability." In doing so, the Law Commission stated that fairness among defendants was not relevant to fairness to the injured party. German regulators seem to have taken a different view on this issue. Although German law specifies the disciplinary procedures against auditors, they are not always strictly implemented due to an overall tendency to focus on damage to the reputation of the profession rather than on the extent of the individual culpability of the auditor. Australia and Canada have introduced systems that recognize proportionate liability for auditors. The Companies Act of 2006 in the United Kingdom removed the long-standing bar on auditors limiting their liability to the companies they audit. Accordingly, limits for auditor liability may be agreed upon between the company and the auditor. From an international perspective, although the current UK regime is less favorable to auditors compared to those in Australia and Germany, a reasonable degree of protection is possible.

Statutory Cap

The use of a statutory cap is yet another approach that has been suggested to limit auditors' liability. The purpose of a statutory cap is to reduce the amount of money that an audit firm would have to pay if found liable for negligence. In Germany, this has been the practice for many decades. In 1931, an explicit limit on auditors' maximum exposure to legal liability damages was introduced to relieve the auditor of an overwhelming worry of unlimited liability and to limit the premiums for liability insurance.[39] In the United Kingdom, the auditors

---

[36] Among the ASEAN countries, in Thailand and Vietnam, auditing firms may be organized as limited liability companies. See M. Favere-Marchesi, "Audit Quality in ASEAN," *International Journal of Accounting* 35, no. 1 (2000), pp. 121–49.

[37] Liz Fisher, "Firms on the Defensive," *Accountancy,* July 2004, pp. 24–26.

[38] *Accountancy Age,* October 5, 1995, p. 1.

[39] C. R. Baker, A. Mikol, and R. Quick, "Regulation of the Statutory Auditor in the European Union: A Comparative Survey of the United Kingdom, France and Germany," *European Accounting Review* 10, no. 4 (2001), pp. 763–86.

are legally prevented from limiting their liability to their client company arising from negligence, default, breach of duty, and breach of trust.[40] As an example of the extent to which auditors may be expected to pay, damages of £65 million were awarded against the accounting firm Binder Hamlyn in 1995. The case involved a careless acknowledgment of responsibility for a set of audited accounts made to a takeover bidder by the firm's senior partner.[41]

Disclaimer

UK auditors often include disclaimers of liability in their audit opinions to protect themselves from unintended liability. In March 2003, in response to a proposal put forward by the Institute of Chartered Accountants in England and Wales (ICAEW) to promote the capping of unintended auditor liability by changing the wording in audit opinions to illustrate to whom an opinion is given, the U.S. SEC clearly stated that this would not be acceptable in the United States and that disclaimers of liability placed in audit opinions by UK auditors would have no validity if placed on U.S. financial reports.

Auditor Independence

One of the main principles governing auditors' professional responsibilities is independence, in particular, independence from management. However, reports of independence rule violations by major international accounting firms have appeared with increasing frequency. As an example, in January 2000, the SEC made public the report by an independent consultant who reviewed possible independence rule violations by one of the Big Four firms arising from ownership of client-issued securities. The report revealed significant violations of the firm's, the profession's, and the SEC's auditor independence rules.[42] Following the corporate collapses at the beginning of this century in many countries, a series of such reports appeared, and auditor independence became the subject of much debate at the international level.

The IFAC Code of Ethics for Professional Accountants identifies two different categories of independence: independence in mind and independence in appearance. Independence in mind requires auditors to be in a state of mind that allows them to express opinions about the auditee without feeling that they are under pressure due to independence issues and to feel that they are allowed to act with integrity, conducting their audits objectively and with professional skepticism. Independence in mind is also referred to as "independence in fact." Independence in appearance relates to a third party's perception regarding the auditor's independence. If the third party doesn't think that the auditor appears to be independent, even though the auditor is independent in his or her mind, the third party doesn't trust the auditor due to certain circumstances or relationships that are incompatible with independence, and the promise of the assurance that the auditor is supposed to provide is lost.

The NYSE Euronext Corporate Governance Guidelines require, among other things, that the board will have four committees: an Audit Committee, a Human Resources and Compensation Committee, a Nominating and Governance Committee, and an Information Technology Committee. The guidelines also require that all of the members of these committees, except for the Information Technology Committee, should be independent directors.

The PCAOB requires public accountancy firms to communicate to an audit client's audit committee about any relationship between the firm and the client that may reasonably be thought to bear on the firm's independence. The communication is required both before the firm accepts a new engagement pursuant to the standards of the PCAOB and annually

---

[40] C. J. Napier, "Intersections of Law and Accountancy: Unlimited Auditor Liability in the United Kingdom," *Accounting, Organizations and Society* 23, no. 1 (1998), pp. 105–28.

[41] *Financial Times*, December 7, 1995, p. 1.

[42] The full report is available at www.sec.gov/pdf/pwclaw.pdf.

for continuing engagements. The remainder of this section reviews various attempts to strengthen auditors' independence.

Auditor Appointment

Having stockholders involved in the auditor appointment process is expected to strengthen the independence of auditors from management and to improve audit quality. Generally, the law, for example, the UK Companies Act of 1989 (Section 384), requires that the registered (or statutory) auditor be appointed by the shareholders in an annual general meeting. However, in practice, it is the company's managers who actually select the auditor, after negotiating fees and other arrangements. The auditor often considers the managing directors of the company as the client, and hence the auditor's contractual arrangement is with the management of the company, not with the individual shareholders.

Restricted or Prohibited Activities

Another issue related to auditor independence is restricted or prohibited activities, including relationships with client companies. Mandated activities such as communication between auditors could also strengthen auditor independence. On the issue of the auditor's relationship with client companies, the Sarbanes-Oxley Act includes specific provisions prohibiting certain nonaudit services from being provided by external auditors. However, the large audit firms point out that certain consulting work in fact helps improve audit quality. For example, they argue that consulting on information systems and e-commerce puts them on the cutting edge of business, and as a result, they can (1) start to measure items, such as a company's customer service quality, that are not on balance sheets even though investors consider them to be crucial assets; (2) develop continuous financial statements that provide real-time information instead of historical snapshots; and (3) explore ways to audit other measures of value that investors use, such as website traffic and market share locked up by being first with a new technology.

Regulatory Oversight

In many countries, the regulation and oversight of auditors have expanded to incorporate external monitoring and oversight of auditor competence and independence. The PCAOB in the United States and the Professional Oversight Board for Accountancy (POBA) in the United Kingdom are two examples. In October 2002, the IOSCO issued a document titled *Statement of Principles for Auditor Oversight,* which requires that "within a jurisdiction auditors should be subject to oversight by a body that acts and is seen to act in the public interest." In its *Statement of Principles of Corporate Governance and Financial Reporting,* IOSCO recommends the following:

- Auditors should be independent, in line with international best practice.
- Auditors should make a statement to the board concerning their independence at the time the audit report is issued.
- The audit committee should monitor the auditor's appointment, remuneration, and scope of services and any retention of the auditor to provide nonaudit services.
- The board should disclose the scope of the audit, the nature of any nonaudit services provided by the auditors, and the remuneration for these.
- The board should disclose how auditor independence has been maintained where the auditor has been approved to provide any nonaudit services.
- An independent oversight body should monitor issues of audit quality and auditor independence.

At the international level, the PIOB oversees the work of IFAC committees on auditing, ethics, and education standard-setting.

Mandatory Rotation

Mandatory rotation of audit firms often has been advocated as a means of strengthening auditor independence, ensuring that potential conflicts of interest are avoided. A government inquiry into auditor independence in the United Kingdom resulted in a recommendation for mandatory auditor rotation as a way to restore investor confidence in the market in response to investor and public concerns in the wake of corporate scandals like the one involving Enron. However, the United Kingdom's largest audit firms overwhelmingly opposed proposals for mandatory rotation. They argue that such a change would only serve to bring down the quality of the audit and that there is no evidence that rotation will prevent corporate collapse.[43]

In revising its code of ethics for professional accountants, IFAC has specified that, for audits of listed entities, the lead engagement partner should be rotated after a predefined period, normally no more than seven years, and that a partner rotating after a predefined period should not participate in the audit engagement until a further period of time, normally two years, has elapsed.[44] A provision of the Sarbanes-Oxley Act imposed mandatory rotation of lead partners after five years. This was copied in many countries, including Japan, France, and Germany. Such a requirement is harder to implement in countries where there may be few partners with a sufficient understanding of the particular industry involved or a particular set of accounting rules (such as U.S. GAAP or SEC regulations).

The biggest stride in mandatory audit rotation occurred in 2016 when the EU began to impose mandatory audit firm rotation. All *public interest entities,* a category composed of listed companies, banks and insurance companies, are required to change audit firms after 10 years. This window can be extended for an additional 10 years if the company conducts a public tender process that puts its audit up for competitive bidding, the United Kingdom was a member of the EU at the time these rules were adopted and has maintained the requirement after Brexit. As of May 2020, 13 members of the FTSE 350 were required to rotate firms and another 21 were required to conduct a tender process. For example, Bellway plc was required to replace KPMG, its auditor since 1979.[45]

Splitting Operations

To address the independence issue, the large accounting firms have taken more drastic action, splitting into separate entities, each dealing with a specific operational area. This allows auditing and consulting arms to deal with the same customer. In 2000, Ernst & Young, PricewaterhouseCoopers, and KPMG LLP announced the split of their businesses into separate entities. Ernst & Young sold its management-consulting business to CAP Gemini Group SA for around $11 billion. One reason was to reduce SEC concerns about lack of independence. PricewaterhouseCoopers separated its audit and business advisory services from its other businesses (e.g., e-commerce consulting) in a decision that was "encouraged" by the SEC. KPMG incorporated KPMG Consulting, to be owned by KPMG LLP and its partners (80.1 percent) and Cisco Systems Inc. (19.9 percent), which in August 1999 agreed to invest $1 billion in the new company.

Stringent Admission Criteria

In the United Kingdom, the Companies Act of 1989, which implemented the EU Eighth Directive, introduced stronger statutory arrangements for the regulation of auditors. It restricted qualifications for appointment as a statutory auditor to those who held a

---

[43] By contrast, in Singapore, the law requires the rotation of audit partners for publicly listed companies.

[44] International Federation of Accountants, *Revision to Paragraph 8.151 Code of Ethics for Professional Accountants* Ethics Committee.

[45] Audit Analytics, "Mandatory Audit Firm Rotation in the FTSE 350," May 26, 2020.

recognized professional qualification and were subject to the requirements of a recognized supervisory body. It also made specific provision for the independence of company auditors; for example, an officer or employee of the company being audited should not act as auditor.

A Principles-Based Approach to Auditor Independence

In an auditor independence standard, the Canadian Institute of Chartered Accountants (CICA) made a shift to a more rigorous "principles-based" approach.[46] The standard reflects features of the relevant requirements included in IFAC, the U.S. SOX, and the SEC for public companies. Its applicability goes beyond any specific situation and mandates a proactive approach based on clearly articulated principles. The core principle of the CICA standard is that every effort must be made to eliminate all real or perceived threats to the auditor's independence. It requires auditors to ensure that their independence has not been impaired in any way. In a set of specific rules for auditors of listed entities, the standard

- Prohibits certain nonaudit services (bookkeeping, valuations, actuarial, internal audit outsourcing, information technology system design or implementation, human resource functions, corporate finance activities, legal services, and certain expert services).
- Requires rotation of audit partners (lead and concurring partners after five years with a five-year time-out period; partners who provide more than 10 hours of audit services to the client and lead partners on significant subsidiaries after seven years with a two-year time-out period).
- Prohibits members of the engagement team from working for the client in a senior accounting capacity until one year has passed from the time when they were on the engagement team.
- Prohibits compensation of audit partners for cross-selling nonaudit services to their audit clients.
- Requires audit committee prior approval for any service provided by the auditor.
- Stipulates that the rules for listed entities apply only to those listed entities with market capitalization or total assets in excess of $10 million.

A Conceptual Approach to Auditor Independence

In Europe, the Fédération des Experts Comptables Européens describes its approach to auditor independence as a conceptual approach.[47] By focusing on the underlying aim rather than detailed prohibitions, it combines flexibility with rigor in a way that is unavailable with a rules-based approach. It is argued that this approach

- Allows for the almost infinite variations in circumstances that arise in practice.
- Can cope with the rapid changes of the modern business environment.
- Prevents the use of legalistic devices to avoid compliance.
- Requires auditors to consider actively and to be ready to demonstrate the efficiency of arrangements for safeguarding independence.

An example of this approach would be the two-tiered corporate governance structure that exists in many continental European countries, such as Germany, France, and the Netherlands, and its perceived impact on auditor independence. Under that structure, because the supervisory board monitors the activities of the management board, and the

[46] Canadian Institute of Chartered Accountants, "Chartered Accountants Adopt New Auditor Independence Standard," news release, December 4, 2003.

[47] Fédération des Experts Comptables Européens, *The Conceptual Approach to Protecting Auditor Independence* (Brussels: FEE, February 2001).

auditors report to the supervisory board, the auditors may be more independent compared to their counterparts in the United Kingdom or the United States.

In reviewing these various attempts to strengthen auditor independence, a clear distinction can be made between the final two approaches described—the principles-based and conceptual approaches—and the earlier entries. Whereas the former approaches rely on a list of specific prohibitions, the principles-based and conceptual approaches avoid making such a list.

Audit Committees

An audit committee is a committee of the board of directors that oversees the financial reporting process, including auditing. The subject of audit committees has drawn increased attention in recent years.[48] In a 1999 report, the U.S. Blue Ribbon Committee, which made recommendations on improving the effectiveness of audit committees, describes the role of the audit committee as first among equals in supporting responsible financial disclosure and active and participatory oversight.[49] It defined the oversight role as "ensuring that quality accounting policies, internal controls, and independent and objective outside auditors are in place to deter fraud, anticipate financial risks, and promote accurate, high quality and timely disclosure of financial and other material information to the board, to the public markets, and to shareholders."[50]

In general, the audit committee responsibilities are to

- Monitor the financial reporting process.
- Oversee the internal control systems.
- Oversee the internal audit and independent public accounting function.

SOX contains specific provisions dealing with issues related to audit committees, expanding their role and responsibilities. For example, it requires the audit committee to be responsible for the outside auditor relationship, including the responsibility for the appointment, compensation, and oversight of a company's outside auditor. It also requires that members of the audit committee be independent from company management.

In January 2003, responding to Section 301 of SOX, the SEC proposed new rules for audit committees to prohibit the listing of companies that fail to comply with SOX's and SEC's requirements.[51] The SEC's requirements relate to the independence of audit committee members, the audit committee's responsibility to select and oversee the issuer's independent accountant, procedures for handling complaints regarding the issuer's accounting practices, the authority of the audit committee to engage advisers, and funding for the independent auditor and any outside advisers engaged by the audit committee.

One of the key responsibilities of an audit committee is oversight of the external auditor. It is now widely accepted that the external auditor works for and is accountable to the audit

[48] Each of the Big Four firms has issued audit committee guidance. See, for example, Pricewaterhouse-Coopers, *Audit Committee Effectiveness: What Works Best,* 2nd ed. (Altamonte Springs, FL: Institute of Internal Auditors Research Foundation, 2000); Blue Ribbon Committee, *Report and Recommendations of the Blue Ribbon Committee on Improving the Effectiveness of Corporate Audit Committees* (New York: New York Stock Exchange and National Association of Securities Dealers, 1999); American Institute of Certified Public Accountants, *Audit Committee Communications,* SAS No. 90 (New York: AICPA, 2000).

[49] Blue Ribbon Committee, *Report and Recommendations of the Blue Ribbon Committee on Improving the Effectiveness of Corporate Audit Committees* (New York: New York Stock Exchange and National Association of Securities Dealers, 1999), p. 7.

[50] Blue Ribbon Committee, *Report and Recommendations of the Blue Ribbon Committee on Improving the Effectiveness of Corporate Audit Committees* (New York: New York Stock Exchange and National Association of Securities Dealers, 1999), p. 20.

[51] Securities and Exchange Commission, *Standards Relating to Listed Company Audit Committees,* SEC Release No. 33-8173, January 8, 2003. This is available at www.SEC.gov/rules/proposed/34-47137.htm.

committee and board of directors (in some cases, the supervisory board). The regulatory bodies in many countries now require listed companies to establish audit committees.

Understanding how the accountability relationship through audit committees is supposed to work effectively is very important for all parties interested in corporate reporting in an international context. One of the potential problems, at least in some countries, would be the unavailability of individuals with the desired skills to be independent directors.[52] Another concern is that, as a result of the expanded responsibilities given to audit committees, suitable individuals may now be reluctant to take on the position of audit committee member.

INTERNAL AUDITING

Internal auditing is a segment of accounting that uses the basic techniques and methods of auditing and functions as an appraisal activity established within an entity. The Institute of Internal Auditors (IIA)[53] defines *internal auditing* as "an independent, objective assurance and consulting activity designed to add value and improve an organization's operations."[54] The internal auditor is a person within the organization and is expected to have a vital interest in a wide range of company operations. SOX specifically recognizes the importance of internal auditing in restoring credibility to the systems of business reporting, internal control, and ethical behavior. The SEC requires listed companies to have an internal audit function. The IIA is a main source of feedback to the SEC regarding implementation of the internal control provisions of SOX.

The role of internal auditing is determined by management and its scope and objectives vary depending on the size and structure of the firm and the requirements of its management. In general, the objectives of internal auditing differ from those of external auditing. As stated in ISA 610, internal auditing activities include the following:

- *Review of the accounting and internal control systems.* The establishment of adequate accounting and internal control systems is a responsibility of management that continuously demands proper attention. Internal auditing is an ordinarily assigned specific responsibility by management for reviewing these systems, monitoring their operations, and recommending improvements thereto.

- *Examination of financial and operating information.* This may include review of the means used to identify, measure, classify, and report such information, and specific inquiry into individual items, including detailed testing of transactions, balances, and procedures.

- *Review of the economy, efficiency, and effectiveness of operations.* These operations include nonfinancial controls of an entity.

- *Review of compliance with laws, regulations, and other external requirements, as well as with management policies and directives and other internal requirements.*

Risk management is directly related to corporate governance and is an area in which internal auditing can make a significant contribution. Monitoring risks and providing assurance

[52] M. Favere-Marchesi, "Audit Quality in ASEAN," *International Journal of Accounting* 35, no. 1 (2000), p. 142.

[53] The Institute of Internal Auditors (IIA) was founded in the United States in 1941. For more details, see S. Ramamoorti, *Internal Auditing: History, Evolution, and Prospects* (Altamonte Springs, FL: IIA Research Foundation, 2003).

[54] Institute of Internal Auditors, *Internal Auditing's Role in Sections 302 and 404 of the U.S. Sarbanes-Oxley Act of 2002* (Altamonte Springs, FL: IIA, May 2004).

regarding controls are among the main internal audit functions (refer to Exhibit 11.1). The IFAC defines an internal control system as follows:

> An internal control system consists of all the policies and procedures (internal controls) adopted by the management of an entity to assist in achieving management's objective of ensuring, as far as practicable, the orderly and efficient conduct of its business, including adherence to management policies, the safeguarding of assets, the prevention and detection of fraud and error, the accuracy and completeness of the accounting records, and the timely preparation of reliable financial information. The internal control system extends beyond these matters which relate directly to the fairness of the accounting system.[55]

As shown in Exhibit 11.5, there are competing demands on internal audits from corporate management and audit committees. On the one hand, corporate management requests, among other things, assistance in designing controls, self-assessment of risk and control, and the preparation of reports on controls. On the other hand, an audit committee requests assurance regarding controls and independent evaluation of accounting practices and processes.

The PCAOB's Auditing Standard No. 5, *An Audit of Internal Control over Financial Reporting,* which is integrated with *An Audit of Financial Statements* (approved by the SEC), requires registered audit firms to use the new standard for all audits of internal control no later than for fiscal years ending on or after November 15, 2007. The new standard reflects a principles-based approach and allows auditors to apply professional judgment in determining the extent to which they will use the work of others. It is less prescriptive and easier to read. It directs auditors to focus on what matters most and eliminates unnecessary procedures from the audit.

EXHIBIT 11.5
Competing Demands on Internal Audit Function

Source: A. D. Bailey, A. A. Gramling, and S. Ramamoorti, *Research Opportunities in Internal Auditing* (Altamonte Springs, FL: IIA Research Foundation, 2003).

Management requests of internal audit function
- Independent evaluation of controls
- Assistance in preparing report on controls
- Evaluation of efficiency of processes
- Assistance in designing controls
- Risk analysis
- Risk assurance
- Facilitation of risk and control self-assessment

Internal Audit Function

Audit committee requests of internal audit function
- Assurance regarding controls, including an independent assessment of the tone at the top
- Independent evaluation of accounting practices and processes, including financial reporting
- Risk analysis primarily focusing on internal accounting control and financial reporting
- Fraud analysis and special investigations

[55] IFAC, *Handbook of International Auditing, Assurance, and Ethics Pronouncements,* p. 122.

In June 2008, applying the extensive experience of its members and member bodies, IFAC drew out a set of globally applicable statements of principles. These principles should (1) guide the thought processes of professional accountants in business when they tackle the relevant topic, and (2) underpin the exercise of the professional judgment that is important in their roles. They provide professional accountants in business (and those served by them) with a common frame of reference when deciding how to address issues encountered within a range of individual organizational situations.

The PCAOB's audit standards require auditors of public companies to examine an entity's internal control over financial reporting that is integrated with an audit of its financial statements. It is expected that by following these standards the auditor will be able to obtain an understanding of the internal controls of the entity being audited in order to plan and perform the audit, for example, determining the nature, extent, and timing of substantive tests to be performed. However, the ISAs do not require an integrated audit that expresses an opinion on the effectiveness of the client's internal controls over financial reporting. ISAs simply require an auditor to test the internal controls of the organization being audited to ensure that they are adequate and functional. In Europe, the emphasis is on voluntary internal controls rather than enforcement of controls by statutes. The government does not prescribe by law because the board structure appears to have inherent checks and balances, which prevent the directors from making decisions that may be to their own advantage.

The Demand for Internal Auditing in MNCs

In a global competitive environment, internal auditing has become an integral part of managing MNCs. The Committee of Sponsoring Organizations of the Treadway Commission (COSO) has issued its Guidance on Monitoring Internal Control Systems. The guidance is designed to help organizations better monitor the effectiveness of their internal control systems and to take timely corrective actions if needed.

Currently, there is a trend for independent registered public accounting firms to either include comments on internal controls of the company audited in their audit report (e.g., Sumitomo Corporation's 2012 audit report) or provide a separate report on internal control (e.g., Cadbury PLC's 2012 audit report).

There is a growing demand for risk management skills, as MNCs face an increasing array of risks due to the fact that their control landscape is more extensive and complicated compared to purely domestic enterprises. The demand for internal auditing has been growing internationally during the past four decades, particularly due to regulatory and legislative requirements in many countries, such as the U.S. Foreign Corrupt Practices Act.

U.S. Legislation against Foreign Corrupt Practices

The Foreign Corrupt Practices Act (FCPA), which became law in December 1977, requires companies to establish and maintain appropriate internal control systems so that corporate funds are not improperly used for illegal purposes. Following the FCPA internal control requirement, the SEC Act of 1934 was amended and, as a result, all the registrants of the SEC have been required to install internal control systems to prevent or detect the use of firm assets for illegal activities.

The FCPA makes it illegal for U.S. companies to pay bribes to foreign government officials or political parties in order to secure or maintain business transactions or secure another type of improper advantage. Violation of the FCPA could result in large fines being levied against the corporation, and the executives, employees, and other individuals involved could also be fined or jailed, or both. U.S. companies may be subject to liability for FCPA violations by their foreign subsidiaries or joint venture partners.

Following the FCPA, U.S. companies are required to include in their 10-K report a report on internal control on financial reporting. An example taken from 2021 10-K of the Coca-Cola Company is provided in Exhibit 11.6.

EXHIBIT 11.6

Extract from the Coca-Cola Company's 10-K Report for 2021 **Report of Management on Internal Control over Financial Reporting**
Management of the Company is responsible for establishing and maintaining adequate internal control over financial reporting as such term is defined in Rule 13a-15(f) under the Securities Exchange Act of 1934 ("Exchange Act"). Management assessed the effectiveness of the Company's internal control over financial reporting as of December 31, 2021. In making this assessment, management used the criteria set forth by the Committee of Sponsoring Organizations of the Treadway Commission (2013 Framework) ("COSO") in *Internal Control — Integrated Framework*. Based on this assessment, management believes that the Company maintained effective internal control over financial reporting as of December 31, 2021. The Company's independent auditors, Ernst & Young LLP, a registered public accounting firm, are appointed by the Audit Committee of our Company's Board of Directors, subject to ratification by our Company's shareowners. Ernst & Young LLP has audited and reported on the consolidated financial statements of The Coca-Cola Company and subsidiaries and the Company's internal control over financial reporting. The reports of the independent auditors are contained in this annual report.

The FCPA grew out of the revelations of widespread bribery of senior officials of foreign governments by American companies. In particular, the Lockheed and Watergate scandals in the mid-1970s triggered the enactment of the FCPA. The Lockheed scandal involved kickbacks and political donations paid by Lockheed, the American aircraft manufacturer, to Japanese politicians in return for aid in selling planes to All Nippon Airways. The scandal forced Tanaka Kakuei to resign as prime minister and as a member of the ruling Liberal Democratic Party. Lockheed had paid a total of $22 million to Japanese and other government officials.

In an investigation launched by the SEC following the Watergate scandal in the 1970s, it was discovered that American companies were engaged in large-scale bribery overseas. According to the report from that investigation, by 1976 more than 450 American companies had paid bribes to foreign government officials, made contributions to political parties, or made other questionable payments. A considerable amount of "slush funds" were generated for this purpose by falsifying their accounting records. Thus, the original intention behind the enactment of the FCPA was to improve corporate accountability and transparency.

The FCPA has two main components—accounting provisions and antibribery provisions. The SEC plays the main role in enforcing the accounting provisions, which require a company to fairly maintain books, records, and accounts reflecting the transactions and dispositions of the assets. In addition, a company must devise and maintain an appropriate internal accounting controls system, execute transactions in accordance with the management's authorization, prepare financial statements in conformity with accounting principles, and record transactions to maintain accountability for assets. These requirements apply to SEC-regulated public companies—both U.S. and foreign companies—including their overseas branches.

The FCPA's accounting provisions require that a company holding a majority of a subsidiary's voting securities must cause that entity to comply with the FCPA accounting requirements. With regard to cases in which the parent holds less than a majority interest, the act requires a parent entity to "proceed in good faith to use its influence, to the extent reasonable under the circumstances" to cause compliance.

The Report of the National Commission on Fraudulent Financial Reporting in the U.S. (Treadway Commission Report, 1987) and the Report of the COSO of the Treadway Commission (1992) also placed particular emphasis on internal controls. The 1987 Treadway Report made several recommendations designed to reduce financial statement fraud by improving control and governance. The report made it clear that the responsibility for reliable financial reporting "resides first and foremost at the corporate level, in particular at the top management level." Top management "sets the tone and establishes the financial reporting environment." The idea is that good record-keeping and internal control make it more difficult to conceal illegal activities.

The International Anti-Bribery and Fair Competition Act of 1998 expanded the scope of the FCPA for application to foreign companies (other than those regulated by the SEC) and foreign nationals, if their corrupt activity occurs within the United States. A U.S. company can be prosecuted not only when it directly authorizes an illegal payment by its foreign affiliate, but also when it provides funds to that affiliate while knowing or having reason to know that the affiliate will use those funds to make a corrupt payment.

In June 2004, the SEC approved the PCAOB Release No. 2004-003: "An Audit of Internal Control over Financial Reporting Performed in Conjunction with an Audit of Financial Statements." Accordingly, companies were required to include in their annual reports two audit opinions: one on internal control over financial reporting and one on the financial statements (e.g., Microsoft Corporation annual report 2017).

For an MNC, an important task of monitoring risks is to develop a plan to systematically assess risk across multinational activities within the organization. In addition, the MNC needs to:

- assess the existing risk of the audited area and reporting of that assessment to management or the audit committee, or both;
- lead the risk management activities when a void has occurred within the organization;
- facilitate the use of risk self-assessment techniques;
- evaluate risks associated with the use of new technology; and
- assist management in implementing a risk model across the organization covering operations in different countries

Exhibit 11.7 shows several evaluative frameworks that have been proposed for internal control.

However, in regard to internal controls, a question remains: What if the top management was involved in the illegal transaction? After all, the top management is responsible for internal control and has discretionary power to override or restructure the internal control system. Managers can commit fraud by overriding internal controls, and audits conducted

EXHIBIT 11.7
Evaluative Frameworks for Internal Control

Source: Deloitte & Touche, "Moving-forward: A Guide to Improving Corporate Governance through Effective Internal Control—A Response to Sarbanes-Oxley," January 2003.

- United States – Integrated framework developed by the Committee of Sponsoring Organization (COSO) of the Treadway Commission and sponsored by, among others, the AICPA, the FEI, and IIA. It is believed to be the dominant framework chosen by the vast majority of U.S.-based public companies.
- Canada – The control model developed by the Criteria of Control Committee (COCO) of the CICA. It focuses on behavioral values rather than control structure and procedures as the fundamental basis for internal control in a company.
- England and Wales – Turnbull Report developed by the ICAEW, in conjunction with the London Stock Exchange. It requires companies to identify, evaluate, and manage their significant risks and to assess the effectiveness of the related internal control systems.
- Australia – Australian Criteria of Control (ACC) issued by the Institute of Auditors – Australia, emphasizes the competency of management and employees to develop and operate the internal control framework.
- South Africa – The King Report by the King Committee on Corporate Governance promotes high standards in corporate governance in SA. It goes beyond the usual financial, ethical, and environmental concerns.

in accordance with auditing standards do not always distinguish between errors and fraud.[56] Evidence suggests that, although better internal controls prevent or discourage fraudulent conduct on the part of employees, it is more difficult to prevent fraud at the top level.

For effective governance, the ultimate responsibility for internal control should be vested in the board, which represents shareholders. The board is responsible for achieving corporate objectives by providing guidance for corporate strategy and monitoring management. The board is effective only if it is reasonably independent from management. Board independence usually requires a sufficient number of outsiders; adequate time devoted by the members; and access to accurate, relevant, and timely information.

Because the board is usually not engaged in its work on a full-time basis, it needs to rely on experts for necessary information, such as the internal auditor and the external auditor. Being employees of the company, internal auditors are faced with a built-in conflict in regard to their allegiance. This makes the role of the external auditor crucial. External auditors are normally required to make an assessment of the internal control. If the external auditors are to attest to the "fair representation" or "true and fair view" of the financial position of the firm, they need to be able to form their opinion independent of the board and management. However, the issue of auditor independence is complicated by the fact that the auditors are paid by the auditee company—more specifically, its management—and often the auditors provide consultancy services to the auditee company.

So far in this chapter, we have discussed various auditing issues that are important to MNCs. In the next section, we provide some thoughts on likely future developments. We identify them in terms of consumer demand for auditing, increased competition in the audit market, the Big Four firms' continued high interest in the audit market, increased exposure of the Big Four firms, a tendency toward a checklist approach, and the possibility that auditing may not be the external auditor's exclusive domain.

Building robust corporate governance systems and processes, managing risk on a global scale, and complying with an increasingly vast web of regulatory requirements is difficult, costly, and time-consuming for MNCs.[57] Top management seems to be concerned about the costs, in terms of money and time, of implementing the extensive audit requirements. Audit committee chairs seem to be feeling the pressure of increased accountability of the required financial reporting process.

FUTURE DIRECTIONS

Consumer Demand

Historically, the assurance opinion of the statutory auditor has been led by legislation rather than by consumer demand. However, the growth of sustainability reporting radically upended this relationship. Sustainability reporting is largely voluntary. To enhance the credibility of their sustainability reports, a large majority of corporations *choose* to have the reports externally assured. We will discuss this topic in greater detail in Chapter 12.

Many sustainability reports are now exclusively web-based, as are a variety of financial disclosures that investors would find materially relevant. Thus, another area of consumer demand for assurance services comes from the sprawling and often chaotic nature of web-based reporting itself. Auditors will be expected to find new ways of giving assurance on that information, which is not limited to financial information, and on a real-time basis.

---

[56] D. Capalan, "Internal Controls and the Detection of Management Fraud," *Journal of Accounting Research* 37, no. 1 (1999), p. 101.

[57] More details about the rating of companies from different countries can be obtained at https://www.msci.com/esg-integration.

A report published by the International Accounting Standards Committee (IASC) in November 1999 concluded that there is a need for a generic code of conduct for Internet-based business reporting.[58] The report suggested that such a code should include conditions clearly setting out the information that is consistent with the printed annual report, which contains the audited financial statements. It also pointed out that the users of Internet-based reports are likely to be confused as to which part of the website relates to the audit report signed off on by an auditor.

Increased Competition in the Audit Market

In the current global environment, the market position of traditional audit firms is becoming increasingly threatened by companies with valuable technical expertise. This is especially true in the area of sustainability reporting. Bureau Veritas and other experts in supply chain assurance have leveraged their expertise to win 40% of the business of auditing sustainability reports. (Chapter 12 discusses sustainability reporting and the auditing of sustainability reports in greater detail.)

More generally, the whole area of systems, particularly technological systems, demands an assurance of their effectiveness. These new demands will require new skills. Nonaccountants with expertise in areas such as the environment and technology have developed into a competitive force. In other words, nonaccounting groups are entering the audit market, which traditionally has been the domain of the accounting profession, protected by statutory franchise.

The accountant firms have one key advantage in this competition. They are governed by stringent independence standards, including significant restrictions on the delivery of audit and nonaudit services to the same client. The Big Four international auditing firms need to ensure that this independence in maintained in fact as well as in perception. This is critical because the perception of a lack of independence will reduce the quality premium that the Big Four firms are able to charge their clients and will open the audit market to even more competition.

Continued High Interest in the Audit Market

Because they have a virtual monopoly of the traditional large-firm audit market, the Big Four firms have been able to use this market to build their brands. The audit market will remain central to the Big Four firms' operations because it helps them to maintain their brands. This will continue to be the case in the future, as it will be more difficult for the large firms to develop a reputation for perceived quality and build brands in the nonaudit market, given that they are competing against recognized competitors with their own brands, such as McKinsey & Company and Boston Consulting Group. Thus, even though the audit market is not extremely profitable, it will be in the interest of the Big Four to protect this market from the encroachment of competitors.

Increased Exposure of the International Auditing Firms

Becoming more global also means becoming more visible. The Big Four international auditing firms audit MNCs listed in numerous jurisdictions, and as these companies grow and become more globalized, the Big Four are increasingly coming under the watchful eye of global financiers and regulatory institutions.

The Big Four accounting firms, which together audit more than 90 percent of the world's largest businesses, can expect a more intense focus on their activities in the future. There will be renewed interest in what users can expect from an audit. The audit firms need to

---

[58] A. Lymer, R. Debreceny, G. Gray, and A. Rahman, *Business Reporting on the Internet* (London: IASC, 1999).

recognize that the nature of business has changed. It is quicker, more connected, more global, and very different from the nature of business in the last century. Questions such as these will be the subjects of discussion and debate:

- Have auditors kept pace with changes in the nature of business?
- Do auditors, like rating agencies, suffer from a potential conflict of interest because they are paid by those they judge?

Summary

1. Corporate disasters, particularly in the United States, have prompted regulatory measures that emphasize the importance of assurance services as an essential ingredient in establishing and maintaining investor confidence in markets through corporate governance.

2. The enactment of the Sarbanes-Oxley Act (SOX) was one of the most important milestones in the history of governance and auditing. SOX stimulated a waive of governance and auditing reforms around the world.

3. MNCs are realizing the need to pay attention to corporate governance issues in their efforts to succeed in increasingly competitive global markets.

4. The role of the external auditor can vary in different countries. For example, the role of the statutory auditor in Germany is much broader than that of his or her counterpart in the United Kingdom or the United States.

5. Corporate structure is an important factor that determines the purpose of an external audit. For example, some European countries have a two-tiered corporate structure, with a supervisory board and a management board. The supervisory board has a general oversight function over the performance of the management board, and the basic function of the statutory auditor is to assist the supervisory board. This is different from the situation that exists in Anglo-Saxon countries.

6. Audit quality is likely to vary in different audit environments, and the audit environments in different countries are determined by cultural, legal, financing, and infrastructural factors.

7. The PCAOB demands the right to inspect the auditors of foreign companies in their home countries. China is the only country that has not reached an agreement with the PCAOB to create a framework for these inspections.

8. The approaches taken to regulate the audit function in different countries range from heavy reliance on the profession (e.g., in the United Kingdom) to heavy reliance on the government (e.g., in China).

9. The nature of the audit report varies depending largely on the legal requirements in a particular country and the listing status of the company concerned.

10. The responsibility for harmonizing auditing standards internationally rests mainly with the International Federation of Accountants (IFAC), which oversees the International Auditing and Assurance Standards Board (IAASB).

11. Most countries have adopted or partially adopted the IFAC's International Standards on Auditing (ISAs).

12. Different approaches have been taken in different countries to deal with the issues concerning the auditor's liability to third parties and the principle of joint and several liability.

13. Recently many countries have turned increased attention to audit committees as an important instrument of corporate governance.

14. Currently, regulators in the United Kingdom, the United States, and some other countries have placed greater emphasis on public oversight bodies to monitor issues of auditor independence.

15. Large auditing firms have adopted a policy of splitting the auditing and nonauditing work into separate entities as a way of demonstrating independence.

16. Internal auditing is an integral part of multinational business management, as it helps restore or maintain the credibility of the business reporting system. The demand for internal auditing has grown during the past three decades, particularly due to regulatory and legislative requirements in many countries.

Questions

1. Why should MNCs be concerned about auditing issues?
2. What is the link between auditing and corporate governance?
3. What provisions of the Sarbanes-Oxley Act were aimed at improving auditing and corporate governance?
4. What provisions of the Sarbanes-Oxley Act inspired governance and auditing reforms in other countries?
5. What determines the primary role of external auditing in a particular country?
6. What is audit quality? What determines audit quality in a given country?
7. What is the PCAOB? What is its role in audit regulation?
8. What is the PIOB? What is its role in audit regulation?
9. What was the impact of the European Union's Eighth Directive on the regulation of auditing in the United Kingdom?
10. In what ways do company audit reports vary in different countries?
11. What are the main benefits of international harmonization of auditing standards?
12. What determines whether or not to issue an unqualified audit opinion on the compliance of a set of financial statements with IFRS?
13. How does the PCAOB supervise the work of auditors of U.S.-listed multinationals that takes place in foreign counties?
14. What are some of the strategies adopted internationally to limit the auditor's liability?
15. What are the main factors that complicate the issue of auditor independence?
16. What is the oversight role of an audit committee?
17. What are the main differences between internal auditing and external auditing within an MNC?
18. Describe the many aspects of the audit expectation gap.

Exercises and Problems

1. Refer to the Independent Auditors Reports of BHP Group's 2021 Annual Report to answer the following questions. (https://www.bhp.com/-/media/documents/investors/annual-reports/2021/210914_bhpannualreport2021.pdf?sc_lang=en)

   Required:
   a. Did the external auditors issue an unqualified opinion?
   b. Which audit standards did the external auditors use in conducting the audit?
   c. What key audit matters did the auditors list in their opinion?

2. ISA 700 describes three types of audit opinions that can be expressed by the auditor when an unqualified opinion is not appropriate: qualified, adverse, and disclaimer of opinion.

   Required:
   What are the circumstances under which each of the above three opinions should be expressed? ISA 700 is accessible from the IFAC website (www.ifac.org).

3. In June 2003, IFAC issued an IAPS providing additional guidance for auditors internationally when they express an opinion on financial statements that are asserted by management to be prepared in either of the following ways:

   - Solely in accordance with IFRS.
   - In accordance with IFRS and a national financial reporting framework.
   - In accordance with a national financial reporting framework with disclosure of the extent of compliance with IFRS.

   Required:
   Identify the additional guidelines under each of the three categories of audit opinion.

4. Auditing is likely to be affected in the future by the changing conditions in the world economy.

   Required:
   Identify some of these changing conditions in the world economy and their likely effect on auditing.

5. Internationally, legislators and professional bodies have focused on corporate governance issues in making recommendations for restoring investor confidence, and auditing is an essential part of corporate governance.

   Required:
   Explain the link between auditing and corporate governance.

6. Some commentators argue that the two-tiered corporate structure, with a management board and a supervisory board, prevalent in many Continental European countries, is better suited for addressing corporate governance issues, including the issue of auditor independence, compared to a corporate structure with one board of directors, prevalent in Anglo-Saxon countries.

   Required:
   Evaluate the merits of the above argument.

7. Germany's Corporate Governance Code (CGC) makes several recommendations related to gender diversity:

   - The Management Board should consider diversity when making appointments to executive positions. (Recommendation A1)
   - The Supervisory Board should consider diversity when making appointments to the Management Board. (Recommendation B1)

   As noted in the chapter, German companies are required to file declarations that lay out the degree to which they comply with the CGC. Under the comply or explain model, if they do not comply with a particular provision of the code, they must provide an explanation.

   Required:
   Download the 2021 declarations of the following two companies in the German wind energy sector:

   - Nordex SE (http://ir.nordex-online.com/download/companies/nordex/Corporate Governance/DCGK-Compliance_Declaration_2021_updated_EN.pdf)
   - Siemens Energy (https://assets.siemens-energy.com/siemens/assets/api/uuid:4a0482de-bb8f-47e8-afba-2004470bac3b/2021-september-declaration-of-conformity.pdf?ste_sid=4a6876d90c7d5e257b073fa9807fb41b)

   To what degree do the two companies comply with Recommendations A1 and B1?

8. This chapter refers to a unique ownership structure of many former state-owned enterprises in China, which have been redefined to create new economic entities.

   Required:
   Describe the uniqueness of the ownership structure of the entities mentioned above, and explain its implications for auditing.

9. The establishment of the PCAOB in 2002 was a major step toward strengthening the auditing function in the United States.

   Required:
   Provide examples of two key steps the PCAOB has taken to strengthen the auditing function in the United States.

10. In Anglo-Saxon countries, mechanisms are put in place to regulate auditors within the framework of professional self-regulation, whereas in many Continental European countries, quasi-governmental agencies play a major role in this area.

    Required:
    a. Briefly describe the main differences between the audit regulation mechanisms in the United States and Germany.
    b. Compare the audit regulation mechanisms in the United States and the United Kingdom.

11. The responsibility for harmonizing auditing standards across countries rests with IFAC.

    Required:
    Comment on some of the problems faced by IFAC in achieving the above goal.

12. There is no agreement internationally on how to address the issue of auditor liability.

    Required:
    Describe the approach taken in your own country in addressing the issue of auditor liability, and explain the rationale behind that approach.

13. The UK Corporate Governance Code takes the "comply or explain" approach.

    Required:
    a. Describe the main features of the comply or explain approach to corporate governance.
    b. Why do you think this approach seems to be popular internationally?

14. The following incomplete sentences (when completed) relate to aspects of corporate governance:
    a. _____ should be supplied in a timely manner with information in a form and of a quality appropriate to enable it to discharge its duties.
    b. _____ should explain in the annual report their responsibility for preparing the annual report and accounts, and state that they consider the annual report and accounts, taken as a whole, to be fair, balanced, and understandable and to provide the information necessary for _____ to assess the company's position and performance, business model, and strategy. There should be a statement by the _____ about their reporting responsibilities.
    c. The board should satisfy itself that at least one member of the _____ has recent and relevant financial experience.

    d. One of the main responsibilities of the _____ is to monitor and review the effectiveness of the company's internal audit function.

    e. _____ should have primary responsibility for making a recommendation on the appointment, reappointment, and removal of the external auditors.

    f. The annual report should include a statement from the _____ explaining the recommendation and the reasons why the board has taken a different position, where the board does not accept the _____ recommendation on the appointment, reappointment, or removal of _____.

Required:
Complete the above sentences.

Case 11-1

Mazda Motor Company

Mazda Motor Company publishes a separate Corporate Governance Report (CGR) that supplements the corporate governance section of its 2021 Annual Report. Access Mazda's 2021 CGR (https://www.mazda.com/globalassets/en/assets/investors/library/governance/files/cg211220_e.pdf) and use it to answer the following questions.

Required:

a. Compare Mazda's governance structure to that required of U.S. companies by the provisions of the Sarbanes-Oxley Act that are discussed in the chapter.

b. Historically, Mazda has been a member of the Sumitomo keiretsu. A keiretsu is a group of companies with interlocking business and financial relationships, traditionally organized around a main bank. Although keiretsu ties have weakened over the years, they still exert influence in many sectors of the Japanese economy. Do you find any evidence of a connection to the Sumitomo group of companies in the 2021 CGR?

c. The chapter discussed the risk that related party transactions pose, particularly in traditional Asian societies. Identify explicit policies to deal with these risks.

CASE 11-2

Mercedes-Benz Group

The 2021 Annual Report of the Mercedes-Benz Group (MBG) is available at the investor relations section of the company's corporate website (https://group.mercedes-benz.com/documents/investors/reports/annual-report-2021-incl-management-report-mbg.pdf). Use this report to answer the following questions.

Required:

a. Refer to the *Independent Auditor's Report*. Which firm was the external auditor? Did the external auditor issue an unqualified opinion?

b. Which audit standards did the external auditor use in conducting the audit?

c. List and briefly describe the *key audit matters* identified by the external auditor.

d. Review MBG's *Declaration on Corporate Governance pursuant to Sections 289 f, 315d of the German Commercial Code (HGB)*. As discussed in the chapter, MGB is allowed to comply with this code or explain deviations from it. Did MGB fully comply with the code or did it report one or more deviations? Explain.

e. Review the report of Mercedes-Benz Group's supervisory board. List and briefly describe three activities of this body related to corporate governance and auditing.

f. How does the size and composition of Mercedes-Benz Group's Supervisory Board differ from that of the typical board of directors in the United States?

Chapter **Twelve**

International Sustainability Reporting

Learning Objectives

After reading this chapter, you should be able to:

- Explain the meaning of sustainability reporting.
- Explain why companies publish sustainability reports.
- Describe the difference between traditional and socially responsible investors and discuss why each group would have an interest in the information conveyed by sustainability reports.
- Explain how companies use standards promulgated by the Global Reporting Initiative (GRI) to prepare and organize information in a sustainability report.
- Explain the concept of nonfinancial materiality and its importance in sustainability reporting.
- Describe the differences between the GRI and the Sustainability Accounting Standards Board (SASB).
- Explain the general approach to measuring carbon dioxide equivalent greenhouse gas emissions.
- Distinguish between Scope 1, Scope 2, and Scope 3 greenhouse gas-producing activities.
- Identify activities that are included in Scope 3 emissions.
- Understand the role that limited assurance plays in auditing sustainability reports.

INTRODUCTION

Sustainability reporting augments traditional financial reporting by providing information about an enterprise's environmental and social policies and practices. The development and expansion of this augmented reporting framework over the last 20 years is arguably the most important trend in modern accounting. Today, most large public companies around the world practice some form of sustainability reporting. Most commonly, they publish a separate stand-alone *sustainability report* that is roughly analogous to the traditional annual report in that it documents the enterprise's performance on an array of environmental and social performance metrics during the just-concluded fiscal year. In the United States, 92 percent of the companies in the S&P 500 published such reports in 2020. Another method of disseminating sustainability information is through an *integrated report,* which weaves sustainability disclosures into the company's annual report. Integrated reporting has grown more common in recent years.

Exhibit 12.1 presents a comprehensive taxonomy of the topics that a reader might encounter in a sustainability report. A cursory glance at the list is sufficient to see that the range of issues covered is potentially very wide and often of critical importance to the entity's stakeholders. Sustainability reports provide information on such widely followed topics as child labor, greenhouse gas emissions, gender and racial equity, animal welfare, and product safety. Most readers find the reports' content informative and interesting. Investors often use it to better evaluate a company's long-term business prospects. Many college students care deeply about one or more of the issues that the reports are designed to address.

The following examples connect topics from Exhibit 12.1 with social and environmental controversies that have received substantial media coverage. As you review the list, try to envision why each issue rose to prominence among the general public and how the issue impacts the company's various stakeholders—investors, creditors, employees, customers, governments, and communities.

- **Human Capital—Fair labor practices at Nike:** Nike has been under fire for decades for allowing substandard labor conditions to persist in its contract manufacturers' overseas factories. As early as 1992, the company introduced a pioneering code of conduct to address hazardous working conditions at these factories and to ban such practices as the use of child labor and forced labor. The company's approach to transparent supply chain reporting has been pioneering as well. In 2005 it published a publicly accessible database of its entire contract manufacturing supply chain. The company's annual sustainability reports regularly provide

EXHIBIT 12.1

The Scope of Sustainability Reporting Topics

Source: Sustainability Reporting Standards Board.

Sustainability Dimension	General Topic
Environment	• Greenhouse gas emissions
	• Air quality
	• Energy management
	• Fuel management
	• Water and waste water management
	• Biodiversity impacts
Social Capital	• Human rights and community relations
	• Access and affordability
	• Customer welfare
	• Data security and customer privacy
	• Fair disclosure and labeling
	• Fair marketing and advertising
Human Capital	• Labor relations
	• Fair labor practices
	• Employee health, safety, and well-being
	• Diversity and inclusion
	• Compensation and benefits
	• Recruitment, development, and retention
Business Model and Innovation	• Lifecycle impacts of products
	• Environmental and social impact on core assets and operations
	• Product packaging
	• Product quality and safety
Leadership and Governance	• Systemic risk management
	• Accident and safety management
	• Business ethics and transparency of payment
	• Competitive behavior
	• Regulatory capture and political influence
	• Material sourcing
	• Supply chain management

statistics on the percentage of the factories in this supply chain that fail to meet Nike's code of conduct. Whereas over half of its factories did not consistently achieve this threshold as recently as 2012, that figure had fallen to 14 percent by 2015 and 6 percent by 2020.

- **Environment—Greenhouse gas emissions at Holcim:** Holcim is the world's largest building materials company, and its primary product is cement. The critical step in cement production is the heating of large kilns to about 2,700 degrees Fahrenheit, a process that requires cement plants to burn very large quantities of fossil fuels—coal, petroleum coke, and natural gas—thereby producing similarly large amounts of greenhouse gases (GHGs). Holcim's sustainability report discloses that it is one of the world's largest direct emitters of GHGs, producing 126 million tons of carbon dioxide equivalent gases (CO_2-e) in 2021. As ominous as this sounds, the report also documents a 29 percent improvement since 1990 in its emissions per ton of cement produced and outlines reduction targets of 33 percent by 2025 and 39 percent by 2030.

- **Social Capital—Access and affordability at GlaxoSmithKline plc:** Pharmaceutical companies control valuable drug patents and are regularly criticized for using this control to raise prices and restrict access to life-saving drugs. As a corollary, they are also criticized for neglecting diseases that disproportionately affect poor nations and thus have low profit potential. GlaxoSmithKline (GSK) uses its sustainability report to outline a variety of programs that have led to its number-one ranking in the Access to Medicine Index, an independent ranking developed with support from the Bill and Melinda Gates Foundation. For instance, GSK has capped the prices of patented medicines sold in the world's poorest countries at 25 percent of the prices at which the products are sold in the European Union. It also has pledged to deliver 720 million doses of *Synflorix*, its pneumococcal vaccine, at deeply discounted prices through 2024.

- **Business Model and Innovation—Product quality and safety at McDonald's:** McDonald's faced criticism over the nutritional content of its Happy Meals, as well as for how it markets these meals to children. The company used sustainability reporting to highlight the extent to which it has added fruit, vegetable, and low-fat dairy options to its Happy Meal menu while deemphasizing soft drinks in menu presentations. McDonald's uses sustainability reporting to publicly announce consumption statistics for these items. For instance, the company reported that it provided 31 million clementine oranges in children's meals between November 2014 and March 2015.

In addition to the area's vast scope, a stumbling block for students approaching sustainability reporting for the first time is the wide array of reporting structures and inconsistently used terms that they encounter. This variety and inconsistency are a natural consequence of the system's largely voluntary and unregulated nature. Sustainability reporting is the most common name used for this type of reporting outside the United States. American companies often refer to it as *corporate social responsibility (CSR) reporting*. The *triple bottom line* was a phrase commonly used in the 1990s to describe the system's method of combining social and environmental performance metrics with traditional financial metrics. *ESG (environmental, social, and governance)* reporting is another popular variant, emphasizing the close connection between social responsibility and the way an organization is governed.

THEORIES TO EXPLAIN THE EMERGENCE OF SUSTAINABILITY REPORTING

Sustainability reporting experienced explosive growth in the first decade of the millennium. This growth is best illustrated by the number of companies publishing annual sustainability reports with the framework established by the Global Reporting Initiative (GRI). (The GRI is the world's most widely used voluntary reporting framework and is discussed later in this chapter.) Between 2001 and 2010, the number of GRI-based reports grew from less than 100 to more than 2,000, a 44 percent annual increase.[1] It is fair to say that over this decade, sustainability reporting was transformed from an experimental system employed by a few pioneering companies to a standard part of the stakeholder relations practices of most large corporations.

A number of theories explain this dramatic growth, among them stakeholder theory and legitimacy theory. The stakeholder theory posits that companies make social and environmental disclosures in response to the stakeholder demands for social and environmental information. Management responds to public pressure by stakeholders by voluntarily disclosing this information. A major problem with this theory, considered apart from other motives, is that it fails to explain why firms from similar industries operating in the same geographic area provide different disclosures.

According to legitimacy theory, sustainability reporting is a tool that assists companies in dealing with exposure to political, economic, and social pressures. Firms behave in a way that is considered to be congruent with the society's perceived goals to legitimize their performance. Accordingly, legitimacy is "a condition or a status which exists when an entity's value system is congruent with the value system of the larger social system of which the entity is a part."[2]

The society's perceived goals are represented by various interest groups—for example, environmental public interest groups. If the members of the community are becoming more interested in the social and environmental impact of the activities of companies, it is likely that the senior management will be called upon to explain such activities. For example, researchers examined the effect of the *Exxon Valdez* oil spill in March 1989 on the disclosures within the annual reports of petroleum firms other than Exxon and concluded that threats to a firm's legitimacy do entice the managers to include more social responsibility information in the annual reports.[3]

Applied specifically to reporting, legitimacy theory covers situations in which companies use sustainability reporting to report accomplishments that their stakeholders might not otherwise learn about. For instance, LafargeHolcim's stakeholders are certainly aware that as the world's largest cement producer, it necessarily has a large carbon footprint. However, through the sustainability report, they may learn of the company's accomplishments in reducing its footprint. The report may also assist them in benchmarking LafargeHolcim's environmental performance with that of other cement producers.

Investors' Demand for Sustainability Information

The most important users of traditional financial reports are the company's owners, which, in publicly traded corporations, are the shareholders. While sustainability reporting is generally aimed at a wider set of users, the emphasis that investors give to social and environmental performance has grown dramatically in recent years. A widely reported illustration of this trend was the announcement in January 2018 by Larry Fink, CEO of BlackRock, the world's largest asset manager, that his company would factor social and environmental performance into its investment decisions company-wide.[4]

---

[1] Based on data downloaded from the Global Reporting Initiative's database.

[2] C. K. Lindblom, "The Implications of Organisational Legitimacy for Corporate Social Performance and Disclosure." Paper presented at the Critical Perspectives on Accounting Conference, New York, 1994.

[3] For example, D. Patten, "Intra-industry Environment Disclosures in Response to the Alaskan Oil Spill: A Note on Legitimacy Theory," *Accounting, Organizations and Society* 15, no. 5 (1992), pp. 471–75.

[4] Andrew Ross Sorkin. "BlackRock's Message: Contribute to Society, or Risk Losing Our Support," *The New York Times,* January 15, 2008.

To understand the investment community's demand for the information contained in sustainability reports, it is useful to separate investors into two classes—traditional investors, who focus on a company's profitability and stock performance, and socially responsible investors (SRIs), who make social and environmental performance a significant factor in their decisions. The distinction between these groups is not clear-cut, and it would be inaccurate to label traditional investors as "socially irresponsible." It is best understood by defining SRIs as those who give a large weight to social and environmental factors. In many cases, but not all, they are willing to accept a lower long-term investment return in exchange for superior performance in the social and/or environmental areas that they care about.

The Information Needs of Traditional Investors

Many published academic studies in economics, finance, and accounting provide support for the view that companies with superior social and environmental performance also outperform their peers financially over the long run. This outperformance has been found in studies of both accounting metrics, such as GAAP profit and operating cash flow, and stock market returns. Explanations for this outperformance that fit traditional investment frameworks posit that social and environmental factors are correlated with the many traditionally recognized success factors. These include:

- Governance issues like executive compensation, board structure, and procedures for long-range planning.
- Successful investments in intangible assets, including marketing intangibles, such as brands, and scientific intangibles, such as those related to energy conservation.
- Efficient cost-cutting that reduces the consumption of energy, water, packaging, and so on.
- Better identification of emerging business opportunities, for instance, those associated with organic foods.
- The avoidance of declining products and industries, for instance, tobacco and soft drinks.
- Risk mitigation, including how the company deals with threats to workplace and product safety.

While traditional investors would be interested in environmental and social performance generally, the above list suggests that they have a special interest in information on corporate governance, new product development, and operating issues, such as energy efficiency or workplace safety. With respect to governance, in one of the most widely cited academic studies linking good corporate behavior with stock returns, Harvard's Paul Gompers and his coauthors documented an 8.5 percent annual risk-adjusted (abnormal) return during the 1990s based on an investment strategy that took long positions in companies with high governance scores while shorting those with low scores.[5] Abnormal returns of such a magnitude justify a substantial resource expenditure to both produce and consume the governance-related information in both traditional financial reports as well as sustainability reports.

The Information Needs of Socially Responsible Investors

Socially responsible investors (SRIs) accounted for $16.6 trillion of $51.4 trillion of investments under professional management in the United States in 2020.[6] Thus, of every $3 invested through mutual funds, pension funds, insurance companies, and so on, approximately $1 was invested using explicit social and environmental performance criteria.

---

[5] Paul Gompers, Joy Ishii, and Andrew Metrick, "Corporate Governance and Equity Prices," *Quarterly Journal of Finance* (2003), pp. 107–55.

[6] Forum for Sustainable and Responsible Investment, Report on U.S. Sustainable, Responsible and Impact Investing Trends (2020).

Moreover, the rate of growth of SRI investments has exceeded 15 percent annually over the last 25 years, a higher rate than for investment assets overall. Larry Fink's announcement that BlackRock would use social and environmental performance to evaluate its investments, although reported with much fanfare, should be viewed as part of a larger trend that has been gaining momentum for some time.

The Forum for Sustainable and Responsible Investment, an interest group comprised of SRI-focused institutional investors, categorizes SRI investment strategies as (1) those that screen for negative attributes that the investor tries to avoid and (2) those that are identified as promoting a *positive impact.* An example of a screen for negative attributes would be a pension fund for medical professionals prohibiting investments in tobacco stocks. Other common screening criteria include the avoidance of investments in particular industries, such as gaming or coal mining, or in companies accused of objectionable business practices, such as using child labor or purchasing conflict minerals. Investments to promote positive impact might select companies that are active in alternative energy development or energy conservation.

Much of the content of sustainability reports will be of interest to SRIs. One area of particular interest that is difficult to untangle from other data sources is the social and environmental performance of supply chain partners. Nike and IKEA are examples of companies that have weathered criticism regarding working conditions and the use of child labor in their supply chains. Both companies have effectively used the sustainability reporting framework to provide data on these issues to activist investors, as well as other stakeholders.

THE STRUCTURE OF THE SUSTAINABILITY REPORTING SYSTEM

As sustainability reporting has become more widely accepted and relied upon, certain sustainability disclosures have become mandatory in the United States and other countries. We will discuss mandatory sustainability reporting later in this chapter. At its core, however, the system is still largely voluntary. A voluntary disclosure system lacks the legal structure and sanctions of, say, the financial reporting system in the United States, established by acts of Congress and overseen by the Securities and Exchange Commission. In their place, the sustainability reporting system relies on trust developed between the reporting parties and stakeholders who use the information that the system provides.

A common misconception is that because sustainability reporting has been largely voluntary, the disclosures produced by the system are necessarily propaganda, sometimes referred to as *greenwashing.* This viewpoint overlooks fundamental requirements of the voluntary disclosure process. The goal of the system is to provide a communication channel by which companies can convey information about their social and environmental performance to stakeholders. These stakeholders include activists, investors, interest groups, and industry officials and, on the whole, they are a sophisticated, sometimes skeptical, set of users. For the company's communications goals to be met, these users must find the reports to be credible and a worthwhile investment of their time. While some reports undoubtedly fall short of this goal, the system's robust growth over the last 20 years is itself evidence of the information's value to stakeholders.

The Global Reporting Initiative

Just as financial reporting systems are organized around generally accepted accounting principles, the evolution of the sustainability reporting system has been facilitated by the development of sustainability reporting standards. At present, the most widely accepted set of standards is that promulgated by the Global Reporting Initiative (GRI). As of 2020, 84 percent of the Fortune Global 250 companies used the GRI reporting system, an indication of its dominant role in global reporting.[7] Even some of those that do not use the

---

[7] The KPMG Survey of Corporate Responsible Reporting, 2020.

GRI reporting system borrow certain elements, a process known as *GRI-informed* reporting. IKEA, the world's largest home furnishings retailer, is an example of the latter type of reporter. It explicitly discloses this looser relationship with the GRI in the following passage from its 2016 sustainability report:

> We use the Global Reporting Initiative guidelines to inform our reporting, though we do not report against the guidelines. We are inspired by the GRI's G4 focus on materiality and reporting of impacts across the value chain.

The GRI framework was developed through a consensus-seeking process, with participants drawn globally from business, civil society, labor, and professional institutions. It was initially published in 2000 and has undergone several iterations. Through 2013, it was published as a set of guidelines. The most recent version of these, the G4 guidelines, was released in 2013. In 2018, the GRI implemented GRI Sustainability Reporting Standards based on the G4 guidelines. In a related development, it created the Global Sustainability Standards Board (GSSB). The transition from *guidelines* to *standards* and the formalization of standard-setting under the aegis of a standards board were both important landmarks in the evolution of sustainability reporting.

The Organization of GRI Standards

GRI standards are organized into four broad categories: universal, economic, environmental, and social. Universal standards, numbered 101 to 103, provide users with general information about the entity's reporting policies. For instance, GRI 101 covers basic reporting issues, such as reliability, timeliness, and comparability. Economic standards, numbered 201 to 206, provide basic economic data about the entity but also address the ethical issues of corruption and anticompetitive behavior. Environmental standards, numbered 301 to 308, cover topics such as energy and water consumption, biodiversity, and the emission of pollutants. Social standards, numbered 401 to 419, cover a broad array of topics related to labor practices, human rights, product responsibility, and so on. Each standard mandates a set of numbered disclosures. For instance, GRI 304, *Biodiversity,* mandates that companies provide four specific disclosures, 304-1 to 304-4, presented in Exhibit 12.2 and discussed below.

Many of the required disclosures under GRI standards are quantitative. For instance, Disclosure 305-6 (the sixth disclosure mandated by GRI 305, *Emissions*) requires the company to report the volume of ozone-depleting emissions by weight. Others are more qualitative. For instance, Disclosure 405-1 requires the entity to identify operations or suppliers that are at risk of employing child labor. Students accustomed to reading traditional financial reports often must adjust their expectations for quantitative precision when they first begin to read sustainability reports. Many of the most important social and environmental problems that society faces are best described by a mixture of quantitative and qualitative metrics. Exhibit 12.2 provides examples of disclosures set out in several environment and human rights standards. Disclosures related to recycling and the emission of pollutants are more amenable to precise quantitative reporting than are disclosures related to biodiversity and human rights. Obviously, the latter topics are no less important simply because they are harder to quantify.

The Global Sustainability Standards Board

The Global Sustainability Standards Board (GSSB) is a deliberative body that exercises authority over GRI standards in much the same way that the IASB exercises authority over IFRS. As of March 2022, the board was composed of 15 members resembled the IASB in its geographic diversity. It was chaired by Judy Kuszewski from the United Kingdom. The rest of the board consisted of members from Australia (two members), Hong Kong, India (two members), the EU (three members), Switzerland, South Africa, the United Kingdom,

EXHIBIT 12.2
Examples of Specific Disclosures Required by Several GRI Standards

Source: *GRI Standards 2016.*

Environment - Materials (GRI 301)
301-2   The percentage of recycled materials used to manufacture the entity's primary products and services.

Environment - Biodiversity (GRI 304)
304-1   Location and size of land owned, leased, managed in, or adjacent to, protected areas and areas of high biodiversity value outside protected areas.
304-2   Description of significant impacts of activities, products, and services on biodiversity in protected areas and areas of high biodiversity value outside protected areas.
304-3   Habitats protected or restored.
304-4   International Union for Conservation of Nature (IUCN) Red List species (i.e., endangered species) with habitats in areas affected by the entity's operations.

Environment - Emissions (GRI 305)
305-1   Direct greenhouse gas emissions by weight.
305-6   Emissions of ozone-depleting substances by weight.
305-7   Emissions of nitrogen oxides and sulfur oxides (acid rain-related emissions).

Human Rights - Nondiscrimination (GRI 406)
406-1   Total number of incidents of discrimination and corrective actions taken.

Human Rights - Freedom of Association (GRI 407)
407-1   Operations and suppliers identified in which the right to exercise freedom of association and collective bargaining may be violated or at significant risk.

Human Rights - Child Labor (GRI 408)
408-1   Operations and suppliers identified as having significant risk for incidents of child labor.

---

and the United States (three members). Several of the board members themselves have multinational backgrounds, having gained professional experience in different regions of the world.

In addition to being geographically diverse, the board is *multi-stakeholder* in representation, meaning that board members represent various societal constituencies by design. Of the aforementioned 15 members, six represented *business enterprises,* four represented *civil society organizations* (including academia), two represented *labor organizations,* one represented *investment organizations,* and two represented *mediating organizations.* The latter category includes public accounting firms, such as Deloitte.

Nonfinancial Materiality

Exhibit 12.1, presented in this chapter's introduction, illustrates the very broad array of topics that can be addressed in sustainability reports. This variety poses a challenge for both reporting entities and readers. How does one sift through the many possible topics and focus on those that are most relevant for a given company? This problem of information overload, widely recognized as a threat to the usefulness of traditional financial reporting, is, if anything, an even bigger threat to the usefulness of sustainability reporting.

The GRI system addresses this concern by explicitly introducing *materiality* as a reporting criterion. In traditional financial reporting, materiality is viewed as a threshold. A general rule of thumb is that companies should disclose material information. This is often defined as information that reasonable investors would want to know in making their investment decisions. In the GRI system, materiality is defined in two dimensions—a particular issue's materiality is scored in terms of its importance to stakeholders as well as its importance in the internal reporting used in the day-to-day management of the business. Companies that use the GRI system generally present materiality disclosures using two-dimensional graphs constructed from these rankings.

Holcim's materiality disclosures in its 2020 sustainability report provide an example of how entities disclose materiality assessments under the GRI framework. The report scores topics along two dimensions, *Importance to external stakeholders* (broadly speaking, society at large) and *Importance to internal stakeholders* (management, employees, etc.). Employee health and safety, business ethics, and greenhouse gas emissions are among the most important topics in both sets of rankings. Topics that are material but receive somewhat lower scores in both rankings included employee development and employee diversity and inclusion. Perhaps the most interesting and informative cases are topics with divergent rankings. For example, consider the following:

Topics with high internal stakeholder rankings but comparatively lower external stakeholder rankings:

- Customer relations and customer satisfaction
- Pricing integrity and anti-trust compliance

Topics with high external stakeholder rankings but comparatively lower internal stakeholder rankings:

- Water management
- Biodiversity management and quarry rehabilitation

It should be noted that the company ranked all of the above topics as material to both sets of stakeholders to at least a medium degree. Just because a topic scored comparatively lower in internal stakeholder rankings does not mean that it is deemphasized by the company's management. Rather, such divergent rankings should be interpreted as an acknowledgment by the company that special measures may be necessary to adjust the company's sustainability performance to society's expectations.

Other Sustainability Reporting Frameworks

A large number of reporting frameworks have developed alongside the GRI as global sustainability reporting has evolved over the last two decades. Some resemble the GRI in that they provide a comprehensive set of benchmarks against which sustainability performance can be measured. Others address particular issues, such as climate change or labor standards. The following list provides brief descriptions of several of the most important frameworks in common use:

- *Sustainability Accounting Standards Board (SASB).* The SASB is a U.S. nonprofit organization that has developed a comprehensive sustainability reporting system designed to meet the expanding information demands of investors, as well as the growing sustainability reporting requirements of U.S. securities laws. (The SASB's reporting model is discussed more fully in the next section.)
- *Carbon Disclosure Project (CDP).* The CDP is a system of voluntary reporting of carbon emissions established by a critical mass of institutional investors acting in concert. A key component of the project is the Climate Disclosure Standards Board, created through the aegis of the CDP in 2007. This board has worked to standardize climate disclosures. In 2020, 790 institutional investors were signatories to the CDP disclosure system, representing $114 trillion in assets under management. In 2021, more than 13,000 companies reported on their greenhouse gas emissions through the CDP. These companies accounted for 64 percent of global stock market capitalization, 96 percent of the FTSE 100, and over 80 percent of the S&P 500. In recent years, the CDP has used its expertise

in measurement and reporting to expand its scope to include sustainability issues related to water, supply chains, and forests.

- *Task Force on Climate-related Financial Disclosures (TCFD).* The TCFD has developed a widely adopted framework for disclosures related to the financial risks and opportunities presented by climate change. The framework includes requirements to disclose the explicit impact of climate events on companies' financial statements. The TCFD was created by the Financial Stability Board of the G20 in collaboration with the CDP. Among the entities considering adopting the TCFD framework is the U.S. SEC.
- *Sustainability-related standards published by the International Standards Organization (ISO).* The ISO has developed a variety of standards related to sustainability issues. ISO 26000 explicitly relates to social responsibility and is often used in conjunction with GRI reporting. In addition, a large number of ISO standards address sustainability topics such as environmental management (ISO 14001), medical device quality (ISO 13485), occupational health and safety (ISO 45001), and anti-bribery management systems (ISO 37001).
- *The ESG ratings system of Institutional Shareholder Services (ISS).* A growing number of entities provide ESG ratings to institutional investors. These are scoring systems, not reporting frameworks per se. However, because so much of sustainability reporting is voluntary, these systems influence the scope and structure of the system through *demand-pull effects.* Among the many scoring systems that have arisen over the last decade, ISS's ESG rating system stands out. ISS is a proxy advisory service. It assists fund managers, such as Vanguard and Fidelity, in deciding how to vote on shareholder resolutions. ISS ESG ratings have become influential in deciding the outcomes of several high profile proxy battles. Most famously, ISS provided critical support to a successful campaign that replaced three members of ExxonMobil's board of directors with climate activists in 2021.[8]

TOWARD MANDATORY SUSTAINABILITY REPORTING

Sustainability reporting is still best characterized as a voluntary reporting system. Even if compelled to issue a report by law or market pressure, companies generally choose the standards that they will use, their degree of compliance with those standards, the formats that their reports will take, and whether to seek third-party verification of the assertions made in their reports.

Calls from many sources to move to a mandatory system of sustainability reporting have increased dramatically in recent years. Many proponents see mandatory reporting as the only way to achieve the levels of reliability and comparability in sustainability reporting that stakeholders require. The investment community, in particular, has been especially vocal, demanding that ESG information be of the same quality as the financial information that has traditionally ungirded its models. After all, if ESG performance truly influences a business's future long-run profitability, real money is at stake when trying to comb through the many pieces of disparate information in the sustainability report.

While the system has remained largely voluntary, virtually every securities regulator in the world is actively considering whether and to what degree to require some form of sustainability reporting in the future. Most of these initiatives will eventually fall within the

---

[8] Svea Herbst-Bayliss, "Exxon under pressure as ISS backs Engine No.1 nominees in board fight," Reuters, May 14, 2021.

reporting framework of the International Sustainability Standards Board (ISSB), which was launched in November 2021 and is discussed at the end of this section. Before turning to the ISSB, we will cover several important mandatory schemes that have been in place for several years and have track records. These are examples of regulatory schemes that businesses should expect to encounter in the future, imposed by governments, transnational bodies, and stock exchanges.

Mandatory Sustainability Reporting in the European Union

The most far-reaching mandate is the European Union's Directive 2014/95/EU, also called the *Non-Financial Reporting Directive (NFRD)*, that requires member nations to implement mandatory sustainability reporting for large entities, generally those with at least 500 employees. Under the directive, acceptable reporting frameworks include the GRI, the OECD's Guidelines for Multinational Enterprises, and the International Standards Organization's ISO 26000. Enacted in 2014, the directive applies to all 27 countries of the EU. In 2021, the directive covered approximately 11,700 institutions, including listed companies, banks, and insurance companies.

EU directives are implemented through national legislation enacted country by country. This system has led to slight differences in how the sustainability reporting mandate is applied. These differences are visible when comparing the reporting requirements in Germany and France, the two largest member states. In Germany, a large company is defined as one with 500 employees or annual net sales of at least €40 million. The report must be published within four months of the balance sheet date. The government may levy significant financial penalties for violations of the nation's sustainability reporting law. France's definition of a large company is identical to Germany's. However, its version of the law imposes no fines and gives companies an eight-month window from the end of the fiscal year within which to file their sustainability reports.

In April 2021, the European Commission adopted a proposal for a new *Corporate Sustainability Reporting Directive (CSRD)* that would replace the NFRD. As proposed, the CSRD would enhance advance mandatory reporting through the following provisions:

- Extending sustainability reporting mandates to all listed companies, regardless of size, with a carve out for micro-enterprises.
- Requiring an external audit of sustainability reports.
- Requiring adherence to EU sustainability standards.

With respect to the last provision, the European Commission charged the European Financial Reporting Advisory Group (EFRAG) to develop and publish a set of EU sustainability standards to be adopted by October 2022. Ultimately, these will be subsumed under new standard promulgated by the International Sustainability Standards Board, a project of the IASB Foundation (see below).

Sustainability Reporting Required by the Hong Kong Stock Exchange

The Hong Kong Stock Exchange (HKEX) is the third largest exchange in Asia and the sixth largest exchange in the world. For many international investors, it is the primary venue for trading the shares of prominent mainland Chinese companies. At the start of 2022, the largest companies by market capitalization included Tencent Holdings, the Industrial and Commercial Bank of China, China Merchants Bank, China Construction Bank, PetroChina, and Meituan Dianping.

In 2015, HKEX enacted a set of comprehensive sustainability reporting rules that came into force in 2016. The rules follow a *disclose-or-explain* approach. The HKEX's rules lay out a robust set of sustainability-related key performance indicators (KPIs). Disclose-or-explain means that companies must either report their performance for a given KPI or explain why they are not able to do so. Strictly speaking, the application of disclose-or-explain to each KPI makes the HKEX a form of mandatory reporting. However, the system is flexible enough to allow a company to forego disclosure of a particular KPI if it is willing to publicly present its reasons for nondisclosure. In effect, the system mixes mandates with stakeholder pressure to preserve a measure of reporting flexibility for the entity.

The following list of KPI categories used by the HKEX illustrates why its sustainability reporting requirements should be viewed as among the world's most comprehensive:

- Air pollution and greenhouse gas emissions.
- Amounts of hazardous waste produced.
- Consumption of energy, water, and packaging material.
- Work hours, workplace safety, and workplace discrimination.
- Supply chain risks, including practices to detect and eliminate child and forced labor.
- Product health and safety.
- Measures to prevent bribery, fraud, extortion, and money laundering.
- Descriptions of community engagement initiatives.

For each KPI in the above categories, HKEX guidelines specify metrics taken from the GRI, the Climate Disclosure Project, ISO 26000, or the Dow Jones Sustainability Index survey that will satisfy the reporting requirements.

In addition to disclosures of performance according to specific KPIs, HKEX rules also set forth a variety of governance-related mandates with reporting implications. For instance, governance rules require companies to discuss their environmental policies in the business review section of the corporation's directors' report, included in the annual report.

Mandatory Sustainability Reporting in the United States

U.S. law sets forth many specific reporting requirements pertaining to issues also covered in sustainability reports. These often flow from laws enacted to regulate the business practices of a specific industry. Once sustainability data are collected by a particular government agency, they are generally published or at least made available under the Freedom of Information Act. The public dissemination of mine safety data is typical of this process. Mine safety laws require the disclosure of detailed mine safety statistics to the Mine Safety and Health Administration (MSHA). Once obtained, the data are published on the MSHA website.[9]

Less common are rules explicitly requiring companies to publicly disclose data themselves. An example of such a rule is a provision in the Dodd-Frank Wall Street Reform and Consumer Protection Act of 2010 requiring a disclosure based on the above-mentioned MSHA mine safety data to be included in Form 10-K. A more expansive and politically controversial example is a rule jointly published by the U.S. Department of Defense and the General Services Administration in 2016 requiring federal contractors to publicly disclose greenhouse gas emissions.[10] In 2021, the President Biden issued an executive order requiring the federal government study extending the emissions reporting mandate to all large federal contractors.

---

[9] Hans B. Christensen, Eric Floyd, Lisa Yao Liu, and Mark Maffett, "The Real Effects of Mandated Information on Social Responsibility in Financial Reports: Evidence from Mine-Safety Records," University of Chicago, Booth School of Business working paper (September 2016).

[10] Federal Register, Vol. 81, No. 223 (Friday, November 18, 2016), Rules and Regulations.

The U.S. SEC's Climate Change Reporting Requirements

In February 2010, the U.S. Securities and Exchange Commission (SEC) issued Release No. 33-9106, *Commission Guidance Regarding Disclosure Related to Climate Change,* a widely publicized pronouncement that had the effect of expanding sustainability reporting requirements within already-existing disclosure regulations. Technically, the guidance was an *interpretative release.* It did not change existing disclosure law so much as it revised how existing laws should be interpreted. However, the release had the practical effect of expanding climate-related disclosure requirements for many companies. It also paved the way for the U.S. securities laws to be reinterpreted to require more expansive sustainability reporting in other areas.

In effect, Release No. 33-9106 requires the threats and opportunities posed by climate change and climate change regulation to be explicitly incorporated into the following sections of the 10-K:

- *Business Description* (Item 101 of Regulation S-K): The company must include the cost of complying with environmental laws, including anticipated required capital expenditures.
- *Legal Proceedings* (Item 103 of Regulation S-K): The company must include litigation related to emissions and violations of environmental rules.
- *Risk Factors* (Item 503c of Regulation S-K): The company must include descriptions of risks to the business posed by climate change and climate-related legislation.
- *Management Discussion and Analysis* (Item 303 of Regulation S-K): Management must incorporate the effects of climate change and climate regulation into required disclosures of "known trends, events, demands, commitments and uncertainties that are reasonably likely to have a material effect on financial condition or operating performance."

Since the publication of Release No. 33-9106, many stakeholder groups have criticized the SEC for not enforcing the release's provisions more vigorously. However, the document's potential to affect corporate disclosure over time is best illustrated by a settlement reached in November 2015 between the New York State Attorney General, Eric Schneiderman, and Peabody Energy, the world's largest coal mining company. Schneiderman had accused Peabody of using overly optimistic forecasts of world coal consumption in its 10-K disclosures, in effect downplaying the consequences of increasingly restrictive regulations on coal worldwide. As part of the settlement, the company agreed to revise its approach to forecasting coal demand.[11]

The Sustainability Accounting Standards Board

The most important development in U.S. sustainability reporting over the last decade has been the founding and subsequent expansion of the Sustainability Accounting Standards Board (SASB). The SASB is a nonprofit body modeled on its counterpart in traditional financial reporting, the Financial Accounting Standards Board (FASB). The SASB has developed a comprehensive disclosure framework that resembles those of its international counterparts in many respects. Exhibit 12.1, included in this chapter's introduction, was based on this framework. However, the SASB differs from its international counterparts by focusing on investors' information needs and linking its framework to the reporting requirements of U.S. securities law. Exhibit 12.3 compares the mission and intended audience of the SASB reporting system with that of the GRI. Whereas the GRI's intended audience is a broad cross-section of stakeholder groups, the SASB's intended audience is explicitly the investment community.

---

[11] Assurance of Discontinuance. Investigation by Eric T. Schneiderman of Peabody Energy Corporation pursuant to Article 23-A, Section 352, of the New York General Business Law. Assurance No. 15-242.

EXHIBIT 12.3

The SASB and the GRI: Alternative Audiences and Approaches to Materiality

Source: Sustainability Accounting Standards Board, 2018.

	SASB	GRI
Definition	Information is material "if there is a substantial likelihood that the omitted fact would have significantly altered the total mix of information available to the reasonable investor."	"The Materiality Principle states that the report should cover Aspects that: reflect the organization's significant economic, environmental and social impacts; or substantively influence the assessments and decisions of stakeholders."
Whose perspective is considered	The reasonable investor.	Broad range of stakeholders.
What kind of decisions are affected	Investor decisions to buy, hold, or sell a security or how to vote on a corporate matter.	Not identified.
Threshold for disclosure	Whether the information would have assumed significance in the deliberations of the reasonable investor.	Whether the information would be considered important by a broad range of stakeholders.

The SASB establishes a linkage between its metrics and the disclosure requirements of U.S. securities law through its own application of the concept of *nonfinancial materiality.* As discussed in the prior section, the GRI framework uses the concept of materiality as a way of sifting through the broad array of possible sustainability concerns to identify those that are most important to the organization and its stakeholders. SASB's approach is to focus explicitly on what disclosures might affect the information available to investors when they make investment decisions about the company. Using the language of prior court cases that define financial materiality, a nonfinancial disclosure is said to be material if it alters the information mix that a reasonable investor would consult in making the investment decision. The SASB's reporting framework can be interpreted as *mandatory* in the sense that it is designed to elicit disclosures that may satisfy the legal definition of what is, or should be, material to investors.

One of the SASB's most significant contributions to sustainability reporting is the development and publication of its *materiality map.* This map ranks the level of importance a particular sustainability topic has for a given industry from an investor's perspective. Under the GRI, materiality rankings are developed by companies and based on the perspectives of both stakeholders and internal management; in contrast, the SASB's materiality map is an objective study of materiality viewed through its more focused investment lens. Readers are invited to explore the map in greater detail on the SASB's website.[12]

The International Sustainability Standard Board

In November 2021, the IASB Foundation announced the creation of the International Sustainability Standards Board (ISSB), a deliberative body that will play roughly the same role in sustainability reporting that the IASB has heretofore played in traditional financial reporting. The IASB and ISSB are designed to be separate, co-equal boards that will operate in parallel, but collaboratively. The IASB will oversee the continuing development and promulgation of IFRS, while the ISSB will oversee the development and promulgation of *IFRS Sustainability Disclosure Standards.* (See Chapter 3 for a detailed description of the IASB and its role in the promulgation of IFRS.)

[12] The SASB Materiality Map™ is available at https://www.sasb.org/materiality/sasb-materiality-map/.

In designing the ISSB, the IASB Foundation assembled a task force that included the SASB, the Task Force on Climate-related Financial Disclosures, and the Climate Disclosure Standards Board. Going forward, the work of the SASB will be subsumed under the aegis of the ISSB. As part of this process, the SASB transferred legal ownership of its standards to the ISSB, which will use them as the basis for the new IFRS system.

The IASB Foundation organized the ISSB to take a capital-markets perspective, in contrast to the GRI's multi-stakeholder perspective. This lays the groundwork for it ISSB's standards to become mandatory under traditional, investor-focused securities law. In March 2022, the Foundation and the GRI announced an agreement to collaborate in creating a global sustainability reporting system with two pillars. One pillar is the ISSB's reporting system with a capital markets focus, while the other is the GRI's system with a multi-stakeholder focus.

The ISSB is still in its infancy. However, it is already possible to predict that its creation will be one of the most important events in the modern history of accounting. As stated earlier, most national capital markets regulators have launched initiatives aimed at making sustainability disclosures mandatory, particularly those related to climate change. Most of these regulators also mandate IFRS or use IFRS as benchmarks to set national standards. It is highly likely that they will adopt the same posture to IFRS Sustainability Disclosure Standards as these are rolled out by the ISSB.

CARBON EMISSIONS REPORTING

Climate change and how society should respond to it have become politically controversial topics, especially in the United States. What is beyond doubt, however, is that it is important for future business leaders to understand societal pressures on entities to report on, and ultimately reduce, their carbon emissions. Ironically, this knowledge is especially important to students planning to pursue careers in industries associated with the production or large-scale consumption of fossil fuels, such as oil and gas, power generation, mining, and heavy manufacturing. Taking oil and gas as an example, each of the world's major oil companies factors climate change considerations into its internal analyses of future capital investments, often explicitly incorporating an internal carbon price into capital budgeting models. Chevron provided insights into its approach in the following response to a Carbon Disclosure Project questionnaire in 2017:

> We integrate climate change risks into strategic and business planning processes. These are examples of major business decisions resulting from this process:
>
> - We have made significant progress in reducing flare gas volumes in Angola through the execution of various projects. For example, our Nemba Enhanced Secondary Recovery Project reduced flaring at the South and North Nemba fields by almost 34 million standard cubic feet per day in 2016.
> - Chevron Australia's Gorgon Project incorporates facilities to safely inject reservoir carbon dioxide more than 1.2 miles (2 km) below the surface of Barrow Island. Carbon dioxide occurs naturally in the gas being produced and is extracted as a routine part of the processing operations. In most gas processing plants, these gases are vented to the atmosphere. When fully operational, it is anticipated that greenhouse gas emissions from the Gorgon Project will be reduced by up to 4 million metric tons per year, or 100 million metric tons over the life of the project.
> - In Alberta, Canada, Chevron is a co-venture partner of the Quest Carbon Capture and Storage (CCS) project—the first CCS project in the Canadian oil sands. This innovative project is designed to capture and safely store more than a million metric tons of carbon

dioxide each year—equivalent to taking 250,000 cars off the road annually. Commercial operations at the Quest CCS project began in November 2015.

Source: Chevron Corporation's response to the 2017 Climate Change Information Request of the Carbon Disclosure Project.

Chevron's disclosure goes on to state that "since 2008, our internal carbon price has been considered in the economic evaluations supporting major capital project appropriations." Clearly, a young cost accountant or financial analyst at Chevron would need to understand the nuances of carbon accounting better than most of her peers outside of the energy sector.

Measuring Carbon Emissions

There has been a large degree of international convergence in arriving at a framework to measure and report carbon emissions. Key contributors in this process have included the U.S Environmental Protection Agency, the World Resources Institute, the Carbon Disclosure Project, the Climate Disclosure Standards Board, the Task Force on Climate-related Financial Disclosures, and representatives from industry. The measurement portion of the system, termed the *Greenhouse Gas Protocol,* forms the basis for reporting used by virtually all of the world's sustainability reporting frameworks, including the GRI.

The basic unit used to measure and report greenhouse gas (GHG) emissions is the *carbon dioxide equivalent* (CO_2-e), based on the protocol's formula for incorporating the relative effects of various greenhouse gases on climate change. After carbon dioxide, the next most common greenhouse gas is methane, which is given a weight of 25 times CO_2. Thus, emitting one metric ton of methane would be measured as emitting 25 metric tons of CO_2-e. Other greenhouse gases receive even greater weights, for example, nitrous oxide (295 times CO_2) and sulfur hexafluoride (23,900 times CO_2).

The consideration of supply chain effects runs throughout the sustainability reporting model. However, nowhere is this more explicitly captured than in carbon emissions reporting. A company that burns fuel oil directly emits CO_2-e. However, what of a company that uses electricity produced by a coal-fired electricity plant? The Greenhouse Gas Protocol captures the company's indirect responsibility for CO_2-e emissions as well. Accountants do this by categorizing carbon-producing activities into one of three *scopes,* defined as follows:

- *Scope 1 Emissions:* Direct emissions of the entity. (GRI Disclosure 305-1)
- *Scope 2 Emissions:* Indirect emissions traceable to the purchase of electricity, heat, or steam. (GRI Disclosure 305-2)
- *Scope 3 Emissions:* Other indirect emissions. (GRI Disclosure 305-3)

Scope 3 emissions are defined relative to the entity's place in the supply chain. They are the hardest to categorize and account for, and their measurement is potentially the most controversial. They include the emissions of both upstream and downstream supply chain partners, but they exclude Scope 2 power providers. An example of an upstream Scope 3 activity would be the transportation of raw materials by a supplier. An example of a downstream Scope 3 activity would be emissions caused by using the company's products. The following is a list of Scope 3 categories contained in the Greenhouse Gas Protocol:

1. Purchased goods and services
2. Capital goods
3. Fuel- and energy-related activities not included in Scopes 1 and 2
4. Upstream transportation and distribution
5. Waste generation in operations
6. Business travel

7. Employee commuting
8. Upstream leased assets
9. Downstream transportation and distribution
10. Processing of sold products
11. Use of sold products
12. End-of-life treatment of sold products
13. Downstream leased assets
14. Franchises
15. Investments, including investments in associates and joint ventures accounted for under the equity method

Note that whereas petroleum- and coal-producing companies are often accused by activists of bearing a special responsibility for climate change, a significant portion of their carbon emissions would be classified as Scope 3. In other words, other entities, including drivers of autos for personal use, are actually responsible for the Scope 1 emissions linked to their products. The world's largest Scope 1 emitters include LafargeHolcim, profiled earlier in this chapter, along with electric utilities that burn substantial quantities of fossil fuels.

Carbon Emissions Intensity

As discussed in Chapter 4, Holcim was created by the 2015 merger of Holcim Ltd. of Switzerland and Lafarge SA of France. Because the main product of each is cement, both were among the world's largest direct (Scope 1) emitters of CO_2-e before their acquisition. In 2013, for instance, Holcim and Lafarge ranked 11th and 12th in the world, respectively, among corporate emitters. Had their operations been combined in that year, they would have been the world's largest corporate Scope 1 emitter of greenhouse gases by a comfortable margin.[13]

Of course, merely combining the operations of Holcim and Lafarge should not automatically hurt their environmental performance scores. In fact, such mergers may very well enhance environmental performance by streamlining operations, accelerating the closure of outdated facilities, and pooling R&D insights. More generally, accountants are aware of the necessity of adjusting performance metrics for scale effects. In carbon accounting, this is accomplished by introducing a set of intensity metrics. Specifically, GRI 305-4 discloses greenhouse gas emission intensity using one or more of the following deflators:

- Production volume (resulting in a calculation of metric tons of CO_2-e produced per unit manufactured or per unit of services rendered).
- Size (e.g., a retailer may report metric tons of CO_2-e produced per square foot of floor space).
- Number of employees.
- Sales revenue.

In preparing its sustainability reports, Holcim chooses to measure intensity using a production volume metric specific to its industry—units produced plus "mineral components consumed for blending."

Carbon Emissions Disclosures at BASF

BASF, based in Ludwigshafen, Germany, is the world's largest chemical company. The company publishes a comprehensive annual greenhouse gas emissions report, from which data

---

[13] The Carbon Disclosure Project database, which includes publicly accessible data on greenhouse gas emissions through 2013.

EXHIBIT 12.4
BASF 2021 Greenhouse Gas Inventory Emissions by Scope

Scopes and Categories	Metric Tons CO$_2$-e	Percentage of Scope 3 Emissions	Primary	Secondary
Scope 1: Direct emissions from owned/controlled operations	17,484,734	–	–	–
Scope 2: Indirect emissions from the use of purchased electricity, steam, heating, and cooling.	3,182,000	–	–	–
Upstream Scope 3 emissions.				
Purchased goods and services	47,753,000	52%	83%	17%
Capital goods.	1,722,000	2	92	8
Fuel- and energy-related activities (not included in Scope 1 or Scope 2)	3,119,000	3	92	8
Upstream transportation and distribution	2,462,000	3	0	100
Waste generated in operations	1,343,000	1	100	0
Business travel.	34,000	0	100	0
Employee commuting.	147,000	0	15	85
Upstream leased assets.	169,000	0	85	15
Downstream Scope 3 emissions				
Downstream transportation and distribution	1,237,000	1	100	0
Use of sold products.	5,951,000	7	100	0
End-of-life treatment of sold products.	23,911,000	26	74	26
Investments	3,438,000	4	100	0

in this section have been taken. BASF's direct (Scope 1) emissions were 17,485 thousand metric tons of CO$_2$-e in 2021. Of these emissions, almost 100 percent was carbon dioxide. Emissions of nitrous oxide, methane, etc., were immaterial.

The biggest challenge BASF faces in developing its emission disclosures is measuring Scope 3 emissions in its supply chain, which are largely outside of its control and sometimes unobservable. Therefore, it categorizes Scope 3 measurements as either primary or secondary. Primary measurements are based on company-specific observations and are of relatively high quality. Secondary measurements refer to data supplied by third parties or extrapolated based on various assumptions. Emissions resulting from employee business travel are estimated from the company's own records and are therefore 100 percent primary. Emissions resulting from employees commuting to work are unobservable and outside the company's direct control. These are 97 percent secondary.

Exhibit 12.4 presents BASF's 2021 emissions calculations by category. The most significant emissions categories are all in Scope 3: emissions traceable to purchased goods and services, the use of BASF's products by customers, and the end-of-life treatment of sold products. Each is larger than the company's direct emissions, highlighting the importance of supply chain relationships in the current carbon accounting framework.

SUSTAINABILITY REPORTING PRACTICES OF MNCS

Up to this point, our discussion of sustainability reporting has been mainly descriptive and conducted at a high level. To complete the picture, we now include examples of sustainability disclosures made by four prominent corporations:

- Comprehensive reporting within the GRI framework (Mazda).
- GRI-informed reporting (IKEA).

- The link between sustainability reporting and traditional financial reporting (Baxter International).
- Mandatory sustainability reporting required by SEC Release No. 33-9106 (ExxonMobil).

These examples illustrate the variety of reporting choices and formats that students can expect to encounter when they begin reading sustainability reports on their own.

External Assurance in Sustainability Reporting

External assurance refers to the practice of hiring an outside party to assure, or verify, the claims made in a sustainability report. A key difference between traditional financial reporting and sustainability reporting is that the reporting entity voluntarily chooses whether or not to have its sustainability reporting externally assured. In addition, there is much greater flexibility in designing the scope of the assurance services to be performed. Nevertheless, approximately half of the sustainability reports in the GRI database are externally assured, including a large majority of reports issued by Global 250 companies. This is an important point of which accounting students should take note: The robust growth of external assurance in the sustainability reporting arena demonstrates that demand for such services stems more from the information needs of the market than the rules imposed by securities laws and regulators. Some of the benefits of external assurance are:

- Enhanced credibility of the entity's sustainability disclosures.
- Better communications between the entity and its stakeholders.
- A reduction in the risk of a misstatement that could later lead to controversy between the entity and its stakeholders.
- Improvement in the internal processes by which sustainability initiatives are managed.

Another key difference between sustainability reporting and traditional financial reporting is the wider use of third-party assurers that are non-accounting firms with specific expertise in engineering or sustainability topics. Of the third-party assurers used by companies in the GRI database, 36 percent are non-accounting firms. For instance, Baxter International's 2020 sustainability report was externally assured by Apex Companies, LLC, an engineering and consulting firm that leverages its technical capabilities to also provide assurance services.

Exhibit 12.5 presents KPMG's independent assurance report for Mazda for the 2020 fiscal year. Readers of Mazda's sustainability report can readily identify disclosures that were evaluated by KPMG because they are marked with checkmarks.[14] Whereas KPMG's coverage of disclosures in the Mazda report was quite comprehensive, assurance may be limited to fewer areas in the reports of other companies. Assurers may offer *reasonable assurance,* but more commonly they will offer *limited assurance.* KPMG clearly states that its assurance level falls short of reasonable assurance. This is a common arrangement given the large range of disclosures being made about widely scattered operations.

Mazda's 2020 Sustainability Report

Mazda is an internationally prominent automaker based in Hiroshima, Japan. The company's fiscal year ends on March 31st. In addition to its annual financial report, it publishes a separate sustainability report covering the most recently completed fiscal year. The following discussion is based on its 2020 sustainability report, available on Mazda's website.[15]

---

[14] Mazda's 2017 sustainability report was based on the GRI G4 system. Therefore, KPMG refers to social performance *indicators.* From 2018, these will be labeled disclosures.

[15] The 2021 Mazda sustainability report is available at https://www.mazda.com/globalassets/en/assets/sustainability/download/2021/2021_all.pdf.

EXHIBIT 12.5
Independent Assurance Report of Mazda Provided by KPMG AZSA for the 2020 Fiscal Year

Independent Assurance Report

To the Representative Director, President and CEO of Mazda Motor Corporation
We were engaged by Mazda Motor Corporation (the "Company") to undertake a limited assurance engagement of the social performance indicators marked with "☑" (the "Indicators") for the period from April 1, 2019 to March 31, 2020 included in its SUSTAINABILITY REPORT 2021 (IN-DEPTH VERSION) (the "Report") for the fiscal year ended March 31, 2020.

The Company's Responsibility

The Company is responsible for the preparation of the Indicators in accordance with its own reporting criteria (the "Company's reporting criteria") as described in the Report.

Our Responsibility

Our responsibility is to express a limited assurance conclusion on the Indicators based on the procedures we have performed. We conducted our engagement in accordance with the 'International Standard on Assurance Engagements (ISAE) 3000, Assurance Engagements other than Audits or Reviews of Historical Financial Information' issued by the International Auditing and Assurance Standards Board. The limited assurance engagement consisted of making inquiries, primarily of persons responsible for the preparation of information presented in the Report, and applying analytical and other procedures, and the procedures performed vary in nature from, and are less in extent than for, a reasonable assurance engagement. The level of assurance provided is thus not as high as that provided by a reasonable assurance engagement. Our assurance procedures included:

- Interviewing with the Company's responsible personnel to obtain an understanding of its policy for preparing the Report and reviewing the Company's reporting criteria.
- Inquiring about the design of the systems and methods used to collect and process the Indicators.
- Performing analytical reviews of the Indicators.
- Examining, on a test basis, evidence supporting the generation, aggregation and reporting of the Indicators in conformity with the Company's reporting criteria, and also recalculating the Indicators.
- Making inquiries and reviewing materials including documented evidence of the Company's headquarter selected on the basis of a risk analysis, as alternative procedures to a site visit.
- Evaluating the overall statement in which the Indicators are expressed.

Conclusion

Based on the procedures performed as described above, nothing has come to our attention that causes us to believe that the Indicators in the Report are not prepared, in all material respects, in accordance with the Company's reporting criteria as described in the Report.

Our Independence and Quality Control

We have complied with the Code of Ethics for Professional Accountants issued by the International Ethics Standards Board for Accountants, which includes independence and other requirements founded on fundamental principles of integrity, objectivity, professional competence and due care, confidentiality and professional behavior. In accordance with International Standard on Quality Control 1, we maintain a comprehensive system of quality control including documented policies and procedures regarding compliance with ethical requirements, professional standards, and applicable legal and regulatory requirements.

KPMG AZSA Sustainability Co., Ltd.
Osaka, Japan
December 14, 2020

In conformity with the GRI's materiality framework, Mazda ranks the importance of sustainability topics along two dimensions: (1) their effect on stakeholders, and (2) the degree to which they present risks or opportunities for the Mazda Group. Topics receiving the highest ranking along both dimensions are:

- Energy
- Water source in community
- Emissions, including greenhouse gas emissions
- Effluents and waste
- Occupational health and safety
- Diversity and equal opportunity
- Customer health and safety
- Indirect economic impacts

Exhibit 12.6 presents company-wide data for the environmental topics ranked as material (corresponding to the first four bullet points above). The data presented here is for the Mazda Group worldwide, whereas KPMG's assurance is limited to operations at four of Mazda's Japanese plants and five of its overseas plants. The company reported marked improvement in several areas—particularly, in water consumption, Scope 1 and 2 greenhouse gas emissions, direct-to-landfill waste, and chemical discharges. However, these reductions must be viewed against the backdrop of the decline in business activity. (Because the 2020 fiscal year ended on March 31, 2020, the onset of the Covid-19 pandemic may have contributed modestly to this decline.) Year-over-year unit sales volume dropped 9.1 percent, while sales revenue declined 3.8 percent. Using unit sales volume as a proxy for physical productivity, many of the metrics did not show an improvement on a per unit basis. This brings up interesting issues about the degree to which ESG metrics contain both fixed and variable costs, an issue that students of cost accounting have encountered elsewhere.

One area that showed only sluggish year-to-year improvement is one of the most important: Scope 3, Category 11, greenhouse gas emissions related to the use of Mazda's products. In essence, this is an estimate of emissions from Mazda cars and trucks that are driven worldwide and is closely linked to their fuel economy. These indirect emissions dwarf the company's direct emissions, and Mazda discusses its long-term strategy for reducing them at length in the sustainability report. The strategy calls for refinements to traditional internal combustion technologies, such as eco-drive systems, as well as advances in electric vehicles, hybrids, and the use of alternative fuels. The report sets forth goals of reducing *well-to-wheel* CO_2 emissions, or total emissions from all sources over the car's life-cycle, to 50 percent of 2010 levels by 2030 and 90 percent of 2010 levels by 2050.

IKEA Group's 2021 Sustainability Report

IKEA is the world's largest furniture retailer. The company was founded in Sweden but is currently headquartered in Leiden, Netherlands. As noted earlier in this chapter, IKEA does not report within the GRI framework but explicitly describes its reporting as *GRI-informed*. In the past, Ikea's sustainability reports were externally assured by Ernst & Young. However, the scope of the assurance engagement was limited to assessing IKEA's disclosures of Scope 1, 2, and 3 carbon emissions. Left outside of the engagement's scope was the much more difficult task of evaluating disclosures about social and environmental conditions in IKEA's far-flung global supply chain. The 2021 report contains no assurance statement from a third-party.

EXHIBIT 12.6
Mazda Group: 2020 Sustainability Data

	GRI Standard	YoY % Change	2020	2019 Units	Units
Energy consumption..........................	302	−3.36%	12,069	12,488	thousand gigajoules
Water consumption..........................	303	−7.28%	8,626	9,303	thousand cubic meters
GHG emissions, Scopes 1 and 2..............	305	−8.08%	648	705	thousand tons CO_2-e
GHG Scope 3, Category 11 (use of sold products)........................	305	−2.46%	31,068	31,853	thousand tons CO_2-e
Wastewater................................	306	+2.62%	7,321	7,134	thousand cubic meters
Direct-to-landfill waste......................	306	−16.02%	1,557	1,854	tons
Chemical discharges........................	306	−10.70%	876	981	tons
Recycling - vehicles collected – flourocarbons..	301	+1.94%	133,798	131,255	units
Recycling - weight collected – flourocarbons ...	301	−4.66%	31,810	33,365	kilograms
Sales volume...............................		−9.10%	1,419	1,561	thousands of units
Sales revenue..............................		−3.77%	3,430	3,565	billions of yen

IKEA is one of the world's largest purchasers of wood. Therefore, procuring wood from sustainably managed forests is one of the company's most material sustainability issues. A number of other supply chain issues are also material to IKEA, including assuring that its suppliers adhere to internationally recognized labor standards in India and China. Verifying the conditions under which wood is produced is particularly daunting. The supply chain is fragmented across many small producers, often operating in remote locations. In addition, 30 percent of its wood is sourced in what IKEA labels *priority areas.* It defines priority areas as regions "where there is a higher risk of illegal or irresponsible forestry practices, such as China, Russia, South and Southeast Asia and Southeast Europe."

When faced with difficult supply chain challenges, companies that need to buy large quantities of a particular product sometimes use a two-tiered system of standards—a basic set of standards that assures a minimum level of compliance with established norms and a more advanced set of standards toward which the company hopes to move over the long run. The basic standards help companies minimize reputation risks while allowing them to meet their short-term sourcing needs.

IKEA has traditionally followed such an approach in sourcing wood. Its basic standards are an internally developed code of conduct, known as the IKEA Way on Purchasing Products and Services (IWAY). The IWAY wood sourcing standard has stipulated that "wood must come from legally harvested forests free from social conflict, and not from high conservation value natural forests, converted tropical and sub-tropical forests or genetically modified tree plantations." All of IKEA purchases have met this basic standard for a number of years. However, the company also established a stricter benchmark, which it has labeled sourcing from "more sustainable sources." The more sustainable sources category includes wood certified by the Forest Stewardship Council (FSC), as well as wood obtained from recycling. IKEA's 2015 sustainability report disclosed that only 20 percent of its wood was purchased from more sustainable sources. As of 2021, the company had achieved its goal of boosting that figure to 100 percent, 14 percent of which came from recycling. Ikea's sustainability reporting system has provided a useful vehicle through which stakeholders could monitor the company's progress toward this important goal.

Baxter International's 2020 Sustainability Report

Baxter International is a large medical products company based in Deerfield, Illinois. Baxter generally receives high marks for its corporate governance policies, as well as for its social and environmental performance. However, the company has also weathered controversies related to the safety of its products. The most well-known was a scandal in 2001 attributing a series of fatalities to the use of its Althane line of hemodialysis equipment. Like other companies that manufacture health care–related products, product safety is among its most material sustainability issues.

Baxter was one of the founding partners of the GRI and still reports using the GRI system. As noted above, its annual sustainability report is externally assured by Apex Companies, LLC. GRI 416, *Customer Health and Safety,* covers product safety and requires two disclosures, 416-1 and 416-2. Disclosure 416-1 requires companies to report "the percentage of product and service categories for which health and safety impacts are assessed for improvement." As part of its disclosure in this area, the company described a new program that improves its response to customer complaints:

> As of the end of 2020, we had reduced product complaints by 19% compared with 2015 (surpassing our goal of a 15% reduction).

Disclosure 416-2 requires companies to report the "total number of incidents of noncompliance with regulations and/or voluntary codes concerning the health and safety impacts of products and services." Baxter's response to this requirement illustrates the importance of establishing connections between sustainability reports and traditional financial reports. In addition to providing noncompliance information in its sustainability report, Baxter referred readers to its 2016 Annual Report on Form 10-K. The section of the 10-K most relevant to Disclosure 416-2 is *Certain Regulatory Matters,* part of the Management Discussion and Analysis section, shown in Exhibit 12.7. There, Baxter provided links to Warning Letters issued by the U.S. Food and Drug Administration. It also provided the following description of an unresolved noncompliance case originating at a plant in Ahmedabad, India:

Climate Change Disclosures in ExxonMobil's 2021 Form 10-K

ExxonMobil Corporation is one of the world's largest oil companies, with 63,000 employees and operations in most countries of the world. The company publishes an annual sustainability report based on standards developed by the International Petroleum Industry Environmental Conservation Association (IPIECA), based in London, and the American Petroleum Institute Oil and Gas Industry Guidance on Voluntary

EXHIBIT 12.7
Extract from the Management Discussion and Analysis Section of Baxter International's 2020 Form 10-K

CERTAIN REGULATORY MATTERS

The U.S. Food and Drug Administration (FDA) commenced an inspection of Claris' facilities in Ahmedabad, India in July 2017, immediately prior to the closing of the Claris acquisition. FDA completed the inspection and subsequently issued a Warning Letter based on observations identified in the 2017 inspection (Claris Warning Letter). FDA has not yet re-inspected the facilities and management cannot speculate on when the Claris Warning Letter will be lifted. However, we are continuing to implement corrective and preventive actions to address FDA's prior observations and other items we identified and management continues to pursue and implement other manufacturing locations, including contract manufacturing organizations, to support the production of new products for distribution in the United States. As of December 31, 2020, we have secured alternative locations to produce a majority of the planned new products to be manufactured in Ahmedabad for distribution into the United States.

Sustainability Reporting. The greenhouse gas emissions portion of the 2020 report was externally assured by Lloyd's Register Quality Assurance, Ltd. Like IKEA, ExxonMobil has in the past stated that its reports are GRI-informed, but not "prepared in accordance with a particular GRI model." Its 2020 report included links to GRI standards in its content index.

In addition to its sustainability report, as discussed earlier in the chapter, the SEC's Release No. 33-9106 requires ExxonMobil to include in its Form 10-K a variety of climate-related disclosures. While this requirement potentially affects many areas of the report, the primary disclosures appear in the Business Description, Risk Factors, and Management Discussion and Analysis (MD&A) sections.

Consistent with SEC guidelines, ExxonMobil's 2021 10-K provided disclosures of environmentally focused capital expenditures in the Business Description section. Here, the company reported spending $4.6 billion worldwide on environmental initiatives and projected that it would spend $5.3 billion in 2022 and an unspecified higher amount in 2023. Seventy percent of these costs consisted of SG&A expenses and 30 percent of capital expenditures. The spending included "a significant investment in refining infrastructure and technology to manufacture clean fuels, as well as projects to monitor and reduce nitrogen oxide, sulfur oxide and greenhouse gas emissions, and expenditures for asset retirement obligations."

The Risk Factors section of the 10-K is sometimes criticized for being an uninformative laundry list of topics, in which highly important risk factors are hidden among those unlikely to be material to most investors. However, ExxonMobil 2021 10-K included four important climate-related risk factors. Two, *net zero scenarios* and *greenhouse gas restrictions,* describe the downward effect that governmental energy transition policies will have on demand for hydrocarbons, as well as the company's costs of doing business. These policies include cap and trade schemes, carbon taxes, trade tariffs, and minimum renewable usage requirements. The third risk factor is the threat posed by government support for alternative energy technologies. However, ExxonMobil also used the Risk Factors section as a platform for highlighting its leading role in developing some of these technologies, in effect hedging its oil-related risks through investments in alternative technologies.

> ExxonMobil has established a Low Carbon Solutions (LCS) business unit to advance the development and deployment of these technologies and projects, including CCS, hydrogen and advanced biofuels, breakthrough energy efficiency processes, advanced energy-saving materials, and other technologies. The company's efforts include both in-house research and development and collaborative efforts with leading universities as well as commercial partners involved in advanced lower-emission energy technologies.

Companies may potentially make a variety of sustainability-related disclosures in the MD&A section. One disclosure that ExxonMobil makes stands out:

> Our Energy Outlook seeks to identify potential impacts of climate-related policies, which often target specific sectors. It estimates potential impacts of these policies on consumer energy demand by using various assumptions and tools—including, depending on the sector, and, as applicable, use of a proxy cost of carbon or assessment of targeted policies (e.g., automotive fuel economy standards). For purposes of the Energy Outlook, a proxy cost on energy-related CO_2 emissions is assumed to reach about $100 per metric ton in 2050 in OECD nations.

Forecasts of future energy market trends are fraught with reporting risk for companies. It was for being overly optimistic in the MD&A section of the 10-K that Peabody Energy was sued by New York State's Attorney General's Office (a case discussed earlier in the chapter). The New York Attorney General (NYAG) also sued ExxonMobil over disclosing an $80-per-ton 2040 carbon proxy cost in earlier regulatory filings. The NYAG alleged that the company actually used an internal carbon proxy cost that was higher than $80 per ton. According to the lawsuit, the public disclosure of the lower figure may have misled investors about the seriousness of the threat posed by climate change. Former Secretary of State Rex Tillerson is reported to have approved this reporting discrepancy when he was the company's CEO, illustrating the senior level at which carbon accounting decisions are made.[16] ExxonMobil ultimately won the case in New York's Supreme Court. However, the controversy over ExxonMobil's carbon cost disclosures illustrates the heightened legal and regulatory risks that companies and auditors are likely to face as sustainability reporting moves closer to traditional financial reporting in terms of legal mandates and the precision of its requirements.

Summary

1. Sustainability reporting augments the traditional financial reporting model by providing information on the entity's social and environmental performance.

2. Because social and environmental performance is closely associated with good governance, many sustainability reporting frameworks incorporate governance metrics. This has led to the widespread use of the label *ESG reporting* to describe the sustainability reporting system.

3. There are two theories that are often used to explain sustainability reporting: stakeholder theory and legitimacy theory. Stakeholder theory posits that sustainability reporting is in response to the stakeholder demand for such information, while according to legitimacy theory, sustainability reporting is a means of dealing with firms' exposure to political and social pressures.

4. Both traditional investors and socially responsible investors increasingly demand the information produced by the sustainability reporting system.

5. Sustainability reporting arose as a largely voluntary reporting system.

6. The Global Reporting Initiative (GRI) has emerged as the world's most important sustainability reporting framework and is used by over 80 percent of the world's largest 250 companies. The GRI migrated from the *guidelines* to a set of formal *standards* in 2018.

7. GRI materiality disclosures require companies to rank the importance of sustainability topics to their stakeholders as well as to company management.

8. Other voluntary reporting frameworks may be used in conjunction with the GRI, including those of the Carbon Disclosure Project and the International Standards Organization.

9. The European Union and the Hong Kong Stock Exchange both require companies to engage in comprehensive sustainability reporting.

10. Disclose-or-explain is a flexible approach to imposing sustainability reporting mandates that allows companies to refrain from making a particular disclosure if they explain their reasons for doing so.

11. The sustainability reporting framework developed by the Sustainability Accounting Standards Board (SASB) is focused on the information needs of investors and requirements to disclose material information inherent in U.S. securities law. The most explicit of these requirements is the SEC's requirement to include climate change–related disclosures in 10-Ks.

[16] "Exxon Emissions Cost Accounting 'May Be a Sham,' New York State Says," *New York Times*, June 2, 2017.

12. In November 2021, the SASB was absorbed into the International Sustainability Standards Board (ISSB). The ISSB was created by the IASB Foundation. It will develop and promulgate IFRS Sustainability Reporting Standards.

13. IFRS Sustainability Reporting Standards will also have an explicit investor focus and are positioned to become the benchmark sustainability reporting standards used by securities regulators as they begin imposing mandatory sustainability reporting requirements on companies around the world.

14. Greenhouse gas emissions are categorized into Scope 1 (direct), Scope 2 (mainly indirect emissions caused by purchasing electricity), and Scope 3 (other indirect emissions).

15. External assurance increases the value of sustainability disclosures and plays an increasingly important role in the sustainability reporting model. To date, companies have used the limited assurance model. This contrasts with reasonable assurance model used by auditors of traditional financial statements.

Questions

1. What is sustainability reporting?
2. What are the theories often used to explain the sustainability reporting practices of firms?
3. What is the Global Reporting Initiative (GRI)?
4. What is GRI-informed reporting?
5. What are the four categories into which GRI standards are divided?
6. What is materiality and how is it measured within the GRI framework?
7. What is the comply-or-explain approach to mandatory reporting?
8. In February 2010, the U.S. SEC issued Release No. 33-9106, *Commission Guidance Regarding Disclosure Related to Climate Change.* Name three sections of the Form 10-K potentially affected by this disclosure rule.
9. What is the primary difference between the GRI and the Sustainability Accounting Standards Board (SASB)?
10. What is a carbon dioxide equivalent and how is it measured?
11. What is a proxy cost of carbon?
12. What are Scope 1 emissions and how do they differ from Scope 2 and Scope 3 emissions?
13. What industry dominates the list of the world's largest Scope 1 emitters?
14. Why do auto companies have larger Scope 3 emissions than Scope 1 emissions?

Exercises and Problems

1. Nestlé is the world's largest food producer and is headquartered in Switzerland. In addition to its annual sustainability report, the company publishes a separate GRI content index, which allows users to navigate within the main body of the report to see where specific GRI standards are being addressed. Nestlé also publishes a separate assurance statement for the report. Links to the 2019 versions of these documents are provided below. Use these to answer the following questions about Nestlé's sustainability reporting practices.

   • Creating Shared Value and Sustainability Report 2019
   • Creating Shared Value and Sustainability Report 2019 - GRI Content Index
   • Bureau Veritas Independent Assurance Statement 2019

Required:

a. What sustainability issues are disclosed as most material to stakeholders? To Nestlé? Is there a general alignment between the two sets of materiality rankings?

b. How does the report's information contribute to your understanding of the material issues that you identified above?

c. The content index lists a number of *omissions*. These are reporting gaps where Nestlé determined that it did not fully respond to a GRI disclosure requirement. How concerning do you believe these omissions to be?

d. Bureau Veritas's external assurance of Nestlé's sustainability report identifies material disclosures that were not externally assured. Why do you think that these were excluded from the assurance report's scope? How concerned are you about their exclusion?

2. Marks and Spencer (M&S) is a multinational retailer headquartered in London. Its 2021 sustainability report, known as Plan A, is at http://planareport.marksand spencer.com.

Required:

a. The report lists *commitments,* performance targets, and reports on the extent to which those commitments were met. List three commitments that were substantially met.

b. List three commitments that were substantially unmet or for which progress cannot be documented.

3. Continue to refer to Marks and Spencer's (M&S) 2021 Plan A report in answering the following questions about the company's carbon accounting.

Required:

a. M&S has asserted that it is the only retailer in the world with "carbon neutral global operations." How did the company achieve this milestone? What carbon accounting conventions underlie this claim?

b. Were Scope 1 emissions greater than Scope 3 emissions in 2020/21?

c. How does M&S measure carbon emissions intensity? Did this metric improve between 2019/20 and 2020/21?

d. By how much has M&S reduced its emissions compared to the baseline emissions level of 2006/07?

4. Apple Inc.'s 2018 Supplier Responsibility Report was one of the most widely read sustainability reports at the time it was published due to persistent allegations of human rights abuses in its Chinese supply chain. Use the report to answer the questions below. https://images.apple.com/supplier-responsibility/pdf/Apple_SR_2018_Progress _Report.pdf.

Required:

a. Compare Apple's Supplier Responsibility Report with those of Nestlé and Marks and Spencer in terms of depth, transparency, and adherence to recognizable reporting standards. What differences in reporting approach do you see?

b. Most of Apple's suppliers are themselves large, publicly traded companies with independent governance structures of their own. Critically discuss whether Apple should assume any responsibility for the working conditions of these suppliers. Should it be responsible for reporting on working conditions at these companies?

5. Imperial Petroleum plc is a multinational oil and gas company based in the United Kingdom with substantial offshore production and exploration activities. Imperial prepares an annual sustainability report using the GRI framework in which it identifies issues that are material to its stakeholders. Only one of the issues below is designated as material by company. Use your knowledge of the oil and gas industry to identify this issue.
   a. Workplace health and safety.
   b. Child and forced labor.
   c. Fair disclosure and labeling.
   d. Product quality.
   e. Data security and customer privacy.

6. Garner Pharmaceuticals is a U.S. drug company that manufactures eye medications. Based on research conducted at the SASB, one of the following sustainability topics is substantially more likely to be highly material for Garner than the others. Use your knowledge of the pharmaceutical industry to identify this topic.
   a. Fuel management and transportation.
   b. Child and forced labor.
   c. Air pollution.
   d. Product quality and safety.
   e. Biodiversity impacts.

7. Clarion Bank and Trust (CBT) is a local bank based in a small town in the American Midwest. The town's only other bank, a branch of a large multinational, recently closed. Based on research conducted at the SASB, one of the following sustainability topics is substantially more likely to be highly material for CBT than the others. Use your knowledge of the banking industry to identify this topic.
   a. Biodiversity impacts.
   b. Child and forced labor.
   c. Air pollution.
   d. Workplace health and safety.
   e. Access and affordability.

8. Joliet 29, owned by NRG Energy, was the largest emitter of CO_2-e in northern Illinois in 2015. The plant's emissions during that year were as follows:

	Metric Tons
CO_2	5,656,485.0
CH_4 (methane)	642.4
N_2O (nitrous oxide)	93.4

Required:
   a. Use the factors set forth in the Greenhouse Gas Protocol to compute Joliet 29's CO_2 equivalent (CO_2-e) emissions in 2015.
   b. NRG Energy converted Joliet 29 from burning primarily coal to natural gas in 2016. Assume that the conversion reduced the facility's GHG emissions by 40 percent. How much lower would 2015 emissions have been had Joliet 29 primarily burned natural gas during that year?

9. The following link takes you to Mazda's sustainability report for fiscal 2021. As is the case for virtually all Japanese companies, Mazda's 2021 fiscal year ran from April 1, 2020 to March 31, 2021.

    https://www.mazda.com/globalassets/en/assets/sustainability/download/2021/2021
    _all.pdf

    Recall that we reviewed the company's 2020 report earlier in the chapter and documented 2019 versus 2020 performance for a set of environmental metrics in Exhibit 12.6.

    Required:
    a. Use the data on page 126 of Mazda's 2021 sustainability report and the 2020 figures from Exhibit 12.6 to determine whether Mazda's performance rose or fell between fiscal 2020 and fiscal 2021 for the following list of environmental metrics.
       - Energy consumption
       - Water consumption
       - Greenhouse gas emissions - Scopes 1 and 2
       - Greenhouse gas emissions - Scope 3, Category 11 (use of sold products)
       - Wastewater

    b. The scale of Mazda's operations was significantly effected by the Covid-19 pandemic in fiscal 2021. Unit sales volume declined by 132,000 vehicles, or 9.3 percent. Net sales revenue declined by ¥548 billion, or 16.0 percent. Measured against each of these sales benchmarks, did Mazda's environmental performance actually improve? Explain.

10. Carbon accounting standards allow companies to use several methods of determining the boundaries between Scope 1/Scope 2 and Scope 3 activities. Similar to most large companies, BHP Billiton (BHP) uses a GAAP-based definition: Scope 1/Scope 2 includes emissions at facilities that the company *controls* (i.e., consolidates). *Equity-accounted joint ventures* and *equity-accounted associates* are companies over which the reporting company has significant influence, but not control. Emissions by these companies are placed in Scope 3, Category 15 (investments).

    Required:
    The following activities of BHP, the Anglo-Australian mining company, result in greenhouse gas emissions. Classify them as contributing to Scope 1, Scope 2, or Scope 3. For Scope 3 emissions, identify in which of the 15 categories they should be placed.
    a. BHP operates mining equipment powered by diesel fuel.
    b. Coal mined in BHP's operations in Western Australia is sold to Australian utilities, which burn it to produce electricity.
    c. BHP sends a high-level executive team to Seoul to negotiate an iron ore sales contract with Pohang Iron and Steel Corporation (POSCO). Flights and rental cars used by the team burn, respectively, aviation fuel and gasoline.
    d. BHP ships iron ore from Port Hedland to POSCO via a tanker, which burns fuel on its journey. The sales contract specifies FOB shipping point. Thus, title passes to POSCO in Port Hedland.
    e. POSCO uses the aforementioned iron ore to manufacture steel at its Gwangyang plant. This plant uses oil to fire its blast furnaces.
    f. BHP is a 47 percent joint venture partner with Alcoa in an aluminum smelter in São Luís, Brazil. The smelter purchases large quantities of electricity to power the Hall-Héroult process, which extracts aluminum from bauxite through electrolysis.

g. BHP is also a 47 percent joint venture partner in an aluminum smelter in Maputo, Mozambique, that also consumes large quantities of electricity. BHP's partners have much smaller stakes: Mitsubishi Corporation (25%), the Industrial Development Corporation of South Africa (24%), and the Government of Mozambique (4%). Applying IFRS 10, BHP's accountants have determined that the company has effective control of the joint venture because it has the largest stake and exercises managerial control over day-to-day operations.

CASE 12-1

The Case of Modco Inc.

Company Profile

Modco was founded in 1960, with the opening of the first Modco discount store, and was incorporated as Modco Stores Inc. in January 1970. The company's shares were listed on the NYSE in 1975. Modco has a full range of groceries and general merchandise in a single store. Modco is proud of the fact that it offers its customers a one-stop shopping experience and is one of the largest private employers in the United States and one of the world's largest retailers. It has more than 8,000 retail units under several banners in 15 countries. They all share a common goal of promoting the idea, "Better life for people by helping them save money." Modco has 2 million employees worldwide and generated net sales of $200 billion during fiscal year 2017.

Since 2005, Modco has published its annual report on its website. According to its CEO, Modco's annual report reflects the social and environmental dimensions of its activities and its constant and progressive work toward social responsibility issues. Modco's 2017 annual report states how its emphasis on sustainability has helped the company to be the retail leader in the market. According to the report, Modco has investments in education, health, commitments to fight hunger, support for local farmers, and access to healthier and affordable food. Such reports portray an image of the company as a role model on corporate social responsibility (CSR).

Company Conflicts

There is a national class action against Modco which started nearly a decade ago. Plaintiffs allege that female employees in Modco retail stores were discriminated against based on their gender, regarding pay and promotion to top management positions. In 2011, the relevant U.S. District Court issued a judgment in favor of the class action. Modco unsuccessfully appealed to the U.S. Court of Appeals. Later Modco appealed to the U.S. Supreme Court, which reversed the Appeals Court's decision in May 2017, concluding that the millions of plaintiffs and their claims did not have enough in common. In September 2017, the plaintiffs' lawyers filed an amended lawsuit limiting the class to female Modco employees in the district where the company head office was located. The new lawsuit alleges discriminatory practices against approximately 100,000 women regarding pay and job promotion, as well as requiring nondiscriminatory pay and promotion criteria.

At the end of 2016, it was announced on the local radio that Modco was using child labor at two factories in Bangladesh. Children aged 10 to 14 years old were found to be working in the factories for less than $50 a month, making products of the Modco brand for export to the United States.

Modco's annual report, called "Global Responsibility Report," covers the three dimensions of "People, Planet, Profit." This report emphasizes gender equality and a diverse workforce. In 2015, Modco took the commitment one step further with the incorporation of the Advisory Board on Gender Equality and Diversity, with the specific function of providing equal and enhanced opportunities for all in top leadership roles. Modco has also committed itself to selling products that sustain people and the environment.

Required:

Assume that you are part of a research team examining the sustainability reporting and stakeholder relations policies of large companies. Evaluate the policies of Modco.

Index

Note: Page numbers followed by *n* indicate source notes or footnotes.